DAVID CROCKETT IN CONGRESS

The Rise and Fall of the Poor Man's Friend

bright sky press

2365 Rice Blvd., Suite 202 Houston, Texas 77005

10   9   8   7   6   5   4   3   2   1

Library of Congress Cataloging-in-Publication Data

Boylston, James R., 1954-
David Crockett in Congress : the rise and fall of the poor man's friend /
by James R. Boylston and Allen J. Wiener.
p. cm.
Includes bibliographical references and index.
ISBN 978-1-933979-51-9 (hardcover)
1. Crockett, Davy, 1786-1836. 2. Legislators–United States–Biography. 3. United States. Congress. House–Biography.
4. United States–Politics and government–1825-1829. 5. United States–Politics and government–1829-1837.
6. Tennessee–Politics and government–To 1865. 7. Land reform–United States–History–19th century.
I. Wiener, Allen J., 1943- II. Title.

F436.C95B796 2009
976.8'04092–dc22   [B]   2009024431

Book and cover design by Marla Garcia and Ellen Cregan
Edited by Tom Kailbourne
Printed in Asia through Asia Pacific Offset

DAVID CROCKETT IN CONGRESS

The Rise and Fall of the Poor Man's Friend

JAMES R. BOYLSTON

AND

ALLEN J. WIENER

With Collected Correspondence, Selected Speeches and Circulars

bright sky press

HOUSTON, TEXAS

TABLE OF CONTENTS

ACKNOWLEDGEMENTS

The authors are indebted to many generous individuals and institutions, who provided immeasurable help in researching and writing this book.

We are very grateful to William C. Davis for giving generously of his time and advice.

We extend our special gratitude and appreciation to our editor, Tom Kailbourn, for his expert workmanship and sound judgment.

Special thanks to Christine Blackerby, archives specialist in the Center for Legislative Archives, U.S. National Archives and Records Administration, for the time she took to provide detailed information on congressional documents and use of the Library of Congress's website, *A Century of Lawmaking for a New Nation* (http://memory.loc.gov/ammem/amlaw/lawhome.html). Christine also located Crockett's letter to Senator David Barton. Thanks to Kenneth Kato, also an archives specialist in the Center for Legislative Archives, for help in understanding how early nineteenth-century congressional sessions were recorded.

Daniel Feller and Thomas Coens of the Andrew Jackson Papers project, University of Tennessee, Knoxville, gave generously of their time and knowledge.

We appreciate the valuable assistance of the following individuals and institutions: the staff of the Daughters of the Republic of Texas Library at the Alamo; Nathaniel King of the Perkins Library Reference Department, Duke University; Travis Westly, Teri Sierra, and Lia Apodaca at the Library of Congress; Allison DeFriese, Gary Ferguson, and the staff at the Tennessee State Library and Archives; Ann Toplovich, Tennessee Historical Society; William B. Eigelsbach, Special Collections Library, Hoskins Library, University of Tennessee at Knoxville; Tracy Luna, University of Tennessee at Knoxville; Kristi Moffitt of www.gensearch.org; Stephen R. Young and Vida Engstrand, Beinecke Rare Book & Manuscript Library, Yale University; Steven Smith, Historical Society of Pennsylvania; Heather Cole, Leslie A. Morris, Rachel Howarth, and Susan Halpert, Houghton Library, Harvard University; Kimberly Reynolds and Sean Casey, Boston Public Library; David Frasier, Lilly Library, Indiana University; Olga Tsapina and Sue Hodson, Huntington Library; Maurice C. York and Kacy Guill, J. Y. Joyner Library, East Carolina University; Alan Wallace, University of Tennessee Libraries, Knoxville; Geri E. Solomon, Hofstra University; James B. Jones Jr., Tennessee Historical Commission; Ted O'Reilly, Jody Cary, and Tammy Kiter, New-York Historical Society; Alyson Barrett-Ryan, Gilder Lehrman Collection, New-York Historical Society; Becky W. Livingston, Panhandle-Plains Historical Museum; Brenda McClurkin, Special Collections, University of Texas at Arlington Library; Robin Davies Chen, University Library, University of North Carolina at Chapel Hill; Diana Franzusoff Peterson and John F. Anderies, Haverford College Library; Cynthia M. Van Ness, Buffalo and Erie County Historical Society; Christine De Groot, Archives of American Art, Smithsonian Institution; Mary M. Huth, University of Rochester Library; Declan Kiely and Christine Nelson, Morgan Library and Museum; John D. Tilford, University Archives and Special Collections, Sewanee: The University of the South; Margaret Downs Hrabe and Edward Gaynor, University of Virginia Library; Jennifer B. Lee, Rare Book & Manuscript Library, Columbia University; Jenny Namsiriwan, Maryland Historical Society; Martha Briggs and Alison Hinderliter, Newberry Library; Bryan McDaniel, Chicago History Museum; Elizabeth C. Denlinger and Charles C. Carter, Carl H. Pforzheimer Collection of Shelley and His Circle, New York Public Library; Laura Ruttum, Manuscripts and Archives, New York Public Library.

We are very grateful to Phil Collins; David Zucker; Bruce Gimelson; Todd and Julian Canaday; and Thomas W. Akin of the Arthur Maury Corporation for their generosity in sharing Crockett materials and for their encouragement of this project.

Many thanks to Anne Skilton, Ted Allen Belue, Jeffrey Eger of Auction Catalogues, Bruce McKinney of Americana Exchange, Susan Rabiner, Gary Foreman, William R. Chemerka, Thomas E. Scruggs, Fred Koller, Mark Michel, Stuart Reid, Bob Durham, Mark Lemon, Herb True, and Ken Sutak.

Finally, we extend our heartfelt thanks to Rue Judd, Lucy Chambers, Ellen Cregan, and the staff of Bright Sky Press.

INTRODUCTION

In the mythology of America, the legend of Davy Crockett looms large. As a pioneer, Indian fighter, congressman, and martyr of the Alamo, Crockett's remarkable life has been the subject of biographies, novels, comic books, plays, songs, movies, and television shows. The image of the coonskin-capped, buckskin-clad hero swinging his rifle like a Louisville Slugger atop the Alamo is iconic; to most folks, Davy Crockett really is the King of the Wild Frontier.

While Crockett certainly was a pioneer and hardscrabble farmer, a soldier under Andrew Jackson in the Creek War, and a hero who gave his life in the fight for Texas independence, he was also an inveterate entrepreneur and a career politician with a talent for hardball campaigning. More Will Rogers than Daniel Boone, more broadcloth than buckskin, David Crockett began his political career as a justice of the peace and magistrate, and served two terms in the Tennessee State Legislature before being elected to the U.S. House of Representatives for three terms, one of them nonconsecutive. Always popular in his district, Crockett nevertheless was a hard-fighting campaigner, as he faced the formidable political machine of Andrew Jackson in virtually every engagement.

While the one-dimensional image of the mythological Davy Crockett is predominant in the public mind, the historical personage on whom this image was based has not been completely forgotten. Attempts to separate the "real" David Crockett of history from the "Davy" of legend began in earnest with James Atkins Shackford's doctoral dissertation in 1948, which provided the research for *David Crockett, the Man and the Legend,* Shackford's landmark 1956 biography of Crockett, published posthumously and edited by Shackford's brother, John B. Shackford. Virtually every David Crockett biography written since then has leaned heavily on Shackford's study. So impressive was the depth of his research that most subsequent Crockett biographers accepted Shackford's theories and conclusions uncritically, and the Shackford interpretation of Crockett has become as pervasive in the historical sector as is the mythological "Davy" to the general public.

Though the debt owed to Shackford's research is indisputable, some of his conclusions about Crockett are questionable. In fact, what may be considered the primary thrust of Shackford's vision of Crockett, that his public image was largely a construct of an anti-Jacksonian Whig conspiracy, merits much closer examination.

William C. Davis, author of the fine triple biography *Three Roads to the Alamo: The Lives and Fortunes of David Crockett, James Bowie, and William Barret Travis,* took Shackford's conspiracy theory to task, but embraced some of his conclusions regarding Crockett, especially Crockett's alleged political naïveté. However, Davis gave Crockett far more credit for political astuteness and purpose than did Shackford. Mark Derr's Crockett biography, *The Frontiersman,* also provided evidence to refute Shackford's image of Crockett, as did Thomas E. Scruggs in "Davy Crockett and the Thieves of Jericho," an essay for the *Journal of the Early Republic,* but for the most part, Shackford's theories have been taken at face value and repeated ad nauseam.

Scholars have sought to separate the real Crockett from the legendary figure mainly by focusing on how the fictional "Davy" arose and what forms he has taken. Walter Blair's "Six Davy Crocketts," from the July 1940 *Southwest Review,* is one of the most often quoted sources taking this approach, and Michael Lofaro's anthology, *Davy Crockett: The Man, The Legend, The Legacy, 1786–1836,* continued and expanded upon this direction of study. However, the real David can best be resurrected through his own words and a careful review of the political issues that were most important to him. Though the importance of Crockett's 1834 autobiography, *A Narrative of the Life of David Crockett of the State of Tennessee,* cannot be overstated in attempting to "get inside" the David of history, Crockett's letters, speeches, and political circulars provide a unique, long-ignored approach to discovering the real man.

The purpose of this book is to retrieve the real Crockett through a careful review of those documents and to correct inaccurate views of him in earlier works. Crockett was a masterful campaigner among his frontier neighbors, an amusing jokester, storyteller and speaker. His jokes and stump speeches helped him win elections, but once in office, he proved himself an astute politician and parliamentarian. Crockett understood the issues under discussion and how his colleagues stood on them; thus, he was able to maneuver effectively among them, sometimes gaining victories for himself.

Crockett's most important political objective was to secure for his poorer constituents legal title to the land they had worked and improved. He never achieved that goal, but his exhaustive efforts to do so illustrate Crockett's devotion to the people who elected him and his insistence on serving them rather than his political party or its leaders. Throughout his career he remained an advocate for the poor, whom he viewed as constantly pushed aside or ignored by wealthier, more influential interests.

Crockett's initial support for Andrew Jackson deteriorated quickly as he found himself at odds with the Jacksonians on many matters, including the land issue, Jackson's brutal Indian removal policy, and his war on the Second Bank of the United States. Most Crockett scholarship has portrayed his increasing opposition to Jackson as either an irrational obsession or merely cynical politics by anti-Jackson operatives, who simply used Crockett as a viable Jackson rival in Old Hickory's own state. But Crockett was far more politically aware than such a theory suggests, and that view of him ignores his genuine opposition to many of Jackson's policies and what Crockett saw as Jackson's expansion of executive power, which he viewed as a threat to the political system and to the Union.

His compassion for the Cherokee and other eastern tribes was genuine and continued long after the battle over removal had ended. He saw cruelty and injustice toward a helpless people in Jackson's Indian policy, similar to the unfairness he saw in the government's lack of concern for the poor.

Crockett's alliance with members of the embryonic Whig Party and eastern business interests may seem anomalous for an uneducated man from the backwoods and defender of the poor, but he found himself increasingly politically isolated in Tennessee. Jackson's forces and the wealthier landed gentry controlled the government and had little interest in the needs of their poorer cousins on the frontier, and Crockett was forced to recruit allies where he could find them, regardless of their political affiliation or regional interests. He often found himself in agreement with eastern factions on some issues, including Jackson's war on the Bank. While Jackson hated banks and paper money, and the Bank was guilty of corrupt practices, Crockett knew that the poor depended on easy credit in order to survive. Similarly, along with the Whigs, Crockett supported internal improvements that could benefit frontier economies, but which Jackson opposed.

Crockett made no secret of his views and openly expressed them verbally and in writing. Rather than a simple-minded pawn in the hands of more adept politicians, he was a staunch activist for his agenda and allied himself with those who shared his views. The older political parties that emerged from the Revolution were fading, and new affiliations were only beginning to materialize. Jacksonians were coalescing into the new Democratic Party, while the remnants of the National Republicans were drifting into a loose coalition of anti-Jackson forces. Many members of Congress, including one time Jackson supporters like Crockett, eventually listed their affiliation simply as "Anti-Jacksonian." These forces would merge into the new Whig Party in 1834 and Crockett would be allied with the Whigs during his final term in Congress, although he never formally became a Whig. He resisted affiliating himself too closely with any faction and believed that party loyalty should never be placed above principle or duty to his constituents. Crockett came to view strict party discipline as a threat to democracy that distanced elected officials from those they represented. In fact, although party cohesion was growing, discipline over members was never a sure thing for any faction, and what has been portrayed as Crockett's stubborn independence can be seen instead as political maneuvering to gain support for his views from politicians outside of his own state. Crockett believed that his political jockeying in Washington would not hurt him at home if his constituents remained assured that he was earnestly working on their behalf.

Crockett emerges as a strongly independent figure at odds with powerful Jacksonian forces, which repeatedly sought to unseat him in favor of someone more pliable. His three election victories and two narrow defeats attest to his personal popularity among his own people and the degree of anti-Jackson sentiment in the western part of Tennessee. Crockett's popularity is also a tribute to his loyalty to the people who elected him. His defeats can be largely attributed to the strenuous efforts of the Jacksonians, who spared no expense in their attempts to blacken his name among his constituents. They seemed to fear that any Crockett success would cement him as a fixture in Tennessee politics indefinitely, creating a long-term headache for them, especially as they sought to reelect Jackson, and later elect his handpicked successor, Martin Van Buren, to the presidency and maintain discipline among their congressional delegation.

The search for the real Crockett, often lost behind a haze of movie and other fictional images, reveals an independent spirit who rebelled against injustice and government cronyism. He spoke for the poor, a class from which he had barely emerged through determined effort, despite chronic debt and a lack of education. He was an egalitarian who bristled at the idea of class privilege and held the Lockean belief that people had a right to land they had worked and fed with the sweat of their brow. His roots endeared him to his neighbors and won him elections, and he sought to work for his supporters. In opposing Indian removal, Crockett was, for once, out of step with his constituents, but he made no secret of his views and defended his actions as a matter of conscience, which, he said, outweighed other loyalties. Where others have seen self-defeating stubbornness and pride, a more careful look at the record reveals a man who simply would not compromise his core beliefs or stray from his objectives. As his motto suggests, when he was sure he was right, he really did go ahead.

Crockett's final campaign for reelection ended in defeat, and though he was outspoken about his disgust with the government and Van Buren's impending presidency, he looked to his own future with optimism. His 1834 autobiography had been a bestseller and contributed immeasurably to his already growing celebrity. A promotional tour of the northeast was a huge success, and Crockett, always comfortable as the center of attention, enjoyed the limelight. Two more books were published under his name and, although neither achieved the success of the *Narrative,* he remained hopeful of continuing his career as an author.

Texas too, had been on his mind for some time. A land of seemingly limitless opportunity for someone with Crockett's tenacity, Texas offered a chance for recreation, recuperation, rehabilitation, and a respite from the taxing political environment in the United States. Relocating to Texas also enabled Crockett to make good on his promise of refusing to live under a Van Buren administration.

When David Crockett died in the Alamo, his legendary alter ego took on new life and very quickly transcended the man. Although "Davy" is a beloved American legend, the real David was a more complex, interesting, and admirable figure. A careful reading of Crockett's own words can restore him and give back to America an even larger hero than the legendary man in buckskins.

The first part of this book consists of a set of chapters that can be read independently, but which are interrelated and form a chronological account of Crockett's years in office, the issues he dealt with, and his political campaigns. The chapters are largely based on his own words, contained in his letters, circulars, and speeches, including those he delivered on the House floor, and those of his contemporaries. The letters and other documents, which are annotated, form the second and third sections of the book and can be read independently. We have included every extant letter and circular of Crockett's and a selection of his speeches. In a few cases, we have also included letters to Crockett, to lend better context to his own correspondence, and a few third-party letters that lend context to the issues he faced. Although there are many other documents that bear Crockett's signature, such as receipts, transmittal notes, and various legal documents, they are not included. Taken together, the book provides an up-to-date analysis of Crockett's political career, while presenting most of the primary documents on which that analysis is based.

A note on the text: All quotations from Crockett's letters and our transcriptions of the letters retain his original spelling and lack of punctuation. Letters of his that appeared in newspapers, his circulars, and printed speeches were enhanced by editors and others before their original publication, but reflect his position on issues, as evidenced by his actions and personal correspondence. We have presented these quoted materials as originally published, including archaic spelling and punctuation that were in use at the time.

DEDICATIONS

For Sandy—my anchor and my compass.
James R. Boylston

For my mother, to whom family was all.
Allen J. Wiener

PART I

— DAVID CROCKETT IN CONGRESS —

Chapter 1

"I Will Not Set Silently"
The Early Years

David Crockett, the newly elected representative from the Western District of Tennessee, arrived in Washington City on December 7, 1827, to begin his first term in the U.S. Congress. His trip to the capitol city had been a stressful journey, and he counted himself lucky to be alive. His wife Elizabeth and son John Wesley accompanied him as far as Swannanoa, North Carolina, where they planned to spend some time visiting Elizabeth's relatives, but Crockett was stricken with an illness shortly after arriving. Most likely it was a recurrence of the malaria that had plagued him since his service in the Creek Indian War, and Crockett spent four weeks bedridden and suffering before regaining enough strength to continue his travels.[1] Elizabeth and John did not join him, but instead returned to Tennessee with three slaves given to them by Elizabeth's father, Robert Patton. Elizabeth may have been anxious to put the slaves to work on one of the small business enterprises she and her husband were continually attempting to launch in order to put their ever increasing debts to rest.

It had only been five years since the couple had seen their family business ruined when a flood destroyed the grist mill the Crocketts had constructed on the banks of the river near their homestead. Hoping to profit from a small industrial complex, they also had built a powder mill and a distillery, but the loss of the grist mill rendered the distillery useless, and the Crocketts found themselves with little cash on hand and three thousand dollars in the hole. Not one for hand wringing, the ever pragmatic Elizabeth simply stated that they would pay their outstanding debts one way or another and start over as soon as they were able. Crockett remarked that he "thought it better to keep a good conscience with an empty purse, than to get a good opinion of myself with a full one."[2] He would never really experience the weight of a full purse, as financial troubles would plague him throughout his career, but his entrepreneurial spirit remained undiminished to the end.

Once Crockett was back on the road to Washington, his troubles continued. Traveling by stage, he stayed at taverns along the route, and at one inn he was bilked by the owner, a man named Briceland. Crockett claimed that he and six other men with whom he was traveling were charged for lodging at the tavern, though none of them "ever saw a bed in his house." Incensed, Crockett argued with Briceland and promised to take his business elsewhere in the future. Likely, Crockett was on a tight budget and was watching his expenses closely.[3]

Once in Washington, his health continued to deteriorate. Tall, robust, and ruddy by nature,[4] but now pale and underweight, he was put under a doctor's care and diagnosed with pleurisy. Settling into rooms at Mrs. Ball's Boarding House on Pennsylvania Avenue, he underwent the prescribed treatment of bloodletting and, after losing two quarts of blood at one session, Crockett began to fear that death was imminent.[5] Slowly, however, he regained his strength and eventually began to familiarize himself with the city and get to know some of his peers.

Mrs. Ball's was located across the street from Brown's Indian Queen Hotel, one of Washington City's most prestigious hostelries, and just down the street from Capitol Hill. At the rooming house, Crockett shared meals and accommodations with nine other congressmen, including Nathaniel Claiborne[6] of Virginia; three Kentuckians; representatives from Alabama, North Carolina, and Connecticut; and two members from New York. During the second session of Crockett's first congressional term, Thomas Chilton, a representative from Kentucky who would figure prominently in Crockett's future, moved into Mrs. Ball's as well. The men ate at a common table, and some probably shared beds, a common practice at the time. Crockett apparently found the situation agreeable, as he boarded at Ball's during every session of Congress save his last, when he moved across the street to Brown's Hotel.[7]

Crockett served during the Golden Age of Congress, where he rubbed shoulders with oratorical giants like Daniel Webster, Henry Clay, Thomas Hart Benton, and John C. Calhoun. Along with fellow Tennessean James K. Polk, Crockett's contemporaries in the first session of the Twentieth Congress included Senators and future Presidents William Henry Harrison, John Tyler, Martin Van Buren, and Congressman James Buchanan. Crockett was suitably impressed with the fast company and wrote that he was "getting along very well with the great men of the nation."[8] He began his first term in the House of Representatives with some campaign debt, a taste for alcohol, a fondness for the gaming tables, and a solid reputation for independence in the service of his constituents.[9] Crockett had already been in public service for over ten years, and the freshman congressman was an old hand at politics and running for elected office.

In 1816, Crockett was a thirty-year-old war veteran and head of a fairly large household. He had recently remarried after the death of his first wife Mary (Polly) Finley, and his blended family now consisted of five children, three from Polly (John Wesley, William, and Margaret) and two stepchildren, George and Margaret Ann, from his new wife Elizabeth, who had lost her husband in the Creek War. Later that year they would add to the family another son, Robert Patton.[10] Though the marriage may have been largely one of convenience,[11] he and Elizabeth were certainly fond of one another, and Elizabeth provided financial, managerial, and moral support for his business and political ventures throughout their long relationship.

Success in business and politics seemed the best avenues to social advancement, and Crockett was determined to better himself. Affable, honest, and renowned as a skillful bear hunter, he possessed natural leadership abilities that had begun to emerge during the Creek War when his men elected him sergeant and later lieutenant, signifying the confidence they had in him.[12] After building a small homestead in Lawrence County, Tennessee, in 1817 Crockett served as a magistrate and justice of the peace, and the following year as a town commissioner.[13]

Though he wrote and spoke often about his lack of formal education, what Crockett missed in schooling he more than made up for with street smarts and common sense, and he was known for fairness and honesty. These were the traits upon which he built his reputation and his political career. He boasted that as a magistrate his decisions were never appealed,[14] and his rapid rise in local office is a testament to his character. During this period Crockett was elected a colonel of the militia. The circumstances surrounding this election give some insight into his early, freewheeling campaign style.

Captain Matthews, a candidate for the post of colonel (actually, lieutenant colonel), encouraged Crockett to run for the rank of major of the regiment. After voicing some reluctance, Crockett nevertheless agreed to seek the position and naturally assumed that Matthews would endorse his candidacy. Upon attending a campaign frolic sponsored by the captain, Crockett found that Matthews' son was opposing him for the position of major. Taking the captain aside, Crockett confronted him about this change in events. Matthews offered the patronizing comment that his son was hesitant to run against Crockett and was concerned about his chance of victory. Crockett replied that his son needn't worry, he'd decided to seek the position of colonel instead, and straightaway took to the stump, soundly defeating the elder Matthews in the election.[15] Crockett's jump in rank from lieutenant to lieutenant colonel was a big one, and he would carry the title "colonel," a real rank, not an honorary salutation, for the remainder of his life.

His success in achieving public office increased his political ambition, and in 1821 he decided to run for the General Assembly, the lower house of the state legislature. His candidacy, like that of William Carroll, a former merchant and respected war veteran with no political bona fides who was running for governor, represented the rising tide of popular democracy that was sweeping the South and West. Crockett hit the campaign trail at a time that was made for him. He resigned as town commissioner in order to begin electioneering and, after driving some horses to the Patton's home in Swannanoa, a task that took three months, took to the stump.

Crockett identified with Carroll and supported his progressive platform of regulating the banking industry and reforming the harsh state penal code. He also echoed Carroll's call for a state constitutional convention in order to address the underrepresentation of the growing western districts of the state in the U.S. Congress and the state legislature, and to establish a more equitable and progressive property tax structure. All of these propositions would bring relief to Crockett's primary constituency: subsistence-level farmers, local merchants, and small-scale, middle-class planters. The financial instability that had brought on the Panic of 1819 worked in Carroll's favor, as voters, feeling intense economic stress, increasingly gravitated toward a change candidate sympathetic to debtors.

Crockett's support of Carroll put him firmly in league with a Tennessee political faction led by Andrew Erwin,[16] and opposed by the conservative banker and speculator John Overton,[17] whose powerful political machine backed Edward Ward for governor. Ward, a wealthy, well educated native Virginian with an aristocratic bearing, had served as speaker of the state Senate from 1815 to 1819, and was generally seen as a friend of the banks and an advocate for the rich.[18] Despite an endorsement from Andrew Jackson, the popular native son and hero of the War of 1812, Ward lost the election to Carroll in a landslide. It would not be the last time that Crockett would find himself opposed to Jackson.

On the campaign trail, Crockett joined the locals in barbecues, squirrel hunts, and dances, and cast himself as a man of the people, which he certainly was, pretending ignorance of the law and formal politics in his speeches.[19] Though unlettered, Crockett's record as a magistrate illustrated that he was familiar with statutes, depositions, and the rules of order, and knew how to conduct himself in government. Although he had taken pains to educate himself and had even worked in exchange for lessons in the "three Rs," he hid that side of his character on the stump.[20] His exaggerated backwoods demeanor and self-deprecating humor provided a stark contrast to the usual verbose, stuffed-shirt, politician that his audience had come to identify with the ruling class.

In this new Age of the Common Man, Crockett was the perfect choice to represent frontier settlers. Up until then, government had been dominated by eastern elites and wealthy southern planters, who chose candidates from their own class, while ordinary citizens, especially the poor, had little influence. Westward expansion created new districts that demanded representation in the legislature, and citizens became empowered, seeking candidates who lived among them and understood their world.

Crockett's competitors underestimated him at their peril. He had the rare ability of connecting with voters on a personal level, remembering names and faces and asking after wives and children.[21] While his early stump speeches were short on content and long on anecdote, they were effective. He was careful to avoid taking definitive stands on controversial issues, lest he offend one side or the other, as in a dispute over where to locate the Hickman County seat,[22] but he endeared himself to the voters, and they came to believe that he could be trusted to represent them and their interests. His campaign delivery included scathing satire directed at his competitors (more often than not playing the poor against the wealthy), exaggerated stories about bear hunting, a healthy dose of "aw shucks" self-directed humor, and speeches that generally ended with an offer to treat the crowd at a nearby liquor stand. The audience identified with this backwoods raconteur, and after Crockett spoke, his opponents were likely to find themselves staring down from the stump into a very sparse assembly.[23] From this broad caricature in the early campaigns, another character would emerge that would grow into a fictional, larger-than-life figure, and eventually become the legendary "Davy" Crockett.

With homespun wit counterbalanced by a serious populist message, and an unfailing desire to legislate for his constituents, his electioneering style paid off, and he won a seat in the legislature by a two-to-one margin in August of 1821. Crockett simply knew what kind of people he would represent better than his opponents did.

On September 17, 1821, the first session of the Fourteenth General Assembly convened in Murfreesboro,[24] and Crockett was put on the Committee of Propositions and Grievances. Foremost among his concerns, however, was the issue of land ownership. Many of his constituents did not hold legal title to their land, although they had staked out homesteads and improved their plots. As mere occupants, or squatters, their existence was precarious. The issue was complicated by the fact that eastern Tennessee had been ceded to the United States by North Carolina, which had issued to its Revolutionary War veterans land warrants that Tennessee was required to honor, many of which wound up in the hands of land speculators. Few occupants in Crockett's district could afford the speculator's inflated price for a warrant, which would provide them legal title to their land. Speculators, then, were able to use the warrants to displace occupants who had improved the plots and increased the property values, and sell the claims to the highest bidder. Crockett would spend his entire career in government attempting to rectify this situation.

His votes in his first term showed his determination to give voice to the concerns of the poor farmers like himself who made up a large part of his constituency. He introduced legislation that would reform the way land-grant surveys were issued, to prevent a small number of wealthier buyers from obtaining the best plots. This eventually became law. He voted to eliminate heavy penalties on overdue property taxes, which fell disproportionately on the poor.[25] He voted against a bill authorizing courts to hire out insolvent defendants to work off costs charged against them in criminal trials, and voted against a number of petitions for divorce, including one from former Governor Joseph McMinn.[26] He continued to support bills that offered relief for the poor and underprivileged, including legislation that provided help for widows and orphans, and voted against repealing a law that allowed the redemption of slaves from bondage. He cast a vote for the relief of Mathias, a free black man. Crockett generally considered individual requests for relief on a case by case basis, taking into account the needs of the individual and the merits of each request. He consistently favored broad relief measures designed to help his constituents as a whole.

Crockett argued against legislation that prohibited gaming, an activity for which he had a particular fondness. In an 1831 letter to the editor of the Southern Statesman, a critic of Crockett writing under the pseudonym "Junius Brutus" recalled that during Crockett's tenure in the state legislature he had "lost a part and sometimes the whole of his wages at the gaming table, and sometimes had to borrow money to bring him home, and some of that money is not paid yet."[27] Crockett's gambling seems indefensible in light of his constant debt and his obligations to his family, but author Robert Morgan, in his biography of Daniel Boone, attempted to explain the problem. "Debtors, like gamblers, live in an uneasy state of hope and despair but try to dwell on hope. The qualities that made Boone such a legendary man of the frontier also contributed to the mire of debt he never seemed to struggle out of, for by the time he paid off one debt he had already acquired others. His hopefulness, his curiosity, his forward looking faith in himself and others, his confidence in his destiny—characteristics that made him a successful hunter and explorer and leader—seemed to cripple him when it came to business."[28] The same might be said of Crockett.

Despite being a newcomer to state government, Crockett was assertive and showed no reluctance to debate, though his rough-around-the-edges demeanor and tenuous grasp of proper grammar surely caused eyes to roll on occasion. After he made a statement in session that likely showcased his colorful vernacular, James C. Mitchell[29] rose and, in reply, referred to Crockett as the "Gentleman from the Cane." Crockett was insulted and angered at this epithet, which was tantamount to calling him a hick from the sticks. He called Mitchell aside after the session and demanded satisfaction. Mitchell demurred, and claimed that he had meant no disrespect. Crockett cooled off and accepted Mitchell's apology, but some time later, after a confrontation with another member of the legislature, Mitchell lost a ruffle from the front of his shirt. Crockett found it on the ground, pinned it to his own homespun cotton shirt, and strutted into the session, taking a seat next to Mitchell. The members of the house found the burlesque hilarious, and roared their approval. Crockett appropriated the "Gentleman from the Cane" sobriquet as well, turning a liability into an asset, and now saw the stereotype as a political device that would work in his favor.[30]

It was during this first session that Crockett's mill was destroyed and he was forced to request a leave of absence to travel home and see to his business. Upon his return to the legislature, he voted twice to table resolutions calling for a state constitutional convention, although he supported the idea of a convention. Since he had voted for the resolution in September, on the surface this seems like a political flip-flop on the issue, but it was an astute move on Crockett's part. He favored postponing the resolution until Governor Carroll could call a second session to address the issue, which proponents of the convention thought would provide a more favorable setting for passing the bill. They were, however, mistaken and the opposition carried the day. Crockett's vote illustrates an understanding of the political maneuvering that was sometimes necessary to get things done, and shows that he knew how to "play the game" as well as the next fellow.

Crockett also cast his vote in favor of a bill that encouraged the building of iron works in the state. This support of manufacturing interests was an early indicator of a pro-business stance he would resume later in his career.

His experience as a justice of the peace served him well when a motion was made to overturn a prohibition on justices of the peace receiving fees for their services. Crockett argued that allowing the practice encouraged corruption, and he couched his remarks in familiar populist rhetoric. He said that since militiamen or men who worked on roads were not paid for their services, and that magistrates were exempt from both of these jobs, that was compensation enough. He then took a more personal shot at those who asked for compensation, claiming, "I know many of these gentry, who would rather serve forty years as a justice of the peace, than to serve one six month's tour of duty fighting the battles of their country. The dull pursuits of civil life is much more congenial to the taste of some of these gentlemen than wild war's deadly blasts." He went on to state that "there is no evil so great in society—among the poor people—as the management and intrigue of meddling justices and dirty constables." Crockett's position carried the day, and the bill was rejected. Of the remainder of his first term in the legislature, Crockett simply stated that he served out his time, likely preparing for his run for reelection.[31]

In 1823, Crockett ran against Dr. William Butler, and it was during this contest that he put a keener edge on the electioneering skills he had begun to hone in 1821. He said that Butler was "the most talented man I ever run against for any office,"[32] but he quickly developed a campaign strategy to take him on. Butler was married to Andrew Jackson's niece, and was wealthy and well-connected. On the stump, Crockett played up Butler's wealth, depicting him as out of touch with the populace. He ridiculed Butler's lifestyle, pointing out that the carpets in Butler's home were made of material finer than any worn by the wives and daughters of the common people.[33]

Crockett continued to utilize his "Gentleman from the Cane" persona, and told Butler at one stump meeting, "I have just crept out of the cane to see what discoveries I could make among the white folks." It was during this conversation that Crockett came up with a tall tale that has been misrepresented as fact ever since; he told Butler that he planned on campaigning while wearing a hunting shirt with two oversized pockets, one holding a liquor bottle and one a twist of tobacco. When he met a potential supporter, he'd offer him a drink and, if the man spit out his chaw to imbibe, Crockett would offer him another plug of tobacco, thus leaving him no worse off than when they first met. Drawing on his prodigious reputation as a hunter, he also mentioned that despite Butler's financial superiority, he thought he could finance his own campaign by selling wolf pelts for bounties. By all accounts, the campaign was good-natured, and when Crockett was victorious, Butler harbored no ill will. Crockett might not have been so lucky where Andrew Jackson was concerned. Standing up to Old Hickory or one of his allies was a risky proposition.[34]

During his second term, Crockett continued to push legislation that would enable his constituents to own the land they occupied and improved, opposing measures that would require cash-only sales and raise the price of land to as much as $2.00 per acre, while favoring a measure to allow widows to keep their land. Most of these measures were adopted. He also tried to frustrate the efforts of speculators, who sought to buy up the parcels for cash and resell them at higher prices to the occupants.[35] Crockett became distrustful of the legislature as he watched the passage of most of these measures, which worked against the interests of the poor. He typically found himself at odds with James Polk and Felix Grundy,[36] who would soon be numbered among Andrew Jackson's staunchest supporters.

In 1823 Crockett struck another blow at Jackson and the Overton alliance. When John Williams[37] was up for reelection as senator from Tennessee, Jackson ran against him. Crockett backed Williams, further alienating Jackson and the Overton men. Though Williams was defeated, Crockett later defended his support as "the best vote I ever gave," and claimed that it proved early on that he was an independent thinker and not a weak-willed Jackson crony.[38]

Throughout his second term, Crockett continued to advocate legislation that protected the poor, including voting in September of 1823 for a bill that would abolish imprisonment for debt, which passed on the first reading. He again voted against hearing petitions for divorce, saying that he was opposed to "all divorces in general," and thought that it was a poor use of the legislature's time to consider divorce complaints. He also introduced a bill that would give traveling entertainers licenses that were recognized statewide rather than require them to apply for permits in individual counties.[39]

Crockett sided with James Polk in supporting a bill that would pay trial jurors for their services. Felix Grundy supported an amendment to the bill, proposed by Representative Williams, which would have included paying road workers for their services, and claimed that road workers "had as hard a time as those who lounged about a court-house and heard lawyers speak, where they could derive some information." Grundy mentioned that he really opposed the entire measure and thought the expense incurred would result in the insolvency of some counties. Crockett argued against the amendment, adding a bit of humor and a dig at Grundy and other legal professionals in the process. He said that men who worked on the public roads benefited from their own labors and weren't inconvenienced, since the jobs were close to home and scheduled in advance. Trial jurors, however, were tapped for that job while visiting the courthouse on other business and were expected to sit with no prior notification. They not only had to put their personal affairs on hold or face heavy fines, but were also subjected to "hearing lawyers talk, and there was not much ease or information in listening to some of them."[40] Crockett further commented that he thought the amendment was proposed only to destroy Polk's original bill. He supported the bill, but opposed the amendment. The amendment failed.

On October 30, Crockett spoke against a bill to "preserve the purity of elections" that would have prohibited candidates from treating voters to drinks at campaign events. Since this bill would seriously cramp Crockett's electioneering method and could not really be enforced, he opposed the measure, stating plainly that "he could get along as well with this bill as without it." If treating was banned, he could always get a friend to treat, thus serving the same purpose, and "he was in favor of letting every man treat as he pleased." Others disingenuously argued that the treating at these events was social drinking and not intended to influence the voters either way, but Crockett cut right to the chase: candidates treated to get votes. It has been suggested that this bill was intended as a referendum on the relatively new style of electioneering of which Crockett was a practitioner: taking to the stump to get the votes of the commoners in a manner that political elites thought was beneath them and denigrating to the political system. This freewheeling campaigning was a departure from the old aristocratic pattern of the office seeking the man and elites choosing the candidates in private. Proponents of that old style found the new practice of overtly seeking an office crass and distasteful. The electorate, however, ate it up. They'd much rather get lubricated and listen to demagoguery and anecdote than suffer through boring oration from the upper class.[41]

In September of 1824, Crockett sponsored additional legislation that attempted to protect his constituents from dishonest warrants held by land speculators, and proposed a bill that would improve the navigation of waters in the Western District, as easier access would reduce prices of goods in the west.[42] During the same session he introduced a bill to establish a chancery court in the Western District, and proposed "a bill to deal out justice more equally," which advocated an increased apportionment of funds to his district due to the increase in population. He explained that "the people being new settlers generally had use for a little money until they could get fairly underway." All measures passed on the first reading.[43]

By the time Crockett completed his second term in October of 1824, he had an established track record as a consistent champion of the people in his district. He issued a circular to his constituents dated October 25, 1824, in which he delineated his accomplishments in the last session and urged his supporters to vote for Andrew Jackson for president. Crockett managed quite a balancing act in his home state. Although he had voted against Jackson for the Senate and continued to be affiliated with the Erwin group, Crockett, always attuned to the sentiments of his constituents, claimed to be a Jackson man. Despite his differences with Jackson and the Overton men, Crockett still found much to admire in Old Hickory, a westerner who stood in opposition to the eastern intelligentsia who had dominated national politics since the Revolution. Although Jackson was from an economic sector far removed from Crockett's own lower-middle-class status, there was much about the man to which Crockett could relate. He and Jackson relied largely on personal popularity to carry them to political victory.[44] Both were self-made men who rose from poverty and hardship and aspired to positions on the national stage. Both achieved acclaim during their military service; Jackson's defeat of the British at New Orleans in the War of 1812 had earned him the gratitude of the nation and, while Crockett's military accomplishments were comparatively minor, his militia service accounted for much of his initial popularity and served as a springboard for his political aspirations.[45] Both men claimed a kinship with the common man that resonated with the people, and, to the electorate, Crockett's support of Jackson wasn't much of a disconnect: they too had a tendency to vote for the man rather than identify with any particular ideology.

Crockett no doubt expected that Jackson's bid would have long coattails, as he also used the circular to announce his own candidacy for the U.S. Congress in the forthcoming election. His opponent was the incumbent Adam Alexander, an established politician with a distinct monetary advantage over the financially strapped Crockett, who had returned to his home in Gibson County and was scratching out a living hunting and trying to make a success of the family farm. Alexander was experiencing a wave of unpopularity in the district because of a vote in favor of the 1824 tariff law, and Crockett thought he could ride the issue to victory, but he miscalculated. Alexander not only had deep pockets but, more importantly, the backing of the Overton alliance. John Overton was still looking for some payback for Crockett's support of John Williams over Jackson for senator and, writing under the pseudonym "Aristides," Overton penned a series of attack articles that were published in the Jackson Gazette in July of 1825. Overton accused Crockett of negligence or incompetence in allowing an East Tennessee militia brigade to be attached to the Western District rather than raising a brigade locally, and argued that Crockett had voted to change the time the county and circuit courts would sit without notifying the citizens. Crockett's supporters blamed the militia issue on a clerical error, but Overton's accusations had traction. The Overton editorials, Crockett's under-financed campaign, and a rise in cotton prices which undercut his argument against Alexander's support of the tariff, all contributed to his loss in the 1825 election, and the relentless assaults in the press were a harbinger of what he would experience from the Overton alliance in future elections.

Crockett's hopes for an 1824 Jackson presidency were also dashed. Among the many people Andrew Jackson despised, he reserved a special hatred for Henry Clay, whose name had been inscribed on Jackson's enemies list since he had criticized Jackson for his 1818 invasion of Florida. But Clay earned Jackson's eternal enmity in 1824, when Jackson lost his first bid for the presidency to John Quincy Adams. After a campaign season that featured a crowded field of candidates, including Clay, the election of the president was thrown into the U.S. House of Representatives when none of the candidates received a majority of electoral votes. When the House awarded the presidency to Adams, Jackson, who had won the popular vote, accused Clay, then serving as house speaker, of using his influence to convince the House to back Adams in return for Adams' naming him secretary of state. Jackson and his supporters thereafter referred to this incident as the "corrupt bargain" that had cheated Old Hickory of the presidency, despite the will of the people.

Crockett's identification of himself as a Jackson man was somewhat incongruous in light of his continued affiliation with the Andrew Erwin faction in Tennessee. While he certainly related to the Jackson party's anti-aristocratic rhetoric, Crockett's economic status was far below that of the eastern and middle Tennessee contingency Jackson represented. Though Crockett and many of his constituents were slaveholders, they generally owned fewer than ten slaves, and were considered middle- to lower-middle-class farmers. Jackson however, was a member of the landed gentry; a large-scale planter with considerable land holdings who owned over a hundred slaves to work his plantation.[46] Though Jackson paid lip service to the poor and middle classes, his policies were not always in their best interests, and Crockett had differences with the Jacksonian ideology. Although he criticized the recklessness of independent state banks, many of which were run by land speculators, Crockett recognized the necessity of credit to enable the small farmer to be competitive in the market and in purchasing land. Jackson, on the other hand, favored a hard currency policy that gave the advantage to wealthier investors who had readily available cash. Crockett worked tirelessly to ensure that small businesses and farmers got a fair shake in the marketplace. Crockett's addresses on the stump and in print had pounded home the idea that the poor needed protection from the wealthy, and that he, a poor man himself, would be their most reliable defender.

Crockett wasted no time nursing his wounds after his loss, and instead jumped into an entrepreneurial enterprise in 1826 that was perhaps more ill-advised than his premature run for Congress. He tried his hand at a business that manufactured barrel staves, likely using his slaves for the labor, and loaded the cargo onto two flatboats for transport downriver to New Orleans for sale. Crockett's experience as a boatman was limited to some canoeing during his hunting trips, and the pilot he hired was woefully inadequate as well. Shortly after casting off he found his venture in deep trouble. Once his boats were on the powerful Mississippi River, pilot and crew completely lost confidence in their abilities, and the vessels began to drift uncontrollably. The neophyte crew decided to lash both craft together in an effort to gain some semblance of control, but that only made matters worse. Observers in other boats and on the shore attempted to shout instructions to the panicked crew, but they were unable to land the overloaded boats, which were caught in the river's current. They drifted until finally hitting a snag in the middle of the river, where both boats began to take on water and break apart. Thirty thousand barrel staves dumped into the roiling river, but Crockett was more concerned with his immediate survival than his lost investment. Trapped below deck in one of the sinking craft, he was pulled to safety through a porthole, and spent a long night clinging to the debris with the other deck hands until a passing boat picked up the shipwrecked crew the next morning and carried them to Memphis. The calamity would, however, prove to be a lucky break for Crockett.[47]

Marcus Winchester, a successful local merchant, took pity on the bedraggled party and outfitted them with new clothes and enough pocket money to get them home. Winchester was a progressive thinker who, as a slaveholder, paid his slaves for their services so they might one day purchase their emancipation. He was also a frequent advocate for local widows seeking assistance with their estates, and was held in high regard in Memphis and said to be "above cast and prejudice."[48] Winchester was well-connected politically and, after spending some time talking with Crockett, encouraged him to try again for the Ninth District congressional seat and offered to finance his campaign anonymously.[49]

In September, Crockett announced his candidacy in the Jackson Gazette, taking a swing at the current administration in Washington City and his rival, the incumbent Tennessee representative Adam Alexander, writing, "I am opposed to this man from the Yankee states called John Q. Adams; I am opposed to the conduct of the Kentucky orator, H. Clay; I am greatly opposed to our present Representative's vote on the Tariff. If I should be your choice, Fellow Citizens, there is one thing that I will promise—that I will not set silently, and permit the interest of my district to be neglected, while I have got a tongue to speak and a head to direct it. . . . I am the rich man's safe guard, and poor man's friend."[50]

Crockett thought Alexander was vulnerable because cotton prices had dropped again since his reelection, and calculated that he could use that to his advantage. He also hoped to benefit from a third party, William Arnold, entering the race, as it was expected he would drain votes away from Alexander rather than Crockett. A fourth candidate, John Cooke, tried to compete for a while as well, and launched accusations of insobriety and philandering against Crockett. When Crockett countered by upping the ante and leveling even more outrageous lies against his opponent, Cooke called him out on the stump for his prevarications. Crockett owned up to the slander, but defended his actions by claiming he'd only responded to Cooke in kind; that they were both lying, but at least he'd admitted it and certainly that made him the more trustworthy of the two. The electorate, charmed by Crockett, bought his explanation, and Cooke was so incensed he dropped out of the race.[51]

On the hustings, Crockett resumed his standard practice of treating, but made a point of mentioning, with tongue firmly in cheek, that he supplied the booze to be sociable, "not to get elected, of course—for that would be against the law."[52] Aside from the usual crowd-pleasing anecdotes and hijinks, Crockett's stump speeches became more issue oriented. He relied heavily on anti-Adams rhetoric and incorporated the perceived injustice of Clay's "corrupt bargain" into his oratory, hoping to score some points with incensed Jackson supporters. More importantly, he continued to voice his identification with the poorest people of society and promised to protect them and advocate their common cause. Land ownership remained his central issue, and he promised, given the chance, to deliver legal ownership to those occupants who had worked so hard to better themselves by putting their blood and sweat into improving their little homesteads.

After the drubbing he had taken in the press from Overton/Aristides during his failed run for Congress in 1825, Crockett was more media savvy this time around and in September issued another circular, hitting hard at Alexander's support of the tariff and taking a general anti-protectionist stance. He articulated his opposition to the Adams presidency and stoked the flames of regional loyalty by reminding readers that their interests were being undermined by those of the "Yankees" in power. He also took the opportunity to champion Jackson's war record and personal integrity, and wrote, in conclusion, "I go for him; I do not pretend to be a great politician; you have my ideas in a plain homespun manner."[53]

When Crockett's opposition published pseudonymous editorials in the Jackson Gazette, he was quick to respond, both in print and in personal appearances. In a letter to the editor of the Gazette in December of 1826, Crockett wrote, "I am the Dave Crockett who volunteered and shouldered his knapsack and gun, and served twelve months under the immortal Old Hickory, in endeavoring to put down the enemies of our country, who spared neither age nor sex; I am the same Dave Crockett who had the honor of representing in the legislature of this state, in 1821 and '22, the people of Lawrence and Hickman counties, and that their rights were strictly attended to and they [were] pleased, I must believe, as I have heard no complaints; I am the same Dave Crockett who had the honor and pleasure of representing the counties of Madison, Henderson, Perry, Humphreys, Carroll, Gibson, Haywood, Tipton, and Dyer, in the years 1823 and '24, in the legislature of this state, and who stood firm and unshaken, upon the political watch tower of his country's rights—I call upon the people of this District to examine the journals and judge for themselves; I am the self same Dave Crockett who has had, and now has the daring impudence to oppose the immaculate Adam R. Alexander, or anybody else, for a seat in the next Congress of the United States."[54]

Crockett's references to himself as "Dave" may indicate either a transitional stage in the development of the "Davy" persona, or may be a phonetic spelling of Davy (this is the only example of him referring to himself thusly), and the cadence of the address is certainly similar to the braggadocio style of the riverboat men he must have heard during his barrel staves adventure on the Mississippi and incorporated into his oratory. On the stump, he was also claiming the ability to "whip his weight in wildcats, jump up higher, fall down lower, and drink more liquors than any man in the state,"[55] to the delight of most of his audience.

In May of 1827, he struck at Alexander directly in an open letter published in the Gazette, questioning his support of the Tennessee land bill's provisions to use funds raised in the sale of the public lands to finance colleges rather than common schools. He drove his message home in the press, and again utilized the overt language of class warfare to get his point across. "Very few of our citizens, even those who are well to do in the world, can afford to pay two or three hundred dollars a year, (besides all the necessary expenditures incidental to the distance) to send their sons to these Colleges. I am not opposed to liberal education; on the contrary, I wish most sincerely that we were all able to give our sons College educations. But as matters now stand, my maxim is let the rich men educate their own sons with their own means, without imposing directly or indirectly any part of the burthen by public donations out of the common stock, be they in land or money, upon the poor yeomanry of our country, who are the last bone and sinew of the great body politick: its support in peace and its safeguard in war: unless the poor themselves can stand an equal chance for an equal participation in the measure."[56]

In June, Crockett, stumping in McNairy County, attacked his opponent in his usual manner, but also began to complain about the press. He was particularly bothered by the unsigned editorials and letters that opposed him, and was openly critical of the editorial policies of the Jackson Gazette. The editors responded by reminding him, "When men become candidates for office, the people of this country will enquire into their merits, and speak and act freely about them; and so long as we conduct a public journal we will be their organ, notwithstanding we may be traduced by many or few; whether candidates for office or their undertrappers."[57] Sometimes Crockett could dish it out better than he could take it.

Adam Alexander and William Arnold hammered each other on the campaign trail and tried to ignore Crockett, probably hoping to render him insignificant. It proved to be a failed strategy. At one gathering, Arnold's speech was interrupted by the racket generated by a nearby flock of guinea fowl. Crockett jumped up and claimed that the birds were calling out for him, crying, "Crockett, Crockett, Crockett." Arnold seemed, Crockett wrote, "mighty bad plagued. But he got more plagued than this at the polls in August."[58] He certainly did. Crockett handily defeated Alexander and Arnold by a plurality of 2,223 votes.[59] He borrowed another hundred dollars from Winchester for travel expenses and packed his bags, ready to take "Davy" onto the national stage.

Not everyone was enamored with Crockett's alter ego. Some constituents found "Davy" too outrageous and over-the-top for their taste. Henry Clay was warned about Crockett's imminent arrival by his son-in-law James Erwin, who told him, "Col. Crockett is perhaps the most illiterate Man, that you have ever met in congress Hall he is not only illiterate but he is rough & uncouth, talks much & loudly, and is by far, more in his proper place, when hunting a Bear, in a Cane Brake, than he will be in the

Capital, yet he is a man worth attending to, he is independent and fearless & has a popularity at home that is unaccountable. . . ." Despite the caveat, Erwin and his faction still valued Crockett's allegiance and encouraged Clay to agree to Crockett's request for a meeting upon his arrival in Washington. Erwin told Clay, "He is the only man that I now know in Tennessee that Could openly oppose Genl. Jackson in his District & be elected to Congress."[60]

Another Tennessean wrote to North Carolina Governor William Graham, "Our Representation in the next Congress will be characterized by dullness, imprudence and blackguardism."[61] Clearly, not everyone was a fan of the Gentleman from the Cane, and though Crockett had ridden the character to victory, he would soon find that "Davy" was indeed a ring-tailed roarer, half-horse, half-alligator, who would prove to be extremely hard to manage.[62]

---

[1] Crockett to James Blackburn, February 5, 1828, Tennessee Historical Society, Tennessee State Library and Archives (hereinafter, TSLA).

[2] David Crockett, *A Narrative of the Life of David Crockett of the State of Tennessee*, ed. James A. Shackford and Stanley J. Folmsbee (Knoxville: University of Tennessee Press, 1973), 144–45.

[3] Crockett to *Telegraph and Intelligencer*, December 12, 1829, published in *Boston Patriot*, December 17, 1829. Crockett explained that the men were forced to leave the premises early due to a storm but were nevertheless charged in full for their stay, and complained that Briceland had taken advantage of him on several occasions.

[4] For a thorough analysis of Crockett's height, see Thomas E. Scruggs, "The Physical Stature of David Crockett: A Re-analysis of the Historical Record," *Journal of South Texas* 9, no. 1, (Spring 1996): 1–29.

[5] Crockett to Blackburn, February 5, 1828.

[6] Nathaniel Claiborne was a six-term congressman from Virginia who, like Crockett, ran as a Jacksonian but eventually left the Jackson ranks. He was the author of *Notes on the War in the South* (Richmond: William Ramsay, 1819), a history of the War of 1812, and may have provided some encouragement or minor input during the composition of Crockett's *Narrative*.

[7] Perry M. Goldman and James S. Young, eds., *United States Congressional Directories: 1789–1840* (New York: Columbia University Press, 1973), 277.

[8] Crockett to Blackburn, February 5, 1828.

[9] Crockett's chronic debt is well documented. For more information on his gambling and drinking, see *(Jackson) Southern Statesman*, July 9, 1831, and Crockett to Jacob Dixon, April 11, 1834, Christie's Auction Catalog, June 17, 2003. The *New York Sunday Morning News*, December 6, 1835, cited in Gary Zaboly, "Crockett Goes To Texas: A Newspaper Chronology," *Journal of the Alamo Battlefield Association* 1, no. 1 (Summer 1995): 10, also cast aspersions on Crockett for his alleged gambling habit, and stated, "If there be, however, such a thing as a faro-bank to be found in Texas, we fear Davy will forget all his prudential maxims." During his 1834 tour of the northeast, Crockett was reported to have lost $160 to a pickpocket in Philadelphia, and was quoted in the *(Portsmouth) New Hampshire Gazette* (quoting the original report in the *(Washington) National Intelligencer*, May 20, 1834, as having said, "Gentlemen, this is not the heaviest loss I have met with. Not long since I was coaxed to go to the Faro table in Washington, and (would you believe it?) I lost $1500!" Other newspapers picked up the report, prompting a response from Crockett. "I did, when I first came to Congress, several years ago" he wrote, "indulge in betting against that game, (Faro) and it is the only game I ever did bet at, and I am ashamed that I ever saw that played: for I do not know any other game in the world. Indeed, I cannot say that I ever *knew* that game, for it has injured me, but not to the extent stated in the Commercial Intelligencer for the best of all reasons, that I never had fifteen hundred dollars at one time in my life. Nor did I ever lose the sixth part of that sum in one night." Crockett to Editor, *National Intelligencer*, cited in *New Bedford Mercury*, May 30, 1834.

[10] James Atkins Shackford, *David Crockett: The Man and the Legend*, John B. Shackford, ed. (Chapel Hill: University of North Carolina Press, 1956), 34. The Crocketts continued to add to their family. In 1818, Elizabeth gave birth to Rebecca Elvira, and in 1821 to Matilda.

[11] Crockett, *Narrative of the Life*, 127.

[12] An extended examination of Crockett's Creek War service is beyond the scope of this book; the reader is referred to the Shackford-Folmsbee edition of Crockett's *Narrative*, cited above. Crockett tends to amplify and, in some instances, misstate his activities during the war, and the annotations by the editors provide a necessary corrective to Crockett's original text.

[13] Ibid., 133–34.

[14] Ibid., 135.

[15] Ibid., 137–38.

[16] Andrew Erwin was a merchant and native Virginian who had moved to North Carolina, where he helped establish Asheville, before relocating to Tennessee. Erwin's animosity toward Andrew Jackson dated at least from 1806, when Jackson killed Charles Dickinson, Erwin's son-in-law, in a duel. Andrew Jackson, *Memoirs of General Andrew Jackson*, (Auburn, New York: James C. Derby & Co., 1845), 157. In 1811, Erwin brought suit against Jackson in a land dispute and in 1819 he published a protest alleging Jackson and his friend John Eaton were involved in illegal land speculation. This charge nearly resulted in a duel between Eaton and Erwin.

Erwin had hoped to be appointed West Tennessee district marshal, but Jackson, determined to get even, charged Erwin with slave trading and took his complaint to President James Monroe in order to stop the appointment. Attorney General William Wirt investigated the charges, and eventually Erwin was found culpable. Thomas P. Abernethy, *From Frontier to Plantation in Tennessee* (Chapel Hill: University of North Carolina Press, 1932), 262–64; Andrew Burstein, *The Passions of Andrew Jackson*, (New York: Vintage, 2004), 140–43.

In 1828, during Jackson's second presidential campaign, Erwin leveled the same charge at Jackson and published a pamphlet with the provocative title "Gen. Jackson's Negro Speculations, and His Traffic in Human Flesh, Examined and Established by Positive Proof" (Nashville: n.s., 1828), Miscellaneous Pamphlet Collection, Library of Congress. In the publication, Erwin and officials of the Bank of Nashville (including bank president Boyd McNairy) produced bank ledgers showing that Jackson and two business partners had purchased and sold slaves in 1811. Jackson claimed that he had not been an active partner in the enterprise, just the financial guarantor. A heated and lengthy public exchange followed, during which Erwin publicized Jackson's 1806 involvement with Aaron Burr and did his best to tie Jackson to an obscure Burr conspiracy allegedly designed to remove western states and the Louisiana Territory from the Union (*Baltimore Patriot*, August 29, 1828).

The bad blood between Jackson and Erwin continued for the rest of their lives.

[17] John Overton was a native Virginian who came to Nashville circa 1789. He was a roommate of Andrew Jackson's, and the two men subsequently became business partners and political allies. A prominent banker, land speculator, lawyer, and one of the wealthiest men in Tennessee, he served on the Tennessee Supreme Court from 1804 to 1816, and was one of the founders of Memphis. From 1803 to 1806, Overton helped negotiate a settlement with North Carolina regarding the cession of lands in the Western District of Tennessee, and agreed to recognize warrants issued by North Carolina to Revolutionary War veterans redeemable for land in the Western District. Overton formed an alliance within the state that was instrumental in Jackson's political ascendancy. Philip R. Langsdon, *Tennessee: A Political History* (Franklin, Tennessee: Hillsboro Press, 2000), 21; *Tennessee Encyclopedia of History and Culture* online, http://tennesseeencyclopedia.net

[18] Robert E. Corlew, *Tennessee: A Short History*, (Knoxville: University of Tennessee Press, 1981), 162.

[19] Crockett, *Narrative of the Life*, 140–42.

[20] Ibid., 49.

[21] James Strange French, *Sketches and Eccentricities of Col. David Crockett of West Tennessee* (New York: J. & J. Harper, 1833), 57.

[22] Crockett, *Narrative of the Life*, 139–40.

[23] Ibid., 143.

[24] Spelled Murfreesborough in Crockett's time, later changed to the current spelling.

[25] Stanley J. Folmsbee and Anna Grace Catron, "The Early Career of David Crockett," *East Tennessee Historical Society's Publications*, no. 28 (1956): 72–73.

[26] Joseph McMinn was a Revolutionary War veteran and governor of Tennessee from 1815 to 1821. McMinn's third marriage, to Nancy Williams, was troubled. Mrs. McMinn accused the governor of abandoning her family for long periods of time while he lived with Indians, and she subsequently left him. McMinn filed for divorce, and his wife was represented in the case by Felix Grundy. The Tennessee House of Representatives voted against granting the divorce, but the couple remained separated. Langsdon, *Tennessee*, 50–51.

[27] *(Jackson) Southern Statesman*, July 9, 1831.

[28] Robert Morgan, *Boone: A Biography* (Chapel Hill: Algonquin Books, 2007), 79.

[29] James C. Mitchell went on to serve as a Jacksonian in the U.S. House of Representatives in the Nineteenth and Twentieth Congresses, and later ran unsuccessfully for governor of Mississippi as a Whig. Biographical Directory of the United States Congress online, http://bioguide.congress.gov.

[30] French, *Sketches and Eccentricities*, 57–59.

[31] Crockett, *Narrative of the Life*, 155.

[32] Ibid., 167–68.

[33] Ibid., note, 166.

[34] Ibid., 168–69.

[35] *Nashville Whig*, September 29, 1823.

[36] Felix Grundy moved to Tennessee in 1807 from Kentucky, where he had served as chief justice of the Kentucky Supreme Court. Grundy represented Tennessee in the U.S. Congress from 1811 to 1814 and served in the Tennessee State Legislature from 1814 to 1819 and as a U.S. senator from 1829 to 1838. He was appointed U.S. attorney general by President Martin Van Buren in 1838, and served one year before resigning and returning to the Senate. He was reelected in 1839 and served until his death in 1840. Langsdon, *Tennessee*, 82.

[37] John Williams served in the U.S. Senate from 1813 to 1823. The Overton alliance, hoping eventually to elect Andrew Jackson president, realized that Jackson needed a high-profile spot in the political arena prior to making a bid for the nation's highest office. The group initially considered running Jackson against William Carroll for governor, a risky proposition considering Carroll's popularity. Were Jackson to lose, his chances for the presidency could have been dashed, so the Overton alliance targeted Williams' Senate seat instead. (Langsdon, *Tennessee,* 62–63.)

[38] Crockett, *Narrative of the Life,* 171–72.

[39] *Nashville Whig,* September 22, 1823.

[40] Ibid., October 6, 1823.

[41] Guy S. Miles, "David Crockett Evolves, 1821–1824," *American Quarterly* 8, no. 1 (Spring 1956): 56–57.

[42] *Nashville Whig,* September 27, 1824.

[43] Ibid.

[44] For an interesting contemporary analysis of voter's preferences in the Jacksonian era, see Francis J. Grund, *Aristocracy in America,* (London: Richard Bentley, New Burlington St., 1839), 239–41.

[45] French, *Sketches and Eccentricities,* 55.

[46] Joseph John Arpad, "David Crockett: An Original Legendary Eccentricity and Early American Character," Ph.D. dissertation, Duke University, 1969, 156.

[47] Crockett, *Narrative of the Life,* 195–200.

[48] James D. Davis, *History of the City of Memphis,* (Memphis: Hite, Crumpton, & Kelly, 1873), 70–71.

[49] Ibid., 150.

[50] Crockett to Republican voters of the Ninth Congressional District, *Jackson Gazette,* September 16, 1826.

[51] Davis, *History of the City of Memphis,* 150–51.

[52] Crockett, *Narrative of the Life,* 165.

[53] September 29, 1826 circular, printed in *Jackson Gazette,* October 7, 1826.

[54] Crockett to Editor, *Jackson Gazette,* December 23, 1826.

[55] Arpad, "David Crockett," 43.

[56] Crockett to Adam Alexander, *Jackson Gazette,* May 5, 1827.

[57] *Jackson Gazette,* June 23, 1827.

[58] Crockett, *Narrative of the Life,* 204–205.

[59] Ibid., note, 202.

[60] James Erwin to Henry Clay, September 30, 1827, *The Papers of Henry Clay, Vol. 6, Secretary of State 1827,* Mary W. M. Hargreaves and James F. Hopkins, eds. (Lexington: University Press of Kentucky, 1981), 1098.

[61] Arpad, "David Crockett," 34.

Chapter 2

"To Make of Your Citizen a Landholder"
The Tennessee Land Bill (1821–1829)

*T*hroughout his political career, one major issue preoccupied Crockett: the disposition of public lands in *his West Tennessee district. There, many poor, small farmers had scratched out a living and built homes on land to which they either had no formal title or which they had obtained with land warrants that were later challenged, sometimes through corrupt practices. Most paid for that land on credit and often found it difficult to make timely payments or to pay property taxes. At times they were the victims of tight money policies, particularly during the Panic of 1819, and at others of fraudulent warrants.*

———————

Squatters were settlers who occupied and built improvements on land to which they held no legal title. The practice was illegal, since squatters were trespassers on federal land, but had been tolerated for years due to the government's inability to stop the wave of settlers who migrated westward to seize new lands. Western states supported the practice, while others urged speedy sale of land to force squatters to either buy or leave. Squatters, or "actual occupants," and many westerners, including Crockett, claimed that they had taken risks by moving to the frontier to populate the land, fight Indians and the British, and cultivate and improve the land, and were entitled to keep it, either for free or at a minimal price. The dispute was partly an extension of the broader fight over the disposal of federal land, which pitted different sections of the country against one another. Westerners favored cheap land and encouraged migration from the East, while other regions resisted that approach for various reasons.[1]

Tennessee's land headache began with the very creation of the state, which had been carved out of territory ceded to the federal government by North Carolina in 1789. The deal required the new state to satisfy countless North Carolina land warrants that had been issued to its Revolutionary War veterans for their wartime service, and warrants the state had issued to redeem specie certificates, which the state had issued to help defray the costs of the war. Holders of those warrants would claim much of Tennessee's land.

In 1806 the United States, North Carolina, and Tennessee concluded a compact that permitted Tennessee to locate and grant the warrants for the state of North Carolina. To sweeten the pill, the agreement stipulated that out of every six square miles set off for that purpose, 640 acres should be set aside by the state to sell to raise funds for common schools, which was standard government practice regarding public lands. However, the 1806 compact stipulated that the school lands be set aside "where existing claims will allow the same."[2] Thus, although Tennessee might have obtained an estimated 444,444 acres to fund common schools, the actual amount of school lands depended on how much remained after the warrants were satisfied. The law also established a north-south line through the state, called the Congressional Reservation Line. It separated approximately three-fourths of the state lying to the east and north of the line from the remainder of the state, west and south of it.[3] The warrants were to be satisfied with land in the eastern part of the state, which was ceded to Tennessee and where the state's allotment of school land also would be located. The western portion was to remain federal public land. However, the process was derailed when it became obvious that there were so many North Carolina warrants it would be impossible to satisfy them all in the eastern section.

Tennessee also claimed that satisfying the North Carolina warrants reduced the land actually available for schools to less than 23,000 acres.[4] Eventually there proved to be insufficient land in the eastern part of the state, and in 1818 Congress opened the western portion of the state to continue satisfying the warrants, even though that land had been acquired from the Chickasaw, not from North Carolina. No provision was made for setting aside lands to fund schools.[5] Tennessee argued that, unless that western land was ceded to the state, it would not realize any money for schools, since it would quickly be taken up by warrants. However, Tennessee had been negligent in setting aside school lands in other instances, and the federal government still felt obliged to honor the warrants, regardless of how much land that might consume, or how little might be left for schools.

Multiplying Tennessee's burden was the degree of fraud connected with these warrants. Many of the Revolutionary War veterans, for whom the warrants were intended, were dead and their warrants had passed to their heirs. Other warrants were simply issued in the name of those who had already died. Many were sold to land speculators, who stood to profit from their resale; some were simply forgeries. Making matters worse was a nefarious practice of "removing entries," which permitted multiple uses of the same warrant. Under this arrangement a person who had obtained poor-quality land, or land that he no longer wanted, in East Tennessee with a warrant, could buy his warrant back from the state for a mere 12½ cents per acre and use it again to obtain better land in the Western District. While the state was no doubt happy to enjoy these revenues, this practice went beyond the intent of the warrants, and it would wreak havoc on the poor farmers in the West. In many cases the warrants were used to bump squatters from land that they had improved, but to which they held no legal title, on the gamble that they would be able to eventually make it pay, but many never earned enough to buy the land.[6]

The two-time warrant holders could make a tidy profit by selling their restored warrant for a dollar or two per acre. They might extend generous terms to buyers, who could only afford to purchase on credit, perhaps giving them a year to pay and agreeing to accept crops or livestock as payment. Meanwhile, the warrant, which acted as a kind of mortgage, may have been sold to someone else, again at a profit, and the new owner might require a good deal more than livestock as payment. In order to meet those payments, some farmers might be forced to sell their last possession and even the land itself or simply default and move away, after which the warrant could be sold again. And there were more costs. Landowners were required to pay for official surveys in order to establish a legal claim to their land, and the surveyors charged hefty fees for that service. Some settlers were forced to sell their few possessions to pay those fees. Most had to borrow, which is why Crockett worked to establish more banks and easier credit in his district and to abolish penalties for delinquent property taxpayers. It is also why these farmers were hit so hard by restricted credit and hard-money policies.[7]

The tangled situation was further complicated by the liberality that was extended to warrant holders. The 1806 law required that warrants be satisfied with land "fit for cultivation," but much of the vacant land did not meet that requirement. To protect the warrant holders from getting stuck with poor-quality land, they were permitted to pick and choose which parcels they wanted until their entitlement was satisfied. Thus, someone with a warrant for one thousand acres could choose a number of separate plots of any size, say twenty acres or one hundred acres, in different places in order to obtain only lands that were "fit for cultivation." The best plots were soon snapped up under this practice, leaving a patchwork of poor lands scattered among the better-quality plots. No other public lands in any state were treated this way. Elsewhere, land was laid out in townships and single plots of specific sizes, and the landowners had to accept poor land along with the good on the plots they purchased.[8] Because of the wording in the 1806 law, Tennessee's public lands were treated in this unique, somewhat bizarre manner, which made a jumble of the state's land records and created uncertainty for occupants. Even those farmers who had obtained land with North Carolina warrants might find their titles challenged. Many plots were not clearly laid out, and two different parties might claim the same parcel of land without knowing it. In such cases, the warrant with the earliest date was honored, and the other party was left to search elsewhere for a place to live. This might happen to a farmer several times. Many of these earlier warrants were postdated or outright forgeries.

Land speculation was a lively enterprise at the time, and many politicians involved in the public lands issue were themselves speculators or large landowners, including Andrew Jackson. The wealthier landed gentry, planters and land speculators, many of whom lived in East and Middle Tennessee, enjoyed greater influence and representation in the state and federal governments than the farmers in the West did.

Crockett would represent this large Western District in Congress for three terms between 1827 and 1835. At that time only one congressional district in the entire country had a larger population, giving Crockett more constituents to answer to than any other member of Congress but one, most of them poor farmers, who became his most important constituency.[9] In truth, Crockett never asked for much. Most of his proposals simply called for the government to give the land outright to those farmers who lacked legal title, or at least extend them a fair chance to purchase it at a reasonable price. He also sought to protect those who had obtained their land legally, but who were being challenged by warrants, some of them fraudulent.

During his years in the Tennessee legislature and his first year in Congress, Crockett was allied with James K. Polk, who represented a nearby Tennessee district, and the two generally agreed on land policy. Later, however, Crockett came to distrust Polk and the legislature, doubting that they would ever grant relief to his poor constituents, and he began to pursue his own objectives in opposition to his colleagues. Polk would become one of Andrew Jackson's most devoted supporters, and the Jackson political organization would increasingly isolate Crockett. A careful consideration of the history of the land issue shows that it quickly became secondary to the Jacksonians' determination to marginalize and then eliminate Crockett, whom they came to view as disloyal and unreliable. They were aware of Crockett's growing popularity in his district and feared that any success by him in Congress would cement his standing there, making him a permanent threat to the Jackson machine. Thus the debate over the land bill must be seen as one of political maneuvering rather than a simple matter of how best to dispose of public lands. The land issue itself would revolve more around who would gain financially from its outcome, rather than justice for occupants.

LAND LAW AND THE TENNESSEE LEGISLATURE

When Crockett entered the state legislature in 1821, he and Polk worked with other delegates to establish a deadline after which no more North Carolina warrants would be honored, crafted legislation to give occupants the first opportunity to buy their land, and sought federal cession of the western land to Tennessee so that it could be sold by the state to raise funds for schools. Although deadlines on warrants were set, they were invariably extended.

In 1823 Congress removed the restriction in the 1806 law that prevented Tennessee from selling public land at less than the minimum price set by law. This allowed Tennessee to sell the refuse lands in the *eastern* part of the state that had not been taken up by North Carolina warrants, for a minimal price, which was set at 12½ cents per acre, with the proceeds to go to a new, permanent fund for common schools. The law also gave occupants of refuse lands first chance to buy them. Crockett supported the measure, hoping that the same policy might be adopted for the western part of the state, and he would continue to back the funding of common schools with revenues from public-land sales, provided that occupants of the land were protected and school funds equally disbursed throughout the state. Before long, however, he would conclude that his own state did not share his concern for the poor, and he began to doubt that he could rely on the legislature to protect his constituents' interests. When Felix Grundy, an influential politician, proposed to sell the public lands in the Hiwassee District at prices as high as $1.50 per acre, for cash only, Crockett opposed the proposal because "if the sale was made for ready money, poor people would get but very little if any of the land" and, as the representative of a district dominated by poor farmers, he had not "come here to legislate for ready-money men." Polk opposed Crockett and spoke for the proposal, which was adopted. Despite Polk's later protestations that Tennessee had been deprived of school lands due to the many North Carolina warrants, the Hiwassee District was not open to those warrants, yet no provision was made to fund schools from land sales there. Polk also attempted to raise the top price to $2.00 per acre, which Crockett opposed, and the amendment failed. Crockett also voted to allow widows to keep the land they occupied, but Polk opposed that too, and the measure was defeated.[10] These efforts by Polk, Grundy, and others to sell land for the highest prices possible, and only for cash, clearly disadvantaged the poor and raised Crockett's suspicion of the legislature. Later, while in Congress, he would break with Polk over the idea of turning the western vacant lands over to the state for disposition because he did not trust the state to protect his constituents.[11]

Meanwhile, North Carolina had turned over to its university all of the land grants that remained unclaimed by Revolutionary War veterans who had died and left no heirs. Tennessee protested these warrants, which were clearly a departure from the original intent of compensating veterans. However, in 1822 Tennessee had accepted some of the warrants under the condition that they would be shared with two Tennessee colleges. The following year, when the University of North Carolina presented more warrants, Polk and Crockett managed to stop them, at least temporarily, arguing that the public lands in West Tennessee should be reserved for funding education. This objective was based on the hope that Congress would eventually cede the western land to Tennessee.[12] Meanwhile, other warrant holders continued to make claims in the Western District. The legislature did succeed in giving squatters the first opportunity to purchase land that they had improved from warrant holders who claimed it or to be paid for their improvements if they were legally displaced. However, prices were typically out of reach for the squatters. Since the federal government had not ceded the land in the Western District to Tennessee, only those who held warrants profited from the transfer or sale of land in that district, whether they were the original grantees or parties to whom they sold their warrants. The grantees were given warrants for free as an entitlement, but they could sell them at any price. Speculators who bought warrants from them could resell them, often at a considerable profit. Squatters who had worked and improved their land remained at their mercy. Ironically, the squatters' improvements often were all that gave much of this land sufficient value to be of interest to speculators.

Crockett came to believe that the wealthier land speculators in Eastern and Middle Tennessee would continue to control the legislature. He later pointed out that his large district held only five seats in the legislature, while the rest of the state held thirty-five.[13] Thus, he saw no chance that the state would agree to sell land to his constituents at affordable prices, let alone donate it to them.

During Crockett's first term, the legislature requested Tennessee's congressmen and instructed its senators (who were chosen by the legislature) to pursue cession of the vacant lands in the Western District to the state, which would dispose of them "at such a price as may be thought prudent by the legislature for the purpose of education."[14] Although there is no record of Crockett opposing this action, he may have unsuccessfully sought a provision that would have offered squatters a guaranteed low price for their land. Later, while in Congress, he was unable to persuade Polk to include such a provision in a Tennessee land bill.

In 1825, both Polk and Crockett were gone from the legislature when it voided the existing deadline on North Carolina warrants and approved the sharing of revenues with two Tennessee colleges, not the common schools. The warrants held by the University of North Carolina were consolidated and reissued in twenty-five-acre certificates, which were largely snapped up by speculators. Although occupants were given preference in purchasing the twenty-five-acre certificates for fifty cents an acre, in addition to surveying fees, many were unable to meet that price or obtain sufficient credit to do so. Crockett later described the costs as prohibitive, saying that he had "seen the last blanket of a poor, but honest and industrious family, sold under the hammer of the sheriff, to pay for that survey."[15] He added that the revenues derived from the sale of these certificates and the taxes on the land claimed were used to fund colleges and schools in the eastern part of the state, rather than in his district, where the lands were located, thus depriving his constituents of tens of thousands of dollars in educational funds. Such actions by the legislature were at the heart of Crockett's distrust of that body, and he would carry that distrust with him into Congress.[16]

CROCKETT GOES TO CONGRESS: THE EARLY LAND BILLS

Polk entered Congress in 1825, two years before Crockett did, and one of his priorities was to push through legislation that would cede the Western District lands to the state. However, since he was in the minority in a Congress dominated by allies of President John Quincy Adams, and because a majority in Congress was resistant to giving away public land, his first attempt to introduce a bill was frustrated, and it never came up for debate.[17] However, with far more Jacksonians in the next Congress, and Jackson himself on the verge of winning the presidency a year later, Polk felt more confident when he presented a bill on December 24, 1827, that would cede to the state all vacant lands in West Tennessee that remained after the North Carolina warrants were satisfied and which would partially make up for the deficiency in school lands. Polk's bill would authorize Tennessee to "dispose of the lands . . . by sale or otherwise, at such price as she may deem expedient; the proceeds of which, or the interest thereon, shall be appropriated for the use of Schools, for the instruction of children forever."[18]

Crockett later accused Polk of ignoring him while drafting this bill and working behind his back during the illness Crockett suffered when he first arrived in Washington. "Mr. Polk took the advantage of me," he charged, "while I was confined to my bed with the indisposition, and made a motion to dispose of the government land in the District, and had it referred to a Select Committee of which he was Chairman. I found his object was to have the whole of the land south and west of the congressional reservation line relinquished to the State of Tennessee, to be disposed of by the Legislature of the State."[19] This alarmed Crockett, who was certain that the state would sell the land for more than his constituents could afford. He also felt sure that the land would quickly fall into the hands of speculators, who would enjoy profits, along with the state, while the occupants in his district would be ignored. This was the seed of the dispute that would erupt between Polk and Crockett a year later.

Polk's refusal to accept Crockett's provision to protect occupants could only have increased Crockett's suspicion of his colleague.[20] However, for the time being, he continued to support the bill and emphasized his cooperation with Polk, cheerfully writing the *Jackson Gazette* that "Mr Polk and myself are getting along very well with our vacant lands bill; and I have no doubt but we shall effect a relinquishment early this session."[21] Despite his expressed optimism, Crockett clearly was at odds with Polk over the language in the land bill, but he wanted to avoid an open break with his state delegation. It is possible that he still believed that an acceptable compromise could be achieved, despite his later, more critical reflection on this period. He consistently wrote optimistically to constituents and the press, expressing confidence that Congress would relinquish the land to Tennessee, but complained that the discussion of the tariff was dragging on and suppressing all other business. Crockett's impatience with the snail's pace of House business would increase with the years. He also continued to praise Jackson: "I can here from all quarters of the union," he wrote, "and the cry is that Jackson will be the next president."[22]

Debate on the bill began on April 24, 1828, when Polk argued that he was simply asking for justice, since the federal government owed the lands to Tennessee to make up for the deficiency in school lands. He emphasized the unique nature of the state's public-land policy compared to that maintained throughout the rest of the country. He claimed that the only remaining Tennessee lands were of such poor quality that the federal government could not earn enough on them to cover surveying costs, but Tennessee could realize something on them since it already had land offices, surveyors, and boundary records in place. Poor as the land was, the state could sell it at low prices if only for the timber or access routes it might provide to owners of adjacent parcels. Polk estimated that most of the land would bring no more than 12½ cents per acre, with a minor amount bringing twenty-five to fifty cents. Crockett supported Polk and told the House that, having lived in the area for years, he could personally confirm that a good deal of it would not bring one cent. Only in passing did Polk mention that "In a few cases, poor persons, residing on these refuse lands, might be enabled to secure homes for themselves and families," indicating how minor this issue was to him. For Crockett, of course, it was the entire issue.[23]

In speaking for the bill, Crockett went a bit beyond its provisions by making a reasonable argument for private land ownership at any price. He echoed Thomas Jefferson when he said that "to make of your citizen a landholder, you chain down his affections to your soil." He suggested that a man defends a country "because in so doing he fights for his home—for the spot upon which all his affections are fixed," adding that a landowner maintains "a pride and elevation of character, which fires his heart with patriotism, and nerves his arms with strength." While he agreed with Polk's aim of using land revenues to improve education, Crockett emphasized that, for him, this meant "to educate the poor man's child. It is to snatch from the vale of poverty and obscurity many a youth, and dispel that gloom of ignorance which shrouds him by inviting him to enter the doors of a respectable country school." He couldn't help mentioning that "I never, myself, had the good fortune to behold the inside of one, which I trust will plead an apology for the plain and unvarnished manner in which I address you. I am, sir, but a farmer, destitute of those advantages of education which others possess. I thank heaven I know their worth, from having experienced the want of them; and on that account, I am the more anxious to extend them to those who will come after me."[24]

Unlike Polk, Crockett spoke primarily for the poor, many of whom had "seen their little farms, which had afforded bread for their children, taken from them by warrants held in hands more fortunate than their own." He pleaded that they now looked to Congress "as children would to a parent, for assistance and protection," wishing to no longer remain tenants but to become owners. This, for Crockett, was clearly more important than the income Tennessee might realize from the land. There was no mistaking the class element in this struggle, and Crockett addressed it openly. "I say, emphatically, the measure will benefit the poor, nor am I ashamed to acknowledge that they constitute the very class of your population, among whom I have met many brave and meritorious men; the class upon whom I should delight to bestow a benefit." He was already showing that he did not really share Polk's agenda, which was simply to persuade Congress to cede the land to Tennessee, and Polk may have viewed Crockett's speech as a distraction from his own plea. Crockett departed even further from Polk, and many in Congress, by proposing that the price of *all* public lands in the United States be reduced because "The rich require but little legislation. We should, at least occasionally, legislate for the poor."[25] For Polk, the land was a commodity; for Crockett it was a potential instrument of social reform.

Polk and Crockett had walked into a larger national argument over the use of public lands. Much of the public domain lay within the borders of new western states, which craved cheap land prices or outright cession in order to populate their states, boost their economies, and increase their representation in Washington. Crockett would have found himself philosophically closer to most other westerners than to Polk. They complained that the federal government set too high a price on public land and thus depressed sales, and they resisted attempts to discourage or remove squatters. Eastern states tended to resist the westward migration, already in full force, which resulted in a loss of their population and labor force as well as a drop in their land values. The South was strongly opposed to westward expansion, which could bring in more free states and threaten slavery. States' rights advocates feared an expansion of federal power through control of land sales that might lead to reduction of state power. Although western states made increasingly belligerent demands for cheap or free public land, Congress resisted those pressures and became increasingly concerned about losing control of the public domain and the revenues that it might bring. States and the federal government also looked to land sales as a means to fund education and internal improvements. Many wanted to use land revenues to pay off the public debt, particularly in the South, because elimination of the debt also could lower the tariff. These sectional differences, as well as some partisan politics, dominated the debate over public land for years.[26]

Polk's bill ran into stiff opposition on the House floor, and the debate dragged out for days, some of it reflecting the broader public land issue. Opponents of the bill doubted Polk's figures and suspected that there was considerably more vacant land than he had suggested and that its value was greater than he stated. They were supported by a report from the General Land Office confirming that there was far more vacant land than Polk claimed, although the quality and value of the land could not be determined. Many in Congress feared setting a precedent by giving away federal land to states.[27] Some doubted that the federal government had any legal obligation to make up the school lands and blamed Tennessee for having failed to set aside the land *before* it issued grants to the North Carolina warrant holders. Polk might have responded to that charge by citing the 1806 law's requirement that the amount of school land depended upon how much, if any, was left after the warrants had been honored. Polk's silence on this point left the impression that Tennessee had been negligent. He had offered the testimony of Tennessee land surveyors as verification for his description of the land and its probable value, but some congressmen found this to be unreliable conjecture, and they wanted to see the records from the Tennessee land offices. Polk assured them that the records were so complicated, due to the odd division of the land, that it would be virtually impossible to make any useful calculations from them. However, he agreed to an amendment that would confine the amount of land ceded to the acreage necessary to make up the deficiency in school lands, a significant concession. Still, the House remained unconvinced, and the bill was eventually tabled by the lopsided vote of 113-63, meaning it was dead for that session.[28]

Following the bill's defeat, Crockett made a further departure from Polk by introducing a resolution that the Public Lands Committee look into the feasibility of donating 160 acres to each settler. Apparently nothing came of this suggestion, but Crockett's increasing assertiveness and independence from the state delegation already raised their suspicions of him.[29] Crockett's thinking was rapidly moving toward the idea of circumventing the Tennessee legislature, which he did not trust, by having the federal government sell or grant lands directly to squatters. This would put him in direct opposition to Polk and the other Tennesseans in the House.

"I CHOOSE TO OBEY MY CONSTITUENTS": THE BREAK WITH POLK

Even before Congress reconvened the following December, Crockett had concluded that Polk's bill would never pass, but that the Congress might be more receptive to one that sought to protect squatters or others whose land titles might be open to challenge. Perhaps, he reasoned, Congress might agree to a proposal that separated the squatters' situation from the larger vacant-land issue. Crockett approached the rest of the Tennessee congressional delegation seeking their support for the idea, but they rejected him.[30] They were adamant in their insistence that the land go to the state and that Crockett trust the legislature to provide for the squatters, despite the resounding defeat Polk's bill had suffered and the holes that had been exposed in Polk's arguments. They did not want Crockett muddying the waters. Although he had gone along with Polk and publicly maintained solidarity with his delegation, Crockett never fully trusted them or the legislature. Nothing short of a provision for the occupants in his district would satisfy him. When he failed to gain any concession from Polk, he decided to break with him openly, and on December 11, 1828, he introduced his own amendment to Polk's bill, which contained the provisions he wanted, but which Polk had rejected.[31] Crockett wrote to the *Jackson Gazette,* announcing his amendment, an open slap at Polk.[32]

Crockett's suspicions of his own state representatives went back to his years in the legislature and were reinforced by Polk's stonewalling. He continued to suspect that, should the state gain possession of the land, it would sell it at prices that his constituents could not afford and that any resulting funding for education would go to schools and colleges for the wealthy, not to common schools in his district. Even those of his constituents who could afford to buy the land contributed to the funding of those schools, rather than schools in their own district, due to their lack of proportional representation in the legislature.[33] Crockett's amendment made no mention of schools because he believed they would not be built in his district. The situation rapidly escalated into mutual distrust between Crockett and Polk, and each became convinced that he could not trust the other.[34]

Polk may have been sincere in his attempt to provide education funds for Tennessee, but he could not guarantee what the legislature would do once the land was in its hands, and the state had a poor record in that regard. When Tennessee had obtained Cherokee lands in the eastern part of the state, the legislature failed to reserve more than 22,705 acres to support schools. Again, when the state was authorized to honor warrants in the Western District in 1818, there was no mention of school lands, and Tennessee never raised the issue. Polk and Crockett had worked together in the legislature to slow the hemorrhaging of public lands and succeeded in temporarily holding off the North Carolina warrants. But after they left that body, it reversed those efforts and opened the West to more warrants, again without making any provision for schools, while agreeing to share revenues with North Carolina for universities and colleges, not common schools. Regardless of Polk's intentions, Crockett had good reason to oppose him and distrust the legislature.

Essentially, Crockett's proposed amendment virtually deleted Polk's entire bill and replaced it with one that differed from the original in four important respects. First, it would give to established settlers on vacant lands, who had built homes and otherwise improved their plots, title to their land, up to 160 acres, free of charge except for the required surveying fees. Second, title to the land would pass directly from the federal government to the occupants, rather than to the state of Tennessee. Third, only the lands then occupied by settlers were affected, rather than the entire Western District, the balance of which would remain in federal hands. Fourth, the bill made no reference to funds for education, since in this case, no funds would accrue from the land transactions. Nor did the bill mention the North Carolina warrants except for one vague reference that stipulated that the federal government would not be accountable to grantees "for any lands, or the value thereof, in case a better title should be in any other person."[35] Virtually everything in Crockett's amendment was unacceptable to Polk, who sought state revenues from the sale of the land for schools, not a giveaway to squatters. Crockett's amendment would eliminate the state government from the process entirely, and he would incur the full wrath of his colleagues in response to his bold move.

Crockett's proposal that the federal government grant up to 160 acres to individual occupants reveals a significant hidden agenda. Although he had urged Congress to simply grant occupants legal title to the land they had cultivated, 160 acres was considerably more than a single family farm could work. Crockett knew that small farmers and occupants aspired to become speculators themselves. He saw nothing wrong in this and, in fact, viewed it as a way for the poor to improve their lot by acquiring additional lands that they might sell or lease, placing them in a position to improve their economic and social standing, and on a more level playing field with their wealthier neighbors. Crockett believed that the poor could not, on their own, elevate themselves regardless of how hard they worked and that the government ought to provide them a leg up by giving them the means to move up the economic and social ladder. The key to such upward mobility lay in the possession of land.[36] For that reason, each of Crockett's own legislative land proposals would call for cessions or sales of 160 or 200 acres per occupant.

Crockett was forced to find allies outside of Tennessee to support his proposal, and he made no secret of his intentions. As early as December 13, 1828, having failed to win over the Tennessee delegation, he wrote to the *Jackson Gazette* announcing that he intended to introduce his own amendment to Polk's bill, which he did that same month, thus sealing his estrangement from the Jacksonians.[37] "True it is," he wrote, "my colleagues, as I believe, are almost unanimously opposed to my proposition, alleging that they feel themselves constrained to obey the Legislature of Tennessee, which seeks to have this land subjected to its control. To this argument, I have only one reply to make, which is, that others may obey the Legislature, but I choose to obey my constituents, who have placed me in office, and whose servant I am. I am decidedly opposed to placing it in the power of the Tennessee Legislature, or any tribunal, to speculate on their labor."[38] He was frank about the opposition from the other Tennessee representatives and confirmed Polk's later charge the he consorted with, or was "operated on," by the anti-Jacksonians, adding "In this I may be disappointed, as the opposition of my colleagues throws a fearful weight in the scale against me—but I have the strong assurance of a great many members in my favor, who I know will not flinch when they are put to the test."[39]

Crockett even went so far as to warn Polk and the others that, if his amendment did not pass, he would work to defeat the entire bill. He openly boasted that the United States would never be able to sell the land and that if it were kept from the state, "his people could have the use of it for nothing."[40] In short, Crockett told Polk and the other Tennesseans that his people would be better off with no bill than being placed at the mercy of the legislature, and that if adequate provision were not made for the occupants, he would introduce his own amendment, knowing the entire delegation would oppose him, and seek votes wherever he might find them.

Debate on Crockett's amendment began on January 5, 1829, and continued a week later.[41] He argued forcefully and passionately for his proposal, repeating many of the points that he had expressed during the earlier debate. He pulled no punches and painted the situation in Tennessee as little more than a scheme to defraud the poor in order to benefit the rich. He was certain that, if the land were given directly to the state, the legislature would dispossess the squatters and sell their land to the highest bidder, and that any revenues devoted to education would be used to build schools in East and Middle Tennessee, not in his district. He mentioned that his district had been deprived of as much as $100,000 in school funds that the state had earned on land transactions and fees in the Western District, revenues that had funded colleges and schools in the eastern part of the state. To him, it was a matter of class warfare, creating "a line of demarcation between the two classes of society—it separated the children of the rich from the children of the poor. The children of my people never saw the inside of a college in their lives, and never are likely to do so." Nor did he mince words, insisting that "if a swindling machine is to be set up to strip them of what little the Surveyors, and the Colleges, and the warrant-holders have left them, it shall never be said that I sat by in silence, and refused, however humbly, to advocate their cause."[42]

Crockett did his best to convince the House that his bill would not set the dangerous precedent for land giveaways that concerned many of his colleagues. However, any proposed donation of federal land was bound to meet with resistance from those strongly opposed to such grants. But those forces had little opportunity to attack Crockett's proposal, since his own state delegation heavily dominated the debate with attacks on him. Crockett responded with equal passion to those challenges, and the general tone of the debate suggests that he had gained considerable support and might well have carried the day had a vote been taken at that time. However, Pryor Lea, another Tennessee congressman and Polk ally, succeeded in halting his momentum by hastily calling for an adjournment, allegedly in deference to the death of Jackson's wife, which was granted.[43] Crockett would never again come so close to success for this bill. He wrote to his constituents, frankly explaining that he could garner no support from the state's other representatives, but felt he was on the verge of victory and had gained the backing of many congressmen from other regions. His speeches in Congress and his circular letter home both show unwavering commitment to the poor of his district. While both documents may have been polished by someone else to correct Crockett's grammar, there is no mistaking the authenticity of his sentiments.

Crockett's amendment had totally derailed the Tennessee delegation's objective, which was to get the land based on an argument related to justice. Crockett openly stated that he doubted his colleagues had much of a case, that by originally asking for all the land, they had entered into the area of broad public policy on the disposition of federal lands, and that many in Congress saw it as a risky precedent that would result in other states asking for free land. Reducing the demand to only enough land to make up the school deficit hadn't changed anyone's mind. He, on the other hand, merely wanted to secure his constituents' titles, also basing his argument on justice, but pitching it on a human, rather than a legal basis. He pled the poor farmer's cause, saying "they had mingled the sweat of their brows with the soil they occupied," and asked if it was "fair for the General [federal] Government to take away these humble cottages from them, and make a donation of the whole to the Legislature of the State for the purpose of raising up schools for the children of the rich?" His voice must have filled the chamber as he implored his colleagues to give the occupants legal title to their land. "Let it be their own. While they bedew it with the sweat of their faces, let them at least have the consolation of knowing that they may leave it to their own children, and not have it squandered on the sons of a stranger."[44]

Crockett's argument clearly resonated with many in the House, and several members rose to say they supported his idea, while objecting to Polk's for the reasons Crockett had expressed. Polk (and some of Crockett's biographers) thought that Crockett was being naive if he believed that these supporters, mostly anti-Jackson men, were sincere in their support for his bill, rather than just using the issue to create disaffection among the Jacksonians. In a broad sense, Crockett may have been naive to think that he could survive in politics while remaining so fiercely independent, but his actions in this case were, in his view, necessary, regardless of the pitfalls or the motivations of those who might support him. Crockett may have sounded more optimistic in his letters on this debate than the facts warranted, but he often wrote in upbeat terms intended to sustain confidence in him among his constituents. Also, when several House members openly endorsed Crockett's limited plan and just as strongly objected to Polk's more sweeping bill, Crockett had every reason to believe that his strategy was working. In any case, votes on the various Tennessee land bills show a general objection to land giveaways that cut across party lines and more closely reflected regional differences, which is at odds with the view that anti-Jackson conspirators sought to use Crockett. The naive image of Crockett was at least partly the result of his disaffected Tennessee colleagues repeatedly spreading that image of him in the press in order to tarnish him at home.[45]

The Tennessee delegation had been taken somewhat by surprise during the January 5, 1829 debate, particularly by the extent to which Crockett was willing to oppose his colleagues on the House floor and to cultivate support from Jackson's enemies. Although debate was to have continued the following day, Pryor Lea again rose to plead for a delay, "influenced by considerations of a character too delicate for public disclosure here, yet sufficiently intelligible to all considerations affecting peculiarly the sensibilities of the whole Tennessee delegation, who are particularly interested in the pending discussion."[46] Crockett clearly had struck a nerve with his colleagues and, unfortunately for him, Lea's motion was granted. Debate would not resume until January 12, nearly a week later, providing sufficient time for Polk, Lea, and the others to marshal their forces against Crockett.

When it resumed, the debate resembled an ugly family fight that had been dragged out onto the House floor and unfolded in front of "outsiders." The arguments of the Tennessee delegation, particularly Polk and Lea, were largely directed at Crockett for his "betrayal" of his own state delegation and ignoring the memorial from the Tennessee Legislature.[47] They attacked his amendment as unworkable and challenged it on legal and practical grounds, but in doing so contradicted some of their own arguments. For example, one of Polk's strongest points in defending his bill was that the state had land offices and surveyors on the scene as well as the land records, which would enable them to survey the land at minimal cost, whereas the federal costs for setting up such an operation from scratch would be prohibitive. But now he and Lea took a states' rights stance and claimed that, under Crockett's plan, the federal government would be compelling a state to carry out surveys for it, insisting that the government had no right to do so, especially when it would be in direct contradiction to Tennessee's stated desire to obtain all of the land, or at least enough to make up the deficiency in school lands. In other words, it was all right for Tennessee to ask for a donation of huge quantities of federal land, but unreasonable to ask Tennessee to survey lands that might be donated or sold to Tennessee settlers by the federal government. Similarly, Polk initially suggested that most, if not all, of the North Carolina warrants had been satisfied, leaving little land for the state to use for schools, but in rebutting Crockett, the other Tennesseans claimed that his plan made no allowance for those warrants and could leave the state vulnerable to legal action by warrant holders. Ironically, the same argument was made against Polk's bill, since the federal government was legally bound to satisfy the warrants. Crockett pointed out that his amendment asked only for land already occupied, leaving plenty to satisfy any remaining North Carolina warrants.

Anti-Jackson forces reveled in the fight. Rollin Mallary of Vermont had expressed sympathy for Crockett's proposal early in the debate, but could not resist pointing out that "the gentlemen from that state [Tennessee] seemed to be quarrelling among themselves about the mode of dividing the spoils."[48]

Polk tried to return to his original bill, brushing aside Crockett's amendment, and offered his own amendment that would give the occupants preference of entry—first chance to buy the land—but he did not stipulate at what price, nor could he have guaranteed what price the legislature might set for the land. Charles Wickliffe, a Jacksonian representative from Kentucky, proposed that Polk's amendment add a provision that guaranteed that the occupants would have a preference of entry "without charge," which was adopted, although Polk and other Tennesseans objected to it, confirming Crockett's fear that the bill would do nothing to protect the squatters from the legislature. Others thought it was not clear whether the phrase "without charge" meant that the land itself would be free, that the costs of surveying or filing would be eliminated, or referred to something else. In any case, Crockett called the offer "a perfect trap," asserting that Polk's amendment "says, to be sure, that the Legislature shall give a preference to the settlers now upon the land, and no doubt they will do so; but, my word for it, the Legislature will fix their own price upon it; and if they cannot afford to pay, what good will the preference do these poor settlers?"[49]

Nor was Crockett impressed by the addition of the phrase "without charge," since he believed that Polk's bill would be defeated and the provision for occupants along with it. Crockett said as much in the debates over Polk's bill. The *Register of Debates* paraphrased Crockett's remarks, noting that he admitted that he had "supported the original measure of his honorable friend, [Mr. Polk] while at the same time he perfectly knew that it would not be carried; he [Crockett] supported it under the hope that it would subsequently unite his colleagues of the Tennessee delegation with him in the support of his favorite measure—that of providing for the poor settlers of the western district," repeating for emphasis that "he was well aware at the time that it could not succeed in passing the House."[50] He thought the only measure that had a chance of success was one that addressed *only* the occupants and avoided being seen as a precedent affecting broader U.S. land policy. Crockett suspected that Polk's amendment regarding the occupants was an effort to doom his idea by adding it to Polk's bill in the hope that the entire proposal would be defeated, as it had been once already, thus ending Crockett's effort to address the occupants separately, hence his description of the idea as a "perfect trap."

Perhaps Polk considered defeat preferable to the idea of being trumped by a disloyal colleague, while hoping for a chance to bring the issue up again at a later date, especially if Crockett could first be removed from office in the upcoming election. In any case, Polk was sure to place blame for the bill's defeat squarely on Crockett, who had supported the same measure in the previous session but now opposed it, in violation of the legislature's memorial. Polk, somewhat disingenuously, wondered what had changed Crockett's mind, asking rhetorically, "What could justify the remark that fell from him the other day, that it was a trap?" Nor could Polk resist leveling another condescending slur at his colleague, suggesting that Crockett "did not at all times speak in measured language," and concluded that Crockett "did not fully comprehend the import of that remark, and many others that he had made against his own State." Polk also suggested that Crockett's disloyalty extended to "co-operating by his course with the enemies of this bill, and contributing to its defeat."[51] While Crockett suspected Polk of trying to kill the idea of providing for the squatters, Polk had countered that Crockett was trying to defeat his bill.

Since Polk and Lea had decided to air their dirty linen on the House floor, Crockett did not hesitate to do likewise. He repeated his charge that he had asked Polk to include in his original bill a provision that would protect squatters, but that Polk had refused. He added that, after Polk's bill had been sternly rejected in the last session, he had again approached his Tennessee colleagues with the suggestion that they address only the squatters' land, but that they had roundly rejected his idea.[52] This, he said, left him isolated from his own state if he was to serve his constituents as he felt he must. In his January 15, 1829 circular, he made sure his constituents knew who was to blame for the failure of his bill, noting that "while gentlemen from other States were aiding me in what I consider so humane an attempt—an attempt to shelter the heads of defenceless widows and poor little orphans from the peltings of the pitiless storm—my own colleagues were bending all their powers against me."[53]

Nonetheless, even though many who spoke in the House seemed supportive of Crockett's amendment, others raised doubts about it similar to those expressed about Polk's bill. Some questioned the claim that there was so little land or that it was all of poor quality, since no reliable information about the land existed. Others again raised the federal obligation to ensure satisfaction of the North Carolina warrants. Although it was thought that all or most of the warrants had been redeemed, there was no certainty that more of them would not be forthcoming; giving land to squatters might prevent warrant holders from claiming land to which they were legally entitled and which the federal government had guaranteed to them.

It was argued that the federal government might realize something from the land and that Tennessee had even estimated its value at no less than $100,000. It was suggested that the federal government should not make a practice of giving away land that could be sold to pay for internal improvements, which many on the frontier wanted; retire the national debt; or for other purposes. In all fairness, the tariff and sale of public land were the only real sources of revenue available to the federal government. Although the odd dispersal of federal plots in West Tennessee may have been unique, and a reasonable exception might have been made for the occupants there, many in Congress may have justifiably objected to setting a precedent for giving away public lands, much of which had already been lost through practices like the redeeming of North Carolina warrants, and the potential federal revenues that they might have brought.

In any event, the momentum Crockett had built on January 5 began to slip by January 12, and it became clear that the House was not likely to support any bill that would give away public land. When the debate finally wound down on January 13, the bill was tabled by a vote of 103-63, ending discussion for the moment.[54] By then the political infighting, which had been dragged into the open on the House floor and into the press, had become as important to the Tennessee delegation as the fate of the public lands. Crockett's independent move had sabotaged the state's carefully crafted offensive. Worse, Crockett had publicly admitted that, proclaimed his distrust of the Tennessee Legislature, and expressed no regret for doing so. For that, his Tennessee colleagues would never forgive him.

While Polk fixated on what he saw as his colleague's disloyalty, Crockett was acting on the clear instructions of his constituents, including those from Haywood County who had petitioned Crockett to press for direct cession of land to the Western District rather than to the state, and complained about the lack of school funding there.[55] Like Crockett, they did not trust the legislature. The petitioners feared that school funds would continue to elude them if the western lands were ceded to the state, and they noted that the Western District remained woefully underrepresented in the legislature, boasting no more than five or six members. Crockett had made the same case himself and intended to carry out the petitioners' instructions.[56]

Crockett wrote to the *Gazette* on January 14, 1829, reporting on the debate and blaming the failure of his amendment on the Tennessee delegation. He said that he would introduce the Haywood County petition the following week and refer it to the Committee on Public Lands "with a hope that I can get the chairman to report a bill for the benefit of the Western District." Crockett mentioned several representatives who had spoken in support of his amendment, almost all of them Adams men, adding to the suggestion that he was being used by them to create dissension among Jackson's forces. Crockett must have seen through this, but he didn't care who his supporters were, or what their motives might be, if they could help pass his amendment. He vowed to "keep on kicking with a hope of success," promising that "If I am whipped, I will not stay whipped." He presented the petition on January 19, as promised, but no bill was forthcoming from the Committee.[57]

Polk immediately moved to direct the General Land Office to report to the next session of Congress exactly how much federal land there was in western Tennessee, how much of it had been taken by North Carolina warrants, how much remained that could be sold, its quality, whether it was in large sections or detached parcels, and if it could be surveyed and sold for enough to cover the surveying costs or to bring any profit. Crockett would later use the report that emerged from Polk's request.[58]

Crockett's speeches and spontaneous statements during these debates show a man well versed in this issue, in command of the facts, able to push his own agenda, both openly and subtly, and capable of holding his own with his far better educated colleagues. The public record puts the lie to the characterization of Crockett as a virtual illiterate and naive bumpkin. That image seemed to grow with the larger-than-life "Davy" caricature that Crockett had created for himself during his campaigns. The press advanced the image, partly as good copy and partly with material generated by the Jacksonians, who sought to turn it into a negative image of Crockett and portray him as an embarrassment to his constituents, who might be shamed into voting him out of office. They would use this strategy in an effort to unseat him in the 1829 election, but Crockett retained the confidence of his constituents and easily won reelection. Although his land bill had appeared doomed, Crockett would resurrect it and even succeed briefly in uniting the Tennessee delegation behind a compromise bill hammered out by a select committee that he chaired. In the end, he would fail, but his efforts showed considerable political skill and clear understanding of the issue and the conflicting parties involved in it, contrary to the common image of Crockett as an inept congressman who found himself continually in over his head. But Crockett was also revealed to be something of a long-shot gambler in risking all on the success of his bill, regardless of the political fallout at home.

---

[1]   Daniel Feller, *The Public Lands in Jacksonian Politics* (Madison: University of Wisconsin Press, 1984), 16–17.

[2]   *An Act to authorize the state of Tennessee to issue grants and perfect titles to certain lands therein described, and to settle the claims to the vacant and unappropriated lands within the same, U.S. Statutes at Large* 2 (1806): 381. For convenience, these areas will be referred to simply as the eastern and western portions of the state

[3]   Ibid.

[4]   Thomas B. Jones, "The Public Lands of Tennessee," *Tennessee Historical Quarterly* (Spring 1968): 26–27, 32. Jones clearly blames the state for ignoring the school set-aside, but he does not mention the "where existing claims will allow the same" clause in the 1806 law. Tennessee continued to claim it never realized a fraction of the school lands to which it should have been entitled due to its obligation to satisfy the warrants *before* school lands could be set aside. When Polk later claimed that Congress owed Tennessee the deficit school lands, some members responded that no promise of any school land had ever been made to the state, which a close reading of the 1806 act confirms.

[5]   *An Act supplementary to the act, entitled "An act to authorize the state of Tennessee to issue grants and perfect titles to certain lands therein described, and to settle the claims to the vacant and unappropriated land within the same," passed the eighteenth of April, one thousand eight hundred and six, U.S. Statutes at Large* 3 (1818): 416; Stanley J. Folmsbee and Anna Grace Catron, "The Early Career of David Crockett," *East Tennessee Historical Society's Publications*, No. 28 (1956): 72–73.

[6]   Although Tennessee actually had adopted laws to protect squatters on federal land, the state had no legal right to do so. When those lands were opened to satisfy North Carolina warrants, occupants found themselves at risk of being dispossessed. Jones, "The Public Lands of Tennessee," 25-26, 32.

[7]   Stanley J. Folmsbee and Anna Grace Catron, "The Early Career of David Crockett," *East Tennessee Historical Society's Publications* No. 28 (1956): 72–73, 82–83.

[8]   Feller, *The Public Lands in Jacksonian Politics*, 6, citing Thomas Donaldson, *The Public Domain* (Washington: GPO, 1884).

[9]   James Atkins Shackford, *David Crockett: The Man and the Legend*, (Chapel Hill: University of North Carolina Press, 1956): 81; Stanley J. Folmsbee and Anna Grace Catron, "David Crockett: Congressman," *East Tennessee Historical Society's Publications* No. 29 (1957): 50. Crockett's district also included wealthier farmers with large land holdings as well, undoubtedly those who had been able to claim the choicest land with North Carolina warrants. Because cotton production was booming in West Tennessee, many held large numbers of slaves. In fact, Crockett's district had a higher ratio of slaves to whites than Tennessee as a whole did, and nearly thirty percent of the state's slaves. The ratio of slaves to whites in East Tennessee, for example, was about one to twelve; in Middle Tennessee it was one to three; in West Tennessee it was three to five. However, these slaves were heavily concentrated on the larger plantations and the vast majority of West Tennesseans held few, if any, slaves. *Abstract of the Fifth Census of the United States, 1830*, Compiled by the Department of State (Washington: Printed at the Globe Office, by F. P. Blair, 1832): 28–29; Samuel Cole Williams, *Beginnings of West Tennessee: In the Land of the Chickasaws, 1541-1841* (Johnson City, Tenn.: The Watauga Press, 1930): 202–14.

[10] Folmsbee and Catron, "The Early Career of David Crockett," 77.

[11] *Nashville Whig*, September 29, 1823; Folmsbee and Catron, "The Early Career of David Crockett," 76–77.

[12] Ibid., 76, 83–84.

[13] *David Crockett's Circular*, February 28, 1831, Rare Books Division, Library of Congress, 6.

[14] Shackford, *David Crockett*, 70.

[15] *Register of Debates in Congress*, January 5, 1829, 163.

[16] Folmsbee and Catron, "David Crockett: Congressman," 46–47.

[17] House Resolution (hereinafter, H.R.) 95, 19th Congress, 1st Session, February 9, 1826; *House Journal*, February 9, 1826, 240. The committee report on H.R. 95 is found at "Application of Tennessee for a Grant of Certain Lands," House Document 494, 19th Congress, 1st Session, 530–32. The bill was reported out of a select committee chaired by Polk.

[18] H.R. 27, 20th Congress, 1st Session, December 24, 1827. This was essentially the same as the bill Polk had introduced in the 19th Congress (H.R. 95, February 9, 1826). The committee report that accompanied Polk's bill does not appear to have been printed in the American State Papers. Unlike the U.S. Congressional Serial Set, the American State Papers were cobbled together years after the original dates of the papers, and included only those items that the printers, Gales and Seaton, were able to locate. Not all congressional documents were included. However, the manuscript version of Polk's report has survived, and it is identical to the one that accompanied his 1826 bill. It consists of an introductory statement glued to a copy of the printed February 9, 1826, report. Information provided by the Center for Legislative Archives, U.S. National Archives & Records Administration; "Report of the select committee on the memorial of the legislature of Tennessee, December 24, 1827," Committee reports and papers, other select committees (HR 20A-D25.3), 20th Congress, Records of the United States House of Representatives, Record Group 233, National Archives.

[19] *David Crockett's Circular*, February 28, 1831, 5.

[20] *Register of Debates*, January 12, 1829, 199; Shackford, *David Crockett*, 90.

[21] *Jackson Gazette*, February 16, 1828.

[22] Crockett to James Blackburn, February 5, 1828, courtesy of the Tennessee State Library and Archives; *Jackson Gazette* April 5, 1828.

[23] *Register of Debates*, April 24, 1828, 2499.

[24] *Register of Debates*, April 29, 1828, 2520.

[25] Ibid.

[26] Feller, *The Public Lands in Jacksonian Politics*, is a thorough discussion of the land issue during this period and the related sectional differences over the tariff and internal improvements.

[27] *Register of Debates*, April 29, 1828, 2514–39. A report from George Graham, commissioner of the General Land Office, called some of Polk's claims into question. The report concluded that it was not possible to ascertain the exact amount of land that had been taken up by North Carolina warrants. Thus, the amount of remaining vacant land was equally uncertain. However, Graham concluded that some 8.5 million acres of vacant land lay in the Western District, far more than Polk had claimed. Graham, however, supported Polk in part by noting that, while the Western District "contains a large portion of lands of very superior quality," much of it must, he guessed, "contain much land of an inferior quality, and as the locations which have been made within it will very generally have been confined to the lands of the best quality, the residuum subject to be disposed of by the United States will generally be of inferior quality." Report of George Graham, General Land Office, to the House of Representatives, January 18, 1828, on "Vacant and Unappropriated Lands in Tennessee," American State Papers, House Document 624, 20th Congress, 1st Session, 395–96. Reports sent to Polk by state surveyors from the various Tennessee districts are found in House Document 669, 20th Congress, 1st Session, 510–12. See Jones, "The Public Lands of Tennessee," 26–27, 30–31. Jones concludes that the evidence "confirms the fact that Polk and the Tennessee delegation were not being completely honest with their fellow congressmen regarding the land situation in the Congressional Reservation."

[28] The *Register of Debates* gives the vote tally as 131–64, but does not include the actual roll call vote, which is found in the *House Journal* and gives the tally as 113–63. *Register of Debates*, May 1, 1828, 2550; *House Journal*, May 1, 1828, 659–61.

[29] *House Journal*, May 10, 1828, 721. There is no mention of Crockett's resolution in the *Register of Debates*. Also see Folmsbee and Catron, "David Crockett: Congressman," 49.

30 See Polk to Davison McMillen, January 16, 1829, and Polk to Pryor Lea, February 17, 1829, in Herbert Weaver, ed., and Paul H. Bergeron, assoc. ed., *Correspondence of James K. Polk, Volume I, 1817–1832* (Nashville, Vanderbilt University Press, 1969), 229–30, 240–43; Lea to *United States Telegraph*, February 23, 1829, reprinted in *Jackson Gazette*, March 28, 1829. Polk acknowledges that Crockett did formally present this idea to the Tennesseans, but said they unanimously rejected it and told Crockett that it would doom the entire bill. They reminded him that he was now opposing a bill he had previously supported and violating the memorial of the legislature. Crockett was aware of this, but saw those points as minor compared to his mandate to secure a land bill. Crockett confirms that he requested support from his delegation before introducing his own amendment, to no avail. See Crockett to *Jackson Gazette*, December 13, 1828, published January 3, 1829, regarding his opposition to Polk's version of the land bill, and Crockett to *Gazette* January 14, 1829, published February 7, 1829, in which he denounced his own delegation and said he was going his own way and introducing his own land bill. Crockett's political sense seems to have been that he didn't need the Jacksonians or the rest of the Tennessee delegation, if he could get his own bill passed. That event would have solidified his standing in his district and ensured his reelection indefinitely. Crockett later explained his doubt that Polk's bill could pass and his confidence in his own limited measure. *David Crockett's Circular,* February 28, 1831, 15.

31 H.R. 27, Amendment, December 11, 1828.

32 Crockett to *Jackson Gazette*, December 13, 1828, published January 3, 1829.

33 Crockett's suspicion of the legislature was well founded. The eighteen counties that comprised his congressional district were underrepresented in the legislature, with approximately one representative in the General Assembly for every 20,211 residents. By contrast, East Tennessee counties elected one representative per 12,940 residents; Middle Tennessee one representative per 16,599; East and Middle Tennessee combined elected one representative per 15,121 residents. West Tennessee held approximately 18 percent of the state's population, but elected only 14 percent of the General Assembly; Middle Tennessee held 49 percent of the population, with 46 percent of the representatives; while the eastern part of the state, which contained 33 percent of the population, held 40 percent of representatives. The wealthier landowners and speculators were from East and Middle Tennessee, and they enjoyed additional influence through political and business connections that were relatively uncommon in the Western District. The legislature's history of selling land at high prices, which benefited the land speculators, and that body's failure to set aside adequate land for support of common schools, gave Crockett and his constituents good reason to doubt that the legislature would follow a different course in West Tennessee. *The Abstract of the Fifth Census of the United States, 1830* (Washington: F. P. Blair, 1832), 28–29; *Journal of the House of Representatives of the State of Tennessee, 1829* (Knoxville: F. S. Heiskell & A. A. Hall, 1829), 3–5, courtesy of the Tennessee State Library and Archives.

34 Polk and the Jacksonians had made it clear that they would not support any bill Crockett might introduce that conflicted with Polk's. See Polk to McMillen, January 16, 1829, and Polk to Pryor Lea, February 17, 1829, in Weaver and Bergeron, *Correspondence of James K. Polk, Volume I,* 229 and 240. In his letter to Lea, Polk confirms that Crockett did show his proposed amendment to his delegation prior to introducing it, only to be strongly rebuked. Polk's point of view is understandable. He was far more interested in maintaining solidarity among the Jacksonians against the "Adams men" than Crockett's small agenda of securing land for squatters. Polk's letters indicate that he saw little chance of his own bill passing, but believed that Crockett's actions in seeking support from pro-Adams forces to be treacherous and unforgivable disloyalty to his own state and the Jacksonians. He is also correct in accusing Crockett of disregarding the memorial from the Tennessee legislature and of opposing Polk's original bill after having supported it, but this view clearly ignores the fact that Polk's bill was defeated and Crockett felt he had to make his own effort to secure land title for his constituents. Polk seems far more upset with Crockett's disloyalty to the Jacksonians than the specific provisions of Crockett's bill.

35 H.R. 27 Amendment, December 11, 1828; *Register of Debates,* January 5, 1829, 162.

36 Authors' interview with Daniel Feller, February 2, 2009. Also, for a balanced view of speculators and settlers, see Daniel Feller, *The Public Lands in Jacksonian Politics* (Madison, Wisconsin, University of Wisconsin Press, 1984), 30-31.

37 The bill was actually dated December 11, but it was rewritten before being brought to the floor for debate in January. The full text is found in Crockett's circular, *Address of Mr. Crockett, to the Voters of the Ninth Congressional District of the State of Tennessee; Together with His Remarks in the House of Representatives, January 5, 1829.* (Washington: Printed by Gales & Seaton, January 15, 1829), Rare Books Division, Library of Congress.

38 Crockett to *Jackson Gazette*, December 13, 1828, published January 3, 1829.

39 Ibid.

40 Jones, "The Public Lands of Tennessee," 33–34, quoting statement of Hugh Lawson White, February 17, 1829. Also see *Register of Debates,* January 5, 1829, 163; Lea to *United States Telegraph*, February 23, 1829, reprinted in *Jackson Gazette,* March 28, 1829; and Polk to McMillen, January 16, 1829, in Weaver and Bergeron, *Correspondence of James K. Polk, Volume I,* 229.

41 During the January 5 debate, John Bell of Tennessee proposed his own amendment to Polk's bill, which was printed up as "Intended to be proposed," but was never formally introduced. It would have given all the land to Tennessee, to be sold for cash only, at 37½ cents an acre, with the money going to public road construction, not schools. Occupants would be given preemption for land they had improved at the same price, with six months to claim the preemption, for cash only. This could not have been welcome to Polk or Crockett, and it fizzled before it materialized.

42 *Register of Debates,* January 5, 1829, 163. Crockett's January 15, 1829, circular includes some of his remarks in the House on January 5, also found in the *Register of Debates,* January 5, 1829, 161–67; the circular includes a few minor word changes, such as "on" instead of "upon." The only noticeable alteration is to the statement, "Sir, I have seen the last blanket of a poor, but honest and industrious family, sold under the hammer of the sheriff, to pay for that survey," rephrased in the circular to read, "Sir, I have seen the last article of property, which was subject to execution, of a poor, but honest and industrious family, sold under the hammer, by the Sheriff, to

pay for that survey." The excerpt from his January 12 speech, however, differs considerably from the one found in the *Debates* (January 12, 1829, 199–200) and has clearly been rewritten, although the essential meaning is unchanged.

43 Crockett's circular, January 15, 1829, 10, said that Lea called for the adjournment out of respect for the death of Jackson's wife.

44 *Register of Debates*, January 5, 1829, 162–63.

45 Folmsbee and Catron, "David Crockett: Congressman," 56–57.

46 *Register of Debates*, January 6, 1829, 168.

47 *Register of Debates*, January 12, 1829, 195–202, and January 13, 1829, 203–211.

48 *Register of Debates*, January 5, 1829, 165.

49 Ibid., 164; Crockett circular, January 15, 1829, 12.

50 *Register of Debates*, January 12, 1829, 200.

51 *Register of Debates*, January 13, 1829, 210.

52 Polk confirms this in his letter to McMillen, January 16, 1829; Weaver and Bergeron, *Correspondence of James K. Polk, Volume I*, 229; *Register of Debates*, January 12, 1829, 199.

53 Crockett circular, January 15, 1829, 13.

54 *Register of Debates*, January 12 and 13, 1829, 195–211.

55 Crockett introduced his amendment before he received the Haywood County petition and said as much in a letter to the *Jackson Gazette* dated January 14, 1829. However, the petition was only an affirmation of his constituents' strong views on the subject, of which Crockett was already well aware.

56 *Jackson Gazette*, December 27, 1828, includes both the constituents' letter to Crockett and the petition, dated November 18, 1828, sent from Brownsville, Tennessee. The petition was devoted mostly to the need for school funds in the Western District and mentioned the occupants only in one brief section. The petitioners claimed that the Northwest Ordinance of 1787, North Carolina's 1789 Act of Cession of its western lands to the United States, and the 1806 compact between the United States, North Carolina, and Tennessee imposed a responsibility on the Federal government to directly protect and act for inhabitants of Federal lands, including a guarantee that 640 acres out of every six square miles would be set aside to raise funds for schools. Thus, it was their right to have lands in their district ceded directly to them, not the state, and to ensure that funds derived from the sale of those lands be used to support schools in that district only. In the House, Crockett spoke mainly about the occupants and mentioned the related lack of school funds only secondarily. His proposed amendment made no provision for schools and focused more narrowly on securing land titles for his constituents. Perhaps he had seen that the school funding issue was tied too closely to Polk's effort to have all of the land ceded directly to the state, which was not going anywhere in the House. By focusing only on the limited issue of land occupied by squatters, Crockett may have seen a better chance of success. *Jackson Gazette* December 27, 1828; *Text of the Northwest Ordinance*, Archiving Early America website: http://www.earlyamerica.com/earlyamerica/milestones/ordinance/ text.html, taken from *Supplement to the First Volume of the Columbian Magazine*, Philadelphia, 1787.

57 *Jackson Gazette*, February 7, 1829; *House Journal*, January 19, 1829. Polk never doubted that the Adams men had supported Crockett's amendment disingenuously. He wrote that they had "seized upon the opportunity to use *Crockett*, and to operate upon him through this measure, for their own political purposes, and *hence* you see such men as Buckner of Ky., *Woods* of Ohio, Mallary of Vermont, Culpepper of N.C. making speeches for his proposition absurd as it was." Polk to McMillen, January 16, 1829, in Weaver and Bergeron, *Correspondence of James K. Polk, Volume I*, 229.

58 *House Journal*, January 15, 1829, 165–66, and January 20, 1829, 184–85.

Chapter 3

"Compelled to Stand Alone"
The 1829 Election

Crockett was disappointed by the failure of the land bill, but he remained confident of reelection. His optimism was well founded, since he was still popular at home, but that did not deter Polk and his allies from going after him. The campaign to unseat Crockett began almost as soon as debate on the land bill ended. Polk wasted no time in rounding up opposition and turning the Jacksonians loose on him. Crockett began with the disadvantage of having accomplished little in Congress, but this was not unusual for a first-term rural member of the House of Representatives.[1] He would find himself attacked for breaking ranks with Polk and the rest of the state's delegation, who blamed him for the defeat of the land bill, even while acknowledging that it had little chance of success to start with. For Polk, the issue was not the land bill, but what he viewed as Crockett's unforgivable disloyalty.

Crockett's years in Congress began when the Era of Good Feelings, during which there were no real parties but only loose factions or coalitions, was ending. Parties and regional factions were beginning to form around individuals, like Jackson and Clay, and the survival or growth of these parties required loyalty and discipline. Moreover, regional loyalties and divisive issues between regions caused people like Polk to insist on a united front if their region was to increase its political power or see its policies adopted. The rise of Jackson offered a golden opportunity for the southwest to increase its national influence, while casting a particularly bright light on Tennessee, Old Hickory's home state. By the end of Crockett's first term in Congress, Polk saw him as a potential threat to the unity he sought. Polk also was aware of Crockett's growing popularity in his district and the likelihood that he would become increasingly difficult to unseat, which would create a long-term challenge to Jacksonians. That concern was stoked by a letter Polk received from a West Tennessee friend earlier in the year notifying him that, should the vacant-land bill pass, "Crockett will be invincible, whether he aids in the cause or not."[2]

The campaign to sabotage Crockett may have begun as early as November 1828, when a belittling lampoon of him appeared in the *Jackson Gazette,* accusing him of uncouth, boorish behavior at a White House dinner hosted by President John Quincy Adams. The story was phrased in the first person, giving the impression that Crockett was telling it himself, and referred to him as "Davy," one of the earlier uses of that sobriquet in print. Crockett is seen drinking from finger bowls and accusing a waiter of stealing his food when the plates were cleared. He is quoted as shouting to the waiter, "'Hello mister, bring back my plate.' He fetch'd it back in a hurry as you may suppose, and when he sat it down before me, how do you think it was? Licked as clean as my hand. *If it was'nt, I wish I may be shot.*" It was an early appearance of the mythical, backwoods "Davy" Crockett, used in a way that undermined him and converted the positive effect it had on voters into a negative intended to portray him as an embarrassment to his constituents.[3]

The story could have been planted by Polk and the other Tennessee representatives, who may have already seen Crockett as a potential problem and thought it wise to unseat him before he became "invincible." Six months had passed since Crockett proposed the idea of giving land directly to squatters under a plan that would eliminate any federal land cession to the state, in contradiction to Polk's plan. In December 1828, Crockett introduced his amendment to Polk's land bill and wrote to the *Jackson Gazette* about it.[4] By then he also had received the petition from Haywood County demanding relief for squatters and more school funds for the Western District. Polk would have known Crockett's intentions by midyear and could have been responsible for planting the lampoon, or getting someone else to do it. Others have suggested that the story was planted by Jackson's enemies to ridicule a congressman from Old Hickory's own state. However, it is unlikely that the Adams forces had taken much notice of Crockett during his first months in office. Although Clay was aware of him and had been told that Crockett might be a potential anti-Jackson ally who was very popular in Tennessee, he had not had sufficient time to evaluate Crockett's views. Thus, there was no motive for the Adams forces to undermine Crockett, whose image was, at most, a mixed one among Jackson's enemies.[5]

Crockett was clearly humiliated. When he got wind of the lampoon, he wrote to two other congressmen who had attended the dinner, James Clark, an Adams man from Kentucky, and Gulian Verplanck, a Jacksonian from New York, asking that they write letters contradicting the story. Although he claimed to have initially ignored it, Crockett concluded that subsequent republication of the story in several Tennessee newspapers was intended "as in its origin it evidently was, to do me an injury. I can submit to it no longer without calling upon gentlemen who were present, to do me justice." He added, somewhat tellingly, that "I would not make this appeal, if it were not that, like other men, I have enemies who would take much pleasure in magnifying the plain rusticity of my manners into the most unparalleled grossness and indelicacy."[6] Clark and Verplanck responded the following day with testimonials on Crockett's behalf. Verplanck recalled "Your behavior there was, I thought, perfectly becoming and proper, and I do not recollect or believe that you said or did anything resembling the newspaper account." Clark called the newspaper article "absolutely destitute of every thing like truth," adding that he had "observed nothing in your behaviour but what was marked with the strictest propriety."[7]

The *Jackson Gazette* also rushed to Crockett's defense, noting "the mild, dignified, and forbearing manner, in which Mr. Crockett has noticed the rude and slanderous insult which has been offered him. His noble bearing on the occasion, has convinced us that he is not only more of the *man*, but more of the *gentleman*, than the miserable caricaturist who has attempted to render him ridiculous in the eyes of a virtuous and intelligent community."[8] For his part, Crockett confessed discomfort with the formal setting of the dinner. "I was wild from the backwoods. . . and I didn't know nothing about eating dinner with the big folks of our country; how should I, having been a hunter all my life? I had eat most of my dinners upon a log in the woods, and sometimes no dinner at all. I knew whether I ate dinner with the president or not, was a matter of no consequence, for my constituents were not to be benefitted by it. I did not go to court the president, for I was opposed to him in principle, and had no favours to ask at his hands. I was afraid, however, I should be awkward, as I was so entirely a stranger to fashion; and in going along, I resolved to observe the conduct of my friend, Mr. Verplanck, and to do as he did; and I know . . . that I did behave myself right well."[9] Although the matter blew over, it was only the opening volley in what would become a more brutal and sustained attack on the gentleman from the cane.

Crockett had already set out on his own course by asking the Public Lands Committee to explore the idea of donating 160 acres to each settler.[10] During debate he had irritated Polk by distracting attention from his objective by raising the separate idea of providing for squatters and later defied the Tennessee delegation by moving ahead with his amendment to Polk's bill. The bloody floor fight that ensued drove a sputtering Polk to round up his Tennessee political allies and begin a concerted effort to defeat Crockett in the coming election. His point man was to be Pryor Lea.[11]

Before Polk left Washington following the adjournment of Congress, he dashed off a vitriolic letter to several Tennessee Jacksonians condemning Crockett as untrustworthy and treacherous, and blaming him for the defeat of the land bill. "At the commencement of the Session we had some little hope of succeeding in the measure," Polk wrote, perhaps overestimating the bill's chance of success, before laying blame for its failure squarely on Crockett, charging that "its defeat is to be attributed in a great degree to the course taken by our man *Crocket,* who I regret to say opposed the very Bill at this Session, which he himself had agreed to in committee and supported and voted for in the House at the last Session of Congress." Polk did not mention Crockett's unsuccessful attempts to address the occupants in that bill, or the fact that it had been soundly defeated. Polk then stoked the fires of suspicion against Crockett: "He associated himself with our political enemies, and declared in presence of Mr. Blair of Ten.[12] and others, that he would vote for any measure any member wished him to vote for, provided he would vote for his foolish amendment and against the original Bill." Polk was sure to point out Crockett's disloyalty to his own state, while neglecting to mention the reasons behind Crockett's suspicions of the legislature and advocacy for his own constituents. "He took a course directly opposed to the interest of the State," Polk charged, "opposed to the whole of the balance of the delegation, and in direct violation of instructions given by our Legislature, (although he himself had been in the Legislature and voted for similar instructions) and one as we believed and so advised him before hand, well calculated, if not certain to defeat the whole measure. . . . I forbear to comment in detail, on the disgraceful and disrespectful terms in which *Crockett* was in the habit of speaking of his own State and her Legislature, further than to say that the whole delegation feel humiliated and can but regret that any one from our own country, should have Cooperated with some of our bitterest and most vindictive political enemies." Polk painted a conspiracy surrounding Crockett that included Joseph Gales and William W. Seaton, anti-Jackson publishers of *The National Intelligencer* newspaper and *The Register of Debates in Congress,* whom he accused of "dressing up and reporting speeches for him, which he never delivered as reported, & which all who know him, know he never did," an unfair swipe at Crockett, since Polk knew quite well that all members of Congress were free to submit speeches ahead of time or to edit them before they were published. Beyond that, Polk warned that "It is whispered that he intends to vote for *Gales* and *Seaton,* for public printers," rather than the pro-Jackson Duff Green.[13] "Rely upon it," Polk huffed, "he can be and has been opperated upon by our enemies. We cant trust him an inch."[14]

Having presented his damning case against Crockett, Polk then alerted his allies to be prepared to launch a counter-attack on Crockett should he attempt to explain himself to voters. "I have understood and think it probable that he may have a letter dressed up by some of *his friends,* and send home, to save himself if he can," an overreaction to what Polk must have known was a normal part of campaigning. "If so," he cautioned, "and any thing he writes requires correction in my absence you have the facts by which to do it. If it shall hereafter become necessary in consequence of any thing he may write or say, the balance of the delegation will notice him, under their own signatures." But Polk cautioned against striking first, preferring instead to wait and respond to Crockett. "We do not wish in advance to do so," he wrote, "for that would give him consequence, and might have the appearance with those unacquainted with the facts of an attack upon him, and thus excite a sympathy in his behalf which he does not deserve. This letter therefore is not written for publication in the newspapers but is addressed to you as a known friend, to furnish you with the facts, to meet any thing that may be said, until we can have an opportunity of meeting him personally, and exposeing his conduct if necessary."[15] Polk's letter was clearly the cornerstone of a conspiracy to unseat Crockett.

Polk must have discussed this strategy with others, including Pryor Lea, who, despite Polk's caution about striking first, opened a blistering attack on Crockett with an anonymous letter to the *Knoxville Register,* written only days after Polk's letter. Lea took issue with Crockett for voting against a proposal to change the method of voting in the House for "a printer and other officers" from anonymous paper ballots to a voice vote (*viva voce*), designed to make each member's vote public. The politicization of the press practically mandated that any administration choose a friendly publisher—thus, the Jacksonian preference for Duff Green over Gales and Seaton—and both sides might want to know who voted for or against them. As Lea noted, the vote was pretty much along party lines, with Crockett the only Tennessean voting to table the measure. Although he acknowledged that a few other Jacksonians voted the same way, he singled out Crockett for disloyalty to his state delegation. By implication, he accused Crockett of trying to conceal his votes from the public by favoring the secret paper ballot, rather than *viva voce*. Lea also claimed that Gales and Seaton curried favor with congressmen by "good dinners and speeches served up to his liking," pointing out that "Col. Crocket is one of these."[16]

Lea also blamed Crockett for the vacant-land bill failing but, like Polk, saw Crockett's perceived disloyalty to his state as his main transgression, saying that he "is estranged from his colleagues, associates chiefly with the other side, and has openly set himself up in market, offering to vote for anything in order to get votes by it. He declared his object to be to defeat the whole bill, if he could not succeed with his amendment, so as to get all for the benefit of a few of the people of his own district," summing up by charging that "He has changed his course, abused his State, and co-operated with her enemies. Where he may land I cannot say." Lea noted that Jackson was soon to take office as president and that Henry Clay and the anti-Jackson forces were organizing to frustrate the new administration's plans, implying that Crockett's disloyalty would aid in that effort. "We may look out for breakers," he warned.[17]

Crockett was quick to express his outrage toward the unidentified author of the letter, calling him a "scoundrel," a "contemptible sneak," a "paltroon" and a "puppy;" and he offered to "take some further notice of him" if he identified himself. He called all of Lea's charges "wicked falsehoods," particularly the suggestion that his vote was "in market" or that he worked against the interests of his constituents regarding the land issue. He suggested the author was among those "sitting by their firesides at home, while with the immortal Jackson, I was putting my *life 'in market,'* and fighting to defend my country."[18] He hinted at his willingness to confront his anonymous attacker by adding that "He will not find me backward in putting it 'in market' again in defence of my reputation."[19] In short, Crockett was insulted and offended, denied all of Lea's charges, and dared his attacker to reveal himself.

Despite his earlier caution not to strike first, Polk wrote to Lea praising his letter and barely took notice of Crockett's response. He confirmed Lea's charges, including the rumor that Crockett planned to vote for Gales and Seaton over Duff Green.[20] Regarding the land bill, Polk said Crockett was the "principal cause" of its having been tabled. "Whether we could have succeeded or not at the present Session in passing the Bill if he had harmonized and acted with the ballance of the delegation, I do not pretend to say, but after he took the course he did, all hope of success was lost."[21]

Polk confirmed Crockett's claim that "Before he offered his amendment, he showed it to several of the Tennessee delegation," but that "all expressed our decided disapprobation of his project, as being well calculated, if not certain to defeat the whole measure."[22] Of course, that had been Crockett's objective, since his amendment was, in fact, an entirely new bill, with all of Polk's language deleted, that would give the squatters their land, but cede none to Tennessee, which was the primary objective of the other Tennesseans. Polk mentioned that Crockett had told Judge Hugh Lawson White,[23] a U.S. senator from Tennessee, "that his object was to *kill the Bill,* if he could and carry his amendment," confirming Crockett's objection to ceding the land to the state. Polk made much of his bill's provision for the land occupants, making Crockett's objection to the bill sound almost nonsensical at that point, but he failed to mention Crockett's concern that no one in Congress, including Polk, could give any assurance that occupants would be charged a price for their land that they could afford.[24]

Polk told Lea that he could not attest to Crockett's bargaining for votes. "I know nothing personally," he said, "of his declaration, that he would do any thing that any member wished him to do, provided he would vote for his amendment," but added that "the fact that he did make such a declaration in the presence of Mr Blair of Tennessee, and others, was communicated to me shortly afterwards, and I suppose will be remembered by them."[25] Polk added a bit of condescension, saying, "I had ever as I believe the whole delegation had, treated him with the utmost kindness, and was more disposed to conceal than to expose his folly," concluding that "I have no other feelings towards Col. Crockett, than those of pity for his folly and regret that he had not consulted *better advisers,* when he suffered himself to give his sanction to the rude and very intemperate publication of this morning." Clearly, Polk found nothing rude or intemperate in Lea's attack on Crockett.[26]

Lea wasted no time in responding and revealed himself as the author of the original letter, repeating his charges and raising some new ones. Crockett, he said, had not only offered to vote for anything in exchange for a vote in favor of his amendment, but was willing "to do any thing for any gentleman who would favor his amendment, even so far as to get on his knees before him."[27] Crockett's disloyalty had been shown, Lea said, in his response to someone who asked if he would vote for the *viva voce* resolution along with the rest of the delegation, to which Crockett is said to have replied "there is no party now." Lea boasted that, while he had not personally witnessed all of Crockett's unforgivable transgressions, he had received written statements from others that attested to them. He included a thinly veiled threat to use those statements against Crockett if he attempted to question their veracity. "These statements are now in my possession to be used according to my own discretion," he claimed, "which dictates forbearance from exhibiting them, until there shall be a greater necessity than is imposed on me by the Colonel's random, indiscriminating negatives. If he can be induced to hazard a positive and public denial of the whole or of any specified part, I will as positively and publicly prove its punctilious correctness." Lea tossed in the same condescending tone as Polk in referring to the way Crockett had been treated by the rest of the delegation. "Having, in common with my colleagues, assiduously cultivated kind feelings for Colonel Crockett, as long as his conduct would permit, I was compelled at length to regard him as the willing instrument of political, sectional and personal malignities, affecting prejudicially the interests and character of my State, my constituents, and myself, through his resort to means unworthy of his situation." In short, the other Tennesseans would tolerate Crockett, a crude backwoodsman among a delegation dominated by more sophisticated lawyer-politicians, as long as he knew his place and didn't step out of line.

Crockett responded by raising the heat of the debate considerably. While Lea had addressed his letters to newspaper editors, rather than to Crockett personally, Crockett addressed his replies directly to Lea. He accused Lea of deception and underhandedness, claiming that he had thought they were warm colleagues and that he believed he could rely on Lea even if all the other Tennesseans abandoned him. He agreed that he told Lea and the others of his plan to introduce his own amendment, noting that if Lea found that unacceptable, he could have told Crockett that at the time. He not only accused Lea of betraying him but of having practiced underhanded duplicity while doing it, noting that if Lea believed these charges, he "should have closed your friendly intercourse with me, at a much earlier period. But was it so? No Sir—to the very last hour that your attempt to ruin me was sealed in secrecy, you seemed to meet me friendly—to converse with me as a friend!!!—affording in your conduct not the *slightest index to the feelings of your heart.*"[28]

Crockett gave his assessment of the land bill's defeat. Rather than a conspiracy among Crockett and Jackson's enemies, he saw it clearly as a conspiracy among the Tennessee delegation against him. "I had a favorite measure before Congress," he said, "a measure which was intended to bless many a poor and helpless family, and afford them shelter from the chilling blast of winter. You, sir, and others, had fixed your affections upon a different system of policy, and because I endeavored to prevail upon *administration* men to stay the merciless hand of the swindling speculators, you cried out, that I had joined the enemies of my party. Because I was unwilling to trust the labour and carings of my constituents in the hands of the Tennessee legislature, you raised the cry that I had abused my state; and indeed, to defeat my proposition, piteous appeals were made of Jackson men; many of whom voted with you on account of the subtlety used to convince them, that their political opponents had taken me up to break down the remainder of the delegation. I did not defeat you—your proposition, your self, and my other colleagues, defeated me."[29] He denied that he caused the bill's defeat and found nothing wrong in seeking votes from anti-Jackson forces. "You attempted to bring me into suspicion, and for the moment, you succeeded; but you should blush (if your cheeks be not of marble) to discover that the period has already passed which tested my political firmness, and your baseless jealousy. Its restless spirit so disordered your brain, that though you formerly concealed it, it now appears you could not see me associate with a gentleman of different politics, without awful apprehensions that there was dander of my apostacy; so frantic was your imagination, that it pursued me to *dinner parties,* where God knows I never went; and even fancied me on my knees imploring votes for my measure, when in fact I never bowed unless it was before my Creator."[30]

Crockett denied Lea's charges and showed his awareness of the condescension that Lea and the others had shown him. "You know that I was but a humble farmer, with but an humble education, and doubtless supposed that I would *tamely* submit to any indignity which you might offer. You supposed your cold array against me a sufficient weight of law and of talent, to crush with me a single effort. But, Sir, in each conclusion you are mistaken. I will resent your insults nor will a magnanimous community ever permit an individual, who is compelled to stand alone, to be condemned without trial, or to suffer without crime. I call upon you, sir, for your testimony and in return, I pledge myself to disprove by gentlemen of the highest respectability, each and every charge which you may attempt to establish injurious to my character." He concluded by throwing down the gauntlet and daring Lea to pick it up. "I retract no sentiment advanced until you do me justice," he wrote. "But if as you intimate, they inspire you with 'personal feelings,' and require *'private satisfaction,'* you know where to find me."[31]

Newspapers picked up the ongoing dispute, especially Crockett's closing lines, and reported the likelihood of a duel between the two. One paper said the duel would take place "immediately on the rising of Congress," adding its disapproval of the whole affair with the sour hope that "May God send them both an ignominious death."[32]

Crockett again sought support from other members of Congress, writing to two Washington boarding houses, the "Mess" at Dowson's and the "Mess" at J. Davis's, asking members to deny Lea's charges. "I request of each of you the favour to say whether I am the Character described by him," he asked, "and what has been my Conduct Sence you have Known me and also the manner in which I have discharged my official duties." No response to the plea has survived, but Crockett noted on the letter to Dowson's, "To which the 'Mess' made no reply."[33]

Lea had the last word in the duel of letters in a very long, final rebuttal to Crockett, consisting almost entirely of Lea's quotations from anonymous sources that confirmed his charges, responding to Crockett's challenge that he produce such proof. Lea quickly brushed off the suggestion of a duel with Crockett and turned to one of his sources, who claimed Crockett had visited him and told him he had dined at Seaton's house and was very pleased with the revised version of his House speech that had appeared in the *Register of Debates.* Crockett is alleged to have remarked "I like Gales prime, for he has made me a much better speech than I made in the House or ever could make and I will get 1000 or 1500 and send them home to my people, and they will think I have made a great speech" or "words to that effect."[34] The source appears to have been James C. Mitchell, who had once dubbed Crockett "the gentleman from the cane," and was now a Tennessee congressman.[35] Lea's sources confirmed all of his charges against Crockett, which is not surprising, since all of them seem to have been members of the Tennessee delegation to whom Polk had written. One source quoted Crockett as saying that his aim was to defeat the entire land bill if he could not pass his amendment, because he feared the land getting into the hands of the legislature. Asked what he hoped to gain by that, Lea's source quoted Crockett as saying that "the United States could never sell the land, and if the State did not procure it, his people could have the use of it for nothing," a cynical, and quite possibly accurate, assessment by Crockett.

Much of what Lea's sources related merely confirmed what Crockett himself had said, including the fact that he openly promised to do what was necessary to get the amendment passed, because his constituents came before any consideration of party loyalty, including cultivating votes from Adams supporters. "He said he would do what his constituents wished," Lea's source claimed, "and that he did not expect either me or any other member from the State to support his amendment; but that we would see he would carry it without any of us; that he had been very industrious in trying to make friends out of doors, and he intended to be more industrious than I ever heard of any other person being."[36] Lea's source also believed that the anti-Jacksonians were using Crockett by pretending to support him in order to cause dissension in the Jackson ranks. Some of Lea's material is taken directly from Polk's February 17 letter, including Polk's claim that Crockett voted for the adjournment motion put forth by Lea, when Crockett seemed on the verge of getting his bill approved, despite Crockett's claim that the adjournment was a ploy to derail his efforts just as he seemed on the verge of success. Crockett did make that claim in his circular of January 15, 1829.

Gales and Seaton also got into the act with a denial that they had anything to do with writing Crockett's material. They also denied that Crockett had dined at either of their homes, although they admitted that Seaton "has had the pleasure of seeing him, with other members of Congress at his house."[37]

Although the affair nearly led to a duel between Crockett and Lea, that outcome was avoided. Crockett was determined to resolve the issue before he returned home, and a peaceful resolution was finally reached, although the specific terms are not known. Crockett's recent turn to religion was credited for the nonviolent end of the incident. As one newspaper put it "It is whispered that a great change has been produced in the character of Mr. Crockett since the last session, and that he has become religious, and the pacific termination of this affair is attributed to that circumstance."[38]

There is evidence to support this explanation in a letter Crockett wrote to his brother-in-law, George Patton, in which he expressed his grief over the death of a young niece. "I hope she is this day in eternal happiness whare I am endevouring to make my way," he wrote. "I have altered my cours in life a great deal sence I reached this place I have not taisted one drop of Arden Sperits since I arrived here nor never expects to while I live nothing stronger than Cider I trust that god will give me fortitude in my undertaking I have never made a pretention to Relegion in my life before I have run a long race tho I trust that I was called in good time I have been reproved many times for my wickedness by my Dear wife who I am certain will be no little astonished when she gets information of my determination". Crockett closed "with a hope that the protecting hand of the almighty may Bless guard & protect you and all our conections is the Prayer of your affectionate Brother Farewell".[39]

The Lea affair may have ended, but the campaign went on. Despite his efforts to undermine Crockett, Polk soon realized that the Colonel was still very popular in his district, where his constituents appreciated the stand he had made on their behalf and his fidelity in following the instructions in the Haywood County petition. They distrusted the legislature as much as Crockett did and for the same reasons. Crockett had kept faith with them and might yet secure a land bill for them, so there was every reason to return him to Congress. Polk also had his hands full in other Tennessee House races, where Lea and John H. Marable, another Tennessee congressman and Polk ally, were in danger of losing their seats. There was little time for Polk to waste battling a popular Crockett, who seemed a shoe-in. Archibald Yell, one of Polk's Tennessee confidants, cautioned that Crockett was likely to remain in office for some time, even while lamenting "the fate of your land bill and the part which *Davy Crockett* took in it. It is a misfortune to the state that such a man should be one of her delegates. But it is so and I fear will so continue for a while at least &c."[40]

Several potential candidates were mentioned as possible opponents for Crockett, most of whom quickly saw no chance to defeat him and backed out. These included Pleasant Miller,[41] a one-time Jackson supporter who turned against the president and saw no reason to oppose Crockett, with whom he strongly agreed on the issue of squatters' rights.[42] The Polk faction finally turned again to Adam Alexander, who had lost to Crockett in 1827. Alexander agreed to run, but frantically requested from Polk any information that might help in his attempt to blame Crockett for the lost land bill, asking specifically what provision had been made for the land occupants in Polk's original bill. He asked Polk to provide him "Anything that you may deem necessary . . . as all will be necessary for me to meet the powerful objections and strong efforts of my personal & political enemies all of whome are paradeing in full relief before the people." Alexander added a bit too optimistically, "If I am not mistaken I will ultimately be able to Triumph over my unprincipled enemies and again find my friends in Congress in support of the peoples President."[43]

Polk told Alexander that his bill had been amended to make "ample provision for the occupants— 'without charge'—and yet Col. Crockett opposed the Bill, as thus amended and adhered to his own amendment," failing to mention that he had not favored such a provision but was forced to accept it.[44] He also either failed to understand or chose not to mention the virtual certainty that his bill would be defeated, as it had been once already, leaving the occupants without relief.

Crockett kicked off the campaign with a circular letter to his constituents on January 15 that clearly blamed the land bill's failure on Polk and the other Tennessee representatives. He noted that, while he nominally supported Polk's original bill, he never believed it had a chance of passing and, when it failed, he was determined to keep the Western District lands out of the legislature's hands. He accused the state of forcing occupants to pay double fees, which many could not afford, for unnecessary surveys in order to force them to sell their land just to pay the surveyors. "The effect was," he summarized, "that it was placed in the power of a few deputy Surveyors to defraud you, by charging double prices for their labor, and often to sell the poor man's all to pay the fee. Seeing what I have seen, and feeling what I have felt, on account of this legislative error, I was unwilling to trust your homes to their mercy. I moreover knew that the weight of the State Legislature would stand, in a great measure, as the Tennessee delegation stands in Congress; that is, opposed to my proposition, which has been, and still is, dear to my heart. To make a short story of the whole affair, I wished you to have your homes directly from the hands of Congress, and then you could, with certainty, call them your own." Crockett appended a copy of his bill and text of his speech in the House defending it, a speech that also raised the point of the inequity of Tennessee funding for schools. He noted that revenues from land sales in the Western District were used to fund colleges elsewhere in the state, with a large amount going to the University of North Carolina under an agreement with that state, rather than funding common schools in the Western District. Thus, his constituents were not only losing their land, but also the schools to which they should have been entitled.[45] Crockett made it clear that, in his view, the other Tennessee representatives had conspired behind his back to destroy his amendment. He ended with a promise to continue his fight, and the voters cheered him on.

Nonetheless, anonymous letters appeared in the local press criticizing Crockett's strategy on the land bill, suggesting Congress would never give away land and that the occupants' best bet lay with the legislature. This outcry was clearly generated by the Polk faction, since the legislature was powerless to act unless Congress relinquished the land to the state, which is what Polk wanted, but which Congress had refused to do.[46] At least one parody ridiculing Crockett as an underhanded, slippery politician and bumpkin was published under the fictitious name "Dennis Brulgrudery," which criticized Crockett for announcing his candidacy before being invited to run again, in keeping with the custom of the "office seeking the man." The letter suggested that Crockett would say or do anything to appeal to any constituent, without regard to principal, and suggested that Crockett's pursuit of office was cynical: "If I am not qualified, the scripture says *the bigger the fool, the better the luck.*"[47] Crockett was also attacked for having cast unfair aspersions on Alexander regarding an outstanding debt he'd left in Washington in 1828, and which Crockett helped to pay. Crockett was forced to write an explanation of what had actually taken place, which amounted to no more than he and Jacob C. Isacks, another Tennessee representative, having posted a bond for Alexander's debt (perhaps to uphold the honor of their state) and Alexander himself later paying it off.[48]

Crockett's enemies dragged out another event from his past in an effort to cast him in a dishonorable light. Crockett later explained that he had sought to help a neighbor, Rev. David Gordon, a preacher, who held a warrant for 236 acres, find vacant land of good quality. Without asking a fee, Crockett located the man and his family on a good site near his own farm, hauled water to them until they dug a well, and even rode forty miles twice for a doctor when the entire family became ill. Meanwhile, Crockett had hired David C. Phillips to build a horse mill, paying him fifty dollars up front. Phillips owed Gordon twenty-five dollars, and Crockett offered to pay off Phillips' debt in lieu of further payment for completing the mill. Phillips, who apparently was completely incompetent at his professed trade, constructed a shabby excuse for a mill that was, in Crockett's view, "a mere Rattle box unfit for any other use than to scare the crows with, for which purpose it unfortunately stood in the wrong place, so that in the end it answered no purpose at all."[49] Crockett refused to pay Phillips' debt, leaving Gordon to deal with Phillips on his own. Crockett's opponents had learned about the incident and persuaded Gordon to accuse Crockett of reneging on a promise, but without fully explaining what had happened. Apparently, the story had little traction with voters, but it showed the limits to which Crockett's enemies were willing to go.[50]

Crockett was so confident of reelection that he wrote a longtime friend that he expected "no opposition in my next Contest," adding perhaps a bit too confidently, "I do expect I could come here [to Congress] as long as I could wish."[51] By April he was predicting that he would win by five-thousand votes. "I have backed out three opponents and Colo[nel] Alexander has lately been entered against me Tho my own opinion is that he will back out before August if he does not I will beat him five thousand votes So says the people."[52] He reminded John H. Bryan, a North Carolina congressman, that he had beaten Alexander two years earlier, adding, "I have no doubt of getting a much larger Majority in very next Race."[53] He felt secure enough to even spend time campaigning against Polk, Lea, and Marable and predicted that all three would be defeated, sarcastically mentioning that he had visited Polk's district "and done what little I could for him."[54]

Crockett's confidence was justified, and he easily won reelection. When the votes were tallied in August, he polled 6,773 to 3,641 for Alexander, not the five thousand-vote margin he had predicted, but still nearly doubling his opponent's total and a far larger victory than some of his struggling Tennessee colleagues had managed. Lea may have regretted the time he had squandered attacking Crockett instead of campaigning when he found himself in a race so close it was only decided by a recount that gave him a slim margin of victory. Marable did even worse, losing to Cave Johnson, but Polk easily won reelection, so Crockett had judged the political winds with some accuracy. His lopsided victory could only have encouraged him to continue his independent course without fear of Polk and the Jackson machine.[55]

The press acknowledged that Crockett had overcome deficiencies in education and refinement with a clear honesty and candor that appealed to his neighbors.[56] He had continued to charm voters from the stump with jokes, stories, and language laced with local flavor. He may not have joined in the drinking, having undergone the religious awakening that had helped him avoid a duel with Lea, but he made sure the people he addressed from the stump were generously "treated."[57] Crockett was able to maintain the image of a plain local farmer, while also reassuring his constituents that he was respectable and never an embarrassment to them in office.

The image Crockett had carefully crafted as a campaigner was, however, beginning to grow into something larger than the humorous stump speaker. During his first term in Congress, newspapers had already begun to run stories that cast Crockett as a fictional, nearly superhuman backwoodsman. Shortly after he took his seat in Congress, newspapers wrote that "It was reported before his arrival there, that he was wading the Ohio towing a disabled steamboat and two keels. He says there was more truth in it, than in the report that Adams would get the vote of his district."[58] This image could be seen as entertaining or comical, but it also could be used against Crockett by making him seem out of place in Washington and unsuited to his office. It may have contributed to the bogus account of his behavior at the White House. During his tour of the United States, Alexis de Tocqueville heard of Crockett and came away with an unflattering impression of the frontier congressman. "When the right of suffrage is *universal*," he observed, "and when the deputies are paid by the state, it's singular how low and how far wrong the people can go. Two years ago the inhabitants of the district of which Memphis is the capital sent to the House of Representatives in Congress an individual named David Crockett, who has had no education, can read with difficulty, has no property, no fixed residence, but passes his life hunting, selling his game to live, and dwelling continuously in the woods."[59] Obviously, Tocqueville was badly misinformed about Crockett's capabilities and living conditions, as well as the electoral system, but his description of Crockett shows how such erroneous images of him were emerging throughout the country and even becoming accepted as factual.[60] Crockett's opponents had sought to portray him as boorish and uncouth during the campaign and would continue their efforts to use the wild man "Davy" image against him.

During the 1829 campaign, newspapers beyond Tennessee had already begun to take pot shots at "Davy" Crockett, attributing bogus speeches to him that cast him as an illiterate bumpkin. At least one seems to have been recycled, at least partly, from the 1827 campaign. "Friends, fellow-citizens, brothers & sisters," it began, "Carroll's a statesman—Jackson's a hero and Crockett's a *horse!!* Friends, fellow-citizens, brothers and sisters—they accuse me of adultery, its a lie. I never ran away with any man's wife that was'nt willing in my life. They accuse me of gambling; its a lie—for I always planks the cash. Finally, friends, fellow-citizens, brothers and sisters, they accuse me of being a drunkard; its a d__d eternal lie, for whiskey can't make me drunk."[61] Although the *Jackson Gazette* reprinted this story, it continued to support Crockett and published a defense of the congressman from such attacks: "All his friends admit that he is somewhat eccentric and that from a defect in education, his stump speeches are not famous for polish and refinement—yet they are plain, forcible and generally respectful. That he ever uttered the expressions contained in the following article from the Missouri Republican, we presume none of his constituents will believe; and we would not now touch upon the subject but to correct any error, which the wise acre who wrote the article, evidently intended to lead strangers into, relative to Col. Crockett's character and abilities. The free people of the Western District have again elected him their representative, and as such is the case, we hope these Missouri folks will endeavor to look to some other quarter for objects to poke their fun at. At the request of several of Col. Crocket's friends we publish the article, and feel a pleasure in saying that his *friends* in this District do not believe him capable of such a pitiful course."[62] Despite the *Gazette's* protestations, it is likely that, at least on the campaign trail, Crockett continued to adopt a persona not unlike the one found in the Missouri newspaper.

The backwoods image that Crockett had so carefully crafted as a campaigner began to slip from his control as that image spread beyond Tennessee. In 1829, William Moncrieff wrote a play titled *Monsieur Mallet; or, My Daughters Letter,* which featured a character named Jeremiah Kentuck, described as "a bragging, self-confident, versatile, and vigorous frontiersman" who also was a "Congressman, attorney-at-law, dealer in log-wood, orator, and 'half-horse, half-alligator, with a touch of the steamboat, and a small taste of the snapping turtle.'"[63] Although that is an image that would become associated with Crockett, he was not sufficiently well known in 1828, when the play was written, to have inspired the character. But Kentuck's appeal signaled a growing public taste for such characters, and a real-life backwoodsman in Congress, about whom such tales were starting to circulate, was sure to draw attention. It would not be long before similar characters would be patterned after that growing image of Crockett.

Even as Crockett injected humor into his campaign, he remained keenly aware that his enemies were afoot. After his reelection he charged that he had been the victim of vicious attacks in each of his campaigns. "I have been a candidate for the last eight years of my life, and it has so happened that once every two years of that period, just before August, I have been charged upon with all the artillery which malice hatred and envy, could bring into the field to bear against me, for the purpose of laying me out, and establishing my character and standing in society, in the odious position of a scoundrel, without having ever once in the course of my life, so far as has come to my own knowledge or belief, either directly or indirectly, deserved the imputation." He claimed that he preferred to ignore malicious stories directed at him, but he was willing to make an exception in the case of the good Reverend Gordon, noting that "when we consider that the author of the present one is a preacher of the Gospel, whose very calling is calculated to cloak his falsehoods, and inspire confidence in the truth of his statement, it is presumed this fact would of itself be a sufficient apology for troubling the public with the present communication." He still found room for humor and assured the Baptist church that "nothing but necessity could have induced me to assail one of their body—but if in doing so I have marked out a black sheep belonging improperly to their flock, I am sure they will not feel unthankful for the favour."[64]

After the election Crockett continued to proclaim himself a Jackson man, but with reservations. "To General Jackson I am a firm and undeviating friend," Crockett wrote. "I have fought under his command—and am proud to own that he has been my commander. I have loved him, and in the sincerity of my heart I say that, I still love *'him';* but to be compelled to love every one who for purposes of self aggrandizement, *pretend* to rally around the 'Jackson standard,' is what I never can submit to. The people of this country, like the humble boatsman on the Mississippi, ought to begin to look out for *breakers!* The *fox* is about! let the *roost* be guarded!"[65] The term "fox" was a reference to Jackson's secretary of state, Martin Van Buren, who was sometimes called "the Red Fox."

The Jacksonian efforts to unseat Crockett in 1829 were merely a dress rehearsal for more intensified future attacks on him. He would find himself increasingly isolated in his own state and forced to rely on the personal appeal he held among his constituents.

The gloves were clearly off, and Crockett knew he would remain an outcast in Tennessee politics. Nonetheless, he decided to reach out to his colleagues once more and seek a reconciliation with them—and he would do it by compromising with them on his most important priority; the land bill.

———————

1   See, for example, the dismal, nearly nonexistent record of William Fitzgerald, who defeated Crockett in 1831, during his sole term in the House. He never even mentioned the land issue, nor much of anything else.

2   Nathaniel Steele to James K. Polk, March 2, 1828, in Herbert Weaver and Paul H. Bergeron, *Correspondence of James K. Polk, Volume I, 1817–1832* (Nashville: Vanderbilt University Press, 1969), 158.

3   *Republican Star and General Advertiser,* January 13, 1829; the story appeared in the *Jackson Gazette* on November 15, 1828, taken from the *Lexington Bulletin.*

4   *Jackson Gazette,* January 3, 1829.

5   *(Easton, Maryland) Republican Star and General Advertiser,* January 13, 1829; the story first appeared in November 1828 in several newspapers. See Stanley J. Folmsbee and Anna Grace Catron, "David Crockett: Congressman," *East Tennessee Historical Society's Publications,* No. 29 (1957): 54; James A. Shackford, *David Crockett: The Man and the Legend* (Chapel Hill: University of North Carolina Press, 1956), 125; Mark Derr, *The Frontiersman* (New York: William Morrow and Company, Inc., 1993), 145. Also see William C. Davis, *Three Roads to the Alamo: The Lives and Fortunes of David Crockett, James Bowie, and William Barret Travis* (New York: Harper Collins, 1998), 134–36; Davis concludes that the lampoon was probably written by a Democrat surrogate of the Jacksonians, reflecting a growing fear of Crockett's independence.

6   Crockett to James Clark and Gulian Verplanck, January 3, 1829, from *Augusta Chronicle,* January 14, 1829. A partial holograph of the letter to Clark is in the Charles Hamilton autograph auction catalog, September 22, 1966, item 60. It appears to be in Crockett's handwriting, but includes some punctuation, typically missing from his correspondence.

7   *Augusta Chronicle,* January 14, 1829; the letters from Clark and Verplanck are dated January 4, 1829.

8   *Jackson Gazette,* February 14, 1829, reprinted from the *Savannah Mercury,* n.d.

9   James Strange French, *Sketches and Eccentricities of Colonel Crockett of West Tennessee* (New York: J. & J. Harper,1833), 166.

10 *House Journal,* 20th Congress, May 10, 1828, 721.

11 Pryor Lea was a lawyer and congressman from Knox County, Tennessee, and a Polk ally. Like Crockett, he had served in the Creek War in 1813 and as United States attorney for Tennessee in 1824 before being elected to two terms in Congress, losing his bid for a third term. He moved to Jackson, Mississippi, in 1836 and to Goliad, Goliad County, Texas in 1846. He engaged in railroad building and management, and was a member of the Texas State People's Convention in January 1861, which passed the ordinance of secession. He died in Goliad September 14, 1879. His brother, Luke Lea, also served in Congress. Biographical Directory of the United States Congress online, http://bioguide.congress.gov.

12 John Blair was a Tennessee lawyer, congressman and supporter of Polk and Jackson. Biographical Directory of the United States Congress online, http://bioguide.congress.gov.

[13] Duff Green was editor of *The United States Telegraph,* which was the principal Jackson newspaper during the early years of the administration and had opposed the administration of John Quincy Adams, placing Green at odds with the pro-Adams Gales & Seaton. Under Jackson, Green replaced Gales & Seaton as printer of government documents. When Jackson and his vice president, John C. Calhoun, had a falling-out with each other, Green backed Calhoun, and his newspaper lost its contract as government printer. W. Stephen Belko, *The Invincible Duff Green: Whig of the West* (Columbia: University of Missouri Press, 2006), 102.

[14] Polk to Davison McMillen, January 16, 1829, in Weaver & Bergeron, *Correspondence of James K. Polk, Volume I,* 229–31.

[15] Ibid. The letter was dictated, and is not in Polk's handwriting; the recipients were Davison McMillen in Fayetteville, Dr. John H. Camp in Pulaski, Archibald Yell at Shelbyville, and Andrew C. Hays in Columbia, all prominent Polk supporters.

[16] *Knoxville Register,* February 4, 1829, reprinted in *Jackson Gazette,* March 14, 1829.

[17] Ibid.

[18] Crockett was mistaken, for, like him, Lea had served in the Creek War in 1813. Crockett probably knew this, since he was well acquainted with Lea, but he did not know that Lea had written the letter.

[19] *United States Telegraph,* February 17, 1829, reprinted in the *Jackson Gazette* March 14, 1829.

[20] Polk could not have known for sure how Crockett voted, unless Crockett told him, because Duff Green, more loyal to John C. Calhoun than to Jackson, was chosen as public printer on February 10, 1829, by the very secret paper ballot that Polk had opposed in favor of *viva voce.* The vote was close, with Green receiving 107 ballots and Gales and Seaton 95; 4 ballots were cast for others and 2 were blank. Given Crockett's friendly relations with Gales and Seaton, and his expressed admiration for the way they had improved his speeches for print, as well as Crockett's general independence, it would not be at all surprising if he had cast his ballot for them. *Journal of the House of Representatives of the United States,* Volume 22, 20th Congress, Second Session, February 10, 1829, 270–71.

[21] Polk to Pryor Lea, February 17, 1829. Weaver & Bergeron, *Correspondence of James K. Polk, Volume I, 1817–1832,* 240–41.

[22] Ibid.

[23] Hugh Lawson White, a Tennessee lawyer, had held many official posts, including state senator, before being elected to the U.S. Senate in 1825 as a Jacksonian, filling a vacancy caused by the resignation of Jackson himself. White was reelected in 1829, but by 1835, when he was reelected again, he had turned against Jackson. He was supported by many Tennessee Jacksonians and former Jacksonians, including Crockett, in his unsuccessful run for the presidency in 1836. Biographical Directory of the United States Congress online, http://bioguide.congress.gov.

[24] Weaver & Bergeron, *Correspondence of James K. Polk, Volume I, 1817–1832,* 240–41.

[25] Ibid.

[26] Ibid.

[27] *United States Telegraph,* February 19, 1829, reprinted in the *Jackson Gazette* March 14, 1829.

[28] *United States Telegraph,* February 21, 1829; reprinted in the *Jackson Gazette,* March 21, 1829.

[29] Ibid.

[30] Ibid.

[31] Ibid.

[32] *(Providence, Rhode Island) Cadet and Statesman,* February 28, 1829; *Baltimore Patriot,* February 19, 1829.

[33] Crockett to the "Mess at Dowsons," February 23, 1829, Rare Book and Manuscript Library, Columbia University; Crockett to the "Mess at J. Davises," February 23, 1829, Department of Rare Books and Special Collections, University of Rochester Library.

[34] *United States Telegraph,* February 25, 1829; reprinted in the *Jackson Gazette,* March 28, 1829. One of the speeches that were inserted into Crockett's January 15, 1829, circular was a heavily rewritten version of a speech he had given in the House on January 12, 1829. That may be the speech that Lea and his sources claim was rewritten by Gales and Seaton, who did print the circular and may have printed the same speech in their newspaper. The original version of the speech survives in the *Register of Debates,* January 12, 1829, 199–200.

[35] James C. Mitchell to Lea, February 17, 1829, cited in Thomas B. Jones, "The Public Lands of Tennessee," *Tennessee Historical Quarterly* 27, No. 1 (Spring 1968): 33. Mitchell, who had once dubbed Crockett "the gentleman from the cane," was clearly one of Lea's sources. Jones also refers to a similar anti-Crockett statement from Hugh Lawson White, another of Lea's sources, also dated February 17, the same day Polk had written to Lea, goading him on, which suggests that the Tennesseans were working in concert to build their case against Crockett.

[36] *United States Telegraph,* February 25, 1829; reprinted in the *Jackson Gazette* March 28, 1829.

[37] *Jackson Gazette,* March 21, 1829.

[38] *U.S. Gazette,* February 20, 1829, reprinted in (Hartford) *Connecticut Courant,* March 3, 1829.

[39] Crockett to George Patton, January 27, 1829, courtesy of the Tennessee State Library and Archives.

[40] Archibald Yell to Polk, February 14, 1829, in Weaver and Bergeron, *Correspondence of James K. Polk, Volume I,* 238.

[41] Pleasant Moorman Miller held several public offices in Tennessee and was elected to Congress in 1809, where he was a strong supporter of national expansion. He was a delegate to the Tennessee legislature from 1817 to 1823, where he became, like Crockett, a strong advocate for squatters' rights. Although he introduced a resolution nominating Andrew Jackson for president

in 1822, he turned against Jackson in 1829, refusing to run against Crockett that year, and became a dedicated Whig Party organizer. *Tennessee Encyclopedia of History and Culture* website, http://tennesseeencyclopedia.net/imagegallery.php?EntryID=M098.

42 *National Intelligencer,* reprinted in *Norwich Courier,* May 13, 1829.

43 Adam R. Alexander to Polk, April 25, 1829, in Weaver and Bergeron, *Correspondence of James K. Polk, Volume I,* 258–59.

44 Polk to Alexander, May 1, 1829, in ibid, 259–62.

45 *Address of Mr. Crockett, to the Voters of the Ninth Congressional District of the State of Tennessee; Together with His Remarks in the House of Representatives, January 5, 1829,* (Washington: Printed by Gales & Seaton, January 15, 1829), Rare Books Division, Library of Congress, 9. Crockett sent copies of the circular and his speech to friends at home, asking that they be distributed as widely as possible; Crockett to Capt. Seat, January 26, 1829, courtesy of the Tennessee State Library and Archives.

46 *Jackson Gazette,* March 7, 1829.

47 Ibid.

48 *Jackson Gazette,* August 15, 1829. Crockett's letter is followed by a rejoinder from B. G. Stewart, disagreeing with Crockett's account, which is not surprising, since Crockett accused Stewart of spreading the false rumor that he had lied about Alexander. Jacob C. Isacks, often referred to as "Judge Isaacks" by Crockett, was an influential Jacksonian congressman from Tennessee who served five consecutive terms in the House of Representatives (1823–32), but was defeated in his bid for a sixth term. Biographical Directory of the United States Congress online, http://bioguide.congress.gov.

49 *Jackson Gazette,* September 26, 1829.

50 Ibid. Crockett did not even respond to the story until after the election, at which time he provided testimony from William Edmonson and John Ryen in support of his account. Gordon raised the issue again during the 1831 election and tried to censure Crockett's witnesses. Gordon's timing casts doubt on his charges. He had waited nearly two years to respond to Crockett's 1829 letter, and each time he raised the issue Crockett happened to be engaged in a re-election campaign, suggesting that Crockett's opponents had coaxed Gordon to come forth on both occasions. *Southern Statesman,* May 14, 1831.

51 Crockett to Boater Canaday, February 3, 1829, from Canaday family website, http://www.geocities.com/canadayfamily/davy/davyandboater.htm. Although the website includes a copy of the original holograph, its present location is unknown.

52 Crockett to Gales & Seaton, April 18, 1829, David Crockett Miscellaneous File, Manuscripts and Archives Division, The New York Public Library, Astor, Lenox and Tilden Foundations. Crockett also mentions that Sam Houston had resigned as Tennessee governor and was leaving for Indian country.

53 Crockett to John H. Bryan, May 26, 1829, original in the John Heritage Bryan Papers (#147), Special Collections Department, J. Y. Joyner Library, East Carolina University, Greenville, North Carolina, USA; transcript and holograph images are found online at http://media.lib.ecu.edu/spclcoll/staffpick.cfm?id=38.

54 Crockett to Gales & Seaton , April 18, 1829.

55 David Crockett, *A Narrative of the Life of David Crockett of the State of Tennessee,* ed. James A. Shackford and Stanley J. Folmsbee (Knoxville, University of Tennessee Press, 1973), 205 n. 7.

56 *Jackson Gazette,* August 15, 1829.

57 Crockett to George Patton, January 27, 1829, courtesy of the Tennessee State Library and Archives; Davis, *Three Roads to the Alamo,* 168–69, citing J. J. B., "Crockett's Electioneering Tour," *Harper's Magazine,* April 1867, 610.

58 *Jackson Gazette,* January 27, 1829.

59 George Wilson Pierson, *Tocqueville in America* (Baltimore: Johns Hopkins University Press, 1938), 608. Pierson was no more accurate in his own assessment of Crockett than Tocqueville. He wrote, "Celebrated from Washington to the reaches of the frontier for his ignorance, his bad language, his lack of modesty, decorum and respect for his elders, even in that day of backwoods democracy Crockett was considered a reproach to American politics." He added that Crockett's death at the Alamo enabled "this troublemaker to end a dubious career in heroism."

60 Tocqueville's information also was dated. He wrote this in 1831, two years after Crockett's reelection and on the eve of defeat in his bid for a third consecutive term. Tocqueville also wrote of meeting Sam Houston aboard a riverboat around the same time.

61 *Jackson Gazette,* August 15, 1829, reprinted from the *Missouri Republican,* n.d.

62 Ibid.

63 Joseph John Arpad. "David Crockett, An Original Legendary Eccentricity and Early American Character," Ph.D. dissertation, Duke University, 1968, 85.

64 *Jackson Gazette,* September 26, 1829.

65 *Jackson Gazette,* May 27, 1830.

Chapter 4

"The Best Provision I Could Make"
The Tennessee Land Bill (1829–1830)

Back in Washington, on the heels of his election victory, Crockett wasted no time renewing his efforts to secure a land bill. When he took his seat in the House of Representatives he had changed his party affiliation from "Jacksonian" to "Anti-Jacksonian," leaving no doubt as to where he stood regarding the popular president. Nonetheless, Crockett would enjoy a brief rapprochement with his Jacksonian Tennessee colleagues.

However, in December 1829, Crockett was still rubbing Polk the wrong way by securing formation of a select committee, chaired by him, to deal with the land issue. Polk insisted that the issue belonged in his Standing Committee on the Public Lands, but Crockett prevailed. After winning this procedural duel, Crockett further irritated Polk by having all of the records on the issue transferred from Polk's committee to his, which was heavily loaded with anti-Jackson easterners, but included Polk as well. Crockett made no attempt to excuse the geopolitical makeup of his committee and explained that he needed the records because most of the committee members were easterners who were unfamiliar with the issue, a clear indication that he was continuing his quest for support from outside of his state.[1]

Despite this acrimonious beginning, Crockett's committee worked out a compromise land bill that Polk and the other Tennesseans approved. This is a little-known or -discussed chapter in the saga of Crockett's land bill, but a significant one. In its report to the House that accompanied the bill, Crockett's committee cited a new report from the General Land Office that provided an inventory of the Tennessee vacant lands. This was the report that Polk had requested the previous January after his own bill had failed. It found that, while there were still more than two million acres of vacant land in West Tennessee, "there can be no doubt that very nearly all the lands of the best quality have been appropriated, and that a very small portion of the residue could be sold at the minimum price . . . until further progress shall have been made in the settlement and improvement of the country, and a greater demand thereby created for the inferior lands."[2] It would be of little value to the federal government, but might bring some revenue to Tennessee for its school fund, although nothing like what might have been realized from the better-quality lands, had Tennessee been able to set some of it aside for schools. The report found it was probable that only "one-twentieth part would be granted at 12½ cents per acre, and perhaps one-fifth of the residue at one cent." Thus, the Land Office report supported the description of vacant lands that Polk and Crockett had made during earlier debates, although the report relied on information provided by the Tennessee secretary of state.[3]

The committee report recommended that a portion of the remaining vacant land be donated to the state to make up for the deficiency in school lands, that occupants be given a preemption (a provision that would have allowed them to buy their land at a minimal price before anyone else could claim it), and that the state be allowed to tax the land. It denied that the "cession might operate injuriously as a precedent in other quarters of the Union."[4]

In drafting the bill itself, Crockett had to yield on several points that he must have found distasteful, but he had clearly seen that his original amendment to Polk's bill would not succeed and concluded that any bill that gave his constituents a fair chance to secure land titles was better than none. Like Polk's bill, Crockett's would cede land in the Western District to the State of Tennessee only equal to the amount that was to have been set aside for schools, in addition to any tracts already set aside for schools throughout the state. Tennessee would be empowered to sell the land at any price, but not less than 12½ cents per acre, and sales would be made only in cash, with the proceeds used for a permanent fund for the establishment of common schools.[5] None of these provisions could have been welcomed by Crockett or completely palatable to Polk, whose original bill had called for the cession of *all* land in the Western District to the state, which could then be sold at any price.

On the brighter side for Crockett, the bill also provided that all occupants who had made improvements to their land "shall be secured in a right of pre-emption of at least two hundred acres of vacant land, including his or her improvement or dwelling." Occupants would be given twelve months to receive these preemption rights at a cost of "not less nor more than twelve and one half cents per acre."[6] This provision was much closer to what Crockett wanted, although he preferred that occupants not be charged for the land.

Congressman Daniel Laurens Barringer, a Jacksonian from North Carolina, submitted an amendment, which Crockett accepted, stipulating that North Carolina warrants would be treated first, for a period of twelve months, before Tennessee could benefit from the sale of these lands.[7] This, too, could not have been palatable to Crockett, since it might have again put his constituents at the mercy of warrant holders, but he needed all the support he could get. In any case, it is not certain that this provision would have interfered with the securing of occupants' titles. The House debates indicate a consensus of belief that most, if not all, of the North Carolina warrants had been satisfied, but the extent of previous fraud regarding these warrants left open the possibility of continued abuse. Still, Crockett believed that his constituents would be given the best opportunity possible to secure their titles and eliminate the uncertainties under which they had been living.[8]

In January, Crockett wrote to Hugh D. Neilson,[9] a supporter from Trenton, saying that the entire Tennessee delegation was now behind him, that they had reached agreement in committee on a new bill that Senator Felix Grundy, a leading Tennessee Jacksonian, had approved. He sounded disappointed, almost apologetic, since he had been forced to give in on so many key points. "I can say to you," he wrote, "that this is the best provision I could make for the occupints placed as I was in the powar of a majority of the committee against me their being four eastern members on my Committee . . . ." He boasted of having "united my whole Delegation in my favour," but he sounded regretful in adding that "I hope this is as good a law as the occupants could expect me to draft for them you may say to them that this is the best that I could do for them."[10]

It is puzzling that Crockett would blame the easterners on his committee for the bill's unwelcome provisions, since he chose them himself in an effort to circumvent his Tennessee opponents who had undermined him a year earlier. Polk should have been the harder sell for him, and Crockett must have sought to placate him by restoring much that Polk had asked for. He had insisted that the land go to the state, which would profit from its sale, and that the revenues go to schools, all provisions that were in the new compromise bill, unlike the amendment to Polk's bill that Crockett had floated in the previous session. Perhaps he was trying to maintain his repaired but fragile relationship with Polk and the other Tennesseans by blaming outsiders for the bill's negative features, or he may have felt a need to apologize to his constituents for some of the bill's features without laying blame on the Tennesseans. In any case, some eastern members of the committee did oppose the bill.[11]

The compromise bill was formally introduced on January 29, 1830, but did not come to the floor for debate until May 3, illustrating again why Crockett had become so irritated by the slow pace of action in Congress. He was used to the shorter sessions and faster pace of the legislature and cringed in Congress when weeks might pass during which a single issue, in which he had no interest, might occupy the House from morning till night. It must have been even more galling that debate on his bill was noticeably short. No one from Tennessee except Crockett spoke for the bill.[12] Gone were the lengthy speeches Polk, Lea, and others had made in attacking him during the previous session. Now they sat silently, neither hurting nor helping him, while others attacked the bill. George Grennell, an anti-Jacksonian from Massachusetts and one of the unsympathetic eastern members of Crockett's committee, spoke "at considerable length in opposition to the bill." Samuel Vinton, an Ohio Whig, objected to the loss of federal revenue that could be realized from sale of the land and attempted to table the bill. His motion was defeated 86-75 with all the Tennessee delegation voting against it, indicating that Crockett's coalition was holding. However, the bill itself was then voted on and defeated, 90-69, with the entire Tennessee delegation again voting with Crockett, harsh evidence that congressional opposition to ceding public land ran deeper than Crockett realized.[13] But, the Tennesseans had kept their bargain by backing Crockett, although they had done nothing to help him push the bill and did not speak a word in its defense. Polk may simply have given up hope of any land bill passing the House and benignly went along with Crocket in order to placate him and remove any blame for failure from the Tennessee delegation. The Jacksonians had hoped to unseat Crockett, only to see him easily win reelection. Polk may have lost hope of defeating him and sought instead to neutralize him as a potentially strong anti-Jackson force in the state, or perhaps hurt him by watching his bill go down to defeat.

The vote on the bill was nonpartisan, contradicting theories that Whigs had manipulated and then abandoned Crockett. Whigs opposed it (33-21), as did Jacksonians (53-45). A majority of North Carolinians seemed to remain skeptical, voting against it (7-4). Most westerners voted for it and southerners against it, with New England and the mid-Atlantic states more evenly divided, but with majorities opposed, reflecting the broader sectional alignment on land policy. The vote indicates a general lack of support for the concept of giving away Federal land, rather than any partisan political motives.

Crockett refused to quit and worked feverishly into the late hours of May 3 in a last-ditch effort to get his bill back on the floor. He approached Grennell and Vinton, who persuaded Crockett to accept an amendment, drafted by Vinton, which provided for sale *only* of the occupants' land, with revenues going directly to the Federal government instead of Tennessee. The remaining vacant lands would remain in federal hands. Tennessee would receive no land and no revenue, and there was no provision for school funds. This was very close to the amendment Crockett had proposed in the previous session and bound to again enrage the Tennessee delegation. Grennell agreed to ask for a reconsideration of the bill the next day, with Vinton's amendment in place. Crockett knew this would shatter his frail coalition with the other Tennesseans, but he was desperate for a victory of any kind.[14]

As arranged, Grennell moved the next day for a reconsideration of the amended bill. Crockett said that he was willing to accept the new provisions because he "had become convinced that the State had no legal claim to the lands." Then he made a tactical error that would cost him any votes he might have gotten from North Carolina's delegation. He "proceeded, at some length, to explain the condition of the occupants, the necessity of granting the relief proposed, and to animadvert on the conduct of North Carolina, and the University of that State, in relation to the land titles in Tennessee."[15] Several North Carolinians, including Barringer, heatedly rose to object to Crockett's disparaging remarks about their fair state. Others, including John Bell of Tennessee, argued against reintroducing the bill. Bell, no doubt reflecting the disapproval of most of the state delegation, "Submitted, at considerable length, his objections to the reconsideration and his dissent from some of the views of Mr. Crockett" (probably his tactless remarks about North Carolina). Only Cave Johnson from Tennessee came to his aid and "zealously supported the reconsideration of, and policy of the bill," but Crockett got no further. A motion to table the bill was approved by voice vote; thus, no record exists of how each member voted.[16] The devil's bargain that Crockett had made with Grennell and Vinton had not paid off and surely sealed his alienation from the rest of his delegation.

Crockett was not being fair when he later claimed that the Tennesseans went back on the deal they had made with him.[17] In fact, all of them had voted with him on both recorded roll calls. Their support was clearly lukewarm to start with, but what tipped them against Crockett in the end was his inclusion of Vinton's amendment. Other congressmen who voted against the bill may have feared that there were insufficient guarantees to ensure that the federal government would receive all the revenues it might if the land were sold for higher prices, certainly more than 12½ cents per acre.[18] They may have greeted the General Land Office report with skepticism and believed the land was more valuable than the report suggested. Others may still have seen possible violation of federal guarantees to North Carolina that all of its warrants would be satisfied. In the end, many may have seen it simply as little more than a camouflaged and unacceptable giveaway of public land. Crockett found himself trapped between those who objected strongly to donating land to states and the staunch refusal of the Tennesseans to settle for anything less. Still other states saw a different, but equally alarming precedent in the federal government's sale of public lands. These were states' rights advocates, who believed that states should control and profit from all lands within their borders and feared any intrusion in state affairs by the central government. In the swirl of this multifaceted debate, Crockett and the poor occupants he represented were of little concern to proponents of any of these views.

Apparently, a majority in the House believed that the fate of Tennessee's vacant lands had been debated long enough and resisted all of Crockett's subsequent attempts to resurrect the issue. However, he came very close to bringing the bill up again on January 6, 1831, when he lost by the slim margin of 92-89.[19] Although this vote was close, it should not be interpreted as an indication of how a vote on the bill itself might have gone. Crockett had won procedural votes like this before, only to be defeated when the actual question was posed to the House. There is no reason to believe that the result would have been different this time.

Nonetheless, Crockett blamed the Tennesseans for this bitter defeat and wrote to the *Jackson Gazette*, declaring his independence entirely from the Tennessee delegation, which signaled the final falling-out between Crockett and the Jacksonians.[20] He claimed that many members were absent during the vote on his bill, having "gone to the Races a few miles from the city." He said that he had asked other Tennessee representatives to support a reconsideration of the bill, but that they had flatly refused and remained opposed to it. "I declared Independence against them, & stated that I would quit the whole of them and 'set up shop for myself,' and do the best I could for my constituents."[21] In his February 28, 1831, circular Crockett staked out a broad anti-Jackson position covering a number of issues, including Jackson's Indian Removal Bill, which Crockett unsuccessfully opposed when it came to a vote only a few weeks after his land bill was defeated. Crockett would increasingly attack the president during his remaining years in Congress, banking his career on joining the ranks of the anti-Jackson forces, who were not an inconsiderable number even in Tennessee.

He also defended his efforts to secure a land bill for the occupants, saying that he had done all that was humanly possible for them. He repeated his conviction that Congress would never pass a sweeping bill like Polk's and that the legislature could not be trusted with the responsibility of disposing of public lands. "I am certain in my own mind," he wrote, "that Congress never would have passed the proposition of my colleagues," which he called "a trick, to try to make you believe that you would have been secure in your homes if I had agreed to their arrangement."[22] He concluded by reminding his constituents that he was one of them and had acted in what he believed to be their best interests. "You know that I am a poor man; and that I am a plain man," he wrote. "I have served you long enough in peace, to enable you to judge whether I am honest or not—I never deceived you—I never will deceive you. I have fought with you and for you in war, and you know whether I love my country, and ought to be trusted."[23] There was a degree of desperation in his plea, and he must have realized that his many upbeat promises of success on this issue had fallen flat and may have begun to ring hollow. He was left only to argue that he had done his best on behalf of his constituents and to emphasize again his bond with them.

In his circular Crockett made a point of noting that the entire Tennessee delegation deserted him on this 92-89 vote, emphasizing that only two votes from the Tennesseans would have swung it in his favor. He did not mention that a few more North Carolina votes would have achieved the same result, and he might have gotten them if he had not made those disparaging remarks about that state. All of the Tennesseans, including Cave Johnson, Crockett's sole Tennessee ally during the May 4, 1830, debate, opposed him, as did all but two North Carolinians. Although this was *not* a vote on his bill, which probably would have been defeated again, but rather on a motion to again bring it to the House floor for debate, Crockett made much of it in his circular, obviously trying to make the close vote seem more important than it really was.

Crockett's may have sensed that his land bill was doomed. He had now compromised on most of the key points that appeared to raise misgivings among House members and still had failed. In winning over those who favored giving revenues to the federal government, he had completely alienated his Tennessee colleagues. However, bending to the wishes of the state would have alienated those who opposed donating public lands to the states, which seems to have been uppermost in the minds of a majority of members. The Congress was doing exactly what Crockett had feared the Tennessee legislature would have done: refuse to donate land or sell it at affordable prices to the occupants. This left him nowhere to turn.

Crockett attempted several more times to bring his bill up for debate, without success, although he continued to speak optimistically about it to his constituents.[24] No doubt the other Tennesseans had given up trying to compromise with him and felt betrayed (if they ever seriously meant to help him). However, Crockett may have reasoned that, with the Vinton amendment and perhaps a smoothing over of the ruffled feelings of North Carolinians, the House might yet be more receptive to selling the land to the squatters at an affordable price. The evidence suggests otherwise.

Had Crockett embraced a broader agenda in Congress, he might have been able to boast of other accomplishments or stressed his views on other issues. But, he had put all his cards on the land issue, and its defeat left him with little to show for his years in Congress, beyond good intentions.

Crockett was defeated in the 1831 election, but he regained his seat in 1833. He introduced a new bill on January 2, 1834, that was virtually identical to the bill that was defeated on May 3, 1830, asking that land equal to the school deficiency be ceded to Tennessee and giving occupants a preemption on two hundred acres for 12½ cents per acre, with proceeds to go to a common-school fund. It was, perhaps, an attempt to win back Polk and the other Tennesseans, but it had come too late to repair the breach with them. A motion to bring the new bill up for discussion was defeated on February 20, 1835, by a vote of 77-52, on which occasion Crockett was shouted down and denied the opportunity to even speak about his bill. The issue was never raised again during Crockett's tenure.[25]

Clearly the bill that was debated on May 3, 1830, was not the bill Crockett wanted, but it was all he could get and, in the end, it too failed. However, his efforts showed a willingness to compromise and a clear understanding of the issue and the diverse views held by members of Congress. His action in this instance flies in the face of the widely held image of Crockett as an inept political novice. However, he showed a distinct lack of political savvy in alienating his delegation by accepting Vinton's amendment. A more manipulative, farsighted politician might have accepted defeat, hoping to find victory at a later date, and found an effective way to explain that to his constituents. But, Crockett's failure to secure the bill should not reflect on his leadership or skill in the House, since neither Polk nor those who replaced Crockett in Congress were able to secure passage of a land bill either. Indeed, Polk seemed to have given up hope of securing a land bill, since neither he nor any other Tennessee representative attempted to introduce one during the Twenty-Second Congress, when Crockett was out of office. That lack of action strengthens the conclusion that it was Crockett's alleged disloyalty, not his version of the land bill, that most troubled his colleagues. Had Polk believed that it was Crockett's persistence that prevented such a bill from passing, it must be asked why he didn't attempt to introduce a bill to his liking during Crockett's two-year hiatus.

Only Crockett's son, John Wesley, a Whig working with Congressman Issac Crary of Michigan, a Democrat, finally achieved passage of such a bill in 1841, very much like the one produced by Crockett's committee. Priority was given to the remaining North Carolina warrants for one year, after which any remaining claims would be paid in cash for two years and no further claims would be considered after that. After the first year, occupants with preemption rights would be entitled to purchase up to two hundred acres for 12½ cents per acre. Other lands would be sold at *not less* than 12½ cents per acre. Any lands remaining after that would be sold at any price they might bring. All revenues after expenses went to the U.S. Treasury, not to Tennessee, which merely acted as the agent of the federal government. In a different time, absent the high-stakes politics that Crockett was forced to play, John Wesley was able to secure passage of a bill that his father could have supported.[26]

―――――――――

[1]   *Richmond Enquirer,* December 21, 1829; *Register of Debates,* December 15, 1829, 474, and December 22, 1829, 480. The other members were Evans (Maine, Whig), Tracy (New York, Anti-Masonic), Hawkins (New York, Anti-Jacksonian), and Grennell (Massachusetts, Anti-Jacksonian); *House Journal,* December 15, 1829, 44. On the same day, Polk successfully moved to refer the Tennessee legislature's memorial on the vacant lands to his Committee on Public Lands, but Crockett would have it transferred to his select committee a few days later, despite Polk's objections. *House Journal,* December 15, 1829, 41; *Register of Debates,* December 22, 1829, 480–81. At the same time, Jacob Isacks of Tennessee introduced a resolution calling for Polk's committee to look into the expediency of permitting North Carolina warrants to be located on *any* public lands of the United States. *House Journal,* December 15, 1829, 44.

[2]   The General Land Office report relied almost entirely on information provided by the Tennessee secretary of state, allowing for some concern about conflict of interest, since Tennessee stood to gain considerably from a relinquishment of federal land. The report found that there was a total of 6,864,000 acres in West Tennessee, 4,510,176 of which had been used to satisfy North Carolina warrants, and that this acreage had consumed most of the quality land; 2,353,824 acres remained, mostly of lesser quality, in scattered, noncontiguous parcels. The total did not include 91,000 acres claimed by the University of North Carolina and colleges and common schools of Tennessee, divided up by the legislature into twenty-five-acre parcels sold at fifty cents per acre, for cash only. Although the report found that "In very few instances could it now be found that an entire section of 640 acres could be laid down on vacant land that would sell, in cash, for as much as would pay the expense of surveying," it still maintained that, whatever disposition might be made of the land, "a quantity of land equal to one thirty-sixth part of the whole district should be appropriated for the use of schools." The reference was to the standard practice regarding public lands set aside for schools in other western states, which was surveyed into townships six miles square, subdivided into square-mile (640-acre) lots numbered from 1 to 36 in each township and later called "sections," with one section in each township reserved for schools. The lands were sold at auction at a minimum price of one dollar per acre. Tennessee had laid out townships in the Western District in units of *five* square miles, although that plan had been torn asunder by the patchwork warrant claims. "Quantity of Public Land Remaining Unsold in Tennessee in 1829," December 17, 1829, transmitted to the House January 7, 1830 by S. D. Ingham, Secretary of the Treasury, and attachment "B," report of Daniel Graham, Secretary of State, Tennessee, to George Graham, Commissioner of General Land Office, August 20, 1829, *American State Papers,* Public Lands 6: 30–32. Crockett's committee report is found in "Disposition of the Public Lands of Tennessee," *American State Papers,* Public Lands 6: 128–29. Also see Daniel Feller, *The Public Lands in Jacksonian Politics* (Madison: University of Wisconsin Press, 1984), 6, citing Thomas Donaldson, *The Public Domain* (Washington: GPO, 1884).

[3]   An exact estimate of the land's value could not be determined; anecdotal evidence included one 5,000 acre tract that had sold for 12½ cents per acre. The report considered that the minimum price and noted that "smaller quantities have uniformly sold proportionably higher whenever a purchaser could be found, though cash sales are seldom effected at any price." "Quantity of Public Land Remaining Unsold in Tennessee in 1829," attachment "B," report of Daniel Graham to George Graham, August 20, 1829, 32.

[4]   "Disposition of the Public Lands of Tennessee," 128–29.

[5]   H.R. 185, January 29, 1830. The wording in the bill is convoluted and somewhat confusing. The bill would give Tennessee "out of the vacant and unappropriated lands within the limits of said State, and lying South and West of the line designated in the said act, which this is intended to amend, a quantity of land, which shall, together with the six hundred and forty acre tracts of land, which have already been laid off in said State for the use of schools [under provisions of the 1806 Act], be equal in acres to the sixteenth section in each township, or the one thirty-sixth part of the district of country authorized to be appropriated by said act, North and East of said line, in said act mentioned, and, also, to the one thirty-sixth part of the district of country lying South and West of said line in said State; and said lands hereby granted, by surveys, and in tracts of such sizes as she may select; and the said State shall dispose of the same . . . and apply the proceeds of such sale as a permanent fund for the establishment of common schools, for the instruction of children in said state, for ever."

6   H.R. 185, January 29, 1830.

7   H. R. 185 Amendment, April 13, 1830.

8   Crockett said that he had been told by Henry Connor of North Carolina that his entire state delegation would vote against Crockett's bill. Crockett then threatened to introduce a resolution calling for the federal government to sue the University of North Carolina for unpaid taxes on every acre of land it owned in Tennessee's Western District. Crockett claimed that Barringer's amendment was an attempt to resolve this dispute. Crockett to *Jackson Gazette*, April 15, 1830, published May 8, 1830. Isacks' resolution of December 15, 1829, supports the general opinion that either the warrants had been satisfied or that a deadline ought to be imposed for accepting them in the future.

9   Hugh D. Neilson was a merchant from Trenton, Gibson County, Tennessee and a Crockett supporter. *(Jackson, Tennessee) Southern Statesman*, March 16, 1833.

10 Crockett to Hugh D. Neilson, January 24, 1830, courtesy of the Tennessee State Library and Archives.

11 Ibid. If Crockett was trying to maintain improved relations with Polk, he would soon abandon that effort. In his February 28, 1831, circular he clearly blamed the ultimate failure of the land reform effort on Polk and the other Tennessee members of Congress, not easterners. *David Crockett's Circular*, February 28, 1831, Rare Books Division, Library of Congress, 6–7.

12 Crockett later made a point of mentioning this to his constituents as evidence that the Tennessee delegation had sabotaged him. Crockett circular, February 28, 1831

13 *Register of Debates in Congress*, May 3, 1830, 869–70.

14 *David Crockett's Circular*, February 28, 1831, 6.

15 *Register of Debates*, May 4, 1830, 873.

16 Ibid. Vinton's amendment was not printed, and the only record of it is the reference made to it during the May 4 debate. Crockett included a copy of the bill, with Vinton's language, in his circular of February 28, 1831.

17 *David Crockett's Circular*, February 28, 1831, 6–7.

18 Westerners had complained that the Federal government had set too high a price on public lands, but Congress had resisted the call for lower prices, and those sentiments were doubtless raised against Crockett's bill.

19 *Register of Debates*, January 6, 1831, 418. All of the other Tennesseans voted against Crockett, as did nine of the ten North Carolinians, Barrington being the only exception. All but one Anti-Jacksonian voted with Crockett, while 90 of 119 Jacksonians opposed him. In a letter to Daniel Pounds written the same day, Crockett again blamed the defeat on the other Tennesseans, and again expressed confidence that he would get the bill passed before the session ended. He also said that his old nemesis, Pryor Lea, actually voted with him during at least one unrecorded vote, although Crockett added, "I cannot till what made him vote for my proposition as we have never spoken to each other Since we had our controversy," a reference to their acrimonious public exchange of letters in 1829. Crockett to Daniel W. Pounds, January 6, 1831, Courtesy, the Lilly Library, Indiana University, Bloomington, Indiana.

20 Crockett to *Jackson Gazette*, May 7, 1830, published May 29, 1830.

21 Ibid. Crockett mentioned that both Cave Johnson and John Blair had expressed some support for his bill, but failed to mention that they, too, deserted him when he sought to have the land sold directly by the Federal government, thus eliminating any revenue the state might realize. The *Gazette* supported Crockett, noting that "If the proposed bill does not become a law, we repeat that the fault will not rest with our representative; on the contrary he deserves the thanks of his constituents, for his zeal in the cause of that portion of our population so vitally interested in the success of the measure." *Jackson Gazette*, May 15, 1830.

22 *David Crockett's Circular*, February 28, 1831, 15.

23 Ibid., 16.

24 Crockett to William Rodgers, January 8, 1834, courtesy of the Tennessee State Library and Archives. Crockett's subsequent unsuccessful attempts to bring his bill up for debate, and the vote tallies, included: December 23, 1830 (86-74), December 31, 1830 (97-69); January 6, 1831 (92-89; see discussion of this vote that follows in this chapter); he introduced his final bill, H.R.126, on January 2, 1834. *Register of Debates*, December 23, 1830, 383; December 31, 1830, 391; January 6, 1831, 418; and February 13, 1835, 1354–55.

25 Ironically, only weeks after Crockett's bill was defeated, Congress passed a preemption act that gave squatters on all federal land the right to purchase up to 160 acres at a minimum price to be established. It was the very thing Crockett had fought so hard for. Unfortunately, the Preemption Act excluded "any land, which is reserved from sale by act of Congress, or by order of the President, or which may have been appropriated, for any purpose whatsoever." *An Act to grant pre-emption rights to settlers on the public lands* (May 29, 1830), *U.S. Statutes at Large* 4, 420. Because of the federal commitment to honor all North Carolina warrants, many of which might still have been extant, Tennessee's occupants could not take advantage of the Preemption Act, and Tennessee never came under the federal land system.

26 Polk was then governor of Tennessee, and he anxiously followed the progress of the younger Crockett's bill, ironically throwing his weight behind it and advocating for the West Tennessee squatters. Although the law did not yield any revenues to Tennessee, the state worked the system over the next five years until Congress finally gave the state all of the West Tennessee lands and allowed the state to keep all of the proceeds from land sales since 1841. Tennessee was to use $40,000 from land sales to build a college in Jackson. H.R. 528, December 17, 1840; H.R. 607, February 15, 1841; *House Journal*, February 15, 1841, 287–90; *An Act to amend an act entitled "An act to authorize the State of Tennessee to issue grants and perfect titles to certain lands therein described, and to settle the claims to*

the vacant and unappropriated lands within the same," passed the eighteenth day of April, one thousand eight hundred and six, (February 18, 1841), *Statutes at Large* 5, 412–13; *An Act to surrender to the State of Tennessee all Title the United States have to Lands in Tennessee, south and west of the Line commonly called the Congressional Reservation Line, and to release to said State the Proceeds of such of said Lands as may have been sold by the State of Tennessee, as the Agent of the United States* (August 7, 1846), *Statutes at Large* 9, 66–67; Thomas B. Jones, "The Public Lands of Tennessee," *Tennessee Historical Quarterly,* 28: 34–35.

Andrew Jackson, however, remained a Crockett hater to the last, continuing to oppose his son, John Wesley, with as much vitriol as he once leveled at Crockett. In 1839, when John Wesley was up for reelection, Jackson wrote to his nephew, General Samuel J. Hays, "You must not permit that hypothetical [?] scamp Crockett to be elected—he is the mere tool of [John] Bell & J. Q. Adams, without principle or talents & has become a good Whig by learning the art of Lying & Slandering good & honest men." John Wesley Crockett won reelection despite Jackson's efforts to unseat him. Jackson to Hays, June 16, 1839, ArtFact auction website, http://www.artfact.com/auction-lot/jackson,-andrew.-autograph-letter-signed-andrew-81-p-lbasx5842n, Lot 56.

Chapter 5

"A Good Honest Vote"
The Indian Removal Bill (1830)

Andrew Jackson may not have hated Indians, but many tribes would come to hate him. When the man they called Sharp Knife won the presidency in 1828, he embarked on a campaign to move eastern tribes from their native lands, opening them to white settlers and land speculators. Jackson began at once to secure a law that would require that tribes sell their lands to the federal government and move west of the Mississippi River, where new land would be provided to them. In 1830 he would succeed. The Indian removal policy was one of the most brutal and disgraceful in U.S. history. Among those who opposed it was Congressman Crockett.

From the beginning of the republic, U.S. Indian policy was somewhat contradictory. There was always strong sentiment to remove the Indians and seize their lands, often for financial gain or for security from the tribes. British troops were still located on the country's borders and had retained alliances with some Indians. Although earlier presidents had favored removal, they pursued it largely by covert means and none of them advocated it as openly or forcefully as Jackson did. President George Washington and his secretary of war, Henry Knox, pursued an honorable policy that would have protected Indian land from white encroachment and opted to deal with Indians as foreign nations through treaties. The policy failed primarily because the federal government lacked the resources to enforce it, and many in the states and Congress simply opposed it. As Washington's secretary of state, Thomas Jefferson, had supported this approach, but later, as president, he favored a constitutional amendment requiring relocation of the Indians to the new Louisiana Purchase territory. He also tried to cajole some tribes into selling their land. President James Monroe tried twice, unsuccessfully, to secure removal legislation, and, during his tenure in the White House, John Quincy Adams also explored removal options.[1]

However, there was also a strong movement to "civilize" or assimilate Indians, convert them to Christianity, and grant them some form of citizenship. The hope was that, given time, these measures would remove the Indians' attachment to their land and bring them into the mainstream population. Missionaries, humanitarian organizations, and some religious groups defended the Indians' right to remain on their land. The United States, somewhat paradoxically, followed both approaches, but the desire to remove the tribes would ultimately hold sway, regardless of the degree to which Indians had been assimilated or "civilized." This was especially true of the Cherokee, many of whom had adopted white customs, government, religion, and land-use methods, but were removed anyway.

Jackson's Indian removal policy was the predictable culmination of many years of that contradictory approach. Jackson had long advocated complete removal of the tribes and the forced sale or expropriation of their lands, while insisting that the government was badly misguided in making treaties with the tribes or recognizing them as independent nations with any right to their traditional lands. He denied that the tribes held such status and said they were aliens who were subject to the will of Congress and the states in which they resided. Countless Indians died on forced marches to the west. Those who refused to leave were forcibly evicted from their homes at the point of a bayonet and then marched west with little more than the clothes on their backs, often in the harshest weather.

Andrew Jackson was a leading proponent of Indian removal long before he became president. Initially, he openly regarded Indians as wild, dangerous savages, but he later adopted a paternalistic approach and claimed to have the Indians' best interests in mind by recommending their removal. Most tribes were coerced into signing questionable treaties that ceded their land to the United States and were typically obtained through threats and bribery, often without the knowledge or consent of tribal leaders. Eventually, despite considerable efforts to challenge such coercion, virtually all of the southeastern tribes would be forced to relocate to areas west of the Mississippi, and their lands would be taken over by whites. The compensation, or bribes, paid to the tribes was minuscule compared to the actual value of the land and often went only to a few corrupt tribal leaders.

Jackson achieved national prominence following his 1815 defeat of the British in New Orleans. Among the political advantages he gained from that victory was his appointment as a commissioner who negotiated with southern Indians during the six years following the War of 1812. Through a combination of threats, bribery, and occasionally fraud, Jackson concluded the sale of a large portion of prime agricultural tribal lands to the United States, including large portions of Georgia and Mississippi, and most of Alabama. In the decades that followed, he and his allies would use the same means to force the sale of more Indian lands, and Jackson and his friends often had a personal financial interest in the land obtained. There was an intense drive to obtain fertile Indian lands once established agricultural plots became scarce or were becoming exhausted, especially in the cotton-growing areas of the South at a time when there was a great global demand for cotton and about half the world's cotton goods were made from cotton grown in the United States. When he took office in 1829, President Jackson made Indian removal a top priority and laid out his plans and justification for it in his first annual message to Congress.[2]

Both rich and poor whites wanted more land for farming or speculating, and Indians held much of the agriculturally fertile land in the southern states. The rationalizations for removing Indians varied over time, but always supported the basic idea that they simply *deserved* to be removed from their native lands, which should then be made available to white settlers. The reasons given included numerous claims: All Indians were wild savages who represented a danger to white settlers. All Indians were, by nature, roving hunters who could not adapt to the farming life, when in fact most Eastern tribes had been practicing this life style for centuries before Europeans arrived in America. Indians could never coexist side-by-side with whites. The government could not protect the Indians from white encroachment, and they would be better off somewhere else. And, the Indians claimed to be autonomous foreign nations within U.S. territory, which the federal government could not tolerate. In fact, the Cherokee made the latter claim, which would help seal their fate. Racist arguments claiming that Indians were by nature inferior to whites were also put forth and found a receptive audience among many Americans, especially those with the greatest desire for Indian land or who feared their proximity. Indeed, recent wars with Indians in the South had fueled the argument that the Indians could not be trusted and would remain a threat unless removed.

States' rights played a crucial role in formulating the policy. Georgia was particularly angry that the federal government had not removed the Indians long ago. In 1802 Georgia agreed to relinquish to the United States its claim to land in the Mississippi Territory in exchange for $1.5 million and the federal government's pledge to extinguish Indian title to lands within Georgia, which Georgia interpreted as a promise to remove the Indians and turn the land over to the state.[3] By 1830, when Congress finally passed Jackson's Indian Removal Bill, that pledge had remained unfulfilled, and Georgia decided to act.

In 1817, the Cherokee had established a representative form of government, including a legislature, chief executive and judiciary, as well as a small army of its own. A decade later the tribe adopted a constitution modeled on that of the United States, which included a bill of rights. However, their constitution claimed that the Cherokee were a "sovereign and independent" nation, a claim that Georgia refused to accept.[4] In fact, the state claimed that it held sovereignty over the Cherokee by virtue of the tribe occupying state territory. The ensuing fight would center in large part on the question of whose land it really was and who had jurisdiction over the Cherokee: the state or the federal government.

In December 1828 Georgia's legislature extended the state's authority over the Cherokee living within its borders, terminating the Cherokee right to self-government. Georgia thus challenged federal authority over Indian tribes and rejected Cherokee claims to sovereignty, which was consistent with Jackson's views that states held jurisdiction over Indians within their borders and that Indians had no legal claim to sovereignty. Georgia postponed enforcement until June 1, 1830, to give the federal government time to remove the Indians, but harassment of them had already begun. Eventually, Georgia would make it illegal for the Indians to pass or enforce laws. Tribal assemblies were banned, and Indians were subjected to Georgia's taxes and required to serve in the militia. Nonetheless, Georgia's policy hypocritically deprived Indians the right to vote, to bring suit or testify in trials of whites, make contracts with whites or work for them. It became a crime to discourage any Cherokee from leaving his homeland or to prevent them from negotiating an agreement to leave. White intruders were encouraged to settle on their land and, after gold was discovered there, the Indians were barred from mining it, while hordes of white miners swarmed over their land and carried away all the gold they could find. Georgia even raised a militia to "protect" the gold and arrest any Cherokee found mining it. The state also initiated surveys of Cherokee land in order to conduct a lottery that would give the land to whites. Neither Jackson nor the Congress interfered with Georgia.[5]

In his first annual message to Congress, Jackson strongly backed Georgia and rejected Indian claims to sovereignty. To him it was the states, not the Indians, who were threatened. He cited Article IV, Section 3 of the Constitution, which prohibits any new state being formed within the jurisdiction of any state without the consent of that state's legislature and Congress. Anticipating opposition to removal from northeastern states, Jackson challenged them to apply equal standards to all states. "Would the people of Maine," he asked rhetorically, "permit the Penobscot tribe to erect an independent government within their State?" Or, "Would the people of New York permit each remnant of the six Nations within her borders to declare itself an independent people under the protection of the United States?"[6] If those states would not, Jackson reasoned, the United States would be obligated to act in their behalf, as it was in the case of Georgia.[7]

Jackson told Congress that he had informed the Cherokee that he would not tolerate their attempt to establish an independent government and advised them to move beyond the Mississippi River, or submit to the laws of Georgia. He expressed sympathy for other tribes that had been badly treated in the past, many of which had become extinct while trying to hold on to some portion of their traditional lands. If the southern tribes were to avoid that fate, Jackson suggested, their best option was to move far away from the whites, where they could preserve their cultures. Jackson suggested that, in their new lands, tribes "may be secured in the enjoyment of governments of their own choice, subject to no other control from the United States than such as may be necessary to preserve peace on the frontier and between the several tribes. There the benevolent may endeavor to teach them the arts of civilization, and, by promoting union and harmony among them, to raise up an interesting commonwealth, destined to perpetuate the race and to attest the humanity and justice of this Government."[8] Jackson must have realized that this was a pipe dream and that, sooner rather than later, whites would encroach on new Indian lands too. His suggestion that they might be taught "the arts of civilization" hints at a vague idea of destroying tribal civilization over time by bringing Indians into the white mainstream, rather than creating some sort of "interesting commonwealth."

The Cherokee, then, were either to move or become individual property owners within Georgia, subject to that state's law. Traditional Cherokee land that was not settled would become public property that could be sold, since the Cherokee could claim no ownership of lands "on which they have neither dwelt nor made improvements, merely because they have seen them from the mountain or passed them in the chase."[9] Jackson rounded out his vision for Indians by fancifully imagining that by "Submitting to the laws of the States, and receiving, like other citizens, protection in their persons and property, they will ere long become merged in the mass of our population,"[10] another vague reference to assimilation, which flew in the face of the discriminatory policies Georgia would invoke on Indians.

The Removal Bill, "An act to provide for an exchange of lands with the Indians residing in any of the States or territories, and for their removal west of the Mississippi," was passed by the Senate on April 23, 1830, by a vote of 28-19 and in the House of Representatives on May 24 by a vote of 102-97, where a change of only 3 votes would have defeated it. Jackson signed the Indian Removal Act the same day. He would later refer to Indian removal as the "most arduous part of my duty" as president.[11]

The Removal Act did not actually require that the Indians move from their homelands, but only authorized the president to offer the "tribes or nations of Indians as may choose to exchange the lands where they now reside" other lands to the west in exchange for theirs. Jackson even told Congress that removal was to be voluntary, "for it would be cruel and unjust to compel the aborigines to abandon the graves of their fathers and seek a home in a distant land."[12] However, despite Jackson's soothing words, his intent was to force the Indians to sell their land and move away, by whatever means might be necessary to achieve that end, or surrender their sovereignty to Georgia.[13]

Jackson's strategy was to encourage Georgia to exert its authority over the Cherokee, no matter how brutally. Shortly after taking office he told a Georgia congressman to "Build a fire under them [the Cherokee]. When it gets hot enough, they'll move."[14] Some officials saw this as a violation of the Commerce Clause of the Constitution, which reserved regulation of commerce with Indian tribes to Congress, by permitting a state to preempt federal authority. Jackson's plan also marked a departure from Washington's long-standing policy of dealing with the tribes as foreign nations through treaties. However, the Constitution was vague on Indian rights and left Jackson free to ignore these precedents unless Congress or the courts acted to stop him. Congress clearly had failed to do so; the courts would soon get their chance."[15]

Crockett openly supported the Indians and voted against the removal bill, and his vote was recorded in the *House Journal*. He spoke against the bill on the floor of the House of Representatives on May 19, 1830. His tone was measured, although he expressed strong sympathy for the Indians and found the idea of removal both cruel and unfair. He did not oppose removal in principle, but took issue with Jackson's proposed method of carrying it out. He objected to what he saw as an irresponsible use of federal funds and a reckless approach to removal, and said he could support it only if the Indians agreed through a legitimate treaty and only after the lands to which they would be relocated were examined and deemed acceptable. He would oppose removal unless it was achieved in a humanitarian way, which was not assured in Jackson's Removal Bill. He also cited U.S. treaty obligations to Indians, precedents that recognized Indians as sovereign nations, and the clear unwillingness of the tribes to remove. He acknowledged that his constituents would undoubtedly oppose his vote, but said that he believed that they had placed him in a position of trust that obligated him to make just decisions according to his own conscience.[16]

Crockett also had said that "He knew many of their tribe; and nothing should ever induce him to vote to drive them west of the Mississippi. He did not know what sort of a country it was in which they were to be settled. He would willingly appropriate money in order to send proper persons to examine the country. And when this had been done, and a fair and free treaty had been made with the tribes, if they were desirous of removing, he would vote an appropriation of any sum necessary; but till this had been done, he would not vote one cent. . . . No man could be more willing to see them remove than he was, if it could be done in a manner agreeable to themselves; but not otherwise."[17] The final decision, he believed, should rest with the Indians, not the government.

The next day the *United States' Telegraph* reported that Crockett had told the House that "although four counties of his Congressional district adjoined the Chickasaw nation of Indians, he was opposed in conscience to the measure, and such being the case, he cared not what his constituents thought of his conduct."[18]

Crockett's support for the Indians and his vote against removal have often been seen as merely part of his consistently strong anti-Jackson stand and just one more swipe at Old Hickory, which lacked real commitment. This view of Crockett's motives stems largely from the fact that the speech he gave in the House does not appear in the *Register of Debates in Congress,* suggesting to some that he tried to conceal his defense of Indians from voters. However, the speech was reported in the *United States' Telegraph* and published elsewhere in full, including in the *Jackson Gazette* in Crockett's home district, and it was mentioned or summarized in newspapers throughout the country. It also appeared in a compilation of speeches on Indian removal.

Crockett read the reports about his speech in the press and took exception to the way it had been paraphrased in the *Telegraph.* He wrote to the newspaper to correct its errors, particularly the report that he had said "he was opposed in conscience to the measure; and such being the case, he cared not what his constituents thought of his conduct." Crockett denied having said anything of the kind and insisted "I never hurl defiance at those whose servant I am. I said that my conscience should be my guide. . . and that I believed if my constituents were here, they would justify my vote."[19] The published speech actually paraphrased him as saying "He had his constituents to settle with, he was aware; and should like to please them as well as other gentlemen; but he had also a settlement to make at the bar of his God; and what his conscience dictated to be just and right he would do, be the consequences what they might. He believed that the people who had been kind enough to give him their suffrages supposed him to be an honest man, or they would not have chosen him. If so, they could not but expect that he should act in the way he thought honest and right."[20]

Crockett knew that he could not keep his vote or such a speech secret from his constituents, and he was keenly aware that his position on the issue was unpopular with many of them. Newspapers back home criticized his vote, and he defended it openly in his letters and circulars, which were widely read by his constituents. He also boasted proudly of his vote in his autobiography, published in 1834, and insisted that it was a matter of conscience and his obligation under the trust that voters had placed in him. "I had been elected by a majority of three thousand five hundred and eighty-five votes," he wrote, "and I believed they were honest men, and wouldn't want me to vote for any unjust notion. . . . I voted against this Indian bill, and my conscience yet tells me that I gave a good honest vote, and one that I believe will not make me ashamed in the day of judgment."[21]

Apparently Crockett had even stronger words in support of the Indians that were cut from his original autobiography manuscript. According to John Gadsby Chapman, who painted Crockett's portrait in mid-1834, "There were, moreover, many portions of his manuscript, cancelled by the counsel of his advisers, that gave him special vexation—chiefly such relating to inhuman massacres of indian women and children, which if he wrote of with half the intensified bitterness of reprobation that I have heard him express towards the perpetrators of such attrocious acts, and the officials by whom they were permitted, suppression of their narrative may have been better for the credit of the nation and humanity."[22]

Crockett continued to defend his vote even after he was defeated in his bid for reelection in 1831. Writing to a supporter in his district, he condemned Jackson on several counts and showed no regret for his vote in opposition to Indian removal, proclaiming that "I also condemned the Course parsued to the Southern Indians I love to sustain the honour of my Country and I will do it while I live in or out of Congress . . . ."[23]

In any event, passage of the Removal Act was only the beginning of the struggle for the Cherokee. Although removal was to be voluntary, Georgia, with Jackson's support, began pressing enforcement of its anti-Cherokee laws and extending its authority over Indian territory, which soon led to a showdown with the Supreme Court.

The Court weighed in on the Cherokee case three times in the years immediately following passage of the Removal Act. All of its decisions were significant, but none would alter the Cherokee's fate. The first followed the arrest of a Cherokee named Corn Tassels (Americanized to "George" Tassels in official court records) by Georgia officials for the murder of another Cherokee, which had occurred on Cherokee land during the summer of 1830. The case should have fallen under tribal jurisdiction, but Georgia now claimed authority over Indian land. The case was brought to the Supreme Court under a claim that Georgia lacked jurisdiction and Chief Justice John Marshall served a writ of error on Georgia's governor, George Gilmer, on November 22, 1830, and ordered Georgia to appear before the Court. Gilmer simply ignored Marshall, declaring that the state, not the federal courts, had jurisdiction over the case and proclaimed that federal actions aimed at interfering with Georgia's courts would be ignored. Tassels' trial took place the same day. He was found guilty and sentenced to be executed two days later, when he was hung in public.[24]

Crockett was outraged by Georgia's defiance of the Court and continued to express his support for the Cherokee, writing to a friend, "I have no doubt but you will see the proceeding of georgia before this reaches you on the Case of hanging the Cherikee Indian the Chief Justice Marshel issued his mandate or writ of error against the State of georgia to bring the Case up to the Supreme Court of the united States and the notice was served on the goverer on the 22 of Decr and the Indian was to be hung on the 24 the goverer refused to pay any respects to the order and the legislature of georgia passed a joint Resolution inforsing the execution of the Indian and bidding defiance to the powar of the Supreme Court of the united States this is what we call going the whole hogg to nullify the whole powar of the Supreme Court of the united states this case took place with in the Cherikee nation and the object of the Chief Justice was to bring the Case before the Supreme Court and decide whether georgia has the powar to extend her laws over the Indians or not and when the attempt was made the goverer & legislature flew into flinders[25] and we Consider they have thrown the gantlet and that the Chief Justice marshel at this time holds a Civil war in his own hands It is believed that he will persue a firm and desisive Course to Sustain the honour and dignity of his Court"[26]

Marshall would not push things that far, although he did continue to seek ways to curb Georgia. Crockett saw Georgia's action and Jackson's acquiescence in it as a serious threat to the Constitution and the survival of the Union, should that state succeed in flouting the authority of the federal government.

The Supreme Court had another chance to resolve the situation in *Cherokee Nation v. Georgia*. In that case, the Cherokee asked for an injunction to prevent Georgia from extending its jurisdiction onto Indian territory and affirm the Cherokees' right to self-government as a foreign nation. The claim was based on the history of U.S. treaties with native tribes. Georgia again refused to recognize the Court's jurisdiction and boycotted the hearing. On March 18, 1831, the Court dodged the issue by ruling that it lacked jurisdiction in the case, which it said more properly belonged with the judicial department. However, Marshall took the opportunity to rule that the Cherokee were not a sovereign nation, while also rejecting Jackson's assertion that they were subject to state law. He said that Indians were "domestic dependent nations," subject to the United States, whose function toward them was that of a guardian and whose territory was part of the United States. Thus, they could not be subject to the individual states. However, Marshall stopped short of finding Georgia's new laws unconstitutional, saying only that "If it be true that the Cherokee nation have rights, this is not the tribunal in which those rights are to be asserted. If it be true that wrongs have been inflicted, and that still greater are to be apprehended, this is not the tribunal which can redress the past or prevent the future."[27]

Georgia ignored the decision and rejected the Court's characterization of Indians as "domestic dependent nations." The state legislature already had passed a law requiring white males who lived on tribal land to take a loyalty oath that affirmed Georgia's sovereignty over the Indian land. The law also prohibited white men from entering Indian territory after March 1, 1831 without a license from the state. The law was intended to drive out missionaries who had encouraged the Indians to pursue their case against Georgia. Samuel Worcester, the missionaries' leader, thought the oath "unjust and oppressive" and a violation of Cherokee rights.[28] He and another missionary were jailed for refusing to obey the law, but a state court dismissed the case, citing the defendants' status as federal employees, since they were subsidized by the federal government, and Worcester also served as postmaster to the Cherokee. Although the state court may have been trying to avoid another showdown with the Supreme Court, Governor Gilmer intervened by requesting that the postmaster general remove Worcester, due to his "influence" over the Cherokee. The postmaster general was only too happy to comply, while Jackson chipped in by declaring that the missionaries were no longer federal employees. Georgia then gave them ten days to either take the loyalty oath or be arrested. Eleven missionaries refused and were arrested, beaten, hastily tried, and sentenced to four years at hard labor. Nine finally agreed to take the oath, but Worcester and Elizur Butler applied to the Supreme Court for a writ of error.[29]

In *Worcester v. Georgia,* the state again boycotted the session, continuing its refusal to recognize federal authority. Nonetheless, on March 3, 1832, the Court struck down Georgia's anti-Cherokee laws and ruled that Indian tribes had always enjoyed the status of "distinct, independent, political communities, retaining their original natural rights, as the undisputed possessors of the soil, from time immemorial." Chief Justice Marshall ruled that Georgia's laws were preempted by federal authority and treaties with the Cherokee, and thus the imprisonment of the missionaries was unconstitutional. His ruling established the federal government's sole authority to deal with the tribes.[30]

No action was taken to carry out the Court's order, and Horace Greeley later claimed that Jackson said, "Justice Marshall has made his decision, now let him enforce it." Greeley cited Massachusetts Congressman George N. Briggs as the source of the quote, but it is doubtful that Jackson actually said it, although it certainly sounds very much like Old Hickory, since there was no legal requirement that he act on the Court's decision at the time. Nonetheless, Jackson actively supported Georgia's harsh code, which was intended to intimidate the Indians into agreeing to sell their land and remove to the West.[31] Although the missionaries were finally released in 1833, Marshall's decision would do little to help the Cherokee. When Jackson was reelected by a landslide in 1832, Marshall echoed Crockett in lamenting, "I yield slowly and reluctantly to the conviction that our Constitution cannot last. The union has been prolonged thus far by miracles. I fear they cannot continue."[32]

The issue was further muddled by an internal Cherokee dispute over whether or not the tribe should sell their land and move west. In 1817 a small group of Cherokees did exchange their lands for new ones in the West and formed the Cherokee Nation West. This prompted the Eastern Cherokee to adopt a law that made any further land sales punishable by death. Following adoption of the Removal Act, an overwhelming majority of Cherokees opposed selling and supported their chief, John Ross, in his long campaign to reverse the government's policy. However, after years of legal actions and petitions to Congress, Ross ultimately failed.[33] By 1839 the Cherokee were forced to leave their homeland and relocate beyond the Mississippi.

In his February 28, 1831, circular Crockett expressed genuine outrage over Jackson's egregious Indian policies and portrayed the Indians as helpless victims who had been abused and deceived by the government, pointing out that Georgia had denied "to the weak Indians all the lands and rights secured to them by treaties made by every President since the commencement of the government. . . . Georgia passes her jurisdiction and laws over them, drives them from working their own lands for gold, tries an Indian by her own laws for an offence committed within the limits of an Indian nation and against an Indian, and hangs the offender; and will not permit them to give evidence in a court of justice. . . . The President, disregarding all the treaties made with them, the voice of humanity, and the honour of his country, flatters the pride and views of Georgia, by declaring to the Indians—'You must go, or submit to Georgia.' . . . The Indians petitioned Congress, stating these grievances: it was referred to the Committee on Indian Affairs, the friends of General Jackson, and they have made no report upon it. It would seem that the sufferings of a hungering people excites no pity with our President; and that all the miseries of famine, brought on by his own acts, are to be used as the instruments for their extermination or removal."[34] Crockett placed Jackson's Indian policy within the larger context of grievances he leveled at the president, whom he saw as a tyrant who was trampling on the Constitution and getting away with it. However, there is no doubt that he was very proud of his opposition to Indian removal and made no attempt to conceal it. Rather, he sought to explain his reasons for the vote and defend it on both moral and constitutional grounds. He called Jackson's policies both cruel and duplicitous and noted that he had "said much about this because I feel much about it."[35]

In January, 1831, Crockett sought justice for three Cherokee Indians whose land had been stolen by whites, but who had been denied relief and could not afford legal representation. He asked that the Congress provide them relief, and he succeeded in having the Cherokees' petition referred to the House Committee of Claims. In pleading the case of the dispossessed Cherokees, Crockett was as moved by their poverty and inability to afford legal counsel as he was by the clear racial injustice that they had suffered as a result of Jackson's policy. He told the House that "by treaties concluded between the United States and said Cherokee nation in the years 1817 and 1819, the petitioners became entitled each to a reservation of 640 acres of land, that they were forcibly dispossessed of said land by white men, that they sued out writs of ejectment, but from poverty were unable to prosecute said writs, and that judgments have gone against them by default; and praying indemnity for their losses from the Government of the United States."[36] He emphasized that they "were too poor to employ counsel. They had thrown themselves on the State of Tennessee for the benefit of the pauper law, so as that counsel might be employed for them; but the benefit of that law was refused."[37]

Finally, Crockett corresponded with Cherokee chief John Ross, who expressed his gratitude to him for his unwavering support of the Cherokee, although Ross was mistaken in thinking that Crockett's constituents approved. "It is gratifying," he wrote, "to hear that your vote on the Indian Bill has given general satisfaction to your constituents—that it has or will produce for you among the friends of humanity & justice a just respect and admiration, I can not doubt. Cupidity and avarice by sophistry intrigue and corruption may for a while prevail—but the day of retributive justice must and will come, where integrity and moral worth will predominate and make the shameless monster hide its head. Whether this day will come in time to save the suffering Cherokees from violence and frauds, it is for the wisdom, magnanimity & justice of the United States to determine. To those gentlemen who have so honorably and ably vindicated the rights of the poor Indians in Congress at the last session, this nation owes a debt of gratitude which the pages of history will bear record of until time shall be no more—and for which they will receive a just reward in the Courts of Heaven."[38]

Crockett continued to support Indians in ways that had nothing to do with Jacksonian policies but were simply clear advocacy for people who he believed were victims of injustice. In April, 1834, nearly four years after the Indian removal debate, he again took the House floor to petition on behalf of a Cherokee citizen whose land had been taken from him by underhanded means, this time through the machinations of a corrupt Indian agent.[39] Several months earlier, Crockett had written to Lewis Cass, Jackson's secretary of war, recommending the appointment of James Rodgers, a Cherokee, as an agent to the Seminoles of Florida, who were preparing to remove from their lands. Crockett had confidence in Rodgers' honesty, noting that the "high merit of this individual recommends him to your consideration."[40]

Others have found Crockett's pro-Indian position not credible due to his service in the Creek War and his being a man of the frontier, where there was little love for Indians and strong support for their removal. Indeed, Crockett's own grandparents had been killed by Indians, but he had often befriended them, fought beside Indian allies in the Creek War, and occasionally found himself in their debt. Once, when Crockett fell seriously ill on a hunting expedition, Indians rescued him and carried him to a nearby farm, where he was nursed until he was able to return home.[41] During the Creek War, friendly Indians had traded food to Crockett for his hungry comrades.[42] He also seems to have viewed the expropriation of Indian land for the benefit of speculators as similar to the plight of the settlers in his district, who also stood to lose their lands due to government actions that favored the influential, including wealthy speculators. Crockett continually objected to what he saw as unfair or abusive treatment of the poor and disadvantaged, and he sought to give them a voice in government. To Crockett, who often viewed issues in terms of class, Indian removal may have seemed no more than another government policy aimed at benefiting the rich at the expense of the poor and helpless.[43] His lonely, unpopular defense of Indians stands out in an era dominated by racism, greed and injustice.

---

[1] For an examination of early U.S. policy toward Indian tribes, see Francis Paul Prucha, *American Indian Policy in the Formative Years: The Indian Trade and Intercourse Acts 1790–1834* (Lincoln: University of Nebraska Press, 1962), 26–50; Joseph J. Ellis, *American Creation: Triumphs and Tragedies at the Founding of the Republic* (New York: Alfred A. Knopf, 2007).

[2] Andrew Jackson's First Annual Message to Congress, December 1829, eJournal Website, http://www.synaptic.bc.ca/ejournal/ JacksonFirstAnnualMessage.htm. For a discussion of Jackson and Indian Removal, see Robert V. Remini, *The Legacy of Andrew Jackson: Essays on Democracy, Indian Removal, and Slavery* (Baton Rouge: Louisiana State University Press, 1988), 45–82. Also see Remini's *The Life of Andrew Jackson* (New York: Penguin Books, 1988), a condensed edition of his three-volume biography of Jackson.

[3] Prucha, *American Indian Policy in the Formative Years: The Indian Trade and Intercourse Acts 1790–1834*, 227–28, citing Clarence Edwin Carter, ed., *The Territorial Papers of the United States*, vol. 5 (Washington, D.C.: Government Printing Office, 1934–1962), 142–46.

[4] Anthony F. C. Wallace, *The Long, Bitter Trail: Andrew Jackson and the Indians* (New York: Hill and Wang, 1993), 62–63.

[5] Ibid., 75; Gerard N. Magliocca, *Andrew Jackson and the Constitution* (Lawrence: University Press of Kansas, 2007), 22–23. The gold strike appears to have been a large one and word of it quickly spread. One miner wrote to a friend in Connecticut "The Gold mines of Georgia. . . far exceed in value what I had anticipated." The unidentified writer estimated the value of one mine "at the enormous sum of $90,000." *(Jackson, Tennessee) Southern Statesman*, August 20, 1831.

[6] Andrew Jackson's First Annual Message to Congress.

[7] The Hopewell Treaty of 1785 recognized Cherokee claim to land in Georgia below the Tennessee River, although specific boundaries between Creek, Cherokee and Chickasaw land was unclear. Jackson himself presided over a number of questionable negotiations with tribal parties, some of which were boycotted by tribes, employing bribery as well as threats, between 1814 and 1817, that resulted in land cessions by some Cherokees, although many others did not approve of them. Wallace, *The Long, Bitter Trail*, 51–52.

[8] Andrew Jackson's First Annual Message to Congress.

[9] Ibid.

[10] Ibid.

[11] *House Journal*, May 24, 1830, 711–12; Wallace, *The Long, Bitter Trail*, 70.

[12] Andrew Jackson's First Annual Message to Congress.

[13] Wallace, *The Long, Bitter Trail*, 25; John Ehle, *Trail of Tears: The Rise and Fall of the Cherokee Nation* (New York: Anchor Press/Doubleday, 1988), 224.

[14] Ehle, *Trail of Tears*, 220.

[15] Article I, Section 8 of the U.S. Constitution stipulates that "The Congress shall have power to regulate commerce with foreign nations, and among the several states, and with the Indian Tribes." However, beginning with President Washington, the power to deal with Indians had been widely interpreted as falling under Article 2, Section 2, which gives the president the power to make treaties "with the advice and consent of the Senate." See Joseph J. Ellis, *American Creation: Triumphs and Tragedies at the Founding of the Republic* (New York: Alfred A. Knopf, 2007), 128. For detailed histories of the evolution of U.S. policy toward Indians see Prucha, *American Indian Policy in the Formative Years: The Indian Trade and Intercourse Acts 1790–1834* and Angie Debo, *A History of the Indians of the United States* (Norman: University of Oklahoma Press, 1970). For assessments of Jackson's policy by his leading biographer, Robert V. Remini, see his "Andrew Jackson Versus the Cherokee Nation," *American History* (August 2001): 48–56 and *The Legacy of Andrew Jackson*. Remini largely condemns Jackson's removal policy, but provides a thoughtful defense of Jackson's response to the Supreme Court decisions, while also noting, and condemning, Jackson's obvious encouragement of Georgia's anti-Indian policies. Remini concludes that Jackson became "obsessed" with Indian removal, which blinded him to the policy's shortcomings and ultimate horrors. This seemed to be a habit with Jackson. A similar obsession seemed to drive his relentless effort to kill the Second Bank of the United States. For a discussion of how new generations of political leaders bring about change by overturning long-held legal precedents or understandings, see Magliocca, *Andrew Jackson and the Constitution*.

[16] Crockett's limited support for the Indians and opposition to removal was as far as he could go, given his constituents' clear support for removal. He expressed more sympathy for the Indians, and more anger over Georgia's actions, in his personal correspondence and was clearly out of step with his own district. See *Jackson Gazette*, April 10, 1830.

[17] The entire speech appears in Louis Filler and Allen Guttmann (eds.), *The Removal of the Cherokee Nation: Manifest Destiny or National*

Dishonor? (Lexington, Mass.: D. C. Heath & Company, 1962), 39–41. It also appeared, with minor alternations, in the *Jackson Gazette,* June 26, 1830, which mistakenly gave the date of the speech as May 20, 1830.

The *Register of Debates* is thus neither definitive nor complete and described itself only as "a summary of the 'leading debates and incidents' of the period." Not until 1850, when the Pitman shorthand system made verbatim reporting possible, did truly accurate congressional reporting begin. Many speeches published in the *Debates* were paraphrased and based only on reporters' notes and printed in the second person. Others were given to Gales & Seaton in written form and published in the first person, so that they appeared exactly the way speakers wanted them to look, not necessarily reflecting what they actually said on the floor. Thus, congressmen and senators could make themselves look as eloquent as they liked in print. It was common practice for members of Congress to visit the offices of Gales & Seaton to edit their speeches and to even review and correct proof sheets before the speeches were actually published in the *Debates.* The press also was permitted to attend House sessions, take notes, and print their own versions of debates in their newspapers.

Debates could last for days, and one speaker might take the floor for hours at a time. Thus, the reporter for the *Debates* might not be present at all times, and accounts that appeared in newspapers might contain information that was not included in the *Debates.* This could result from nothing more complicated than a reporter answering the call of nature during a particular speech, or skipping one because the speaker had already given him a written version for publication. In fact, Crockett's statement on May 19 was preceded by two very long speeches by Massachusetts representatives Issac Chapman Bates, who spoke for nearly four hours, and Edward Everett, whose speech took up twice the space of Bates' speech in the *Debates* and ran until five p.m. Both speeches appear in the first person in the *Debates,* indicating that reporters were furnished written copies and thus may not have sat through the speeches themselves, possibly missing Crockett's speech entirely. Or Crockett's speech was so brief compared to the others that it may have been skipped or forgotten by the *Debates* reporter. The House had engaged in a marathon twelve-hour debate the previous day, which went long into the night. It would not be surprising to find that Crockett's relatively insignificant remarks were simply lost in the avalanche of paper. *United States' Telegraph,* May 25, 1830; *Macon (Georgia) Telegraph,* June 5, 1830; *Register of Debates,* May 19, 1830, 1049–79. On November 19, 1863, Everett gave a two-hour address at the dedication of the Soldiers' National Cemetery in Gettysburg, Pennsylvania, shortly before President Lincoln delivered his Gettysburg Address, which lasted a mere two minutes.

Crockett's speech appears in the second person, indicating that he did not produce a written version of it, but rather that it was summarized and paraphrased by a reporter who worked either for the *Debates* or a newspaper. The style of the published version is very much like that used in the *Debates,* referring to Crockett as "Mr. C.," for example, which was common practice in the *Debates* for all speeches reported in the second person. That version simply could have gotten lost in the *Debates* press room among the countless pages of far longer speeches that day. The reporter for Gales & Seaton may simply have missed the speech, since it did not appear in the *Debates* or the *National Intelligencer,* both published by Gales & Seaton, but it was reported in the *United States' Telegraph,* which seems to have been the source for many other newspaper summaries. Several days could pass between the time a speech was given and its appearance in print. Reporters had to go through their notes, make sense of them, and write them up. Typesetting, proofreading, and printing required additional time. It would not be surprising if Crockett's speech, which added no new points to the debate, was forgotten, ignored or simply lost by the *Debates.* Meanwhile, Crockett himself or someone else could have secured a copy and had it printed for distribution to the press, which is how it came to appear in the *Jackson Gazette* and was summarized in other newspapers. It is doubtful that Crockett deliberately had the speech withheld from the *Debates* or thought that he could conceal it from his pro-removal constituents, because he did nothing to prevent its publication elsewhere and knew he could not prevent word of the speech from leaking out, nor did he ever deny making the speech and, in fact, boasted about it. Finally, Crockett knew he could not conceal his vote against the Indian Removal Bill, and publication of the speech at least offered him the opportunity to explain and defend his vote. Crockett likely sent the speech to the *Gazette* himself to head off his political enemies, who would surely have exposed any effort to conceal it. They never did, although they used it against him in the 1831 election. For a discussion of the *Register of Debates* see Donald A. Ritchie, *Press Gallery* (Cambridge: Harvard University Press, 1991), 7–34. Also, our thanks to Christine Blackerby, archives specialist in the Center for Legislative Archives, U.S. National Archives & Records Administration, for information regarding the history of the *Debates.*

[18] *United States' Telegraph,* May 20, 1830. The *Telegraph's* short paraphrase was repeated or mentioned in other newspapers, including the *Pittsfield (Massachusetts) Sun,* May 27, 1830; *Augusta Chronicle & Georgia Advertiser,* May 29, 1830; *(Keene) New Hampshire Sentinel,* June 4, 1830; and *Macon (Georgia) Telegraph,* June 5, 1830.

[19] *United States' Telegraph,* May 25, 1830.

[20] *Jackson (Tennessee) Gazette,* June 26, 1830.

[21] David Crockett, *A Narrative of the Life of David Crockett of the State of Tennessee,* ed. and annotated by James A. Shackford and Stanley J. Folmsbee (Knoxville: University of Tennessee Press, 1973), 206.

[22] Curtis Carroll Davis, "A Legend at Full-Length: Mr. Chapman Paints Colonel Crockett— and Tells About It," *Proceedings of the American Antiquarian Society* 69 (1960), 169–70.

[23] Crockett to James Davison, August 18, 1831, DRT Library at the Alamo.

[24] Magliocca, *Andrew Jackson and the Constitution,* 36; "Elias Boudinot Editorials in the *Cherokee Phoenix* 1829, 1831" at website: http://www.cerritos.edu/soliver/Student%20Activites/Trail%20of%20Tears/web/boudinot.htm.

[25] Flinders is an archaic word meaning bits, fragments, splinters, etc. "Flew into flinders" means burst or exploded.

[26] Crockett to Daniel W. Pounds, January 6, 1831. Courtesy, the Lilly Library, Indiana University, Bloomington, Indiana.

27   Indian Land Cessions website: http://www.tngenweb.org/cessions/18310100.html.

28   Magliocca, *Andrew Jackson and the Constitution*, 22–23, 39.

29   Ibid., 39–40.

30   Ibid., 42, citing Marshall's decision.

31   See Remini, "Andrew Jackson Versus the Cherokee Nation." Remini describes legal technicalities surrounding the Worcester deci-
     sion. The Supreme Court adjourned immediately after handing down the decision without ordering Georgia officials to appear
     before it on a charge of contempt, nor did it order a writ of habeas corpus for the release of the two missionaries. The law required
     that the state formally respond to the court's ruling, expressing its unwillingness to comply, before further federal action could be
     taken. Thus, Remini concludes that Jackson would not have made the remark about enforcement, since there was nothing to
     enforce. He did write to his loyal crony John Coffee that the court's decision "has fell still born" and that the court found "that it
     cannot coerce Georgia to yield to its mandate." The Constitution does not clearly define Native American legal status. Article One,
     Section Eight only states that Congress has the authority to "regulate Commerce with foreign Nations, and among the several states,
     and with the Indian Tribes." See Magliocca, *Andrew Jackson and the Constitution*, 49–51; he argues that Marshall went beyond the issue
     of Georgia's loyalty oath in his decision in order to rouse public opinion against the Removal Act and to oppose Jackson's argument
     that Indians had no sovereign rights and that the states could establish policies toward tribes within their boundaries. Although
     Georgia refused to comply with the court's order to release the two missionaries, the state did release them after Wilson Lumpkin
     became governor and gave in to widespread criticism of their incarceration by Georgia and perhaps some pressure from Jackson,
     who did not want another constitutional crisis. Lumpkin pressured the legislature to repeal the law the missionaries had violated.
     They accepted a pardon and were finally released in January 1833. See *New Georgia Encyclopedia* website: http://www.georgiaencyclo-
     pedia.org/nge/ Article.jsp?id'h-2720. Also see Remini, *The Life of Andrew Jackson*, 217–18; which draws attention to the broader con-
     stitutional issues Jackson was facing. While favoring strong federal authority in some instances, especially that of the president,
     Jackson was cautious about taking action against states that could result in a secession crisis. Resistance to strong central government
     and insistence on states' rights were prominent and volatile issues at the time and would remain so until boiling over into the Civil
     War in 1860. In addition to the crisis with Georgia, Jackson soon faced an equally alarming states' rights crisis brought on by South
     Carolina's attempt to nullify the federal tariff. Jackson would not tolerate secession, but was reluctant to act too forcefully against
     the states, lest such crises escalate dangerously. He managed both crises successfully, partly by pacifying Georgia with his removal
     policy, but at a cost of terrible suffering by the Cherokee and other tribes.

32   Marshall to Joseph Story, September 22, 1832, quoted in Magliocca, *Andrew Jackson and the Constitution*, 59.

33   John Ross was only one-eighth Cherokee, but he had fought alongside Jackson, Sam Houston, and possibly Crockett with their
     Cherokee allies during the Creek War. He was educated in white schools, but became the tribe's only elected chief, serving until
     his death in 1866, and led a relentless fight against removal, basing persuasive arguments on a long history of U.S. treaties with
     the Cherokee. For more on Ross's struggle to save the Cherokee homeland, see Walter H. Conser, Jr., "John Ross and the
     Cherokee Resistance Campaign, 1833–1838," *Journal of Southern History* 44, no. 2 (May, 1978): 191–212

34   Crockett circular, February 28, 1831.

35   Ibid.

36   *Journal of the House of Representatives*, January 31, 1831, 233.

37   *Register of Debates*, January 31, 1831, 544

38   John Ross to Crockett, January 13, 1831, with enclosure (report, ca. March 1814), Ayer MS 782, Edward E. Ayer Manuscript
     Collection, the Newberry Library, Chicago; Gary E. Moulton, ed., *The Papers of Chief John Ross, Volume 1* (Norman: University of
     Oklahoma Press, 1985), 210–12. Crockett's December 16, 1830, letter to Ross has not been located, but in a letter to David L.
     Child, dated February 11, 1831, Ross mentions that he had received Child's letter of October 6, 1830, "thro Colo. [David]
     Crockett" (Ibid., 214). Ross remained an admirer of Crockett and as late as 1834 wrote to William H. Underwood regarding his
     efforts to maintain Cherokee land, commenting, "And in the language of Colo. Crockett, being convinced that we are right, I say
     'Go a head,'" thus invoking Crockett's own familiar motto (Ibid., 298).

39   *Journal of the U.S. House of Representatives, 23rd Congress, 1st Session,* April 10, 1834, 517. Crockett "presented a petition of Joseph M.
     Lynch, a native born citizen of the Cherokee nation of Indians, praying to be indemnified in the amount of his claim against a citi-
     zen of the said Indian nation, which he lost by the unlawful and improper interference of Mr. Montgomery, the United States agent
     stationed in said nation; which petition was referred to the Committee of Claims."

40   Crockett to Lewis Cass, November 28, 1833, Courtesy of the Pierpont Morgan Library, New York.

41   Crockett, *Narrative*, 129.

42   Ibid., 121.

43   For a summary rebuttal to commonly held views of Crockett's pro-Indian stance and other views see Thomas E. Scruggs, "Davy
     Crockett and the Thieves of Jericho: An Analysis of the Shackford-Parrington Conspiracy Theory," *Journal of the Early Republic* 19
     (Fall 1999): 488 n. 25.

Chapter 6

"Determined To Persevere"
The Elections of 1831 and 1833

Crockett had done himself little political good, and considerable harm, during his years in Congress. His vote against Jackson's Indian removal policy, his failure to secure relief for occupants on Tennessee vacant lands, and his break with the Tennessee delegation and the Jacksonians combined to create a perfect storm that severely handicapped his bid for reelection in 1831. He clearly saw the trouble brewing and did his best to apply preemptive damage control.

Despite his earlier protests about unfair treatment in the press, the *Jackson Gazette* was, at this point, still supportive of many of Crockett's positions. In April of 1830 the editors applauded his efforts to abolish the U.S. Military Academy at West Point and agreed that the institution was a "depot for favoritism."[1]

Crockett held that the academy was primarily a school for the sons of the wealthy and titled, who had political influence and were educated at public expense. Probably drawing on his own militia experience and resulting bias against professional soldiers, he argued that the heroes of the Revolution and the War of 1812 were ordinary soldiers, not West Point graduates, and that the institution was unnecessary. Furthermore, he pointed out that "No one could ever gain an admittance who had not rich or influential friends to aid him. A poor, friendless young man, however worthy, might beg a full century at the doors of the Academy, and never be permitted to enter, or partake of its benefits."[2] He also noted that even if appointments were granted to poor young men, the costs of transportation to and from the academy would be prohibitive.

Crockett's position was not altogether unusual. The academy at West Point was seen by many as elitist, and the Tennessee legislature had debated sending a memorial directing its representatives in Washington to oppose any further funding of the institution. Though the memorial was voted down, Crockett claimed that during his canvass his district had made its opposition to the academy clear, and he found it a matter of conscience to vote for its abolishment.[3]

In his remarks to Congress on February 25, 1830, he said that the establishment was indulging in favoritism, "the extent to which it was calculated to advance the aristocracy of a *country* which I love, and which I have fought to defend." He told his fellow congressmen, "If, Sir, you can so arrange it, as to feed 'the rich upon the rich,' I have not a word to say; but when you attempt to feed the 'RICH' upon the ruins of the poor, I cannot be satisfied to hold my peace." He went on to say, "I have another and I may say it, a serious objection to this institution. It is that though the POOR contribute their portions, and often unjust portions, for the support of the government, they seem to have *'no rights.'* Wealth, sir, carries with it, from its superior advantages, its own wreath of victory and triumphs over the POOR; but shall that wreath be embroidered at the cost of those who solemnly protest against awarding it? Surely not; unless in truth *power* is to prevail over justice; and falsehood over truth, unless *usurpation* is the watchword of the day." Crockett argued that the taxation imposed upon the poor that was used, in part, to pay for West Point, was "literally calculated to pick the pockets of the poor to educate the sons of the *rich*."[4]

Crockett complained that "our western men choose, when they are compelled to fight, to elect their own commanders. They are wholly unwilling to trust themselves amid the fury of the battle, under the command of a *'Boy,'* not of their own choosing—untried, except at the famous place called "West Point," where, like the ancient story, they march up the hill, and down again, but smell no powder . . . this, Sir, is ARISTOCRACY with a vengeance."[5]

In March, the *Jackson Gazette* lost its public printing contract to publish the laws of the United States, an appointment that had netted the newspaper a profit of about $400 per year, to the *Memphis Advocate*. The *Gazette* editors wrote to Crockett, asking if he knew why the business had been taken elsewhere. President Jackson may have been penalizing the *Gazette* for what he saw as a lack of enthusiastic support, although the paper was pro-Jackson. Crockett responded in a March 5 letter, noting that although the *Gazette* had "opposed me in all my elections," he thought the reassignment was unfair. He blamed the change on partisan politics, an issue that would remain central to his argument whenever he defended his departure from the Jackson ranks. "I am a party man in the true sense of the word," he wrote, "but God forbid that I should ever become so much a party man as obsequiously to stoop to answer party purposes."[6]

He had written to Martin Van Buren, Jackson's secretary of state, on behalf of the paper and complained about the loss of the contract despite the fact that he considered the *Gazette* a Jackson paper, while the new recipient was not. He wrote "You have removed a man who was the first Editor of a newspaper within that District, and a warm friend to the present Chief Magistrate, and appointed one who had junior claims. I am friendly to each, but I protest against such an unwarranted interference." Furthermore, Crockett wrote, "I had supposed that before you would make material change in my district, you would according to custom condescend to consult, me."[7] Van Buren never responded to him.

Throughout the year, Crockett wrote to the *Gazette*, outlining his ongoing efforts to secure for his constituents legal title to their lands, but the electorate was losing patience with him, and his opponents were quick to take advantage of his vulnerability on the issue. Pleasant Miller, a wealthy eastern Tennessean and a John Overton ally, penned an article critical of the handling of the vacant land bill in Congress, and Crockett wasted no time in firing off a heated response. He wrote, "I wish to inform Mr. Miller, that if it be his desire to become a candidate against me, that he need not make any apology nor try to lash me, over the shoulders of my colleagues." He referred to Miller's "stupidity" in trying to alarm constituents and called his position "a downright insult on common sense." Crockett sarcastically offered to school Miller on the issue, and donned his "Davy" persona, declaring, "I will endeavor to explain it to him; that is, if he will *condescend* to be advised by the *Bear hunter*—who is always ready to aid the needy." He concluded with the now familiar caveat, "I do not profess to be a grammarian or a scholar, nor have I any inducement to dispute the palm of erudition with Mr. Miller; but there is a palm which I will not yield to him; it is that of honesty, and devotion to the interests of those who have kindly honored me with a seat in Congress."[8] In fact, it would not be Pleasant Miller who would oppose Crockett, but William Fitzgerald, a lawyer who had served as clerk of the circuit court of Stewart County, Tennessee, and as a member of the state legislature. In a May letter to the *Gazette*, Crockett confessed his failure to pass a land bill, put most of the blame on the other members of his delegation, and promised to "set up shop" for himself, something he'd already largely done. This admission was a bitter pill to swallow, as Crockett was fully aware that his hopes for reelection hung largely on his ability to get the land-occupant bill through, or at least convince people that he could. He wrote that "as disappointment is the lot of man I will reconcile myself to my fate. I have labored earnestly to promote the interest of poor Occupants, in my district, who I know were looking with a fond anticipation to this Congress." Crockett promised to continue to promote the cause in his next session, should he be reelected, but he knew the effort would be an uphill climb and he'd be going it alone.[9]

Sometime during his second term Crockett sat for the first of what would become a number of portraits, this one painted by an artist he identified only as Mr. Hincley. Before departing for his home at the recess, he rolled the canvas up in some newspapers for transit, labeling it a map of Florida. The portrait must have been a treasured possession, maybe a mark of his rising status as a person of consequence, and probably a pricey investment, but it was lost somewhere along the stage route back to Tennessee during a transfer. Crockett wrote to Michael Sprigg and asked him to look for it at the transfer station and forward it to him if it was found.[10] If Sprigg ever located the painting, it has never been positively identified.[11]

Crockett had more pressing difficulties, particularly his bid for reelection, which hit rough waters from the start. By June the *Gazette* was reporting Crockett's speech in opposition to the Indian Bill, criticizing his position and claiming, "We regret that our representative tho't as he did on this question, for we are sure a large majority of his constituents will be found opposed to his vote on that subject, and differing in opinion with him to its bearings on the Indians themselves."[12] The paper also stepped up its negative reports about Crockett's departure from the Jacksonian fold and pointed to his roommate Thomas Chilton, who had recently made public his own departure from the ranks, as the culprit behind Crockett's apostasy.[13]

On Independence Day, Crockett appeared at a barbecue in his home district, where he proclaimed his support for Henry Clay. In a letter printed in the *Gazette,* a pro-Crockett constituent reported, "There was a very large collection of the citizens of the county present. From the spirit of the toasts you will discover that Mr. Clay has many warm admirers here, and that 'Jackson and Reform' are not in so high regard as they once were." Crockett, the writer claimed, "sees the many inconsistencies of Gen. Jackson— he knows the principles now advanced by the President and his partisans during the last contest for the Presidency—and that every solemn promise made by himself and his partisans has been violated, except *one* and *that* he will violate if he finds there is any chance for his reelection to the Presidency."[14] The editors amended the letter by declaring that "the course pursued by Col. Crockett during the late session of Congress, puts it entirely out of the power of his friends to defend him. He certainly *voted* with the *enemy* on very important occasions, and as far as we could learn, but one opinion prevailed on the subject at Washington, and that was that the Col. had, in reality, *bolted.*"[15] Henceforth the *Gazette* editors were openly critical of Crockett, but they continued to publish letters from his supporters as well.

A series of articles by someone writing under the name "Madison" defended Crockett's independence and echoed his claims that he had not changed, but Jackson had. "Madison" cited Crockett's votes in favor of internal improvements and Jackson's reversal of his own position on the issue, and wrote that Crockett was ostracized "because he chose to adhere to what he believed to be the interest of the nation, and would not change with those who changed." He also pounded the populist drum for Crockett, declaring that "*He is, say the big men about the little towns,* to be beaten shamefully, but I will not believe it 'till I hear it from the hardy and independent freemen of the district—from the working class of the people—from the Occupant; from all those who constitute the bone and marrow of the country. I cannot believe the people of the district will be gulled by the Lawyers, land speculators, Merchants, (some of them) who dwell about our little towns, and are continually crying out, 'Crockett has no standing in Congress'—he has changed his politics—he is opposed to Gen. Jackson. . . . They know that Jackson has changed his politics on some subjects of importance and that Col. Crockett, not being so *plyant* as themselves, would not follow . . . ."[16] The open attack on Jackson confirmed that there was significant opposition to Old Hickory in West Tennessee.

In addition to railing against Crockett's vote on Indian removal, the Jacksonian press had taken him to task for voting against awarding the widow of Stephen Decatur remuneration for service that Decatur had rendered in Tripoli in 1804, years before they were married.[17] "Madison" defended

Crockett for that vote and launched a salvo against Jackson's increasing attempts to consolidate more power in the executive branch of government, a topic that Crockett would embrace with a passion. He wrapped up his letter by reiterating the idea that all of Crockett's opponents, primarily lawyers, were in collusion and conspiring to bring about his defeat.[18]

By December of 1830, the *Rhode Island American* was already proclaiming that Crockett was "no longer a half-horse, half-alligator Kentuck; but has become a whole hog Clay man."[19] Polk and the Jacksonians were keeping tabs on Crockett as well. Archibald Yell[20] wrote Polk that Crockett had stayed the night with Dr. James Armstrong, an anti-Jackson man, while traveling to Washington City.[21] Back in Washington, Crockett wrote Henry McClung, another Clay supporter, "I still am of the opinion that Mr. Clay has as many frinds in Congress as Genl Jackson tho we have had no chance to try the test." Crockett enclosed five dollars he had borrowed from McClung to help with expenses on his way back to the capitol, a clear indication that he was still experiencing dire financial straits.[22]

Crockett's reputation (or notoriety) in Washington City had grown during his first two terms in Congress, and the press had found that the exploits, misadventures, and quips emanating from the eccentric "Davy" could be counted on to provide popular public-interest stories in national newspapers. One person who took particular notice of the trend was James Hackett, a well-known actor and producer. Hackett saw potential in Davy Crockett, and pictured himself in a role based on the character, stalking the stage in a buckskin jacket and wildcat fur hat. He offered a cash prize of $300 to the playwright who could come up with the best script, and soon James Kirk Paulding's *Lion of the West* was on Hackett's desk.[23] Paulding had done some research on the congressman, embellished a great deal, and created Nimrod Wildfire, a western wild man with a heart of gold, as one of the play's central characters. Hackett was overjoyed, and production on the play soon began.[24]

Word leaked to the press, and Paulding took it on himself to write Crockett and apologize, lest he take offense at the character. Crockett quickly responded and assured Paulding that he was certain no offense had been intended and so none had been taken. In fact, when the production proved to be successful, Crockett went on to ride *Lion of the West* to even greater fame than did Hackett.[25]

James Strange French also acknowledged Crockett's growing fame, and the young writer began contemplating a biography of the colonel. Crockett had little time to bask in his growing celebrity, as he was ever aware of the tough reelection bid he faced back home. His correspondence reflected his gloomy disposition. In January he fretted over an incident involving the Georgia Cherokee, and worried that the Jackson administration would bring about both a civil war and possibly ignite an international conflict. "These are times that is new to me," he wrote, but he could not find a way to use these issues to energize his campaign.[26]

A letter from Crockett to the *Southern Statesman* carried the same uncharacteristically defeatist tone. He reported again that his efforts to secure a land bill were going nowhere and again blamed the other Tennesseans. Despite his attempt to end the letter on a positive note, his blue mood was evident. "I am determined to persevere," he wrote, "so long as I retain a seat in Congress, encouraged by the hope that other times and other men will do justice to the cause of suffering humanity. I have done all that mortal man could do for the District; days of toil, and sleepless nights have I spent, in endeavoring to soothe the palpitating hearts of our population, by procuring for them the protection and liberality of the government—and I thank God that the people know it, and will charge the failure to those who caused it, and not to me; certainly not to one who has had an array against him, even from the bosom of his own country and his own household." The letter is sincere, but carries none of the humor or fire that was so common to his earlier campaigns.[27]

Crockett's personal correspondence reflected his growing anger with the Jacksonians. "I would see the whole of them hung up at the devil before I will submit to such carryings on as this I did not come to Cloke their extravagancy to let them make a speculation of this governmint," he wrote. He was also planning to take his case directly to the public in a circular he was writing.[28] Clearly, his campaign was beginning to take on an overtly anti-Jackson tone that sought to direct anger toward the president and distract voters from Crockett's own failures in Congress.

William Fitzgerald issued his own circular in March that was printed in the *Southern Statesman*. He outlined his positions on the issues: against nullification, against the tariff, for internal improvements if financed by the states rather than the federal government, and, of course, he addressed the vacant-land bill that was stalled in Congress. Fitzgerald reminded the electorate that he had served in the state legislature in 1825 and had a hand in drafting the memorial asking Congress to donate the vacant lands to the state. He wrote, "What has caused the failure of this desirable measure, I shall not pretend to say, but one thing is certain, that the occupants seem to be further from the title to their lands, than they were four years ago. Should I be your representative, I will pursue the same course that I did in 1825. I shall not represent the occupants as a set of sturdy beggars, asking scraps and crumbs at the federal table." Fitzgerald did not explain how he intended to convince the federal government to cede the lands, but instead jumped ahead and voiced his confidence that the state legislature would distribute the ceded lands fairly. He complained of the partisanship in Washington, but then immediately pledged his loyalty to Jackson, "so long as he acted on the principles by which he has heretofore been guided."[29] Fitzgerald's less-than-overwhelming endorsement of Jackson suggests that Crockett was correct in his estimation of the extent of anti-Jackson sentiment in his district and that Fitzgerald was aware of it too.

Though somewhat vague on how he would implement his ideas, Fitzgerald did not attack Crockett and only mentioned him once in closing, remarking that when Crockett issued his circular, the two of them would likely have more to discuss.

Crockett's lengthy circular came out the following week and it was incendiary.[30] He dropped the "Davy" persona completely and adopted a combative posture toward Jackson and his followers from start to finish. He accused the administration of reneging on the promise to reform the government and retrench expenses, claiming that Jackson had increased spending, wasted federal funds, and expanded the government. He condemned Jackson's Indian removal policy, calling it inhuman, and said that Jackson's actions brought "shame and reproach on the American name." Crockett stepped his constituents through issue after issue and laid out his case against the administration: Jackson's reversal on internal improvements, desperately sought by Westerners; his appointment of friends of Martin Van Buren to cabinet positions, thereby attempting to corrupt Congress; and Jackson's broken promise to serve only one term as president.

He then turned to the issue most dear to him, the vacant lands, and outlined all he had done on behalf of his constituents to get them title to their homesteads. He railed against Polk, Pryor Lea, and the other "great Lawyers of Tennessee" who conspired to ensure his failure. He claimed that while he had been looking out for the interest of the occupants of his district, his colleagues "made it a party question" and voted against him "merely to gratify the ambition of partizans." As to the squatters, he acknowledged that "It is asked why have I not done something to save them? Why have I not entered into some arrangement with my colleagues to secure the land to them? I can only reply that I have done so . . . Heaven knows I have done all that a mortal could do, to save the people, and the failure was not my fault, but the fault of others." He reminded his readers that the other members of the Tennessee delegation "were unwilling to let you have the land in any way except you got it from the Legislature of Tennessee, and to this I was opposed, because I knew that advantage would be taken of you, and that your rights would be sacrificed . . . I know, and you know too, that the Legislature has imposed upon you before, and I was afraid to trust them again." Crockett closed by asking for another chance and suggesting that a new Congress might include more members friendly to his views. "Fellow citizens, I am once more a candidate to represent you in Congress. I have met many disappointments since I have been in your service, but I am not discouraged. I firmly believe that if I am again your choice, I shall meet a set of men in Congress, who will know how to feel for your situations and will do you justice; and that I shall have the unspeakable pleasure of seeing you seated by firesides you can safely call your own. You know that I am a poor man; and that I am a plain man. I have served you long enough in peace, to enable you to judge whether I am honest or not—I never deceived you—I never will deceive you. I have fought with you and for you in war, and you know whether I love my country and ought to be trusted. I thank you for what you have done for me, and hope that you will not forsake me to gratify those who are my enemies and yours."[31]

The impact of Crockett's circular was explosive, and was the focus of biting criticism in the Tennessee press. The *Southern Statesman* blasted him for his open rebellion against Jackson and blamed Chilton and Daniel Webster, among others, for his defiant stance, suggesting that he was either incapable of forming such opinions himself or that he was far too easily influenced by others. They took "Davy" to task, writing, "Strayed or stolen from the Jackson ranks, a certain Member of Congress from the Western District, named David Crockett. Davy is upwards of six feet high, erect in his posture, and has a nose extremely red, after taking some spirits. He possesses vast bodily powers; great activity, and can leap the Ohio, wade the Mississippi, and carry one steam and two flat boats on his back. He can vault across a streak of lightning, ride it down a honey locust; grease his heels, skate down a rainbow, and whip his weight in wildcats and panthers. Davy took the bounty in the Western District, enlisted in the Jackson ranks, and performed prodigies of valour, in divers engagements, between the Jacksonites and the Adams boys . . . the last that has been heard of him, he was riding towards Yankee land upon a broken down poney called OCCUPANT."[32]

Crockett's growing fame was wearing thin on some in his district as well. One constituent wrote, "The name of this gentleman, like the Sunday mails, has been repeated so often and in such a diversity of ways, that it has become disgusting, or is considered as a matter of no importance by a large portion of individuals . . . the conduct of this gentleman, as a man who represents 50 to 60 thousand souls in the Congress of the Nation, one of the first offices within the gift of a free and enlightened people, has been such as is calculated to disgrace the district he represents." The same writer attacked Crockett for his failure to secure the vacant lands and ridiculed him for referring to himself as "the poor man's friend" while on the stump. He ripped into Crockett for joining the Clay ranks and criticized his support of internal improvements and his position on Indian removal. In a venomous conclusive paragraph, the writer mocked Crockett's plea for reelection in his circular, claimed Crockett was insincere in his support for and identification with the poor people of his district, and charged him with using the land bill as a proverbial carrot-on-a-stick to get reelected.[33] Although clearly written by a Jackson proponent, it must have resonated with many voters.

Some of the most excoriating editorials were published in the *Statesman* under the name "Junius Brutus" and focused exclusively on Crockett's charges against Jackson. Brutus warned Crockett that "If it should turn out that you are guilty of this crying sin against your country for the motives which influenced you, you will be accountable to your God, but for the consequences, you will be accountable to your constituents."[34]

Despite the decidedly contrary reception to his circular, Crockett repeated his attacks on Jackson while on the hustings, using most of the arguments he had published, and adopted the same hostile posture toward his opponent. Frustrated and feeling the heat, Crockett went completely negative. He continued to utilize his tried and true method of casting his opponent as an elitist who was out of touch with the common man and attempted to use Fitzgerald's legal pedigree against him, stereotyping him as a typical wealthy lawyer looking to fleece the public. He insinuated that Fitzgerald had pitched in with other lawyers in a cabal, conspiring against him in his effort to retain his congressional seat.[35] His speeches were increasingly acrimonious, and he gave full vent to his contempt for Fitzgerald, engaging in unabashed character assassination that shocked even the editors of the *Statesman*. They wrote, "Statements were made, as facts, which are of too serious a nature to publish without better authority, for their truth, than the Col. had to offer. Mr. Fitzgerald was depicted, as a man, void of principle, corrupt and unworthy of confidence, or respect. We must confess that, our astonishment was extreme at the language, which the

Col. thought proper to adopt, in reference to this Gentleman." They warned that Crockett's campaign behavior "should it be imitated by others, will form a new era in the history of canvassing for public office." The *Statesman* also reported that the crowd response to Crockett's invective was less than enthusiastic, and commented, "How far the Col. may succeed, in supporting his claims, to public confidence, by retailing slanders against his rival, we cannot say; but for our own citizens, in this quarter, we will venture to assert, that, if he thus seeks, to gain their support, he has mistaken his men."[36]

Fitzgerald mounted an able defense. When appearing in tandem with Crockett on the stump, he brought up witnesses to vouch for his character and contradict Crockett's defamatory claims. Fitzgerald also was helped by an endorsement from the *Southern Statesman,* which provided a steady flow of anti-Crockett press. The paper published a lengthy article outlining all the votes Crockett had missed during his tenure in Congress and claimed that, since he received a per diem for those days, he had effectively ripped off the taxpayers.[37] The *Statesman* dredged up an old complaint about some alleged outstanding personal debts,[38] and accused him of flip-flopping in his current support of the Second Bank of the United States. They charged that he had abused his franking privilege by shipping personal items back to Tennessee at public expense.[39] In short, Crockett was under fire on almost every pertinent issue. "Indeed," Crockett wrote, "they were ready to print any and every thing the ingenuity of man could invent against me."[40]

Crockett was not above engaging in some invention of his own. In what would become a standard campaign tactic whenever he sensed he was losing ground, Crockett leveled charges against his opponent based on hearsay and half-truth, and succeeded in keeping Fitzgerald on the defensive for a good portion of the summer. He accused Fitzgerald of chicanery during his tenure as solicitor general, implied that his opponent was susceptible to bribery, and trotted out depositions from witnesses in an attempt to corroborate the charges, but his efforts were little more than a distraction. Fitzgerald's skillful refutation of the allegations called Crockett's honesty into question, and he was eventually forced to backpedal and return to a defensive position.[41]

Even Crockett's trademark electioneering style was being appropriated. Adam Huntsman, writing as "Black Hawk," released a popular satirical pamphlet entitled "Book of Chronicles, West of Tennessee and East of the Mississippi Rivers" wherein he used Biblical language to lampoon Crockett's public image. "David was a man wise in council," he wrote, "smooth in speech, valiant in war, and of fair countenance and goodly stature; such was the terror of his exploits, that thousands of wild cats and panthers did quake and tremble at his name. . . . In those days there were many occupants spread abroad throughout the river country: these men loved David exceedingly, because he promised to give them lands flowing with milk and honey."[42]

Huntsman did an effective job of skewering Crockett for his failure to pass the land bill and took him to task for his alliance with Clay and the Adamsites. He was probably all the more persuasive because he used comedy as a vehicle to deliver his message; a tactic that had served Crockett well in the past. Crockett saw little humor in the tract, dismissing it as "foolish stuff," but the *Statesman* picked up the piece in July, and it reached a wide audience.[43]

Fitzgerald also got in on the action, pulling a stunt that would have made Crockett envious in less stressful times. Fitzgerald and his cronies advertised personal appearances by Crockett, but didn't inform him of the dates, and when crowds showed up to see the celebrated Gentleman from the Cane, they were met by a cadre of Jacksonian campaigners and candidates vociferously attacking Crockett for failing to show up, and vying for their votes. Crockett wrote, "All this intrigue was kept a profound secret from me, 'til it was too late to counteract it."[44]

The barrage of attacks in the media also took their toll, and Crockett sensed that the mood of the electorate was not trending in his favor. In June, the *Southern Statesman* reported that at a log rolling in Crockett's neighborhood, twenty-two voters were polled, and Fitzgerald had bested him eighteen votes to Crockett's two, with two abstaining.[45]

He was tapped out financially as well, running his campaign on borrowed money and whatever cash he managed to realize from selling off his property. His brother-in-law, George Patton, paid him $100 for a parcel of land and $300 for a slave girl named Adeline, but Crockett's diminishing finances and the heat of the campaign created a lot of stress, and he was off his game.[46]

The strident back-and-forth in the press between Crockett and Fitzgerald continued, often sinking into pettiness. Fitzgerald, thirteen years Crockett's junior, baited the Colonel by continually referring to him as an old man, while Crockett took to calling his opponent "Little Fitz" or even "this little thing," and claimed in a speech at Jackson that he would "grease the little fellow's head and swallow him,"[47] but his tone was angry rather than mischievous. He told his constituents, "Whether you will sacrifice an old and as far as his capacity extends a faithful servant, to gratify the ambition of this man and satisfy the malevolence of his sycophants, your votes at the coming election will show . . . In the name of Heaven fellow citizens, what have I done that I must be treated with such contumely and glaring injustice? I appeal to your justice, your honor, and your magnanimity. If you re-elect me I will endeavor, as I have hitherto done, to discharge my duty faithfully—but if it be your will that I shall be sacrificed as a victim on the altar of conscience, be it so. I shall retire to private life with the proud consciousness of having done my duty."[48]

Realizing he faced likely defeat, Crockett set about getting his personal affairs in order and sold the rest of his land holdings in an attempt to pay off his outstanding debts. He wrote to Calvin Jones asking for a land lease so that he might start anew, building a cabin, digging a well, and planting a small orchard.[49]

On the 18th of August, Crockett wrote to a friend, "I am sorry that I cannot give you a full account of the result of my election, however I have hird from enough of the countys to sattisfy me that I'm beaton something like five hundrid votes."[50] He wasn't far off. When the final tally came in, Crockett was defeated by only 586 votes out of 16,482 cast.[51] Bitter over the loss, and convinced that he had been the victim of a concerted Jacksonian effort to unseat him, Crockett commented, "My Competitor is a little County Court lawyer with very little standing he is what we call here a perfect lick spittle . . . there is four newspapers published in the district and I had to bare the slang and pole-cat abuse of every one of them . . . the truth is the Jackson worshipers became desperate and had to resort to any and every thing in order to have me beaton . . . I was beaton this time intirely by managemint and rascality."[52]

Crockett made a half-hearted attempt to contest the election results, but the effort went nowhere. In a letter to the editor of the *National Intelligencer* he stated his belief that the election had been stolen from him, and his disdain for Fitzgerald had reached the point where he refused to even mention him by name, referring to him as "the thing that had the name of beating me."[53]

Back in Tennessee after his defeat, Crockett concentrated on his homestead, constructing a simple dirt-floor cabin and laying-in subsistence crops. With no slaves left to help them, the Crockett family labored together with axe, saw, and plough, and held fast to the hope of a brighter future. Crockett resumed his favorite pastime, bear hunting, and stocked up in preparation for a severe winter.[54] Sometime after setting up his new place, he received a visit from James Strange French, who was working on his biography of Crockett. French found the Colonel in better spirits and conversed with him about his recent loss and the strength of the Jackson political machine in his district. When French commented that he had doubts as to whether Crockett could ever regain his congressional seat in such an environment, Crockett responded that he didn't care and held that "If they won't elect me with my opinions, I can't help it."[55] His attitude towards the jests in the press had mellowed somewhat as well, and he told French that "Those who publish them don't intend to injure me."[56]

While Crockett toiled at home, Congressman William Fitzgerald seemingly did very little. The *Register of Debates* for the Twenty-Second Congress records him speaking only four times from the floor during the first session, all of his remarks short and none of them pertaining to securing the land bill for his constituents. During one of the few times he did speak, he admitted that "It was not a very common thing for [me] to engross the attention of the House."[57] During the second session, no comments from him were recorded at all.

During Fitzgerald's term, the Jacksonians gerrymandered Crockett's old district, splitting it in two, and included Madison County, where Crockett had lost in 1831, in his new district. Crockett accused Fitzgerald of promoting the fix, claiming "It was done to make a mash of me."[58]

While Crockett played the farmer and contemplated his comeback, his "Davy" alter ego continued to grow. On April 25, 1831, James K. Paulding's play based on Crockett, *The Lion of the West*, opened at the Park Theatre in New York to strong box office, and actor James Hackett's Nimrod Wildfire character was a sensation. Despite glowing reviews, however, Hackett was unhappy with the script and called for a rewrite, preserving only Wildfire's character from the original. Once revised, the production was soon on the road, playing to packed houses in Boston, Philadelphia, and other cities, before returning to New York on November 12.[59]

Hackett took the production out west for a stint, but the play was not well received there. Westerners found the broad parody of themselves evidenced in Wildfire to be offensive and over the top, and they threatened to throw Hackett "up Salt River if he ventured a repetition of the objectionable performance." Hackett hightailed it back east at the earliest opportunity.[60] By 1833 however, after still another revision, Wildfire was delighting audiences in far-away London.[61]

In January 1833, James French applied for a copyright for his now completed Crockett biography. Originally titled *The Life and Adventures of Colonel David Crockett of West Tennessee*, with subsequent editions titled, *Sketches and Eccentricities of Col. David Crockett of West Tennessee*, French's book cobbled together personal observations and anecdotes from his visits with Crockett along with jokes, hunting and electioneering stories, and exploits credited to him. French also included a liberal sampling of Nimrod Wildfire's dialogue copped from Paulding's play, but attributed it to Crockett.[62]

The book was an immediate best seller and, coupled with *Lion of the West*, provided Crockett a national stage from which to relaunch his political career. Excerpts from the book appeared in newspapers throughout the country, fueling a national acceleration of the "Davy" caricature, which would soon grow beyond Crockett's control.

Largely a positive portrait, *The Life and Adventures* also included Huntsman's "Book of Chronicles" parody and the unflattering Adams dinner story which, when coupled with the outlandish Paulding material, tended to give a somewhat fractured depiction of Crockett. The colonel was not pleased.

Though Crockett supplied much of the material that appeared in *The Life and Adventures*, it is possible that he was unaware of French's intention to publish. French's name is not on the title page, and Crockett later claimed that he did not know the author of the work and that the book was unauthorized.[63] He angrily wrote to newspapers complaining that the book "in many respects, does me great injustice," insisting that the author "should at least have obtained my permission to publish, if he even thought it unnecessary to submit for my inspection a copy of the work before it went to press."[64] Crockett received no royalties from the book, though French reported substantial earnings, which must have been particularly vexing given Crockett's problematic financial situation.[65]

When he began his next campaign for Congress in the spring of 1833, Crockett toned down his rhetoric and addressed the issues rather than launching personal attacks on Fitzgerald. The land bill remained his primary focus, but he also voiced his support for the Second Bank of the United States and continued to back internal improvements. His opposition to the Jacksonians was undiminished, and he repeatedly trumpeted his hatred of Martin Van Buren from the stump. To Crockett, Van Buren was the embodiment of partisan politics and the puppeteer who pulled Jackson's strings.

Early on he had approached Fitzgerald through Adam Huntsman and suggested a truce of sorts. Both men agreed to turn down the intensity and try to remain civil during the campaign, but both Huntsman and Fitzgerald expressed doubts as to whether Crockett would hold up his end of the bargain. Toward the end of the campaign, Crockett seemingly breached the agreement by leveling unsubstantiated charges against Fitzgerald. In May, he was reported to have produced an anonymous letter accusing Fitzgerald of "swindling the government out of a good deal of money," apparently by overcharging for mileage to and from Tennessee to Washington City.[66] The accusation was followed by a firestorm in the press, with both sides attacking tooth and claw, and the same charges were leveled against Crockett. Somewhat disingenuously, Crockett claimed, "I never charged Mr. Fitzgerald with swindling, I only asked him if it was true or false . . . ."[67]

Crockett also took a shot at Jackson operative Huntsman. Still smarting from the "Book of Chronicles" series, and probably irritated all the more by the expanded audience the articles received from their inclusion in French's popular book, he said that he had originally thought the piece had originated from "some poor little possum headed lawyer. I have cut open many possum's heads to hunt for brains and I never found any; therefore, I considered some little pin hook lawyer without brains was the author of the piece . . . I did think that Adam Huntsman had more sense than to ever let such insignificancy come from his pen."[68]

Anti-Jackson sentiment in Tennessee was also more apparent than it had been in 1831, and Henry Clay had many supporters in the district, so Crockett wasn't painted as quite the pariah he was in the previous contest. It was also increasingly difficult for the opposition to depict Crockett as a buffoon. French's biography had helped much more than it hurt, and bolstered by the book and *Lion of the West*, Crockett's popularity was again on the rise.

Both sides continued sniping as the campaign drew to a close, but despite the gerrymandering, Crockett won the election in a squeaker. When all the ballots were counted, his margin was a mere 173 votes.[69]

Crockett certainly felt vindicated. He had survived another onslaught from the Jacksonians and came out on top. He had regained the trust of a majority of his constituents, and his star shone again. He would return to his rooms at Mrs. Ball's Washington boarding house and learn to juggle his duties as a congressman with a new role he would savor even more: celebrity.

---

[1] *Jackson Gazette,* April 10, 1830; *Register of Debates,* January 21–22, 1830, 551–54; ibid., February 25, 1830, 583–84. Crockett entered a resolution to abolish the academy on February 25, 1830, apparently taking over the lead on the issue from James Blair of South Carolina, who had in January pressed for an accounting to determine if admissions to the school were weighted in favor of the wealthy and well-connected. Crockett certainly felt that to be the case and saw the institution as another example of the few gaining advantage at the expense of the many.

[2] *Jackson Gazette,* April 10, 1830.

[3] *Register of Debates,* February 25, 1830, 583.

[4] *Jackson Gazette,* March 27, 1830.

[5] Ibid.

[6] Crockett to *Jackson Gazette,* March 5, 1830, printed in *Jackson Gazette,* March 27, 1830. Crockett's old adversary John Overton commented on the printing contract in a July 3, 1831 letter to Crockett's Memphis benefactor, Marcus B. Winchester. Overton wrote, "I see from the last Memphis *Gazette* that a majority of the people from Memphis will vote for Crockett for congress. Be it so, as they are freemen, though Mr. C is known to be, and professes to be, opposed to the present administration. It can't be because the last administration promoted the growth of Memphis. But for the present administration it would not have risen as it has. Don't your citizens sometimes think of this? What administration was it that made it the great leading road East and West throughout the United States to Mexico by the establishment of three stages a week, and besides speaking of it as it deserves? Is there no consideration of these things? besides giving the public printing to the editor of your newspaper?" Throughout the year, Overton continued in his attempts to undermine Crockett in the Memphis area. He pressured Winchester , the acting postmaster, to drum up subscribers for the *Globe,* in hopes that he paper's anti-Crockett stance would have influence in the district. It's doubtful that Winchester complied, since he had always supported Crockett, albeit anonymously. Overton was, however, suspicious of Winchester's allegiance and finally wrote to him, "In the north, where generally people are minutely informed, it was stated to me that you yourself was not in favor of this administration." J. M. Keating, *History of the City of Memphis, Tennessee* (Syracuse: D. Mason & Co., 1888), 178–79.

[7] Crockett to Martin Van Buren, March 3, 1830, printed in *Jackson Gazette,* March 27, 1830.

[8] Crockett to *Jackson Gazette,* March 24, 1830, printed in *Jackson Gazette,* April 17, 1830.

[9] Crockett to *Jackson Gazette,* May 7, 1830, printed in *Jackson Gazette,* May 29, 1830.

[10] Michael Sprigg was a Maryland congressman who served with Crockett in the Twentieth and Twenty-First Congresses. Sprigg was

born in Frostburg, Maryland, the location of the transfer station where Crockett lost his portrait.

11 Crockett to Michael Sprigg, May 5, 1830, David Zucker Collection. William C. Davis has convincingly argued that this letter was actually written in 1831, but misdated by Crockett. See William C. Davis, *Three Roads to the Alamo: The Lives and Fortunes of David Crockett, James Bowie, and William Barret Travis* (New York: Harper Collins, 1998), 624 n. 51. The letter was written from Maysville, Kentucky, while Crockett was on his way home, but he remained in Washington until after Congress adjourned on May 31, 1830. "Hincley," the artist to whom Crockett referred, has not been identified and it is uncertain if this portrait was ever recovered. Frederick Voss has argued that a Crockett portrait that has been routinely attributed to Rembrandt Peale is more likely the Hincley portrait and not the work of Peale. See Frederick S. Voss, "Portraying an American Legend: The Likenesses of Davy Crockett," *Southwestern Historical Quarterly* 91, no. 4 (April 1988): 459–61.

12 *Jackson Gazette,* June 26, 1830.

13 Ibid., August 14, 1830.

14 Ibid., August 21, 1830. Jackson had promised to serve only one term as president.

15 Ibid.

16 Ibid., November 20, 1830.

17 Stephen Decatur led a daring raid during the U.S. war against the Barbary pirates in which he and his crew successfully destroyed the captured American frigate *Philadelphia* in the harbor at Tripoli, depriving the enemy of a valuable resource. Ordinarily, the crew who captured an enemy ship was entitled to the prize money after the ship and its contents were auctioned, but since the *Philadelphia* was an American vessel and was burned, no prize was realized.

Congress presented Decatur with a commemorative sword, and he and his crew were awarded two months' pay in lieu of a prize. The decision was controversial and, after Decatur's death in 1820, his wife asked Congress in 1826 to readdress the idea of more lucrative compensation for the surviving crew members and their dependents. An award of $100,000 was suggested, a share of which would have gone to Mrs. Decatur, but it was tabled after debate. The bill was brought up again on February 4, 1831, but House members refused to hear it, and it was reintroduced on February 11, when Crockett and others successfully contested the award. In 1837, Mrs. Decatur was awarded a pension of $50 per month, which was cancelled in 1842. She tried unsuccessfully to bring the matter before Congress again in 1849. *Register of Debates,* May 3, 1826, 2593–2600; February 4, 1831, 614–15; February 11, 1831, 680–82; Mary W. M. Hargreaves and James F. Hopkins, *The Papers of Henry Clay, Vol. 6, Secretary of State 1827* (Louisville: University Press of Kentucky, 1981), 1038–39; James Tertius De Kay, *A Rage For Glory: The Life of Commodore Stephen Decatur, USN* (New York: Free Press, 2004), 45–60, 75, 210.

18 *Jackson Gazette,* November 20, 1830. Another lengthy Madison editorial in support of Crockett appeared in the *Gazette* on November 27, 1830, and a critical reply was published under the signature "A Farmer of Madison" on December 4, 1830. Crockett addressed the Decatur issue throughout the campaign. In an April 13, 1831 speech, reported in the April 30, 1831 issue of the *Southern Statesman,* Crockett argued that "Gen. Jackson, whilst thousands of other poor soldier's widows were more needy, and equally deserving the charity of the government, had singled out Mrs. Decatur as the peculiar object of national bounty, proposing to lavish large sums of the public money upon her and at the same time objecting to the donation of *pittances* to the widows of other poor soldiers." Crockett may have also been aware that Decatur, upon his death in 1820, had left his wife an estate worth $75,000, which had been lost through profligacy and mismanagement.

Crockett showed some inconsistency on the issue of awarding compensation to individuals. In 1828 he voted against providing federal funds for the relief of the widow of General Brown, a veteran of the War of 1812. Though he opposed the use of federal funds, Crockett was sensitive to Mrs. Brown's plight and offered to contribute to a private fund for the widow's relief.

In December of 1832 however, when Crockett was out of office, he wrote to U.S. Senator Daniel Webster and requested that federal relief be granted to the family of Colonel Henry Dyer, a Tennessee and war veteran who was also a friend of Crockett's. It is unclear why Crockett viewed Dyer's situation differently from that of Mrs. Brown. Crockett may have simply been showing favoritism to an old friend. De Kay, *A Rage For Glory,* 210; *Register of Debates,* April 2, 1828, 2086; Crockett to Daniel Webster, December 18, 1832, Courtesy of Bruce Gimelson, Garrison, New York.

19 *(Providence) Rhode Island American,* December 28, 1830.

20 Archibald Yell was a Jackson supporter who had served under Jackson in the Creek War and at the Battle of New Orleans. Jackson appointed him judge of the Territory of Arkansas in 1832, and he later served in Congress (1835–38, 1845–46) and as governor of Arkansas (1840–44). Biographical Directory of the United States Congress online, http://bioguide.congress.gov.

21 Archibald Yell to James Polk, December 1, 1830, Herbert Weaver, ed., and Paul H. Bergeron, assoc. ed., *Correspondence of James K. Polk, Volume I, 1817–1832* (Nashville: Vanderbilt University Press, 1969), 349.

22 Crockett to Henry McClung, December 21, 1830, Historical Society of Pennsylvania.

23 Nelson F. Adkins, "James K. Paulding's Lion of the West," *American Literature* 3, no. 3 (November, 1931): 249.

24 Joseph John Arpad, "David Crockett: An Original Legendary Eccentricity and Early American Character," Ph.D. dissertation, Duke University, 1969, 92–93, citing undated letter from Paulding to John Wesley Jarvis in Ralph M. Alderman, ed., *The Letters of James Kirke Paulding* (Madison: University of Wisconsin Press, 1962), 113.

25 *Baltimore Gazette and Daily Advertiser,* December 7, 1830; James Kirke Paulding to Crockett, December 15, 1830, New-York Historical Society; Crockett to Paulding, December 22, 1830, courtesy of the Phil Collins Collection.

26 Crockett to Daniel Pounds, January 6, 1831, courtesy of the Lilly Library, Indiana University, Bloomington, Indiana.

27 Crockett to *(Jackson) Southern Statesman*, dated January 6, 1831, published February 12, 1831

28 Crockett to A. M. Hughs, February 13, 1831, Tennessee State Library and Archives (TSLA).

29 *(Jackson) Southern Statesman*, March 19, 1831.

30 *David Crockett's Circular*, February 28, 1831, Rare Books Division, Library of Congress. Although Crockett's circular is dated February 28, 1831, it doesn't appear to have received widespread distribution until after Fitzgerald's circular was published in the *Statesman*.

31 Ibid.

32 *Southern Statesman*, March 26, 1831.

33 Ibid.

34 *Southern Statesman*, April 9, 1831.

35 David Crockett, *A Narrative of the Life of David Crockett of the State of Tennessee*, ed. James A. Shackford and Stanley J. Folmsbee (Knoxville: University of Tennessee Press, 1973), 207.

36 *Southern Statesman*, April 16, 1831.

37 Crockett, *Narrative of the Life*, 207.

38 *Southern Statesman*, May 14, 1831.

39 Ibid., July 9, 1831.

40 Crockett, *Narrative of the Life*, 207.

41 In a speech given at Huntingdon on April 13, 1831, reported in the May 7, 1831, *Southern Statesman*, Crockett made two accusations against Fitzgerald. First, he claimed that in 1827, while Fitzgerald was serving as solicitor general, he had inappropriately dropped charges against William Fore, who had been convicted of counterfeiting, during the appeals process. Crockett also claimed that Fitzgerald was then living on land formerly owned by Fore and implied that he'd received the land as a bribe in exchange for Fore's release. Second, he accused Fitzgerald of dereliction of duty for failing to prosecute or testify against some fellow attorneys accused of gambling at Trenton, in Gibson County, when Fitzgerald was serving as state's attorney.

Fitzgerald was present in Huntingdon and denied the charges in Crockett's speech relating to the Fore case. He pointed out that he was not solicitor general when the original case had been tried, and had nothing to do with the charges against Fore being dismissed. He promised to counter Crockett's second charge at a later date.

Crockett took his accusations to the press and, on May 14, 1831, provided a partial transcript of the Weakley County records of the Fore case to the *Southern Statesman* along with a statement from A. M. Hughes, an attorney for the defense, in an effort to bolster his claims. Hughes wrote, "Whatever compromise was made, (and there was one) was made, to the best of my knowledge (in fact I am certain) by Mr. Fitzgerald."

The copy of the record Crockett provided was in his own handwriting, and he stated that the clerk, Colonel Warner, refused to certify his copy. Warner claimed that Crockett was attempting to take parts of the record out of context and offered to make a full transcript available, but Crockett declined, saying he had "all that he wanted." (These details appeared later in a deposition by William H. Johnson, printed in the *Statesman* on June 11, 1831).

Crockett's copy of the record stated that the solicitor general and the defendant appeared "in proper person" before the court and that by assent of the court, no further action would be taken against Fore. The Hughes deposition stated that Fore was tried and convicted *before* Fitzgerald was solicitor general, and that Fore's council had moved for an arrest of judgment due to "some defect in the indictment."

As the appeal was not heard until some time later, two different attorneys, H. W. Dunlap and a General Cook, defended the prisoner; the prosecution was handled by D. S. Jennings. Judge Joshua Haskell heard the case, overruled the appeal, and sent the case to the solicitor general, who was now Fitzgerald. The defense council met with Fitzgerald, who subsequently declined to pursue the case against Fore.

The June 11, 1831, issue of the *Statesman* carried Fitzgerald's response to Crockett's charges published on May 14. He pointed out that if Hughes had any evidence to corroborate the charges, he failed to provide them, and claimed that Hughes' equivocating statement, "to the best of my knowledge," was proof that he had none and was just covering himself legally. Fitzgerald then besmirched Hughes' character by claiming that Hughes had bet a "large amount of money" on Crockett winning the election, and therefore had a vested interest in Fitzgerald's defeat.

The June 11 *Southern Statesman* carried a statement provided by Fitzgerald, signed by seven people, attesting that Crockett's copy of the Weakly County record was inaccurate and claiming that the phrase "in proper person" never appeared in the original record. The same issue carried a statement by Judge Haskell, requested by both Crockett and Fitzgerald, claiming that, to the best of his recollection, Fitzgerald had nothing to do with the case. Haskell wrote, "While this suit was under examination, a proposition I think, was made by defendant's counsel, for defendant to pay or secure all the costs, which were considerable in this cause, if the state would accept of the terms so offered, that being considered all the punishment that could properly and humanely be inflicted on him at that time, owing to the low and prostrate condition of his health and constitution, which proposition being accepted by Mr. Jennings, as the most advisable upon a view of all the circumstances of the case, and the course it seemed to be taking; the result of these arrangements being made known to the court, and being considered by the court most for the advantage and honor of the state, so to dispose of it, I cheerfully assented to it, without which no *nolle prosequi* could have been entered."

In addition, statements were presented from John B. Fonville, who claimed to hold the paper on four bets made by Hughes, totaling $40, on Crockett to win the election over Fitzgerald.

Fitzgerald also answered Crockett's charge about his failure to prosecute or testify in the gambling case involving other attorneys. Fitzgerald said that, had these parties been prosecuted and convicted, as state's attorney he would have benefited financially, as he received a $10 bounty for each conviction. Thus, he recused himself and the grand jury concurred. He said that, had he done otherwise, Crockett would surely have accused him of conspiracy in that instance as well. Fitzgerald included corroborating statements to disprove Crockett's allegations.

In the July 9 issue of the *Southern Statesman*, A. M. Hughes answered the charges Fitzgerald had made against him. Hughes also pointed out that in charging him with betting on the election, Fitzgerald omitted the names of the people Hughes had wagered with, one of whom, Col. Willie Bayliss, was a close personal friend of Fitzgerald. Furthermore, Hughes claimed that he also had a side bet (for a hat) with his accuser, Dr. Fonville!

Hughes also included an affidavit from William Fore, who gave his version of the whole affair. Fore claimed that Fitzgerald, as solicitor general (though not prosecuting the case), proposed to Fore that if he settled part of the costs incurred, he would enter a *nolle prosequi* and the matter would go no further. Fore said that Fitzgerald made the offer due to Fore's illness and said that he had accepted Fitzgerald's offer.

Crockett's charges do not appear to have had much traction with the electorate. While there are conflicting reports as to Fitzgerald's involvement in the Fore case, it seems clear that even if he was the man who released Fore, he did nothing illegal. Seemingly, the mercy shown Fore was based on his infirmity, and the actions of the solicitor general were approved by all involved parties.

In the long run, this sort of campaigning hurt Crockett far more than it helped. In a letter published in the July 7, 1831, issue of the *Southern Statesman*, a reader who signed himself "A BEAR HUNTER" wrote, "On last Saturday, I was at Capt. Joseph Nicholson's Muster-ground, where the company had assembled to pay taxes—after the business was over, it was proposed to take the vote of the company between Col. Crockett and Mr. Fitzgerald. There were present 72 persons—64 of whom voted for Mr. Fitzgerald and not one for Crockett—8 would not vote; three of whom said they should vote for Mr. Fitzgerald and one for Col. Crockett. In this company at the last election Crockett lost but four votes; so then you see that the Col's old friends are forsaking him in this strong hold, which used to be his hunting ground; and if the Col. Does not get more votes in other companies, in this county, Mr. Fitzgerald must beat him *sixty to one*. The reason assigned for leaving Crockett, is his abuse of General Jackson and the ungentlemanly advantage he wished to take of Mr. Fitzgerald about the gambling business at Trenton. They are all acquainted with that affair, and know Fitzgerald's conduct to be correct and not at all censurable."

42 James Strange French, *Sketches and Eccentricities of Col. David Crockett, of West Tennessee*, New Edition (New York: J. & J. Harper, 1833), 130.

43 Crockett, *Narrative of the Life*, 207.

44 Ibid., 208.

45 *Southern Statesman*, June 4, 1831.

46 Crockett, *Narrative of the Life*, 207, n. 13.

47 *Southern Statesman*, June 25, 1831.

48 Crockett to Fellow Citizens, undated, published in *Southern Statesman*, July 2, 1831.

49 Crockett to Calvin Jones, August 22, 1831, Emma Inman Williams, *Historic Madison, The Story of Jackson and Madison County Tennessee, from Prehistoric Moundbuilders to 1917* (Jackson, Tennessee: Madison County Historical Society, 1946), 422.

50 Crockett to James Davison, August 18, 1831, DRT Library at the Alamo.

51 Crockett, *Narrative of the Life*, 208, n. 14.

52 Crockett to Davison, August 18, 1831, DRT Library at the Alamo.

53 Crockett to *(Washington) National Intelligencer*, reprinted in *Brattleboro Messenger*, February 18, 1832; Crockett to Richard Smith, January 7, 1832, Historical Society of Pennsylvania.

54 Crockett to *National Intelligencer*, reprinted in *Brattleboro Messenger*, February 18, 1832.

55 French, *Sketches and Eccentricities of Col. David Crockett*, 118.

56 Ibid., 127.

57 *Register of Debates*, April 16, 1832, 2543.

58 Crockett, *Narrative of the Life*, 209.

59 Adkins, "James K. Paulding's Lion of the West," 253.

60 Ibid., 254.

61 Melvin Rosser Mason, "The Lion of the West: Satire on Davy Crockett and Frances Trolloppe," *South Central Bulletin* 29, no. 4, Studies by Members of SCMLA (Winter 1969), 143.

62 James S. French contract with Harper & Brothers, January 5, 1833, for "The life and adventures of Col. David Crockett of West Tennessee," signed by William Miner, copyright clerk of the Ohio District, and endorsed by French, who assigned the copyright to the publisher; Miner's January 18, 1833, letter to French; also see French's contract dated September 9, 1833, with J. & J. Harper of New York for a second printing or edition, titled "Sketches and Eccentricities of Col. David Crockett of West Tennessee," to which French maintained the copyright, All three documents are found in the Rare Book and Manuscript Library, Columbia University. Because *Life and Adventures* was published anonymously, probably due to its unauthorized release,

controversy has surrounded the authorship of the work. Some Crockett biographers have attributed the book to Matthew St. Claire Clarke, but there is no evidence to suggest that Clarke was the author. Edgar Allan Poe also attributed the work to French in a review of another French work, *Elkswatawa,* in *Southern Literary Messenger* 2, no. 9 (August 1836): 589.

[63]   Crockett, *Narrative of the Life,* 3–4.

[64]   *Daily (Washington) National Intelligencer,* December 31, 1833.

[65]   *(Portland, Maine) Eastern Argus Tri-Weekly,* November 22, 1833, cites the *Boston Gazette* as reporting that the author shared earnings with Crockett, who also authorized the book. Crockett claims that he never received any remuneration for the work, which seems likely.

[66]   Huntsman to Wm. R. Harris, June 19, 1833, published in *Southern Statesman,* June 29, 1833

[67]   Crockett to *Southern Statesman,* July 13, 1833, published in *Southern Statesman,* July 20, 1833.

[68]   Ibid.

[69]   Crockett, *Narrative of the Life,* 210 n. 18.

Chapter 7

"The Government of One Man"
The Second Bank of the United States (1834–1835)

*A*ndrew Jackson, the hero of New Orleans, was no stranger to war, but as president he would find himself *in a far different sort of conflict, one nearly as volatile as battlefield combat. This "war" was over the rechartering of the Second Bank of the United States and became one of the defining issues of Jackson's presidency. The clash pitted a president mistrustful of banks and eager to consolidate power in the executive branch of government, against the formidable strength and influence of the Bank's president, Nicholas Biddle.*

Much of the ground fighting in the "war" over the Second Bank occurred during the Twenty-Second Congress, while David Crockett was sidelined following his 1831 loss to William Fitzgerald. At home in Tennessee and still smarting from what was a particularly nasty campaign, Crockett nevertheless immediately began planning his political comeback.

While Crockett would continue for the balance of his days to proclaim himself a true Jacksonian and accuse Jackson of being a Van Burenite,[1] he henceforth dropped all pretense of support for the administration and became increasingly vitriolic in his public opposition to the president's policies.[2] The Tennessee vacant lands remained his top priority, but while in political exile, he was also quick to voice his support for the renewal of the Bank's charter.

Crockett was to represent a peripheral figure in the long, often brutal war over the Bank, but his alarm about how the issue unfolded was genuine and shows that his abandonment of Jackson was motivated by real issues and concerns, not a blind allegiance to Jackson's political enemies. He had already seen the danger in the growth of factional and party loyalties in the defeat of his land bill. He lost the support of his own state delegation largely because he had refused to subdue his objectives to what Polk and others saw as a greater need for group discipline. As the Bank war evolved, Crockett saw an even greater danger in Jackson's expansion of executive power and genuinely feared for the survival of the Constitution.

In the early nineteenth century, the United States had no central banking system. There was no United States currency other than gold and silver coin, and each state had its own banks that issued their own paper currency and operated independently of one another. Deposits of gold and silver, known as *specie*, ostensibly backed bank notes issued by these state banks, but, due to a lack of regulation, many banks were undercapitalized, with well under one-fifth of their assets in specie.[3] As long as economic times were good and the bank notes were kept in circulation, the banks reaped the benefits of large profit margins, but an economic slowdown or an overwhelming demand for redemption of the inflated notes in specie were potentially disastrous.

The Second Bank of the United States (SBUS) was established in Philadelphia in 1816 with a twenty-year charter, in part as an attempt to control the inflationary practices of the state banks. As the repository, collection, and disbursing agency for the U.S. government, the Bank controlled enormous revenues and quickly became the nation's largest lending institution, exercising powerful control over credit throughout the country. By expanding and contracting loans made to the smaller state banks, the SBUS was able to force many of the weaker, overextended state banks out of business by calling in loans or refusing credit, thus providing a more stable U.S. economy. Though this practice benefited the national welfare, it was, in the short run, harmful to businesses and landowners that relied on credit to survive. In 1819, the contraction of lending by Bank President Langdon Cheves (in part necessitated by poor SBUS lending practices under its first president, William Jones), coupled with a precipitous drop in the price of cotton, led to a national depression commonly known as the Panic of 1819.

During the economic boom following the War of 1812, two banks were formed in Tennessee, one in Knoxville, the other in Nashville. The Nashville operation was headed by Stephen Cantrell, with directors including John H. Eaton, a U.S. senator from Tennessee; Ephraim Foster; and William B. Lewis.[4] All of these men were members of a political alliance headed by John Overton, a wealthy Nashville lawyer and land speculator said to be the richest man in the state. Overton's group was part of a coalition formerly headed, until his death in 1800, by William Blount, a founder of the state and a powerful land speculator who had dominated Tennessee politics since its territorial days.[5] Andrew Jackson was also a Blount protégé and a long-time friend and former law partner of John Overton. Other members of this Blount-Overton faction included Hugh Lawson White, Overton's brother-in-law, and Pleasant M. Miller, Blount's son-in-law, both of whom were major players in Tennessee politics. White was president of the Knoxville Bank, which had a branch in Nashville under the personal direction of Overton.[6] Despite some competition between the two banks, they typically acted in concert on major issues.[7] Since most of the principals were land speculators drawn to banking in hopes of increasing investment capital, naturally both banks were heavily involved in land speculation.

There was, of course, a party that opposed the Overton group. Led by Andrew Erwin and including Congressman Newton Cannon[8] and Senator John Williams[9], this alliance was forged primarily because each of these men had personal disputes with Andrew Jackson.[10] Another player, acting as a free agent rather than a member of either faction, was Felix Grundy, a Nashville lawyer. Grundy had a long political pedigree, including terms in the Kentucky state legislature, a short tenure as chief justice of the Kentucky Supreme Court, and service as a U.S. congressman from Tennessee from 1811 to 1814.[11] Grundy had an uncanny ability to gauge public opinion and throughout his career rode this talent to elected office, sometimes siding with one faction, sometimes another, depending upon the prevailing political winds. In fact, all of these alliances were, to a degree, fluid. Since the dissolution of the Federalist Party, there was only one political party in the country, the Democratic-Republicans, to which all these men belonged. Factions formed around personalities rather than different parties, and at times political expediency demanded that loyalties either broaden or change.

Given their governance, it's no surprise that the two Tennessee banks doled out credit to parties friendly to them, usually personal securities to friends of the bank's directors. Inevitably, those with whom the bank refused to deal, including many members of the mercantile community who were vocal in their opposition to the bank's land-speculation deals, were left angered and out in the cold.[12] This show of favoritism prompted Felix Grundy and William Carroll, a Nashville merchant sympathetic toward the Erwin group,[13] to lobby in 1817 for a branch of the SBUS to be located in Nashville.[14]

In an effort to block the SBUS branch and protect the profits of the Overton banks, Hugh Lawson White, now in the state legislature, pushed through a blatantly protectionist tax of $50,000 on any bank that wasn't chartered by the state. Offering a "compromise" in exchange for the legislature's approval of the tax, White cut a deal and agreed to open ten additional state chartered banks, with the provision that these new banks could become branches of the two Overton banks, mollifying some of the credit-seeking merchants who sided with Grundy and Carroll, while at the same time keeping the competition at bay and sowing the seeds of a state bank monopoly.

Nashville merchant John P. Erwin[15] attempted to follow through with the SBUS deal himself, but was unsuccessful. The merchants opposed to the Overton banks even briefly opened their own bank in Nashville, which ultimately failed due to the fierce competition from the Overton banks.[16]

Even though the Overton faction managed to thwart the efforts to place a SBUS branch in the state, they nevertheless had regular dealings with the Bank. Since there was no federal income tax, revenue was generated through sales of federal lands and tariffs levied on imported goods. The state banks collected these tariffs locally, which they then remitted to the SBUS for federal disbursement. State banks also borrowed funds regularly from the SBUS.

Though many wealthy plantation owners were able to finance their own operations and had no real need of the services offered by banks, small farmers depended on loans to get their goods to market. Large-scale planters like Andrew Jackson could afford to ship their crops (predominantly cotton) directly to New Orleans and sell them with minimal middleman involvement. Though it could take four months to complete the shipping and sales transactions, the profits were much higher than those from selling locally, and the men with the deeper pockets had the advantage. Small farmers needed a much faster return on investment. They were forced to consign their crops to local cotton merchants, who then offered them for sale in New Orleans. The local merchant would advance the farmer money, borrowed from the bank, against the impending sale of the crop. The bank's fees and interest were added to service fees and additional interest charged by the merchant, all passed on to the farmer. Typically, this advance ate up half the income from the sale of the crop. The balance would be paid to the farmer when the crops were sold, after even more charges and commissions were deducted.[17] Clearly, it was difficult for the smaller planter to be competitive, and margins were slim. This precarious system worked as long as markets were good and the profits were larger than all the interest and handling charges. In 1819 though, the price of cotton dropped.

Farmers who had borrowed heavily against their crops were ruined, and the value of notes issued by the banks plummeted. The undercapitalized and overextended banks, which had invested large sums in land speculation, were unable to back their notes, and the reverberations were felt through the entire economic spectrum. The Nashville and Knoxville banks were among those caught in the squeeze. The banks petitioned the state for relief, asking for a moratorium on specie payouts, which would stabilize the situation, a short-term solution at best. At the same time, the banks mercilessly pressed their debtors for repayment of loans in hard cash, often foreclosing on homesteads and leaving families, a great number of whom were from the western part of the state, destitute.[18] It was hypocrisy of biblical proportions.

Debtors responded by pleading for new laws that would delay debt collection or force creditors to accept property as payment instead of specie.[19] Overton's nemesis Erwin was quick to advocate this option, while the banking interests loudly voiced their opposition, but it was Felix Grundy who opportunistically rode the controversy into the election for state legislature as a voice for the debtor class. Once elected, he straddled the fence and crafted a law that provided some relief to debtors, but also gave the banks a break by extending the use of the inflated bank notes as currency.

Despite this stopgap measure, by 1820 the downturn had worsened and the calls for a bailout increased. Public sentiment toward the banks was hostile, with many blaming the economic collapse on speculators and free-lending practices. The voters weren't predisposed to offering public funds or relief to institutions that had been profligate in their business practices, all in the name of seemingly endless higher profits, while at the same time making draconian demands for repayment in specie from their poor and working-class debtors. Plus, the favoritism the banks had shown in lending was not lost on the public.

Grundy championed the people's cause by advocating issuing loans of treasury notes backed by the state for relief of debtors, a move that infuriated the Overton faction, which now conveniently opposed government intervention in the state banking industry still under its control. Treasury notes would likely further devalue the state bank notes, causing the bankers' profits to drop even more. Unsurprisingly, the Erwin faction also endorsed this plan. After Grundy's reelection, the new plan was modified and adopted. Rather than the state issuing the notes directly, the New Bank of the State of Tennessee, ostensibly a loan office owned and operated by the state, was established to issue them. These notes would be backed by revenues from land sales in the Hiwasee District of the state.[20] A law was enacted whereby any creditor that refused to accept the notes from the New Bank as payment for debt would be required to wait two years before collection could be enforced.[21] Though the establishment of the New Bank was something of a victory for the debtors, Overton's alliance, through some slick maneuvering, managed to get John Eaton and a couple of other Overton cronies put on its board of directors.[22] However, despite some attempts by the Overton operatives to subvert the bank's efforts, the New Bank of the State of Tennessee stood firm.

In 1821, the Erwin faction backed William Carroll, the former Nashville merchant, now broke due to the panic, in his run for governor. Carroll's platform was heavy on social reform, including a more progressive penal code that included building a state penitentiary and sentencing that relied more on incarceration than barbaric practices like branding and whipping that were common at the time, establishing a public school system, internal improvements, and state care for the insane.[23] Carroll was a military veteran and war hero who had served with Jackson (who was backing Edward Ward, the Overton group's opposition candidate) in the War of 1812. Among the Carroll supporters in the Erwin group was David Crockett, finishing up his first term in the state legislature and who, like Carroll, had recently faced tough financial times. The flash flood that had destroyed Crockett's milling operation[24] left him standing empty-handed before his creditors, and consequently numerous lawsuits were filed against him for collection of debt. Crockett's small landholdings, including his homestead, were eventually auctioned by the court to satisfy his outstanding obligations, and he and his family were left homeless and living with relatives.[25] During the previous legislative session, Crockett had also cast his vote for a constitutional convention, an item high on Carroll's agenda during the gubernatorial race.

Carroll favored a convention in order to rectify what many rural Tennesseans saw as a huge injustice. Large landholders in East and Middle Tennessee enjoyed a great tax advantage because the 1796 constitution (drafted in part by Andrew Jackson[26]) declared that all land in the state should be taxed equally, with no consideration given to the actual value of the property. Therefore, subsistence farmers on less valuable land in the western part of the state carried a tax burden that was equal to that of the wealthy plantation owners. The commoners opposed this regressive tax, and they rallied behind Carroll's populist call for a realignment. West Tennesseans were proportionally under-represented both in Congress and the state legislature, and it was hoped that the convention would address this inequity. Citizens also wanted county officials elected by voters rather than the existing practice of appointment by the state legislature. Unsurprisingly, the wealthy planters and landholders fiercely contested the idea of a convention, and they managed to stave off a new convention until 1834.[27]

Carroll's military record, populist message, and measured anti-bank stance had wide appeal in a state reeling from the effects of the depression. It didn't hurt that Ward was seen as another wealthy friend of the banks: a status quo candidate who would not answer to or represent the *vox populi*. Carroll trounced the Overton-sponsored opposition, raking in nearly three times as many votes as his competitor.[28] As governor, Carroll continued his campaign against the Overton banks. Believing that an eventual return to hard currency would stabilize the economy, he enacted legislation in 1821 that required the banks to resume specie payments by April of 1824.

In 1823, the Overton group attempted to repeal the 1821 law. Crockett, again siding with Carroll against the Overton alliance, opposed repealing the law, and one newspaper reported that he "considered the whole Banking system a species of swindling on a large scale and it seemed to him that in all cases when any difficulty or loss was created by the Banks, that the farmers suffered most".[29] He later sponsored legislation requiring the New Bank of the State of Tennessee (the bank created by the state to aid the debtors) to open branches in every county.[30] Clearly, Crockett's earlier anti-bank statements applied to the unregulated state banks that had preyed upon his constituents and ruined the economy. Though both men were very vocal in their criticism of banks, Carroll publicly blaming them for the depression, he and Crockett saw banks as a necessary evil and realized that the availability of credit was essential to merchants, farmers, and small planters.[31] Crockett believed that additional, more regionally accessible branches of the New Bank of the State of Tennessee would level the playing field for his constituents, and was quoted in the *Nashville Whig* as saying he was "decidedly in favor of selling on credit, at least for the greatest part of the purchase money." He further commented that his reason for being there was "to legislate for the encouragement of the poor."[32]

Crockett further cemented his alliance with the Erwin faction with his support for incumbent John Williams over Andrew Jackson for the U.S. Senate in 1823.[33] Jackson was victorious, however, and among his supporters was James K. Polk, who, though currently a member of the Carroll group, would become an indispensable Jackson ally. Crockett defended his vote by saying that Williams had served the state well and deserved to be returned to the Senate. But he was now seen as an enemy among Jackson's supporters, who planned to run him for president the following year. Old Hickory, of course, regarded any opposition as disloyalty and never forgave it.

Later in the year the Overton faction mounted yet another attempt to repeal the hard-money law, this time with more success. A compromise was reached, with Polk leading the Carroll group, whereby specie payments would be resumed gradually over a two-year period.[34] Crockett opposed this compromise agreement.[35] Ultimately, the banks were unable to comply by the stated deadline, and by 1827 both the Knoxville and Nashville branches of the Overton banks folded. Governor Carroll eventually prompted the legislature to close the New Bank of the State of Tennessee as well,[36] but in 1826 efforts were again underway to repeal the prohibitive state tax laws and bring a branch of the SBUS to Nashville. Despite attempts by Andrew Jackson and others to block the repeal and keep the SBUS out, the repeal passed and the Bank began operations in Tennessee in 1827.[37]

The Second Bank of the United States was often the primary target of public animosity toward banks after the Panic of 1819, and there were some provocative issues unique to that particular institution. The Bank was a problematic entity from its inception. Modeled after Alexander Hamilton's design for the First United States Bank and established as a repository for federal funds, the bank was a private corporate enterprise with limited accountability to the federal government. The constitutionality of such an enterprise had been debated since the establishment of Hamilton's bank, and arguments over the issue continued. Of its twenty-five-member board of directors, only five members were government representatives. The Bank paid no interest to the government on the federal funds in its coffers, but was authorized to invest the monies to generate profits for its stockholders, both foreign and domestic. It could issue its own bank notes, and was exempted from state taxes. In return, the Bank was required to pay the government a bonus of $1.5 million and conduct federal financial transactions at no charge.[38] Perched precariously between the worlds of private commerce and public welfare, the Bank was looked upon by many with suspicion and antipathy, particularly after the 1819 panic.

Upon Langdon Cheves' resignation in 1826, Nicholas Biddle, a prominent member of the bank's board of directors, was appointed president of the Bank. Biddle was a renaissance man and an aristocrat, a child prodigy who entered university at the age of ten and was graduated from Princeton at fifteen. In London, in his first public post, Biddle served James Monroe, then the American minister to Great Britain, as a temporary secretary. After returning to America, in 1807 he began a law practice and in 1810 was elected to the Pennsylvania state legislature.[39] A lover of Greek art and architecture, and a man of letters, Biddle also edited the journals of Lewis and Clark for publication.

A man of towering intellect and immense ego, Biddle expanded the Bank's operations, and by the 1830s it was effectively a central bank - a financial and political power. Biddle continued to use the bank's lending power to regulate the nation's economy (and raise the bank's profits), but also made a practice of extending generous personal loans to politicians and media outlets that were friendly toward the bank. Among the long list of recipients of Biddle's largesse were Senators Henry Clay from Kentucky (already near the top of Jackson's enemies list) and Daniel Webster of Massachusetts (who was also an executive with the Boston branch of the bank), and Crockett, who had graduated from local to national politics in 1827 by winning a seat in the U.S. Congress.

The bank's twenty-year charter was due to expire in 1836, and President Jackson had made no secret of his dislike for the institution, evidenced by his earlier opposition to the Nashville expansion. In fact, Jackson expressed opposition to banking in general, supported a return to hard currency, and was opposed to buying on credit. Jackson's opinions of banking were colored by personal experience—opinions not shared by his allies in the Overton group, but their united animosity toward the Erwin faction overshadowed their disagreements on banking. Jackson had remained relatively silent through much of the battle over Overton's banks, interjecting only in opposition to Grundy's implementation of the New Bank of the State of Tennessee and the opening of the Nashville branch of the SBUS, in both cases conveniently opposing Overton's competition.

Though Jackson had made a fortune through land investment and speculation in Tennessee, he very nearly lost it in 1797 when he accepted promissory notes as payment for property (some of which he co-owned with Overton). Jackson used the notes to start a business, stocking a trading post on the Cumberland River. Unfortunately, Jackson's buyer defaulted, leaving the future president holding the bag on the store's inventory and scrambling for money to pay his creditors. Though he managed to square his debts over the next several years through a combination of selling off property and savvy deal making, Jackson never again trusted promissory or paper currency of any kind, and was adamantly opposed to buying on credit.[40] In 1825, Jackson put forward a measure that would have outlawed private banking in Tennessee, but the effort was defeated by the Erwin-Carroll group, which worked against the Overton faction in two ways. First, Andrew Erwin's son-in-law, Thomas Yeatman, had opened a private bank in competition with the Overton banks and was offering credit to a number of Nashville merchants sympathetic to Erwin and Carroll, and second, the bill's defeat was another strike against Jackson.[41]

Jackson was antagonistic to the banking industry in general, but the SBUS especially offended him. Supporters of the president had informed him that Biddle's branch banks had granted loans to opposition candidates while refusing loans to Jackson Democrats; that the bank was, in effect, attempting to manipulate the outcome of elections. Formal complaints were lodged against a number of the branches, with the offices in Louisville, Kentucky (Henry Clay's home state) and Portsmouth, New Hampshire cited as major offenders. An investigation of the alleged corruption was requested. Biddle recoiled at the allegations and took an aggressive defensive posture. Rather than agreeing to let an independent party conduct the investigation of the Louisville branch, he assigned the job to an internal committee. Instead of making an honest appraisal of the situation, Biddle engaged in what appeared to his critics to be a cover-up and whitewash, and in so doing let a major opportunity to circumvent an impending crisis slip away.[42]

His response to the charge against the Portsmouth branch was equally ill-considered. Although the office had a history of mismanagement, Biddle categorically denied the charges of discriminatory lending. Again he decided to handle the accusations with an internal investigation, but this time conducted the operation himself. In a show of force from the administration, Secretary of War John Eaton notified the Portsmouth branch manager that all funds and documents relating to a Revolutionary War soldier's pension fund on deposit with the branch were to be transferred to another bank of the government's choosing, and that said funds and documents should be surrendered on demand. Jeremiah Mason, the branch manager, contacted Biddle and asked for instructions. Biddle told him to refuse the request and shortly thereafter announced that he had found the charges against the bank "groundless."[43] It was an arrogant and foolish move.

Jackson might have been content, at least for a while, to have the Bank's discriminatory lending practices acknowledged and corrected. The issue of the Bank was, after all, highly controversial and politically volatile. Had Biddle deferred to Jackson and assumed a penitent posture, he might have been able to continue operations under some degree of regulation. Jackson had implied as much in remarks to John Overton in an 1829 letter. The Bank, Jackson wrote, needed to be "curbed,"[44] but now Biddle had thrown down the gauntlet, and Jackson was never one to back away from a challenge. Biddle's actions inflamed the president, turned the issue into a personal conflict, and made Jackson even more determined to undermine him and put his Bank out of business. "The bank," Jackson later told Martin Van Buren, "is trying to kill me. But I will kill it."[45]

In October of 1829 more charges of discrimination were leveled, this time against the New Orleans branch of the Bank, and Jackson requested another inquiry. Biddle, beginning to realize that the administration was playing hardball, immediately sent an emissary from the Bank directly to the president to answer the charges. Assurances were again proffered that the Bank was not engaging in any political favoritism, and Jackson, at least outwardly, seemed to accept the explanation. Biddle, however, wanted to more accurately gauge the president's attitude and decided to call on Jackson himself.

Jackson greeted Biddle with civility, but after playing the gracious host for a time, the president informed Biddle of his true intentions regarding the Bank. He told Biddle that he considered the Bank's charter unconstitutional, an old argument that dated back to the foundation of the Hamilton bank, and that he intended to take the issue up with Congress.[46]

Jackson laid out his case during his next annual Congressional address. He questioned the Bank's constitutional right to exist, and accused the Bank of failing its mission to provide the nation with a sound currency. Jackson also included a vague reference to the possibility of Congress considering the foundation of some other institution to take the place of Biddle's Bank that would avoid the "constitutional difficulties" that beset the SBUS.[47] Jackson made no mention of the real driving force behind his ire: the Bank's support of his rivals.

Biddle calculated that Jackson's address would do the Bank more good than harm. The charges that the bank had failed to produce a sound currency were groundless, a fact of which the public was well aware. Currency issued by the bank was "more sound and uniform than that of any country in the world," and Biddle was sure the people wouldn't accept Jackson's sketchy ideas about a replacement for his institution.[48] Public opinion about the bank was divided, but Biddle was confident that the numbers were on his side.

In the House, Jackson relied on James K. Polk, chairman of the Ways and Means Committee, to marshal support for his measures and build a solid case against the Bank.[49] Despite Polk's best efforts, the Ways and Means Committee and the Senate Finance Committee both disagreed with Jackson's opinions regarding the Bank, and Biddle rushed their conclusions into print in newspapers he subsidized.[50] Jackson and Polk were quick to counterattack in the administration's press, and a media war ensued.

The official Jackson media outlet during the bank war was the *Washington Globe,* edited by Francis Blair. Blair had come highly recommended for the position by Amos Kendall, one of Jackson's most trusted advisors and a newspaperman himself who likely authored the anti-Bank portion of Jackson's congressional address.[51] Blair was just the man Jackson needed: a master mudslinger whose pen spit poison.[52] Kendall and Blair were both defectors from the Clay camp: hard-money men who didn't pull any punches in print. Blair issued a series of scathing editorials against the Bank that served more to elicit fiery responses from the pro-Bank press than to turn public opinion.

Determined to force Jackson's hand on the re-charter issue, Biddle considered asking for a renewal in 1830, a full six years before the current charter was due to expire. Calculating that both congressional and public opinion were favorable to the Bank, he contacted inside sources, asked for advice, and weighed his options.

Henry Clay initially advised against pressing the issue. Unsure that Biddle had the requisite support in Congress to ensure a renewal of the charter and equally certain that if the charter passed, Jackson would veto it, Clay wrote, "I think the Session immediately after the next Presidential election would be the most proper time . . . but suppose Gen'l Jackson should be again elected? If that should be the case, he will probably have less disposition than he has now to avail himself of any prejudices against the Bank. He will then have also less influence, for it may be loosely asserted, at least as a general rule, that the President will have less popularity in his second term than in his first term. And that I believe would emphatically be the fate of the present President. At all events, you will be in a better condition by abstaining from applying to renew the charter during his first term than you would be in if you were able to make the application and it should be rejected."[53]

Biddle, however had ideas of his own,[54] and soon brought Clay around to his way of thinking,[55] an easy job once Clay had been nominated to oppose Jackson in the upcoming election. Biddle had been advised that Jackson did not want the Bank question to be a central issue during the 1832 election season. Biddle met with Secretary of the Treasury Louis McLane, who was sympathetic to the Bank, who cautioned him that Jackson would see an attempt at recharter during the election year as hostile, and that the president would fight back. In pressing the issue, McLane warned, Biddle would be playing into Jackson's charges of using the Bank to interfere in politics. He urged Biddle to wait and suggested a deal. McLane offered to recommend that Jackson take a public position that he would leave the decision on the Bank in the hands of Congress. This compromise was win-win; Jackson could save face and avoid controversy during the election cycle, and Biddle would get his recharter, since both houses of Congress favored renewal.[56] In his 1831 address to Congress, Jackson held up his end of the bargain and pitched the issue to the legislative branch. While he insisted that his personal attitudes about the bank had not changed, he was willing to back off and let Congress decide the issue.[57] Political expediency, it seemed, had given Biddle his victory. All he had to do was wait.

Biddle should have heaved a sigh of relief that a major crisis had been averted and gone about his business until 1836 or whenever addressing a renewal was agreeable to Jackson. Instead, he misread the situation and overplayed his hand. Feeling that Jackson's desire to avoid controversy was a sign of weakness and that the president feared the Bank's power, Biddle upped the ante. He demanded that Jackson personally support the recharter, and then forged ahead with his campaign to put the issue to a vote before the election.

On January 9, 1832,[58] the recharter bill was submitted to Congress. It was met with bitter opposition from the Jackson forces, who faced equally stiff resistance from the Biddle contingent. The battle raged for months, culminating in wins for the Bank on June 11, 1832,[59] when the Senate renewed the charter, and then on July 3,[60] when the House approved the renewal. For Biddle, the victory was sweet but short lived. A week later, on July 10, Jackson vetoed the bill to recharter the bank. His lengthy address to the Senate was, in reality, a passionate and direct appeal to the electorate, an unprecedented move for a sitting President.

Jackson's veto message couched the Bank issue in terms of class warfare and xenophobia. The president continued to levy the complaint that the Bank had failed its mission of stabilizing the nation's currency, and reiterated the charge that the Bank was unconstitutional. He claimed it to be a monopoly and warned that its foreign investors were a threat to national security. Presenting himself as the standard-bearer of Jeffersonian agrarianism and the representative of the common man, Jackson cast Biddle as the voice of the aristocracy: the personification of the moneyed ruling class, out of touch with the people and having far too much unregulated influence over national affairs through his control of public funds. The Bank, Jackson claimed, was "dangerous to the Government and country."[61]

At the conclusion of his message, Jackson threw himself on the mercy of the public. "I have now done my duty to my country," he said. "If sustained by my fellow citizens, I shall be grateful and happy; if not, I shall find in the motives which impel me ample grounds for contentment and peace."[62] "It is to be regretted that the rich and powerful too often bend the acts of government to their selfish purposes,"[63] wrote Jackson. He could just as well have been referring to himself.

Jackson's use of the veto as a political device, rather than limiting his argument to the strict constitutionality of the issue, was unprecedented. Hereafter, Congress had to consider the political desires of the president during the legislative process or face a possible veto. The balance of power shifted.[64] In what has been called the "most important veto ever issued by a president,"[65] Jackson not only attacked Biddle's Bank, he expanded the power of the executive branch of government and changed the presidency forever.

Biddle found the veto message ludicrous. Jackson's charges that the bank had failed to stabilize the nation's currency were patently false, and the bank's constitutionality had been debated since its inception and had always been upheld. The balance of the message was a mass of contradictions. Biddle was confident that public sentiment would fall his way, and wrote to Henry Clay that he was "delighted" with the president's address. "It has all the fury of a chained panther biting the bars of his cage. It is really a manifesto to anarchy . . . and my hope is that it will contribute to relieve the country from the dominion of these miserable people."[66] Concluding that Jackson was his own worst enemy, Biddle had thousands of copies of the veto message printed and distributed.

The Bank's supporters in Congress wasted no time is lashing out at the administration. Daniel Webster, Biddle's friend and an attorney retained by the Bank, delivered a blistering retort in the Senate the day after Jackson's message was received. Webster deconstructed the veto point by point, calling attention to the inaccuracies and speculation within the message. His summation, like Jackson's, laid the issue before the electorate. Webster charged that "This message calls us to the contemplation of a future which little resembles the past . . . It denies first principles; it contradicts truths, heretofore received as indisputable. It denies to the judiciary the interpretation of law . . . It extends the grasp of executive pretension over every power of government . . . It presents the chief magistrate of the Union in the attitude of arguing away the powers of the government over which he has been chosen to preside . . . It appeals to every prejudice which may betray men into a mistaken view of their own interests . . . It sows, in an unsparing manner, the seeds of jealousy and ill-will against that government of which its author is the official head . . . It raises a cry, that liberty is in danger, at the very moment when it puts forth claims to powers heretofore unknown and unheard of. It effects alarm for the public freedom, when nothing endangers that freedom so much as its own unparalleled pretenses . . . It manifestly seeks to inflame the poor against the rich; it wantonly attacks whole classes of people, for the purposes of turning against them the prejudices and the resentments of other classes . . . Such is this message. It remains now for the people of the United States to choose between the principles here avowed and their government. These cannot subsist together. The one or the other must be rejected."[67]

Clay also spoke against the veto, but despite the best efforts of the Biddle contingent, they were unable to garner the two-thirds majority necessary for an override, and the president's veto stood. The bank, however, was not dead yet. There was still an upcoming election and the possibility of unseating Jackson. The bank had just shy of four years left on its charter and a lot of money still under its control. The game remained afoot.

In 1832 the second-party system began to coalesce in the United States. The monolithic Democratic-Republican Party continued the fragmentation that had begun in 1828 when Jackson challenged John Quincy Adams for the presidency. During that election the Adams supporters began to refer to themselves as National Republicans, while the Jackson men retained the Democratic-Republican tag. Soon the two parties would abbreviate their titles to simply "Democrat" and "Republican," and the Democrats began to hold conventions to nominate candidates for the presidency.

One of the chief architects of this new "party spirit" was New York political maven Martin Van Buren. He had created an effective political machine in New York, and hoped to repeat his success on a national scale. In the 1824 election season Van Buren had been the de facto campaign manager for one of Jackson's opponents, William Campbell, but by 1828 he was firmly in the Jackson camp. An energetic and ambitious politician with a talent for organization, Van Buren built for Jackson a platform and a national party. He made deals, forged alliances, traded favors, and promoted patronage, most of the time conducting his business in proverbial smoke-filled rooms. Though he quickly gained a reputation as rainmaker, many saw

Van Buren as a sinister figure—a puppet-master pulling Jackson's strings. Jackson, however, trusted Van Buren completely, valued his council, and supported him as the vice presidential candidate in 1832.

As the election season heated up, Nicholas Biddle poured money into newspapers friendly toward the candidacy of Jackson's nemesis Henry Clay, the Republican presidential nominee. The Jackson press, led by Francis Blair's *Globe,* counterattacked with a vengeance. Both sides depicted the struggle as one in which the very survival of the country was at stake. Jackson's Democrats characterized the contest as a battle between the common people and the aristocracy, while Clay and Biddle painted Jackson as a power-mad despot seeking to subjugate every branch of government and rule as a monarch. They tapped into a very real fear in an age when the Revolution was not yet a distant memory. Martin Van Buren concurred with the strategy and told Jackson, "The ground, that this is in truth a question between Aristocracy and Democracy, cannot be too often or too forcibly impressed upon the minds of the people."[68]

Subsidized editors cranked out the rhetoric. "Andrew Jackson and the people against an overbearing monied aristocracy!" claimed the *Blairsville (Pennsylvania) Recorder.*[69] The *Globe* declared, "The people of this country are at last invoked to decide whether they will have for President, Andrew Jackson, or the Bank of the United States."[70]

Biddle's press responded by dismissing the barrage. "It is thus that people are deceived and imposed on by hirelings, who cry 'God Save King Andrew,' whether he bear the constitution aloft in his hand, or trample it under his feet."[71] A political cartoon captioned "King Andrew the First" appeared in 1832, and depicted a regal Jackson sporting a crown and ermine robe, scepter in one hand and the veto in the other, trampling the constitution on the floor beneath his feet.[72]

For his part, Biddle believed that he could beat Jackson on the bank issue if people knew the facts, and he did his best to disseminate information in the press to that effect.[73] Unfortunately, he committed the grave error of letting the Jackson forces frame the argument, and was too often put in a defensive posture.

Crockett weighed in on the election from back in Tennessee, writing to the *National Intelligencer,* "I am strongly solicited to offer for Elector, to vote for Henry Clay. The truth is, I do believe Mr. Clay is gaining friends in these parts. The people are beginning to find out the true worth of Jacksonism; they are beginning to find out that Davy Crockett is not alone to raise his voice against the reelection of Andrew Jackson."[74]

When interviewed by James Strange French for his soon-to-be-released biography, Crockett reiterated his opposition to Jackson in measured language and said he "admired Mr. Clay, but had objections to him," likely referring to their differences on tariff issues. He stated, probably with tongue firmly in cheek and taking a jab at Martin Van Buren, a preference for Philip Pendleton Barbour, a former speaker of the House from Virginia, for president over either Jackson or Clay. Barbour, a Jacksonian, briefly entered the 1832 race for vice president opposing Jackson's choice, Van Buren, but dropped out and was subsequently awarded a seat on the Supreme Court. Crockett also proclaimed himself a supporter of the Bank.[75]

In January of that year, Crockett had written Richard Smith, a cashier of the Washington branch of the Bank, asking for an extension on a loan he had received earlier, probably to offset expenses from his losing campaign against Fitzgerald. He had sold his land and at least one slave[76] to pay some of his debts[77] and remarked that "times is hard in this country." He also indelicately reminded Smith that, unlike his opponent, during the campaign he had been in favor of rechartering the Bank and intended to continue his support once he was reelected.[78] The Tennessee press noted Crockett's pro-Bank stance as early as 1831,[79] and it would become a major issue in his upcoming campaign to unseat William Fitzgerald.

Though Biddle was criticized for forgiving notes written to those friendly to his cause, his practice of writing off bad debt was not limited to politicians, and included "hundreds of others."[80] Biddle's actions were all "on the record," so the charges of favoritism in this situation may be unfounded. A certain amount of debt retirement was expected in the course of regular bookkeeping. Crockett's loan was relatively small, around $500, and though he received several extensions on the note, there is no evidence that Biddle forgave the debt. As late as February 1835, Crockett was still making arrangements for payments.[81]

Though public opinion about the renewal of the Bank's charter was divided, a majority of voters may have actually favored the Bank.[82] Old Hickory, however, was a favorite son, and the electorate tended to vote for the man over the issue. "General Jackson," said an anonymous senator, "has a peculiar way of addressing himself to the feelings of every man with whom he comes in contact." He continued, "When the people give their suffrages to a man, they never do so on a rigid examination of his political principles; for this task the labouring classes of any country have neither the time nor the disposition, and it is wholly needless to attempt to persuade them to a different course by a long and tedious argument. The large masses act in politics pretty much as they do in religion. Every doctrine is with them, more or less, as a matter of faith; received, principally, on account of their trust in the apostle. If the latter fail to captivate their hearts, no reasoning in the world is capable of filling the vacancy: and the more natural and uncorrupt the people are, the less they are to be moved by abstract reasoning, whether the form of government be republican, monarchical, or despotic."[83]

Jackson, then, could count on the people, even if voting for him might not have been in their own best interests. The Bank served a useful function, and Jackson had offered no clear alternative to the current system. He had, however, managed to dominate the dialogue on the issue, adopting the voice of the common man railing against the ruling class who were out to destroy democracy. The people loved Jackson's public image, his rough-around-the-edges manner, and his plain talk. They seemed to forget that Jackson himself was wealthy and lived in a world far different from their own. Historian Thomas P. Abernethy wrote of Jackson, "He thought he was sincere when he spoke to the people, yet he never really championed their cause. He merely encouraged them to champion his."[84]

Champion him they did. The president's personal popularity carried the day, and in a stinging rebuke to Biddle and Clay, Jackson was reelected and Van Buren carried the vice presidency. Crockett wrote, "I proclaimed it far and wide that I never would vote for Andrew Jackson for reelection; that I would vote for anyone in preference who was spoken of as a candidate. And I now say, that I never will vote for Jackson nor any man that will vote for him."[85]

His second term won and his veto upheld, Jackson could have been content to let the Bank's charter run out over the remainder of his term as president. Instead, with impatience and malevolence, he charted a course that would more rapidly bring about the Bank's destruction and, as a result, galvanized his opposition and nearly wrecked the national economy. He set the issue aside for a time to deal with the more pressing Nullification Crisis in South Carolina[86], but the Bank issue was never far from his mind. Jackson was certain the pro-Bank forces would mount another attempt to recharter, so in 1833, he resumed his crusade to destroy Biddle's "hydra of corruption."[87]

The president targeted the primary weapon in Biddle's arsenal, his supply of money. Jackson determined to disarm Biddle and enervate the Bank by withdrawing the federal funds on deposit with the Bank and placing them instead in state banks of his own choosing: "pet" banks that were friendly toward the administration. By cutting Biddle's purse strings, Jackson predicted that Biddle would be hamstrung and the Bank would wither and die. He outlined the plan to his cabinet in a private meeting, and the response was less enthusiastic than he had hoped. Nearly all of the cabinet objected to the removal of the deposits. They argued that the action would jeopardize the economy, given the state banking system's history of instability when unregulated by the SBUS, and they saw no danger in leaving federal funds in the care of Biddle's institution. Members cautioned that the move would be seen as entirely political, one of Jackson's primary complaints against Biddle's Bank. They also questioned the legality of removing the deposits. The president, however, forged ahead with his plan, claiming that since the Bank had been a campaign issue, his reelection signified a mandate to take action against the Bank.[88] Jackson declared himself the representative of the electorate, and insisted that the people had spoken.

He directed Amos Kendall to provide him with a list of state banks that were sympathetic to Democrats and willing and strong enough to take over the government's business. Kendall, always a staunch opponent of the Bank, was only too happy to comply. Once Jackson had Kendall's list, he planned to act before

Congress convened.[89] Legally, Jackson could not remove the deposits himself, as that responsibility lay with the secretary of the treasury alone, so the president began pressuring Secretary of the Treasury William Duane to remove the funds forthwith. Duane argued for waiting until the administration could bring the issue before Congress, as he felt he had a legal responsibility to report his decision to the legislative branch. Jackson, predictably, was intolerant of any dissent or obstruction, and consequently fired Duane and appointed Roger Taney as treasury secretary. Taney had already given Jackson assurances that he was more than willing to do the president's bidding even before Congress confirmed his new position. Jackson then went public, publishing an announcement of his plan in the *Globe*.[90] He restated all his usual complaints against the Bank, and by the end of September the national press had picked up the story. Jackson directed that the withdrawal of the deposits was to begin by October 1. In a scathing editorial the *National Intelligencer* commented, "This is the summary mode by which the Executive of a free country evades the provisions and the inhibitions of the law. Are we to see a Cromwell in our day? Surely if there be a redeeming spirit in the country, this last act of Executive aggression must rouse it into action."[91]

Biddle was certainly roused. In a quick response to Taney's removal order, the Bank's board of directors authorized Biddle to stop making loans and start tightening credit. While the action was necessary to meet the demands for relinquishment of the federal funds, it was also designed to squeeze the economy and bring public pressure to bear on Jackson to reverse the order.[92] The economic effects of the contraction were immediate, and the outcry for relief was universal. Credit was unavailable to get goods to market, money was short, and debts were being called in. Since the SBUS was no longer a source of capital, lenders were forced to scramble for financing elsewhere, and the shortage of available funds raised the discount rate.[93] The nation plunged into a recession, and Biddle kept turning up the heat.

When Congress reconvened in December, Henry Clay was in fighting form. Joined by Daniel Webster and John C. Calhoun, Clay led the Senate's assault against Jackson. On December 3 the Senate received Taney's mandatory report to Congress explaining his actions, and seven days later Clay demanded that Jackson hand over the personal notes he used when he addressed his cabinet on the removal of the deposits. Confident that he could prove the removal order was at Jackson's command and that he had abused his executive authority by bullying the secretary of the treasury to do his bidding and then fired him when he refused, Clay insisted upon a full Senate investigation into the affair.[94] The Senate debated the propriety of Clay's request for Jackson's papers on the following day, but the measure passed the Senate by a vote of 23 to 18. Jackson wasted no time in thumbing his nose at the decision. On the following day, he issued a statement to the Senate refusing the request and claiming that the legislative branch had no authority "to require of me an account of any communication, either verbally or in writing, made to the heads of departments acting as a cabinet council."[95]

Crockett, who had regained his seat in the House for the Twenty-Third Congress, wrote to a friend, "You have seen I suppose the Genl refusal to comply with the resolution of the senate and I do believe the house will order the deposits back in to the united states bank and I also believe the president will tell us to go to hell that he knows his bussiness and ours too."[96]

On December 26, 1833, Clay delivered a long speech in the Senate outlining his charges against the president, and offered two resolutions that censured his actions. In firing Duane and appointing Taney, Clay charged, Jackson "has assumed the exercise of a power over the treasury of the United States, not granted to him by the constitution and laws, and dangerous to the liberties of the people."[97] He further proposed that Taney's explanations for removing the deposits were "unsatisfactory and insufficient."[98] As to Jackson's claims of being the representative of the American people in justification of his own actions, Clay asked, "By what authority does the President derive power from the mere result of an election? . . . He was re-elected from his presumed merits generally, and from the attachment and confidence of the people, and also from the unworthiness of his competitor. The people had no idea, by that exercise of suffrage, of expressing their approbation of all the opinions which the President held. . . . The election of a President, in itself, gives no power, but merely designates the person who, as an officer of the Government, is to exercise power granted by the constitution and laws."[99] Clay warned of a chief executive who controlled both sword and purse.

In January, Crockett wrote, "By this you see we have the government of one man That he puts forward his will as the law of the land If the American people will seanction this we may bid farewell to our Republican name it is nothing but a shaddow our once happy government will become a despot I consider the present time one that is marked with more danger than any period of our political history. You see our whole circulating medium deranged and our whole Commercial Community destroyed all to gratify the ambition of King Andrew the first becaus the United States Bank refused to lend its aid in upholding his corrupt party."[100]

For months, the debate raged. Spectators filled the Senate chamber to watch the Great Triumvirate of Clay, Webster, and Calhoun tag-team against the president's defenders, led by the formidable talents of Thomas Hart Benton. In the House, James K. Polk did his best to hold the Jackson party together as angry constituents lobbied their Congressmen for relief from the economic downturn brought on by the war between Jackson and Biddle. On February 24, Crockett went on record saying, "They know very well in my district the character of the man who, when he takes anything into his head, will carry it into effect. They know how I should act in this Bank business, for I told them, before I was elected, how I should vote—that I would recharter the bank and restore the deposites. Sir, I get letters every day, from all parts, which tell me these acts are disapprobated. The question is, now, whether we shall continue to live and do well under the old and happy state of things, or have a despot."[101]

The fight also continued in the press, with both sides spitting and spinning. The anti-Jackson men were beginning to be referred to as Whigs and quickly adopted the name, with all its implications of opposition to the monarchy. Finally, on March 28, 1834, the Senate adopted Clay's resolutions by a vote of 26-20, sending a clear message to Jackson that he had overstepped his bounds.[102]

Jackson, insulted and fuming, composed a formal protest that his nephew and private secretary, Andrew Jackson Donelson, delivered to the Senate on April 17. Jackson charged that the Senate proceeding against him was unlawful and tantamount to an act of impeachment, but that impeachment was the purview of the House of Representatives, not the Senate. He reasserted his right to fire members of the cabinet at will, and also proclaimed it the duty of the executive branch to oversee the protection of public property, which included public funds. He wrote, "But where is the difference in principle, whether the public property be in the form of arms, munitions of war and supplies, or in gold and silver or bank notes? None can be perceived—none is believed to exist. Congress cannot, therefore, take out of the hands of the executive department the custody of the public property or money without an assumption of executive power, and a subversion of the first principles of the constitution."[103] The cabinet secretaries, he argued, were members of the executive branch who served at the president's pleasure. While the secretary of the treasury must be the legal instrument by which the funds were transferred, the ultimate decision lay with the chief executive.

Jackson also used the protest as another opportunity to attack the Bank, renewing his charges that the institution was corrupt and had used its funds to control public opinion in the 1832 election by investing in the pro-Bank press. More important, though, he continued his argument that the president was the "direct representative of the American people."[104] His summation, another call to arms for the electorate, again drew the distinction between his "plain system, void of pomp" and the government of his critics, "supported by powerful monopolies and aristocratical establishments."[105]

The remarks were met with immediate disdain in the Senate, and Senators George Poindexter and Clay both chastised the president on his shameful attempt to use the Senate as a court of public appeal. Jackson's claim that the president was the direct representative of the people met the most aggressive response. Daniel Webster excoriated Jackson's claim in an address on May 7. Piece by piece, Webster tore apart Jackson's protest message, repeatedly illustrating how Jackson's claims to power amounted to little more than monarchy. He pointed out that by proclaiming himself the personal protector of the people's liberty, protecting them from, in fact, the Congress, Jackson was upending every conventional idea about the process of preserving freedom. Throughout history, Webster avowed, "executive power has been regarded as a lion which must be caged. So far from being the object of enlightened popular trust—so far from being considered the natural protector of popular right, it has been dreaded, uniformly, always dreaded, as the great source of its danger."[106] Webster also reminded Jackson that he had not been elected president by the votes of the people, but by electors, some of whom were elected by the people, others of whom were appointed.[107] Furthermore, Jackson's claims that he was responsible to the people above all else were also ill considered. The president was obliged first and foremost to protect and defend the Constitution and the law, not to be manipulated by public opinion.

After a lengthy rebuttal by Thomas Hart Benton, the Senate voted to reject Jackson's protest message and uphold its resolutions condemning the president's actions.[108] It was, however, a hollow victory.

In the House, Polk had managed to hold his Democrat majority together, and on April 4 the House voted in support of Jackson's veto and the removal of the deposits. Crockett voted against all of the measures.[109] Jackson's propaganda machine was also beginning to have an effect on the public, who were still suffering financial hard times. The message of the aristocracy controlling the money was repeated ad nauseam until public support for the Bank dwindled. The president's protest message, though rejected by the Senate, resounded with the electorate, who rallied to the support of their old hero.

Jackson remained steadfast in his refusal to either recharter the Bank or restore the deposits, and Biddle could only hang on until his money ran out and the "pet" banks, now holding the federal monies, gained strength. The bickering about the issue continued, but the Bank War was effectively over. The newly empowered electorate had spoken. Jackson's test of the limits of executive power had been decided in his favor, and the presidency gained strength as a result. In 1837 a Democrat majority in the Senate voted to expunge Jackson's censure from the record, vindicating Old Hickory on the record if not in history.

Crockett's opposition to Jackson intensified, and he continued to hold out hope that the federal deposits would one day be restored to the Bank. In June of 1834 another joint resolution was put forward in the House claiming that the reasons given for the removal of the deposits were unsatisfactory, and Polk immediately moved to have the resolution tabled. Crockett, incensed, jumped to his feet and ripped into Polk. He shouted that Polk "had been dodging around this question all the session." He hoped that now the members could "stand up to the rack and say to their constituents, that we have supported the laws and constitution. This question is to test that fact, and I hope to meet it upon its merits, and say to the country, by our votes, whether we have a government or not."[110] He was shouted down and called to order, but despite Crockett's impassioned outburst, the resolution was tabled. Two days later he wrote to a friend, "on the day before yesterday the house rejected Mr. Clays resolutions by laying them on the table and I consider the last hope gone of retaining the laws and constitution I now look forward to our adjournment with as much intrest as ever did a poor Convict in the Penatintiary."[111]

Crockett continued to speak and write about Jackson in increasingly harsh terms, but he reserved a large portion of his invective for Vice President Van Buren, on whom he blamed most of Jackson's shortcomings. Crockett's letters of the period are filled with slurs directed at the vice president, and he lent his name to a hack-job biography of Van Buren that was released in 1835, when Van Buren began his campaign for the presidency. Crockett threatened to move to Texas if "Little Van" won, and made good on his threat soon after.[112]

Biddle continued to lobby for the Bank's recharter, but his efforts were in vain. He remained politically active and continued to correspond with Webster, Clay, and other leading Whig figures, using his ever waning influence to support their causes when he could. He negotiated a charter with the state of Pennsylvania for the Bank's main branch, but remained intractable when it was suggested that the state charter should include prohibitions on the bank's involvement in politics.[113] He defended the Bank until it sputtered to an end in 1841.

The "pet" banks operated in much the same way they had in the past, but, with more capital on hand and no accountability to a regulatory source, they floated more paper than ever. By 1837, new President Martin Van Buren found himself in charge of a country mired in another major depression.[114]

The divisiveness of the Bank War also helped realize Van Buren's goal of strengthening and organizing a national party system, changing the face of U.S. politics forever. Factionalism and party loyalty often supplanted true patriotism, and professional politicians eclipsed statesmen in the corridors of power.

The Second Bank of the United States served a useful purpose, both in its role as a federal depository and in its efforts to curb the speculative tendencies of the state banks; it strengthened and stabilized the U.S. economy. There is no question that Biddle's bank needed regulation, and a compromise leading to a recharter would have been attainable had either Jackson or Biddle been willing to put their egos aside for the good of the country.

Although Crockett's involvement in the Bank crisis was peripheral and of small consequence, it illustrates his genuine concern for Jackson's expansion of executive power. While much Crockett literature suggests that his support of the Bank was motivated either by knee-jerk anti-Jacksonism or personal debt to the Bank, his concerns clearly transcended such motivations and were genuine. Crockett continued to claim he was a "Jackson man" and accused the president of betraying his own views. Jackson's behavior regarding the Bank, and his apparent disregard for the broader public good, were, to Crockett, clear signs of a power-hungry executive. "Is it possible," he asked, "that the blood and treasure of our forefathers can have been shed in vain? Can it be, that they resisted the crook of king George's finger, and that we, like pups, will crouch under king Andrew's whip? I hope not; and that the redeeming spirit of the people will show, that, although the harlot has been among them, their locks are still unshorn; and, feeling their own power, will exercise it like freemen . . . the day is fast approaching when truth and justice will prevail over intrigue and party discipline."[115]

---

[1]   *Register of Debates*, February 24, 1831, 788–89.

[2]   Crockett's circular of February 28, 1831, was openly critical of Jackson and provoked even more forceful negative campaigning in the Jackson press. Ample evidence of this can be seen in issues of the *Southern Statesman* from this period.

[3]   Thomas P. Abernethy, "The Early Development of Commerce and Banking in Tennessee," *Mississippi Valley Historical Review* 14, no. 3 (Dec. 1927): 314.

[4]   John Eaton was a staunch supporter of Jackson, a close personal friend, and a seven term U.S. senator. Eaton's 1829 marriage to Peggy O'Neal Timberlake, a woman of controversial repute, caused a scandal in the Jackson cabinet. See Robert V. Remini, *The Life of Andrew Jackson* (New York: Harper and Row, 1988), 174, 190–92, 204. Ephraim Foster served in the Creek War and acted as Jackson's private secretary from 1813 to 1815. He later left the Jackson ranks and represented Tennessee as a Whig in the U.S. Senate in the Twenty-fifth and Twenty-eighth Congresses. Biographical Directory of the United States Congress online, http://bioguide.congress.gov. William B. Lewis was a Nashville neighbor of and close advisor to Jackson.

[5]   Charles Grier Sellers, Jr., "Jackson Men with Feet of Clay," *American Historical Review* 62, no. 3. (Apr. 1957): 539. William Blount served as one of Tennessee's first U.S. senators, but was expelled in 1797, having been found guilty of attempting to incite the Creek and Cherokee Indians to assist the British in conquering Spanish West Florida. Still popular in Tennessee, he subsequently served as president of the Tennessee State senate. Biographical Directory of the United States Congress online, http://bioguide.congress.gov.

[6]   Charles Grier Seller, Jr., "Banking and Politics in Jackson's Tennessee," *Mississippi Valley Historical Review* 14, no. 1 (June 1954): 62–65.

[7]   Ibid., 65.

[8]   Newton Cannon was a four-term Tennessee congressman.

[9]   John Williams was a U.S. senator who lost his seat to Jackson in 1823.

[10] Sellers, "Banking and Politics in Jackson's Tennessee,", 63.

[11] Biographical Directory of the United States Congress online, http://bioguide.congress.gov.

[12] Sellers, "Banking and Politics in Jackson's Tennessee," 65.

[13] Carroll later became a Jackson supporter.

14 Sellers, "Banking and Politics in Jackson's Tennessee," 65.

15 John P. Erwin was Andrew Erwin's son and in 1824 became one of the editors of the *Nashville Whig*. John Y. Simon, "In Search of Margaret Johnson Erwin," *Journal of American History* 69, no. 4 (March 1983): 932.

16 Sellers, "Banking and Politics in Jackson's Tennessee," 65–66.

17 Abernethy, "The Early Development of Commerce and Banking in Tennessee," 316–18.

18 Thomas P. Abernethy, "Andrew Jackson and the Rise of South-Western Democracy," *American Historical Review* 33, no. 1 (Oct. 1927): 67.

19 Sellers, "Banking and Politics in Jackson's Tennessee," 67.

20 St. George Leakin Sioussat, "Some Phases of Tennessee Politics in the Jackson Period," *American Historical Review* 14, no. 1 (Oct. 1908): 61.

21 Abernethy, "Andrew Jackson and the Rise of South-Western Democracy," 67.

22 Sellers, "Banking and Politics in Jackson's Tennessee," 70.

23 Robert E. Corlew, *Tennessee: A Short History* (Knoxville: University of Tennessee Press, 1981), 162.

24 David Crockett, *A Narrative of the Life of David Crockett of the State of Tennessee*, ed. James A. Shackford and Stanley J. Folmsbee (Knoxville: University of Tennessee Press, 1973), 144.

25 James Atkins Shackford, *David Crockett: The Man and the Legend*, John B. Shackford, ed., (Chapel Hill: University of North Carolina Press, 1956), 55–56.

26 Remini, *The Life of Andrew Jackson*, 29.

27 Corlew, *Tennessee*, 164–65.

28 Sellers, "Banking and Politics in Jackson's Tennessee," 73.

29 *Nashville Whig*, October 13, 1823.

30 Mark Derr, *The Frontiersman* (New York: William Morrow & Co., 1993), 127.

31 Sellers, "Banking and Politics in Jackson's Tennessee," 73.

32 *Nashville Whig*, September 29, 1823.

33 Crockett, *Narrative of the Life*, 170-71.

34 Sellers, "Banking and Politics in Jackson's Tennessee," 74.

35 Derr, *The Frontiersman*, 127.

36 Sioussat, "Some Phases of Tennessee Politics in the Jackson Period," 62.

37 Ibid., 62–63.

38 Bernard A. Weisberger, "The Bank War," *American Heritage Magazine* 48, no. 4. (July/August 1997), viewable at www.americanheritage.com; George Rogers Taylor, "A Brief History of the Second Bank of the United States," in *Jackson versus Biddle: The Struggle Over the Second Bank of the United States* (Boston: D. C. Heath and Co., 1949), 1–2; Bray Hammond, "The Second Bank of the United States," *Transactions of the American Philosophical Society*, New Ser., 43, no. 1. (1953): 80–85.

39 Robert V. Remini, *Andrew Jackson and the Bank War* (New York: W. W. Norton & Co., 1967), 32–33.

40 Idem, *The Life of Andrew Jackson*, 33–35.

41 Sellers, "Banking and Politics in Jackson's Tennessee," 78.

42 Remini, *Bank War*, 51.

43 Ibid., 55.

44 Jackson to Overton, June 8, 1829, Jacob Dickinson Papers, Tennessee State Library and Archives (TSLA), cited in Remini, *Bank War*, 45.

45 *The Autobiography of Martin Van Buren*, ed. John C. Fitzpatrick (Washington: U.S. Government Printing Office, 1920), 625.

46 Remini, *Bank War*, 58–59.

47 Ibid., 64–65.

48 Biddle to John McKim, Jr., Jan. 18, 1830; Nicholas Biddle, *Correspondence of Nicholas Biddle*, ed. Reginald C. McGrane (Boston and New York: Houghton Mifflin Co., 1919), 96–97.

49 John Seigenthaler, *James K. Polk* (New York: Times Books, Henry Holt & Co., 2003), 50.

50 Remini, *Bank War*, 67.

51 Richard B. Latner, "A New Look at Jacksonian Politics," *Journal of American History* 61, no. 4 (March 1975): 952; Remini, *Bank War*, 61.

52 Erik McKinley Eriksson, "President Jackson's Propaganda Agencies," *Pacific Historical Review* 6, no. 1 (March 1937): 53.

53 Clay to Biddle, Sept. 11, 1830, in Biddle, *Correspondence*, 112–13.

54 Biddle to Clay, November 3, 1830, in ibid., 115–16.

55 Clay to Biddle, December 15, 1831, in ibid., 142.

56 Remini, *Bank War*, 72–73.

57 Ibid., 72–74.

58 *Register of Debates*, January 9, 1832, 53.

59 Ibid., June 11, 1832, 1073.

60 Ibid., July 3, 1832, 3852.

61 Andrew Jackson, "Veto Message," in George Rogers Taylor, ed., *Jackson vs. Biddle's Bank* (Lexington, Mass.: D.C. Heath and Co., 1972), 27.

62 Ibid.

63 Ibid.

64 Remini, *Life of Andrew Jackson*, 230.

65 Ibid., 229.

66 Biddle to Clay, August 1, 1832, in Biddle, *Correspondence*, 196.

67 *Register of Debates*, July 11, 1832, 1221–23, 1225–29, 1239, 1240.

68 Ted Widmer, *Martin Van Buren* (New York: Henry Holt, 2005), 85–86.

69 Reprinted in *Pittsfield (Massachusetts) Sun*, August 16, 1832.

70 Reprinted in *(Newport) Rhode-Island Republican*, October 30, 1832.

71 *Baltimore Chronicle*, reprinted in *(Hagers-Town, Maryland) Torch Light and Public Advertiser*, August 2, 1832.

72 "King Andrew the First," American Cartoon Prints, Call No. PC/US-1833.A000, no. 5, (A size) [P&P], Library of Congress. The references to royalty must have been particularly offensive to Jackson, who had fought the British Crown both as an adolescent in the Revolutionary War and in the War of 1812. As a youth, he had lost most of his immediate family in the struggle for independence. Comparisons of Jackson to a king would likely have been highly insulting to him.

73 Biddle to Joseph Gales, March 2, 1831, in Biddle, *Correspondence*, 125; Biddle to James Hunter, May 4, 1831, in ibid., 126.

74 *National Intelligencer*, reprinted in *Brattleboro Messenger*, February 18, 1832.

75 James Strange French, *Sketches and Eccentricities of Col. David Crockett, of West Tennessee*, New Edition (New York: J. & J. Harper, 1833), 117–18.

76 Shackford, *David Crockett*, 136.

77 Crockett to Doctor Jones, August 22, 1831, Emma Inman Williams, *Historic Madison, The Story of Jackson and Madison County Tennessee, from Prehistoric Moundbuilders to 1917* (Jackson, Tennessee: Madison County Historical Society, 1946), 422.

78 Crockett to Richard Smith, Esq., January 7, 1832, Historical Society of Pennsylvania.

79 *Southern Statesman*, June 18, 1831.

80 Ralph C. H. Catterall, *The Second Bank of the United States* (Chicago: University of Chicago Press, 1903), 254–55.

81 Crockett began an exchange of letters with Nicholas Biddle in October of 1834 attempting to work out an arrangement to pay off an outstanding loan. After some confusion at the Nashville branch that resulted in branch president Poindexter listing Crockett as a bad credit risk, Crockett wrote Biddle and asked him to write directly to Poindexter to vouch for him and get the matter straightened out. Biddle did so, and Poindexter subsequently extended Crockett's loan. In a letter to Crockett dated December 19, 1834, Biddle comments, "The note has been discounted and the old draft paid." Some Crockett biographers have interpreted this as Biddle writing off the debt, but that is not the case. The bank simply renewed Crockett's loan and relisted it. It is obvious that Crockett still had an outstanding balance as of February 16, 1835, as Biddle wrote informing him of his account balance and asked for at least partial payment before the note came due in March. Biddle wrote, "Let me know how much you can pay and I will send you the notes for renewal with the proper calculations." It is not known how much of this debt Crockett was able to reconcile before his death a little over a year later. It is possible, of course, that Biddle cleared his books after learning of Crockett's demise, but it is clear that while Crockett was alive he stayed in contact with Biddle about the debt and made every effort to pay it off.

82 *Register of Debates*, February 24, 1834, 2782.

83 Francis J. Grund, *Aristocracy in America* (London: Richard Benley, New Burlington St., 1839), 239–40.

84 Abernethy, "Andrew Jackson and the Rise of South-Western Democracy," 76.

85 Crockett to *National Intelligencer*, reprinted in *Brattleboro Messenger*, February 18, 1832.

86 South Carolina claimed the right as a state to nullify any federal law with which it didn't agree. The state threatened to secede from the Union in a dispute over federal tariffs, and Jackson threatened to use force to bring South Carolina into compliance. Eventually, a compromise agreement was reached.

87 John Spencer Bassett, *The Life of Andrew Jackson* (New York: MacMillan, 1911, reprinted 1925), 604.

88 Remini, *Bank War*, 109–14.

89 Ibid., 116–17.

90 Ibid., 122–24.

91 *National Intelligencer*, quoted in *Portsmouth (New Hampshire) Journal*, September 28, 1833.

92 Robert V. Remini, *Henry Clay: Statesman for the Union* (New York: W. W. Norton & Co., 1991), 444.

93 Peter Temin, *The Jacksonian Economy* (New York: W. W. Norton & Co., 1969), 63.

94 *Register of Debates*, December 10, 1833, 27.

95 Ibid., December 12, 1833, 37.

96 Crockett to Albert Waterman, December 15, 1833, Haverford College Library, Haverford PA, Special Collections, Charles Roberts Autograph Letters Collection.

97 *Register of Debates*, December 26, 1823, 58.

98 Ibid., 59.

99 Ibid., 66.

100 Crockett to William Rodgers, January 8, 1834, TSLA.

101 *Register of Debates*, February 24, 1834, 2782.

102 Ibid., March 28, 1834, 1187.

103 Ibid., April 17, 1834, 1327. Jackson was wrong in this assertion and later attempted to clarify his position by issuing an explanatory message to the Senate on April 23, 1834.

104 Ibid., 1333.

105 Ibid., 1335.

106 Ibid., May 7, 1834, 1682.

107 Ibid., 1688.

108 Ibid., 1712.

109 *Register of Debates*, April 4, 1834, 3474–77.

110 Ibid., June 13, 1834, 4467.

111 Crockett to William Yeatman, June 15, 1834, Haverford College Library, Haverford PA, Special Collections, Charles Roberts Autograph Letters Collection.

112 Crockett to Charles Schultz, December 25, 1834, Gilder Lehrman Collection, GLC01162.

113 Biddle to William B. Reed, January 15, 1836, Biddle, *Correspondence*, 261.

114 There were other factors that also contributed to the Panic of 1837. For a more detailed analysis see Temin, *The Jacksonian Economy*.

115 David Crockett, *An Account of Colonel Crockett's Tour to the North and Down East* (Philadelphia: Carey and Hart, 1835), 109.

Chapter 8

"They Came To See a Bar"
Celebrity and the Election of 1835

*W*hen Crockett returned to Washington City in December1833 for the start of the Twenty-Third Congress, *he found the political climate in the capitol changed. During his hiatus, the anti-Jacksonians, under the able guidance of Henry Clay, had formed the Whig party. Though never officially registered as a Whig, the avowed anti-partisan Crockett and the newfound party enjoyed a symbiotic relationship.[1] Still alienated from his own delegation, Crockett's early alliances with the Erwin group in Tennessee and his open opposition to the Jackson administration made him a prime candidate for Whig recruitment, and his burgeoning celebrity was all the more reason for Clay's group to fete him. Davy Crockett, the Poor Man's Friend, the champion of the under-privileged, and now the Lion of the West, was a perfect counterbalance to the image of the typical Whig: a stuffy, northeastern businessman, out of touch with the common man. With Crockett as a mouthpiece, the Whigs could more ably take down the Jacksonians by appealing to the masses already captivated by the Colonel's fame. Crockett saw the alliance as an opportunity to use the Whig platform (and the Whig purse) to advance his own agenda on his own terms. For him, it was a win-win situation.*

Crockett reveled in all the attention. He certainly realized the important role the media played in his celebrity status, but having been burned by the press in the past, he also knew he needed to control the message. He was getting plenty of mileage out of Paulding's Nimrod Wildfire and French's book, but he wasn't making money from either, and some of the broad characterizations rubbed him the wrong way. He'd worked hard to overcome the backwoods stereotype, and there was a danger that too much "Davy Crockett" silliness would undermine his efforts to be taken more seriously by his colleagues. Still, he'd managed earlier to turn an insult into a trademark when he'd been branded the "Gentleman from the Cane," and there was no reason why he couldn't do it again. He could appropriate the elements of *Lion of the West* that appealed to him and jettison everything else. And why let French have the last word on his life when he could write his own story?

On December 12, Crockett attended a Washington performance of *Lion of the West*, by then retitled *The Kentuckian; Or a Trip to New York.* The theater managers gave him his own box and, to the delight of the crowd who responded with deafening applause, Crockett and Wildfire (played by James Hackett) acknowledged one another by exchanging bows. The event was such a hit that the production company offered to pay Crockett's expenses to Philadelphia to repeat the performance.[2] Though there is no evidence he ever took them up on the offer, the warm reception strengthened his resolve to get a tighter grip on "Davy" and use him to advance his own cause.

Hackett wasn't the only thespian making money off of Crockett. Another actor, J. C. Mossie, was touring the theater circuit doing impressions of Clay, Webster, Van Buren, and Crockett, charging fifty cents admission, with children under fifteen admitted free.[3] Mossie's program included "Crockett's protests against the dandified, the soft talkers, and the ef-fected," and contrasted the "finished Intellectual Gladiatorship of the late Hon. John Randolph,[4] and the rough but effective knock-me-down oratory of David Crockett of Tennessee."[5]

Crockett's rough oratory was also appearing semi-regularly in newspaper columns by Seba Smith, who had invented Major Jack Downing, a character who rivaled the colonel for humor and plain speaking. The Downing articles offered political and social commentary written in the vernacular of a New England naïf, and were enormously popular. Nobody missed the similarity between Downing and Davy, and the two characters were soon connected in the press. "We understand from good authority (says the Pennsylvanian) that Major Jack Downing of Maine intends to visit Colonel Crockett of Tennessee—cholera or no cholera."[6]

In September of 1833, a Downing letter addressed Crockett directly, and a Crockett response, penned by Smith and signed "Davy Crockett," followed.[7] Composed in the same outlandish dialect as the Downing letters, the exchanges between the two characters proved popular and continued throughout Crockett's congressional term. Crockett was quick to embrace the Downing connection. In November of 1833, he jokingly told John Quincy Adams, now serving in the House of Representatives, that he was sharing rooms with Major Downing at Ball's boarding house and that Major Jack was "the only person in whom he had any confidence for information of what the government was doing."[8]

The popularity of the Smith columns encouraged Crockett to pursue his idea about writing his auto-biography. The French book continued to sell, and he was certain he could turn out a better product. However, he wasn't as sure that he could handle the work on his own, so he turned to his old friend and fellow boarder Thomas Chilton, another defector from the Jackson ranks, for assistance. Crockett could provide the content, but he needed Chilton's literary skill to pull the project together and help him market it to a publisher. He knew exactly what he wanted, "a plain and singular production. It will afford, I have no doubt, much amusement every where, as my life has been full of strange and laughable incidents."[9] Crockett was perturbed that French had released an unauthorized work, which paid him nothing, and was straightforward about the potential financial benefits of the project. His campaign had driven him deeper into debt, and he hoped to reap some profits from the new book. "If I can sell the copy right for a respectable sum," he wrote, "I shall . . . accomplish two objects. First, I shall vindicate myself from the spurious work sent abroad; and secondly shall get the means of going ahead, just now."[10]

Chilton sent out several inquiries to publishers on Crockett's behalf. "If I was not a poor man," Crockett wrote, "I shouldn't need anything for the work at all. But I am poor, with a large family, and as the world seems anscious for the work, I know they would want me to have the profits of it."[11]

Crockett spent most of his spare time on the project, and by January 10 had written over a hundred pages, with Chilton editing and correcting as he wrote. He was entertaining offers from a couple of publishers and expected the completed work to run about two hundred pages. He was already planning a promotional tour of the eastern states to help sell the book during the congressional recess, writing "I in tend never to go home until I am able to pay all my debts and I think I have a good prospect at present and will do the best I can."[12]

Though Crockett was concentrating primarily on writing the autobiography, he was still speaking out against Jackson's "kingley powar" and the removal of the deposits from the Second Bank of the United States. "It is plainley to be discovered," he wrote, "that old Jackson is determined to Carry his point or Sacrifice the nation It has been said by Some of his worshipers that he has been the Savior of the country . . . the truth is if he had been dead and at the devil four years ago it would have been a happy time for this country."[13]

Crockett's high-profile anti-Jackson rhetoric caught the attention of many, and on January 12, a delegation from Plymouth, Lowndes County, Mississippi, sent him an interesting proposal. They wrote, "We have, with much regret, noticed that most of the recent struggles, and threatening dangers in our Government, have been brought about by selfish individuals, ambitious, not for the welfare of our country, but for the loaves and fishes. We have recently heard several names mentioned in connection with the subject of the next Presidential election, and among them we have heard yours, which is the only one we can cheerfully support. We have every confidence in your integrity and ability to conduct the Ship of State safely through the threatening storm of party spirit, and steer her smoothly into the harbor of uninterrupted happiness and prosperity. There is nothing wanting, in our opinion, to make you our next President, but your own consent. Impressed with this belief, and confidant of your success, we respectfully ask permission to lay your name before the people as a candidate for our next President, and *we go the whole hog for you.*"[14]

It was a heady offer, and from his somewhat tongue-in-cheek reply, declining the invitation, it is unclear whether Crockett took it seriously, though the thought was surely in the back of his mind. He took the opportunity in his response to promote his alter ego, however, saying, "If I am elected, I shall just seize the old monster, party, by the horns, and sling him right slap into the deepest place in the great Atlantic sea."[15]

Crockett surely felt as though things were finally coming together for him, although he professed to find being a celebrity somewhat unsettling. "I know, that obscure as I am, my name is making considerable deal of fuss in the world," he wrote. "I can't tell why it is, nor in what it is to end. Go where I will, everybody seems anxious to get a peep at me . . . there must therefore be something in me, or about me, that attracts attention, which is even mysterious to myself."[16]

The end of the month brought more good news. The Philadelphia house of Carey and Hart offered to publish Crockett's now completed autobiography. Henry Carey, one of the principal partners, was likely enthusiastic about the proposal because of his own Republican political leanings. Carey was a supporter of manufacturing interests, an investor in the iron and coal industries, and a respected economist.[17] Crockett's well-known anti-administration sentiments found a receptive audience at the firm, and he accepted their offer. On February 3, Crockett mailed them the only copy of the manuscript, written in Thomas Chilton's hand, accompanied by the certified copyright and a letter with some specific instructions. He was adamant that the book be printed in large type "as to make it very open and plain . . . as in that way it will easily spread over more than two hundred pages." He also directed them that "it needs no correction of *spelling* or *grammar,* as I make no literary pretensions." The success of the use of vernacular in the Downing columns had not been lost on Crockett, and he made liberal use of the technique in his manuscript.[18]

He expressed his confidence that the work "will exceed any calculation you have made. All along the Mississippi, where the counterfeit work sold rapidly, I have been urged by the people generally, to publish. There, very many copies will sell. I have also rec'd a letter from a Bookseller in Louisville Ky—informing me, that it will sell rapidly there. That more than 500 copies of the other work, had been sold at his single house in that place, and that many more of the genuine work would find ready market."[19] The initial acceptance letter is written in Chilton's hand, but Crockett signed it.

The reference to a Louisville bookseller illustrates that Kentuckian Chilton was helping Crockett market the book as well as providing his services as a scribe and editor. Chilton also had a vested interest in the project, as Crockett had generously offered him half of the proceeds in payment for his contributions. Crockett made Carey and Hart aware of this arrangement on February 23 in a letter written in his own hand. He explained, "The letters which you have heretofore received from me were also in his hand writing as I was unwell and not able to write at their dates."[20] While it is possible that Crockett was ill at the time, it is doubtful. There is extant correspondence in Crockett's hand from February 3, the same date Chilton penned the acceptance letter,[21] and none of Crockett's personal correspondence from the period mentions that he was ill. More likely, Crockett was self-conscious about his own handwriting and grammar and thought Chilton's would make a more professional impression on the publishers. Once he had the contract in hand, he wasn't as concerned.

With the book deal now sewn up, Crockett hired Samuel Osgood to paint his portrait, which was completed by the end of February. He scratched off an endorsement for the young artist's resume,[22] praised the picture as "the only correct likeness that has been taken of me,"[23] and wasted no time in having lithographic reproductions of the portrait issued by Childs and Lehman to be sold alongside the book.[24] He also made the sly comment, "Some men are immortalized by their painters—but the painters are to be immortalized by me."[25]

Crockett took a personal interest in marketing his autobiography, now titled *A Narrative of the Life of David Crockett of the State of Tennessee*. He kept up an active correspondence with the publishers, sending them leads on booksellers interested in carrying the book or even directing interested parties to the Philadelphia offices of the publisher. He was determined to make the book a success. Most mornings in Washington, he met with admirers in the Library of Congress or near the post office to chat and probably promote his upcoming project.[26]

The autobiography was released in March, and Carey and Hart took out ads in newspapers all over the country announcing its arrival. Prominently displayed under the book's title in the advertisements was Crockett's motto, "I leave this rule for others when I am dead—Be always sure you're right, then go ahead." A nationwide marketing campaign had begun.

Crockett claimed in his introduction the need to set the record straight, to offer a more realistic portrayal of himself than the image projected by the earlier, unauthorized biography, and he did a masterful job in the *Narrative*. He toned down the half-horse, half-alligator characterizations that were predominant in French's book and focused instead on the story of pulling himself up from adversity, being his own man, and making sure he was right before going ahead. He told of his early years on the frontier, of his courtships and two marriages, and featured lively adventure tales of bear hunts and exploits in the backwoods. He devoted much space to his service in the Creek War, a subject French had altogether avoided, and painted a harrowing picture of the Indian massacres and battles in which he had participated. He told of his rise in politics, from the local level to the national stage, and he interjected biting criticism of Jackson and his minions throughout the work. He also made some fleeting references to his possible presidential aspirations, so the letter from the Mississippi delegation had clearly had at least a minimal effect. Crockett's heavy use of good natured humor in the book blunted the sting of his often vitriolic political attacks on the campaign trail and helped to reestablish him as an entertaining raconteur who knew a good deal more than he was letting on.

The *Narrative* was evidence of Crockett taking control of his own public image. He embellished or omitted details from his story that didn't further the persona he wanted to project, and, though the Crockett presented in the book wasn't a complete reinvention, he developed a character he could slip into with comfort. This Crockett was still homespun, but he was no fool; he might feign ignorance, but it was done with a nudge and a wink so that the reader was in on the joke. Above all, though, this character was a self-made man, beholden to no party, and steadfast in his support of the common man.

The public loved the book. If the French depiction of Crockett was popular, his own version was even more so, and the *Narrative* flew off the shelves. Publishers in Britain inquired about options, and Crockett was the toast of the town in Washington. Basking in the attention, he nevertheless anxiously awaited his royalty payments from Carey and Hart and wrote them asking for an accounting. "I am hard pressed in money matters," he said, and "wish barely to forme some opinion of the aid I may expect from the source."[27]

Feeling the pressure of an empty purse, Crockett wrote an irate letter to Jacob Dixon on the following day demanding that he settle a $200 debt incurred during a faro game. "Now I tell you to go and settle this," he demanded, "as you know you have got a great deal of money from me for no thing and I will not be imposed on in this way I have written plain and I will act as plain with you if you do not Settle this note I will be damned if I don't give you the bennefit of the law."[28]

Crockett made the Washington social scene at night, at one point accompanying his old acquaintance Sam Houston to a private function, while spending his days at his chair in the House tending to the nation's business. He still spoke up, but he was beginning to tire of the seemingly endless back-and-forth and looked forward to the recess. His anti-Jackson sentiments were as strong as ever, and his personal correspondence from the period lacks any attempt at levity. He railed about Jackson's removal of the deposits, compared Jackson to a dictator, and referred to Martin Van Buren as a "political Judas" and the president's followers as "imps of famine."[29] Though his anger is evident, there is also a note of despondency in some of his writing. In May he wrote "our long and happy mode of government is near at an end we may from present appearances soon bid fare well to our republican libertys we have completely the government of one man and he has tools and Slaves enough in the house of reprisentatives to sustain him in his wild carear I do believe his whole object is to promote the intrest of a set of scoundrals that care nothing for the good of the country."[30] He even expressed his fear that the country would be thrown into a civil war.[31]

He continued to hold to the hope that he would get his land bill passed, but was unable to get a hearing and, frustrated, told a constituent, "I have been trying for some time to get up my land Bill but we have not even passed the appropriation Bills and there is no chance to do any thing."[32] His dream of securing the lands for his poor constituents was still alive, but the hard reality of the situation was disheartening. Legislation was stalled, and Crockett felt he was being sandbagged. Earlier in the session he had formed a select seven-member committee, with himself as the chair, to review the disposition of the Tennessee public lands, but even that action had failed to move the process forward.[33] Crockett's frustration must have been reinforced by the knowledge that Congress had little interest in the issue. Many members had become as tired of the subject as Crockett was of much day-to-day business in the House.

Disgusted with the gridlock and partisanship in Washington, on April 25, well before the scheduled congressional recess, Crockett packed his bags and left town on a promotional tour of the northeastern states in support of his book. All along the way he was wined and dined by the Whigs, who were attracted by his fiery anti-Jackson rhetoric and happy to have him as a standard bearer for their cause. They needed someone like Crockett to connect with the common people in the West if they were to have any hope of defeating the Jacksonians in the 1836 presidential election. He might have seemed the perfect opposition for the stuffy, effete Martin Van Buren, Jackson's hand-picked successor and the likely nominee. Crockett's plain-spoken message and rugged individualism, now trumpeted by virtually every media outlet due to the overwhelming success of the *Narrative,* would surely continue to resonate with the people. At the very least, the Whigs might get up a few viable candidates, Crockett among them, and split the vote, again throwing the election into the House of Representatives, where they might enjoy a majority and secure the presidency. Either way, Crockett was a valuable asset and worth courting.

Crockett's long association with the Clay group was well established, and Whig sponsorship of his northeastern tour would elevate his public profile, sell more books, and put some much-needed money in his pocket. Despite his strong opposition to partisanship and his tendency to go it alone, he probably reasoned that an alliance with the Whigs might also help push his land bill through Congress. He certainly couldn't count on anyone in his own delegation to assist him in that regard. He believed that it was simple party politics that had cost him his last election, and he balked at the efforts of Polk, Van Buren, and their ilk to enforce party discipline on members of Congress, who he felt should have placed greater emphasis on representing their districts than party loyalty. Crockett continued to stress that he had been a Jackson man in principle, but that he reserved the right to chart his own course when he disagreed with the president, or anyone else for that matter. If anyone questioned his stance on partisanship, they needed only to refer to the closing lines of his autobiography to acquaint themselves with his position: "I am at liberty to vote as my conscience and judgment dictates to be right, without the yoke of any party on me, or the driver at my heels, with his whip in hand, commanding me to go-wo-haw, just at his pleasure. Look at my arms, you will find no party hand-cuff on them! Look at my neck, you will not find there any collar, with the engraving 'MY DOG. Andrew Jackson.' But you will find me standing up to my rack, as the people's faithful representative, and the public's most obedient, very humble servant."[34]

Crockett's attacks on Jackson in the *Narrative* were somewhat tempered by the adventure tales and humorous anecdotes he relied on to tell his life story, but the speeches he had on hand for his road show were more pointed. He felt that the president's removal of the deposits from the Second United States Bank, his inexcusable treatment of the Indians, his broken promise to serve only one term if elected, his reversal on internal improvements, and his dangerous and continual attempts to consolidate power in the executive branch of government provided conclusive evidence that Jackson had abandoned his principles. The congressman planned to deliver that message to the cities of the northeast, and he didn't intend to use subtlety.[35]

Crockett's first stop on the tour was Baltimore, a city he had visited as a youth when he dreamed of escaping the boredom of his backwoods existence and setting sail for London on one of the ships anchored in the harbor.[36] He stayed the night at Barnum's Hotel and set off the next morning for Philadelphia, no doubt looking forward to a face-to-face meeting with his publishers Carey and Hart. The first edition of the *Narrative* had sold out, and he was in constant contact with them, renegotiating prices for new editions and offering more bookseller leads. Before departing from Washington, he had asked for an advance of $150 to $200, likely needed to help finance his travels, and still cited the previous election's expenses as the cause for his financial problems. "I was beaten the election before last and it gave me a back set in money matters an election costs a man a great deal in my Country," he told them.[37]

He crossed the Chesapeake Bay in a steamboat and then boarded a railroad train, a new experience for him. He marveled at the speed of the train; "the whole distance is seventeen miles and it was run in fifty-five minutes," he remarked. At Delaware City he embarked on another steamboat for the remainder of the trek to Philadelphia.[38] An enormous crowd awaited him at the wharf, waving their hats and shouting, hoping for a handshake or at least a glimpse of the nation's newest celebrity. He was shuttled through the throng and pushed into a carriage, where he waved to the fans crowding the curbs all the way to his Chestnut Street hotel. The enthusiastic mob pressed around the front doors, doing their best to gain entrance to the lobby, and Crockett's handlers quickly herded him to a balcony overlooking the street, hoping to restore some sense of order by giving the crowd a taste of what they wanted: some small connection to the Lion of the West. Crockett finally quieted the gathering and said a few words, promising to entertain them with prepared remarks the following day, then disappeared inside the hotel. Later that evening, when the crowd had disbursed, he tried to unwind by taking a walk around the area before retiring for the night. He was anxious over the prospect of speaking to what promised to be a huge crowd the next day, and the huge reception at the harbor had been a little overwhelming. When he finally went to bed, he tossed and turned all night.[39]

The next morning Crockett had breakfast with some old friends from Washington, Judges Baldwin and Hemphill, and John Sergeant (who had run as a vice presidential candidate with Henry Clay in 1832), before being hustled around to some of the city's popular sites.[40] He was taken to the waterworks and the mint, but after observing the asylum for the mentally ill, he came away in a somber mood. "I felt monstrous solemn," he wrote, "and could not help thanking God I was not one of them; and I felt grateful in their stead to that city for caring for those who could not take care of themselves, and feeding them that heeded not the hand and heart that provided for them."[41]

He was still nervous about delivering his promised speech at the Philadelphia Exchange and wrote, "I had made stump speeches at home, in the face of all the little office yelpers that opposed me; but, indeed, when I got within sight of the Exchange, and saw the streets crowded, I most wished to take back my promise; but I was brought up by hearing a youngster say, as I passed by, 'Go ahead, Davy Crockett.' I said to myself, 'I have faced the enemy; these are friends. I have fronted the savage red man of the forest; these are civilized. I'll keep cool, and let them have it.'"[42]

Before an estimated crowd of five thousand, Crockett walked out on the balcony overlooking the street, took a deep breath, and delivered a blistering harangue against Jackson that must have delighted every Whig in attendance. He closed with the cautionary remark, "The stars and stripes must never give way to the shreds and patches of party,"[43] then paused and awaited the crowd's reaction. Cheers sprang up all around. When Crockett exited the Exchange, he was mobbed and spent nearly an hour shaking hands.

In the evening, he went to the Walnut Street theatre to see Thomas Rice in a minstrel performance as Jim Crow. Crockett's name had recently become associated with minstrel performances, where blackface musicians began adding verses about him to the already rambling structure of the song "Zip Coon."[44] Rice followed suit and improvised, incorporating Crockett's "Be always sure you're right, then go ahead" motto into the conclusion of one of his song and dance numbers, prompting tremendous cheers from the full house. Rice then bowed to Crockett, who, to the delight of the audience, repeated his famous *Lion of the West* performance with James Hackett by returning Rice's gesture.[45]

The next day Crockett was presented with a watch seal emblazoned with his "Go Ahead" motto and was promised a custom-made rifle by James Sanderson and the young Whigs of Pennsylvania. He was especially enthusiastic about this offer and provided all the specifications necessary for the production of the firearm. He then toured the Navy Yard and, at the end of the day, made his way back to his hotel to ready himself for the following morning's travel to New York.

The visit to Philadelphia set the template for the remainder of the tour. Crockett would arrive in a city, be greeted by admiring crowds and then whisked off to a hotel for lunch and a meet-and-greet with prominent Whig politicians. Speeches would be scheduled, and he'd spend his days visiting popular local sites and his nights at dinners and theatre performances. Newport, Providence, and Boston were all on the itinerary, and Crockett gave some variation of his excoriating anti-Jackson speech at each stop.

In Boston he took a break to sit for artist Chester Harding, who painted a beautiful portrait that was subsequently displayed in his gallery. During the sessions, Harding might have told Crockett about an earlier subject of his, Daniel Boone. The artist had searched out the elusive frontiersman some years earlier and found him near death in Missouri, consequently becoming the only artist to paint both Boone and Crockett from life.[46]

He spent a day touring the factories at Lowell, Massachusetts, came away with an increased appreciation for the manufacturing industry, and hoped that some day the South might embrace such a system. He marveled at the quality of the goods and the attitudes of the workers and, at the end of the visit, was presented with a broadcloth suit, of which he was very proud.[47] He also claimed to have changed his mind about protectionism and the tariff; that he had been enlightened after seeing Lowell and realized he had been wrong in thinking that the West was being taxed for the benefit of New England. "I saw I was opposing the best interest of the country, especially for the industrious poor man," he wrote.[48]

On a stop in Baltimore during the trip back to Washington, Crockett delivered his usual anti-Jackson tirade and reiterated his independence and disdain for political parties. In front of Barnum's Hotel, he railed at Jackson's despotism, voiced his support for the Bank, and reminded the crowd, "I broke off with Jacksonism whenever I found I could not be a freeman. I could not stand the lash of the whippers-in. 'Go with the party, go with the party,' was the everlasting argument. I got disgusted, and knew that the less you handle rotten eggs, the better chance you have of coming off with clean hands: so I cut loose."[49]

Crockett wrapped up the first leg of his tour and was back in Washington by May 15. The trip had been a high point of his career. After the embarrassing defeat in 1831 and his hard-fought, narrow victory in 1833, he must have felt a certain amount of validation in the sight of the large, adoring crowds and the attention lavished on him by the Whigs. His book was a bestseller, he was celebrated in song, portrayed on the stage, and his name was known far and wide. He was a national celebrity, the brightest star in the firmament, at least by popular standards. Some enterprising sculptor in Cincinnati had even cast his likeness in wax, setting the figure in a "beautiful forest room surrounded by a great number of wild animals," creating a striking, if unsettling, tableau.[50]

None of this went unnoticed by the Jacksonians, who were more determined than ever to stop the Crockett juggernaut in its tracks. They stonewalled him in Congress[51] and ridiculed him in the pro-administration press. Crockett's decision to leave Washington and begin his tour before the recess left him open to the same charges brought against him in the earlier campaigns: that he was derelict in his duty, as evidenced by his many absences. He offered a somewhat disingenuous excuse for his absenteeism, claiming, "As for retrenchment I have always wint for that I voted for it in committee of the whole but when the final vote was taken I was not there I had been for some time labouring under a complaint with a pain in my breast and I concluded to take a travel a couple of weeks for my health."[52] Crockett also argued that his record of attendance was no worse than that of any other congressman.

His detractors again floated accusations that Crockett had abused his franking privilege by shipping copious amounts of anti-Jackson material home to his district at public expense.[53] The opposition also attempted to use his fame against him. They asked "if his constituents elected him to a seat in Congress for the purpose of his there writing his life, instead of watching over and advocating their interests."[54] The old charges of ignorance and buffoonery were relaunched as well: "it is evident he is a most illiterate, profane, and disgusting simpleton," wrote a Deacon Boylston after speaking with Crockett in the rotunda of the capitol. "He is himself a complete burlesque—a laughing-stock for the whole nation. I am satisfied he is unfit for and unworthy of the place he holds. I am astonished at the notice that was taken of him on his journey—he is wholly unworthy of it."[55]

Washington likely seemed dull and stifling after the warm welcome he'd received on the tour, and Crockett was anxious for the session to end. He wrote to a friend, "There was nothing done while I was gone, more than to pass the Appropriation bill, which was obliged to pass as a matter of course. I was highly gratified with my trip. I had a great many fine present made to me. One rifle gun that must have cost at least $150, and a watch seal of fine gold that cost $40, and a fine suit of broadcloth from the woolen manufactory at Lowell, and many other smaller presents."[56] He wrote Carey and Hart of his plans to return to Philadelphia at the close of the session, but added, "I fear we are to have a long session and do but little good for the country."[57] Crockett's contributions to debates in the house were now liberally salted with overt anti-Jackson rhetoric, usually pertaining to Bank War issues, and his outbursts were often disruptive.[58] He made no secret that he was tired of the proceedings and the endless oratory that seemed to go nowhere, and some days he had his fill and simply walked out. He remarked, "I can stand *good nonsense*—rather like it—but *such nonsense* as they are digging at up yonder, it's no use trying to—I'm going home."[59]

It was probably during this period between the tour and the congressional recess that Crockett sat for yet another portrait, this time for Washington artist John Gadsby Chapman.[60] Crockett enjoyed Chapman's company and was glad to be away from the House chamber. He was still excited about his reception in the Northeast, and talked a good bit about the success of the *Narrative* and his efforts to promote the book. The adulation he'd experienced on the tour was in stark contrast to the hostility and rejection he received at the hands of his Washington colleagues. His vernacular and twisted syntax made for an entertaining read, but his rough grammar could be a stumbling block when trying to express himself before the erudite members of Congress. Crockett had focused on managing his public image, but there was little he could do to change the attitudes of some of the stuffed-shirts in Washington who looked upon him as an uneducated, low-class clown, unworthy of their attention. Their prejudice grated on him. Some in Congress may simply have been jealous of his status as a national celebrity, or resented it in a person on whom they looked down.

Chapman's first effort was a bust of Crockett, with the subject in a typical, static pose, gazing off to his left, the beginnings of a smile on his slightly parted lips. It was a nice enough portrait, but Crockett was unsatisfied and had hoped for something more from Chapman. "It's like all the other painters make of me," he complained, "a sort of cross between a clean-shirted member of Congress and a Methodist Preacher." Fresh from his travels around the country, Crockett had a better idea of what he wanted: an iconic image that would capture the essence of Davy Crockett, and yet retain the dignity of the real man that he had worked so hard to protect. He suggested that Chapman start over and think bigger. "If you could catch me on a bear-hunt in a 'harricane,'" he told the artist, "with hunting tools and gear, and a team of dogs, you might make a picture worth looking at."[61]

Chapman was enthusiastic, and the two began to collaborate on preliminary sketches; Chapman at his drawing board, Crockett looking over his shoulder, offering corrections and suggestions for better positioning of weapons and the all-important hunting dogs. They worked quickly, both excited by the prospect of something new and different. Crockett left the studio energized and spent the next couple of days scouring the city for wardrobe and accoutrements. He left no detail to chance. Since Chapman knew little to nothing about hunting in the wild, Crockett took complete charge and rustled up a well-worn hunting frock, buckskin leggings, and moccasins from some cobwebbed corner of the bustling city. He borrowed a rifle, a plain affair with no ornamentation that would reflect light and frighten off prey while on the hunt, and added a butcher knife and tomahawk to the package. Probably thinking of Nimrod Wildfire, he opted out of the over-the-top wildcat skin cap and topped off the outfit with a more practical wide-brimmed brown felt hat. All he needed was some dogs, but not just any dogs would suffice. These needed to be mixed-breed hounds, preferably showing some battle scars, so Chapman joined Crockett on a quick trip around the neighborhood to corral some likely candidates. Once all the elements were gathered together in the studio, Crockett slapped his hat on his head, cradled his rifle, and struck a pose amid the unruly hounds. Chapman settled in front of his easel, sketched out the scene, and began to paint.

The sessions went on for a few days, and, while Crockett made no negative comments, Chapman got the distinct impression that he was uncomfortable with the progress. He asked the colonel what was bothering him, but received a shrug in reply before Crockett shuffled out for the day. The next morning Crockett burst into the studio with a whoop, waving his hat over his head, and illustrating for Chapman what was wrong with the near-finished portrait: it needed energy and motion. The artist agreed completely and dug back into the painting, making modifications. When he was finished, the picture was a full-length work of art of which both men could be proud. It was a perfect merging of Davy and David, and exactly what Crockett desired. Chapman relocated to New York in November of 1834 and took the portrait with him.[62] In the spring of 1835, he exhibited the painting at the annual show at the New York Academy of Design. One reviewer commented "We are told that it is an excellent likeness. The face has less of a ruggedness than one would expect in the bear-hunter, but whether his fault or the artist's, we are not advised."[63]

This was a common complaint from the many people who stood in line to catch a glimpse of Crockett on his tour, or sought a brief audience with him in Washington. The myth was always bigger than the man. "His appearance disappointed hundreds," wrote one observer. "It was that of a plain, practical, unassuming man. He pretended nothing, and set up claims to nothing, except to be thought an honest man. His history proves that he is just such."[64] Another described him as "an intelligent, well-meaning gentleman, and although there are certain peculiarities in his speech, which are calculated to induce laughter, yet he is by no means so rough and uncultivated as we had been led to suppose."[65] A Pennsylvania paper said that Crockett's appearance at a public event had the effect of "leaving persons who expected to see a wild man of the woods, clothed in a hunting shirt and covered with hair, a good deal surprised at having viewed a respectable looking personage, dressed decently and wearing his locks after the fashion of our plain German farmers."[66] Crockett was well aware of their expectations, and occasionally complied. Chapman tells of the colonel preparing to receive tourists in his rooms at Mrs. Ball's by donning a hat inside, as if he didn't know better, and lounging with his leg thrown over the arm of a chair when the guests entered. He shook hands, still seated, and regaled the visitors with humorous anecdotes delivered in an exaggerated drawl. Once he'd fulfilled his obligations and the party had been ushered out, Crockett threw his hat aside and regained his customary composure. "They came to see a bar," he told Chapman, likely with a wink, "and they've seen one."[67]

Crockett likely sat for another artist, Anthony Lewis DeRose, around the same time, but with a more commercial project in mind. DeRose proposed to paint an image of the congressman that he would then forward to engraver Asher Durand, who would strike a number of lithographs to be offered for sale. DeRose and Durand planned to sell the prints for fifty cents apiece, and DeRose was certain that "many will sell in Baltimore, where Crockett is an especial favorite."[68] The colonel added a personal touch and scratched his now familiar motto, "Be always sure you're right, then go ahead," beneath the image. It is not known how much of the proceeds went to Crockett.

On June 15, Crockett wrote to James Sanderson, who had contacted him to apprise him of the progress on the rifle that had been promised him by the Whigs in Philadelphia. Sanderson had sent Crockett a target used during the gun's first firing exercise, and Crockett offered some suggestions on realigning the sights. He mentioned that he hoped to be in the city for the Fourth of July festivities, and was clearly anxious to get his hands on the new rifle. He asked Sanderson to buy him some canister powder and percussion caps, and promised to reimburse him when they met.[69] Bored to distraction with Washington and the daily grind, he finally bolted a day before the end of the session and headed back out on the road toward Philadelphia and, eventually, Tennessee. On July 1 the Whigs presented Crockett with his rifle, an ornate and beautiful weapon he christened "Pretty Betsey,"[70] and he spent the next day in Camden, New Jersey, trying it out.

On the Fourth of July, he shared a Philadelphia stage with prominent Whig leader Daniel Webster and others in a huge Independence Day celebration. Crockett was called upon to speak and was a bit intimidated in following Webster, one of the great orators of his day.[71] He had reportedly joked with Webster upon meeting him in Washington some years before, "I heard that you were a great man, but I don't think so. I heard your speech and understood every word you said."[72] Crockett began his speech with a deferential tone, and then delivered an abbreviated version of his now standard anti-Jackson screed.

When asked to speak again later in the day at another location, Crockett veered away from his semi-scripted remarks and attempted to explain his alliance with the Jacksonians in the early years of his career. "I was one that was deceived, among many others," he told the crowd, "and was made to believe that Messrs. Adams and Clay were two of the greatest scoundrels on the face of the earth. I joined the band, and raised the war whoop against them; and finally we succeeded in putting them down—thus supposing we were serving the Lord and General Jackson. But I found, by personal acquaintance of those gentlemen, that they had been grossly misrepresented, and saw it was a political speculation—a fuss, kicked up just to promote a certain set of men's own interests."[73]

Crockett moved on to Pittsburgh, Wheeling, and Cincinnati, again giving speeches and meeting with local Whigs. He had begun to close his performances with codas such as, "May the Whigs increase in numbers and grow in strength, and send one to represent them that can serve his country, instead of being the tool of a party."[74] If he was referring to himself, then he was also delivering to his hosts an open caveat that he intended to remain his own man. After quick stops in Louisville, Kentucky, the heart of Clay country, and Indiana, Crockett finally headed for home.

There was no "hail the conquering hero" reception awaiting him upon his arrival in Weakley County; there were no crowds, no formal dinners, no lavish gifts. Back home he was no novelty, but merely another public servant who had, thus far, been unable to keep his promises. His critics continued to point out his shortcomings in the local newspapers, and his constituents were asking hard questions of him.

There were also pressing personal problems during his hiatus. Crockett's father had recently died, and he was named as one of the executors of the small estate. He was facing more legal challenges of his own for old, outstanding debts again as well.[75]

All the traveling had put even more strain on his finances, and he was already hearing rumblings about possible challengers in the next congressional campaign. The Jacksonians were gearing up to unseat him, and by October word was leaked to the press that they had tapped his old nemesis Adam Huntsman, "Black Hawk," the author of the "Book of Chronicles" articles, to oppose him.[76] One paper quipped, "A *skinning* contest may be expected between the *Great Huntsman* of Madison and the *Great Hunter* of Weakley."[77]

Crockett's opposition had urged Huntsman to run against him back in 1829, but the Madison County lawyer had declined, claiming that he found Crockett's style of electioneering distasteful and undignified. "To go up creeks," he wrote, "down valleys, over hills, and into the dales for the purpose of collecting votes, as a tax gatherer would his tax, or a cow driver to buy cattle; and in doing this, frequently propogates or gives currency to lies, slanders and detractions against other candidates, is so far descending beneath the dignity of a man, or the independence of a correct politician, that I would not condescend to such an act of degradation."[78]

Huntsman may have opted out of running, but he was an active participant in the opposition party during the 1831 election, and his "Chronicles" articles certainly helped William Fitzgerald unseat Crockett. In 1833 Huntsman again took a very public stance with Fitzgerald against Crockett, which probably contributed to the closeness of the contest. Crockett's narrow margin of victory left him little room for error, and he would find that "Black Hawk" was a much better campaigner than Fitzgerald had been.

Huntsman was a colorful figure. A war veteran with a wooden leg to show for his service, he was well known in Tennessee for his quick wit, and, despite his protestations, his stump style was a match for Crockett's. He was also riding high in public approval due to his participation and leadership in the long awaited Tennessee constitutional convention, which had finally taken place in the summer of 1834. Huntsman's efforts to more evenly distribute the burden of state property taxes had been of great benefit to poor and middle-class landholders and put him in a good position to cut into Crockett's voter base.[79]

In October, Crockett wrote again to his friends at the Second Bank of the United States and to his publishers, Carey and Hart, for an accounting of his royalties, hoping to find some money to help offset his traveling expenses to Washington for the second session of Congress.[80] In the end, he borrowed another $300 from a neighbor and headed back to Washington in November.[81]

Huntsman began canvassing almost immediately, and by January 1835 had visited nearly every county in the district. He thought his chances were good. "Crockett is evidently loosing ground or otherwise he never was as strong as I supposed him to be," he wrote James Polk. "Perhaps it is both. If my friends take anything of a lively interest in it I think my prospects are as good as usual. He is eternally sending Anti Jackson documents here and it has its effect. If he carries his land Bill it will give him strength. Otherwise, the conflict will not be a difficult one."[82]

Crockett knew that passage of the land bill was his only hope, but his every effort to push it forward had been thwarted. Now, even congressmen who had been nominally supportive were losing interest, and Crockett must have felt a sense of desperation. He was running out of time and had little to show for the three terms he had served. His latest attempt at funding internal improvements to make the Obion, Forked Deer, and Hatchie Rivers more navigable, which would have helped to lower the cost of consumer goods, had failed.[83] He had done his best to protect the poor of his district, but they weren't much better off than they had been in 1827. He was still struggling to repay personal debts and was now facing a tough reelection campaign with an empty war chest and a shallow record of accomplishment. From his perspective, the future of the nation looked bleak as well, as Martin Van Buren's star seemed on the rise. "I have almost given up the Ship as lost," Crockett wrote. "I have gone so far as to declare that if he martin vanburen is elected that I will leave the united States for I will never live under his kingdom Before I will Submit to his Government I will go to the wildes of Texas."[84]

On December 27, Crockett joined other members of the Tennessee delegation, with the notable exceptions of Felix Grundy, Cave Johnson, and Polk, in drafting a petition to promote Hugh Lawson White as an alternative presidential candidate to Van Buren. While Andrew Jackson had expressed a clear preference for Van Buren as his successor, the New Yorker was not a popular figure among most westerners. Crockett, in particular, despised him, seeing in Van Buren everything he hated most about partisanship and backroom political maneuvering. Other Tennesseans had long memories and still resented efforts by northeastern interests to keep the state out of the Union back in 1796 for fear it would support Jefferson over Federalist candidates.[85] Whether the objections to Van Buren were regional or personal, for once a majority of the Tennessee delegates were in agreement: "Little Van" was an unacceptable candidate.

White had an impressive resume, which included serving on the Tennessee Supreme Court and as a U.S. district attorney before being elected to the state legislature and serving in the U.S. Senate. He had been a friend of Jackson's and a prominent member of John Overton's political network in

Tennessee, serving as president of one of Overton's banks. After voting against confirming Van Buren as minister to Great Britain in 1831, however, White had been on the outs with Old Hickory.[86] The typically vindictive Jackson, upon hearing of the plan to encourage White to run for president, issued an angry threat that if White accepted, he would ruin his reputation in the state. White had expressed little interest in the offer until Jackson threatened him and, perhaps as a matter of personal pride, he decided to stand up to the president's bullying and exercise his right to seek the office. "Despotic power has never governed me," White wrote, "and never shall govern me."[87]

Jackson was livid and directed his ire against the men he perceived to be the ringleaders of the movement, Crockett and Congressman John Bell. During his tenure in the House, Bell had opposed Jackson frequently, although never in such a vehement manner as had Crockett, and Jackson already considered him a bitter enemy. He now focused his efforts on crushing both men who dared defy him. Jackson wrote "Mr. Bell, Davy Crockett & Co. had placed judge White in the odious attitude of abandoning principle & party for office. . . . Political demagogues, hypocrites, and apostates, may delude the people for a short time, but the moment the deception, and abandonment of principle, is discovered, the people will hurl them from their confidence, and the recoil is overwhelming. Just so with Mr. Bell, Davy Crockett and Co."[88] It was Jackson's fervent wish to see "Mr Bell Davy Crockett and Co, hurled as they ought, from the confidence of the people,"[89] and he intended to use his considerable influence in the state and as president to bring about that result.

While Jackson plotted Crockett's political annihilation, Richard Lawrence, a thirty-five-year-old Washington house painter, was plotting the assassination of the president. On January 30, Lawrence confronted Jackson on the eastern portico of the Capitol, where the president was attending a funeral, and leveled two pistols at his breast, both of which, miraculously, misfired. Jackson, true to form, raised his cane and shouted that he could defend himself, but was hustled off into a waiting carriage. Crockett, who was in attendance, shouted, "I wanted to see the damndest villain in the world, and now I have seen him," and helped subdue Lawrence until he could be taken into custody.[90] Jackson, his anger edging near paranoia, spared the reputations of Crockett and Bell in this instance and made the ridiculous claim that another of his enemies, George Poindexter, was behind the assault. Lawrence was later found to have been a longtime sufferer of mental illness and was institutionalized.[91]

Crockett, fighting for his political life, continued to flood his district with anti-administration propaganda, taking advantage of his free franking privilege to alleviate the costs,[92] and in February made a last-ditch attempt to get his land bill through the House.

After riding on the fast track during his tour, he had even less patience with the slow pace of business in the capitol and remarked from the floor that "The House was within four weeks of the termination of the session, and many important bills were pressing for consideration, which had been postponed, from time to time, to hear gentlemen make speeches. Look back to last session and it would be seen that seven months were almost entirely consumed in long speeches."[93] His frustration was evident during a debate about relief for citizens of Arkansas who had lost property due to a treaty with the Choctaw. Crockett said that he favored the bill, but then sarcastically remarked that "speaking had become so fashionable on that floor, in this pressing stage of the business of the session, that he began to believe in the doctrine that silence was a virtue."[94]

Finally, on February 20, in an inexplicable show of bipartisanship, William C. Dunlap, a Jacksonian, asked the House to take up the land bill again.[95] Before the motion was considered, Crockett rose and asked to make "a few explanations on the subject" of the bill, but resumed his seat when objections were made. It was apparent that the House had tired of Crockett's interruptions and sarcasm and that the Jacksonian majority, despite Dunlap's gesture, was not about to give him another chance to argue for a bill that could get him reelected. Their goal was to destroy Crockett, and whatever support he had gotten from the Whigs was not enough to overcome that obstacle. The motion to hear the bill failed, and Crockett did not attempt to bring it up again.[96] Unable to claim any real progress on behalf of his constituents in the current term, he desperately needed to find another way to preserve his seat. His only option was to run a totally negative reelection campaign and hope for a miracle.

In December, he had pitched Carey and Hart on an idea for another book, a "history" of his recent, successful northeast tour.[97] While they seemed less than enthusiastic, the publisher likely found it hard to say no to a bestselling author and eventually gave the project the go-ahead. Crockett enlisted fellow congressman William Clark to help him and, over the course of a couple of months, the two men patched together a cut-and-paste scrapbook of anecdotes and speeches culled from various newspapers around the country. Crockett desperately needed money, and book royalties seemed an obvious way to augment the $8 per day he received as a congressman in lieu of a salary. He received a $200 advance on the book,[98] which helped tide him over but, unfortunately, *An Account of Colonel Crockett's Tour to the North and Down East,* released in late March 1835, was not well received. Crockett mistakenly expected the fire-and-brimstone anti-Jackson rhetoric that had excited the crowds during his travels to do the same for the book-buying public, but they wanted adventures about bear hunting and witty stories of backwoods life. *Tour* did not deliver. In the *Southern Literary Messenger,* Edgar Allan Poe wrote, "We see no reason why Col. Crockett should not be permitted to expose himself if he pleases, and to be as much laughed at as he thinks proper—but works of this kind have had their day, and have fortunately lost their attractions. We think this work especially censurable for the frequent vulgarity of its language."[99]

Even while *Tour* was still in the works, Crockett pitched Carey and Hart another idea he hoped would bring in some cash, this time proposing a satirical biography of Martin Van Buren. The publishers were understandably wary about producing the title, fearing libel, but Crockett eventually had his way, and *The Life of Martin Van Buren, Heir Apparent to the "Government" and the Appointed Successor of General Andrew Jackson,* was issued. Crockett had virtually nothing to do with the writing of the book. That was handled by his friend, Georgia senator Augustin Clayton, but if the concept wasn't completely his own, it earned his wholehearted endorsement, and he affixed his name to the title page.[100] Carey and Hart, however, chose to omit their imprint.

The Van Buren "biography" was a hatchet job, a piece of propaganda that was welcomed by the anti-Jackson press and reviled by the administration's supporters, and it did little to increase either Crockett's finances or his literary aspirations. He had more popular success with another round of exchanges in the press with Seba Smith's Major Jack Downing character, but Jackson had taken to playing Crockett's own game and was inundating his congressional district with copies of the official presidential organ, *The Globe,* and other material that depicted the congressman in an unfavorable light, all under the presidential frank.[101]

Upon his return to Tennessee at the end of the session, Crockett barely had time to take a breath before hitting the campaign trail. He had hoped that a third announced candidate, James McMeans, might split the vote to his advantage, but McMeans quickly dropped out of the race. Huntsman had gotten a jump on Crockett on the stump, and the colonel had given him plenty of ammunition. The tour had boosted his image nationally, but at home Huntsman was reminding people that Crockett had gone off on his publicity-seeking venture during the congressional session rather than waiting for the recess. Consequently, Huntsman reasoned, Crockett owed the taxpayers $8 a day for all the time he'd missed. He also charged that Crockett had padded his expense account by overbilling mileage,[102] an accusation Crockett had leveled at Fitzgerald in the last election. Most damaging of all however, was the reminder that despite all his promises, Crockett had failed to deliver on the land bill. He had been given a second and a third chance and, Huntsman argued, his time was up.

The pro-Jackson press revived the old charge that Crockett was a dupe of the Whigs and ignored his long connections with the pro-Clay, Erwin faction in Tennessee. Crockett saw the Tennessee congressional delegation as the political arm of the monied land speculators who preyed on his constituents, a tenable position considering their repeated attempts to defeat his version of the land bill and promote a variation more favorable to investors.[103] The Clay contingent in Washington had given him the opportunity to raise his public profile, which he hoped would bring him greater esteem and, with it, the additional clout to push his land bill through. Unfortunately, Crockett miscalculated. Though the northeastern tour was a personal triumph, it was a political mistake. His absence from the session and his missed votes enabled the competition to portray him as a man more concerned with personal advancement than looking out for the welfare of his constituents.

Despite his own tenuous situation and the strength of his opposition, Crockett continued to put on a brave face. Still hoping to capitalize on literary revenue to support his campaign, he stayed in touch with Carey and Hart and wrote of Huntsman, "I have no doubt of beating him with ease,"[104] but in an earlier personal letter, in which he had expressed a degree of confidence that he would win, he had confessed, "I cannot tell I am determened to do my duty if I should niver See another Congress."[105]

Crockett campaigned as effectively as his empty pockets would allow, throwing around as many charges against Huntsman as he could muster, but there was really little of substance to offer. Huntsman, on the other hand, had only to point out Crockett's failings and his own opposition to the tariff, the U.S. Bank, and his states' rights stance. Ultimately, Huntsman's momentum was too much for Crockett to overcome, and when the August election results came in, Huntsman was the victor, defeating Crockett by a small margin. The Jacksonian press gloated, "The buffoon may now play his antics to the varmints of the forest, or join a caravan and grin for the amusement of 'lookers on.'"[106] Another wrote, "The Colonel can now indulge in literary leisure, and herein the reading public will be vastly benefited."[107] A Connecticut paper said, "Crockett will find the business of 'Coon hunting' which he will now resume, much better suited to his genius than legislation. The Whigs have used him until he is used up."[108]

The colonel did not take the loss well. In a letter to the *National Intelligencer* he blamed his loss on Jackson's intervention and accused Huntsman of buying votes and election tampering. "In fact," he wrote, "I am astonished that I came out near as beating him as I did." He signed off with the foreboding admonition, "I do believe Santa Ana's kingdom will be a paradise, compared with this, in a few years. The people are nearly ready to take the yoke of bondage, and say Amen! Jackson done it—it is all right!"[109]

On August 11 he broke the news to Carey and Hart, repeating the same charges he had publicly leveled, insisting, "I come within 250 votes of being elected not withstanding I had to contend against the greatest & best with the whole powar of the treasury against me . . . if I am never a gain elected I will have the grattification to know that I have done my duty."[110]

Angry and hurt over the rejection, Crockett also may have felt a sense of relief. His last term had been sheer drudgery, the only high points being the popularity of his book and the 1834 tour, and he had learned something on that excursion. What he enjoyed most about politics wasn't legislating, but meeting and interacting with people along the way. He loved to see the faces in the crowd light up when he told another hunting story or spun a yarn that got them laughing and shouting for more. He wasn't in it for the money; the eight dollars a day never stretched very far, and running for Congress had kept him in the hole financially. It was the people. Celebrity had brought him to the center of the crowd, and he liked it there. Now, the crowds had dispersed, and he was back in Weakley County facing an uncertain future, but Crockett had never been a quitter. He had been down before and had always managed to right himself and move forward. There might not be much opportunity left for him in Tennessee, but there was always "Santa Ana's kingdom"—Texas.

"I am on the eve of starting to the Texes," Crockett wrote, "on to morrow morning my Self Abner Burgin and Lindsy K Tinkle & our Nephew William Patton from the lowar Country this will make our company we will go through Arkinsaws and I want to explore the Texes well before I return."[111] He may have been planning to make good on his promise to leave the country rather than live under a Van Buren administration; he may have been seduced by the articles and advertisements that appeared in almost every newspaper reporting riches beyond compare; or he may have simply been looking for another adventure; but, whatever the motivation, Texas beckoned.

Though his political career was over, at least for the foreseeable future, Crockett discovered that his celebrity status was intact, and the press reported his every move as he traveled. He was wined and dined all the way to Texas, and was greeted by enthusiastic crowds hoping to catch a glimpse of the "Lion of the West." In Nacogdoches he told his admirers, "I am told, gentlemen, that, when a stranger, like myself, arrives among you, the first inquiry is—what brought him here? To satisfy your curiosity at once as to myself, I will tell you all about it. I was, for some years, a member of Congress. In my last canvass, I told the people of my District, that, if they saw fit to re-elect me, I would serve them as faithfully as I had done; but, if not, they might go to h-ll and I would go to Texas. I was beaten, gentlemen, and here I am."[112]

Crockett's time in Texas was short, and his death at the Alamo on March 6, 1836, insured his place in history. Eulogists rhapsodized about his glorious demise, and the legend of Davy Crockett, frontier fighter, flourished. Ultimately, despite his own best efforts to control the image during his lifetime, Crockett's mythological persona eclipsed the plainspoken gentleman from the cane, and, while his sacrifice in defense of Texas liberty should never be forgotten, his tireless efforts on behalf of his poor and working-class constituents should also be honored. Before Crockett was lionized, before he was crowned king of the wild frontier, he was the poor man's friend.

---

[1] Crockett's party affiliation during the Twenty-third Congress was listed as Anti-Jacksonian. There is no evidence that he ever formally joined the Whigs, although he clearly grew closer to them during his final term in Congress. Biographical Directory of the United States Congress online, http://bioguide.congress.gov.

[2] *Portland (Maine) Advertiser,* December 24, 1833; *(Portland, Maine) Eastern Argus,* December 23, 1833. It is possible that Crockett saw an abbreviated, two-act version of the play. An advertisement for a December 10, 1833, performance in the *Baltimore Gazette and Daily Advertiser* lists Hackett as Nimrod Wildfire in "a Drama, in two acts, founded on 'The Lion of the West,' and performed with great success in London, New York, Philadelphia and Boston called, THE KENTUCKIAN; or A TRIP TO NEW YORK."

[3] *(Poughkeepsie, New York) Independence,* October 19, 1833; *Salem (Massachusetts) Gazette,* May 6, 1834.

[4] Mossie was paying tribute to the recently deceased John Randolph, a congressman and senator from Virginia known for his oratorical skills.

[5] *Salem Gazette,* May 23, 1834.

[6] *Pittsfield (Massachusetts) Sun,* July 18, 1833, reprinting an article from the *Pennsylvanian.*

[7] *(Jackson) Southern Statesman,* September 14, 1833.

[8] *The Diary of John Quincy Adams,* ed. Alan Nevins (New York: Longmans, Green, and Co., 1928), 444–45, as quoted in Joseph John Arpad, "David Crockett, An Original Legendary Eccentricity and Early American Character." Ph.D. dissertation, Duke University, 1968, 181.

[9] Crockett to Henry Storrs, January 9, 1834, collection of Buffalo & Erie County Historical Society (mss. A00-110). The letter appears to be in Thomas Chilton's hand, but signed by Crockett.

[10] Ibid.

[11] Ibid.

[12] Crockett to John Wesley Crockett, January 10, 1834, Thomas W. Streeter Collection of Texas Manuscripts. Yale Collection of Western Americana, Beinecke Rare Book and Manuscript Library.

[13] Crockett to John O. Cannon, January 20, 1834, courtesy of the Phil Collins Collection.

[14] Plymouth Delegation to Crockett, January 12, 1834, *New-York Spectator,* March 10, 1834.

[15] Crockett to Mississippi delegation, February 24, 1834, *New Bedford Mercury,* March 14, 1834.

[16] David Crockett, *A Narrative of the Life of David Crockett of the State of Tennessee,* ed. James A. Shackford and Stanley J. Folmsbee, (Knoxville: University of Tennessee Press, 1973), 7.

[17] Alexander Saxton, *The Rise and Fall of the White Republic* (London and New York: Verso, 2003), 82.

[18] Crockett to Carey and Hart, February 3, 1834, Tennessee State Library and Archives (TSLA). This letter also appears to be in Chilton's hand, but signed by Crockett.

[19] Ibid.

[20] Crockett to Carey and Hart, February 23, 1834, courtesy of the Trustees of the Boston Public Library/Rare Books.

[21] Crockett to Mr. Reeves, February 3, 1834, The Huntington Library, San Marino, CA.

22 Crockett to S. S. Osgood, February 23, 1834, DRT Library at the Alamo.

23 Inscription on an 1834 Albert Newsam lithograph after Osgood portrait, National Portrait Gallery, Smithsonian Institution.

24 The original Osgood portrait was destroyed in a fire at the Texas Capitol in 1881. Another engraving based on the painting, by T. B. Welch, bears little resemblance to the Newsam print issued by Childs and Lehman, which was criticized for its inaccuracy, so there is no surviving image that gives an adequate representation of the Osgood painting. For more information see Frederick S. Voss, "Portraying an American Legend: The Likenesses of Davy Crockett," *Southwestern Historical Quarterly* 91, no. 4 (April 1988): 459–61, and Jim Boylston, "Crockett, Boone, and the Chester Harding Matrix," *Crockett Chronicle* 1, no. 1 (August 2003): 3–5.

25 *Brattleboro Messenger,* January 24, 1834.

26 Ibid.

27 Crockett to Carey and Hart, April 10, 1834, courtesy of General Collection, Beinecke Rare Book and Manuscript Library, Yale University.

28 Crockett to Jacob Dixon, April 11, 1834, *Christie's Auction Catalog,* June 17, 2003, item 74.

29 Crockett to John Drurey, April 4, 1834, Gilder Lehrman Collection, GLC00931; Crockett to Joseph Wallis, May 26, 1834, typescript in DRT Library at the Alamo.

30 Crockett to T. J. Dobings, May 27, 1834, courtesy of the Lilly Library, Indiana University, Bloomington, Indiana.

31 Crockett to John Drurey, April 4, 1834.

32 Crockett to T. J. Dobings, May 27, 1834.

33 *Congressional Globe,* December 17, 1833, 37.

34 Crockett, *Narrative of the Life,* 210–11.

35 David Crockett, *An Account of Col. Crockett's Tour to the North and Down East* (Baltimore: E. L. Carey and A. Hart, 1835), 68–74.

36 Crockett, *Narrative of the Life,* 36–37.

37 Crockett to Carey and Hart, March 25, 1834, cited in James Atkins Shackford, *David Crockett: The Man and the Legend* (Chapel Hill: University of North Carolina Press, 1956), 152.

38 Crockett, *An Account of Col. Crockett's Tour,* 16–17.

39 Ibid., 17–20.

40 While Sergeant was a Whig, Hemphill had registered as a Jacksonian during his last term.

41 Crockett, *An Account of Col. Crockett's Tour,* 22.

42 Ibid., 22–23.

43 Ibid., 32.

44 *Nashville Banner and Whig,* March 3, 1834.

45 *Pittsfield (Massachusetts) Sun,* May 8, 1834; *Baltimore Gazette,* April 29, 1834. "Colonel Crockett's March," by H. Dielman, also was published by John Cole and Son of Baltimore, followed a year later by "Go Ahead—A March Dedicated to Colonel Crockett" (aka "The Crockett Victory March"), published by Firth and Hall in New York. Both instrumentals may have been simple adaptations of older marches, but reflected Crockett's growing celebrity. See Allen J. Wiener and William R. Chemerka, *Music of the Alamo: From 19th Century Ballads to Big-Screen Soundtracks* (Houston: Bright Sky Press, 2009), 123.

46 Boylston, "Crockett, Boone, and the Chester Harding Matrix," 3–5.

47 Crockett, *An Account of Col. Crockett's Tour,* 91–99.

48 Ibid., 78–79.

49 Ibid., 110–111.

50 *Nashville Banner and Whig,* November 12, 1834.

51 *Register of Debates,* May 16, 1834, 4138, and June 23, 1834, 4701; *Congressional Globe,* June 28, 1834, 465, and December 11, 1834, 31.

52 Crockett to William Hack, June 9, 1834, TSLA.

53 *Richmond Enquirer,* May 30, 1834.

54 *(Nashville) National Banner and Daily Advertiser,* August 1, 1834.

55 *(Concord) New Hampshire Patriot* and *State Gazette,* June 9, 1834.

56 Crockett to a friend in Huntingdon, Tennessee, May 28, 1834, from *(San Francisco) Evening Bulletin,* October 23, 1886.

57 Crockett to Carey and Hart, May 27, 1834, New York Public Library.

58 *Register of Debates,* June 13, 1834, 4467–68.

59 Curtis Carroll Davis, "A Legend at Full-Length: Mr. Chapman Paints Colonel Crockett—and Tells About It," *Proceedings of the American Antiquarian Society* 69 (1960): 173.

60 The painting was done in Washington in 1834 and, according to Chapman, while Crockett was living at Mrs. Ball's. During the second session of the Twenty-third Congress, Crockett moved to Brown's Hotel, so it seems likely that this

stated time period is correct.

61 Davis, "A Legend at Full-Length," 165.

62 Ibid., 165–70.

63 Voss, "Portraying an American Legend," 473.

64 *New Bedford Mercury,* May 9, 1834.

65 *Richmond Enquirer,* May 13, 1834.

66 Stanley J. Folmsbee and Anna Grace Catron, "David Crockett: Congressman," *East Tennessee Historical Society's Publications* 29 (1957): 72.

67 Davis, "A Legend at Full-Length," 172–73.

68 Anthony DeRose to Asher Durand, June 20, 1834, Asher Durand papers, New York Public Library, microfilmed by the Archives of American Art, Smithsonian Institution, Microfilm reel number N19.

69 Crockett to James Sanderson, June 25, 1834, Historical Society of Pennsylvania.

70 Texas Jim Cooper, "A Study of Some David Crockett Firearms," *East Tennessee Historical Society Publications* 38 (1968), reprinted in Herbert L. Harper (ed.), *Houston and Crockett: Heroes of Tennessee and Texas—an Anthology* (Nashville: Tennessee Historical Commission, 1986), 238–39.

71 Crockett, *An Account of Col. Crockett's Tour,* 126.

72 *(Columbus) Ohio State Journal,* May 2, 1855.

73 Crockett, *An Account of Col. Crockett's Tour,* 135–36.

74 Ibid., 157–58.

75 Shackford, *David Crockett: The Man and the Legend,* 170.

76 *Philadelphia Inquirer,* October 28, 1834.

77 *Nashville Banner and Whig,* October 8, 1834, quoting the *(Jackson, Tennessee) Truth Teller.*

78 *Jackson Gazette,* July 5, 1828, quoted in Chase C. Mooney, "The Political Career of Adam Huntsman," *Tennessee Historical Quarterly* 10, no. 2 (June 1951): 115.

79 Robert E. Corlew, *Tennessee: A Short History* (Knoxville: University of Tennessee Press, 1981), 164–65.

80 Crockett to Carey and Hart, October 9, 1834, *Swann Galleries Auction Catalog 1863,* June 8, 2000, Lot 18.

81 *Dallas Morning News,* December 25, 1927.

82 Huntsman to James K. Polk, January 1, 1835, in Herbert Weaver, ed., and Paul H. Bergeron, assoc. ed., *Correspondence of James K. Polk, Volume 3, 1835–1836* (Knoxville: University of Tennessee Press, 1975), 3.

83 *Register of Debates,* December 11, 1834, 781.

84 Crockett to Charles Schultz, December 25, 1834, Gilder Lehrman Collection, GLC01162.

85 Joshua W. Caldwell, "John Bell of Tennessee: A Chapter of Political History," *American Historical Review* 4, no. 4 (July 1899): 652–53.

86 Phillip Langsdon, *Tennessee: A Political History* (Franklin, Tenn.: Hillsboro Press, 2000), 66–67.

87 Powell Moore, "The Revolt Against Jackson in Tennessee, 1835–1836," *Journal of Southern History* 2, no. 3 (August 1936): 336.

88 Jackson to James Polk, May 3, 1835, *Correspondence of James K. Polk, Vol. 3,* 182–83.

89 Jackson to James Polk, May 12, 1835, *Correspondence of James K. Polk, Vol. 3,* 191.

90 *Nashville Banner and Whig,* February 16, 1835; Crockett to R. R. Waldron, February 2, 1835, *Charles Hamilton Autograph Catalog,* September 22, 1966, item 62.

91 Jon Meacham, *American Lion: Andrew Jackson in the White House* (New York: Random House, 2008), 299–300.

92 David Jarrett to James Polk, May 15, 1834, in Herbert Weaver, ed., and Paul H. Bergeron, assoc. ed., *Correspondence of James K. Polk, Volume 2, 1833–1834* (Knoxville: University of Tennessee Press, 1972), 428.

93 *Congressional Globe,* February 4, 1835, 199.

94 *Congressional Globe,* February 13, 1835, 241.

95 There was apparently no love lost between Crockett and Dunlap. In June of 1835, Dunlap wrote Polk asking him to confirm that he had been present in Washington for a period during which Crockett claimed Dunlap had been absent. Dunlap to James K. Polk, June 28, 1835, *Correspondence of James K. Polk, Vol. 3,* 228.

96 *Congressional Globe,* February 14, 1835, 245–47.

97 Crockett to Carey and Hart, December 8, 1834, by permission of the Houghton Library, Harvard University (Autograph File C).

98 Crockett to Carey and Hart, January 8, 1835, Vertical file, H. Furlong Baldwin Library, Maryland Historical Society.

99 *Southern Literary Messenger* 1, no. 8 (April 1835): 459.

100 Crockett to Carey and Hart, April 16, 1835, Haverford College Library, Haverford PA, Special Collections, Charles Roberts Autograph Letters Collection; Crockett to Carey and Hart, January 22, 1835, Rosenbach Museum & Library,

Philadelphia, PA, (AMs 773/3).

[101] Moore, "The Revolt Against Jackson in Tennessee, 1835–1836," 344; *(Brattleboro)Vermont Phoenix,* September 18, 1835, reprinting Crockett letter from the *National Intelligencer.*

[102] *Portsmouth (New Hampshire) Journal of Literature and Politics,* September 12, 1835. This article states that fabricated documents regarding Crockett's mileage reports, in the handwriting of Jackson's secretary, Andrew Donelson, and sent under Jackson's frank, were also introduced into the argument. Huntsman denied Jackson's involvement and said that he had attempted to get reports of Crockett's per diem charges during his tour from John Bell, then a Crockett ally, to no avail. He subsequently asked Donelson for the records. *(Concord) New Hampshire Patriot,* October 26, 1835.

[103] Crockett's opponents urged James Polk to vote against the land bill in an effort to defeat him. "If Crockett gets his land bill through he is Statesman of while he lives under all circumstances & in behalf of our Country, I think it would be best to Voat against it at the preasant Session or postpone the final decision until another Congress." David Jarrett to James Polk, May 15, 1834, in *Correspondence of James K. Polk, Volume 2, 1833–1834,* 428.

[104] Crockett to Carey and Hart, April 16, 1835, Haverford College Library, Haverford PA, Special Collections, Charles Roberts Autograph Letters Collection.

[105] Crockett to John P. Ash, December 27, 1834, University Archives and Special Collections, Sewanee: The University of the South.

[106] *Eastern Argus,* September 1, 1835.

[107] *(Columbus) Ohio State Journal,* August 28, 1835.

[108] *(Hartford) Connecticut Patriot and Democrat,* August 29, 1835.

[109] Crockett to editor of *National Intelligencer,* August 10, 1835, published September 2, 1835.

[110] Crockett to Carey and Hart, August 11, 1835, Vertical File, H. Furlong Baldwin Library, Maryland Historical Society.

[111] Crockett to George Patton, October 31, 1835, courtesy of the David Zucker Collection.

[112] *(Bennington) Vermont Gazette,* April 19, 1836, quoting the *Louisville Journal.*

— ILLUSTRATIONS —

"David Crockett," unknown artist, circa 1830, Courtesy of Carol Campbell, Direct Descendant of David Crockett; Photo From the Collection of Gary Foreman.

This earliest known image of Crockett is sometimes attributed to Rembrandt Peale, but the painting bears little stylistic resemblance to Peale portraits of the same era. The artist may have been the "Mr. Hincley" to whom Crockett refers in his May 5, 1831 letter to Michael Sprigg. An ambrotype of this portrait was made circa 1855.

"David Crockett," by James Hamilton Shegogue, watercolor on paper, 1831, Courtesy of National Portrait Gallery, Smithsonian Institution; Gift of Algernon Sidney Holderness, NPG.84.231.

James Shegogue was a New York portraitist affiliated with the National Academy of Design. Crockett's great-grandson, John W. Crockett, purchased this painting in 1906 from Shegogue's grandson. The younger Crockett praised the portrait as "a fine likeness, one of the best I ever saw." (John W. Crockett to Ben Rudd, January 2, 1907; Courtesy of the Lilly Library, Indiana University, Bloomington, IN.)

"David Crockett," engraving by T.B. Welch, 1834; From the Collection of James Boylston.

This engraving was used as the frontispiece in Crockett's "Tour" book, and is based on an 1834 portrait by Samuel Stillman Osgood. The original painting is no longer extant.

"David Crockett," lithograph attributed to Albert Newsam, published by Childs & Lehman, 1834; Courtesy of Library of Congress Prints and Photographs Division, Washington, D.C.

Also based on the Osgood portrait of Crockett, this lithograph was commercially available and widely circulated.

"David Crockett," by John Gadsby Chapman, 1834; Courtesy of the Alamo.

Painted in Washington in 1834, Crockett was ambivalent about this portrait and encouraged Chapman to paint another that would better capture his essence.

"David Crockett," by John Gadsby Chapman, 1834; Courtesy of the Harry Ransom Humanities Research Center, University of Texas at Austin.

Chapman helped Crockett build his "Davy" image with this life sized portrait of the Colonel dressed in frontier garb and armed for the hunt. The original portrait was destroyed in the Austin Capitol building fire in 1881 but, luckily, Chapman had also painted this much smaller version, which survives.

"Colonel Crockett," mezzotint by Charles Gilbert Stuart, 1839; From the Collection of Gary Foreman.

Based on the full length Chapman painting and published for commercial distribution.

"Davy Crockett," by Chester Harding, oil on canvas, 1834, Courtesy of the National Portrait Gallery, Smithsonian Institution; Future Bequest of Ms. Katherine Bradford, L/NPG.1.88.

Painted in Boston during Crockett's tour, this may be the finest extant likeness of the Colonel.

Painted by A.L. De Rose.   Engraved by A.B.Durand.

I leave this rule, for others when I am dead
Be always Sure, you are right, then go, a head

David Crockett

"David Crockett," engraving by Asher B. Durand, 1834; Courtesy of Library of Congress Prints and Photographs Division, Washington, D.C.

An edition of this engraving, based on the watercolor portrait by Anthony Lewis DeRose (seen on the cover of this volume), was offered for sale at fifty cents per copy during Crockett's last term in Congress.

"Brown's Indian Queen Hotel," Published by W. Endicott & Co., 1832; Courtesy of Library of Congress Prints and Photographs Division, Washington, D.C.

Crockett lived at Brown's during the second session of his last term in Congress.

"West front of the United States Capitol with cows in the foreground," by John Rubens Smith, 1828; Courtesy, Library of Congress, Marian S. Carson collection, LC-DIG-ppmsca-06609.

"The House of Representatives" by Samuel Finley Breese Morse (1822-1823). In the Collection of The Corcoran Gallery of Art, Museum Purchase, Gallery Fund

The House Chamber, now Statuary Hall, as it appeared during Crockett's tenure.

Crockett to Robert Patton; Courtesy Tennessee State Library and Archives.

one drop of Arden Spheruets Sence I arived here nor never expects to while I live nothing Stronger than Cider I trust that god will give me fortetude in my under taking I have never made a pretention to Religion in my life before I have Run a long Race the I trust that I was Caled in good time I have been Reproved many tims for my wickedness by my Dear wife who I am Certain will be no tittle astonished when she gets information of my determenation You write me that Father is gueing to visit our Country and also Brother Trosper I have no doubt but Brother trosper will be well pleased with our Country and it will be a Pleasing Sean to all of us to see father in our Country and also it will be an unexpected one to all his children Brother McWharter has mooved down in my neighbour hood in fact to my old place the old gentle man will find us all close to gether I should like much to be at home when Brother Trosper is thare on several reasins I will be home between the 11 & 20 of March if it is Gods will to keep me in health I shall

---

Crockett to Robert Patton; Courtesy Tennessee State Library and Archives.

C3 187 C

leave here a bout the 4 or 5 of March and if no
Bad luck I will Reach home in eleven days
Brother William wrote to me that John had
Got my mare and coult from that young
man tho he did not write that he paid
twenty Dollars I consider that gentle man
had no busisiness with her except he had
Brought her home as I wrote him I had
no Idea of his getting her to Keep thare
fore I consider the case the same as you and
Brother Trosper does that he had no Right
to make a charge

Brother William Wrote to me that
he wished to By her & the coult and that
he would bring me a negro boy in one year
ten years of age and well grown if I would
give him the mare & coult and send him
one hundred & fifty dollars at this time
I could not do it be caus in the first place
I built a mill last summer and got in
debt and have not the money to spare
& in the second place I can get a negro
here of that discription for less than $150
and Should Rather keep my mare for I
have a fine Sted horse at home a pace tot

which I would like to Breed from that mare
and would like much if Father & brother
Could Bring her out this I wish you to in
forme them I wish you to tender my kindest
friendship to all my connection also except
to your self & Familey my warmest esteem
I must conclude with a hope that the
protecting hand of the almighty may
Bless guard & protect you and all our
Connection is the Prayr of your affectionate
Brother Farwell
                                    David Crockett
George Patton

P S Pleas write imediately on the Receipt
of these lines let me know how all is

Crockett to Robert Patton; Courtesy Tennessee State Library and Archives.

Washington City 22 Decer 1830

Sir your letter of the 15 Inst was handed to me this day, by my friend Mr Wilde – the news paper publications to which you refer I have never Seen. and if I had I should not have taken the reference to myself in exclusion of many who fill offices and who are as unlaught as I am I thank you however for your civility in assuring me, that you had no reference to my peculiarities the frankness of your letter induces me to Say a declaration from you to that effect was not needed to Convince me that you were incapable of wounding the feelings of a Strainger and unlettered man who had never injured you – your Charcter for letters and as a gentleman is not altogather un known to me

I have the honour with great respects &c –

David Crockett

J K Paulding –

Crockett to James Kirke Paulding; From the Collection of Phil Collins.

Lagrange Fayett County 30th Sept. 1835

Gentlemen

In answer to your kind note inviting
me to partake of a public dinner this day
at the planters Hotel I am Compeld to
accept your invitation from a Sence of
Grattetude which I feel at all times willing
to acknowledge to my old friends & constents

I have anounced through the news
papers that I never expect to offer my name
again to the public for any office is one
great reason of my acceptance of your
kind offer I hope to Spend the evaning
in a Social manner leaving politicts out
of the question as I hope, never again
middle my formerly political course is known
to the public and I have not Changed

I am with Great respects your
friend & old serct
David Crockett

Paris A Gorman
R. T Mahaffy
A B Gloster
T Hackney
H Atkinson
I E Moody
E H r Whitfield
Eeaston Morris
R J Sanford
R S Gancy.
Thos B Firth
George Cossett
W. Chase
D Jones

Crockett to Citizens of La Grange, Tennessee; From a Private Collection.

New York, Sept. 9, 1833

This Contract, made this day between I & J Harper of New York, and James S. French, of Mississippi witnesseth, that the said I & J Harper, for the privilege of publishing a book entitled, Sketches and Eccentricities of Col. David Crockett of West Tennessee, bind themselves to print as many copies of said work as may meet with a ready sale, they paying the said James S French, the author, six cents pr copy for whatever number may be printed — and the said James S French on his part covenants that, as owner of the Copyright, he will permit none others to publish the above work

Witness

J S Damant

James S. French

James Strange French's contract for his 1833 biography of Crockett; Courtesy of Harper Brothers Records, Rare Book & Manuscript Library, Columbia University.

PART II

— DAVID CROCKETT CORRESPONDENCE —

1820:

LETTER TO JOHN C. MCLEMORE, OCTOBER 26, 1820.

Lawrance County Tennessee Octr 26, 1820

Dear Sir after my best Respects to you I was speaking to you for a land warrant of three hundred and twenty acres for which I expected to pay you the money for by the first of November and also for the Sixty acres which I got of you but I have been on able [?] have my old Claim Identified and have been detained longer than I expected my powder factory have not been pushed as it ought and I will not be able to meet my contract with [you?] but if you can send me a three-hundred acer warrant by the male I will pay you interest for the money until paid I do not wish to disapoint you I dont expect I can pay you the hole amount until next Spring if you can confide in me you can Sent the warrant by male as soon as posable and my letter can Stand as my note I wish you to write to me [?] imediately whether you can Send me a warrant or not as I have two good ocupants claims to lay them on

I am Respectfully yours Sev. [servant?]
David Crockett
John C. McLemore.

Transcription from DRT Library, the Alamo.

Crockett writes as an occupant who had staked out land for which he had no title. He was trying to purchase a North Carolina land warrant from McLemore, which would give him full legal title to the "ocupants claims" he mentioned. His letter mentions difficulties in securing his claim and in coming up with the money he and McLemore apparently had agreed upon for the purchase of the warrant, as well as delays in completing his powder factory. Crockett clearly had firsthand knowledge of the difficulty occupants (or "squatters") faced in securing legal title to land that they had settled, which motivated his efforts to secure a federal land bill that addressed occupants' concerns. McLemore was a prominent Tennessee land owner and a road commissioner for the state's Franklin Turnpike Company. He also was a surveyor who bought out Jackson's interest in the city of Memphis and a lifelong Jackson supporter. McLemore was married to Jackson's niece. J. M. Keating, *History of the City of Memphis, Tennessee* (Syracuse: D. Mason & Co., 1888), 124.

*   *   *   *   *

1824:

LETTER TO C. MCALLISTER & CO., AUGUST 6, 1824

Nashville August 6th 1824

[illeg., possibly Mssrs.]C McAllister & Co.

Dear Sirs
     you will please send Mssrs Allen & Grant of Pittsburgh a [illeg] on [illeg.] for $400: at sixty or ninety Days [illeg.] and the ballance of Proceeds of Sales of thirty Bales of cotton you will please pay to Mssrs. Wilm B. Wilson & Co. of your place you will much oblige us by giving Wm B. Wilson & Co. your note at whatever time you think you will be in funds from the Sales of Cotton for the Sufficient Ballance 70 pounds of the [illeg.] tot of cotton [illeg.] be glad to be kept advised of the price of cotton in your Market also the price of flower Whiskey etc.

yours Respectfully

G & D Crockett

Courtesy of the Chicago History Museum, David Crockett Collection.

The signature on this document may be authentic, but the balance of the letter does not appear to be in Crockett's hand. It is unclear whether the date is 1824 or 1827, and there is no other known record of Crockett conducting business in the cotton trade. It is possible that this is not the same D. Crockett.

*   *   *   *   *

1826:

LETTER TO THE REPUBLICAN VOTERS OF THE NINTH CONGRESSIONAL DISTRICT OF THE STATE OF TENNESSEE, DATED SEPTEMBER 16, 1826, PUBLISHED IN THE *JACKSON (TENNESSEE) GAZETTE* **OF THE SAME DATE AND REPRINTED IN THE** *GAZETTE* **ON SEPTEMBER 23, 1826.**

Fellow-Citizens:

From a full conviction of the necessity and importance of having this District represented in the Congress of the United States, I have again been induced to submit my pretensions to a generous, high minded and magnanimous people. In thus tendering to my services, I am aware that no man can unite the sentiments of the whole of this great national family, let his talents and acquirements be what they may; for the present suffice it for me to say that my politics are of the republican order; I am opposed to the Administration of this man from the Yankee states, called John Q. Adams; I am opposed to the conduct of the Kentucky orator, H. Clay; I am greatly opposed to our present Representative's vote on the Tariff.

If I should be your choice, Fellow Citizens, there is one thing that I will promise—that I will not set silently, and permit the interests of my District to be neglected, while I have got a tongue to speak and a head to direct it. As an independent man, I have independently offered on my own bottom— deny all combination—ask no favors nor grant none, farther than civility. I am the rich man's safeguard, and poor man's friend.

I am,
DAVID CROCKETT
Gibson County, Sept. 16, 1826

*   *   *   *   *

UNDATED LETTER TO THE *JACKSON (TENNESSEE) GAZETTE*, **PUBLISHED DECEMBER 23, 1826.**

To the Editor of the Jackson Gazette.

When I offered my services for the suffrages of the people of the Ninth Congressional District, I had no such notion that I was lifting the flood gates of malice and abuse, and that through the medium of your very useful paper, be held up to ridicule; it is true, in common with the rest of my fellow citizens, I did believe that I had a right to the enjoyment of my religious, civil and political opinions, rude, wild and uncultivated as they are, without passing through the ordeal of a newspaper scrutiny. I thought the con- stitution of my country secured to me the right of offering for any office in the gift of the people , if I thought proper, even without being solicited by any person. However great my anxiety might have been upon this occasion, my great diffidence would have forbid my becoming a candidate, had I not been warmly and pressingly solicited.

Mr. Editor, permit me here to say, that I have no superior claims upon the people, and I am willing that they vote as they please at all elections. It is nevertheless true, that I am the Dave Crockett who volunteered and shouldered his knapsack and gun, and served twelve months under the immortal Old Hickory, in endeavoring to put down the enemies of our country, who spared neither age nor sex; I am the same Dave Crockett who had the honor of representing in the legislature of this state, in 1821 and 1822, the people of Lawrence and Hickman counties, and that their rights were strictly attended to and they pleased I must believe, as I have heard no complaints; I am the same Dave Crockett who had the honor and pleasure of representing the counties of Madison, Henderson, Perry, Humphreys, Carroll, Gibson, Haywood, Tipton and Dyer, in the years 1823 and 24, in the legislature of this state, and who stood firm and unshaken, upon the political watch tower of his country's rights—I call upon the people of this District to examine the journals and judge for themselves; I am the self same Dave Crockett who has had and now has the daring impudence to oppose the immaculate Adam R. Alexander, or any body else, for a seat in the next Congress of the United States.

Some time since, I noticed a piece in your paper under the signature of some man who spells his name with but one letter, and that letter is truly just like his production, very cross, X is the letter; he promised a continuation, but, for the want of mental funds, he has been forced to desist. I also noticed in your paper of the 18th of last month, a cruel, bitter piece, over the signature of a "W. District Cotton Planter." If I may be permitted to judge from his productions, his cotton fields will not yield more cotton than one good hand can spin in three months; however, let that be as it may, he has a right to disgorge himself, as he has swallowed a political emetic, the tariff.

Mr. Editor, the Cotton Planter and every body else are mistaken if they sappose that I can be made a tool of by any set of men, for any purpose. No, Sir. I told you at first, that I came out on my own footing and deny all combinations. There is no printing office near me, I live in the forest of Gibson county, and have not an opportunity of addressing the people through the medium of your very useful and impartial columns;—nor would my time permit, as I am now engaged in aiding the improvement of my country, by opening the navigation of Obion river into the heart of a rich and fertile country.

Cotton Planters may find time to scribble, and ridicule the common farmers and bear hunters, as they call me, when they attempt to come before the people. I am a poor man, it is true, and it is said that "poor people have poor ways;" the maxim, if true, I cannot alter. I never had the opportunity of college learning, like cotton planters' boys;—No, I have been raised in the humble walks of life—but I have been taught the glorious privileges of American freedom and independence.

Mr. Editor, hereafter, when men write pieces for your paper, let them put their true names to them, and this will save you the trouble of giving up persons names—For feel assured, when unjustly attacked, I will have redress.

DAVID CROCKETT

In part, Crockett was responding to a letter that appeared in the Gazette on November 18, 1826, signed only "Cotton Planter, W. District," which opposed Crockett's anti-tariff views.

*   *   *   *   *

1827:

UNDATED LETTER PUBLISHED IN *JACKSON (TENNESSEE) GAZETTE* MAY 5, 1827.

Col. Adam R. Alexander,

Sir—As a citizen of the congressional District which you have the honor of representing, and a candidate who whishes to supplant you by fair and honorable means only, and as the poor man's friend, I now take the liberty, through the medium of the Jackson Gazette, respectfully to ask of you information on a subject appertaining to your official duties, in which we are real interested, and in respect to which most of your constituents are no doubt anxious to be informed. It is in relation to the memorial of the legislature of this state to the Congress of the United States, praying a relinquishment of the vacant and unappropriated lands in the Western District. We have for two sessions of Congress past been kept in suspense as to the fate of a bill founded on that memorial, without even once being informed what were the provisions it contained. It was natural for in the first instance to have expected that our representative would have asked of Congress this land for the benefit of the Western District, either for the use of schools and academies, or to enable us to improve the face of our country, and open and improve the navigation of our rivers. If such a request should have been considered reasonable and just, it is probable that it would have been granted; & it seems to me that upon a full disclosure of all the facts upon which our claim is founded, together with the great need in which we stand of assistance, that Congress would have deemed such a proposition reasonable had it been made. But should Congress have been disposed to reject an application of this nature, or should our Representative differ with us as to the propriety of making it, it follows that the least we could have expected from the provisions of any bill introduced on the subject, would have been a relinquishment of the vacant soil to the state of Tennessee, generally, without prescribing the uses to which it should be applied. I do not pretend sir, to assert that such are not the provisions of the bill, but as I am in the habit of looking anxiously over the papers, particularly under the head of *Congressional proceedings,* my attention was not long since arrested by a few remarks which appeared to have dropped from Judge Isaacks in relation to this bill. It was called up, it seems, at a late period of the session, and for the want of time to think and act upon it, suffered an abortion. But Judge Isaacks in advocating the bill seems to convey the idea, if my memory rightfully serves me, that its provisions are for the benefit of the Colleges of the East and West Tennessee; in which case it is evident we are not to be benefited by it let it pass when it will.

I profess myself to be the poor man's friend, not only because I am poor myself, but because it accords with the best feelings of my nature to be so. I envy no man his wealth, nor the means which he may have for the education of his children, but when our rights (the rights of the poor) are threatened by monopolizing institutions, for the advantage and convenience of the wealthy, I cannot, either as a man looking up for public promotion, or as a private citizen, remain a silent and submissive spectator. Colleges at Nashville and Knoxville, can be of no advantage to the poor people of the Western District. If we can only get a common country, or as College Gentlemen sometimes deridingly call it, a B-a school, convenient enough to send our Big Boys in the winter and our little ones all year, we think ourselves quite fortunate, especially if we can raise enough *Coon-Skins* and one little thing or other to pay up the teacher at the end of every quarter. Very few of our citizens, even those who are well to do in the world, can afford to pay two or three hundred dollars a year, (besides all the necessary expenditures incidental to the distance) to send their sons to these Colleges. I am not opposed to liberal education; on the contrary, I wish most sincerely that we were all able to give our sons College educations. But as matters now stand, my maxim is let the rich men educate their own sons with their own means, without imposing directly or indirectly any part of the burthen by public donations out of the common stock, be they in land or money, upon the poor yeomanry of our country, who are at last the bone and sinew of the great body politic: its support in peace and its safeguard in war; unless the poor themselves can stand an equal chance for an equal participation in the measure—I have heard of some country or other, either of ancient or modern times, which educated youth, rich or poor, at the public expense. The consequences was that the son of the poorest peasant had an equal opportunity of arriving at the highest honors in the state, with that of the richest. Had we such an institution among us, I would be the last man to oppose donations for its support, but as it is, & as those Colleges have already had liberal donations through Congress and by means of leger-de-main legislation at home, I am not willing to yield one foot of land more, at least on this side of Tennessee river, for their benefit, please or offend whom it may.

I again repeat that I am ignorant of the provisions of the bill, which sleeps among the unfinished business of Congress. It is for the sake of information I make the enquiry, hoping that you will have the goodness to lay it before the people, in the same friendly spirit in which this request is made.

I remain your obedient servant
David Crockett

Adam Alexander had defeated Crockett in his first bid for a seat in Congress in 1825, but Crockett beat him in 1827. In this letter, which was intended for public consumption, Crockett showed that the vacant land issue was a top priority for him even before he arrived in Washington and he emphasized Alexander's lack of action on it. He also notes the lack of school funding in his district. "Judge Isaacks" is Jacob C. Isacks, an influential Jacksonian congressman from Tennessee, who served five consecutive terms in the House of Representatives (1823–1832), but was defeated in his bid for a sixth term.

*   *   *   *   *

LETTER TO JAMES L. TOTTEN, DECEMBER 17, 1827.

Washington City
17th of Decr 1827

Dr Sir
I take the liberty of writing you a line these lins leave me well and I hope will find you enjoying good health we have done but little Business as yet and the oppinion is that thare will be but little done until after Chrisemas holladay we have not Set more than one hour in the day Sence I have been here I have presented the Petition for the Post rout from Troy to Mills Pint and thence to dresden to Tottons Wells Just as Soon as I can get the Rout accomplished I will write to you again and through you Mr. Drabilbass & Esqr Totton can be informed that I will appoint them Post master I have got James M gibson appointed post master at the great town of Fulton I went to Mr. McLane and he promised me that he would gave the appointment to Mr Gibson and after wards he Sent me the recommodations of two more men and it was left to me to gave the appointment to who I pleased and I took the Responsabillity on my Self and gave the appointment to gibson I find a representative have power to appoint who they pleas I have started the subject of our vacant land on the third day after we went into session I have no doubt of the passage of the Bill this session I have given it an erly start I have wrote to my editors a tolerable lengthy letter for Publication I wish to gave my constituents all infermation in my power you shall here from me again on all important matters I wish you to write to me and informe me of the tims in your country gave my best respects to all friends I must conclude with great Respects   your obt Humbl-servt

David Crockett

James L. Totton

Transciption in Emma Inman Williams, Historic Madison, The Story of Jackson and Madison County Tennessee, from Prehistoric Moundbuilders to 1917 *(Jackson, Tennessee: Madison County Historical Society, 1946), 420, which notes "original owned by Curtis Bray."*

James L. Totten (which Crockett misspelled "Totton") was a lawyer and state senator in the Tennessee legislature from West Tennessee. He co-sponsored a resolution calling on Tennessee's congressional delegation to vote in favor of expunging the censure that the Senate had invoked against President Jackson. He and Crockett would have been pro-Jackson allies at the time that this letter was written. The "Esqr Totton" who Crockett planned to appoint postmaster was likely a relative of James L. Totten.

*   *   *   *   *

1828:

PARAPHRASE OF A CROCKETT LETTER OF JANUARY 20, 1828, PUBLISHED IN *JACKSON (TENNESSEE) GAZETTE*, FEBRUARY 16, 1828 (EXCERPT).

We have received a letter from the Hon. David Crockett of the 20th ult. in which he remarks, that "Mr Polk and myself are getting along very well with our vacant land bill; and I have no doubt but we shall effect a relinquishment early this session."

This excerpt from Crockett's letter reflects the brief period of harmony between him and Polk during their first months together in Congress. Polk had reintroduced the land bill he had failed to bring up during the previous Congress and Crockett supported him. By year's end, however, after the bill had failed again, Crockett would propose an amendment that was very much at odds with Polk's objectives.

*   *   *   *   *

LETTER TO JAMES BLACKBURN, FEBRUARY 5, 1828.

Washington City
5th Febry 1828

My Dear old friend
    I have this day Recd your polite and friendly favour of the 19th of Jany and will hasten to answer it These lines leave me in a tolrable state of health and I hope will find you and famaly in good health I have nothing very interesting to write you we are progressing very slow with bussiness owing to the great number of members and the mutiplicity of bussiness that each member has to do we are two hundred and thirteen in number in the house of Representatives and the great party spirit which exists on the great political question makes us progress very slow with business Tho we are on the strong Side our old patriot and friend to his country [tear] Jackson [tear] large majority of friends in both bra[nches] of congress and I can here from all quarters of the union and the cry is that Jackson will be the next presidant I have no doubt but that he is gaining ground Every day our mighty administration that got in to power by bargain and manage ment and not a cording to the inlightened youmenry of the nation begins to look very much down in the mouth we have elected Andrew Stevenson from Virgina a Jackson man for our speaker and the Senate has appointed Genl Duff green public prenter for that boddy having choaked off Joseph Gails and Co. the treasury papp Sucking Editor imployed by the Coalition by this you see that the administration is in the minority and I pray god that thare they may Remain Thare is nothing to prevent our old Hero from receiving the Reward of meret but his [tear] by the [tear] and of pro[tear] and called to [tear] in a better world with our

other political four fathers who are keeping a plentiful crop the Reward of meret he was cheated out of hi political birth Right at his last election tho I hope he will Shine conspictous when his enemies will stand be fore the world un noticed by every Honest Amarican Citizen I have enjoyed the worst health Sence I arrived here that I ever did in my life I was taken the next day after I left your house with the billes feaver tho I traveled until I arrived at my father in laws Thare I was taken down and lay four weeks When I got abel to travel I started on and my wife and Sone returned home I have Recd two letters from my Sone Sence he got home he wrote me that they found all well at home my wifes father gave her three young negros they wrote to me that they got home with [tear] much trouble [tear] with the [tear] I have [tear] down three times Sence I arrived [tear] the last attact was the pluricy the doctor took two quarts of Blood from me at one time I am much reduced in flesh and have lost all my Red Rosy Cheeks that I have carryed So many years I have thought twice that I was never to see my family any more tho thanks be to god I hope that I am Recovering as fast as I could expect I have great hope that I am to Spend the balance of the Session with much better health I can not gave you the information that I would wish to in the lines of a letter I think I am getting along very well with the great men of the nation much better than I expected I have not determened yet whether I will return home through your country or not I will write to you again and I wish you to write to [tear] the Reception of this letter [tear] to all your [tear]s and famileys and all my old Neighbors I remain with high esteem your friend and well wisher

David Crockett
James Blackburn

From the Tennessee Historical Society Miscellaneous Files, courtesy of the Tennessee State Library and Archives.

Tears in the paper of the holograph letter caused gaps, signified by [tear]. Blackburn was a friend of Crockett's and may have hosted the Crockett family as they traveled toward Washington. Crockett relates the attack he suffered later in his journey, while in North Carolina and his continuing poor health after he arrived in Washington.

*   *   *   *   *

LETTER TO JAMES L. TOTTEN, FEBRUARY 11, 1828.

Washington City
11 Febry 1828

Dear Sir
    I Recd your polite favour of 13 Jany and purused it with pleasure and will hasten to answer it these lines leaves me well and I hope will find you in good health we are progressing very Slow with bussiness owing to the great party Spirit that exists here on the great political question tho old hickory is like the dimond in the hill of no vallue until it is Rubed and pollished So with genl Jackson the harder they Rub him the brighter he Shines the adminestration party has made Several attacks on him and they all opperate in favour of Jackson we have all got entirely easy here it is given up from all quarters that I Can here from that the dye is cast and that Jackson will in a Short time begin to Recieve the Reward of his merit I can asure you that those heads of the Cabenet begins to treat the Jackson men with the utmost politeness I have the Subject of our vacant land under train and have but litle doubt of obtaining a ["this" crossed out] Relinquishment this Session I think in a few weeks you will find that I have been Successful I will gave the earliest information of the fate of the bill I have also—the male Rout from Troy to Millses Pointe thence to Dresdon before the proper committee and the Chareman of the committee informed me that they had examened the case and find it Reasonable tho they have not Reported nor will not until near the end of

the Session then they Report one general Bill for all the new Routs in the united Stats thare is no chance of hurrying bussiness here like in the legeslature of a State thare is Such a disposition here to Show Eloquence that this will be a long Session and do no good I will not tier your patience Reading my Scrall you wrote to me to Send you and Esqr white the Tellegraph I went to the office and ordered them you will get them Regular I wish you to write to me often and lenthy tender my best Respects to all friends excuse my Scrall I am in great hast I Remain with high esteem your friend & Humbl Servt

David Crockett
James L Totton

[envelope addressed, Washington City March 1st 1828 D Crockett Mr James L Totten Esqr Trenton Tenn]

Typescript from Emma Inman Williams, Historic Madison, The Story of Jackson and Madison County Tennessee, from Prehistoric Moundbuilders to 1917, *421, which notes, "Original owned by Carlos Dew."*

For more information on Totten, see the letter dated December 17, 1827.

*   *   *   *   *

LETTER TO CAPTAIN ROBERT SEAT, MARCH 11, 1828.

Washington City
11 March 1828

Dr Sir
    You will excuse me for not writing to you earlyer I did wish to have somthing worth your attention tho it is in vain to wait any longer we are ingaged in the Tariff and I expect we will not get Rid of it until the first of April this will be a long session and do but little good Thare is So much party feelings exists here that it is with great dificulty to do anything I did believe that I would have been abel to [to] give infermation to my district that we had procured a Relinquishment from the genl goverment for our vacant land and I can not give you this infermation as yet tho I have a Strong hope that I will give you this news as soon as we get Red of the Tariff I intend to vote against all amendments to the Tariff and finally I will vote against the bill I have no news except that old hickory is Rising Thare is a great many of the adminastration party begins to give up the test I wish you to write me the times in our country also tender my best Respects to all friends I remain your friend and Humble Servt
David Crockett
Mr. Seat

Copy of holograph in San Antonio Express, *March 27, 1904.*

    Robert Seat, a long-time friend of Crockett's, operated a store in Gibson-Port (later renamed Trenton), Tennessee, in the mid-1820s. He later took on a partner, Thomas Fite, and named his firm Fite and Seat. In 1830 Seat received a license to operate a house of entertainment (probably a reference to a tavern). In 1838, he and Hugh D. Neilson, another of Crockett's friends, served on a committee to secure a Bank of Tennessee branch for Trenton. Frederick M. Culp & Robert E. Ross *Gibson County, Past and Present* (Gibson County, Tennessee: Gibson County Historical Society, 1961), 12, 72, 87; *San Antonio Express,* March 27, 1904 (includes a photographic copy of the holograph.)

*   *   *   *   *

EXTRACT OF A LETTER FROM CROCKETT TO THE EDITOR, *JACKSON (TENNESSEE) GAZETTE,* **DATED MARCH 14, 1828, AND PUBLISHED IN THE** *GAZETTE* **ON APRIL 5, 1828.**

Washington, 14th March, 1828

"We are engaged in the discussion of the Tariff, and from present appearances, there is but little prospect of getting thro with it for some time. I used every exertion in my pow[er?] to get my vacant land bill through before we took up this subject, but to no purpose. I yet have no doubt of obtaining a relinquishment, during the present session. I am doing the best I can to promote the welfare and interest of my district. I will vote against all the amendments of the Tariff bill, as reported by the committee, and finally I will vote against the bill."

Quotation marks are included in the printed version. Crockett refers to this as his vacant land bill, not Polk's. In fact, at this point, only Polk's original bill had been introduced and had yet to be debated. No doubt Crockett wanted the credit for any land bill, since he had placed the issue at the top of his agenda and promised his constituents that he would get such a bill passed.

*   *   *   *   *

LETTER TO DR. CAHERN, MARCH 16, 1828.

Washington City
March 16, 1828

To Dr. Cahern

I will now redeem the pledge I gave you when bording with Mrs. Ball, that is to enclose you Genl. Brady's letter to me . . . I have no news, we are doing nothing here worth your attention only discusing the Tariff I have no idea when we will get rid of it it keeps down all other business pleas write me on the Reception of these lines . . . ."

Excerpt from **Charles Hamilton Auction Catalog,** *December 6, 1973, item 117.*

Mrs. Ball operated the boarding house where Crockett roomed during most of his years in Washington. General Brady's identity is not known.

*   *   *   *   *

LETTER TO *JACKSON (TENNESSEE) GAZETTE,* **MARCH 30, 1828, PUBLISHED APRIL 26, 1828, WITH** *GAZETTE* **EDITOR'S COMMENTARY.**

Mail to Perryville. — We some time since addressed a letter to Col. Crockett, and drafted a memorial, which was placed in the hands of a gentleman of Henderson county, for the purpose of *extending* the mail route from this place to Purdy's Office via Mount Pinson, to Lexington, &c. to Perryville.

In answer to our letter we received the following prompt reply.
"Washington City 30th March 1828.
Dear Sir—Your favor of the 9th was received by this morning's mail. You informed me that there would be a petition sent on for a mail route from Jackson to Perryville, via Mount Pinson &c. &c. I have no doubt of the propriety of that route, and shall accordingly introduce a resolution for the committee on Post Offices and Post Roads to enquire into its expediency; and when the petition comes it will strengthen the case."

On the 2d inst. Col. Crockett introduced the following resolution which was referred to the proper committee.

Resolved, That the Committee on the Post Offices and Post Roads be instructed to enquire into the expediency of establishing a post route from Jackson to Mount Pinson, thence to Purdy's office, thence to Lexington, thence to Perryville, Perry County, Tennessee.

We also learn by the same letter that some obstructions have been thrown in the way of Colonel Crockett's vacant land bill, by the "petitions of Joseph B. Porter and Jesse W. Egnew, praying the general government to compel Tennessee to satisfy some claims for lost land. I hope their petition will not injure our cause; and I think it a grand imposition for them to make the attempt."

The newspaper, like Crockett, refers to the land bill as his, rather than Polk's, who was the actual sponsor of the bill. Crockett's protestations regarding the interference of the two petitioners is in keeping with his outward support of Polk's bill at this point, even though he already had serious misgivings about it. By year's end, after Polk's bill had been tabled, Crockett would introduce his own radically different amendment to the bill, much to Polk's consternation.

* * * * *

LETTER TO THE *(WASHINGTON) UNITED STATES' TELEGRAPH,* **APRIL 7, 1828, REPRINTED IN THE** *JACKSON (TENNESSEE) GAZETTE* **MAY 3, 1828.**

Washington City
7th April 1828

Messrs. Green & Jarvis:—

The "Banner and Whig" published in Nashville, contains an article upon the subject of the Presidential election, which I am sure must have been designed to misguide and influence public sentiment abroad. It is said that "a number of the citizens of the western district of Tennessee, have determined upon running a candidate for the office of elector, favorable to the re-election of Mr. Adams."

I consider it a duty which I owe to truth and the people to say, that it is a mere *trick!!!* A *"number,"* may have determined upon the course suggested. Residing, however, as I do, in that district, and having the honor to represent it, I do not hesitate to say that, the "number" is very small indeed. So small that nothing short of the vanity of the FROG, which aspired to be an OX, could kindle the slightest hope of success, in such a project.

The western district is too firm to be shaken by so delusive a breeze. Those who inhabit it, know how to appreciate the benefits of liberty; and while they enjoy it, they will fix a proper estimate upon those who have fought to defend it. Among that number *General Jackson* stands pre-eminent.

I have made these remarks, with a view to remove any impression which might be made by the statement alluded to. It is at best a misrepresentation of facts.

I am, gentlemen, your obedient servant,

DAVID CROCKETT.

Duff Green was editor of *The United States' Telegraph,* **which was the principal Jackson newspaper during the early years of the administration and had opposed the administration of John Quincy Adams prior to that. When Jackson and his vice president, John C. Calhoun, fell out, Green backed Calhoun and found that his newspaper had lost its contract as government printer in 1831. Green hired Russell Jarvis as associate editor of the** *Telegraph* **in 1827. W. Stephen Belko,** *The Invincible Duff Green: Whig of the West* **(Columbia: University of Missouri Press, 2006), 102.**

* * * * *

NOTE TO DOCTOR HUBBERT, TRENTON, GIBSON COUNTY, TENNESSEE, SEPTEMBER 11, 1828.

11 Sept. 1828

Dear Doct I have let Mr Hirom Partee have the amount of twenty five Dollars on you you can be so good as to settle that amount with him and oblige your friend &tc

David Crockett

From the Tennessee Historical Society Miscellaneous Files, courtesy of the Tennessee State Library and Archives.

The exact identities of Hubbert and Partee are not known, but the letter makes it clear that Crockett was settling a debt owed to Hubbert, apparently a doctor in Trenton, Tennessee, and had left the money with Partee.

*   *   *   *   *

LETTER TO THE EDITOR, *JACKSON (TENNESSEE) GAZETTE*, DECEMBER 13, 1828, PUBLISHED JANUARY 3, 1829.

Washington
Dec. 13, 1828

My Dear Sir
    Ever anxious that those for whom I act, may have it in their power to judge of and determine the fidelity with which I attend to their interest, and considering them deeply concerned in my proposition, I have to request of you the favor that you will give publicity through your paper, to the document which I enclose. You will perceive upon a perusal of it, that I propose to give to each individual who on the 1st day of April next, shall be an actual occupant within the boundary described, a quantity of land not exceeding one hundred and sixty acres, and in each instance to include the improvement of the settler. This, I think, due to them, and this I humbly hope I shall succeed in procuring. True it is, my colleagues, as I believe, are almost unanimously opposed to my proposition, alledging that they feel themselves constrained to obey the Legislature of Tennessee, which seeks to have this land subjected to its control. To this argument, I have only one reply to make, which is, that others may obey the Legislature, but I choose to obey my constituents, who have placed me in office, and whose servant I am. I am decidedly opposed to placing it in the power of the Tennessee Legislature, or any tribunal, to speculate on their labor; to avoid which, I am inclined to give each one a home to shelter his wife and little ones. I esteem the proposition both just and reasonable, and therefore I most confidently expect its success. In this I may be disappointed, as the opposition of my colleagues throws a fearful weight in the scale against me—but I have the strong assurance of a great many members in my favor, who I know will not flinch when they are put to the test.
    I am, dear sir, most respectfully your friend and ob't. serv't.

DAVID CROCKETT

Crockett attached his amendment to House Resolution (H.R.) 27, the bill that Polk had introduced a year earlier, but which failed to pass. Before Crockett's amendment came up for debate in the House of Representatives, it had been revised to include additional language; the complete version appears in the *Register of Debates*, January 5, 1829, 161–62, and in Crockett's circular dated January 15, 1829, 4–5. Although this was an amendment to H.R. 27, it was, in effect, an entirely new bill, since Crockett struck out virtually every word of Polk's original bill and replaced it with his own language.

*   *   *   *   *

1829:

LETTER TO REPRESENTATIVES JAMES CLARK OF KENTUCKY AND GULIAN VERPLANCK OF NEW YORK, JANUARY 3, 1829, AND THEIR RESPONSES.

House of Representatives,
January 3, 1829

Dear Sir: forbearance ceases to be a virtue, when it is construed into an acquiescence in falsehoods, or a tame submission to unprovoked insult.

I have seen published, and republished in various papers of the United Stats, a slander, no doubt characteristic of its author, purporting to be an account of my first visit to the President of the Nation. I have thus long passed the publication alluded to with silent contempt. But, supposing that its republication is intended, as in its origin it evidently was, to do me an injury, I can submit to it no longer, without calling upon gentlemen who were present, to do me justice. I presume, sir, that you have a distinct recollection of what passed at the dinner alluded to, and you will do me the favor to say distinctly whether the enclosed publication is not false. I would not make this appeal, if it were not that, like other men, I have enemies who would take much pleasure in magnifying the plain rusticity of my manners into the most unparalleled ["ruthlessness" crossed out] grossness and indelicacy. I have never enjoyed the advantages which many have abused; but I am proud to hope that your answer will show, that I have never so far prostituted the humble advantages I do enjoy, as to act the part attributed to me. An early answer is requested. I am, sir, most respectfully,
Your obt servt

DAVID CROCKETT
Hon. James Clark
    of Ky
[a similar request to the above was communicated to the Hon. Mr. Verplanck, of New York.]

Response from James Clark, representative from Kentucky:

Washington, Jan. 4, 1829
Dear Colonel: In your letter of yesterday, you requested me to say if the ludicrous newspaper account of your behaviour when dining with the President, which you enclosed to me, is true.

I was at the same dinner, and know that the statement is absolutely destitute of every thing like truth. I sat opposite to you at the table, and held occasional conversation with you, and observed nothing in your behaviour but what was marked with the strictest propriety.

I have the honor to be, with great respect, your ob't servant,
JAS. CLARK
Col. D. Crockett

Response from Gulian C. Verplanck, representative from New York:

Washington, Jan. 4, 1829
Dear Sir: I have already several times anticipated your request in regard to the newspaper account of your behaviour at the President's table, as I have repeatedly contradicted it in various companies where I heard it spoken of. I dined there in company with you at the time alluded to, and had, I recollect, a good deal of conversation with you. Your behaviour there was, I thought, perfectly becoming

and proper, and I do not recollect or believe that you said or did any thing resembling the newspaper account. I am yours,
GULIAN C. VERPLANCK
Col. Crockett

Augusta (Georgia) Chronicle, January 14, 1829; Charles Hamilton Autographs Catalog, September 22, 1966, item 60.

Crockett asked Clark and Verplanck to vouch for his good conduct at a White House dinner that President John Quincy Adams had hosted, in response to a scurrilous story that had appeared in the press accusing Crockett of boorish, crude behavior at the dinner. Although the letter appears to be in Crockett's handwriting, it includes some punctuation, which is typically missing from Crockett's letters.

*   *   *   *   *

LETTER TO THE EDITOR OF THE *JACKSON (TENNESSEE) GAZETTE*, DATED JANUARY 14, 1829, AND PUBLISHED FEBRUARY 7, 1829.

TO THE EDITOR
Washington
14th Jan'y. 1829.

Dear Sir: I am sorry to inform you that on yesterday the Tennessee land bill was laid on the table, by a large majority. This, however, I am in hopes may put an end to my colleagues opposition to my measure. I had introduced my amendment, before I received the petition from Haywood county; I therefore considered it best to hold back the petition, until I discovered the feelings of the house on my amendment if our own Delegation had not have opposed me. I was supported by Mr. Mallary, of Vermont, in a speech of some length; also by Mr. Weems of Maryland, Mr. Buckner, of Kentucky, Mr. Culpepper, of North Carolina, Mr. Woods of Ohio. They all supported my amendment with speeches of considerable length. I am really sorry to inform you that there was no opposition to my amendment, except the members from our own state, I was opposed by Messrs. Polk, Bell, Blair, Lea, Mitchell, and Isacks, all come out with long speeches against me. You must know I was overpowered. I made two speeches in support of my measure. I will have them both published, and sent to the District—then my constituents can judge whether I have supported my measure or not. If I am whipped, I will not stay whipped. I shall introduce the petition on Monday next, and refer it to the committee on public lands, with a hope that I can get the chairman to report a bill for the benefit of the Western District. I know of nothing that interests my district, as this subject. I will keep a kicking with a hope of success—if not at this session, I am certain the occupants will be provided for, when the disposition is made. I remain your humble servant, &c.

DAVID CROCKETT

Crockett was referring to the debates of January 5 and 12–13, 1829, in the House of Representatives regarding the Tennessee land bill. Although he had supported Polk's bill, when it failed to pass, Crockett introduced his own amendment that effectively deleted all of Polk's language and replaced it with a direct cession of public land to squatters in the Western District of Tennessee. Those whom Crockett mentions as having supported him were mostly Adams men, who may have been using Crockett's rebellion against his own state delegation to stir up dissension among Jackson's supporters. Although Crockett was probably aware of this, he was more concerned with passing his amendment, regardless of who his supporters were. The individuals named by Crockett all were members of Congress.

*   *   *   *   *

LETTER FROM JAMES K. POLK TO DAVISON MCMILLEN, FAYETTEVILLE, TENNESSEE, JANUARY 16, 1829.

Washington City Jany. 16th 1829

My Dear Sir

We have again had up the Bill to relinquish to Tennessee, the vacant lands in the Western part of the State, & as you will see from the newspapers, after having undergone considerable discussion, it has been laid upon the table. At the commencement of the Session we had some little hope of succeeding in the measure, and the cause of its defeat is to be attributed in a great degree to the course taken by our man *Crocket,* who I regret to say opposed the very Bill at this Session, which he himself had agreed to in committee and supported and voted for in the House at the last Session of Congress. He associated himself with our political enemies, and declared in presence of Mr Blair of Ten. and others, that he would vote for any measure any member wished him to vote for, provided he would vote for his foolish amendment and against the original Bill. He took a course directly opposed to the interest of the State, opposed to the whole of the balance of the delegation, and in direct violation of instructions given by our Legislature, (although he himself had been in the Legislature and voted for similar instructions) and one as we believed and so advised him before hand, well calculated, if not certain to defeat the whole measure. The result has been the one we feared. You may suppose that such a man under no circumstances could do us much harm. In ordinary cases, such would be the fact, but in this instance, many of the *Adams men,* not having forgotten the violence of the recent political struggle and feeling more than willing to disappoint Tennessee and her delegation, seized upon the opportunity to use *Crockett,* and to operate upon him through this measure, for their own political purposes, and hence you see such men as *Buckner* of Ky., *Woods* of Ohio, Mallary of Vermont, Culpepper of N.C. making speeches for his proposition absurd as it was. The balance of the delegation took their stand against him and his new friends. They supported the State, her character & her interests, against the attacks made upon them; and finding an argument, either that they could not vote for his absurd proposition, or that it could not be carried, a Yankee (Mr. Bartlett of N. Hampshire) moved to lay the whole subject on the table and thus with their forces added to those opposed on principal to the whole measure, the quietus has been given to it for the present. I forbear to comment in detail, on the disgraceful and disrespectful terms in which *Crockett* was in the habit of speaking of his own State and her Legislature, further than to say that the whole delegation feel humiliated and can but regret that any one from our own country, should have Cooperated with some of our bitterest and most vindictive political enemies, men, some of them of "Coffin handbill" and "six militiamen" memory, and joined them in denounceing the Legislature of his state on the floor of Congress. Gales and some of the *Adamsites* during the whole discussion, were nursing him, and dressing up and reporting speeches for him, which he never delivered as reported, & which all who know him, know he never did. Rely upon it he can be and has been opperated upon by our enemies. We cant trust him an inch. It is whispered that he intends to vote for *Gales* and *Seaton,* for public printers, against *Duff Green.* I have given you this statement to the end, that if any false impressions should be attempted to be made, you may have the fact to put the matter right. I have understood and think it probable that he may have a letter dressed up by some of *his friends,* and send home, to save himself if he can. If so and any thing he writes requires correction in my absence you have the facts by which to do it. If it shall hereafter become necessary in consequence of any thing he may write or say, the balance of the delegation will notice him, under their own signatures. We do not wish in advance to do so, for that would give him consequence, and might have the appearance with those unacquainted with the facts of an attack upon him, and thus excite a sympathy in his behalf which he does not deserve. This letter therefore is not written for publication in the newspapers but is addressed to you as a known friend, to furnish you with the facts, to meet any thing that may be said, until we can have an opportunity of meeting him personally, and exposeing his conduct if necessary. I have no room in this letter to give you any political news. I will however write you shortly of the movements here, which are not without interest.

James K. Polk

In Herbert Weaver, editor, and Paul H. Bergeron, associate editor, **Correspondence of James K. Polk, Volume I, 1817–1832** *(Nashville: Vanderbilt University Press, 1969), 229–31.*

Polk's use of the terms "Coffin handbill" and "six militiamen" refer to anti-Jackson propaganda that Adams and Clay supporters had used in the 1828 election. They charged Jackson with barbaric cruelty in ordering the execution of six militiamen for mutiny in 1813 during the Creek War, in which Crockett had fought.

Joseph Gales, Jr. and William Winston Seaton were publishers of the National Intelligencer, a pro-Adams, anti-Jackson Washington newspaper, and *The Register of Debates in Congress.* Polk and the Jacksonians supported Duff Green's *United States' Telegraph* in the vote to decide who would be official printer of government documents (Green would ultimately replace Gales & Seaton). Polk's letter shows the degree and causes of his anger at Crockett for what he viewed as his "betrayal" of the Tennessee congressional delegation and the Jacksonians, rather than disagreement over the provisions of the land bill, although the two clearly disagreed about that. The letter is a copy and not in Polk's handwriting, nor does it bear his signature. Polk dictated the letter and had copies sent to several of his Tennessee political allies, including McMillen, Dr. John H. Camp of Pulaski, Archibald Yell of Shelbyville, and Andrew C. Hays of Columbia. McMillan, who lived in Fayetteville, Tennessee, has not been identified, but was clearly a Polk supporter.

*   *   *   *   *

UNSIGNED LETTER FROM PRYOR LEA ATTACKING CROCKETT, DATED JANUARY 19, 1829, PUBLISHED IN THE *KNOXVILLE (TENNESSEE) REGISTER*, FEBRUARY 4, 1829.

Washington City, Jan. 19, 1829.
Dear Sir

You will discover by the newspapers, that on Saturday last, the resolution which had been introduced in the House of Representatives, to change the manner of voting for a printer and other officers, from the ballot to the *viva voce* plan, was laid on the table by a small majority. It was almost a complete party vote, but more than twenty members were absent. All the administration men I believe, and a few Jackson men were in favor of voting by ballot as heretofore; but the remainder desired a change, so that it might be known how every individual would vote on all such occasions. They believed that the people have a right to know how every one of their representatives may vote—that, although it may be very well for a private individual to vote by ballot, and even secretly, if he please, so as to avoid the censure and oppression of him, inasmuch as it is desirable in common elections, to get the free will of every citizen, without any accountability to others, yet in the case of representatives, who ought to be responsible for all their conduct to their constitutes, it would seem that directly the reverse of secrecy ought to be consulted for accountability cannot exist without knowledge of the facts. By the vote on this resolution, you may have some idea of the manner in which things are working here. It is very doubtful whether Green or Gales & Seaton will be elected printer. The administration forces rally to a man, I believe, against Green, who will not be able to unite all the Jackson men in his favor. This election is considered, on both sides, to be of great importance, and it would be impossible for me to give you any proper conception of the arts and contrivances resorted to—but one thing cannot be misunderstood—the Jackson side, with a few exceptions, are for open work, and the other, for the contrary, as this may enable them to have a few votes smuggled in under false colors. Gales is officiously polite to all who will tolerate him, and plies every doubtful man with good dinners and speeches served up to his liking. Col. Crockett is one of these, and voted for laying the resolution on the table. He has been a principal cause, too, of having the western district land bill laid on the table again, as you may see by the papers. He is estranged from his colleagues, associates chiefly with the other side, and has openly set himself up in market, offering to vote for any thing in order to get votes by it. He declared his object to be to defeat the whole bill, if he could not succeed with his amendment, so as to get all for the benefit of a few of the people of his own district, notwithstanding he was a member of the General Assembly, when it asked for the lands for the benefit of common schools throughout the State, and supported the application, as he also did the bill at the last session of Congress, which was brought forward according to the application of the State. He has changed his course, abused his State, and co-operated with her enemies. Where he may land I cannot say. The North Carolina members generally were against his project; but he was sustained in his mischief by Lewis Williams and old Culpepper, who seem to hate every thing belonging to Tennessee, except their own kin. As some of the Jackson members appears "uncertain" —as the Senate will be nearly equally divided after the fourth of March—and as there is now no doubt that Henry Clay and others intend to keep their forces organized, so as to annoy Jackson's administration, and thwart his measures as much as possible, we may lookout for breakers in every quarter where they may calculate on any chance for success in the next election. As the people were cheated in the election of Mr. Adams, it was right to send such representatives as would keep him from mischief as far as possible—but as they have been gratified in Jackson's election, and desire a change in public affairs, it is certainly proper to give him a fair support. If his enemies should succeed in turning out a few of his friends so as to get a majority in either House of Congress, they will be able to defeat him entirely, and prevent him from doing the good which the nation has expected from him. Knowing this, his enemies will resort to every means of flattery, deception, and defiunation in order to succeed, and the real friends of "Jackson and Reform" ought to know the danger, and guard against it. It is vain to have done so much, if we now leave the work unfinished.

This letter was the opening salvo in a prolonged exchange between Lea and Crockett, which nearly led to the two fighting a duel. It also was reprinted in the *(Washington) United States' Telegraph* on February 14 and the *Jackson (Tennessee) Gazette* March 14, 1829. Pryor Lea was a congressman from Knox County, Tennessee, and clearly an ally of Polk's.

*   *   *   *   *

LETTER TO CAPTAIN SEAT, JANUARY 26, 1829.

Washington City
26 January 1829

Dear Capt
     I have taken the liberty of Directing a number of my addresses to to my constetuants to you which I hope you will do me the favour to give them as wide Circulation as posable in your county and you will confer a particular favour on your friend I know of no person in your town better quallifyed to do me this favour than your self we have nothing new here and is doing but little bussiness in Congress I am in as fine health as you ever saw me and I hope these lines will find you enjoying the same Respectfully your obt servant

David Crockett

Capt Seat

From the Tennessee Historical Society Miscellaneous Files, courtesy of the Tennessee State Library and Archives.

     See Crockett's letter to Seat dated March 11, 1828. Although Seat remains unidentified, he was clearly a good friend of Crockett, who trusted him to distribute his speeches among his constituents.

*   *   *   *   *

LETTER TO GEORGE PATTON, JANUARY 27, 1829.

Washington City
27th January 1829

My Dear Brother
    I recieved your favour of the 11 inst and parused its contents with great Pleasure all except that part whare it relates to the disagreeable situation of friends Differing it is certainley the worst of all fuses I recieved a letter on yesterday from John which affected my feelings a great deal that was in consequence of the Death of our Poor Dear little neice Rebecca ann Burgin She had been at my house for two or three days and on the first day of this month She was with my children in my horse Mill walking Round after the oxen and stopped opposite one of the out side Posts and the end of the arm or Brace that which the oxen worked too caught her head a gainst the post and mashed it all to peaces Poor little dear Creature never knew what hurt her I thought almost as much of her as one of my own I hope she is this day in eternal happiness whare I am endevouring to make my way I have altered my cours in life a great deal sence I reached this place I have not taisted one drop of Arden Sperits since I arrived here nor never expects to while I live nothing stronger than Cider I trust that god will give me fortitude in my undertaking I have never made a pretention to Relegion in my life before I have run a long race tho I trust that I was called in good time I have been reproved many times for my wickedness by my Dear wife who I am certain will be no little astonished when she gets information of my determination You write me that Father is going to visit our country and also Brother Trospher I have no doubt but Brother trospher will be well pleased with our country and it will be a pleasing seen to all of us to see father in our country and also it will be an unexpected one to all his children Brother McWharter has moved down in my neighbor hood in fact to my old place the old gentle man will find us all close to gether I should like much to be at home when Brother Trospher is thare on several ocasions I will be home between the 11-26 of March if it is Gods will to keep me in health I shall leave here about the 4 or 5 of March and if no Bad luck I will reach home in eleven days Brother William wrote to me that John had got my mare and Coult from that young man tho he did not write that he paid twenty Dollars I consider that gentle man had no bussiness with her except he had Brought her home as I wrote him I had no idea of his getting her to keep thare fore I consider the case the same as you and Brother Trospher does that he had no right to make a charge
    Brother William wrote to me that he wished to by her & the coult and that he would bring me a negro boy in one year ten years of age and well grown if would give him the mare & coult and send him one hundred & fifty dollars at this time I could not do it be caus in the first place I built a mil last summer and got in debt and have not the money to spare & in the second place I can get a negro here of that discription for less than $150 and should rather keep my mare for I have a fine stud horse at home a[parl let] which I would like to breed from that mare and would like much if Father or Brother could bring her out this I wish you to in forme them I wish you to tender my kindest friendship to all my connection also except to your self & Family my warmest esteem I must conclude with a hope that the protecting hand of the almighty may Bless guard & protect you and all our conections is the Prayer of your affectionate Brother Farewell

David Crockett

George Patton

PS—Pleas write imediately on the recept of these lines let me know how all is DC

From the Tennessee Historical Society Miscellaneous Files, courtesy of the Tennessee State Library and Archives.

George Patton was Crockett's brother-in-law. Crockett mentions several family members in the letter, including his niece, who had met a tragic death.

*   *   *   *   *

LETTER TO BOATER CANADAY, FEBRUARY 3, 1829.

Washington City
3rd Febry 1829

my Dear old Friend,

These lines leave me in entire good Health and I hope will find you and Family in the alike health. We have nothing new here to enform you. it has been many years since I saw you or heard from you until I made an inquire of your Representative the Hon. Wm. Smith about you a day or two since he informed me whare you and your Brothers were settled in his District I then concluded I would Divote a Small Portion of my time in letting you know of my ups & Downs in this world since I saw you tho I expect you had little idea when I lived with you that I was ever to fill a Station in the Congress of the United States tho true it is I fill that Station at this time and have no opposition in my next Contest I Represent 18 counties what is called the western District of Tennessee I beat an honourable gentleman 2748 votes, who had been our former member for four years I have filled a Seat in the Legislature four years I do expect I could come here as long as I could wish I must give you a small history of my life Since I Saw you I moved to West Tennessee and had three Children by my first wife two sones & a Daughter I then had the misfortune to looz my wife I lived a Bachelor life a while I then married a Widdow Patton who had two children and we have three children sence two Daughters and a sone my eldest sone is married—last Summer to the Hon-Judge J C Hambeltons' Daughter, the Judge of the Destrict that I live in and I hope he will do well I have made him a first Rate Schollar that is what you know I never waz tho I have never offered for any office but what I was elected with eaz I should be extreemly glad to See you and family and all your Brothers & their famileys and I fear your father and mother is not living tho I have herd nothing to contrarys in fact I have never herd from any of you for many years until I conversed with Mr. Smith about you he is a fine man and makes a first rate member. I set near him and is well aquainted with him and you Cannot Send a better member here than he is I wish you to write to me how you are all doing on the Reciept of this letter Direct your letter to Trenton gibson County, Tennessee Please present my kindest respects to all your Brothers and families and all Connection and old neighbours if any of them is living in your neighbourhood. I must conclude by subscribing my self, Your Sincere friend & well wisher.

David

Boater Cannaday

Copy of the original holograph at the Canaday Family Website, http://www.geocities.com/canadayfamily/ davy/davyand-boater.htm; present location of holograph unknown.

Crockett misspelled Canaday's name. Part of the end of the letter was torn off and lost, including "Crockett" in the signature. A transcription of the letter made by Julian Canaday, a descendant of Boater, says that part of the letter was lost while it was being repaired and used by a newspaper for a news article. Canaday says that family tradition holds that Crockett was a close friend of Boater and had attended the same school as Boater's son John Canaday, Sr. (1741–1830), when the Canadays lived at Lost Creek, Jefferson County, Tennessee. Crockett had sought to improve his education and paid for lessons by performing labor. The letter indicates that he lived for a time with the Canadays while attending school, and it is one of the few in which Crockett discusses his personal life.

Crockett says little about his education in his autobiography, but credits the family of a Quaker, John Kennedy, for his schooling, which he says lasted about six months. "Kennedy" may well be a simple misspelling of Canaday, although when he wrote this letter, five years before his autobiography was published, Crockett nearly spelled the name correctly as "Cannaday." The Canaday Genealogy website claims that it was their family that Crockett referred to in his autobiography and cites Jim Stokely and Jeff D. Johnson, eds., *An Encyclopedia of East Tennessee* (Oak Ridge, Tennessee: Children's Museum of Oak Ridge, 1981), which says the Canadays lived near Panther Springs in the present Hamblin County. See David Crockett, *A Narrative of the Life of David Crockett of the State of Tennessee*, ed. by James A. Shackford and Stanley J. Folmsbee (Knoxville: University of Tennessee Press, 1973), 46–49.

*   *   *   *   *

LETTER TO THE *(WASHINGTON) UNITED STATES' TELEGRAPH*, FEBRUARY 16, 1829, PUBLISHED FEBRUARY 17, RESPONDING TO PRYOR LEA'S ANONYMOUS LETTER OF JANUARY 19, 1829.

Washington City
16th Feb. 1829.

To the Editor of the U. States' Telegraph.

Sir:

There has just been placed in my hand a copy of the Knoxville Register, under date of the 4th instant, which upon examination, I find to contain a letter addressed by some individual in this city, either to the Editor of that paper, or to some one who has taken it upon himself to procure its publication. The letter bears date the 19th January, and relates particularly to myself—comprising the most unprincipled tissue of falsehoods ever written or published. My patience would not permit me to answer at any considerable length, the production of so *base a scoundrel,* as the author of the letter alludded to, evidently is. I know not who he is, nor do I believe that he has the *courage* to avow himself the author of his *vile calumny.* I should not notice it, if I were not convinced beyond the reach of very rational doubt, that like a *midnight assassin,* he was aiming a secret stab at my reputation and standing in society. Why did he not (whoever he be) say to me or publish in this city, what is contained in this letter? Why, like a *poor contemptible sneak,* send it off to Knoxville for publication? For the simple reason, that he supposed either that it would escape my notice, or perhaps did not calculate that it would be published at all. That those who are with me, and who know me, and who are prepared to detect such *secret villany* may have it in their power to appreciate the *merits* of the article, and its cold blooded author, referred to, I subject it. It is as follows:
[Here Crockett inserts Lea's letter of January 19, 1829.]

Who, to read the foregoing, can fail to shudder for the *corruption* of a heart *so base,* so deranged by malignity, as to embody so many wicked falsehoods; and that, too, without provocation? *My vote in market!! I the cause of defeating a proposition for the benefit of my constituents?!!!* The kindness of my feelings towards the human family in general, would prompt me to give it some other name, if I were not so fully convinced that the author of this WICKED LIE, is some *contemptible wretch,* who seeks to gratify a secret feeling of revenge, which he dares not openly avow. In conclusion, I inform the author of that letter, *whether he be in the city,* or out of it, (I care not,) I consider him a *paltroon,* a *scoundrel,* and a *puppy.* If he will dare avow himself, puppy as he is, I will condescend to take some further notice of him. I would hazard the opinion, that if he is ever known, he will be found to be one of those who were quietly sitting by their firesides at home, while with the immortal Jackson, I was putting my *life "in market,"* and fighting to defend my country. He will not find me backward to putting it "in market" again, in defence of my reputation.

I am, Sir, respectfully,
Your obedient servant,
DAVID CROCKETT

The letter was reprinted in the **Jackson (Tennessee) Gazette** *March 14, 1829.*

*   *   *   *   *

LETTER FROM JAMES K. POLK TO PRYOR LEA, FEBRUARY 17, 1829.

Washington City
Feb. 17th 1829

Dear Sir

My attention has been called to the communication of Col. Crockett, which appeared in the Telegraph of this morning, and to which you allude in your note of this date. I have examined your letter of the 17th of January, published in the Knoxville Register, and so far as the facts come within my knowledge believe it to be strictly true. That col. Crockett did vote with the administration men to lay on the table, the resolution of Mr. Wickliffe, which proposed that all elections in the Ho. Rept. should hereafter be viva voce and not by ballot, the Journal of the House will show. That he was the only member from Tennessee who did so vote the Journal will likewise show.

It is a matter of notoriety that during the discussion of the Tennessee Land Bill and afterwards many of the Jackson members of the House, entertained serious fears that he had been opperated upon through that measure, by our political enemies, & from his conduct, his associations, and apparent intimacy with some of them, fears were entertained that he had gone over to them and would vote for Gales & Seaton for Public printer.[1] This was a matter of conversation among many of the Jackson men at that time. That he was the principal cause of having the Land Bill laid on the table I have no doubt. Whether we could have succeeded or not at the present Session in passing the Bill if he had harmonized and acted with the ballance of the delegation, I do not pretend to say, but after he took the course he did, all hope of success was lost. Before he offered his amendment, he showed it to several of the Tennessee delegation, of whom I remember yourself, Judge White, Genr. Desha and myself were of that number. We all expressed our decided disapprobation of his project, as being well calculated, if not certain to defeat the whole measure, and our regret that any member from the state should take a course which was likely to produce that result. He was reminded that the Legislature of Tennessee, had instructed their Senators and requested their representatives in Congress, to procure the relinquishment to the state, for the purposes of common schools. He was reminded that he himself had been a member of the Legislature and voted for their instructions. He was reminded too that at the last Session of Congress, he had supported the very Bill, that was before the House at this Session, and which he then avowed his intention to oppose. He was admonished that his proposition, would probably have no other tendency, if he persued in it, than the rejection of the whole measure. No importunities would avail any thing, and in answer to an inquiry made by Judge White, he distinctly said that his object was to *kill the Bill* if he could and carry his amendment. Even after the Bill had been so amended as to make ample provision for the occupants, he still (as we suspected under the influence of others) pertinaciously adhered to his proposition, and opposed the Bill even with the provision in it for the benefits of the occupants. That he was estranged from his colleagues, and associated much with our political enemies all who were here known. That he spoke in terms of abuse and great disrespect of the Legislature of his own state, both in and out of the House, he can not deny. I know nothing personally of his declaration, that he would do any thing that any member wished him to do, provided he would vote for his amendment, and against the very Bill he himself at the former Session, had voted for and supported. But the fact that he did make such a declaration in the presence of Mr Blair of Tennessee, and others, was communicated to me shortly afterwards, and I suppose will be remembered by them. Col. Crockett several times, in conversation upon the subject of his amendment, said that he did not expect any member from his own state to vote for it because they had been instructed by the Legislature to procure a relinquishment to the State for common schools. I avail myself of the occasion to express my deep regret of the necessity, which renders it propper to make this statement. I had ever as I believe the whole delegation had, treated him with the utmost kindness, and was more disposed to conceal than to expose his folly. But when he separated himself from us and took council from some of our most rancorous political enemies, associating with apparent intimacy with them and joining with them in slandering and abuseing his own state, we would have been [...] to our duty if we had not vindicated the honour of that state and sustained the measure which she had instructed us to support. Opposed as he was to the whole of his Colleagues, and as we conceived to the interest not only of the state, but of his own immediate constituents, there was but one course left for us to pursue. It was to discharge our duty, and to communicate to our constituents what we had done, and the causes of the failure of the measure. That you have done, and if in telling the truth, any one feels its force & is the more sensitive because it is the truth, that is a matter for himself and his constituents. I have no other feelings towards Col. Crockett, than those of pity for his folly and regret that he had not consulted *better advisers,* when he suffered himself to give his sanction to the rude and very intemperate publication of this morning.

James K. Polk

P.S. I further add, that when pending the discussion on the Tennessee land Bill, you moved a postponement of its further consideration for a few days. I know Col. Crockett did acquiesce with the balance of our delegation in the propriety of [the] motion, and agreed before the motion was made, that it was proper to make it. Since I understand he has complained of the postponement.
J. K. Polk

In Herbert Weaver, editor, and Paul H. Bergeron, associate editor, Correspondence of James K. Polk, Volume I, 1817–1832 *(Nashville: Vanderbilt University Press, 1969), 240–43.*

This letter shows that Polk conspired with other members of the Tennessee delegation against Crockett. Lea, a member of that delegation, had already launched an attack on Crockett in the press and would continue to battle Crockett in writing. This letter and signature are not in Polk's hand; the postscript, however, is in his handwriting and signed by him. Polk mentions several other members of the Tennessee congressional delegation as well.

---

[1] Polk could not have known for sure how Crockett voted, unless Crockett told him, because Duff Green, eventually more loyal to John C. Calhoun than to Jackson, was chosen as public printer on February 10, 1829 by the very secret paper ballot that Polk had opposed in favor of *viva voce*. The vote was close, with Green receiving 107 ballots and Gales & Seaton 95; 4 ballots were cast for others and 2 were blank. (See *Journal of the House of Representatives*, vol. 22, February 10, 1829, 271). Given Crockett's friendly relations with Gales & Seaton, and his expressed admiration for the way they had improved his speeches for print, as well as Crockett's general independence, it would not be at all surprising if he had cast his ballot for them.

* * * * *

LETTER FROM PRYOR LEA TO THE *(WASHINGTON) UNITED STATES' TELEGRAPH*, **FEBRUARY 18, 1829, PUBLISHED FEBRUARY 19, IN REPLY TO CROCKETT'S LETTER TO THE SAME NEWSPAPER DATED FEBRUARY 16 AND PUBLISHED FEBRUARY 17.**

Washington City,
Feb. 18, 1829

To the Editor of the U. States' Telegraph.

Sir:

In your paper of yesterday, I have read Colonel Crockett's answer to a letter recently published in the Knoxville Register. He impugns the correctness of that letter, denounces its author, and threatens to "take some further notice of him," if he dare avow himself." *I am the author of that letter,* and ask you, also, to publish this reply to his communication, concerning the *manner* of which I have but little to say at present, as matters merely personal suit better for private adjustment than for public proclamation; but its *substance* shall be noticed without imitating its indecorum of expression.

My letter was addressed to a particular friend, whose authority for having it published, instead of being questioned, is distinctly admitted. It was written with freedom, to be sure; but, with the strictest regard for accuracy, predicated partly on my own knowledge, and partly on the information of others. If, on revising it, I could discover any error, no man would more cheerfully correct it, with any proper atonement; but, after the closest scrutiny, I refuse to retract a single word, believing the facts alleged to be true, and the speculative suggestions warranted by appearances at the time. To show the utmost particularity, one indifferent circumstance may require a remark of explanation not affecting the substance, especially as it seems to afford the *gravamen* of the Colonel's complaint. In my letter are these familiar expressions among others in relation to the public printer's election: "Gales is officiously polite to all who will tolerate him, and plies every doubtful man with good dinners and speeches, served up to his liking. Col. Crockett is one of those, and voted for laying the resolution on the table." I am since told, though I understood it differently at the time, that the Colonel's dining was at the house of Mr. Seaton, and not at that of Mr. Gales; but they were partners in the printing, which was the object in view, and the act of one to obtain it might be regarded as the act of the other, with something of even legal accuracy. I hasten, however, from this ludicrously important "distinction without a difference," to matters of grave import, and with the foregoing qualification; I *re assert* what is said in my letter, in substance as follows: *Col. Crockett was a doubtful man, and did vote to lay the* viva voce *resolution on the table. Gales or his agent did make speeches for him different from those he delivered, and so as to please him. He was a principal cause of having the Western District land bill laid on the table again. He was estranged from his colleagues, did associate chiefly with the other side, and openly set himself up in market, offering to vote for any thing in order to get votes by it. He did declare his object to be to defeat the whole bill, if he could not succeed with his amendment, notwithstanding he was a member of the Tennessee Legislature when it asked Congress for the lands for the benefit of common schools, and supported that application then and during the last session of Congress. He has changed his course, abused his State, and co operated with her enemies. The North Carolina members generally were against his project, which was supported by the honorable Mr. Williams and the honorable Mr. Culpepper, whose hostility to Tennessee has been too often discovered and felt to be now disputed.*

Having thus *re-affirmed,* as I believe, whatever parts of my letter had particular reference to Col. Crockett, instead of mitigating, I now add some corroborating facts. *He represented his willingness, not merely to vote for, but to do any thing for any gentleman who would favor his amendment, even so far as to get on his knees before him. When I moved the postponement of the Tennessee land bill, to which in part, he has since attributed the failure of his amendment, he acquiesced with all his colleagues in the propriety of the motion. At another time in answer to one of them, who asked him if he would not vote with his political friends on the viva voce resolution, he said "there is no party now." His circular dated 14th January last,* [Note: The actual date of Crockett's circular was January 15] *was printed by Gales & Seaton. Very recently he exhibited to different members of Congress, as containing remarks complimentary of himself an account of his conduct here, a number of the* Knoxville Enquirer, *a paper of most infamous notoriety, which was endorsed with the name of the honorable Lewis Williams.* This fact is given as a *key.* Numerous other circumstances might be adduced corresponding with the general tenor of my letter; but they are unnecessary.

Part of the facts before stated were within my own knowledge, but *all* of them are known to other members of Congress, from a number of whom I have obtained statements, ample and conclusive, to *establish every alleged fact.* These statements are now in my possession, to be used according to my own discretion, which dictate forbearance from exhibiting them, until there shall be a greater necessity than is imposed on me by the Colonel's random, indiscriminating negatives. I cannot suppose that he intended to deny all the allegations of my letter; nor do I understand him as sufficiently distinguishing the exceptionable parts. If he can be induced to hazard a positive and public denial of the whole or of any specified part, I will as positively and publicly prove its punctilious correctness.

It is useless to express any unavailing regrets. Having, in common with my colleagues, assiduously cultivated kind feelings for Colonel Crockett, as long as his conduct would permit, I was compelled, at length, to regard him as the willing instrument of political, sectional and personal malignities, affecting prejudicially the interests and character of my State, my constituents, and myself, through his resort to means unworthy of his situation. If any disclosures were true, and for that I am responsible, they carry intrinsic evidence of the propriety of making them to any or all of my constituents, who have a right to know from their representative, the means by which their just expectations have been disappointed, and their confidence in him attempted to be impaired. If, in doing justice to them and myself by exposing the truth on others, the sensibilities of any should be so affected as to produce collisions, such occurrences must be regarded as casual incidents of political life, always to be deprecated, yet never to be avoided by an abandonment of duty.

PRYOR LEA

This letter was reprinted in the *Jackson (Tennessee) Gazette* **March 14, 1829.**

*　　*　　*　　*　　*

LETTER FROM CROCKETT TO PRYOR LEA, FEBRUARY 19, 1829, PUBLISHED IN THE *(WASHINGTON) UNITED STATES' TELEGRAPH,* **FEBRUARY 21, 1829, IN REPLY TO LEA'S LETTER OF FEBRUARY 18.**

Washington City
Feb. 19, 1829.

Hon. Pryor Lea,

Sir:

I published in the United States' Telegraph of the 17th inst. a few remarks in reply to a most shameful, *unprovoked* and merciless attack made upon my feelings and reputation, by some one who was then to me unknown. I perceive, in the same paper, under date of this morning, that you avow yourself the author of that production, and even endeavored to render your arrows more poignant, and your stab at my reputation more fatal. Sir, when I penned my reply, (and you should blush to hear it.) the world, without your own avowal, could scarcely have aroused in my bosom a suspicion that you were capable of acting towards me such a part. You were the last man on the earth whom I should have singled out as my secret persecutor, or as intending to destroy the humble standing which I have secured to myself, without the advantages of a lofty birth, or wealth, or education, or a numerous train of connexions around to support me. It pained me to the heart to find that I had been so much disappointed in you, and that while I had cherished you in my affections as a friend, you were planning my destruction as a foe. To scenes, however, so sacred as former supposed friendship, it is useless to advert—as they can at best, only be said to be "pleasant yet mournful to the soul" that is deceived. You are called, sir, the representative of many individuals whose names, from early association, are endeared to me; and among whom you have archly attempted to destroy me. Whether your course towards me has been the result of regard for them, or whether it was dictated by the conviction that your own fabric of popularity was tottering upon its base, your conscience, your constituents, and the world must judge. If you needed a victim for *peace offering* to either, I regret that you had not selected one, who, from his former treatment to you, had fewer claims upon your forbearance then myself. Many of your constituents could attest that I have bestowed time and labor upon my feeble attempts to advance your popularity and your wishes little thinking that like the unsuspecting lamb, I was *"licking the hand just raised to shed my blood."* This (*politically*) you have attempted to do. But, Sir, there is a superruling power in Providence, which is able to counteract and neutralize the poison of malice, and to stay the dagger of revenge, usually causing the most unrelenting to suffer the severest pain.

The manner in which you have attempted to destroy me is worthy of remark. You and myself were in daily habits of intimacy, and I again repeat that I looked upon you as one that would do me justice—should all others fail. This confidence I must have enjoyed for near four weeks after you had forfeited every claim to it, by sending forth to the world, and as you intimate, for publication, charges against me which, if you believe them true, should have closed your friendly intercourse with me, at a much earlier period. But was it so? No Sir—to the very last hour that your attempt to ruin me was sealed in secrecy, you seemed to meet me friendly—to converse with me as a friend!!!—affording in your conduct not the *slightest index to the feelings of your heart.* Sir, you complain that my feelings were alienated from my colleagues—and well they might have been so, had they all been like you—had their countenances been lighted with affected smiles of friendship, while their hearts burned with secret flames of ambition. With them, I hope it was not so, as I am sure it should not have been. If you, however, want a stronger and more substantial reason, why some of my colleagues did not fall very near to my heart, you have it in this. I had a favorite measure before Congress; a measure which was intended to bless many a poor and helpless family, and afford them shelter from the chilling blast of winter. You, sir, and others, had fixed your affections upon a different system of policy, and because I endeavored to prevail upon *administration* men to stay the merciless hand of the swindling speculators, you cried out, that I had joined the enemies of my party. Because I was unwilling to trust the labour and earnings of my constituents in the hands of the Tennessee legislature, you raised the cry that I had abused my state; and indeed, to defeat my proposition, piteous appeals were made to Jackson men; many of whom voted with you on account of the subtlety used to convince them, that their political opponents had taken me up to break down the remainder of the delegation. That I was thus treated is too notorious to be disputed. It can be proved, by witnesses, who are fully as reputable as yourself. But after all the stratagems resorted to, you failed; and being, as I suppose, willing to lay the blame resulting from your defeat, upon any one sooner than upon yourself, you adroitly charged me with being the cause of it. No, Sir, you do me injustice; I did not defeat you—your proposition, yourself, and my other colleagues, defeated me. You attempted to bring me into suspicion, and, for the moment, you succeeded; but you should blush (if your cheeks be not of marble) to discover that the period has already passed which tested my political firmness, and your baseless jealousy. Its restless spirit so disordered you brain, that though you formerly concealed it, it now appears you could not see me associate with a gentleman of different politics, without awful apprehensions that there was dander of my apostacy; so frantic was your imagination, that it pursued me to *dinner parties*, where God knows I never went; and even fancied me on my knees imploring votes for my measure, when in fact I never bowed unless it was before my

Creator. Had it been otherwise, you should have pittied a lonely individual, who, as a supplicant for mercy, bowed beneath such a load of law. The truth is, you have endeavoured to sacrifice me to save yourself. This I take to be the prevailing opinion—

Who shall prescribe a limit to wounded pride? Or who count the writhings of the restless worm of vanity?

Sir, you call upon me to deny your statement, and allege your readiness and ability to prove them. I deny each and every allegation contained in your first and last publication, calculated in the smallest degree to impugn my honor or to exculpate yourself from the charge of having wantonly assailed me. You know that I was but a humble farmer, with but a humble education, and doubtless supposed that I would *tamely* submit to any indignity which you might offer. You supposed you could array against me sufficient weight of law and of talent, to crush with me a single effort. But, Sir, in each conclusion you are mistaken. I will resent your insults, nor will a magnanimous community ever permit an individual, who is compelled to stand alone, to be condemned without trial, or to suffer without crime. I call upon you, sir, for your testimony, and in return, I pledge myself to disprove, by gentlemen of the highest respectability, each and every charge which you may attempt to establish injurious to my character.

When my former remarks were made, I knew not that they were applicable to you. You have, however, given them application, and I retract no sentiment advanced until you do me justice. But if as you intimate, they inspire you with "personal feelings," and require *"private satisfaction,"* you know where to find me.

DAVID CROCKETT
of West Tennessee

This letter was reprinted in the *Jackson Gazette* March 21, 1829. Crockett's closing line was interpreted by many as the prelude to a duel, which never took place. Crockett declined to pursue the "affair of honor," as he felt it conflicted with his recent turn to religion, and Lea seemed unwilling to accept what appeared to be a challenge from Crockett. However, neither would Lea let the matter rest. He responded to Crockett in a final letter to the *United States Telegraph*, dated February 23, 1829 and published on February 25.

*　　*　　*　　*　　*

LETTER FROM PRYOR LEA TO THE *(WASHINGTON) UNITED STATES' TELEGRAPH*, FEBRUARY 23, 1829, PUBLISHED FEBRUARY 25, IN REPLY TO CROCKETT'S LETTER OF FEBRUARY 19.

Washington City
Feb. 23, 1829.

To the Editor of the U. States' Telegraph.

Sir—

To protract unnecessarily a public controversy can never be justified, and I am perfectly aware, that the honorable Mr. Crockett's publication in your paper of Saturday, addressed to me by name, is of a character to prelude any rejoinder from me *to him;* but, some may think, I owe a brief statement *to the public,* and it is easier to make it than to discuss the propriety of doing so.

My positions, however may be maintained by recurring to our respective publications, from which the following extracts will be sufficient for the present occasion.

From his of the 16th—"In conclusion, I inform the author of the letter, *whether he be in the city,* or out of it, (I care not,) I consider him a *paltroon,* a *scoundrel* and a *puppy.* If he will dare avow himself, puppy as he is, I will condescend to take some further notice of him. I would hazard the opinion, that if he is ever known, he will be found to be one of those who were quietly sitting by their firesides at home, while with the immortal Jackson, I was putting my *life "in market"* and fighting to defend my country. He will not find me backward in putting it "in market" again, in defence of my reputation."

From mine of the 18th—"In your paper of yesterday, I have read Colonel Crockett's answer to a letter recently published in the Knoxville Register. He impugns the correctness of that letter, denounces its author, and threatens to "take some further notice of him," if he dare avow himself." *I am the author* of that letter, and ask you, also, to publish this reply to his communication, concerning the *manner* of which I have but little to say at present, as matters merely personal suit better for private adjustment than for public proclamation; but its *substance* shall be noticed without imitating its indecorum of expression." From the same—"Having thus *re-affirmed,* as I believe, whatever parts of my letter had particular reference to Col. Crockett, instead of mitigating, I now add some corroborating facts." From the same—"Part of the facts before stated were within my own knowledge, but *all* of them are known to other members of Congress, from a number of whom I have obtained statements, ample and conclusive, to *establish every alleged fact.* These statements are now in my possession, to be used according to my own discretion, which dictate forbearance from exhibiting them, until there shall be a greater necessity than is imposed on me by the Colonel's random, indiscriminating negatives. I cannot suppose that he intended to deny all the allegations of my letter; nor do I understand him as sufficiently distinguishing the exceptionable parts. If he can be induced to hazard a positive and public denial of the whole or of any specified part, I will as positively and publicly prove its punctilious correctness."

From his of the 19th.—"Sir, you call on me to deny your statements and allege your readiness and ability to prove them. I deny each and every allegation contained in your first and last publication, calculated in the slightest degree to impugn my honor or to exculpate yourself from the charge of having wantonly assailed me." From the same,—"I call upon you, sir, for your testimony; & in return, I pledge myself to disprove, by gentlemen of the highest respectability, each and every charge which you may attempt to establish, injurious to my character. When my former remarks were made, I knew not that they were applicable to you. You have, however, given them application, and I retract no sentiment advanced until you do me justice. But if as you intimate, they inspire you with "personal feelings," and require "private satisfaction," you know where to find me."

These last extracts are preceded by a *chapter of lamentations,* concerning former "habits of intimacy," and such soft concerns, applicable only to last winter and the first of this, showing how the roaring and rampant lion can transform himself into "the unsuspecting lamb," but, lest any should suppose, contrary to the fact, that the expressions "personal feeling" and "private satisfaction," were used by me as quoted in the last extract, I brand them with disgrace, as an effort to change relative positions, characteristic of *those* who have participated in making it. Instead of using rude of menacing language, I have studiously refrained from it, as cheap and unbecoming.

Turning to another aspect of the case, it must be observed, that the honorable gentleman has called on me for testimony before the issues are properly joined, I proposed to prove "the whole" or "any specified party," of which he could "be induced to hazard a positive and public denial;" but he says, "I deny each and every allegation contained in your first and last publication, calculated in the slightest degree to impugn my honor, or to exculpate yourself from the charge of having wantonly assailed me." Now, what allegations are denied? and what proof is required? If my exculpation depend on his inculpation, then a question of honor is preliminary for both; what would impugn that of any gentleman could only be matter of opinion, and in the present case, perhaps indefinite uncertainty. If any allegation were established, the honorable gentleman might contend successfully, for aught I know, that his honor remained as safe as before; but I simply asserted facts, and he might easily have admitted or denied them plainly, without referring them to his own standard of honor. With such *barefaced evasions he* cannot be entitled to any thing whatever from me; yet a due regard for myself and for the public may require of me some further explanations, in making which, however, I consider him as laid aside.

Between the public and myself, there shall be no difficulty as to the facts, and all that can be desirable shall be given; but prudence restrains me from occasioning any unnecessary trouble, either to the community or to particular individuals, and, of course, from publishing the *entire* statements, which many know to be in my possession, subject to my discretion. They were all made by members of Congress, who desire no concealment, and whose names, with all they have said, will be at command, as may be proper. At present, it will be sufficient for me, without distinguishing among them, to give some *pertinent extracts, conclusively sustaining the various allegations in question.* This I proceed to do omitting much that would give additional force to the parts exhibited.

"That Col. Crockett, about the time spoken of, had assumed a doubtful political attitude is, in my estimation, but too true." "While the Colonel's amendment to the Tennessee land bill was under discussion, he came to my room," "said he had been, as I understood him, to Seaton's to a dining party. I asked him if any other person of the delegation was there. He answered me in the negative, and said he had happened there rather accidentally." "He replied with some earnestness that he would carry his amendment. But said I, suppose you should, the very men who will aid you in your amendment will turn round and by some side wind defeat both bill and amendment, and thus put the whole to rest. He said, I don't fear that. I continued—but, Colonel, it grieves me to see you acting with and surrounded by our deadly political enemies upon this occasion.—He replied, I could not get enough of friends without them, and I would do any thing upon earth to get votes from any body to carry my measure." "Colonel Crockett commenced hunting the paper with a view to show us his speech. I told him he need be at no trouble upon that head, for I had heard him deliver it in the House. But he replied, I know that—I want to shew how it is in the paper, continuing, I like Gales *prime,* for he has made me a much better speech than I made in the House, or ever could make, and I will get a 1000 or 1500 and send them home to my people and they will think I have made a great speech—or words to that effect.[1] I observed that Gales had nothing to do with the matter—it was Mr. Stansbury, the Reporter for Gales' paper, who had made him the *fine speech.* The Colonel replied that he knew it was *somebody about that paper.* After some hunting about the room, the paper containing the speech was found, and I was requested to read it, which I did out audibly, commenting upon such parts as had not been delivered by the Colonel in the House. He agreed to the justness of my strictures on the report of the speech and the discrepancies between the speech as delivered and the one as reported, saying he had never seen a word of it, until he saw it in the paper." "I became alarmed, lest the Colonel should go over to the enemy; and having my fear, I expressed them to you and the grounds thereof, and to several of our mutual friends. I was enabled to attend the House when the vote was taken to lay Mr. Wickliffe's *viva voce* resolution on the table, and with extreme regret, heard Col. Crockett vote in the affirmative. What before I had only feared, was now in my imagination reduced to certainty. I believed he was not only in market, but had gone over irrevocably to the enemy."

"During the unpleasant discussion upon the Tennessee land bill, I had frequent conversation with Col. Crockett in relation to his amendment, and its probable effects upon the measure, in which he stated that he did not expect his colleagues to vote with him." "I took occasion to express to him my regret, that he had estranged himself from us, and had sought succour from his political opponents. To which he replied that he had his amendment so much at heart, that he would look for support wherever he could get it, seeing that his party would not give it to him; that he would do any thing for any gentleman who would favor his amendment, even so far as to get on his knees before him." "The change which had taken place in his opinion from the last session, when he supported the bill—his declarations that he preferred the rejection of the whole measure to that of his amendment—his apparent confidence in being able to carry his amendment, by the assistance of the opposite party; and the freedom of his remarks in relation to the legislature of our State, excited my suspicions in regard to him. His afterwards voting with the same party against the *viva voce* resolution of Mr. Wickliffe, not only confirmed in my own mind, but all with whom I conversed, the suspicions which had been before entertained."

"I heard the Colonel say publicly, that North Carolina and Tennessee had combined, and had swindled the General Government out of a quantity of lands. I must confess, at the time this measure was before the House (the Tennessee land bill) I thought, and so did a number of my friends, that the Colonel was about to change his political course, for his associations were to a considerable extent, confined to the friends of the administration and he did appear to me to be estranged from his colleagues." "Whilst the resolution submitted by Mr. Wickliffe was under consideration, which was to change the mode of voting by ballot to *viva voce*, I went to Colonel Crockett and asked him if he would not vote with his political friends in favor of the resolution. His answer was "there is no party now." "While the Tennessee land bill was pending before the House several of my friends remarked to me, that Col. Crockett had gone over to the enemy." "On yesterday, I heard Col. Crockett ask some gentleman, if he had seen his publication." "I took occasion to say to the colonel, at the time, that he had said (when the bill was before the House,) that his object was to defeat it, and that he had said that North Carolina and Tennessee had swindled the General Government out of a large quantity of lands, which he acknowledged. I stated to him, also, that a gentleman had informed me that he heard him (Crockett) say, that he would either go for any thing any gentleman wanted, if they would vote for his amendment. This the colonel did not deny." "I saw Colonel Crockett a few days since exultingly shewing, to some of the member of the House, the Knoxville Enquirer, a violent administration paper, with the name of the Hon. Lewis Willliams written on it, to whom I suppose it had been addressed, which paper contained a eulogy on Colonel Crockett, for his conduct on the Tennessee Land bill. I remarked to the Colonel that it was an administration paper, and that I should not like to be pulled by such a paper.

"I felt mortified at even the appearance of disaffection in our delegation, and did participate in the fears which I thought were about that time pretty common among our political friends, that Col. Crockett might not vote with us in the election for printer, and expressed my doubts to others. These doubts were produced from conversations wholly repugnant to my wishes, and I am sure from no unfriendly feeling towards Col. Crockett. Although I regretted that there should be a difference of opinion among us that that might defeat the main object, I had no right to control him, and did not intend to find fault with the fair and zealous support which he might give to his favorite plan. But during the debate he made (if not misunderstood) reflections upon the proceedings of the Tennessee Legislature, which I was extremely sorry to hear from a Representative of the State, in regard to North Carolina University Claims, which were seized upon by others as the authority for indulging in terms which I considered as unjust as they were disreputable to the character of the State."

"The delegation felt great anxiety for the fate of the bill, and suggested to Col. Crockett the effect likely to be produced by his amendment. He said his object was to defeat the bill if his amendment did not carry."

"At the moment, I thought he had said that which he did not intend and put this question to him—is it your wish to *prevent* the bill from passing, if you cannot succeed in your amendment? He answered, *it is*. I then asked him what good that would do his constituents? He answered, that the United States could never sell the land, and if the State did not procure it, his people could have the use of it for nothing." "He said he would do what his constituents wished and that he did not expect either me or any other member from the state to support his amendment; but that we would see he would carry it without any of us; that he had been very industrious in trying to make friends out of doors, and he intended to be more industrious than I ever heard of any other person being." "Before the bill was taken up, and while it was under consideration, and for some days after it was disposed of, I was told by several members of Congress, as well from our own State, as from other States, that Col. Crockett was making statements to the prejudice of the Legislature of his own State. While the bill was under discussion and for some days afterwards, it was the common impression of all those members, who I heard speak of him, that he had actually determined in his future votes to go with those, to whom he had been previously opposed; and most of them expressed very strongly their fears, that in the election for printer he would vote for Messrs. Gales & Seaton. For myself, I believed when the bill was defeated, and still do believe, that the offering of Colonel Crockett's amendment with the disagreement among our own members necessarily produced thereby, was one principal cause of defeating the bill. I then believed, and still do, that some of those who had always been our political opponents, and who seemed most active in favor of Colonel Crockett's amendment were deceiving him, and that their real object was to induce him to pursue a course which would defeat the bill entirely, enable them to speak in disrespectful terms of our State, and induce him to act with them in future. In these opinions I may have done him injustice, but as they are those I really entertained, I hold it my duty to state them when called upon."

"I have examined your letter of the 19th of January, published in the Knoxville Register, and so far as the facts come within my knowledge, I believe it to be strictly true." "It is a matter of notoriety, that during the discussion of the Tennessee land bill, and afterwards, many of the Jackson members of the House entertained serious fears that he had been operated upon thro' that measure, by our political enemies; and, from his conduct, his associations, and apparent intimacy with some of them, fears were entertained that he had gone over to them." "That he was the principal cause of laying the land ill on the table, I have no doubt." "We all expressed our decided disapprobation of his project, as being well calculated, if not certain, to defeat the whole measure, and our regret that any member from the state should take a course which was likely to produce that result. He was reminded that the Legislature of Tennessee had instructed their Senators, and requested their Representatives in Congress, to procure the relinquishment to the State, for the purposes of common schools: He was reminded that he himself had been a member of the Legislature, and voted for the instructions. He was reminded, too, that, at the last session of Congress, he had supported the very bill that was now before the House at this session, and which he then avowed his intention to oppose. He was admonished that his proposition would probably have no other tendency, if he persevered in it, than the rejection of the whole measure. No importunities would avail any thing." "He distinctly said, that his object was to *kill the bill,* if he could not carry his amendment. Even after the bill had been so amended as to make ample provision for the occupants, he still (as we suspected, under the influence of others) pertinaciously adhered to his proposition, and opposed the bill, even with the provision in it for the benefit of the occupants. That he was estranged from his colleagues, and associated much with our political enemies, and was supported in the discussion by several of our political enemies, all who were here know. That he spoke in terms of abuse and great disrespect of the Legislature of his own State, both in and out of the House, he cannot deny." "When pending the discussion of the Tennessee land bill, you moved a postponement of its further consideration for a few days, I know that Col. Crockett did acquiesce with the balance of our delegation in the propriety of the motion, and agreed before the motion was made that it was proper to make it. Since I understand, he has complained of this postponement. Indeed in his circular letter, of the 15th January, printed by Gales & Seaton, he alleges this postponement, to which he himself had agreed, as one cause of the failure of his amendment." "I avail myself of the occasion to express my deep regret of the necessity, which renders it proper to make this statement. I had ever, as I believe the whole delegation had, treated him with the utmost kindness, and was more disposed to conceal than to expose his errors. But when he separated himself from us, embraced and took counsel from some of our most rancorous political enemies associating with apparent intimacy with them, and joining with them in slandering and abusing his own State, we would have been recreant to our duty, if we had not vindicated the honor of that State, and sustained the measure which she had instructed us to support. Opposed as he was to the whole of his colleagues, and as we conceived to the interests, not only of the State, but of his own immediate constituents, there was but one course left for us to pursue. It was to discharge our duty, and to communicate to our constituents what we had done, and the causes of the failure of the measure. That you have done, and if in telling the truth any one feels its force, and is the more sensitive, because of its truth, that is a matter for himself and his constituents."

In addition to the foregoing extracts, I might adduce very many others of similar import, which I now have and could probably obtain; I might advert to the Journal of the House, and to the honorable gentleman's own speeches, to confirm much of what I have advanced; but the danger is, that too much has been presented already.

Having said and sustained, in my own manner, and subject to all just responsibilities, what my own sense of duty dictated as proper, according to the circumstances only partially known to the public, I cheerfully acquiesce in the adoption by others of their own measures, on similar terms.

Magnanimity would now enjoin forbearance, even if my purpose had ever been, what it never was, to pursue or harrass Colonel Crockett, for whom I once entertained the feelings of friendship imputed to me, and against whom I have no disposition to aggravate any thing; but my object, conduct, and justification, have already appeared, I trust, to the entire satisfaction of impartiality, and I designedly refrain from all commentary, as more properly belonging to the intelligence of others.

PRYOR LEA

Lea did not mention any of his sources, but at least some of the statements he quoted were taken from the letter Polk had written him earlier in the month. Hugh Lawson White and James C. Mitchell (both Jacksonian Tennessee representatives at the time) appear to have been among his other sources. The similarity in language among the sources, and correspondence among them at the time, suggest that they had orchestrated a campaign to undermine Crockett and discredit him at home. Charles Anderson Wickliffe was a Jacksonian congressman from Kentucky. Lewis Williams was a pro-Adams congressman from North Carolina. This letter was reprinted in the *Jackson Gazette* March 28, 1829.

[1]   This may be a reference to a rewritten version of Crockett's January 12, 1829 speech in the House, which was heavily rewritten for his January 15, 1829 circular, which was printed by Gales and Seaton, who may have printed the same speech in their newspaper. However, the original version of the speech was printed in the *Register of Debates*, January 12, 1829, 199–200, also published by Gales & Seaton.

*   *   *   *   *

LETTER TO THE MESS AT J. DAVIS'S, FEBRUARY 23, 1829.

Washington City
23 Febry 1829

The Mess at J. Davises

Gentlemen you have doubtless seen and red the correspondance which has unfortunately sprung up between the Hon Mr. Lea of Tennessee & myself you will without explanation from me understand my situation and all I need say is that I – request of each of you the favour to say whether I am the Character described by him and what has been my Conduct Sence you have Known me and also the manner in which I have discharged my official duties your early Compliance will oblige your very obt. Servt
David Crockett
The Mess

Department of Rare Books and Special Collections, University of Rochester Library.

Crockett sent a nearly identical letter on the same day to the "Mess at Dowson's" to which Crockett added the comment, "To which the *'mess'* made no reply". The original of the Dowson's letter is in the Rare Book and Manuscript Library, Columbia University.

*　　*　　*　　*　　*

LETTER TO PRESIDENT ANDREW JACKSON, FEBRUARY 25, 1829.

Washington City
25th February 1829

To the President of the United States;

　　Sir. Presuming that it will shortly devolve on you to appoint an Indian Agent, to supply the vacancy occasioned by the death of George Gray Esq., we take the liberty of recommending most respectfully for your consideration Thomas Griffith Esq. of Kentucky, as a gentleman well qualified to discharge the duties of that station. The appointment was before made from Kentucky, which induces the presumption and the hope that the vacancy may be filled from the same state. The standing of Mr. Griffith is fair and his moral character irreproachable. He was one of those who engaged during the last War in our second struggle for liberty and was six years of his life commencing in 1812, has been devoted devoted [sic] in actual service, and upon the peace establishment. We should be highly gratified to see him advanced; as he is in but moderate circumstances, and was active and faithful in our great political struggle.

Your Obedient Servants.

T P (Thomas Patrick) Moore
Michael Sprigg
David Crockett
Chittenden Lyon
Jos[eph] M. White
Tho[mas] Chilton
Bossa [illeg]
Joseph LeCompte

In the year 1814 I served with Mr. Thomas Griffith in the army at Detroit and have no hesitation in saying he is a high minded honorable man, and that he is well qualified to discharge the duty of Indian agent I have not the least doubt—and Respectfully recommend him to fill the vacancy he aspires to.

Rob[er]t. Desha
Joseph Duncan

　　This letter is not in Crockett's hand and was clearly drafted by one of the other signers. Jackson appointed Griffith to the Red River agency on March 12, 1829. Daniel Feller, Harold D. Moser, Laura-Eve Moss, Thomas Coens, eds., *The Papers of Andrew Jackson: Volume VII - 1829* (Knoxville: University of Tennessee Press, 2007), 136.

*　　*　　*　　*　　*

LETTER FROM GALES & SEATON IN RESPONSE TO LEA, PUBLISHED IN *JACKSON (TENNESSEE) GAZETTE*, MARCH 21, 1829, REPRINTED FROM THE *(WASHINGTON) NATIONAL INTELLIGENCER*.

A newspaper controversy has arisen between two members of Congress from the state of Tennessee, Mr. Crockett and Mr. Lea, in consequence of the publication, in a Knoxville paper, of a letter from Washington, of which Mr. Lea avows himself to be the author, reflecting upon the political course of Mr. Crockett. It is odd enough, certainly, that in such a controversy, the editors of this paper should have been introduced in a manner to oblige them to speak upon it. But so it is. One of the charges against Mr. Crockett, in the Tennessee letter, is in the following terms: "Gales is officiously polite to all who will tolerate him, and plies every doubtful man with good dinners and speeches, served up to his liking. Col. Crockett is one of those, and voted for having the resolution [requiring members to vote in elections *viva voce*] on the table." Without stopping to remark on the spirit which would criminate one man for having broken bread with another, it is no more than justice to Colonel Crockett to rescue him from the imputation here conveyed. 'Gales' never had the honor of Col C's company at his table, or in his house. As to the 'officious politeness' of 'Gales,' he learned the duty of common civility in his infancy, from those who understood it and has endeavored to practice it ever since, without offence, as he had hoped to God or man. It is a new sin under the sun to be accused of. As to his 'dinners,' he does not feel himself called upon to plead to the charge of giving them, further than to exonerate an innocent person from the high misdemeanor of participating in one of them. Neither has 'Gales' or his partner had any concern in Col. Crockett's speeches. They were reported by their able and faithful reporter in the House of Representatives, and committed to the press without being seen by either of us.

In the letter signed with his proper name, and just published, Mr. Lea, with a view to correct an error into which he had fallen in his letter to Tennessee, says he has been since told 'that the Colonel's dining was at the home of Mr. Seaton, & not at that of Mr. Gales. It is not easy to discover of what consequence it can be to the public at whose house Col. Crockett dines. But it is a fact that Mr. Lea's late information is as erroneous as his first; for Col. C. has never dined at the house of Mr. Seaton, any more than at the house of Mr. Gales, though Mr. S. has had the pleasure of seeing him, with other members of Congress at his house. These things are very unfit for newspaper discussion, we are aware, and it is a source of deep regret that they should be made the subjects of it. As for Col. Crockett, he is so far from being any particular friend of ours, we are given to understand, that at the late election in the House of Representatives, he voted an open ticket against us, though we are of opinion that he might have found very substantial reasons for voting otherwise. Whatever other cause of difference of opinion there may exist between him and his colleagues, we do not choose that he shall be hunted down upon a suspicion of intimacy with us. It is true, as Mr. Lea says, that we printed his speech: we plead guilty to that: and, if Mr. Lea pleases to command our services, we will with equal readiness print his also.

This letter was in response to Pryor Lea's claim that the two publishers had curried favor from members of Congress by wining and dining them, and by enhancing published versions of their speeches, including Crockett's. Although Crockett admitted that Gales and Seaton had made some of his speeches read better than they had actually sounded on the floor of House, this was a common practice in the *Register of Debates*. All congressmen and senators were given the opportunity to edit and rewrite speeches before they were published.

*   *   *   *   *

LETTER TO GALES AND SEATON, APRIL 18, 1829.

Huntingdon Carroll City
18 April 1829

Dear Sirs

I arrived home safe and found all well on the 15 of March I am on my way home from a journey of three weeks and am in better health than I have been in for ten years past I have backed out three opponents and Colo Alexander has lately been entered against me Tho my own opinion is that he will back out before August if he does not I will beat him five thousand votes So says the people

I was in Nashville a few days and a Circumstance took place last Saturday which created much exitement Our Governer Houston has parted with his wife and Resigned the governers appointment he told me that he was going to leave the country and go up the arkensaw and live with the Indians as he calls them his addopted Brothers The balance of his days So I expect Wm Carroll will be our next governer with out opposition I hope the Chance is good for Lea and Polk both to be beat and Doct Marable will be Badley Beaton

So Sais the People of his district I have just traveled through the Doctors district and Colo Johnson has the voice of the people at this time I also traveled through Polks district and done what little I could for him

Be so good as to answer this letter informe me how times is in the city and how you are coming on and how every thing is working write lengthy also Pleas to tender my Best Respects to Mr Hyat and old friend Tipee Brown & mr St Clark I must conclude & may god Bless you & familys is the wishes of your friend

David Crockett

Mrsrs
Gailes & Seaton

David Crockett Miscellaneous File. Manuscripts and Archives Division. The New York Public Library. Astor, Lenox and Tilden Foundations

Crockett's correspondence with Gales and Seaton supports the accusations that he was "disloyal" to the Jacksonians and too friendly toward their "enemies." It also shows Crockett's determination to remain independent and free of strict party discipline. He expresses strong confidence that he will be reelected, while suggesting that several of his Tennessee colleagues might be defeated. In fact, Polk was easily reelected, but Lea was declared the winner in his district only after a recount. John Hartwell Marable ("Doct Marable"), another Tennessee Jacksonian, was defeated by Cave Johnson.

"Colo Alexander" was Adam Alexander, whom Crockett had defeated in 1827; he would lose to him again in 1829. "Mr Hyat, Tipee Brown & mr St Clark" appear to be friends of Crockett's.

Crockett refers to Sam Houston's resignation as governor of Tennessee, which resulted from his wife's desertion and caused a scandal in the state.

*   *   *   *   *

LETTER TO JOHN H. BRYAN, MAY 26, 1829.

Dresdon Weakley County
26 May 1829

Dear Sir

    I am Requested by a gentleman who lives on your land to write to you for the Purpose of Soliciting you to give him a leace he Bought a gentlemans improvement and Paid fifty Dollars thare was a Small field & Cabben on it and he has had the use of it two years he wishes you to extend his Privaledges to what would be the Custom of the Country which would be five years to come. I informed the gentelman that I was well acquainted with you and thought you would give him a leace if you give him a leace he will Clear twenty acers and Plant you one hundred fruit trees also Mr Wm L Petty John lives on your land and wishes also to take a leace if you conclude to give these leaces write them and enclose them to Dresdon to me Mr Elisha W Glass is one and Mr Wm L Petty John is the other Please to answer this letter as Soon as Posable I am well and family hoping these lines to find you in the alike

Your friend   David Crockett

John H. Bryan

PS Please to write imediately as these Poor Men is uneasy and wants to know the Result. I have said nothing about my next Election I think if I am not Flattered I will Beat 5000 vots I have Backed out Mr Miller and Mr Alexander has taken the [trail] he Run against me in my last contest I Beat him 27&48 vots and I have no doubt of getting a a much larger Majority in very next Race. I Remain your Sincear friend in hast direct your letter to Trenton

David Crockett

Hon. John H. Bryan
[Mailed from Trenton, June 2, 1829.]

Courtesy of John Heritage Bryan Papers (#147), Special Collections Department, J. Y. Joyner Library, East Carolina University, Greenville, North Carolina, USA.

    Bryan, an Adams man, had been a representative from North Carolina in the previous Congress. Crockett was trying to arrange a land lease from Bryan by the two men mentioned, one of whom had purchased the buildings on the land, but did not have title to the land itself. Crockett refers to having "backed out" Pleasant Miller in the congressional race.

*   *   *   *   *

LETTER TO THE *JACKSON (TENNESSEE) GAZETTE*, JUNE 28, 1829, PUBLISHED JULY 11, 1829.

June 28, 1829:

I am truly sorry that it has so happened, that it becomes necessary for me to make a statement on [illeg.] which, I never did think was becoming to a Candidate. But as I have been informed that Col. B. G. Stewart has made a statement relative to a matter that took place between Col. A. R. Alexander and myself,

I have understood that Mr. Stewart has stated that I had tried to injure Col. Alexander, by telling a lie on him, in relation to a monied matter in Washington City. I now think it my duty to make a fair statement on the subject.

Shortly after I arrived at Washington, I was enquired of by J. C. Letrute, a jeweler, [who knew (?)] Col. Alexander; I told him I was his successor, he informed me that he was like to suffer by him; he had endorsed in the U. States Branch Bank, for Col. Alexander, to the amount of twelve hundred and fifty dollars and was protested on his account, and at the same time shewed me his protest, and give it to me, and wished me to write to him on the subject. I enquired and Judge J. C. Isaacks was also bound, and he told me that he had wrote to the Col on the subject. And after a few days, Judge Isaacks called on me and stated, that he had tried nearly all the balance of my colleagues to aid him, and take up the note or renew it.

I told Judge Isaacks that Col. Alexander was very good for the amount and I would see Col. Blair, and get him to join and done so, and Judge Isaacks executed his note, and Col. Blair and myself were the endorsers. I also spoke to Ovrton Carr, our assistant door keeper, and Mr. Seaton was the other City endorser.

I advanced the money to pay the discounts and expences to the amount of between 80 and 100 dollars, and Judge Isaacks wrote a letter by me to Col. Alexander, stating how my treatment had been to him.

I took the letter to Col. Alexander's [illeg.] house and delivered it to him, he paid me the money that I advanced for him. And some time during the summer, I had a protest sent me from Washington for twelve hundred and fifty dollars, the same [illeg.] that the Col. was protested for when I went to Washington.

I then spoke tolerable rough, tho I never knew any more about the matter until I arrived in Washington at the last session. I then enquired of Judge Isaacks about the matter—he informed me that Col. Alexander had sent on the money and paid it. I immediately wrote a letter to Esq Atchison, that the Col. had sent the money and paid off the debt; this I done because Esq Atchison was in company with myself and Col. Stewart when, I made the statement, on account of being protested. I said no more until in May. I 'meet' Col. Alexander in Jackson, and we both addressed the people on that day. The Col. informed me that the people were talking about that monied matter at Washington. I informed him that I had wrote to Esq. Atchison, that he had paid the money and I requested him to walk with me to the Esq. Atchison, and I would satisfy him that I had acted honorable. We went to the Esq's, and Col. Alexander appeared to be well satisfied. This was the last account I heared of the matter, until I heared Col. B. G. Stewart was trying to circulate a report that I had told a lie on Col. Alexander to injure him.

I conceive Col. Stewart's statement, ungenerous, ungentlemanly and untrue, and I hold myself responsible for this assertion.

David Crockett
June 28, 1829

Bartholomew G. Stewart was an early, prominent resident of Madison County, Tennessee, and held several offices, including county commissioner and judge. Crockett refers to Adam Alexander, whom he succeeded in Congress, and John Blair and Jacob C. Isacks, both Tennessee members of Congress. "Esq. Atchison" is unidentified.

An undated rejoinder from Stewart also was printed with Crockett's letter, disagreeing with Crockett's account. Stewart said that when the others inquired of Crockett whether he and Judge Isacks had paid the debt, or Alexander

had paid it himself, Crockett replied "yes" to both questions and simply walked away without explaining. The end of Stewart's letter is difficult to read, but includes some reference to the likelihood of this being an affair of honor for Crockett and Alexander:

As regards the truth of the charge, I submit it to the public, whether I was not authorized from the circumstances to make it. It was his duty to have explained the matter to me that [illeg.] could have done so, but this I believe he could not do—and [illeg.] still insist he has not been charged wrongfully.

As respects his holding himself accountable, I am well aware that he is not in a [illeg.] to be affected by any process in law, let him say what he may, for it is notoriously known that he is insolvent, and as for any affair of honor, the Colonels business in that way at Washington City, in the affair with Mr. Lea seems to be quite too unsettled to admit of any interference of [mine (?)] without incruing the disgrace of putting myself upon a footing with a man of doubtful courage.

B. G. Stewart

*   *   *   *   *

UNDATED LETTER TO THE *JACKSON (TENNESSEE) GAZETTE*, PUBLISHED SEPTEMBER 26, 1829.

To the Editor of the Jackson Gazette.

Sir:

I am truly sorry now the canvass for Congress is over, to trouble either you or myself with any remarks of a personal nature, but I consider it due to myself, and those who have kindly supported my pretensions to make some explanation relative to a matter which has taken place between myself and the Rev. David Gordon.

I have been a candidate for the last eight years of my life, and it has so happened that once every two years of that period, just before August, I have been charged upon with all the artillery which malice hatred and envy, could bring into the field to bear against me, for the purpose of laying me out, and establishing my character and standing in society, in the odious position of a scoundrel, without having ever once in the course of my life, so far as has come to my own knowledge or belief, either directly or indirectly, deserved the imputation.

Among others, tho' least expected the Rev David Gordon of Gibson county, in the late contest was kind enough to lay down his character of the *divine*, and all his religious notions, & take a set at me. I therefore consider it my duty, to make a full expose of the matter between this worthy Divine and myself by giving an entire and fair statement of the facts which have given rise to this unpleasant difference.

I never wish to boast of my friendship to any man, nor could any thing but necessity ever induce me to do so in regard to any obligation or act of friendship which kind providence has enabled me at any time, to perform towards any man living; but I view this as one of the cases in which it may not be improper to depart from a general rule. Commenting with the history of my acquaintance with Mr. Gordon, it will in the sequel be discovered, that the old gentleman ought rather to have considered me as entitled to his good will than his enmity.

In the fall of the year 1824, the old man came to my house and asked me, if I knew of any vacant land of good quality, informing me at the same time that he had a 236 acre warrant, that he would like to locate for a home. I went immediately without fee or reward, and shewed him a peice of vacant land, upon which he located his warrant. He then returned home, moved out, settled upon it, and became my neighbour, and I am proud to own that I was always pleased with his family and himself, until the old gentleman in the dispensation of providence lost his wife, whom I always considered as one of the finest women and neighbors I ever lived by. But now the good old man has married a young wife, and whether he has become deranged, or is in his dotage, I cannot tell, but certain it is that something is wrong with him, or he would not without any just ground whatever, fall out with, and traduce the reputation of his best friend.

The fall the old gentleman moved out, his family were very industrious, and exposed themselves so much, that they were nearly all taken sick. The good old man himself lay very low, and was considered by all his neighbours nearly past recovery for several weeks during which time, every morning until he got a well dug, I carried a half bushel pail of water to his house from a good spring, (the nearest good water) which was near to where I lived. I also got on my horse as often as twice in the critical hour of extreme danger, and rode to Huntingdon, upwards of forty miles after Dr Nicholson, and brought him once to him and once to his daughter. I was pleased and gratified that I had it in my power to accommodate him, and render what I conceive to be a very essential service to himself and family; and indeed I have often thought, and frequently expressed my opinion, that I did not believe it possible, that good old man could have the sin of ingratitude to answer for, by acting and talking about me in the manner I heard; though I regret that I have to recall it, as I am now satisfied that although ingratitude is a crime of blacker dye, than even heathens are willing to admit themselves guilty of, yet this good old Christian for once has committed it—and I here take occasion to say that if that being who he professes to worship, and to whom alone he is responsible will forgive him, as I sincerely hope he will at a coming day, that I will with all my heart, though I can never forget it.

The great cause of his pretended displeasure towards me arises out of the following facts: A certain David C. Philips who professed himself to be a Mill-wright, was indebted, and had been for a long time to Mr. Gordon, the sum of about twenty-five dollars for which he held his note, with one Nathan Fike, security thereto. Now it so happens as it probably always will, that neither said Philips or Fike, is worth one groat, nor were they at the time of the conversation, between Mr. Gordon, Philips and myself hereafter mentioned. I had contracted with Philips to build me a horse mill, for which when finished in the manner he represented himself to be able, and stated he would do, I was to pay him in trade. I had already in anticipation paid him upward of fifty dollars, (as it turns out for nothing at all) when Mr. Gordon called on Philips at my house, in the month of September last for payment. Philips informed him that I would be indebted to him when the mill was finished. I told Mr. Gordon in the presence of Philips how the matter stood between us, but stated that if Philips would prosecute his work with industry, and finish the mill in the manner which he had promised to do, before I started on to Congress, that I would remit the *money* from Washington City to Esqr. Atchison, for the payment of the debt due him from Philips. Not being able to get Philips to start the mill before I set out for the City. Some time after my arrival there, I received a letter from my brother in law Burgen, informing me that the mill would do no good and was of no account, consequently I did not send the money to Mr. Gordon which Philips owed him, neither could Mr. Gordon have reasonably expected it. But during the late canvass the old man it seems, in order to injure my election, has propagated and circulated a report, stating that I was to have remitted the money (without naming the condition) that I had forfeited my word, and in short, was every thing except a clever fellow, and to establish his statements, has *piously* procured these subborned instruments of his imbecility or malice as the case may be, to swear just as they have sworn about the matter—which is just as Mr. Gordon has said it was, whereas in fact Mr. Gordon as I charitably *would hope,* thro' some derangement of intellect or defect of memory, has omitted stating the truth and mistated the fact, as will be seen by reference to the deposition of credible and totally disinterested witnesses, which I herewith transmit for publication. I have also procured a copy of Philips' affidavit, which I also send you for the like purpose; I have not procured a copy of Fikes' but am informed it is of the same stamp. It is then by the circumstance of the case and the credibility of the witnesses on each side, that the public are to judge between Mr. Gordon and myself. In the neighborhood of the residence of the witnesses, no comments of mine would be necessary—those who are acquainted with them, would not hesitate a moment which side to credit. As for Philips he is well known to be an unprincipled vicious fellow, without standing in society—totally destitute of any thing like moral integrity, and no man is better apprized of this fact than Parson Gordon himself. Fike if possible, is a still more odious character—he has been charged with malicious mischief, for cutting and stabbing two horses in Dyer county, one the property of John W. Needham, the other that of a Mr. White, of which he was convicted—fined and imprisoned in Jackson Jail—besides he is one of the most profane and blasphemous wretches that lives and has been known not unfrequently to curse Jesus Christ, a fact of which the Parson was not ignorant and yet in order to injure my reputation, he has condescended to lay aside *holy orders* for a moment, in order to procure the deposition of this man, in regard to a *fact* which he knew nothing about, for Fike was not present, nor do I suppose within a less distance than three miles of my house when the conversation above referred to took place. From such men, interested as they are as principal and security in the debt which they seem with the Parson to have conspired together to get out of me, the truth could hardly be expected, and yet such are the witnesses relied upon by Parson Gordon. The testimony which I offer to rebut the evidence, is the statements of John Ryen and Wm. Edmondson, who are credible men and entirely disinterested in the affair. They happened to be present at the conversation referred to, and both distinctly recollect the conditions annexed to my promise.

I will now leave it with the public to judge, whether I have forfeited my word and honor, or whether the Parson has not erred in his statements, before the public concerning the affair. If Mr. Gordon looses his debt, it was his own folly or misfortune, to trust a man of so little account—true he took security, but this not being a case which falls within the spirit of Judge Catron's proposition, he wants me who was no security at all in the transaction, & who have a family to support, as well as he has to pay for that which I have never eat nor drank, nor ever will, unless I eat the horse mill—for I can safely say, no man will ever fatten upon the meal it will ever grind, and what is worse still to pay for it, in the absence of any obligation whatever, either moral or legal. It would be a great hardship, & a still greater piece of folly to pay this man Philips or his creditors, any thing more than what I have already for his imposition upon me in receiving my property, destroying my timber—and for disappointing me, and putting myself, family and neighbors, to great inconvenience by constructing in the place of a horse mill, a mere Rattle box unfit for any other use than to scare the crows with, for which purpose it unfortunately stood in the wrong place, so that in the end it answered no purpose at all. It has been usual with me to treat most of the fabricated malicious electioneering stories against me with silent contempt, but when we consider that the author of the present one is a preacher of the Gospel, whose very calling is calculated to cloak his falsehoods, and inspire confidence in the truth of his statement, it is presumed this fact would of itself be a sufficient apology for troubling the public with the present communication. But that is not all; this pious man who professes himself to be the meek and humble follower of our saviour, and to have received a call from the throne of grace, to consecrate himself in the holy ordinances and service of god, to preach the Gospel to a wicked world for the salvation of sinners, instead of confining himself to the object of his holy mission by the conversation of his fellow citizens to the true faith, has I contend most irreligiously, maliciously and industriously, during the late canvass, went about from place to place propogating and uttering falsehoods for the purpose of converting those who were already right, to the end that he might bring them over to vote for my opponent. The Lord has not been pleased in this case to bless the labours of *his* minister with fruition, and I hope his abortion in the attempt, with the little counsel which I am now endeavoring to bestow upon him may be the means of restoring him to his senses, as well his ministerial duties if he is or hereafter may be worthy the office, henceforth abandoning all pretensions to electioneering which neither becomes his calling or abilities.

To the members of the Baptist church generally I can say with truth that I respect and reverence the order to which they belong, and that no church or set of people in the world stands higher in my esteem—nothing but necessity could have induced me to assail one of their body—but if in doing so I have marked out a black sheep belonging improperly to their flock, I am sure they will not feel unthankful for the favour.

DAVID CROCKETT

P.S. I have had the mill inspected and examined by a number of gentlemen and amongst others two millwrights to wit: James Smith and Esqr. Webb—all of whom pronounce it to be as it most unqestienably is, the most abominable horse mill, that ever was put up by the hands of man. D. C.

Crockett was responding to accusations that he had failed to pay a debt. He had hired Phillips (spelled "Philips" by Crockett) to build a mill for him and, in lieu of direct payment, promised to pay a debt that Phillips owed to Rev. David Gordon, a preacher. Because the structure Phillips built was of such poor quality that it was useless, Crockett refused to pay. Crockett believed that his political enemies had persuaded Gordon to make the accusation against him while he was running for reelection. Crockett did not seem concerned about potential political fallout from the issue since he did not bother to address it until the campaign had ended. The issue would be raised against Crockett again in a later election campaign. Crockett's letter in the *Jackson Gazette* of September 26, 1829, was followed by a brief rejoinder from Phillips and the two supporting sworn statements that Crockett mentioned from Edmonson and Ryen.

*   *   *   *   *

UNDATED LETTER TO THE *(WASHINGTON) TELEGRAPH AND INTELLIGENCER,* **PUBLISHED DECEMBER 12, 1829.**

To the Editors of the Telegraph and Intelligencer.

Gentlemen:

On the evening of the 7th inst. I reached Washington City, and should, at an earlier period, have attended to the matter concerning which I now trouble you, but for the fatigue incident to my journey, and the subsequent duties incumbent on me as the representative of a Congressional District.

This matter may, upon a slight view, appear unimportant. I nevertheless feel myself in duty bound to submit the following remarks for public examination.

The facilities for transportation, to this place, both for passengers and the mail, are justly a subject of wonder, yet the frauds which are frequently practised on passengers on the route, are undeniable, and demand exposure. Avarice, in these small matters, operated upon me as lightly, perhaps, as upon any other man; but extortion, even in the smallest matters, arouses my indignation, and in the present case, impels me to do all in my power to correct the abuse and punish the offender. On the line from Wheeling to Washington City, at Washington, (Penn.) resides a landlord. (and as I presume, an agent for the line) whose name is Briceland, who has, on several occasions, misused me, (and as I am informed, many others) in a most improper and disgraceful manner.

As I was coming on in 1828, he charged me, and six other gentlemen, for lodging—when in fact, not one of us ever saw a bed in his house; and when we were all forced out of his house, and exposed to a violent storm, four hours before the regular time.

Much provoked at this, I determined never to stop at his house again. Influenced by this feeling when I came on to Washington City, for the present session, upon reaching this place, I avoided Mr. Briceland's house, and went to the tavern of Mr. Morrison, and there took supper. Upon returning to Mr. Briceland's, and settling for the stage fare to the next place of payment, he charged me with supper and lodging—when I had neither eaten, drunk, nor slept in his house. Upon being reminded by the Hon. Mr. Benton, of Missouri, that he had charged me the same that he had charged those who had supped there, he persisted, insolently remarking—*that his supper was ready, and if I did not partake, it was my own fault.*

This principle would justify, any and every merchant and tradesman in extorting any price for any thing which he chooses to offer for sale, from whomsoever he chooses to charge with it, for it is the *fault* of the *purchaser* if he do not buy what is ready for him.

I shall make no further observation on these circumstances, than to caution travellers against this species of imposition, and to call upon the contractor to consult his own interest by removing the causes of such complaint.

Respectfully,
Yours,
DAVID CROCKETT

Crockett's irate letter indicates that, at the time, even congressmen could be fleeced and put upon by unscrupulous individuals with little redress.

* * * * *

1830:

CROCKETT LETTER TO HUGH D. NEILSON, JANUARY 24, 1830.

Washington City
24th Jan 1830

My Dear Neilson
I received your favor of the 6th inst on this day and will hasten to answer it I have sent you a copy of my ocupent law as my Committee agreed on and I can say to you that this is the Best provision I could make for the occupints placed as I was in the powar of a majority of the committee against me their being four eastern members on my Committee I was compeled to put up a claim and urge the [propriety?] of it also by falling in to this plan I have united my whole Delegation [in?] my favour I showed the bill I have [?] drawn to Mr. grunday and he liked it well and said thare would be no dainger of passing it I hope this is as good a law as the occupants could expect me to pass for them you may say to them that this is the best that I could do for them I have sent on your appointment and wrote to you at home [another?] I am well and Remain your friend & Humble servt

David Crockett

Hugh D. Neilson

From the Tennessee Historical Society Miscellaneous Files, courtesy of the Tennessee State Library and Archives.

The letter, which includes Crockett's hand-written Tennessee land bill, supports his contention that the entire Tennessee congressional delegation had agreed to support his bill in the Twenty-First Congress, despite the acrimony that had occurred among them over the issue in the previous Congress. Having failed to unseat Crockett in the 1829 election, the rest of the state delegation may have thought it prudent not to attempt to block him again, probably knowing that his bill had little chance of success. All of the Tennesseans voted for Crockett's measure, which did fail, but not one rose to speak in its favor. Hugh D. Neilson was from Trenton, Tennessee, and was appointed postmaster on January 18, 1830, which is likely the appointment Crockett referred to in the letter. Frederick M. Culp, and Robert E. Ross, *Gibson County: Past and Present* (Trenton, Tennessee: Gibson County Historical Society Publications, 1961), 99.

* * * * *

LETTER TO *JACKSON (TENNESSEE) GAZETTE,* **MARCH 2, 1830, EXCERPT PUBLISHED MARCH 27, 1830.**

In answer to the numerous enquires, about our friend Col. Crockett's Land Bill, we reply—that we received a letter from him dated the 2d inst. in which he says: "A few days ago I took my land Bill and got it referred to the Committee of the whole on the state of the Union.—I can take it up at any time and act on it. I apprehend no danger of its final passage."

Crockett was not only overly optimistic about the likelihood of his land bill passing, but also was mistaken about being able to "take it up at any time." The bill would not come up for debate until May 3. However, at this point he had reason for some optimism, since he had secured the support of the entire Tennessee delegation for his measure.

*　　*　　*　　*　　*

LETTER TO SECRETARY OF STATE MARTIN VAN BUREN, MARCH 3, 1830. PUBLISHED IN THE *JACKSON (TENNESSEE) GAZETTE,* **MARCH 27, 1830**

Washington City
March 3

Hon. Martin Van Buren, Sec of State.

Sir—

I have recently been much surprised upon the reception of a letter from one of my constituents, informing me that without knowing why or wherefore, the printing of the Laws of the United States had been taken from him and bestowed upon another. I am, sir, the representative of the section of country, most deeply interested in the matter, and therefore feel myself authorised to enter my protest against the manner in which your authority has been exercised. I am not inclined to take part in discussing the relative merits of the individual removed and the gentleman appointed to succeed him. No, sir, I should blush to find myself drawing distinctions *upon mere party grounds.* If I were to do so I should be compelled to approve your choice. The Editor upon whom you have conferred the trust has been uniformly my friend, and to him I acknowledge myself under many political obligations. But to witness so uncertain a state of things, is calculated to weaken the confidence of the citizen in his government or the consistency of those who administer it.

For corruption & crime or for either, an officer should be removed. But, Sir, is the doctrine to be established, that for either a former or an anticipated difference of opinion, a man is to be *proscribed?* If so, the triumph of virtue is wholly doubtful, and the range of favoritism may be made as wide as the universe.

Sir, I had supposed that before you would make material changes in my district, you would according to custom *condescend* to consult me; I surely have more opportunities of understanding the interests of the people of the *Western District in Tennessee* than to yourself; I hope that I am sufficiently devoted to these interests not to misrepresent them.

You have removed a man who was the first Editor of a newspaper within that District, and a warm friend to the present Chief Magistrate, and appointed one who had junior claims. I am friendly to each, but I protest against such an unwarrantable interference.

I am, sir, with due consideration,
Your obedient servant,
DAVID CROCKETT

Crockett included a copy of this letter with his March 5, 1830, letter to the *Jackson Gazette;* both letters were published in the March 27, 1830, edition of the *Gazette,* along with a response from Polk, to whom the Gazette also had written regarding this issue. Crockett never received a response from Van Buren, for whom he developed an increasing loathing. The emphasis on the phrase *mere party grounds* may have been a slightly oblique objection to Van Buren's drive to develop strong party affiliation and loyalty, something that Crockett was never comfortable with, preferring that politicians retain some independence without suffering party reprimands.

*   *   *   *   *

LETTER TO THE *JACKSON (TENNESSEE) GAZETTE,* MARCH 5, 1830, PUBLISHED MARCH 27, 1830.

Washington City
March 5.

Dear Sir:

I received with much astonishment, a notification of your removal as public printer. I know, as is known to others, that you have opposed me in all my elections; nor is it with a view to reconcile you that I have either defended you, or enclosed the evidence of having done so. It is because I wish justice done to every man and under *all* circumstances. On the day of the date of my letter, it was transmitted to Mr. Van Buren, and I delayed writing you, under a supposition that I should obtain an answer. He has, nevertheless, not yet made a reply, nor do I believe that the world can produce the man who is able to reply and successfully vindicate the course of which I complain, in the letter which I enclose you, and which I hope you will publish.

I am a party man in the true sense of the word; but God forbid that I should ever become so much a party man as obsequiously to stoop to answer party purposes. I wish, sir, and indeed it is the principal object of this note, to assure you that I have had neither a direct nor indirect participation in (what I at least consider) the unjustifiable business of withdrawing from you the little bounty heretofore allowed to you, and for the procurement of the necessary services, which in my judgment, you have both promptly and ably rendered. I am indignant at seeing a set of men, whether in elevated or humble stations, pursuing with such madness the very course of intolerance and proscription which they have so long and so loudly (and as they informed me so justly) condemned in others.

To General Jackson I am a firm and undeviating friend. I have fought under his command—and am proud to own that he has been my commander. I have loved him, and in the sincerity of my heart I say that I still love *'him;'* but to be compelled to love every one who, for purposes of self aggrandizement, *pretend* to rally around the "Jackson Standard," is what I never can submit to. The people of this country, like the humble boatmen on the Mississippi, ought to begin to look out for *breakers!* The *fox* is about! let the *roost* be guarded!

I am, sir, with high consideration, most respectfully, the humble servant of yourself, and of the people of my district.

David Crockett

C.D. M'Lean, Esq.

The letter was written in response to a query from the *Gazette* regarding its removal from the list of newspapers designated as publishers of public laws by Secretary of State Martin Van Buren. The *Gazette* wrote to both Crockett and James K. Polk asking why the action had been taken. Crockett wrote to Van Buren, but never received a reply, and enclosed his letter with the above letter to the *Gazette.* The *Gazette* published his letter to Van Buren and his response to the newspaper, along with Polk's, in its March 27, 1830, edition. It prefaced the letters with the following introduction:

"When we learned that our paper had been stricken from the list of those authorized to publish the Laws of the United States, we informed our readers of the fact and at the same time indicated that as we were the advocates of "reform" and "rotation" in office we would not "complain." We, however, addressed a letter to our attentive representative, the Hon. David Crockett, and one to the Hon. James K. Polk, enquiring if any *cause* was alledged for the change on the part of the honorable Secretary of State. From those gentlemen we have received the following answers:"

Polk's response was more circumspect and less supportive than Crockett's, although he did assure the *Gazette* editor that he had no hand in the paper's removal from the list. Polk's reply, in part, responded to the paper's inquiry about the transfer "of the laws of the United States, from your paper to the Memphis Advocate, by whose influence it was effected, and whether 'the whole Tennessee Delegation joined in displacing you.' I can only answer for myself as one of the 'Tennessee Delegation,' that I had no agency in displacing you and indeed did not know that it had been done, until a considerable time after the change had been made; nor do I know 'what induced Mr. Van Buren to make the change,' nor by whose influence or agency it was effected.

"I have known you personally for several years—have often seen your paper, and it is but due to you to say, that had I been called upon to give an opinion, I should not have recommended the change. I have not had an opportunity to converse with the Secretary of State, upon the subject, since I received your letter, but suppose as he is an entire stranger in your section of country, he must have been induced to make the change upon information received, from some source, entitled in his estimation, to confidence. He could have had no object in view, but to give the laws the most extensive circulation, and though he may have acted on mistaken information, (having no personal knowledge of the two presses himself,) he can I doubt not give a satisfactory explanation.—all of the Tennessee Delegation with whom I have conversed, inform me that they had no agency in your removal, or rather in making the change. I have no political information of interest to communicate, other than what you see in the newspapers."

It is doubtful that Polk's closing sentence regarding "what you see in the newspapers" was intended as a tongue-in-cheek reference to the *Gazette's* predicament, since Polk seems to have had virtually no sense of humor, another trait that must have made him ill at ease around Crockett. In any case, the *Gazette* was not amused or satisfied with Polk's reply and followed it with the following commentary:

"Still we are at a loss to account for the change. For some time we feared that our newly elected Senator Felix Grundy, to whose elevation to that station we were opposed, had recommended it. We embraced him in our letter to Mr. Polk, and we presume he informed him of that fact, and that Mr. Grundy disclaimed all interference. We regret that Mr. Polk did not *specify* him, for we still think 'Old Felix,' or some of his understrappers, had a hand in it. If we are mistaken, we will cheerfully make the correction. In relation to the *value* of the appointment we care nothing. For the last two years it has yielded us less than $100 annually, but having held the appointment at Nashville under Madison and Monroe, and in this place under John Quincy Adams, without solicitation, we felt chagrined when Mr. Van Buren displaced us.

"Perhaps Mr. Polk is correct when he says the Honorable Secretary acted from the best confidential information he could obtain, and inasmuch as he is said to be a clever man, and we are known to be the friends of Gen. Jackson, and his administration, he may perhaps justify himself by thinking it good policy to reward his enemies—knowing his friends, who have supported him for fifteen years, would not desert him for trifles."

＊　　＊　　＊　　＊　　＊

LETTER TO THE *JACKSON (TENNESSEE) GAZETTE*, **MARCH 24, 1830, PUBLISHED APRIL 17, 1830.**

Washington City
March 24:

To the Editor of the Jackson Gazette.

Dear Sir.

I discover in your paper of the 6th inst. an article over the signature of P. M. Miller, in which he as an *unwavering* politician takes many exceptions to the course of the members of Congress from Tennessee, in relation to the vacant lands in the District.

Had not this very distinguished gentleman better *atone* to the good people of the Western District of Tennessee for the past sin of trying to gull them on the subject of the proposition which I had the honor to submit to Congress, during the last session, which was to give the land direct from Congress to the *occupant?*

For my own part I am not at all surprised to see this very honorable gentleman beginning to become restless again. I do expect he is beginning to come to his taste again for a seat in Congress. I wish to inform Mr. Miller, that if it be his desire to become a candidate against me, that he need not make any apology, nor try to lash *me*, over the shoulders of my colleagues.

If Mr. Miller had never been in congress his remarks might be excusable on the subject which he has the stupidity to suppose he can gull the good people of the district by trying to alarm them, by holding out an idea that there is a host of Commissioners to be sent out by the General Government, to examine whether Tennessee was about to steal some of her land or not.

I do consider this sentiment of Mr. Miller a downright insult on common sense. Mr. Miller is apprised that there is but one Commissioner of the General Land Office,—Mr. George Graham, who lives in this City. I referred to his report, made to Congress, to ascertain the quantity of land within the Western District.

This distinguished politician must certainly understand this matter, but if he does not and will acknowledge it like an honest man—I will endeavor to explain it to him; that is, if he will condescend to be advised by the *Bear hunter*—who is always ready to aid the needy.

Would this be injurious to the character of the great Lawyer of the Western District of Tennessee? Answer. It is doubtful.

Here I will leave Mr. Miller, for the present, and let him try to gull the good people in the district about routine in office, until I get home, then I will take him under my own special charge, and do as well as I can by him.

Very respectfully,
Your friend,
DAVID CROCKETT.

P.S. I do not profess to be a grammarian or a scholar, nor have I any inducement to dispute the palm of erudition with Mr. Miller; but there is a palm which I will not yield to him: it is that of *honesty* and devotion to the interests of those who have kindly honored me with a seat in Congress.
D.C.

Crockett's letter is in response to Pleasant M. Miller's letter published in the *Jackson Gazette* on March 6, 1830. Miller had agreed to the provisions in Crockett's land bill that pertained to the occupants, but took issue with other aspects of the bill, particularly the manner in which land would have been ceded to Tennessee. Although he did not mention any of the Tennessee representatives by name, Crockett obviously objected to Miller's harsh reprimand of the state's congressional delegation. Ironically, Miller would seem to have been a likely ally of Crockett's, since he, too, had broken with Jackson and supported the occupants. Crockett may have wanted to appear supportive of the Tennessee delegation since he still had its full support for his land bill. Within a few months, they would turn against him following the defeat of his compromise bill and his efforts to offer a radically different one that would give neither land nor revenue to Tennessee. Pleasant Moorman Miller was elected to Congress in 1809 and served as a delegate to the Tennessee legislature from 1817 to 1823. He had been a tentative candidate against Crockett in the 1829 election, but backed out of the race, having turned against Jackson, and proclaimed that he had no reason to run against Crockett. *Tennessee Encyclopedia of History and Culture* website, http://tennesseeencyclopedia.net/imagegallery.php?EntryID=M098.

*   *   *   *   *

LETTER TO SAMUEL D. INGHAM, MARCH 27, 1830

House of Representatives
March 27, 1830

Hon S. D Ingham

I enclose you a letter of Mr William Gillispia Relating to a Claim which I laid before your Department early in the Session of Mr Gillaspies Services as an old Revolutionary Soldier will you examine his letter and inform me of the Disision

I remain with high respects your obt servt

David Crockett

Samuel D. Ingham

Revolutionary War Pension and Bounty-Land Warrant Application Files, U.S. National Archives and Records Administration.

Crockett writes on behalf of William Gillespie, a Revolutionary War veteran and resident of Dyersburg, Tennessee. Gillespie was one of many veterans petitioning the government for a pension. Throughout his public service, Crockett was often called upon to endorse and file claims for veterans seeking remuneration. Samuel D. Ingham was Secretary of the Treasury at the time of Crockett's request.

*   *   *   *   *

LETTER TO THE *JACKSON (TENNESSEE) GAZETTE*, APRIL 15, 1830, PUBLISHED MAY 8, 1830.

Washington City
15th April, 1830.

Dear Sir—
I have delayed writing to you for the last week as well as to many others of my constituents, with a hope that I would be able through your columns to spread the news over my District, that my occupant Bill had passed. I had it taken up on last Thursday and passed through the Committee of the Whole on the State of the Union without opposition. Mr. Barringer, of North Carolina, offered an amendment to the bill, of which I will enclose you a copy. I do not consider that his amendment can injure or affect the provisions of the bill in any way, and I will accept it, by doing so I will unite the whole delegation from that State.
I was told my Mr. *Conner,* of N. C. "that the whole of the members from his State would vote against my bill." My reply to him was that they were of age, and might do as they pleased, but I walked on as high ground as any man in Congress. I informed him that I had stated in my Speeches before the people that if my Colleagues, or the members from N. Carolina, did oppose the passage of such a bill as I could report on that subject, and were the means of defeating my object, that I would introduce a resolution and refer it to the Judiciary Committee to enquire into the expediency of commencing a suit in behalf of the General Government against the agents for the University of North Carolina, for every acre of land that they had in my district. I told him that their lands were lying in that country exempted from taxation, until 1850; I have always considered the University claims as unjustly obtained from the general government, and have always thought that it would be better for the people of the Western District if the Government were yet the owners of the lands.

With these threats I expect that I put them to thinking, and Mr. Barringer offered his amendment and as I know that I am not to be charged with acts of other men, I would accept his amendment; it will not injure the occupants in the district by the provisions of my bill.

The subject is postponed until Wednesday next, and made the special order of the day for that day, and I hope to have no difficulty in passing the bill, as I reported it with his amendment, and a small one that I offered to it myself, that I omitted. In the 18th line I inserted the word select, *"and all land now in the possession of occupants."* I done this to prevent the State from selecting lands that are not settled, to get a higher price than 12½ cents per acre—my object is to provide for the occupants, and my opinion is that if I pass the bill now before Congress, I will effect the object.

We had a discussion of the great National Road on yesterday, from Buffalo in New York, to New Orleans. I offered an amendment to the bill, and to run the road direct from W. City to Knoxville, thence to Memphis, and before we could get the vote the previous question was called for and sustained which cut off all amendments; I then voted for the road, the western route, with a firm belief that when the Engineers laid off the road they would see the propriety of stopping at Memphis.

I made a Speech on the subject, and made a fair and honest statement of facts, which you will see published in a few days. My greatest object was to speak against the duties on such articles of necessity as every poor man in the country is compelled to consume in his family, and to affect my object I was compelled to speak against the expediency of commencing this work at present. Though I have ascertained that it is impossible to reduce duties, and therefore I did believe it nothing but justice to give the western country an equal portion of the money of the country—thereby we would get a circulating medium. These are part of the reasons that I was governed by, and others I will explain when I am heard in person before the people of my district.

Since I have commenced this letter, the house has re-considered the vote of yesterday, and have laid the bill on the table ready to act on next session.

Respectfully yours,
DAVID CROCKETT.

Henry William Connor and Daniel Laurens Barringer were Jacksonian congressmen from North Carolina. Crockett appended Barringer's amendment to his bill, House Resolution 185. Crockett also appended his proposed amendment to the Buffalo road bill, prefaced by the following letter to C. D. McLean.

*　　*　　*　　*　　*

LETTER TO CHARLES. D. MCLEAN, APRIL 16, 1830, PUBLISHED IN THE *JACKSON (TENNESSEE) GAZETTE* MAY 8, 1830.

April 16, 1830.

Dear Sir—

I enclose you the amendment which I offered to the Buffalo Road, contemplated to be made from the State of New York direct to Washington City District of Columbia, then to New -Orleans. This bill was rejected by a majority 17 votes, we then reconsidered it and laid it on the table ready to act on next session.

I am of opinion that it is just in the situation it ought to be. When we return to our Districts we can obtain the sentiments of the people; then we will be able to represent their wishes.

I remain, with high esteem, your ob't humble serv't,

David Crockett

C.D. McLean, Esq.

  Charles D. McLean became publisher of the *Jackson Gazette* in 1824. Prior to that he had published newspapers in Clarksville and Nashville. He was elected to the Tennessee General Assembly, serving one term.

 * * * * *

LETTER TO THE *JACKSON (TENNESSEE) GAZETTE*, MAY 7, 1830, PUBLISHED MAY 29, 1830.

Washington City
May 7.

Dear Sir—

 I am under the painful necessity of informing you that the bill reported by me for the benefit of the People of the Western District, and by your kindness published in the Gazette, has been *rejected,* but as disappointment is the lot of man I will reconcile myself to my fate. I have labored earnestly to promote the interest of the poor Occupants, in my district, who I know were looking with a fond anticipation to this Congress I had every reason to believe that my bill would pass until last Monday, when the vote was taken. There were 69 for and 90 against its passage. A great many members had gone to the Races, a few miles from the city. On the next morning I solicited a gentleman who had voted against the bill, to call for a reconsideration.

 I went to Col. Bell, and he opposed the motion, and said he would not vote for a reconsideration. I then went to General Desha, and he told me that the whole delegation would vote against my substitute, and against a reconsideration. I took this for granted—and in my speech I declared *Independence* against them, & stated that I would quit the whole of them and "set up shop for myself," and do the best I could for my constituents. You will see my remarks at length in a few days. I enclose you a paper in which the Telegraph has attempted to give the debate, though it is incorrect. I will have it corrected and send it to you.

 After I had spoken I found my friend Cave Johnson, Esq. advocating my last bill; and in truth he made an able speech in favor of reconsidering—he said he cared not where the money went so the people got their lands. He is a gentleman of the first respectability, and worth, and a firm friend to the poor people of his country; and is at all times zealous to promote their interest.

 At first I thought that Mr. Johnson and myself would be all the support, my new plan would meet with, but I find on examination that Cols. Blair and Standifer will go with us.

 I must acknowledge that I was never so much astonished at any circumstance, so much as I was at Col. Bell coming out in the manner he did towards me; I had looked upon him as my warmest friend, & the last man in the world that would get up and abuse me for telling what I knew to be the truth. He has great talents and great acquired abilities. Too much I had thought to jump on a man like myself who had risen from obscurity to a seat in Congress by my own exertions without an education or wealth. This is what I never looked for from that gentlemen.

 The ballance had little to say except to vote against the measure—I have enclosed you a copy of the substitute after the enacting clause, which I hope to have adopted in lieu of the first bill, before we adjourn. Then it will be ready to be acted on the next session. I have drawn this bill myself without aid from any person, and I do hope it may please the people; I believe I will pass this into a law at the next session with ease. The whole of the Eastern members tell me that they will vote for this proposition, and I care not where the votes come from, so I get them. We expect to adjourn of the 31st of this month.

I remain, very respectfully,
Your humble servant,
DAVID CROCKETT.

The *Gazette* posted the following comment after Crockett's letter: "We regret that the press of other matter previously in type, compels us to defer Col. Crocket's proposed substitute until our next. Editor Gaz."

In this letter, Crockett was being deceptive and unfair to his Tennessee colleagues. He omitted any mention of the fact that all of them had voted with him while his original bill, H.R. 185, was being debated in its original form, which called for the federal government to cede land to Tennessee. It was only after Crockett completely changed the bill by incorporating an amendment drafted by Samuel Vinton, an Ohio Whig, following discussions with Vinton and George Grennell, an anti-Jacksonian from Massachusetts, that his Tennessee colleagues turned on him. That amendment called for the Federal government to sell individual plots to the occupants directly and gave no land to Tennessee, nor did it provide any land for schools, two key provisions that Polk and the other Tennesseans insisted on. He also exaggerated his role in drafting the final bill in claiming that "I have drawn this bill myself without aid from any person," since the amendment was clearly Vinton's work. He also overstated the degree of support he was getting from easterners, many of whom voted against the bill, when he said "The whole of the Eastern members tell me that they will vote for this proposition." Crockett also continued his pattern of speaking in overly optimistic terms regarding the chances of his bill succeeding, again professing certainty that it would pass during the next session. He was, however, accurate in stating that the other Tennesseans "had little to say except to vote against the measure," since none of them except Cave Johnson spoke a word in its defense, even in its original form, and all voted against the final version. Johnson, John Bell, John Blair, Robert ("General") Desha, and James Israel Standifer all were Jacksonian congressmen from Tennessee.

* * * * *

LETTER TO THE *(WASHINGTON) UNITED STATES' TELEGRAPH*, **MAY 20, 1830, PUBLISHED MAY 25, 1830.**

Washington City
May 20, 1830.

Sir: A sketch of my remarks in opposition to the bill for the removal of the Indians West of the Mississippi river, read in your paper as follows:

"Mr. CROCKETT also spoke in opposition to it, stating that, although four counties of his Congressional district adjoined the Chickasaw nation of Indians, he was opposed in conscience to the measure; and such being the case, he cared not what his constituents thought of his conduct."

I request it, Sir, as an act of justice, that the error be corrected, as I never hurl defiance at those whose servant I am. I said that my conscience should be my guide, regardless of the opposition of my colleagues, or any other consequence as to myself, and that I believed if my constituents were here, they would justify my vote.

Very respectfully,
Your obedient servant,
DAVID CROCKETT

Crockett's letter, correcting the *Telegraph's* paraphrasing of his speech opposing Indian Removal, is the best evidence found to date that Crockett did, indeed, deliver the speech on the floor of the House of Representatives on May 19, 1830. The transcript of the speech, published in the *Jackson Gazette* on June 26, 1830, confirms Crockett's claim that the *Telegraph* misrepresented the meaning of his references to his constituents.

The *Telegraph* prefaced Crockett's letter by saying that the newspaper's editor had not heard the speech, but that its reporter was "confident that the term constituents was used as reported." Reporters from several newspapers noted Crockett's speech and several papers published paraphrased excerpts from it, most of them taken from the *Telegraph*. The fact that no mention of the speech was made in the *Register of Debates in Congress* or the *National Intelligencer,* both published by Gales and Seaton, suggests that their reporter either wasn't present when Crockett gave the speech or lost or misplaced any notes on it among the many hours of speeches delivered on the Indian Removal Bill.

*　　*　　*　　*　　*

LETTER FROM JAMES KIRKE PAULDING TO RICHARD HENRY WILDE, TRANSMITTING A MESSAGE TO CROCKETT, DECEMBER 15, 1830.

New York
15th Dec. 1830

Dear Sir,

If you have any acquaintance with Col. Crockett of Tennessee you will oblige me by delivering the enclosed letter into his hands. It relates to certain malicious and unfounded rumors which lately appeared in the newspapers noting that I had made him the hero of a comedy I lately wrote for Hackett of the theatre. You will also I hope do me the favor to Sp[illeg.], provided your knowledge of me will rectify the [offense?] that I am incapable of committing such an outrage on the feelings of any gentleman.

I do not wish him to publish the letter as I have taken measures to have the whole story contradicted in the newspapers.

I am [illeg.]

Yours Respectfully,

JK Paulding

Courtesy of the New-York Historical Society, BV Francis (Goelet) Collection.

James Kirke Paulding was a playwright who penned the play *Lion of the West* in response to an offer of $300 by actor James Hackett for a script based on the fictional "wild man" persona that had begun to grow around Crockett. Hackett went on to play Nimrod Wildfire in the play, a character that was widely associated with that Crockett image. Paulding's letter to Crockett has not been found, but this letter, transmitting it through Wilde, clearly shows his intention to deny suggestions that he had taken advantage of Crockett or sought to ridicule him through the Wildfire character, although there is little doubt that Paulding was heavily influenced by Crockett. Richard Henry Wilde was a Jacksonian congressman from Georgia.

*　　*　　*　　*　　*

LETTER TO HENRY MCCLUNG, DECEMBER 21, 1830.

Washington City
21st Decr 1830

My Dear Sir

I arrived in the city on the 14th inst but have neglected to write you until this time with a hope that I could give you Some entiligence how the state of party was working on I still am of opinion that Mr Clay has as many friends in Congress as Genl Jackson tho we have had no chance to try the test

I here enclose you the five dollars which you was so kind as to loan me on my way which I consider a particular favour—we are going on with Judge Pecks Trial at preasant public opinion is against the Judge I cannot tel how he may come out it is generley supposed it will consume three weeks of our time If so we will do but little else this session

I remain with high esteem
Your obt servt
David Crockett

Henry McLung

PS pleas write me on the Recept of this

Courtesy of the Historical Society of Pennsylvania (Sventy Case S 19-35).

Henry McClung (whose name Crockett misspelled) was from Staunton, Virginia, a supporter of John Quincy Adams and Henry Clay, and a friend of Sam Houston. In the late 1820s he operated the Eagle Tavern, classified as a "House of Entertainment," in Lexington, Virginia, which he put up for sale in 1829. *Richmond (Virginia) Enquirer,* November 28, 1829; James Atkins Shackford, *David Crockett: The Man and the Legend,* edited by John B. Shackford (Chapel Hill: University of North Carolina Press, 1956), 128.

*   *   *   *   *

LETTER TO JAMES KIRKE PAULDING, DECEMBER 22, 1830.

Washington City
22nd Decer 1830

Sir your letter of the 15 Inst was handed to me this day by my friend Mr. Wildes—the news paper publications to which you refer I have never seen; and if I had I should not have taken the reference to myself in exclusion of many who fill offices and who are as untaught as I am I thank you however for your civility in assuring me that you had no reference to my peculiarites the frankness of your letter induces me to Say a declaration from you to that effect was not needed to Convince me that you were incapable of wounding the feelings of a Strainger and unlettered man who had never injured you— your Charector for letters and as a gentleman is not altogether un known to me

I have the honour with great respects &c

David Crockett
J. K. Paulding

Courtesy of the Phil Collins Collection.

Crockett's gracious letter was intended to assure Paulding that he held no animosity toward the playwright, nor the fictional Nimrod Wildfire, portrayed by James Hackett, in the play *Lion of the West*. Indeed, Crockett attended one of Hackett's performances.

*   *   *   *   *

1831

LETTER TO DANIEL POUNDS, JANUARY 6, 1831.

Washington City
6th January 1831

Dear Sir

I am enjoying the best of health which I feel thankful to the giver of all good for his blessings and hope these lines will find you and family enjoying the Same blessing I hope you will excuse me for not writing oftener this is part neglect and part for want of Something enteresting to write however I will proceed we are doing but little business in Congress on account of the delay which is occasioned by Judge Pecks trial and I fear we are to do but little business during the preasant session

I have no doubt but you will see the proceeding of georgia before this reaches you on the Case of hanging the Cherikee Indian the Chief Justice Marshel isued his mandate or writ of error against the State of georgia to bring the Case up to the Supreme Court of the united States and the notice was served on the governer on the 22 of Decr and the Indian was to be hung on the 24 the governer refused to pay any respects to the order and the legislature of georgia passed a joint Resolution inforsing the execution of the Indian and bidding defiance to the powar of the Supreme Court of the united States this is what we call going the whole hogg to nullify the whole powar of the Supreme Court of the united states this case took place with in the Cherikee nation and the object of the Chief Justice was to bring the Case before the Supreme Court and decide whether georgia has the powar to extend her laws over the Indians or not and when the attempt was made the governer & legislature flew into flinders and we Consider they have thrown the gantlet and that the Chief Justice marshel at this time holds a Civil war in his own hands It is believed that he will persue a firm and desisive Course to Sustain the honour and dignity of his Court if that Should be his course god only knows how Soon we may have a Separation of the union— the Judiciary Committee this day reported a bill to repeal the 25 Section of the Judicery act which will destroy the whole powar of the genl government thin we are no more a united States if that Section should be repealed I do believe it is a political menuver of this administration to [?] throw the blame of the administration upon Congress and to prevent the court from bringing the Cherikees Case before the supreme Court of the united States it has been predicted by many that if Jackson was president he would bring on a war and I can asure you that the preasant aspects looks gloomy all Europe is in Commotion and france is in a State of Revolution these are times that is new to me—

I made two attempts to get up my land bill but proved unsuccesful my whole dellegation went against me with the exception of Mr Lea and I cannot till what made him vote for my proposition as we have never spoken to each other Since we had our controversy I do believe I will be able to get it up and pass it in spite of all their opposition before I leve here.

I have not Sold my horse yet but expects to in a few days he is getting in fine order I will performe my promis to you in my next letter to your sattisfaction I must close may god bless and prosper you I must close in hast I remain your [?] friend obet Servt

David Crockett

Daniel W Pounds

Courtesy of the Lilly Library, Indiana University, Bloomington, Indiana.

No information about Pounds has been found, but the letter suggests he was a close friend of Crockett, perhaps a neighbor. Crockett is quite outspoken in his defense of Indians, but also mentions the personal matter of selling his

horse and fulfilling a promise made to Pounds. Crockett's claim that his old nemesis, Pryor Lea, actually voted with him on at least one occasion on the land bill is puzzling. Although all of the Tennesseans voted with him on May 3, 1830, no roll call vote was taken on May 4, when Crockett failed to have the bill reconsidered. He made three subsequent unsuccessful attempts (December 23, 1830, losing 86-74; again on December 31, 1830, 97-69; and January 6, 1831, 92-89, the same day he wrote to Pounds). Lea voted against Crockett on January 6; neither the *House Journal* nor the *Register of Debates* includes a roll call vote for December 23 or December 31, which are the only votes in which Lea could have backed Crockett, although history remains as mystified regarding his reasons as Crockett was.

*   *   *   *   *

LETTER TO THE EDITOR OF THE *(JACKSON, TENNESSEE) SOUTHERN STATESMAN*, JANUARY 6, 1831, PUBLISHED FEBRUARY 12, 1831.

Extracts of a Letter to the Editor, dated,
Washington City
Jan. 6, 1831.

My Dear Friend—I am reminded, not only of my promise, but also of my obligation to address you, and through you, to address my constituents as often as anything interesting happens, and an opportunity may offer. I have often written you, but seldom indeed under the influence of deeper regret and mortification than at present. If I know my own heart, I am devoted to the interest of those whose servant I am, and such are my feelings towards them, I participate alike in their happiness and their woes.

It is well known to you and to them, that ever since I have been in Congress, I have been engaged in one continued struggle, to secure to the honest poor of my district, to their wives and helpless children, their humble homes, and to afford them the means of subsistence, and shelter from the pitiless storm. So deep has been the interest which I have felt in this matter, that I have from time to time, varied my propositions, in relation to lands held by the humble occupants in the Western District, with a view to render it palatable to my colleagues; but I am at last brought to the conclusion, that it is vain to strive longer with them, as a multitude of circumstances prove that I should continue to strive in vain.

My original proposition, was to bestow the land upon those who had settled upon and improved it, as a donation from the government; believing then, as I do now, that although the little scraps which I sought to obtain, would be of some value to the poor man, who from necessity had toiled upon them, yet they never could be of any material service to the United States. The surveying them and bringing them into market, would cost the Government more than it could ever realize from the sales. In this attempt, I was opposed by my Colleagues, who I hesitate not to say, defeated the Bill, embracing these provisions before stated; and thereby cast a cloud of gloom and anguish over many a family that had listened to hear the joyful tidings, that their little cottage and field was their own. But sad reverse!!! My Colleagues seemed determined to consent to no arrangement, which did not directly grant the land to the State of Tennessee, thereby placing the people of my District, completely at the mercy of the Legislature of the State of Tennessee. To this I was decidedly opposed, and shall remain opposed, while I continue to respect the rights of those who sent me here; and while I have a heart to feel for the calamities, and an ear to hear the groans of the oppressed. What would have been the result, had the proposition of my Colleagues prevailed?—plainly this: the Legislature of Tennessee would have fixed upon the highest possible price which could have been commanded for those lands, a price which the poor settler could not pay: hence, he must have been turned out with has wife and children, a hopeless wanderer through the world, his little farm torn from him—his improvement, the product of many days of toil and labor, thrown into the hands of the merciful [merciless?] speculator, and the fund thus raised, at the expence of the poor expended for the education of the rich. May Heaven defend me against viewing so sorrowful a scene, and my constituents against realizing it.

But they contend as an argument in opposition to my proposition, that the *precedent* would be a dangerous one, and that if a donation were made of the land to the people of the Western District, others would claim a similar bounty from the government!! This argument was perfectly delusive—for I will venture the opinion, that such another case cannot be presented in the United States. To obviate, however, this objection, during the present session of Congress, I proposed a new proposition, which was to pay the general government twelve and a half cents per acre for the land; it not costing them one cent to convey or perfect titles to the same, but paying the fees for those services to the officers of our own state. Upon exhibiting this proposition, I did most fondly hope, that I should have secured the aid of at least the Tennessee delegation. But to my surprise and great sorrow, they moved in a solid phalanx against me, and have thus far baffled all my efforts. Upon three several occasions have I endeavored to bring this matter before the house, the 3d and last effort was made this day. The question, on taking up the subject was decided by ay's and nay's, and eventuated as follows: for the motion 89, against it 92; only a majority in the negative of 3 votes, & as will appear from the journal, every one of the Tennessee delegation, who were present, voting against me. It is almost enough to discourage any man, and cause him to fold his arms and commit his constituents to the care of Heaven; but reflection arms me again with fortitude and increased courage, and I am determined to persevere, so long as I retain a seat in Congress, encouraged by the hope, that other times and other men will do justice to the cause of suffering humanity. I have done all that mortal man could do for the District; days of toil, and sleepless nights have I spent, in endeavoring to soothe the palpitating hearts of our population, by procuring for them the protection and liberality of the government—and I thank God that the people know it, and will charge the failure to those who have caused it, and not to me; certainly not to one who has had an array against him, even from the bosom of his own country and his own household.

Truly, your friend and obt. sevt.
DAVID CROCKETT

The letter has the distinct ring of a campaign document, as Crockett faced a tough fight for reelection in a few months and still had little to show for his efforts to secure a land bill. He placed the blame for failure on others, particularly the rest of the Tennessee delegation, while holding out hope that a new Congress ("other times and other men") might be more receptive to his proposal. He again exaggerated the importance of the narrow 89-92 vote against bringing his bill up for debate again, which had taken place the day he wrote this letter. Despite that, and his laying it on a bit thick in his references to the poor, put-upon occupants, the letter does honestly lay out Crockett's dilemma. The Tennesseans would not accept any proposal that did not cede at least some land to the state, but a majority in Congress opposed such donations of public lands as a bad precedent that would spread to other public-land states and deprive the central government of revenues from land sales. The Tennesseans and a majority of other members of Congress opposed Crockett's proposal that the federal government sell land directly to the occupants.

*   *   *   *   *

LETTER FROM JOHN ROSS TO DAVID CROCKETT, JANUARY 13, 1831.

Head of Coosa Cherokee Na.
January 13th 1831

Hon. David Crockett
Representative in Congress.

Sir— Your favor of the 16th ult. together with the letters enclosed came safe to hand, for which you will please to accept my sincere thanks—It is gratifying to hear that your vote on the Indian Bill has given general satisfaction to your constituents—that it has or will produce for you among the friends of humanity & justice a just respect and admiration, I can not doubt—. Cupidity and avarice by sophistry intrigue and corruption may for a while prevail—but, the day of retributive justice must and will come, when, integrity and moral worth will predominate and make the shameless monster hide its head. Whether this day will come in time to save the suffering Cherokees from violence and frauds, it is for the wisdom, magnanimity & justice of the United States to determine. To those gentlemen who have so honorably and ably vindicated the rights of the poor Indians in Congress at the last session, this nation owes a debt of gratitude which the pages of history will bear record of until time shall be no more—and for which they will receive a just reward in the Courts of Heaven. The effects of this Bill have brought to view the reality of what was anticipated by those who opposed it—the exercise of jurisdiction assumed by Georgia & Mississippi have been exhibited in awful colours to the Indians by the negotiators on the part of the U States, and as a dernier alternative to escape the impending calamity, the generous douceur of the Bill have been introduced to them—but the Cherokees have borne with untiring fortitude and forbearance all those oppressive acts which Georgia have ungraciously heaped upon them, and they have escaped the serpentine movements made against them by her coadjutors. Still entertaining confidence in the justice and good faith of the United States, the Cherokees flatter themselves that the present Congress will do something definitively for the relief of their sufferings. The circumstances under which the U.S. Troops were ordered into this nation, and the manner in which they were employed whilst here, and their sudden withdrawal from the nation, leaves a chasm full of mysteries especially when it is known that the withdrawal of the federal troops has been ordered for the purpose of making room for the militia troops of Georgia, who are ordered into service by the authority of that state for the purpose of dispossessing the Cherokees of their gold mines within their own territory, and for aiding in the execution and enforcement of the laws of Georgia over the Cherokees and for protecting their surveyors in runing out our lands and enforcing possession to those citizens of Georgia who may rent from the state, those improvements which have been abandoned by emigrants and are now in the occupancy of Cherokees. How the President of the U States can reconcile it to his feelings to withdraw from us the protection pledged by treaty and to allow the state of Georgia to usurp from us the rights and liberties of freemen and to keep up a standing military force in our country and in time of profound peace too, I cannot understand. Such a manoeuvre under state authority exhibits a warlike movement and is calculated to destroy the peace and tranquility of our citizens, as there can be no doubt that it is repugnant to the Constitution, statutes and treaties of the United States. I have known Genl. Jackson from my boyhood—my earliest and warmest friends in Tennessee are generally his advocates—during the late war I held a rank in the Cherokee regiment & fought by his side—and so far as common sense will dictate to me that his measures are correct & just I should be among the last to oppose them—but it is with deep regret, I say, that his policy towards the aborigines, in my opinion, has been unrelenting and in effect ruinous to their best interests and happiness. And whatever may be the final result of our present difficulties and troubles, we are prepared to meet it—but never to remove west of the Mississippi upon lands within the limits of the U States. May health and happiness attend you.

I am Sir very respectfully your obt. servt.
John Rosss

P.S. It would afford me pleasure at all times to hear from you and I trust you will do me the honor of giving me occasionaly a line on the sign of the times—.

John Ross, letter to David Crockett, January 13, 1831, with enclosure (report ca. March 1814) Ayer MS 782, Edward E. Ayer Manuscript Collection, the Newberry Library, Chicago.

John Ross, who was only one-eighth Cherokee, led the tribe's fight against Andrew Jackson's Indian Removal policy. He was the Cherokee's only elected chief, serving until his death in 1866. His suggestion that Crockett's constituents supported his vote against removal was incorrect; Crockett's vote was widely criticized in his district. Crockett's letter of December 16, 1830 to Ross has not been found.

*　　*　　*　　*　　*

LETTER TO DAVID BARTON, U.S. SENATE, JANUARY 18, 1831.

My Lodgings Washington City
January 18th 1831

Hon David Barton

Sir

　I have just recieved your note of this date propounding to me under the instructions of the Committee of the Senate of which you are Chairman certain interrogatories relative to Stockley D Hays who you Say has been nominated to Surveyor general of the public lands South of Tennessee &ca

　It is Sir a delicate Matter to Speak of an individual at all when truth forbids that much Should be Said in his favour nor Should I in the present Case respond at all if it were not that the interest of my country demands it as well as the respectable source from whence the call emanates—

　You first enquire whether I am acquainted with Stockley D Hays of Tennessee to this question I answer that I am and have been acquainted with him ever Sence the last war while I was in the Service he was one of the Staff officers of Genl Jackson to whome he is nephew—

　You Secondly enquire relative to his mathematical Skill and whether it is Such as to qualify him for the office named? I answer that if he possesses any Such Skill or knowledge of the Sciences it is to me unknown—

　Your third enquiry relates to his pursuits his habits in reference to industry & Sobriety and his prudence in the management of his own affairs? To this I answer that he is by profession a Lawyer but has Succeeded badly in finding employment for reasons which may be infered from the remainder of this answer whether he is industrious or not I am unable to Say but his want of Sobriety is So great that on the other hand he is notorious for intemperance bordering on Sottishness. From the best knowledge that I have of his Circumstance and hence of his management of affairs I am Compeled to Say that I believe he has been insolvent ever Sence he has lived in my District which has been about Eight or nine years

　You fourthly and Conclusively enquire whether from my knowledge of Mr Hays taking all together I think him qualified and a Suitable person for the office?

　I answer emphaticaly I do not　　Your obt Servt
David Crockett
Hon David Barton, Chr Com Sen Pub Lans

Letter from David Crockett regarding the nomination of Starkley [sic] D. Hays, January 18, 1831. Papers relating to executive nominations (SEN 21B-A4); 21st Congress, Records of the U.S. Senate, Record Group 46, National Archives Building, Washington, D.C. Courtesy of the Center for Legislative Archives, National Archives and Records Administration.

　Senator David Barton was an Anti-Jacksonian from Missouri, and chairman of the Senate Committee on Public Lands. He had written to Crockett on January 18, 1831 asking his views on the qualifications of Stockely D. Hays, President Jackson's nephew, who had been nominated Surveyor General for lands south of Tennessee. Crockett responded in writing on the same day and was criticized in the Jacksonian press for opposing the Hays appointment. Crockett then wrote to the (Jackson, Tennessee) *Southern Statesman* defending his position and enclosed a copy of his letter to Barton. The *Statesman* printed part of Crockett's letter to the editor, the inquiry from Senator Barton regarding

Hays' qualifications, and some of Crockett's reply, partly quoted and partly paraphrased, on June 4, 1831. The following is the portion of Crockett's undated letter to the *Statesman*, published on June 4, 1831; the full letter has not been found:

"If I am to be condemned for acting honestly, let it be so. I considered myself bound to answer the inquiry, in the language of truth, which I yet contend I did. I regret the necessity I am under of giving publicity to the correspondence between the Committee and myself, but I am informed Col. Hays is cursing and abusing me, and misrepresenting the true state of the case. Self justification is the first law of nature. I have never done an act that I am unwilling for the people of my District to know."

Stockley Donelson Hays (1788-1831) was the nephew of Jackson's late wife Rachel. The surveyor general's appointment was for public lands "south of Tennessee," which encompassed Louisiana and Mississippi; Hays was not confirmed for the position. After his nomination was sent to a Senate committee, it was effectively killed by a resolution of Mississippi Senator George Poindexter stating that it was "inexpedient" to make out-of-state appointments "without some evident necessity." Jackson then made a deal with Poindexter, withdrew the nomination for surveyor, and instead nominated Hays for register of the Clinton, Mississippi land office, for which the Senate confirmed him on February 21, 1831 (Volume 4, *Senate Executive Journal*). Hays died shortly thereafter.

Jackson had written to his supporters predicting that Crockett would oppose Hays' appointment and criticize him as an inebriate, which Crockett did. Jackson kept track of these events and scribbled on the back of a copy of a letter he had written to L. McLane on March 8, 1831, the following notation, indicating that he had seen or been told of Crockett's letter to Barton:

"Mr. David Crockett to David Barton chairman &c interrogatories answers he is acquainted—from last war one of the staff &c.

"as to his skill in science as it is to him unknown—That he is intemperate to a degree of sottishness & has been insolvant—and is unqualified for the office." (Library of Congress Jackson Papers collection and on Reel 73 of their microfilm at March 8, 1831 [incorrectly indexed in the microfilm guide as "Crockett to D Bostear"]. Courtesy of Daniel Feller and Thomas Coens of the Andrew Jackson Papers project, University of Tennessee, Knoxville.)

*   *   *   *   *

LETTER TO A. M. HUGHES, FEBRUARY 13, 1831.

Washington City
13th Febry 1831

Dear Sir

Your favour of the 24th Jany came safe to hand by this mornings mail and I will hasten to answer it I am still injoying fine health and hope these lines will find you & family in the alike health

As I am writing a circular which will give a full history of the afairs of the government I deem it unnessacery to mention much a bout politics more than to give you the signs of the times

The Senate is handling the PO general with out gloves Mr Claton has laid that departmint open to the world in its true coulers for refusing to answer the enquire made by the Committee—Mr Grundy has introduced a Resolution in the Senate to prohibit any man who has been reformed out of that office from giving testimony This is carrying proscription to the full extent that a man who has been proscribed for opinion Sake are not to be intitled to his oath This is high times in this besled land of liberty the truth is Mr Barry has expended all the money that Mr McLean made for the country and now we cannot pass the post office & post Road bill for want of money to carry it in to oppiration with out congress makes a large appropriation This is the effect of this glorious sistom of retrinchment & reform this is the efect of turning out men that knows their duty to accommodate a Set of Jackson wor-shipers what they lack in quality must be made up in quantity Can any honist people have the like of this upon them I for one cannot nor will not I would see the whole of them hung up at the devil before I will submit to such carryings on as this I did not come to Cloke their extravigency to let them make a Speculation of this government their partizens here reminds me of some large dogs I have seen here with their collers on with letters engraved on the coller <u>My dog</u> & the mans name on the coller I have not got a coller Round my neck marked my dog with the name of Andrew Jackson on it—because I would not take the coller Round my neck I was herld from their party

There will be an explosion take place this week that will tare their party in to a sunder Mr Calhoun is coming out with a Circular or a publication of the Correspondance between him & the President that will blow their little Red foxe or aleous Martin vanburen in to atoms then you will see Genl Duff Green come out upon them with all of his powars this will rais a fuss in the camps—the truth is I expect we will wind up this remainder of the session in in a fuss and have done nor will do nothing for the country this is the effect of the Strong Jackson congress that were to do so much Bussiness

I must close with high esteem

Your friend and obt servt

David Crockett

AM Hughs

PS You can use this letter as you pleas I stand pledged to sustain this to be a true fact

From the Tennessee Historical Society Miscellaneous Files, courtesy of the Tennessee State Library and Archives.

A. M. Hughes (whose name Crockett misspelled) was a Tennessee attorney and Crockett ally who was involved in the 1831 campaign controversy involving charges Crockett had made against his opponent, William Fitzgerald. James H. Peck, judge in the U.S. District Court of Missouri, was impeached by the House of Representatives for abusing his judicial powers. He was tried in the United States Senate early in January 1831 and was acquitted on January 31, 1831. A rewritten version of this letter, which omitted Hughes' name, appeared in the press (see the following letter).

*   *   *   *   *

LETTER TO THE *(JACKSON, TENNESSEE) SOUTHERN STATESMAN* **FEBRUARY 13, 1831, PUBLISHED MARCH 12, 1831; REPRINTED IN THE** *BRATTLEBORO (VERMONT) MESSENGER,* **APRIL 16, 1831.**

Extract of a letter from the Hon. David Crockett, *to a gentleman in this town, dated*
"Washington City, 13th Feb. 1831.

"Your favor of the 27th ult. came duly to hand, and I would answer it more fully, were it not for the fact that I am preparing a *"Circular,"* addressed to my constituents, which I will send you, and in that will give an account of matters and things generally at the seat of Government.

"The Senate are handling the Post-Master General, pretty roughly, without gloves, for refusing to answer the enquiry made by the Senate upon the score of *removals.* Mr. Grundy's resolution prohibiting, Post Masters who had been removed, from being examined, &c. has caused much excitement, and has been severely exposed by Mr. Clayton, together with the manner in which Maj. Barry has managed the affairs of the department, having expended the whole of the $270,000 surplus Revenue that his predecessor, (McLean) made for the country and left in that Department. He has done this by turning out men that knew their business, to make room for a set of the Jackson partisans, and what they lack in quality, he has to make up in to Quantity. Is this the *retrenchment* that the people expected to see? I am of opinion that any honest man will answer in the negative.

"Congress cannot pass the post office and post road bills without making an appropriation of upwards of $100,000 to carry it into effect, and the truth is, I do not believe we will pass any bill this session to establish new routes. It was put off last session, on account that if we had passed that bill, and made the appropriation, it would have been charged to last year of Gen. Jackson's expenditures. The "Jackson Party," as they call themselves, opposed its passage, and it was laid over; and I do not believe from present appearances, that we shall pass it this session. I am tired of this party question. It is to ruin and destroy the happiness and peace of the Union. Their parties here remind me of some large Dogs, that I have seen in this city, with their Collars on, with letters engraved—"MY DOG; and with the name of the owner on the collar.

"I, for one would not wear a collar round my neck, with *"my dog"* on it, and the name of Andrew Jackson, on the Collar—therefore they will not have me for their partisan.

"I am informed that the vice President will come out this week with a publication with the whole correspondence between him and the President. If so, he will expose the whole intrigue of the *"Little Red Fox,"* alias Martin Van Buren, and sink him into insignificance. I have always believed that he was the sole ground of destroying the peace and harmony of the Jackson party, as they call themselves.

"We are bringing the session to a close, and I am of opinion that we will wind up the remainder in a fuss, and do but little good for the country.

"I was told on yesterday that a majority of the Senate were opposed to the Chickasaw and Choctaw treaties, and that they would not therefore be ratified, as it requires a concurrence of two thirds of the Senate to ratify a treaty."

The letter appears to be a rewritten version of the letter Crockett wrote to A. M. Hughes on the same date. It is not known how the newspaper obtained a copy. The newspaper transcript does not include a signature line or addressee, but does follow the letter with a rebuttal criticizing Crockett's defection from Jackson and noting that the Choctaw treaty had been ratified, despite Crockett's prediction to the contrary. The editor claimed that he did not intend to influence the upcoming congressional election, but the newspaper was clearly not an ally of Crockett.

*   *   *   *   *

LETTER TO MICHAEL SPRIGG, MAY 5, 1831 (MISDATED MAY 5, 1830).

Steam Boat Curier near Maysville
5 May 1830

Dear Sir
    I am getting on well and expects to reach my residance if no axident in ten or eleven days from the City—I am under the necessaty to ask you to do me a favour that is to call at the house whare the Stage Stops and in frostburgh enquire for a portetrate of my own likeness it was taken by Mr Hincley and presented to me—I had it roaled up and some news papers round it and I had called it a map of florida I had tied it up in side of the male Stage and I was in the acomodation Stage and we got parted when I came to frostburgh whare they had changed Stages I enquired for it and was told by the driver that he had put it in to the other Stage tho I came on a few miles and over took the mail Stage and found that the fellow had not told me the truth

    I am confidant that it was left their and it will be of no use to any other person than my self—I will take it as a particular favour of you if you will enquire and find it and enclose it to the care of Foresyth and Dobbings at wheeling then they will send it on to me—I spoke to Mr Hart to enquire for it and he may get it but knowing you live near that place induces me to request this favour of you to assertain what went with it I have thought it posable that some negro might have takin it after the Stage Stopped it might have been left in the Stage and taken before I come up will you be so good as to enquire for it and write me to my post office in tennessee

I remain with high esteem your obt servt

David Crockett

Micheal C Sprigg

Courtesy, David Zucker Collection.

Michael Cresap Sprigg was a Maryland congressman who served with Crockett in the Twentieth and Twenty-First Congresses. He was born in Frostburg, the location of the transfer station where Crockett lost his portrait.

The date on this letter (5 May 1830) is inconsistent with events in Crockett's life and more likely dates from 1831. The letter was written from Maysville, Kentucky, which Crockett had reached after leaving Frostburg, Maryland, on his way home from Washington. However, Crockett was in Washington throughout May, 1830 since Congress did not adjourn until May 31. His land bill had been debated during the previous two days and he participated in the debate on Indian Removal later in the month, casting his vote against it on May 24. Crockett may simply have mis-dated the letter due to his anxiety over the lost portrait. William C. Davis has argued convincingly that the letter was written in 1831 (in *Three Roads to the Alamo: The Lives and Fortunes of David Crockett, James Bowie, and William Barret Travis* [New York: Harper Collins, 1998], 624 n. 51).

*   *   *   *   *

UNDATED CROCKETT LETTER PUBLISHED IN THE *(JACKSON, TENNESSEE) SOUTHERN STATESMAN,* MAY 14, 1831.

Mr. Editor:—I send you for publication the following transcript from the record of the court of Weakly county, together with the certificate of A. M. Hughes Esq. Col. Warner, the Clerk of the court, from some motive of delicacy refused to certify to the correctness of the copy. He, however granted me the use of his book. I pledge myself for the truth of the copy, which I took myself. The procedings which I have copied is in Mr. Fitzgerald's own hand writing. Will the editor of the Palladium publish this or will he wait for *"better authority?"*
DAVID CROCKETT

State of Tennessee
vs.
William Fore   May term 1827
Presentment for Passing Counterfeit Money.

This day came the solicitor General in proper person in behalf of the state, and the defendant in proper person, and upon agreement of the parties, and by assent of the court, the Solicitor says, he will no further prosecute the presentment, and the said William Fore agrees to pay all cost of his presentment and Wm. H. Johnson came into court in proper person, and acknowledges himself security for said costs. It is therefore considered by the court that the state recover of the said Wm. Fore & Wm H. Johnson the amount of the cost in this behalf expended.

––––––

Being called on by Col. Crockett to state what I know relative to the compromise of the suit of the State of Tennessee against Wm. Fore for passing counterfeit money: The Bill and Indictment was found against Capt. Fore, and he was tried and convicted before Wm. Fitzgerald was Attorney General. I was one of the prisoner's council. After the verdict of guilty was brought in against him by the Jury, his council moved an arrest of Judgment for some defect in the indictment; the motion was not decided on at that term of the court, nor do I believe it was at the next, but the motion was at last argued before Judge Haskell, by Mr. H. W. Dunlap, and I think Gen. Cook for the prisoner, and by D. S. Jennings, Esq. in behalf of the state. The motion was over-ruled by the Judge. After the decision of the question at the same term of the court a compromise in some way was made between the State's Attorney, Mr. Fitzgerald, and the defendant or his council. (I did not appear for the defendant in the argument of the motion of arrest &c.) There was something said to the Judge about it, to which the Judge replied in substance about as follows: That unless Judgment was moved by the Attorney General, he could not pas sentence &c. There was no motion made for judgment to be passed upon the prisoner. Whatever compromise was made, (and there was one,) was made, to the best of my knowledge (in fact I am certain) by Mr. Fitzgerald.

A. M. Hughes, April 27th, 1831

TO THE PUBLIC

Fellow-Citizens—On my return from Washington City, I found that my competitor Mr. Fitzgerald, had opened the campaign against me by scrutinizing, rigidly, my course as your Representative. To this I had no objection, whilst he treated me fairly; but when I discovered he was misrepresenting my conduct and misstating fact, I thought that a due respect for my character would not suffer me to forbear any longer. I denied his charges and thought I was fully justified in retorting on him by examining into the manner in which he discharged the duties of the different offices with which he had been entrusted. To this I could see nothing objectionable; every public officer, no matter how humble, or how elevated his station may be, is, or ought to be equally accountable to the people. Among the derelictions of duties with which I charged Mr. Fitzgerald, one was that he, holding the office of States' Attorney after having charged the Grand Jury that it was their binding duty to use every endeavor to detect and bring gamblers to punishment, was *himself* called on to give evidence, and he refused. I asserted this at Huntingdon in the presence of Mr. Fitzgerald, who denied the truth of my statement and pledged himself to disprove it. As he has not yet attempted to do so, I conceive myself bound to state on what authority I made the assertion. I have seen & conversed with as many of those who were at that time Grand Jurors as I possibly could; some of them have moved out of the county since that time—others I have not had an opportunity of seeing. I now repeat that at a county court of Gibson county, town of Trenton, (since Mr. Fitzgerald has held the office of State's Attorney) information was received by the Grand Jury that there had been gambling to a large extent carried on the night before, in which several members of the bar and other persons were concerned. The Grand Jury used every effort to detect them; for which purpose they summon'd Mr. Fitzgerald to give evidence concerning the transaction, and he the said Fitzgerald positively refuse, alledging as a reason, that it would impeach himself, and moreover, that if he became witness there would be no prosecutor.

DAVID CROCKETT

We, the undersigned, members of the Grand Jury at the time of the aforesaid occurrence, certify that the above statement, is according to the best of our recollection, correct.

J. BILLINGSLEY
DANIEL CONLEE.

I, Hardy Hunt, do certify, as one of the Jury, that Mr. Fitzgerald did refuse to give evidence when called on.

HARDY HUNT.

P.S. Comment upon this is unnecessary—let me ask the plain honest farmers of this country what they believe would have been their situation if they had been similarly situated and had unwarily fallen into Mr. Fitzgerald's clutches? Would he have had any qualms of conscience? Would the State have been in want of a prosecutor? D.C.

This exchange of letters highlights the harsh nature of the 1831 campaign between Crockett and William Fitzgerald; see chapter 6, footnote #41. Also see Crockett's letters to A. M. Hughes.

*　　*　　*　　*　　*

LETTER TO JAMES DAVISON, MAY 28, 1831.

Harisburgh Tennessee
28 of May 1831

Dear Sir
　　Your favour of the 2 Inst came safe to hand and I will hasten to answer it I am well and family and I am in high Spirites in my Election I have been through twelve counties and have six more to go through and I have no doubt but that I will be re Elected by a majority of upwards of five thousand votes the Jackson question not with Standing
　　The Jackson feavour is going down here as fast as it ever went up the people is naturly astuned here on account of the explosion of the cabinet they know there is Something rong and I find it will operate in my favour my last majority was three thousand five hundred & 25 votes and I am Satisfyed my present prospects is much brighter then ever it was I have taken the firm independant ground I would rather be politically Buried than to be hypochriticaly imortalized I will Sinque or Swim upon merite I will not go further for any party than I believe to be honist
　　You need not be astonished to here of two Representatives from Tennessee that will have the hardehood to rais their voice against genl Jackson for re Election I do believe this will be the case and perhaps there may be more when I Say two I speak advisedly my opinion is there will be one or two more I do hope to see our country brought back to former days and this party faction Buried and peace and harmony prevail in our land though it has had a Severe Shock
　　I here enclose you one of my pamphlets and it has brought the people to their recollections of genl Jacksons former pledges and it will have its wait will you pleas to tender my kindest respects to my friend Doctor Condet and informe him that I feel safe in my next Election the enquire you made relative to my command in the fort I am not the man   I was born and raised in Tennessee and never had six months Schooling in my life I was one of the first white men that ever crossed the Tennessee river in the last war under genl Jackson and I served two six months towers under him as a volunteer and I voted for him for the presidency and I expected him to be the president of the people and not of a party I must acknowledge I was discieved and I am not alone here I must close with great respects

Your obt. Srvt

David Crockett

James Davison

Courtesy of Hofstra University Libraries' Special Collections Department.

Crockett was overly optimistic about his chances to win reelection, especially his prediction of gaining a margin of five thousand votes. He also over estimates anti-Jackson sentiment in his district and the degree of it among the Tennessee congressional delegation. Davison apparently had confused Crockett with another person of that name who had commanded a fort in the recent war.

The recipient of the letter, James Davison, has not been identified, but he appears to have been a friend and supporter of Crockett's to whom Crockett was anxious to convey his strongest views without fear of Davison's disapproval. Crockett wrote to Davison again on August 18, 1831 and an accompanying typescript of that letter notes that Davison was an ancestor of Dr. Edmund D. Soper of Evansville, Illinois.

＊　　＊　　＊　　＊　　＊

LETTER TO THE (*JACKSON, TENNESSEE*) *SOUTHERN STATESMAN,* **JUNE 16, 1831 PUBLISHED JUNE 25, 1831.**

For the Southern Statesman
Harrisburg, 16th June, 1831

Col. Read, Sir—
    I am on my way home from Brownsville; from thence I will go on to Dresden, and will try to procure a copy of the record of the Court of Weakly county in the Fore case; and if Col. Warner refuses to certify it again, I will know whether he can be removed or not.
    I applied to him at first for a copy, and he refused to give it, and I then asked him to show me the record, which he did; and if he did not show me the whole copy, he did not name any thing about any more except that of the court before, when John L. Allen was acting as pro. tem. Solicitor. I told him all I wanted was the record of the decision Term, when Mr. Fitzgerald was Attorney General; this was all I conceived was necessary, as I know that I had said nothing about Mr. Fitzgerald, nor implicated him in any way, only that I said Fore had been prosecuted and convicted for passing counterfeit money, and that after Fitzgerald come into office, which was at the time the case was compromised, I stated that he compromised it. This is what I attempted to establish, and I conceive I have done so, although Mr. Fitzgerald has paraded such a battalion of names before the public, to prove that I missed a word in copying the record, which it may be possible I did. But this does not alter the importance of the charge, as he has proved the record to be in his own hand writing after his friends attempted to prove he was not Solicitor, at the time the compromise took place.
    I discover he has come out with an answer to that which I never did say—that which appeared in the Southern Statesman, as my speech in Huntingdon, where it purported that Fitzgerald, was called on to do his duty and refused. I never said that. My charge was, that after he had charged the Grand Jury, that it was their binding duty to call on any one who was in company where gambling was going on, and make them give evidence. This is what I did say—and this is what I have proven to all intents and purposes, although Fitzgerald is trying to play it off, by his low cunning on the people. This is his trade—to make every thing appear as favorable to his case as possible. Part of his publication is a perfect tissue of falsehoods.
    I will go on to Paris, and procure Major Jenning's certificate & will enclose it to you and a copy of the record, if there is any way to procure it from the clerk of the Circuit Court of Weakly county, in the Fore Case. I never did design to deceive the people. My object was to act fairly. I went to Col. Warner, and asked him to give me a copy, which he refused to do. If there is an error in it, why did not Fitzgerald publish the record? As he has not, I will; and ask the people to give no credit to his publication until they see the record. Then decide on me accordingly. I never did deceive the people— nor would I for a seat in Congress while I live.
    I hope you will publish this letter in your paper, and oblige your friend and ob't ser't.

DAVID CROCKETT

The letter is another campaign document in which Crockett continued to focus on his charges of improper conduct against William Fitzgerald.

*   *   *   *   *

UNDATED LETTER TO THE *(JACKSON, TENNESSEE) SOUTHERN STATESMAN,* **PUBLISHED JULY 2, 1831.**

FELLOW CITIZENS:

As my opponent Mr. Fitzgerald, in the plentitude of his wisdom, has thought proper to address you another circular, I feel it due both to you and myself to notice it, by exposing the falsehood of his assertions—that they are false I believe I can satisfy any man whose eyes are open to conviction. Of the motives which influenced him and his coadjutors I shall not constitute myself the judge. In relation to any thing applying to me individually, without any bearing upon my conduct as your representative of my course in this electioneering campaign, I shall not speak, leaving him and *his* to enjoy the whole benefit of the sneer attempted to be cast upon my age—not being yet convinced by the arguments of Mr. Fitzgerald or any other lawyer, that there is any thing degrading in being *"old,"* he may chuckle at his success, an intelligent people will fully appreciate it. Whether I have need of false charges to sustain myself in the righteous cause in which I am engaged, I shall also submit to my constituents; but if I have, and shall hereafter incontrovertibly prove those charges which he has been pleased to pronounce *false,* the public will at least justify me in preferring them.

Mr. Fitzgerald is astonished, as well he might be I suppose—did he think that my character both private and public was to be made the theme of the grossest misrepresentation and that I would passively submit to it, without any attempt at vindication? Did you think little Fitz, that I would suffer myself to be squeezed to death like a mouse, without at least a squeak? It was indeed a bold attempt to think I could impose upon the good people of this District such a thing as truth; well done Fitz, you are not accustomed to it I suppose. But to come at once to this certificate, which "will show what a glaring imposition he has attempted to impose on the public, and the certificate which will also show his conduct when he found out that the records would prove him to have made false statements to the people." Well, now fellow citizens, to what does all this amount? I have heard that a mountain was once in labour and when a great multitude had assembled to witness the birth of some wonderful off spring; strange to relate, a little mouse crept out. Mr. Fitzgerald and some of his friends seem to have a great abhorence to the words "in proper person," and whether these *proper personages* do so by a natural instinctive adherance of *propriety* or not, I shall not pretend to assert.

I have already told the public that the Clerk, Col. Warner, refused to give me a copy unless I would agree to take a transcript of the whole record. I had nothing to do with but a very little part of the record; the fact is this, I believed then and still believe they wanted me to publish if I published at all, an article so long that no body would take the trouble to read it; but settling all this a part, as Col. Warner would not transcribe and certify to the correctness of what I wanted, I got William H. Johnson Esq. to read the part of the record which suited my case whilst I wrote it. As to the insertion of the words "in proper person," whether it was his mistake or mine it makes no difference, as it is not material. Mr. Fitzgerald has made a great fuss about this—let me ask you Mr. Fitz do they alter the sense or meaning of the record, or even that particular sentence, one title? The record states: "This day came the Solicitor General in behalf of the State, &c."—Very well now *young Fitz,* if the solicitor general came at all I should like to know how he came unless in proper person, that is in his own person—did you Mr. Fitz assume another shape or another hue? or have you the faculty of doing it as easily as you can change your coat, whether that coat belongs to your ward robe or your politics? Mr. Fitzgerald says that I have "also published a certificate of a certain A. M. Hughes;" who that knows the characters of Mr. Hughes and Mr. Fitzgerald, does not laugh at this epithet of *"certain;"* as if Mr. Fitz was not acquainted with him or had never before heard of him. What will be the surprise of those who do not know either personally, when they are told that Mr. Hughes is better known and Mr. Fitzgerald's superior in every thing, except the admirable talent of magnifying nothing into an extraordinary affair. The certificate of Mr. Hughes upon this subject is conclusive. But it appears, at least so the *young man* would have us believe that because Hughes has bet about forty dollars on the election he is unworthy of credit. Mr. Fitz had better go farther, *he*, might make ten dollars on every bet Mr. Hughes has made. But Mr. Fitzgerald is not going to do this: on the contrary, he gives Mr. Hughes the very wholesome advice of endeavoring to raise the sum of $40 to pay his bets, because Mr. Fitzgerald's election is now reduced to a certainty. The consumate vanity of this Mr. Fitz amounts to impudence. The honest yeomanry of our country need not trouble their heads about the election; Mr. Fitzgerald and the Lawyers have settled the question.

I shall make but a few remarks on Judge Haskell's certificate. Mr. Fitzgerald in remarking on Mr. Hughes' certificate in which he says, "whatever compromise was made and there was one to the best of my knowledge, in fact I am certain was made by Mr. Fitzgerald:" says "if Mr. Hughes was certain that I had made a compromise, what use had he of the cautious language to the best of my knowledge &c." Judge Haskell says, "although Mr. Fitzgerald had in the course of the prosecution been appointed prosecuting Attorney, yet *as far as my recollection serves me*, He had nothing to do in relation to this trial before me;" now why did not Mr. Fitzgerald also state, that if Judge Haskell was certain that he had nothing to do with this case what use had he for saying *"as far as my recollection serves me!"* But enough of Judge Haskell's certificate.

Mr. Fitzgerald asked why I did not procure the certificate of Dudly S. Jennings Esq. because, as he alledges, Mr. Jennings is hostile to him. *This little would be Honorable*, seems to take it for granted that every man who will not worship his honour, would tell a lie to injure him. The people are indebted to him for his good opinion of them. I will however tell him why I did not get the certificate of Mr. Jennings. I had a conversation with Mr. Jennings after I had obtained the certificate of Mr. Hughes, this certificate I shewed him; he said that he was very busy at that time, that Mr. Hughes' statement was correct, and if it would be controverted by Mr. Fitzgerald he would give a certificate, that he was merely employed to assist in conducting the prosecution and not acting in the capacity of Attorney General, and therefore had no power to compromise the matter, and farther that Mr. Fitzgerald was the first person who proposed making the compromise. Since Mr. Fitzgerald's last circular made its appearance, I wrote to Mr. Jennings by my son William, for his certificate but Mr. Jennings had unfortunately gone to Kentucky. So much for Mr. Fitzgerald's nonsense.

As for my voting in Congress every body knows that I have always been in favor of Internal Improvements. One thing however is very remarkable: Mr. Fitz says, that I voted for the Washington Turnpike road one hundred and fifty thousand dollars. What will the people think when I tell them that no such Bill has ever been before Congress since I have been a member. The man who will not scruple at making one misstatement will not stick at many. But he also finds fault of my voting to give Gales & Seaton the printing of the "Old Documents" as they are generally termed. Does he know what they are? as he has asserted that they are of no use to the country I will inform him. Know then wise Mr. Fitz, that they embrace the reports of the Committees of Congress from the time of the Revolution, to the time of the conflagration of the Capital during the last war. Gales and Seaton were then printers to Congress and they alone have the manuscript from which they can be printed. The expense will be about twenty or thirty thousand dollars, which the *veracious* Mr. Fitz has multiplied by four; besides, as to this being for the exclusive benefit of any individuals. If he were as wise as he would have us believe, he would have known that it was left discretionary with the Clerks of the two houses of Congress to select what they considered necessary to be preserved as useful to the country, for which alone the printers are to be compensated. So much for another *lie*.

One word about this tract of land which in the classical language of Mr. Fitzgerald an earthquake or some other convulsion of nature has sunk from the face of the earth. I never said that Mr. Fitzgerald received Fore's house and farm, as a bribe. (This is another one of his facts.) I only said that a short time after the "*compromise,*" he was living in the house and on the same farm that Fore had just left. Is this not true? will he dare deny it? How he came there I repeat is none of my business.

Col. Warner the Clerk of the circuit court of Weakly, requires some notice. It appears from his "want of experience" he was in the habit of getting Mr. Fitzgerald to make up his entries upon the minutes "especially in all difficult and state cases." Now I am not prepared to assert nor do I, that Col. Warner would plead ignorance of his own duty for the purpose of screening Mr. Fitzgerald; but one thing I will say, that Mr. Fitz appears to have a number of *Friends* whom he occasionally finds very convenient and who stand ready to lend their names to any thing. It has been asserted that the clerk refused to certify to the part of the record I had copied, because it was not correctly copied. This is as false as it is malicious. He himself says that he refused to do so "unless I would take a copy of the whole record." He was very much afraid that the "innocent" would appear "guilty." I have now a transcript of the whole affair and I should think it an insult to the good sense of the community to ask them to drudge through five or six pages of stuff, and *law stuff too,* which has nothing to do with the question. I only wanted a history of the transaction, since Mr. Fitzgerald was appointed Solicitor. The idea has been held out and boldly asserted as a fact, that the suit was compromised before his appointment, and I cannot help believing Col. Warner intended to connive at the falsehood, else why give me a copy of the record certified by him to be correct, without any date to the part of it where the compromise was made. He has not been pleased to tell us on what day—in what term or even in what year. Why not date the part: why not begin as he ought "May term 1827?" Oh! no, it is well known that Mr. Fitzgerald was then Attorney General. If we leave out the date it may be passed over without notice.

Although I do not think that Mr. *Fitzgerald's* Circular deserves half the attention I have given it; as I have taken it under consideration I suppose I must notice his principal charges. He makes an appeal to the occupants —charges me with abusing the Legislature &c. The Occupants are already indebted to Mr. Fitz for the aid he gave in letting loose upon them the swarm of warrant holders. I believe that I once gave him the name of a pretty good Country Court Lawyer; I shall be obliged to retract it, if he continues to assert that the Legislature can afford any protection to the occupants. The land belongs to the General Government and the Legislature has no more power to give it to them than Mr. Fitz himself has. I tell the occupants that the Legislature has no power to deprive them of their homes.

Thus, fellow citizens, have I noticed every thing in the late circular of Mr. Fitzgerald which I can conceive worthy of reply. The whole production seems to be in character with the infamous publication which four years ago made its appearance over the ostensible signature of "Yarnell Reece." That scurrilous publication you will recollect appeared on the eve of the election, when I had not time to answer it. By your votes then you put your mark upon the calumny. I have always believed and I still believe that Mr. Fitzgerald was the author. I have charged him with it several times publicly and he has not denied it. For this reason I repeat *that this little thing,* has been yelping at my heels for the last four years.

Whether you will sacrifice an old and as far as his capacity extends a faithful servant, to gratify the ambition of this man and satisfy the malevolence of his sycophants, your votes as the coming election will show. This publication will appear in a newspaper if I can get justice as my competitor did, from the proprietors of newspapers. I have no right to expect any courtesy, to judge by the past, as they will not even grant me justice. We have four in the district, all of which teem with the most unmerited abuse and the grossest calumnies upon my character. They not only misrepresent facts, but some of them are blessed with the genius for coining falsehoods. Col. Read is the only editor who ever publishes any thing from my friends. Even the Clerks of the Courts (or some of them) seem to have joined the conspiracy against me. In the name of Heaven fellow citizens, what have I done that I must be treated with such contumely and glaring injustice? I appeal to your justice, your honor, and your magnanimity. If you re-elect me I will endeavor, as I have hitherto done, to discharge my duty faithfully—but if it be your will that I shall be sacrificed as a victim on the altar of conscience, be it so. I shall retire to private life with the proud consciousness of having done my duty.

I am, Fellow citizens, your
most obedient servant.
DAVID CROCKETT

P.S. Upon examination of Mr. Fitz' Circular, I find something said about my absent votes in Congress, and about my not sending the Journals of Congress to my district—this is unusual to do. I have the Journals of Congress in my house from 1789, up to the last Congress. If any gentleman disputes what I say, they can come and examine for themselves. I say there never has been such a bill as the Washington Turn Pike Road Bill presented since I have been in Congress. The bill perhaps, that he has allusion to, is the Rockville road bill: this is a part of the great Cumberland road, 24 miles in length, and passed Congress by a large majority, and the appropriation was ninety thousand dollars. This shows that Fitz's intention is to magnify every thing he talks or writes about. As for my absent votes, if he had any intention of doing me justice why did he not set out the absent votes of the balance of the delegation from Tennessee, and then compare mine with theirs and contrast the difference, instead of trying to hold out the idea that I was absent one day in each vote. Any man acquainted with the business of Congress knows the vote is taken sometimes a half dozen times in one day, and also that a great part of the session, Congress meets at the same time that the public offices open and all members must attend to their local business, and thereby are compelled to be absent when the vote is taken. I saw I have been as attentive to business as any other member from Tennessee. I have always believed Mr. Fitz furnished that article that made its appearance in the Bolivar Palladium; and nothing is better evidence of that fact, than his taking it in his famous circular. I was told by the gentleman that kept the Post office in Dresden, that Mr. Fitz was well attended to during the last congress, by both the Senators and part of the representatives from Tennessee; they were all franking him documents during the sitting of the last Congress—I would not be surprised if he has trash enough to furnish the newspapers until August.

As Mr. Fitzgerald has made the calculation how much money I have received unjustly for my absent votes, I will ask him if this would be worse than for him to receive fourteen hundred dollars from Mr. Nevils and Aaron Winters for ninety five dollars or thereabouts—I make this as a set off. A few weeks ago I delivered a speech in the upper end of Weakly county, in the neighborhood of Aaron Winters', he then told me that he had come to expose Fitzgerald for his conduct to him. The charge was this: that a man by the name of Richard Cocke, had put a debt in Fitzgerald's hands for collection; the debt was between three and four hundred, on a man by the name of Nevils; and Fitzgerald brought suit against Nevils and got judgment, and Nevils filed a bill of injunction and gave Winters as his security. He got final judgment against both Winters and Nevils, and had his execution levied upon three negroes the property of Nevils, and on the day of sale Nevils forbid the sale. The negroes were sold and Mr. Fitzgerald was the purchaser at $86, or thereabouts. They then run the execution upon Winters' land, and he told Winters not to make any arrangement, and he would get a friend to bid his land off, and it was sold for $9; a plantation worth $7 or $800. Fitz kept the negroes one year or over that time, then sent them down the river and sold them for $750. At the time when Winters' land was to be redeemed, he went to Mr. Bondurant, the man that bid it off, and paid the money to him with interest and took his receipt, and that Fitzgerald refused to receive the money. There was fourteen hundred and fifty dollars worth of property sold, and the execution credited with 95 dollars or thereabouts. This information I received from Aaron Winters, the man who lost his land. Now compare this act of Mr. Fitzgerald with my receiving the public money for my absent votes, as he would have the people believe I did. Mr. F. stands charged as above; I give it as I got it, whether true or false, he has plenty of time to make it appear before the election.

A hint at his official conduct:—Mr. Peter Littaker told me that Joseph Serat had been at his house and told him that himself and his brother John were presented to the grand jury of Obion county, for a fighting scrape with some other persons, and there was a true bill found against them both, and they removed to Gibson county, and that the papers were sent to that county by Fitzgerald, the attorney general. And Joseph Serat went to Fitz and offered him ten dollars, and told him that his brother John would also give him ten more if he would let the case die. Fitz refused to take the ten dollars from either, but told him that if he, Joseph & John Serat, would vote for him and use their influence with the Shults' their connection, that they should hear no more of it. This has been upwards of twelve months ago, and no suit brought as yet. This looks suspicious for a good faithful officer. I give this as I got it, and I want Mr. Fitz to clear himself of this charge for neglect of duty.

He says a great deal in his circular in answer to that which I did not say in my speech in Huntingdon, although Col. Read reported it as saying that Fitzgerald was called on to do his duty and refused. I never made such a charge on him at Huntingdon nor any other place; but he got my printed speech and found that he could raise a fuss, as all other demagogues do, and thereby slip out. I have said that his late circular was a tissue of falsehoods, and I repeat it. He has also got Mr. Wickliff's old letter on the expenditures of the government, where he loaned his imposing name to Gen. Duff Green to help him out with the dispute with him and the editors of the National Intelligencer; Mr. Fitzgerald is trying to impose this on the people for truth. I must call on the editor to publish Mr. Chilton's answer to that letter; it will show what a glaring imposition this little man is trying to put on the public. I enclose Col. Read Mr. Chilton's letter with a special request to publish it, and I do hope the balance of the editors will do me the justice to publish this letter and my answer to Fitzgerald's late circular; I ask this though not with much hope of success. The reason I make this remark, is that they have teemed their polecat abuse on me for the last twelve months, with the exception of Col. Read, who I have no reason to complain of, for withholding justice from me; he has pursued an honorable course. I also send Col. Read the transcript of the whole of the Fore case in Weakly county, as so much has been said on the subject, I must request Col. Read to publish it; then the people can see what a glaring imposition is trying to be palmed upon them by Fitzgerald and his friends. They will see at the decision term his friend Col. Warner the clerk, has neglected to put the date, which I took it, was on Thursday, May term 1827. Now is this not a worse mistake than I made in adding the words "in proper person?" If I did do so, it was done through no motive whatever and would not alter the meaning of the record; perhaps the editor might have made a typographical error. I wish him to examine and inform the public.

DAVID CROCKETT

This very long letter is an example of the personal nature of the attacks made during the 1831 election campaign.

*　　*　　*　　*　　*

UNDATED LETTER TO THE *(JACKSON, TENNESSEE) SOUTHERN STATESMAN*, **PUBLISHED JULY 30, 1831.**

David from the River country to Adam the Chronicle writer.

Adam, David feareth that thou hast wilfully misrepresented David without having the fear of God before thine eyes. Wilt thou recollect that thou hast been a distinguished Senator from Tennessee, and also that thou hast received a letter franked by Andrew the Chief ruler over the tribe of Columbia, enclosing a prospectus of the Globe a Van Buren type for the purpose of procuring subscribers, in order to mislead the people of the District which David has had the honor to represent for the last four years.

Know then Adam, David calleth on thee to explain how this league has been entered into between thyself and Andrew the Chief ruler, and also what is to be thy reward for thy services, and if thou art to be Foreign Minister, and where to—for thy witty Chronicles which thou hast been pleased to furnish to the people of this river country. How is this come to pass, when thee thyself told David of the river country, that at the close of the Legislative council in 1819, when thee was filling the station of distinguished Senator in Tennessee, and after Andrew our Chief ruler, had come before the Legislature and made a speech before them against the People's Bank, which was established at the Session, and that it had kindled thy wrath against Andrew so that thee and thy friend from East Tennessee went down to the Rocky city to fight against Andrew, and avenge thyself for the insult cast upon the body to which thou was a distinguished Senator? Now how has this all happened that the lion is to lie down with the lamb? David is exceedingly anxious to know how this has come to pass? Will thee be so good as to tell David what is to be thy reward for this strange somerset of this distinguished Senator, who was carrying on a correspondence with Andrew the Chief ruler, during the last Congress, and at the same time was writing deceitful letters to David and exhibiting David's letters and Andrew's publicly, and saying that David or the President had one or the other lied. This shows what little reliance can be placed in this distinguished Senator. David charges Adam with dealing deceitfully with him and he will not neglect Adam: no not even when Adam shall make the attempt to go to the great Sanhedrim, David will pay the utmost farthing.

David calls on Adam to retract his statement concerning David's franking books to his friend in Trenton. Here David charges Adam of a wilful misstatement, to deceive the people. Adam states that David franked one hundred and thirty dollars worth of postage on books. David is sorry to say that a distinguished Senator should write down a wilful falsehood to injure David in his election. David never did at any time frank any books to Trenton to his friend, over the two ounce weight, which is given to all members of Congress. The books perhaps, that Adam has allusion to, were the American Biography. These books were franked by the Clerk of the House of Representatives and directed to John W. Crockett, at Trenton. David told the Clerk that if he would frank them, he would bring his Journals of Congress and Diplomatic correspondence, and other books, which he had a right to frank, to the amount of four or five times the weight of what the Clerk did frank. David's name was never on a book sent to Trenton, nor any where else over lawful franking privilege, there fore he does pronounce Adam's late address to William, particularly what relates to the franking books a barefaced falsehood.

David did have a better opinion of Adam than to believe he would have joined the little yelpers, which have been after his heals for the last four years. David has had to bear the slang and pole-cat abuse of every little parasite of a partizan, that could lift a pen, and they have hurt him just as much as the moscheto can hurt the ox, when he lights on his horn to suck his blood. Here David disposes of Adam, by laying him away with the unfinished business for the remainder of his days.

DAVID, *from the river country.*

P.S. I discover another Circular from little Fitz, in which he repeats the President cannot expend any money without it is given to him by Congress. I am sorry to see this little man trying so hard to deceive the people of this district. He must believe the people are the most ignorant of all creation. Does he not know that the President did expend before the first Congress met, after he took his seat, for recalling Ministers and outfits to Ministers, Charge de Affairs, and Secretary of Legations to the amount of one hundred and eighty-four thousand dollars. This he done before the first Congress met after he went into power; and has he not since the last Congress adjourned, called home M'Lane from London and sent out Van Buren at an expense of eighteen thousand dollars, and still he will try to deceive the people? Does not every body know that the President possesses the whole removing power and it always has been the case.

He also parades another batalion of names before the public to prove that I had made a mistake in denying there being such road as the Washington Turnpike road. If Mr. Fitz had said I voted for a Washington Turnpike road, and that the appropriation was ninety thousand dollars I never would have denied the road, but he magnified the appropriation to one hundred and fifty thousand dollars, therefore I did not know of any such a road. I was not at home when I wrote my answer to Fitz's circular—I never examined the journals, but every man that reads the papers knows that the newspapers all took it up and called it the Rockville and Frederick town road, and every body knows too that the appropriation was ninety thousand dollars, which makes my statement part a misstatement & part the truth. Now I ask little Fitz if this is a worse mistake than he made when he charged me with receiving pay for days before I arrived at my post. If Mr. Fitz. had never been a member of the Legislature he might be excused, but as it is he has written down and published a wilful falsehood to deceive the people

Now as he has been taking some trouble to show the people my votes, I will call the attention of the people to Mr. Fitzgerald's vote in the occupant law. His vote stands recorded in the journal of the Session of 1825, in page 351 and 2; he voted against the passage of the occupant law on its third reading, and his name will be found recorded as above. I do hope the people will not be imposed on in the manner Mr. Fitz is trying to play himself off on them. He states in his circular that he toiled night and day for the benefit of the occupants, and any man who will examine will find the above statement to be true! Is this dealing honestly with the people? I do hope that every occupant will examine this vote as above stated, then compare that vote with his public addresses. He says he cannot answer the silly charges that I have made against him, for taking Nevels' negroes and Winters' land for ninety-five dollars, as for my part I do not think this to be a silly charge. I handed Fitz the certificate of Winters at Maryville while he was making a speech, and he read it: that certificate stated that the case was worse if possible, than my statement; Fitz read it and [owned?] to the truth of the charge. Here he received fourteen hundred and fifty dollars worth of property, and credited the expedition with ninety-five dollars, and poor Winters is to be the sufferer for the balance of the debt which will be near three hundred dollars. Now let any honest man take this case to himself and ask himself if it is honest for Mr. Fitz to take Winters' land for nine dollars, a plantation with one hundred and thirty acres well improved, worth $7 or 800. This he got by deceiving Winters; still Mr. Fitz calls this a silly charge, and thinks it unworthy of a reply I published this near five weeks before the election; the truth is he cannot controvert this charge. I will now wash my hands of this subject, but will add that I have always canvassed with a gentleman heretofore. Col. Alexander is incapable of doing a mean act, he is a gentleman, but this is more than I can say of little Fitz as I do not believe he possesses a single qualification belonging to a gentleman. Adieu, to all scriblers hereafter.
DAVID CROCKETT

[The *Southern Statesman* added the following comment to the above letter:]

July 22, 1831.

In reference to the above address, we cannot forbear expressing how disagreeable it is to us to publish a production abounding with invective and detraction. A man should wish to be sustained upon his own merits alone, and not at the expense of another's reputation, unless it can be a recommendation to one man to prove that another is meaner than himself. As to the case of Winters we know nothing, but if as Col. Crockett states, Mr. Fitzgerald publicly admitted the charge as certified by Winters, to be true, we are constrained to suppose there can be nothing very criminal in the transaction, particularly as candidates these times don't seem much disposed to admit things prejudicial to their popularity; however that may be, as Col. Crockett appears to be in possession of Winters' certificate, we should like to have been furnished with a copy of it, accompanying his present address.

Crockett was, in part, responding to a satire written by Adam Huntsman, writing as "Black Hawk," titled "Book of Chronicles, West of Tennessee and East of the Mississippi Rivers," designed to damage Crockett's image and cast him as "David from the River Country." But the bulk of the letter is another attack on the honesty of his opponent, William Fitzgerald.

*   *   *   *   *

LETTER TO JAMES DAVISON, AUGUST 18, 1831.

At home Weakley County 18 August 1831
West Tennessee

Dear Sir

Your favour has been received and I will hasten to answer it and your request shall be attended to   I am sorry that I cannot give you a full account of the result of my election   however I have hird from enough of the countys to sattisfy me that I am beaton something like five hundrid votes   this is a small majority considering the powerful extent of District that I had to canvass through   I had eighteen countys in the district and a poppulation of about 16 thousand voters   I came out too and told the people that I never would vote for genl Jackson for re-election   I could not after his recommendations in both his messages to Congress   he said four years or one term was as long as any man ought to weld the destineas of this mighty nation   the truth is I was one of the first men that ever crossed the Tennessee river in to the Creek war with him and I served two towers of duty with him and voted for him for president and I contend that I supported him as far as he parsued the principles he professed to possess before he was elected   I never did support men and forsake principles nor I never will   I have always parsued one straight forward corse and I ever expect to   It was not the Jackson party strength that beat me   it could not have come with in two thousand votes of beating me   My Competitor is a little County Court lawyer with verry little standing   he is what we call here a perfect lick spittle   he huzzawed for Jackson and he would write down wilful falshoods and publish   and there is four news papers published in the district and I had to bare the slang and pole cat abuse of every one of thim besides the little pin hook County Court lawyers was galloping from one side of the district to the other and where little Fitzgerald would represent anything they would give a Certificate-makers from Circuit Judges down to Clerks of the Court & Shiriffs the truth is the Jackson worshipers became desperate and had to resort to any and every thing in order to have me beaton   If I had been treated as an honist man aught the Jackson question Could not have beaton me   The Jacksonism is going down here as fast as it ever went up   The Jackson partazans here is exulting that they have got me beaton   I thank god I would rather be beaton and be a man than to be elected and be a little puppy dog to yelp after their party   I am gratified at one thing   I beat my oponent in the County we both live and I beat him in nine Countys out of eighteen   the Jackson question   not with standing I had the pleasure of beating in the Countys which will compose the district when it is divided that we both live in   I beat upwards of six hundred votes therefore I shall hold my self in readiness for the next race   I was beaton this time intirely by managemint and rascality I come out independant and told the people of this district that I never would vote for genl Jackson for reelection after his pledges to the people I will vote for either of the other candidates in preferance to him Their party run me as a Clay man my principle is to support a man for president and suport his principles as far as I like them and oppose and expose those that I do not like I am a verry plain man I never had six months education in my life I was raised in obsurity with out either welth or education I have made my self to every station in life that I have ever filled through my own exertions I am a republican in fact not like the Jackson republicans a name with out a substance I would rather be politically burried than to be hypochritically imortalized I have been made a political marter of for being an honest man I love my Country and I would not give one Chaw of tobaco for a man that will not make a sacrifice of him self before he will have his Country imposed on this is my situation at preasant one thing consolates me I have no doubt but the time is not far distant when the american people will see the purity of my motives I have truth on my side and we have high authority for saying it is mighty and will prevail I do consider the time has come when every boddy aught to do his duty I intind to do mine and I still hope to see the Country flourish and the time come when this proscription for opinion sake will cease this is the first act of the presant administration that I condemned I also condemned the Course parsued to the Southern Indians I love to sustain the honour of my Country and I will do it while I live in or out of Congress I must close with great respects your friend & obt servt

David Crockett

James Davison

Holograph and typescript in the Crockett Genealogy file, DRT Library, the Alamo.

See Crockett's May 28, 1831 letter to Davison, above.

*   *   *   *   *

UNDATED LETTER, MID-1831 TO GALES & SEATON.

Dear Friends— . . . I consider the time has come when every man aught to do his duty. I hope the day will soon come when this man worship will cease. I am gratified that I can informe you that I beat in nine Countys out of eighteen and I beat 103 votes in the county that Fitz and myself live in, and I beat him upwards of six hundred in the Countys that will compose the district when divided and of course I will hold myself in readiness for the next race, by that time the people will see the purity of my motive, all the people want is infermation and they will do right. This little Thing [Fitzgerald] has been blowed into Congress by lying and huzzawing for Jackson in fact I had to run against Jackson as well as this mean puppy—he is ready to taike the coller with my dog on it and the name of Andrew Jackson on the Coller he will have the name of beating me on General Jacksons popularity but this is not true, he beat me by writing down wilful lies and publishing to the world, that which ought to sink every honorable man into insignificants. I would rather be beaten and be a man than to be elected and be a little puppy dog. I must close with great respects I remain

your obt servt
David Crockett

Joseph Gailes
and

William Seaton.

PS please to correct errs and publish this letter. You know me.
DC

From Josephine Seaton, **William Winston Seaton of the National Intelligencer: A Biographical Sketch** *(Boston: James R. Osgood & Co., 1871), 184.*

Although the letter is undated, it undoubtedly comes from this period. It shares many common phrases and sentiments found in the August 18, 1831 letter to Davison.

*   *   *   *   *

LETTER TO DR. CALVIN JONES, AUGUST 22, 1831.

Weakley County Tennessee
22 August 1831

Doctor Jones

Dear Sir
       I under stand you are the agent for Calvin Jones for a tract of 2500 acres that lyes adjoining me in the fork between Rutherford fork and main obian and I am informed you are authorised to give a leace on it or to Sell a part of the tract
       I have been compeled to sel my land where I live to try to pay my debts and I wish to take a leace in the north east corner of the tract adjoining the low grounds of the south fork of obian where I wish to take a leace is near the corner of the tract I wish to clear twenty acres and build comfortable Cabbens & Smoke house corne cribs & Stables and dig a well and set out some fruit trees There is no water on it without digging a well if you will give me a good liberal leace I will make you a good improvement I may perhaps clear more than twenty acres it is verry heavy timbered and will take hard work to open a plantation my reason for wishing to take a leace on it, it will be handy to move to it if I get able to buy pleas to write me the terms that I can have a small part in that corner my nephew will call on you and any arrangement you make with him will be sattisfactory with me it may be that I may be able to buy before the leace would be out if so I Should like to know the terms – I have not herd the result of my election from all the countys I expict I am beaton I have one consolation I would rather be beaton and be a man than to be elected and be a little puppy dog I have always supported measurs and principles and not men I have acted fearless and independant and I never will regret my course I would rather by politically buried than to be hypochritically imortalized I contend that if the people of the western District elected me to fill the Station of an honourable Representative I done my best to fill their expectations but if they elected me to be a little puppy dog to yelp after a party I have decived them and would again if elected I have always believed I was an honist man and if the world will do me Justice they will find it to be the case
Respectfully your obt servt

David Crockett

Doctr Jones

Calvin Jones Papers, Southern Historical Collection, Wilson Library, University of North Carolina at Chapel Hill, available on microfilm in University Publications of America, Series J: Selections from the Southern Historical Collection, Part 8, Reel 1; OCLC No. 12894903.

Crockett confusingly seems to refer to "Doctor Jones" as a land agent for Calvin Jones, as if they were two different people, but they appear to have been one and the same. Dr. Calvin Jones, from whom Crockett was seeking a lease on a tract of land, was a physician, North Carolina militia officer, editor of the Raleigh, North Carolina, *Star*, and owner of a plantation near Bolivar, Hardeman County, Tennessee, to which he relocated in 1832. Jones's papers show that he dealt in land sales as well as medicine. Calvin Jones Papers Inventory (#921), Manuscripts Department, Library of the University of North Carolina at Chapel Hill online (http://www.lib.unc.edu/mss/inv/j/Jones,Calvin.html).

Jones was typical of many Tennessee land owners, both resident and absentee, who leased tracts of land to those who were not able to buy it. Note Crockett's phrase "if I get able to buy" and description of the difficult financial straits he was in due to debt that had forced him to sell his own land. Tenant farmers were able to earn a living from crops they cultivated and improvements they made to the owner's land, which they were then entitled to sell.

Jones wrote on the back of Crockett's letter, "This letter was handed me by Mr. Thomas Crockett nephew of Col. Crockett and I have written an answer offering a lease for 6 years commencing next Jany. August 24, 1831."

*   *   *   *   *

PARTIAL TRANSCRIPT OF LETTER TO THE *(WASHINGTON) DAILY NATIONAL INTELLIGENCER*, DECEMBER 25, 1831, PUBLISHED FEBRUARY 3, 1832.

Col. Crockett. We have lately received a characteristic letter from this gentleman, who is well remembered as a Representative in the last Congress from the State of Tennessee, which letter he desires us to publish. . . . The Colonel [says] that it was his intention to have come to the Seat of Government to contest the election of the Member returned from his district. But let us state his intention in his own words:

"I did expect to have been on to the City this winter, but the winter has set in so severe that it will be out of my power to get there. I wished to have gone on to contest that Member's right to a seat in Congress that had the name of beating me [a reference to his opponent, William Fitzgerald, who defeated him in the 1831 election]. I have proof sufficient to break any election in common times; however, I cannot tell how it might have terminated in these times of high party excitement."

Some of the practices at the election, he says, were "contrary to all the laws of Tennessee. In fact," says he, "I do believe there was a combination of rascality throughout the district; I was to be beaten, no matter how many votes I got: they had the Judges, Clerks, and Sheriffs, fixed friendly to him [Fitzgerald]. I know, that the Jackson question will get the name of beating me; but this is not true. The Jackson question would not have come within two thousand votes of beating me."

He complains then bitterly of a Circular of his opponent, in which advantage was taken of some of his votes in Congress, and of his occasional absence on calls of the Yeas and Nays. From some source or other, he says, copies enough were obtained of the Journal of the House, "to place one in almost every little town in the district," and, as he had not the gift of ubiquity, he could not counteract this industry of his opponents. The Colonel says:

"I proclaimed it far and wide that I never would vote for Andrew Jackson for re election; that I would vote for any one in preference who was spoken of as a candidate. And I now say, that I never will vote for J. nor for any man that will vote for him. I am strongly solicited to offer for Elector, to vote for Henry Clay. The truth is, I do believe Mr. Clay is gaining friends in these parts. The people are beginning to find out the true worth of Jacksonism; they are beginning to find out that Davy Crockett is not alone to raise his voice against the re-election of Andrew Jackson. I was one of the first men that ever crossed the Tennessee under the General, and I served under him two tours of duty; and I supported him for President. But I could not follow him any further, when I found the whole object of his administration appeared to be to reward his friends, at the sacrifice of his political opponents. I have heard an old saying, "once a man and twice a child." I think this applicable at the present time."

The Colonel, however, consoles himself, in conclusion with the following reflections, with the quotation of which we close our extracts from his letter:

"I had rather be beaten and be a man, than be elected and be a dog to take the collar on my neck, with "My dog" written on the collar. This I would not do. I told the People that I would rather be politically buried than hypocritically immortalized. I am satisfied that the People in this country are beginning to find out that it is useless to support a name without principle. All the People want is information. Gen. Green's paper is doing much good in this country. It is a well-known fact that no man did more to promote the election of Gen. Jackson than he did; and now to see him horned off, and that —— paper the Globe taken in as the Organ of the Administration, is what cannot be accounted for."

We are somewhat surprised not to find enumerated among the causes of the Colonel's defeat the very serious charge brought against him by one of his late colleagues, that he once dined (or supped, we forget which) with one of the Editors of the National Intelligencer. That, we suppose, is reserved for the next election, when his district, being now very large, will have been divided, and he will again be a candidate for Congress with (as he appears to think) apparently good reason to expect success.

The same excerpts from this letter were published in the *Boston Daily Courier* on February 13, 1832, and the *Brattleboro (Vermont) Messenger*, February 18, 1832.

The letter refers to Crockett's charges that the 1831 election was dishonest and is very much like others Crockett wrote at the time, including his reference to Fitzgerald as "the thing that had the name of beating me" and his claim that he'd rather be beaten and maintain his integrity than to be elected and become subservient to party discipline. "Gen. Green" is a reference to Duff Green, whom the Jacksonians had once favored as official publisher of government records over Gales and Seaton, but who had fallen out of favor due to his loyalty to John C. Calhoun. The closing remarks by the editor mistakenly raise a charge that had been made against Crockett in the 1829 election, that he had gotten too cozy with the anti-Jackson editors Gales and Seaton. Crockett makes a rare reference to himself as "Davy," although it is possible that the editor inserted the name, since Crockett rarely used it.

*   *   *   *   *

1832:

LETTER TO RICHARD SMITH, JANUARY 7, 1832.

at home Weakley County Tennessee
January 7th 1832

Richard Smith Esq

Dr Sir

I have wrote to my securitys in your Bank to try to indulge me until I could make some arrangement I hope you will extend all the liberalitys in your powar I did come out in the late election in favour of the renewal of your charter and the thing that had the name of beating me took the Jackson ground against it I still hope to be in Congress again before there is a vote taken on that subject I have inclosed some Blanks asigned with a hope that my securitys would fill them and get them discounted for me times is hard in this country I will do the best I can

Respectfully your obt servt

David Crockett

Courtesy of the Historical Society of Pennsylvania.

Smith was an official of the Second Bank of the United States. Crockett was requesting an extension on a loan he had taken from the Bank. His reference to his support for the Bank's rechartering while he was in Congress borders on the kind of coziness, if not corruption, that President Jackson had cited as one reason for not rechartering the Bank. Crockett expresses confidence in returning to Congress in the next election and refuses to mention William Fitzgerald, who had beaten him in 1831, by name, referring to him only as "the thing that had the name of beating me."

*   *   *   *   *

LETTER TO DANIEL WEBSTER, DECEMBER 18, 1832, MAILED FROM JACKSON, TENNESSEE.

18th December 1832

Hon Daniel Webster

Dr. Sir

From my personal acquaintance with you and my knowledge of your liberality to the friends of our Country I will make no appology for troubling you with this letter I have been in conversation with my friend Colo Joel Henry Dyer upon a subject which I feel a deep interest

I have advised him to lay the clame of the heirs of Colo Henry Dyer before Congress and I hope you will give your aid to an amiable widdow and creditable family which from the circumstance of Colo Dyer's devoting his whole time to the services of his Country has occasioned Colo Dyer to leave his Family in an imbarised Situation and much oppressed I myself entered the army with Colo Dyer and was acquainted with his Services and can say that the government cannot do a greater act of grattitude than to relieve his family from distress which will be no more than justice from their Country you will please to read this and Show it to other members of your boddy and I hope they will appreciate this request—I must close with great respect

Your friend and obt Servt

David Crockett

Courtesy of Bruce Gimelson, Garrison, New York.

Crockett was out of office when he wrote this letter. His action in this case is at odds with his earlier position against the government providing for survivors of individual officers or veterans, although he occasionally advocated for individuals. His opposition to providing for the widow of Stephen Decatur was used against him in the election of 1831.

Daniel Webster, the well-known orator and leader among anti-Jacksonians, was a Representative from New Hampshire to the Thirteenth and Fourteenth Congresses and from Massachusetts to the Eighteenth, Nineteenth, and Twentieth Congresses. He was elected to the United States Senate in 1827 as an Adams party loyalist (later Anti-Jacksonian) and reelected as a Whig in 1833 and 1839, serving until his resignation in 1841. He was an unsuccessful Whig candidate for president in 1836, was appointed Secretary of State by President William Henry Harrison and again by President John Tyler, serving from 1841 to 1843. He was again elected to the Senate in 1845, but resigned when he was appointed Secretary of State by President Millard Fillmore. Biographical Directory of the United States Congress, http://bioguide.congress.gov.

*   *   *   *   *

1833:

LETTER TO THE *(JACKSON, TENNESSEE) SOUTHERN STATESMAN*, JULY 13, 1833, PUBLISHED JULY 20, 1833.

To the Editors of the Southern Statesman:

Gentlemen:—I enclosed you a few days ago a Circular, and made the necessary apology for having been brought under the necessity of troubling you any more during the present canvass. I have since seen a publication in your paper, signed *"A Citizen of Madison County,"* and also one signed by William Fitzgerald. In justice to myself, I cannot withhold giving each a passing notice—they are both upon the subject of the anonymous letter.

I will, in the first place, inform you that I have received an answer from the Clerk of the House, and the Secretary of the Treasury. The Clerk writes in substance as follows: That he received my letter of the 10th of May, from Haywood county, and one from home, Weakly county, about the first of June, both by the same mail. He transmitted both to the secretary of the Treasury, and received his answer, stating that the information called for in my letter could not be had in his office—that the speaker settled with all the members, and kept his own books, and carried them home with him—and that there was no other source to obtain information from, only through the Speaker; both of which letters I sent by the same mail that brought them, to Paris for publication. I know of my own knowledge that the Speaker lives in Richmond, Virginia, and I have not time to write to him for information before the election. From this the people will see that I have done all that I could to lay this case before them. I have applied to the source I thought the information ought to come from. I have understood that Fitzgerald has written on, and I wish to see his answer. Perhaps he may know what source to apply to, as he appears to be so well versed in legislative matters, and shows laws that I do not know any thing about. I know that all the law that I have been acquainted with, was to give each member just what they charged for mileage. They are considered high-minded, honorable men, and proof is never required of them; and this Committee of Accounts which he speaks of, is to settle their accounts by their charges. —No member is ever required to make proof as to what he may charge for mileage. —The truth is I should never have shown the anonymous letter if Mr. Fitzgerald had not in Denmark told the people in his speech that he had been laying up artillery and ammunition for the political war with me, for the last two years. He said he had got some even in Washington City. I told him that he had none, and to fire the biggest gun he had; that he was holding out insinuations, when in fact he had nothing to tell; and the next day when at Brownsville I took out the anonymous letter and read it, and asked him if it was true or false; he then never pretended to deny the truth of the letter, although it had no name to it; but undertook to justify himself. He said that he was entitled to one thousand miles of mileage at each session, and at the first session, through a mistake, he only received pay for seven hundred miles, and of course he was entitled to three hundred miles of arrearages, which if doubled would make the sixteen hundred as charged in the anonymous letter. I never charged Mr. Fitzgerald with swindling, I only asked him if it was true or false; he then made the above explanation, and now I see he denies the letter in toto; and expresses his fears that some of my friends will commit a forgery, just upon the eve of the election to prove it. The truth is, there is no need of proof, when he admitted, in the presence of at least three hundred people, at Brownsville, last May, when he and myself both addressed the people of Haywood at Brownsville. I cannot tell how any man can write down and have published so palpable a lie, when every man that heard us speak can testify to the truth of this assertion. I do hope Mr. Fitzgerald cannot with impunity lie the people out of their votes a second time. I will dismiss this subject as the certificates of my neighbors annexed to my circular will prove him a liar and ought to convict him before any Court or Jury.

I will now give a passing notice to old Black hawk, as he has taken the credit of the citizens of Madison upon himself. I can only say, that Black Hawk is not the man that I thought he was. I did think that piece emenated from some poor little possum headed lawyer. I have cut open many possum's heads to hunt for brains and I never found any; therefore, I considered some little pin hook lawyer without brains was the author of that piece, and that old Black Hawk believing in his mental powers, took it on himself. I was much surprised, for I did think that Adam Huntsman had more sense than to ever let such insignificancy come from his pen. He talks about my franking a little lawyer to Trenton, and that the little lawyer loaned me some four or five hundred dollars; the truth is, I did travel with the little lawyer from Washington to my residence, but instead of his loaning me money, I loaned him what paid his expenses from the mouth of Cumberland to my home, which was about eight dollars. I did think that the author of the Citizen of Madison was just such a lawyer as the one franked, and I thought that he had an interest in getting Fitzgerald to Congress again, as he has had the franking privilege extended to himself from one session to another, and I suppose he thought that he could get the law extended to frank these little possum headed lawyers from one court to another as they cannot get fees enough to pay their expenses. I have no authority for saying that the Franking privilege is extended only from Mr. Fitzgerald's own word, when I heard he had a speech written down purporting to be his Trenton Speech (and in fact one that he never made,) and published, and was franking them over the district, I did believe it was a violation of the law, for all the law I ever have been acquainted with gives members the franking privilege sixty days before the session commences and sixty after it closes. I heard he had franked a large pair of saddle bags full of his speeches to Madison and Haywood about the 4th of July, which was two months after any law that I had any knowledge of had expired. I went immediately to the post master, Mr. Gardner at Dresden, and asked him what authorized Mr. Fitzgerald to frank his speeches at this time; he said Mr. Fitzgerald had informed him that there was a law passed at the last session giving members leave to frank from one session to another. If this is a law I must think it a bad one, for it must inevitably break down the post office department. I have spoken upon this subject in my circular, and cannot withhold mentioning it again, as I am astonished that such a law should be passed in these times of retrenchment and reform.

Before I close I must turn my attention again to Black Hawk, as he claims the honor of the Citizen of Madison, and was so afraid that the people would not know it, that he told Maj. McLaurine and others, of Gibson county, that he was the author, and that they might tell the people so. I see he goes in to arrangement to expose the anonymous letter writer, he doubles all the member's mileage from this State, and gives Mr. Fitzgerald single to deceive the people. If Mr. Fitzgerald's had only been sixteen hundred miles it would have been no imposition at all, but to double it like the rest it would make 32 hundred miles, and calculate his 91 days session, at $8.00 per day, and the mileage 3,200 miles at 8.00 for every 20 miles would make the precise sum that he is charged with having received in the anonymous letter. As for my receiving more mileage than was due me, I can only say that he has written and had published a barefaced falsehood. I took the same mileage that Col. A. R. Alexander took, which I have the proof at home to show in the books giving the receipts and expenditures for his last session and my first. I must close with a hope that the editor will insert the above mentioned letter, and also give this letter a place in his columns as soon as possible, and oblige his ob't ser'vt.

DAVID CROCKETT
July 13, 1833

P.S. In my last canvass we had four printing presses in the district and but one that ever would publish any thing in my favor, and that one was the Southern Statesman. I see Fitzgerald complains that there was a publication printed in Nashville, and sent over this district by or through me; this I do deny; I had no agency in it.

Can Mr. Fitzgerald say this much about the Chronicles that emenated from Black Hawk?

I hope the editors will give fair play & both papers publish this as this I consider due to me as an American citizen; this will be the last time that I will trouble you during the present canvass.
D.C.

Crockett wrote a follow-up letter, published in the *Southern Statesman* on July 29, 1833, with the letters he referred to appended. In the letter above, Crockett was responding to the oft-traded accusations between him and his opponents that one or the other had charged more for their travel allowances than they were entitled to. His references to "Black Hawk" are to Adam Huntsman, who wrote anti-Crockett material for the press and would defeat Crockett in his final election in 1835. Major McLaurine may be a reference to a Mr. McLaurin, one-time sheriff of Gibson County, Tennessee, who had spoken of Crockett's superiority as a hunter, but boasted of having beaten him in a shooting match for a five-hundred-dollar prize. (Shackford, *David Crockett: The Man and the Legend*, 77).

*　　*　　*　　*　　*

UNDATED LETTER TO THE *(JACKSON, TENNESSEE) SOUTHERN STATESMAN,* PUBLISHED JULY 29, 1833.

To the Editor of the Southern Statesman.
In the piece I lately addressed to the people, I spoke of two letters received by me from Washington, the one from Mr. Burch, one of the clerks of Congress, the other as a letter from the Secretary of the Treasury to Mr. Burch, declining to give the information I desired to obtain, by saying he had not the books in his office by which to give such information, in my understanding of these letters, from a hasty perusal; I find since that I was mistaken.—They were both from Mr. Burch, the one of 24th June was a copy of a letter from him to Mr. Duane, Secretary of the Treasury, requesting of him to give me and Mr. Fitzgerald the information desired; and the other of the 25th June, an answer from Mr. Burch to me, containing the copy from him to the Secretary of Treasury. In consequence of my misunderstanding of this matter, all my remarks about them are wrong. The letters will be published in the papers, and will speak for themselves.—The reason of my making the mistake about them is this: I was at Esqr. Dibrell's when the mail come that brought the letters; I read them, and that hastily, and took no copy, for I had no time to do so, and prevailed on the mail rider to wait a few moments until I could write a few lines to a friend, to whom I enclosed the letters, and did not keep them in my possession but a few moments.

DAVID CROCKETT

[Crockett appended the two letters to which he referred:]

Washington, June 24, 1833
Sir—The enclosed letters from the Hon. David Crockett, the member of Congress from Tennessee, were received at this office to-day.
The information they seek to obtain can only be furnished from the Book of payments kept by the Speaker of the House of Representatives for the two last sessions of Congress.—These books are filed in the Treasury Department; I therefore transmit the letters to you, to take such order upon them as to you may seem proper.
The fact of Mr. Crockett's having received an anonymous letter containing an abstract [& probably an erroneous one] of the account of Mr. Fitzgerald, which he has publicly exhibited, would seem to render it proper, on Mr. Fitzgerald's account, that a correct statement should be forwarded to both gentlemen. I would thank you to inform me of the result of the application.

With great respect Sir,
Your obd't sev't,
S. Burch.

Washington City, June 25, 1833.

Dear Sir: Your letter of the 10th of May, written from Haywood County, and your other letter of the 2d of June, instant, written from home, Weakly county, were received at the same time by yesterday's mail.

Mr. Clark is absent, and the pleasure of affording you an answer devolves upon me.

The Clerk of the House of Representatives has nothing whatsoever, to do with the payments of members of Congress. The law provides that they shall be paid by the Speaker of the House of Representatives; & there is nothing in the office of the clerk that shows how the money is disbursed, or to whom paid, or the amount paid. This is only to be obtained from the Speaker's book of accounts, which book is filed in the Treasury Department as a voucher, when the speaker's account is settled at the Treasury.

I have referred your application to the Secretary of the Treasury; and herewith transmit you a copy of the letter of reference to that officer.

With great respect, I am sir, your ob't serv't.
S. Burch, Chief Clerk
of House of Representatives.

Neither the May 10 nor the June 2, 1833, Crockett letters have been located.

*　　*　　*　　*　　*

LETTER TO UNKNOWN RECIPIENT, AUGUST-SEPTEMBER, 1833. PUBLISHED IN THE *NEW YORK SPECTATOR*, SEPTEMBER 9, 1833.

Dr. Sir—

Went through—tight squeeze—beat Fitz 170—Yours, D.C.

Crockett's very brief note reports his victory over William Fitzgerald in the August 1833 congressional election. His actual margin of victory was 173 votes.

*　　*　　*　　*　　*

LETTER TO GENTLEMEN OF ABINGDON, VIRGINIA, NOVEMBER 18, 1833. PUBLISHED IN THE *(WASHINGTON) UNITED STATES' TELEGRAPH*, DECEMBER 5, 1833.

Abingdon, Nov. 18th, 1833.

Gentlemen, —Your polite note has been handed me, containing an invitation to partake of a public dinner, this day, at 3 o'clock, at the Eagle Tavern. I am at a loss, gentlemen, for language to express my gratitude to you for this mark of respect; but as I am out of my own State, and as I conceive, it can have no political effect, I will do myself the pleasure to dine with you at the appointed hour, although I have declined invitations of the same nature in my own State, for the reason above alluded to.

I remain, gentlemen, with great respect,
Your obedient servant,
David Crockett

To Messrs. John Keller, Peter Mayo, John H. Fulton, Edward S. Watson, John W. Lampkin.

Crockett's letter was in response to a dinner invitation from the four men named, also dated November 18, 1833. The invitation and response appear to have been formalities, since Crockett delivered a prepared speech at the dinner.

*　*　*　*　*

LETTER TO LEWIS CASS, SECRETARY OF WAR, NOVEMBER 28, 1833.

Washington City
28th November 1833

Mr James Rodgers of the Cherokees wishes to be appointed sale agent to the Seminoles of Florida about to remove—the high merit of this individual recommends him to your consideration It will be a most Judicious appointment

My willingness for recommending Mr Rodgers is that I believe he is the first applicant that ever made any pretentions for an agency under the government

Respectfully yours—
David Crockett

The Hon. Lewis Cass—

Autographed letter, signed, from David Crockett to Lewis Cass, November 28, 1833, courtesy of the Pierpont Morgan Library, New York.

Lewis Cass was appointed Secretary of War by President Jackson and served from 1831 to 1836, afterward serving as envoy extraordinary and minister plenipotentiary to France from 1836 to 1842. He was later elected to the United States Senate, was an unsuccessful candidate for president on the Democratic ticket in 1848, and appointed secretary of state by President James Buchanan, serving in that position from 1857 to 1860.

*　*　*　*　*

LETTER TO A. M. HUGHES, DECEMBER 8, 1833.

Washington City
8th Decer 1833

My Dear Friend

Your favour of the 21 inst has just been recd and I will hasten to answer it I am enjoying good health and hope these lines will find you and family in the alike you wrote me that I could see the Congressional Districts by the papers I have not saw a paper from our State since I left it however you know let it be laid off as it may, I go the whole hog for you against any person whatever I never will have the sin of ingrattitude to answer for—

I have wrote you one or two letters on the commencement of the session we disposed of the Contested Election between Moore & Letcher on Thursday and adjourned over untill Monday, we disposed of them by letting neither of them take the Seat until it is decided by the Committee of Elections which is intitled to it This makes a bad apearance for a Jackson [atacks?] Congress and the Globe complains heavily about it the truth is I have no doubt but there is a Considerable majority in both houses apposed to Jackson and his measure

The United States Bank has come out in self defence and have made the clearest defence I ever saw and have informed Jackson and the Kitchen Cabinett out of measure [the next line seems to be missing from the letter] I have but one coppy or I would sent it to you it is a large pamplet and contains more than any thing I ever saw of its size it will sink the administration in the mind of all honest men it proves that the whole hostility of the president to that institution originated from the cause that the bank refused to lend its aid in [proping?] up the preasant power right or wronge when you see the attempts to bring over the Bank to be subservant to the preasant administration it will disgust you and every honest man the truth is I do believe The old Chief is in a worse drive then he ever was before and he is begining to find it out you wrote me to informe you of the insolvency of the post office department the most favourable accounts that it Stated here is that it is upwards of three hundred and seventy five thousand dollars behind hand and it is curtant that the deficiency will amount to one million it is yet unknown but they can hide no longer and the thing has to come before the world in its true coulers

I will deliver your message to Mr Clay and Everett with much pleasure relative to your two sones their namesakes you shall here how we progress often let me here from you as often Mr Clay handled the president with out gloves whin he turned his land

[The third page, which follows, is torn, and only fragments of each line have survived; Crockett's signature has been torn off too, with only most of the letter "D" surviving. Someone has printed "David Crockett" in place of the original signature]

. . . land Bill with his veto message on
and Mr Poindexter was almost as bad
fact the old man is in much
by adhering two much to his
will you please to tender my best
to Mr Ellis and family & W
[line obscured by tear]
from [tear] count
to the Rai [tear] der or
morrow I expect to Comm
land Bill [tear] ver I expect
resolution & appoint the
not Commence until the
was out of the way, we
business on tomorrow
I will go a head I mus[t?]
Respects your friend and ....
A M Hughes
David Crockett [printed]

From the Tennessee Historical Society Miscellaneous Files, courtesy of the Tennessee State Library and Archives.

See Crockett's February 13, 1831, letter to Hughes. The mention of Mr. Poindexter is a reference to George Poindexter, a Jacksonian senator from Mississippi, who eventually broke with Jackson over the issue of rechartering the Second Bank of the United States. Edward Everett, a Whig from Massachusetts, and Horace Everett, an Anti-Jacksonian from Vermont, both served in the House during the Twenty-Third Congress. Mr. Clay is obviously Henry Clay.

*   *   *   *   *

LETTER TO EDMUND DEBERRY, DECEMBER 14, 1833.

Washington City
14th Decr. 1833.

Dear Sir,

Although I am an entire strainger to you, I hope you will excuse my freedom in addressing you. It is entirely on account of my intimate acquaintance with your father, who is at this time a mess-mate of mine. he informed me that you expressed Some anxiety to see me and I take it for granted that if you would feel an intrest in seeing me, that you would not take it a miss to here from me upon matters and things in general.

In the first place, I will say to you that I never saw such a meeting of Congress in my life. Every thing appears to be new to me. In fact, I have no Idea what will be the result of the present Congress. It apears to me that the whole object of the present adminestration is to unite their party. I do believe they care nothing for the good of the country, So they can grattify their ambition. I am confident they are destroying the best intrest of the country for the purpose of promoting their party. I consider the time has come when every lover of his Country must do his duty fearlessly and independantly. We must put down this tyranical powar, claimed by our Chief magistrate, and restore the good old days of Washington & Jefferson and other presidents that have wielded the destinies of this nation. I was once the friend of Andrew Jackson when I thought he was the friend of his country, but when I see him trying to destroy the best intrests of his country to keep up his party, I am off like a pot-leg.* I see his pet Billey Barry, the postmaster genl, has fallen short So, that he sais in his report that he will be compeld to retrench to the amount of two hundred & odd thousand dollars a year. This is getting on slowley. In these days of retrenchment and reforme he can hide no longer. some say he is three hundred and seventy five thousand dollars be hind hand in that department, and some say he is one million behind hand. This is a beautyful Specimen of Retrenchment, and as for reforme they have caried it to the full extent, regardless of any thing like principle.

Your father is in good health, and requests me to say to you to answer this letter. I am, Sir, your obt humble servt,

David Crockett

* Moving rapidly or in a flash.

Mississippi Department of Archives and History (David Crockett Letter, Z/0392.000./F).

The letter illustrates the degree to which Crockett's fame had spread and shows that total strangers had an interest in meeting or corresponding with him. There is some punctuation in the letter, rare for Crockett, and it may have been added by someone else after the letter was written. The recipient's name does not appear on the letter.

Edmund DeBerry was the son of North Carolina Representative Edmund DeBerry, who was serving with Crockett in the Twenty-third Congress and, like Crockett, boarded at Mrs. Ball's Washington boarding house (or "mess"). He had been elected as an Anti-Jacksonian from North Carolina to the Twenty-first Congress (March 4, 1829-March 3, 1831), was defeated in his bid for reelection, but was elected again as an Anti-Jacksonian to the Twenty-third and the Twenty-fourth Congresses, and as a Whig to the Twenty-fifth through the Twenty-eighth Congresses (March 4, 1833-March 3, 1845). He chose not to run again until 1848, when he was elected again as a Whig to the Thirty-first Congress (March 4, 1849-March 3, 1851). He also had served as a member of the North Carolina State senate 1806-1811, 1813, 1814, 1820, 1821, and 1826-1828 and also served as justice of the peace.

*   *   *   *   *

LETTER TO ALBERT G. WATERMAN, DECEMBER 15, 1833.

Washington City
15th Decr 1833

Dear Sir

your polite favour of the 12th Inst has just been rec'd and I will hasten to answer it—

you State that you expect me to visit your city in this month it is true I did intend to have done so when I arrived here but I must Confess it will be Some what uncertain as I Concieve every man must be at his post in those days of King by powars god only knows what the present Congress is to bring a bout there is more expectation than I ever Saw be fore at the meeting of any Congress ("that I ever Saw" crossed out) Sence my acquaintance with the business of the nation I am proud to see the able defence of the Bank of the United States in answer to the paper assigned Andrew Jackson I am determined to distribute that able paper through my district and the State of Tennessee

you have Seen I Suppose the genl refusal to comply with the resolution of the Senate and I do believe the house will order the deposits back in to the United States bank and I also be lieve the president will tell us to go to hell that he knows his business and ours too

you need not look for me this winter I may come on early next fall and go on east to new york I am Sir with respects your obt servt

David Crockett

Albert g Waterman

Haverford College Library, Haverford, Pennsylvania, Special Collections, Charles Roberts Autograph Letters Collection (collection 745).

Albert G. Waterman was born in Virginia and moved to Philadelphia in 1832, where he became a member of the board of managers and also served on the city's Select Council and Common Council. He served as manager of the Institution for the Blind for fifteen years and was active in the preservation of Independence Hall.

*   *   *   *   *

LETTER TO JOHN MCLEAN, DECEMBER 26, 1833 (EXCERPT).

Washington City
December 26, 1833

. . . there has been some several speeches made against the president in fact I have little doubt of Congress ordering the deposits back and I have as little doubt that Jackson will tell us to go to hell. This is in substance what he said to the Senate . . . The Truth is I never saw such times in my life. It appears as if Jackson is determined to destroy the United States Bank or sacrifice the Government. . . .

Charles Hamilton Auction Catalog, *September 22, 1966, item 61.*

According to the catalog, "Crockett continues in this vein, with reference to 'that political Judas, Martin Van Buren.'" The full letter is a page and a half. The catalog adds punctuation that is undoubtedly missing from the original.

*   *   *   *   *

LETTER DATED DECEMBER 30, 1833, PUBLISHED IN THE *(WASHINGTON) DAILY NATIONAL INTELLIGENCER* **DECEMBER 31, 1833.**

Washington City, Dec. 30 1833.

It is not my desire to indulge in censures on the author of a late work, purporting to present a history of my *"life adventures, and eccentricities."* But it becomes my duty to say to the public, that that publication was wholly unauthorized by me, and, in many respects, does me great injustice. I know not who the author is; yet I think, if he designed any thing of a friendly character, so far as I am concerned, he should at least have obtained my permission to publish, if he even thought it unnecessary to submit for my inspection a copy of the work before it went to press. The profit which I can reasonably expect from such an undertaking is but a small consideration, compared with the duty I owe both to myself and the reading community. To myself, in being placed fairly before them—and to them, in placing in their hands a true narrative of my adventures, and the vicissitudes which have marked my obscure history. I know not why my humble name should have excited any general interest; but, so far as it has done so, that interest shall be met by a plain and unvarnished history of myself, prepared under my own notice, and submitted to the public by my own authority.

The object of this note is therefore to give general information, that, as early as the same can be completed. I shall put to press a Narrative of my Life; in which I will carefully endeavor to avoid those refinements of literature which would disrobe my narrative of its greatest interest—and shall strive to represent myself, as I really am, *a plain, blunt, Western man,* relying on honesty and the woods, and not on learning and the law, for a living. I am hopeful the work will be ready for the press before the close of the present session of Congress. It shall not be delayed a moment longer than is indispensable from my public engagements.

The public's most obedient servant.
DAVID CROCKETT

The letter was likely polished by Thomas Chilton, but clearly reflects Crockett's irritation with the unauthorized biography written by James Strange French. It also served as an early promotion for his own forthcoming autobiography.

*   *   *   *   *

1834:

LETTER TO WILLIAM RODGERS, JANUARY 8, 1834.

Washington City
8th January 1834

Dear Sir

Your favour relative to the araingment of your mail was recd on yesterday and I took it imediatly to the P Ms G and left it for his action he promised me to answer me in a few days upon the contents of your letter but he is harased to death upon the deranged state of that department you recollect that the peoples President at the commencement of the present Congress said in his message to both houses of Congress and the nation that the Post office department was in a most flourishing Condition and what do we see now, you per haps have seen the call from the Senate upon the department and Mr Barrys answer he acknowledges that he had Borrowed from their [illeg.] Banks three hundred and fifty thousand dollars and that he had over drawn fifty thousand making in all four hundred thousand dollars that he has borrowed at six per cents and with out any authority from the Government and it is common rumer here and I have no doubt of the truth of the report that he is upward of six hundred thousand dollars be hind with his contractors Glorious reforme and retrenchment under King Andrew the First will the people be blinded always to uphold a name destitute of principle I concieve this a duty that every servant of the people ought to expose all such conduct [illeg.] come from whare it may   I suppose you can see by the news papers that we are Well engaged in discussing the Great question of Jacksons kingley powar exercised in the removil of the deposits and God only knows when this debate will end or what will be the result In the Senate there is a large majority in favour of the restoration but in the house I am unable to say how it will be determined I am of opinion that we are gaining ground to restore the deposits the memoreals are poring in to Congress from all quarters to restore the Country from ruin by replacing the deposits to the United States Bank a few days a go we had a delegation of twenty members from the City of New York with a memoreal of Six thousand merchants and dealers praying that the deposits may be restored and save the Commercial men   They laid their memoreal before Congress and then waited on the President and he got in to a perfect rage and told them that if every one of his party quit him that he never would agree for the deposits to be restored he said that he had determined to put down the United States Bank and By the Eternal he would effect his object By this you see we have the government of one man That he puts forward his will as the law of the land If the American people will Seanction this we may bid farewell to our Republican name it is nothing but a shaddow our once happy government will become a despot I consider the present time one that is marked with more danger than any period of our political history The South Carolina question was nothing to the present for the over throw of our once happy government You see our whole Circulating medium deranged and our whole Commercial community destroyed all to grattify the ambition of King Andrew the first because the United States Bank refused to lend its aid in upholding his corrupt party The truth is he is Surrounded by a set of imps of famin that is willing to distroy the best intrest of the country to promote their own intrest I have spoken free but I write the truth and the world will be convinced I hope before it is too late

My land Bill is among the first Bills reported to the house and I have but little doubt of its pasage during the present session I must close by a request that you present me kindley to your neighbors and receive my best wishes for yourself & family

I am with great Respects your obt servt

David Crockett

William Rodgers

PS will you do me the favour to send me a list of the names of your [illeg.] documents to your post office I am determined to enliten the people if it costs me my salary I will trust to an honist community here after for reward I love my country better than any party or Riches Mr Grundy is well
DC

From the Tennessee Historical Society Miscellaneous Files, courtesy of the Tennessee State Library and Archives.

William Rodgers was from Caledonia, in Henry County, Tennessee. Mr. Barry refers to William Barry, Jackson's postmaster general. Barry was under attack from Henry Clay and others for incompetence and corruption. Robert Remini, *Henry Clay: Statesman for the Union* **(New York: Norton, 1993), 469–70. Crockett's comment about "the South Carolina question" refers to the nullification crisis, in which South Carolina declared federal laws subservient to those of the states and reserved the right of states to "nullify" federal law if they saw fit. The situation between South Carolina and the federal government intensified to the point that the state threatened to secede and President Jackson threatened military action to force the state into compliance. See Richard Latner, "The Nullification Crisis and Republican Subversion,"** *Journal of Southern History* **43, no. 1 (February 1977): 19–38.**

*   *   *   *   *

LETTER TO HENRY STORRS, JANUARY 9, 1834.

Washington City
January 9th 1834

Dear Friend
    Your favour of the 2nd Inst. has been duly received; and if I was to thank you a thousand times over for your kindness, and the interest you take in my affairs, I would still be greatly your debtor. My narrative will be ready for [the] press, in about a month and will be just like myself, a plain, and singular production. It will afford I have no doubt, such amusement every where, as my life has been full of strange and laughable incidents. It will afford [illeg.] for at least a hundred and fifty pages and [illeg.]. I know the demand for the work will be great, but as I am in quite [illeg.] circumstances, if I can sell the copy right for a respectable sum I shall [illeg.] accomplish two objects. first, I shall vindicate myself from the spurious work sent aboad; and secondly shall get the means of going ahead, just now.

    Please ascertain the best price which can be had for the copy right in your city, as many propositions are reaching me—and then I can make a choice among them all. If I was not a poor man, I shouldn't want anything for the work at all. But I am poor, with a large family; and as the world seems anscious for the work, I know they would want me to have profits of it.

    I am well, and hanging on to the true faith, like a puppy to a root. Answer me as soon as possible; and get your book-sellers, and book-printers to send me their propositions.
I am without hypocrisy
yr real friend

D. Crockett

Collection of Buffalo & Erie County Historical Society (mss. A00-110).

    Henry Storrs was a six-term congressman from New York and a staunch anti-Jacksonian. As with many of the letters concerning the publication of Crockett's *Narrative*, this appears to be written in Thomas Chilton's hand, but is signed by Crockett.

*   *   *   *   *

LETTER TO JOHN WESLEY CROCKETT, JANUARY 10, 1834.

Washington City
10th January 1834

My Dear Sone
    I have waited for Several days to get a letter from you but I will not wait no longer it is about three weeks since I recieved a line from you and in fact I have recieved but one since I left home from you I must charge you with neglect but I hope you will do better here after I have but little to add to what I wrote you in my last letter more than to informe you that I am still blessed with good health and doing as well as I can and I hope these lines will find you in the alike health

    We are still engaged in debating the great question of removing the deposits I have no doubt but that we are gaining ground and I do believe we will order the deposits back but the Jackson folks is begining to Bost and say that Jackson will veto any order that congress will make to put them back I must confess that I have never saw such times in my life but I am grattifyed to see the mooves of old virginia She put down old John Adams and she put down young John Adams & I do hope she will dethrone King Andrew the first She is coming out most gloriously and I do hope in time to Save the country I consider this a question between the representatives and their country I do believe in the two years from this time that the man will be hard to find that will acknowledge that he ever was a Jackson man

I have sent you a coppy of my land Bill and report and I want you to show it to the people It will relinquish upwards of seven hundred thousands acres This will secure every occupant in the district and that will effect the object that I have been So long and so anxious to effect my whole Delligation will go with me I have no doubt of effecting this object before this session closes my prospects is much brighter that ever it was at any former session

I am in gaged in writing a history of my life and I have compleated one hundred and ten pages and I have Mr Chilton to correct it as I write it I have had several letters from Philadelphia and New York up on the Subject of publishing it and several have wrote to me to buy the coppy wright I have not yet concluded yet to sell it I expect it will contain about two hundred pages and will fully meet all expectations

I may take a trip through the eastern States during the session of Congress and sell the Book a great many have perswaded me to take a towar through the Eastern States that my presents will make thousands of people buy my book that would not by it and I intend never to go home until I am able to pay my debts and I think I have a good prospect at present and I will do the best I can

I saw a few days ago an account in the paper that Rebeca Alvira was married to Doctor McNeal I did not believe the report to be true I hope you will write me often as you have here to fore done I hope you are doing well and I hope you will present me kindley to my old freind Jack and to my neighbours and recieve my best love for your family and Sisse I remain your affectionate father until death

David Crockett

John W Crockett

PS Mr Barry the P.M.G. has been [illeg.] hundred thousand dollars out of the Banks he has owned this in his recent answer to a call of the senate and it is believed that he is [illeg.] be hind hand no wonder he called the people of Trenton a Stage [illeg.] their town [illeg.] divil take such a government as this is DC

Courtesy of Thomas W. Streeter Collection of Texas Manuscripts, Yale Collection of Western Americana, Beinecke Rare Book and Manuscript Library.

John Wesley was Crockett's oldest son, by his first wife, Mary (Polly). "Rebeca Alvira" was Crockett's daughter, Rebecca Elvira, born in 1818 to his wife, Elizabeth. Crockett's letter of January 15 , 1834, to the *National Intelligencer* attempts to set the record straight about Rebecca's marital status. "Mr. Chilton" refers to Kentucky congressman Thomas Chilton, Crockett's friend and mess mate at Ball's Boarding House in Washington City. Chilton served as editor, scribe, and confidant during the composition of Crockett's *Narrative.*

*   *   *   *   *

ANONYMOUS LETTER FROM "TWO CITIZENS" OF LOWNDES COUNTY, MISSISSIPPI, TO CROCKETT, JANUARY 12, 1834, PUBLISHED IN THE *(WASHINGTON) UNITED STATES' TELEGRAPH*, **MARCH 1, 1834.**

Lowndes County, Mi.
12th January, 1834

Col. David Crockett:

Sir—In compliance with the wishes of a respectable portion of your fellow-citizens in this part of the State, we take a singular pleasure in addressing you upon a subject in which we are deeply interested.

Although we haven't the honor of a personal acquaintance with you, we are far from strangers to your character, and well-deserved popularity. Your fame has travelled far beyond the circle of your acquaintance.—We have long known by report and have greatly admired your straight-forward course, devoted patriotism, and your truly American virtues. We have carefully examined, sir, the course of your undeviating track in relation to political affairs, your votes in Congress, and your decided opposition to every Anti-Republican measure, all of which, together with your open friendly intercourse with your fellow-citizens generally, entitle you to our full approbation, and highest esteem. We are fully convinced that measures, not men, have been the objects of your steady aim.

We have, with much regret, noticed that most of the recent struggles, and threatening dangers in our Government, have been brought about by selfish individuals, ambitious, not for the welfare of our country, but for the loaves and fishes.

We have recently heard several names mentioned in connection with the subject of the next Presidential election, and among them we have heard yours, which is the only one we can cheerfully support.

We have every confidence in your integrity and ability to conduct the Ship of State safely through the threatening storm of party spirit, and steer her smoothly into the harbor of uninterrupted happiness and prosperity. There is nothing wanting, in our opinion, to make you our next President, but your own consent. Impressed with this belief, and confident of your success, we respectfully ask permission to lay your name before the people as a candidate for our next President, and *we go the whole hog for you.*

We wait with impatience for your answer, and hope you will favor us with your views upon the leading topics of the day. We are plain republicans, and can never support little *Van* under any circumstances.

Very respectfully sir, we are your ob't servt's
[Signed "Two Citizens"]

Crockett's reply to this request, dated February 24, 1824, was printed in the same edition of the *Telegraph* **and follows.**

*   *   *   *   *

LETTER TO THE *(WASHINGTON) NATIONAL INTELLIGENCER*, **JANUARY 15, 1834, REPRINTED IN THE** *(BRATTLEBORO, VERMONT) INDEPENDENT INQUIRER*, **JANUARY 25, 1834.**

Washington City
January 15 1834

Gentlemen

I see it is stated in your paper, that a daughter of mine was married at Columbia, Tennessee, a while back. This is a mistake. There's a heap of Crocketts in that part of Tennessee, and from that no doubt, the mistake arose, but none of my family live there.

Yours, &c.
David Crockett

> **Crockett was, no doubt, referring to his daughter Rebecca Elvira. He also mentioned this incident in his January 10, 1834, letter to his son, John Wesley Crockett.**

*   *   *   *   *

LETTER TO G. W. MCLEAN, JANUARY 17, 1834.

Washington City
17th January 1834

Dear Sir

Your favour have been recieved some time and in Justice I ought to make an appology for not answering it before this time but I hope you will excuse me for neglect as I have a great deal of bussiness to attend to besides I am in gaged in preparing a worke that may be of little prophit to me but I consider that Justice demands of me to make a Statement of facts to the amirican people I have no doubt but you have saw a Book purporting to be the life and adventures of my self   that Book was written with out my knowledge and widley Circulated and in fact the person that took the first liberty to write the Book have published a second addition and I thought one inposition was enough to put on the country and I have put down the Imposition and have promised to give the people a Correct Statement of facts relative to my life as I consider no man on earth able to give a true history of my life I have under taken it my self and will compleat it by the last of next week ready for the press and it will Contain about two hundred pages and I hope it will fill expectations I give the truth and I will venture to say it will be as interesting as the Imposition that has been imposed on the people

We are still engaged in discussing the great question of Jacksons kingley powar in the removal of the Deposits I have no doubt of the deposits being ordered back by the houses of Congress and I have as little doubt that Jackson will veto the measure and if he does I hope Congress will teach him a lesson that will be of use to the next Tyrant that fills that Chair

You wrote me to informe you how my eldest sone is doing he is Clerk of the Circuit Court and teaching the accadamy and doing well I have often herd him talk of you the Balance of my family is well or was the last account I herd of them I have been carrying on a correspondence with your Brother ever since I have been here he is at Clarks ferry

I remain with great respects
your obt servt
David Crockett

G W McLean

Courtesy of the Phil Collins Collection.

The unauthorized book to which Crockett refers is James Strange French's *Life and Adventures of Colonel David Crockett of West Tennessee*, also known as *Sketches and Eccentricities of Colonel David Crockett of West Tennessee*. Crockett's eldest son was John Wesley Crockett.

G. W. McLean remains unidentified, but was likely another of Crockett's friends or supporters. McLean's brother, John, lived in Clarks Ferry, Pennsylvania. There is an envelope addressed to him in Crockett's hand, dated December 27, year unknown, in the J. S. Cullinan Family Collection, MC 013, San Jacinto Museum of History, Houston, Texas.

*   *   *   *   *

LETTER TO JOHN O. CANNON, JANUARY 20, 1834.

Washington City
January 20, 1834

Dear Sir

Your favour Came Safe to hand by this mornings mail enclosing six dollars to subscribe for the Intelegencer I went imedeately and had it ordered and enclose you a recept for the Same and I return to you my thanks for your good opinion of me

I can give you but little that is enteresting more than you Can See in the papers we are still engaged in discussing the great question of the removal of the deposits in both houses and god onley knows when it will end or what will be the result I am Clearley of the opinion that the deposits will be ordered back by both houses but it will do no good the Jackson folks is beginning to brag of his vetoeing powar It is imposable for us to get two thirds against the will of King Andrew the first one thing I live in hopes that if he does veto the measure that Congress will teach him a lesson that may be of use to the next Tyrant that will fill that Chair I must Confess that I never saw such times in my life every thing is news to me

It is plainley to be discovered that old Jackson is determened to Carry his point or Sacrafice the nation It has been said by Some of his worshipers that he has been the Savior of the country provided this be true he will retire from the government with the disgrace on him of destroying the Best interests of the Country the truth is If he had been dead and at the devil four years ago it would have been a happy time for this country

He is coming on finely in the great arts of retrenchment and reform that was promised you will See the post master genl reply to a Call of the Senate where he acknowledges that he Borrowed three hundred & fifty thousand dollars out of the Pet banks for which he is paying Six per cent for and also he has over drawn fifty thousand making a greeable to his own showing the little sum of four hundred thousand dollars they Can hide no longer

The world muss see the imposition trying to be plaid of upon the american people by Jackson and his partazans I have been examining the expenditures of the post office department and I find whare they have paid for printing for that department alone to their hireland the globe the moderate sum of forty two thousand dollars in two years Jackson is determened to feed his pets out of a silver spoon I must Close and request you to excuse this rough letter as the management here [is] enough to put any man out of temper that has any love for his country

I remain with great respects your obt servt
David Crockett

John O Cannon

John Cannon was a lawyer living in Madisonville, Tennessee. He later served in the Tennessee General Assembly and was appointed judge in 1844. The "Intelegencer" is the *National Intelligencer*, the anti-Jackson Washington newspaper published by Joseph Gales and William Seaton, which was friendly to Crockett.

*   *   *   *   *

LETTER TO CAREY AND HART, FEBRUARY 3, 1834.

Washington City
February 3rd 1834

Mssrs Carey & Hart

Gentlemen

Your favour of the 31st Inst. came to hand by yesterdays mail and having duly considered its contents, I have determined to accept your proposition to publish my Narrative. I enclose the Manuscript by to days mail, and I hope it may reach you safely as I have preserved no copy of it—nor indeed have I time to have it copied. The Copy right, certified by the clerk is attatched to the Preface and I am too ignorant of the business of printing, to pretend to give you any instructions about the manner of executing it except barely in relation to one thing. I wish it printed in *large* type, and so leaded as to make it very open and plain. Please do not neglect this—as in that way it will easily spread over more than two hundred pages—which I have ascertained by counting the number of words on an average page of the manuscript, and several printed books that I have also examined and counted. It has been hastily passed over for correction, and some small words may have been omitted. If so you will supply them. It needs no correction of *spelling* or *grammar*, as I make no literary pretensions.

The sale of the work, I am satisfied will exceed any caculation you have made. All along the Mississippi, where the counterfeit work sold rapidly, I have been urged by the people generally, to publish. There, very many copies will sell. I have also recd a letter from a Bookseller in Louisville Ky—assuring me, that it will sell rapidly there. That more than 500 copies of the other work had been sold at his single house in that place, and that many more of the genuine work would find ready market. In this place I should be glad to receive 500 copies, at your price to the trade, instead of selling to them. I however[?] mean, that number of the first copies that you send off. The very first moment that you can do so—please send me 10 copies—with a Bill of the cost of printing & binding *per copy* that I may know what the profit for *division* is to be.

Like yourselves, I hope and believe that we will have no difficulty in managing the ultimate settlement of the concern. All I can or do expect, is that the work will be executed by you as cheap as it could be procured to be done by any other printers and that a faithful account of the number of copies printed, will be rendered by you. Your high standing is a satisfactory guarantee, though I am personally unacquainted with you. I reserve your letter, of the date alluded to, as your contract—and you will consider this, as my acceptance of it.

Please inform me immediately, on the acception of this, whether you have safely recd the manuscript, and when I shall get my 10 copies—and such other matters as you may deem important.

Respectfully Gentlemen I am yrs
David Crockett

From the Tennessee Historical Society Miscellaneous Files, courtesy of the Tennessee State Library and Archives.

    Carey and Hart were publishers in Philadelphia. This letter is in Thomas Chilton's hand, but signed by Crockett.

*   *   *   *   *

LETTER TO JOHN COOK REEVES, FEBRUARY 3, 1834.

Washington
3rd February 1834

Will Mr Reeves do me the favour to Send me a recept for Major Wm Claxton Subscription for the Globe and discontinue the paper I will pay Mr Reeves on Sight

Respectfully your obt servt.
David Crockett

The Huntington Library, San Marino, California (HM 20428).

    John Cook Reeves was one of the publishers (with Francis Blair) of the *Congressional Globe,* **the major Jackson media organ.**

*   *   *   *   *

LETTER TO CAREY AND HART, FEBRUARY 23, 1834.

Washington City
February 23rd 1834

Mrssrs Cary & Hart
Gentle men
    For some days I have been anxiously expecting the arival of a copy of my book which you had the goodness to promis to send me so soon as it was finished But as you were mistaken in its length when you Stipulated the time at which I would recieve a copy I suppose its completion has been probably delayed by that Circumstance I desire it early as may suit your convenience—not for the purpose of indiscriminated use but for my own private satisfaction until the time Shall arrive at which you may open a sale of them at the different points to which you may think proper to send them In my former letters I spoke of you sending me 500 copies to this place. As the trade is to be supplied here, and as my public engagements consume all my time I have concluded that it will be unnessacery to do so— and you will therefore decline it unless I should make some subsequent arrangement with you on the subject pleas however send me *ten copies* as I wish that number for distribution among my imediate friends I wish you also to understand that the Hon Thos Chilton of Kentucky is intitled to one equal half of the sixty two and a half per cent of the entire profits of the work as by the agreement between you and my self—and also to half the copy right in any subsequent use or disposition—which may be made of that I have thought proper to advise you of this fact and to request that you will drop him a memorandum recognizing his right as a foresaid that half the said profits, which would otherwise be due to my self may be subject to his order and control at all times here after Enclose such a memorandum to me and I will hand it over to Mr Chilton It is more over proper that this should be done in order that if either or any of us should die our heirs may understand the arrangement This will

therefore be my relinquishment to Mr Chilton of the intirest aforesaid one half of which you are duly notified The manuscript of the Book is in his hand writing though the entire substance of it is truly my own The aid which I needed was to Classify the matter but the style was not altered

The letters which you have heretofore recieved from me were also in his hand writing as I was unwell and not able to write at their dates I deem it necessary to give you this infermation that you may hereafter know my hand writing and his, as it may be necessary that each of us should correspond with you when absent from each other

Several gentle men from London in Great Britain have urged me to secure the Copy right of my Book in that country I wish to consult you on the subject A Mr Jno Barry who is a strainger to me but who has the appearance of a gentleman is anxious to attend to it for me and proposing to do it with out charge he will probably call on you—and you are—authorised to make any arrangement concerning it which you may think advisable I suppose you have agents in London and if so you could if you think it would be profitable make the arrangement through them this letter will always answer you as a guide in Judging of my hand writing as it is written by my own hand Pleas let me here from you on the recept of this, and afford me a bill of cost *per copy* of printing the Book

This whole arrangement as to the interest of my friend Mr Chilton is committed to yourselves as confidential and so will your memorandum to him be considered

I am gentlemen Sincearly your friend and obt servt
David Crockett

Mrrss Cary & Hart

Courtesy of the Trustees of the Boston Public Library/Rare Books.

*   *   *   *   *

LETTER TO SAMUEL STILLMAN OSGOOD, FEBRUARY 23, 1834.

Washington City
23 Febry 1834

I have employed Mr S. S. Osgood to paint a Portrate and Can say with out flatry to the artist or the public that he has completed the work and I am proud to acknowledge that his Success, not only in taking my own likeness but The Hon Henry Clays of Kentucky and many others which I have examined

In fact Mr Osgood deserves in Couragement in the bussiness of fine arts as I Consider him a young man of unseasing industry and good Moral Character

with esteem I am your friend & obt servt
David Crockett

DRT Library, the Alamo.

This letter was Crockett's endorsement of Samuel Stillman Osgood, portrait artist. Osgood's original Crockett portrait was lost in a fire at the Texas State Capitol Building in 1881, but two engravings exist that are based on the painting, one issued by Childs and Lehman, the other by T. B. Welch. Unfortunately, the engravings are not similar, so the true appearance of the Osgood painting, which Crockett endorsed as a good likeness, has been lost.

*   *   *   *   *

LETTER TO THE MISSISSIPPI CONGRESSIONAL DELEGATION, FEBRUARY 24, 1834, PUBLISHED IN THE *(WASHINGTON) UNITED STATES' TELEGRAPH,* **MARCH 1, 1834.**

Washington City
24th Feb. 1834

Gentlemen

After perils by land and water, your highly flattering communication, bearing date 12th January, [h]as been duly received, and its contents, having been considered, your very humble servant, with due respect, answers and says, that if you are really in good earnest about making him President, you are more partial to me than I am to myself. You speak in the strongest possible terms of my fitness for the office of President of the United States, and a discharge of its duties. In this you may be right, as I expect there is likely something in me that I have never yet found out. I don't hardly think, though, that it goes far enough for the Presidency though I suppose I could do as the "Government" has done—make up a whole raft of Cabinet Ministers, and get along after the manner. But wo be unto me, if I should catch a "magician," while fishing for a Cabinet—my Cabinet would soon blow up sky high. It is the way with all great men, never to seek or decline office. If you think you can run me as President, just go a-head. I had a little rather not; but you talk so pretty I cannot refuse. If I am elected, I shall just seize the old monster, party, by the horns, and sling him right slap into the deepest place in the great Atlantic sea.

Gentlemen, I can't give you just now my notions about the great bulk of Government matters, as they hardly stand in any one way long enough to form any opinion about them. Opinions are not the things that they are cracked up to be, no how. They get mightily in a man's way in after times, every once in a while. I believe, therefore, I shall go in for *non-committal* just [a] bit, and you may work the election much more to your notion—as nobody can misinterpret my opinion when I wont express any. Running against the man I do, I can't get along in any other way. Again I say, Go a-head! Most affectionately, yours

David Crockett

See the related letter of January 15, 1834.

*   *   *   *   *

LETTER TO CAREY AND HART, FEBRUARY 25, 1834.

Washington City
25th Febry 1834

Mrrrs Cary & Hart

Gentlemen permit me to introduce to your acquiatnace my esteemed friend the Revrd William H Bigham from my district in Tennessee he informes me that he will be in Philadelphia for the purpose of purchasing goods and I have recommended him to call upon you and examin the Book which you are publishing for me and any araingement that you may make with Mr Bigham in regard to Sale or to Sell on Commission will be punctually performed by Mr Bigham I say this to you with pleasure as I am well acquainted with him

Your favourable attention to Mr Bigham will be thankfully acknowledged by your friend and obt servt

David Crockett

Courtesy of the Historical Society of Pennsylvania.

William Bigham was an early settler in Carroll County, Tennessee.

*   *   *   *   *

LETTER TO COL. THOMAS HENDERSON, FEBRUARY 26, 1834.

To Colonel Thomas Henderson
Washington City
26 Febry 1834

Dear Sir

Your favour of 2nd inst came safe to hand by the last mail and I will hasten to answer it Your request shall be attended to by the Payment of your subscription for the Intelligencer. I handed Mr Seaton your letter, and will in a few days send you a receipt for the amount I am glad to see that you are a candidate for Convention I hope you will beat old Blackhawk to death I do hope the people of Madison will lay him away among the unfinished business.

I now see what occasioned him to come out so unprincipled against me in the last two Elections he thought I was so unpopular in that County that If he would come out against me that it would secure his present Election I have no confidence in him and I wish to see a man that Every Confidence can be placed in to fill that station.

We are still engaged in the political war upon the deposit question There is no doubt of the deposits being ordered back and it is said that Jackson will veto the measure If he does I do believe the people will not submit to it I consider the question now pending before Congress is whether we will surrender up our old long and happy mode of government, and take a despot—I cannot call it any thing else.

I have sent a great many documents to the district I hope the people will read and Judge fore thimselves I do consider it one of the dangerouses periods that have ever been recorded in our political history the South Carolina question was nothing to the present moment.

I must close in hast and
Remain with great respects your friend and obt servt
David Crockett

Colo Thos Henderson
Mount Pinson
Madison Coty Tenn

Transcript published in Emma InmanWilliams, Historic Madison, The Story of Jackson and Madison County Tennessee, *from Prehistoric Moundbuilders to 1917 (Jackson, Tennessee: Madison County Historical Society, 1946), 423.*

Thomas Henderson relocated to Tennessee from North Carolina in the 1820s and was a large landholder in Madison County. "Mr. Seaton" refers to William Seaton, editor (with Joseph Gales) of the *National Intelligencer* and the *Register of Debates.*

The convention to which Crockett refers is the Tennessee Constitutional Convention of 1834. "Blackhawk" was a pen name of Adam Huntsman, a Crockett critic and eventual rival for Crockett's seat in Congress. Huntsman was elected a delegate to the Constitutional Convention from Madison County.

*   *   *   *   *

LETTER TO MRS. MARY BARNEY, FEBRUARY 28, 1834.

Washington City
28 Febry 1834

   Mrs Barney requests me to informe her whether Amos Kindall is dismissed or not If he is dismissed it is unknown to me, in fact I cannot believe The report, for Jackson thinks more of that imp of *famin* than all the ballance of the world
   We have had a controvercy in the Senate this morning between two of the Honourables Mr Poindexter and Mr Forsyth it is believed it will end in a duel I hope they may adjust the (the) matter
   I am in good health and hope these lines find you in the alike health

I am your obt servt
David Crockett

Mrs. Mary Barney

Courtesy of the Chicago History Museum, David Crockett Collection.

Mrs. Barney is likely Mary Chase Barney of Baltimore, Maryland, the editor of *National Magazine, or Ladies' Emporium*, an overtly anti-Jackson publication that was widely distributed until she ended its run in 1831. Mrs. Barney's husband, William, lost his job as a naval officer in 1829 as a result of Jackson's spoils system and, consequently, Mrs. Barney attacked the president with a vengeance. She gained national celebrity when she wrote an incendiary letter to Jackson excoriating the president for his abuse of power, which was published in pamphlet form and distributed by anti-Jackson politicians. Jonathan Daniel Wells, *The Origins of the Southern Middle Class, 1800–1861* (Chapel Hill: University of North Carolina Press, 2004), 119–25. Amos Kendall was one of the founders, with Francis Blair, of the Washington Globe, the official Jackson media organ. He was a member of Jackson's "kitchen cabinet" and was one of the president's closest confidants. Kendall served in an official capacity as the fourth auditor of the treasury until he was appointed postmaster general in 1835. The altercation between Senators George Poindexter (Mississippi) and John Forsyth (Georgia) involved Forsyth disputing a statement made by Poindexter on the Senate floor. Poindexter took offense and asked if Forsyth intended to "impeach his honor or veracity." Forsyth replied, "What I said, sir, I meant." A duel was averted when Henry Clay and some other senators intervened. Both Poindexter and Forsyth had a history of dueling. *(Portsmouth) New Hampshire Gazette*, March 18, 1834.)

*   *   *   *   *

LETTER TO CAREY AND HART, MARCH 8, 1834.

Washington City
8th March 1834

Mrsss Cary & Hart
   Gentlemen permit me to introduce to your acquaintance my particular friend Mr Lewis Levy who lives in my District Mr Levy is a merchant and perhaps he may wish to purches some of the Books that you are publishing I mean my narative any araingments that you may make with Mr Levey will be sattisfactory to me if he wishes to take some of the coppys he can account to me and you and my self can settle here after
Your attention to Mr Levey will be thankfully acknowledged by your friend

David Crockett

Courtesy of the New-York Historical Society, Misc. Mss., Crockett, David.

*   *   *   *   *

LETTER TO CAREY AND HART, MARCH 25, 1834.

Washington City
March 25, 1834

. . . as I am drawn on and am compeld to make some araingment in the early part of next week a mans needcesaty must pleed his apology I was beaten the election before last and it give me a back set in money matters an election costs a man a great deal in my country and I had strength & power to contend against.

Partial typescript from **Anderson Auction Company Catalog,** *December 15, 1914, item 173.*

Crockett, strapped for cash, was requesting money from his publishers.

*   *   *   *   *

LETTER TO JOHN DRUREY [DRURY?], APRIL 4, 1834.

Washington City
4 April 1834

Dear Sir

Your favour of the 13th March came safe to hand by the last mail and I will hasten to answer its contents I am enjoying good health and hope these lines may find you and family in good health I will now give you a history of the times at head quarters we are still engaged in debating the great question of the removal of the deposits This question have consumed almost the whole of the session thus far we have done no other business except to pass some few private Bills I do hope we may dispose of it next week The Senate took the vote last week on Mr Clays Resolutions first resolution was that the secraterys reasons were insufficient and and was not sattisfactory to the Senate and the other was that the President has violated the law and the Constitution the first resolution was addopted 28 to 18 and the Second by a vote of 27 to 19 and there was two absent Senators which would have voted with the majority this was the votes of the Senate and I hope the vote may be taken in the house next week it will be a close vote both partys claim the victory I still am of opinion that the house will addopt similar Resolutions, to that of the Senate, my reasons for these opinions is that in so large and entelegent a boddy of men called Honourable men cannot violate principle so much as for a majority to vote for a measure that every man that knows any thing must acknowledge is contrary to the laws and Constitution I have Converced with some of our own members that has acknowledged that the act was not right that Jackson had not a friend in Congress but what was sorry that the act was done but that they must sustain their party this is what may be—called forsaking principle to follow party this is what I hope ever to be excused from I cannot nor will not forsake principle to follow after any party and I do hope there may be a majority in Congress that may be governed by the same motive these are the reasons that induce me to believe we will gain this great question

I do consider the question now before Congress is one of deep intrest to the american people the question is whether we will surrender up our old long and happy mode of government and take a despot if Jackson is sustained in this act we say that the will of one man shall be the law of the land this you know the people will never submit to I do believe no thing keeps the people quiet at this time only the hope that Congress will give some relief to the country   we have had memorials presented to Congress from more than three hundred thousand people praying for the restoration of the deposits and a renewal of the Charter of the United States Bank they state that the manufacturers have nearly all Stoped and dismissed their hands and that there is men women and children roming over the country offering to work for their victuals you know that such a State of thing cannot be kept quiet long This have never been the case before Since previous to the old war the people petitioned in vain for some time and at length we knew what followed and this is my great dread is a civil war I do consider the South Carolina question nothing to compare with the present moment we see the whole Circulating medium of the country deranged and destroyed and the whole commercial community oppressed and distressed and for what Just to grattify the ambition of one man that he may reek his vengance on the United States Bank and for what Just becaus it refused to lend its aid in up holding his party The truth is he is surrounded by a set of imps of famin that is willing to sacrafice the country to promote their own intrest

I have no doubt of the people getting their eyes open yet in time to defeat the little political Judeas Martin vanburan although they have all chances never was the money of rome more compleat in the hands of Ceasar than the whole purse of the nation is at this time in the hands of our President Jackson in fact he is now in full possession of both sword and purse Ceasar Said to the secretary of rome give me the money and the secratery said no person have a right to ask that but the roman Senate and Ceasar said to him that it would be as easy for Ceasar to take your life as to will it to another   with that the secratery knowing that Ceasar had all powar he steped aside and Ceasar took the money how was it with Andrew Jackson when he asked Mr Duane to remove the deposits and he refused & he was then dismissed and a more pliable one appointed and the act is done and I believe they are sorry for it   no man knows whare the money of the country is Congress has no controle over it This is a new seen in our political history

The Post office department is upwards of one million of dollars behind hand and the Senate is handling the post master genl without gloves they will lay open all their acts to the people you know the president said in his last message to Congress and the nation that the post office department was in a most flourishing condition when at the same time he knew that the Post master Genl had borrowed three hundred and fifty thousand dollars from their pet Banks at ten per cents intrest and he has over drawn upwards of fifty thousand and he is upwards of six hundred thousand dollars behind with his contractors I can show you in ten contracts whare they give one hundred and twelve thousand dollars as extra to favourites   This is Jackson retrenchment I must close pleas to present me kindley to all your neighbours and recieve my best wishes for your self & family

I remain with great respects your friend and obt servt
David Crockett

John Drurey

David Crockett to John Drur[e]y, April 4, 1834, courtesy of the Gilder Lehrman Collection, GLC00931. Not to be reproduced without written permission.

John Drurey may have been John Drury, a resident of Gibson County, Tennessee.

*   *   *   *   *

LETTER TO HIRAM S. FAVOR, APRIL 9, 1834.

Washington City
9th April 1834

Dear Sir

Your favour of the 28 March has been recd by the last mail and I will hasten to answer it You state that you have herd that I intended visiting the eastern States at the close of Congress   I have had a desire to travel through your country mearly for curosity as I have been raised entirely in a frontear country and that it is natural for me to have a desire to become acquainted with the customs and habits of your country as I expect they are greatly differant from my native country

You may rest asured if I do come that I will take great pleasure in calling on you as I will be an entire stranger to every person I meet and will have to forme my acquaintance as I go tho I wish you not to missunderstand me I may not come I am getting anxious to get home and I see no hopes of doing any good by Staying here the house of representatives have determened by a majority that Andrew Jackson shall Wield both sword and purse his will is to be the law of the land

If this is what is called republicanism good god deliver me from all such doctrine

I must close with respects Your obt servt
David Crockett

Hiram S Favor

Courtesy, David Zucker Collection.

Hiram S. Favor was a publisher and native of Eastport Maine. In 1849 he established Favor's Express, a popular postal express company with headquarters in Boston and branches in Eastport, Portland, and St. John.

*   *   *   *   *

LETTER TO CAREY AND HART, APRIL 10, 1834.

Washington City
April 10th 1834

Mrrrs Cary & Hart

Gentlemen

Your note has been recd a day or two Since and I ought to have replied to it earlier but a number of letters had accumulated on me which I was compeld to answer, and in the multitude, yours has Just come up for Consideration

You propose to Sell 500 Copies of my Narrative provided I will agree to have it accounted for at 51 Cents pr Coppy I know might little a bout Such matters But might this not end in a perminent reduction of the trade price, So as to bring the Book down to little more in the end than the mere Cost of printing & binding

I have the most implicit Confidence in you, and that you will do nothing in the whole bussiness with out an equal eye to my intrest as well as your own If you think it advisable to make the arrangement I do not oppose it So far as the 5 Ct Copies Spoken of are Concerned provded you will furnish two other lots of copies each to my self and a friend on the Same terms if hereafter requested

Pleas let me here from you informing me what number of copies have been printed and what number Sold the aggragate price and time of payment. Those inquires I make only because I am hard pressed in money matters wish barely to forme some opinion of the aid I may expect from this Sourse

I hope to visit your City before the adjournment of

I am gentle men most Sincearly your friend and obt servt
D Crockett

Courtesy of General Collection, Beinecke Rare Book and Manuscript Library, Yale University.

*　　*　　*　　*　　*

LETTER TO JACOB DIXON, APRIL 11, 1834.

Washington City
11 April 1834

You asked me to assign my name on a note for two hundred dollars. I then thought you to be good and I put my name on the note and you afterwards told me that you had destroyed the note and made no use of it and I never knew any better until I received a notice from the bank that the note was protested. I then went to you and you told me that you had seen Mr Kerworth and settled it. I tell you that I will be damned if you do not settle it immediately if I dont go right strait to Court and informe against you for dealing farrow. You know that I saw you deal farrow your self one night when the Cardes did not slip well in the Box your Sone and Mr Brown was dealing and you took the Box and delt I can prove this by other witnesses

now I tell you to go and settle this as you know you have got a great deal of money from me for no thing and I will not be imposed on in this way I have written plain and I will act as plain with you if you do not settle this note I will be damned if I dont give you the bennefit of the law

Yours in hast
David Crockett

Partial typescript from **Christie's Auction Catalog,** *June 17, 2003, item 74 (the second page of the letter is reproduced photographically).*

Jacob Dixon, a fervent Clay supporter, appears to have had his hand in all manner of gambling enterprises in and around Washington City. The *Baltimore Gazette* of October 26, 1835, lists him as entering a horse named for Henry Clay in the Kendall Course race. The *Baltimore Patriot* of July 10, 1830, quotes Dixon proposing a toast to Henry Clay at a July 4th Republican Festival in Washington City. Dixon said, "Andrew Jackson, may he be distanced in the next presidential race, and his jockey, Martin Van Buren, be expelled the turf for foul riding." Crockett had apparently guaranteed a $200 note for Dixon, which he thought had been destroyed. Dixon seemingly cashed the note, and the funds were charged against Crockett when the note bounced. Always protective of his own credit and reputation, Crockett fired off this angry letter.

*　　*　　*　　*　　*

LETTER TO CAREY AND HART, APRIL 12, 1834.

Washington
April 12th 1834

Mrrrs Cary & Hart

Gentlemen
    You will receive at the Same time with this a letter from Mr Chilton, who is entitled to the first eight hundred dollars from the Sale of my Book, out of the Sixty two and one half per cent, Coming to me, as by your original agreement with me I enclose an order for that amount, which you will pleas accept and return to Mr Chilton I shal shortly visit your city, when we will make some further regulations a bout distributing the work

I am Sincearly your frind

David Crockett

Photostat courtesy of New York Public Library, Thomas Madigan Collection.

*   *   *   *   *

LETTER OF RECOMMENDATION TO SAMUEL S. OSGOOD, APRIL 20, 1834.

Washington City
20th April 1834

Mr S S Osgood
informs me that he is a bout to leave this city for Boston to his residence and as I consider it due this young gentleman as I have been quite intimate with him during the winter and as he has done me the favour to paint my portrate and as it is due to him that I shall State the masterly manner in which he has performed that work
    I have no hesitation in saying that it is the most perfect likeness I ever saw in fact I consider him more perfect as an artis than any man I ever saw I take much pleasure in this expressing my opinion of his great perserverance in the bussiness he is a young man of good morals and attentive to his bussiness

With great respects I am sir
your friend & obt servt
David Crockett

Samuel S Osgood

Holograph reproduced photographically in **Christie's Auction Catalog,** *December 15, 1997, item 30.*

*   *   *   *   *

LETTER TO GALES AND SEATON, MAY 20, 1834. PUBLISHED IN THE *(WASHINGTON) DAILY NATIONAL INTELLIGENCER*, MAY 22, 1834.

Washington City
20th May, 1834

Messrs. Gales & Seaton

I have seen, with surprise, an article copied from the Philadelphia Commercial Intelligencer, in which I am represented as saying, that I had been coaxed to a Faro-Bank not long since, and that I had lost fifteen hundred dollars in one night at it, and that I am to be pitied on that account.

I am truly sorry that I am compelled to be at the trouble of asking you, through your paper, to correct the error. It is true, I was asked by some gentlemen to partake of a dinner in Camden, where the conversation is said to have occurred, and, while there, a large collection of people being assembled, before I was asked in to the dinner, I was in an adjoining room in the midst of the crowd; at which time, I suppose it was, that I lost my Pocket Book, with one hundred and sixty or seventy dollars in it. Whilst at dinner, I heard it stated, that a gentleman who was present had lost his money, and I felt for my Pocket Book, and I found that I had lost it with its contents. I then stated that I knew another gentleman that had the deposites removed, and I was asked if I had lost my money. I said I had, and stated to what amount, as near as I could recollect.

I had received three hundred dollars through Messrs. Carey & Hart, and had lent a gentleman one hundred and fifty dollars of the money. I was indebted to the Farmers' and Mechanics' Bank of Georgetown in a small sum, and a Mr. George Riston had one hundred and twenty dollars of the money of that Bank, and proposed to sell it for one hundred and two. I exchanged with him to that amount. And when I stated that I had lost the money, several gentlemen said that they were sorry for my loss; and I replied that it might have been worse, if they had got it but a short time before. I said, jocularly, that I had once lost more than that at the Faro-Bank; which was true. I did, when I first came to Congress, several years ago, indulge in betting against that game, and it is the only game that I ever did bet at, and I am ashamed that I ever saw that played; for I do not know any other game in the world. Indeed I cannot say that I ever *knew* that game, for it has injured me, but not to the extent stated in the Commercial Intelligencer—for the best of all reasons, that I never had fifteen hundred dollars at one time in my life. Nor did I ever loose the sixth part of that sum in one night. So that the Editor is under a mistake when he states that I said that I was coaxed to the Faro-table not long since, and lost fifteen hundred dollars in one night. I hope the Editor will do me the justice to correct the error, and that all other papers that have copied the article, will do the same, and oblige their and your obedient servant,

David Crockett

The misinterpreted story of Crockett's $1,500 Faro loss was spread widely, and this letter to Gales and Seaton, publishers of the *National Intelligencer*, was his attempt at damage control. Crockett's April 11, 1834, letter to Jacob Dixon illustrates that he still had a predilection for the game, but here his primary concern seems to be the amount involved. As an advocate of the poor and middle class, Crockett did not want to appear cavalier about the loss of a large sum of money.

*   *   *   *   *

LETTER TO JOSEPH WALLIS, MAY 26, 1834.

Washington City
26th May 1834

Dear Sir

Your favour of the 11 Inst came safe to hand by the last Mail and I will hasten to answer its contents You request me to say to you at what time I will visit the white Sulphur Springs It would give me pleasure to say to you at what time I could be thare But we have set no day for an adjournment of Congress and until that is done it would be imposable for me to say to you that I would be thare on any particular day and again I will be compelled to go imediately home when Congress adjourns I will then make my arangements and come up and see you I have some bussiness that will require my attention when we adjourn

My Post office is called Crocketts P.O—Gibson County whare if you wrote to me at home I will get it imediately I have no Idea when Congress will Brake up But if It does in time I will be at the Springs in August or the first of September If I can come I have no object in view more than to injoy my self I am electionaring for no boddy in the world if I can put Back this political Judeas Martin Vanburan I will do so for I do think him a perfect Scoundrel and in fact he is like the Ballance that Jackson is surrounded with The truth is he is Surrounded by a set of Imps of famin that would destroy the country to promote their own intrest they do not care if Jackson was at the devil So they get the Spoils of victory

The truth is they have prompted the poor old man by Singing glorification to him until he believes his popularity is able to brake down the Constitution and laws of the country in fact he has come to the conclusion that he can make the people believe that no man ever did understand the Constitution until he mounted the throne he has come to the conclusion that not even the men that formed the Constitution understood it

In fact we may say with propriety that we have the government of one man Andrew Jackson holds both the sword and purse and claims it by the Constitution as the arms and amunition and other public property and he has tools and Slaves to his party enough to sustain him in the house of representatives— But we have one hope the Senate will save the Constitution and laws in spite of King Andrew the first.

we have had a warme session and I expect it will get no better until Congress closes we are getting his poor lick spittles almost ashamed of them selves—

I must close and remain your obt servt
David Crockett

Joseph Wallis

Photostat courtesy of the Center for American History, The University of Texas at Austin, Crockett (David) Papers.

Joseph Wallis was a lawyer from Morgan County, Alabama. He may have been a distant relative of Crockett's by marriage, as his wife Elizabeth's maiden name was Crockett. White Sulphur Springs was located in Alabama near the Tennessee border, about thirty-six miles from Chattanooga.

*   *   *   *   *

LETTER TO CAREY AND HART, MAY 27, 1834.

Washington City
27th May 1834

Mrrrs Cary & Hart

Gentle men

when I was in your city I made an arange ment with you to publish me Some of my Books I am written to from all parts of my District to have a number of them sent on and I have concluded to write to you, and get you to Box up Say two thousand if convenient you may have two thousand five hundred in Boxes of a suitable Sise to hold Say five hundred Send them on to Some commissioned merchant at Pittsburgh and write to him to let them a wait my order

I will come on to Philadelphia when Congress Coloses it is unknown when that will be I fear we are to have a longe Session and do but little good for the country

Will you pleas to write to me if it will be convenient for you to send on the Books and if So whether you can do so in time for me to get them as I go on home. Some have wrote to me that I could Sell five thousand So that the half may Sell if you Send me that number you can dispose of the Same number if you wish

I remain your friend & obt servt
David Crockett

PS I have wrote on the wronge page but have not time to correct the err

The Carl H. Pforzheimer Collection of Shelley and His Circle, The New York Public Library, Astor, Lenox and Tilden Foundations.

*   *   *   *   *

LETTER TO T. J. DOBINGS [DOBYNS?], MAY 27, 1834.

Washington City
27th May 1834

Dear Sir

Your kind favour of the 8th Inst came safe to hand and I will hasten to answer it   I am in good health and hope these lines will find you in the alike health

I can give you but little political news more than you can see by the papers you will See that our long and happy mode of government is near at an end we may from present appearances Soon bid far well to our republican libertys we have compleatly the government of one man and he has Tools and Slaves enough in the house of representatives to sustain him in his wild carear I do believe his whole object is to promote the intrest of a set of Scoundrels that care nothing for the good of the country

You recollect that I said in Brownsville in my Speech that the whole object of Jacksons great zeal to get the government money out of the united States Bank was to get it placed whare he could have the control of it to use for the purpose of making that political Judeas Martin Vanburen our next president and you now see my prediction come true you see Andrew the first King hold both Sword and purse and claims it as the other public property by the constitution will the people agree that no man not even those that formed the constitution did not under stand it nor no man that ever wielded the destinees of this nation ever under stood that Sacret article until Andrew Jackson mounted the throne I am much mistaken in the people of this country if they have forgot the Blood and treasure that was lost in relieving this country from a government of one man and will fall back to the kingley powar The truth is the poor Superanuated old mans vanity has promted him to think that his popularity could Slant any thing You State to me that the people is well pleased with my course This is grattifying to me beyond measure and I hope you will tender to my friends my greatful acknowledgement for their complementary letter expressing their sattisfaction at my course as their Servant I never did know any mode of legislating only to go and do what my consience dictated to me to be wright I care nothing for any party more than to do Justice to all

The old man thinks he has put down the Bank of the united States and he has commenced war on the Senate as he thinks that to be the only Barior in his way to kingley powar let him once Conquer the Senate and he will put his foot on the Constitution and tell the Judicial powar to go to hell I do believe this to be his calculation but I hope he may be misstaken The Senate will Save the Constitution and the laws of the country in spite of Andrew Jackson and all his minions around him

I was one of the first men that ever fired a gun under his Command and I Supported him while he Supported his promised principles but when he abandoned them I abandoned him and I have niver [illeg.] my course I have been trying for some time to get up my land Bill but we have not even passed the appropriation Bills and there is no chance to do any thing I know of no opposition to it if we could get to act on it

I must close with great respects
I remain your friend and obt servt
David Crockett

T.J Dobings

Ps we are at the contested election between Moore & Letcher if it is made a party question Moore will get it and if it is desided on Justice Letcher will get it
DC

Courtesy, the Lilly Library, Indiana University, Bloomington, Indiana.

T. J. Dobings may have been Thomas J. Dobyns, a resident of Brownsville, Tennessee. In a typescript of this letter published in S. G. Heiskell's *Andrew Jackson and Early Tennessee History, Vol. 3* **(Nashville: Ambrose, 1921), 18–19, Dobings was listed as T. J. Dobyns. Born around 1802 in Tennessee, in 1835 Thomas J. Dobyns was the part owner of a large lumber mill in the Brownsville area (***Nashville Banner & Whig,*** August 3, 1835), and by the 1840s was operating a daguerreian gallery in Memphis. He subsequently opened a chain of galleries in Louisville, Cincinnati, Nashville, and other cities. Dobyns died in May of 1865. Peter E. Palmquist and Thomas R. Kailbourn,** *Pioneer Photographers from the Mississippi to the Continental Divide: A Biographical Dictionary, 1839–1865* **(Stanford, California: Stanford University Press, 2005), 209–10. Robert Perkins Letcher and Thomas P. Moore were both candidates for the House of Representatives from Kentucky, and were involved in a contested election. The House was unable to reconcile the dispute, and a second election was held in Kentucky, with Letcher, an anti-Jacksonian, the victor.**

*   *   *   *   *

LETTER TO "A FRIEND," MAY 28, 1834.

Washington City
28th May 1834

I can give you little political news since you left. There was nothing done while I was gone, more than to pass the Appropriation bill, which was obliged to pass as a matter of course. I was highly gratified with my trip. I had a great many present made to me. One rifle-gun that must have cost at least $150, and a watch seal of fine gold that cost $40, and a fine suit of broadcloth from the woolen manufactory at Lowell, and many other smaller presents.

Partial letter printed in the (San Francisco) Evening Bulletin, *October 23, 1886.*

Crockett refers to gifts he received during his tour of the northeast. The letter's recipient is unknown.

*   *   *   *   *

LETTER TO CAREY AND HART, JUNE 1, 1834.

Washington City
June 1, 1834

I would like to take four Boxes on to the District as I wish to Send about three hundred to Memphis by the same Boat that I go home on to my friend Major Winchester and I would like to take three Boxes of the Sizes you name which in all will be fifteen hundred.

Partial typescript from Anderson Auction Catalog, *March 13, 1914, item 64.*

This letter contained instructions for Crockett's publishers on orders for copies of his autobiography. Major Winchester is Marcus Winchester, a prominent citizen of Memphis and an early supporter of Crockett, who encouraged him to seek national office and provided financial backing for his early campaigns.

*   *   *   *   *

LETTER TO WILLIAM HACK, JUNE 9, 1834.

Washington City
9th June 1834

Dear Sir

Your favour of the 28th May was recd by this mornings mail and I will hasten to answer its contents—

In the first place I will give you my reason for voting against the Bank Committee being raised I give the vote and have never regreted it in the first place if you will examin the proceedings you will See that a large majority had voted the Bank to death that it never was to be rechartered This was desided well the President had drawn all the governmint money out of it now I would like to know what right Congress had to send a committee to examin it in fact It looked to me Just like taking a man up and hanging him and then [illeg.] a Jury to try whether he was gilty or not So with the Bank they thought they had killed it and they concluded that if they Sent their Committee it would rais an exitement in the Country and prop up Jacksons Sinking popularity who was this Committe that was Sent on to investigate the Bank you know in our country when a Juror once sets and gives his opinion on a Case he is never more a Competent Juror in the Same Case

Here is Frances Thomas from Maryland that was one of the most Clamorous members of the Bank Committee at the last Congress and Said all he could against it and he is now made Chairman of their fameous Committee of which I have Sent you one of their reports and you will See our partee partial Speaker made five Jackson men & two anti Jackson men serve on the Committee you will get Both the reports and you can Judge for your self

As for retrenchment I have always went for that I voted for it in committee of the whole but when the final vote was taken I was not thare I had been for some time labouring under a complaint with a pain in my breast and I concluded to take a travel a couple of weeks for my health I knew they would do no thing more than to pass the appropriation Bill that was all the vote I regretted not being there at But if you will examin you will see the whole delegation voted against it however I have not examined their votes on the ays and nays but they all voted against me on committee We will adjourn if the Senate agree to our Resoltion of the 30th of June So I fear I will have a Bad Chance to get up my land Bill I have Been trying for some time and if I could get it up I have no doubt of its passage I know of no opposition to it [illeg.] whole delegation will go for it [illeg.] are to Close this Congress and [illeg.] more than to establish Andrew Jackson the governmint of [illeg.] he now holds [illeg.] sword & purs and claims it [illeg.] Consititution a powar never [illeg.] of by any other presedent

I must close in hast and remain your friend & obt servt
David Crockett

Wm Hack

From the Tennessee Historical Society Miscellaneous Files, courtesy of the Tennessee State Library and Archives.

William Hack was a resident of Denmark, Tennessee, in Madison County. Francis Thomas was a Jacksonian congressman from Maryland who served a total of nine terms in the House. He was killed by a locomotive in 1876 while walking on railroad tracks near Franklin, Maryland. *Biographical Directory of the United States Congress,* http://bioguide.congress.gov.

*   *   *   *   *

LETTER TO WILLIAM T. YEATMAN, JUNE 15, 1834.

Washington City
15th June 1834

Dear Sir

Your favour of the 11th Inst came safe to hand by this mornings mail and I will hasten to answer it I am well and hope these lines may find you in the alike I am beginning to thing the time long that we are to remain in session as I have not the least hope of doing any act to relieve the country on the day before yesterday the house rejected Mr Clays resolutions by laying them on the table and I consider the last hope gone of retaining the laws & constitution

I now look forward to our adjournment with as much intrest as ever did a poor Convict in the Penatintiary to see his last day come we have done but one act and that is that the will of Andrew the first King is to be the law of the land he has tools & Slaves enough in Congress to sustain him in any thing that he may wish to effect

I thank God I am not one of them I do consider him a greater tyrant than Cromwell Ceasar or Bonepart—I do hope his day of Glory is near at an end If it ware not for the Senate God only knows what would be come of the country I still have hopes that all is not lost while we have Such a guard as the Senate the people will Sustain the Senate and if so they will Save the laws & Constitution

I must Close with great respects your friend & obt servt
David Crockett

Wm T Yeatman

Haverford College Library, Haverford, Pennsylvania, Special Collections, Charles Roberts Autograph Letters Collection (collection 745).

William Yeatman was a steamboat captain and a resident of Cheatham County and Davidson County, Tennessee. This letter was addressed to Fishkill Landing, New York (James D. Davis, *History of the City of Memphis* [Memphis: Hite, Crumpton, & Kelly, 1873], 155), where Yeatman may have been staying with friends. The Tennessee State Library and Archives has a letter from Yeatman, written from Baltimore on April 6, 1834, to William P. Palmer, Fishkill Landing, wherein he tells of his travels to Philadelphia with Sam Houston, whom he says was a "mean fellow . . . he did not treat his wife well." He also mentions plans to visit Washington City and his hopes of visiting Daniel Webster. Yeatman Family Letters, III-G-1, (MS Files), AC No. 125, Tennessee State Library and Archives.

Yeatman appears to have been the son of Thomas Yeatman and Martha Beckwith. Thomas Yeatman was a wealthy Tennessee banker and businessman. Upon Martha's death, he married the daughter of Andrew Erwin, the leader of the anti-Overton faction in Tennessee, with whom Crockett was allied. Upon Thomas Yeatman's death in 1833, his widow married Tennessee congressman John Bell, then serving as speaker of the House, and another Crockett ally by 1834.

*   *   *   *   *

LETTER TO J. M. SANDERSON, JUNE 25, 1834.

Washington City
25th June 1834

Dear Sir
   Your favour enclosing the target of my fine guns first shooting has Been recd and I am much pleased to see that she Bunches her Balls She Shoots two low but that will be altered by Raising the hind Sight
   I have taken passage in the Stage for Baltimore on this day two weeks and expects to be in Philadelphia on Monday The 30 and per haps may spend the 4 of July their
   Will you pleas to procure me Say a half Dozen or a whole dozen of Canister Powder of the Best quality and See Mr Cary & Hart They are Sending me Some Boxes of Books to Pittsburgh and get them to Box it up with the Books and send it on to Pittsburgh I will pay you the money on Sight for it as there is no Chance to get the article in my country I will also want Several Boxes of Caps of the Best quality These are articles cannot be had in my country

I must close with great Respects
I am Dr Sir your friend & obt servt
David Crockett

J. M. Sanderson

Courtesy of the Historical Society of Pennsylvania.

James M. Sanderson was a resident of Philadelphia who worked as a journalist and a printer, and was an avid marksman. That is probably why the young Whigs of Philadelphia asked him to work with Crockett on the specifications for the rifle that they presented to Crockett during a visit to that city. Crockett would christen the rifle "Pretty Betsey." David Crockett, *An Account of Col. Crockett's Tour to the North and Down East* (Baltimore: E. L. Carey and A. Hart, 1835), 35; Sanderson to Editor, *American Turf Register and Sporting Magazine*, September 24, 1829, 208–209. Also see Crockett's February 18, 1835 letter to Sanderson.

*　　*　　*　　*　　*

LETTER TO NICHOLAS BIDDLE, OCTOBER 7, 1834.

Trenton Tennessee
7th October 1834

Dear Sir

I am on my way home from Nashville my Bussiness was to arrange my Bill which I had drawn on my friend Boyd McNeary and Got Mr Poindexter to indorse

But when I got to Nashville I found that he had not accepted it and I was So Compleatly Cowed that I could not ask any person to indorse another I was distressed to find my disappointment

I then concluded to draw a draft on my friends Mrrrs Cary & Hart with a hope that they have Been Successful in the Sale of my Books

If this arangement Should not answer I know of no other way that I can do but to pay you when I get to Washington I am more distressed in having a friend protested in Bank than any thing in the world I will leave home the last of the first week in November and I expect to come through Philadelphia at which time I will See you and I will try and have matters arranged

The Bank question is popular in my district although there is Some talk of my having two opponents if So they cannot Beat me But I am of the opinion I will have no opposition as the Jackson question is dying in this country and no hopes for little Van—I hope these lines will find you & family well

I remain with great respects your friend and obt servt
David Crockett

Nicholas Biddle

Courtesy of the Historical Society of Pennsylvania

Nicholas Biddle was the president of the Second United States Bank. Boyd McNeary was probably Boyd McNairy, a Nashville physician and Clay supporter. McNairy was a member of the anti-Jackson Erwin group with whom Crockett associated in Tennessee, and was president of the Bank of Nashville in 1828. *Southern Journal of Medical and Physical Sciences* (Knoxville: Kinslow and Rice, 1857), 69–70; Thomas P. Abernethy, *From Frontier to Plantation in Tennessee* (Chapel Hill: University of North Carolina Press, 1932), 292–93. Poindexter was the manager at the Nashville branch of the Bank.

*　　*　　*　　*　　*

LETTER TO CAREY AND HART, OCTOBER 9, 1834.

Weakley County Tennessee
9 October 1834

I have through necessity been compeld to draw upon you in favour of my friend Biddle. I do not know how matters stand between yourselves & me. I know you will do right. I wrote to you some time ago and got no answer. I expect to leave home for Washington in the first week in Nover. and will call on you as I go on and I will then appolagise for the freedom I have taken with you. Jacksonianism is dead here and the people will not have the flying doutchman little vann. I must close in hast and remain your obt servt.

Transcript, **Swann Galleries Sale 1863** *(June 8, 2000), Lot 18.*

Crockett attempted to draw funds from the Nashville branch of Biddle's Bank against a guarantee from Carey & Hart, which was denied. See Crockett to Biddle, October 7, 1834.

*   *   *   *   *

UNDATED LETTER TO UNKNOWN GENTLEMAN OF NEW YORK.

My dear Sir:

I give you many thanks for your kindness in forwarding to me the lithographic likeness of myself, painted at Washington last winter; by Mr. De Rose. My wife says it looks precisely as I do after returning from hunting.—By the way, the Tories have just nominated *Mr. Huntsman,* in my district, in opposition to me.—If he "goes ahead," he is a better huntsman than I ever thought he was, and I've know him from a cub. Twenty years ago there was a powerful sprinkle of bears in our district.

Some of my friends express consarn about the New York Election. I tell them not to fear, for says I, was not I among them last summer, and I know there was no doubt that every Whig would do his duty. Still, if this letter reaches you in season it will do no harm to give it a place in some good Whig paper. And I wish you to try to spur up every voter that is lukewarm—just put some inflammable gas into his heels, and tell him to "go ahead" Do not let any of our friends keep open shop on the three days. Tell them to do as I do, and that is, dispatch one thing at a time. As an illustration I will tell you what happened not two weeks ago:—

A young man came up to me while hunting, and asked my consent to give him my daughter. I was just at that moment engaged in a battle with a wolf and a catamount. Hold on a moment, said I; and let me despatch with these fellows, and then I'll attend to you—one thing at a time is my motto. After I got through that job, said I, now young man, "go ahead!" Now you have got both a wolf and a cata-mount to slay, and what I have to say is, do it at once. I am glad to see that you have placed *Sampson* on your ticket. We want all his strength at Washington next winter. He must come *unshorn of his locks,* and take his seat by me. As the Philistines will be upon him, he must bring along with him his *jaw-bone*— and then never fear, we'll all go ahead.

Your friend and fellow citizen
Crockett

Published in the **New Bedford** (Massachusetts) *Mercury, November 14, 1834.*

    This was clearly not written by Crockett, but was published under his name. DeRose was Anthony Lewis DeRose, an artist who had painted Crockett's portrait, but the date of the letter is not consistent with when Crockett sat for DeRose, and the only portrait from life that depicts Crockett in hunting gear was painted by John Gadsby Chapman.

*   *   *   *   *

LETTER TO CAREY AND HART, DECEMBER 8, 1834.

Washington City
8th December 1834

Mrrrs E.L Carey & A Hart

Gentlemen
    will you pleas to make out the accoumpt in ful between you and me and Send it on to me as Soon as you can with convenience make it out plane as it Stands as I am anxious to know how we Stand I expect to be hard pressed and if you think the right will ever be worth any thing more write me what you will give for it as I can never need money worse than at present
    I have talked to Mr Clark upon the subject we was talking about But we have not come to any terms yet I will know in a few days and then I will write you more fully   pleas answer this as soon as posable and oblidge your friend and obt servt

David Crockett

By permission of the Houghton Library, Harvard University (Autograph File, C).

    Mr. Clark was William Clark, an Anti-Masonic congressman from Pennsylvania. Crockett was making preliminary arrangements for Clark to assist him in editing his second book for Carey and Hart, *An Account of Col. Crockett's Tour to the North and Down East.*

*   *   *   *   *

LETTER TO NICHOLAS BIDDLE, DECEMBER 8, 1834.

Washington City
8th Decr 1834

My Dear Sir
    I have talked to Governor Poindexter upon the subject that I was so much destresed a bout when I saw you That was his being protested on the Bill which he indorsed for me with you and I informed him that you Stated to me that if he would indorse a note for me in the bank It could lie over a while he Said he would do any thing he could for me and I wish you to make out the account and enclose a note and Check for the amount and I will get it endorsed and enclose it to you which I hope will keep matters easy until I can pay It for your friendship to me you shall never be for gotten by your friend & obt servt—

David Crockett

Nicholas Biddle

Ps write to Mr Poindexter that It is for the Same Bill that he endorsed for me as he may know that he is not decieved
DC

Courtesy of the Historical Society of Pennsylvania (Grotz case 4 - Box 32).

*   *   *   *   *

LETTER FROM NICHOLAS BIDDLE TO CROCKETT, DECEMBER 13, 1834.

Phila.
Dec. 13 1834

Dear Sir
    I enclose a memorandum of the State of your account, with a new note to be signed by you and endorsed by Mr. Poindexter, and also a check for the proceed to be signed by Mr. Poindexter.
When you have it fixed, send it back to me. I write today to Mr. Poindexter to explain it to him.
With great respect
N.B.
Hon. David Crockett
Wash.

P.S. I enclose your draft from Nashville on Messrs. Carey & Hart which they decline accepting.
N.B.

Manuscript Division, Library of Congress.

*   *   *   *   *

LETTER TO CAREY AND HART, DECEMBER 13, 1834.

Washington City
13th Decr 1834

Mssrs E.L Cary & A. Hart
. . . I would not sell at all if I were not So hard pressed for money and do not no what else to do—pleas to write to me imediately that I may know what to do
I remain with great respects your obt servt
David Crockett

Partial transcription in the **Chicago Sunday Tribune,** *May 29, 1955.*

    The *Tribune* published a partial transcription of the letter and a photograph of the last few lines of the original document, which are quoted above. The accompanying article quotes from the letter that Crockett's "accounts" with Carey and Hart showed him "to be in your debt 332 dollars," and mentions that Crockett proposed a "complex transaction for settlement," but the article does not quote Crockett's proposition. Likely he was again offering to sell his publishers his copyright.

*   *   *   *   *

LETTER TO NICHOLAS BIDDLE, DECEMBER 16, 1834.

Washington City
16th Decr 1834

Dear Sir
    enclosed you will find the note and check endorsed which will give me much relief and I hope will not be any disadvantage to [to] the Bank I hope never again to be so hard pressed as I have often Said poverty is no Crime but it is attended with many inconveniences
    I have good news from my district I am told by a gentle man who have been all over my district that I will get a better vote than I ever got I want to be elected once more to know whether we are to have a king of a President and I am of the opinion that the next Election will deside that matter I do hope this war message will open the peoples eyes The truth is it was only ever minded to Call Public attention from enquiring in to the abominable corruption of this administration which would have been exposed this may hide it and Blind the people a while longer
    I must close pleas to write me on the recept of this let me here if you get those papers Safe as the Post office is so uncertain that I would like to here as I have no confidence in their honisty

I am with high respects your friend and obt servt
David Crockett

Nicholas Biddle

Courtesy of the Historical Society of Pennsylvania.

    Crockett's remark about a "war message" is in reference to President Jackson's demands that France pay the United States for property damage to U.S. shipping incurred during the Napoleonic Wars. Under an 1831 treaty, France had agreed to pay about five million dollars but, in 1834, refused to make restitution. Jackson responded by rattling his saber and brought the countries to the brink of war. Britain finally intervened and brokered a compromise. The French accepted a line in Jackson's 1835 annual message as a de facto apology for threatening war (it wasn't intended as such), and agreed to pay their debt. See Jon Meacham, *American Lion: Andrew Jackson in the White House* (New York: Random House, 2008), 283–85, 292–97.

*   *   *   *   *

LETTER FROM NICHOLAS BIDDLE TO CROCKETT, DECEMBER 19, 1834.

Phila. Dec 19 1834

Dear Sir
    I received this morning your favor of the 16th inst. with its inclosures. The note has been discounted & the old draft paid.
Very respt Yrs
N.B.

David Crockett
Washington, DC

Manuscript Division, Library of Congress.

*   *   *   *   *

LETTER TO CAREY AND HART. DECEMBER 21, 1834.

Washington City
21st Decr 1834

Mrs Cary & Hart
    Gentlemen I have Commenced the new Book and have taken 31 pages to Mr Clark to Correct and I have twelve more written ready for him he is well pleased with what I have done and Sais he can make you the most interesting Book you ever had
    If he could keep way with me I would have it very near or quite done by the first of January or early in February my dread is that our friend Clark will not keep up with me he has Commenced the preface and I am of opinion he will pleas you well I intend to let him make that to Suit him self
    I will endeavor to get him to have as much as posable done and send on to you by the first of January so that you can begin and another reason that hurts [?] me is I owe three hundred dollars that is due the last of this month or the first of next and If I can get you a good Chare of it done I can ask you with Some hope to aid me in getting it out of the Bank It is payable in the Bank here
    I wish you to write to Mr Clark how he likes what I have done and whin he thinks he can have it ready I will asure you that I will do my part pleas to answer this and Say whether If we got on well next week with the work and I was to ask you for an acceptance If I could get it for three hundred dollars, I got a check for the draft you give me I must close in hast I remain your friend and obt servt

David Crockett

David Crockett, ALS: Washington, D.C., to Carey & Hart, 1834 Dec. 21 (AMs 530/2) Rosenbach Museum & Library, Philadelphia, Pennsylvania.

*   *   *   *   *

LETTER TO NICHOLAS BIDDLE, DECEMBER 22, 1834.

Washington City
22 Decr 1834

Dear Sir
    The Casher enclosed me this check for the purpose of endorsing my name on it which was neglected I hope it will make no differance as I have Complyed with request

I am with great respects your obt servt
David Crockett

Nicholas Biddle Esq

Courtesy of the Historical Society of Pennsylvania.

*   *   *   *   *

LETTER TO CAREY AND HART, DECEMBER 24, 1834.

Washington City
24 Decr 1834

Mrsrs Cary & Hart
 Gentle men your favour of the 20th Inst Came Safe to hand and I saw Mr Asgood and obtained his permission a greeable to your request and here enclose his letter to you which I hope will be agreeable to your wish
 I have written and taken to Mr Clark 55 pages of my new Book Mr Clark Sais it will do excelent for him to work upon and he sais he will make you a Book that will fill expectation

excuse hast I am your obt servt
David Crockett

Holograph photographically reproduced in unidentified newspaper article "Letters from Famous Americans," from the Tennessee Historical Society Miscellaneous Files, courtesy of the Tennessee State Library and Archives; also in **Sotheby Parke-Bernet Auction Catalog,** *December 16, 1994, item 42.*

 "Mr Asgood" was probably S. S. Osgood, the artist who painted a portrait of Crockett that the congressman particularly liked. Crockett was arranging to have an etching, based on the Osgood portrait, used as frontal matter in the forthcoming book about his tour of the Northeast. He enclosed a note from Osgood, dated December 24, 1834, granting permission "to have a small engraving for your book taken from the print of which I hold the copyright and am happy to have it in my power to grant so small a favor." Osgood to Crockett, December 24, 1834, auctioned February 26, 1998, Smythe. The engraving used was by T. B. Welch.

* * * * *

LETTER TO JOHN WESLEY CROCKETT, DECEMBER 24, 1834.

Washington City
24th December 1834

My Dear Son
 Tomorrow is Chrismas and I have never received But two letters from You and none from any of the rest. I am begining to think that out of sight is out of mind with you all. I have wrote regularly once a week and expect to do so.
 I am in as good health as I have been in for many years and hopes these lines may find you all well. I am doing the best I can. I did expect to have had it in my power before this time to have conveyed the news of the passage of my land bill to the district,—But the bill to regulate the pay of the officers of the navey came up on tuesday the day before I had got fixed for the order of the day for my Bill and it has remained as the unfinished Business of the house and has kept down every thing else; how ever mine will come up as a matter of course when it is disposed of. I have little or no fears of its passage with but little amindment; the whole delegation from Tennessee will vote for my Bill and they say there is no fears of its passage in a few days.
 I see by the Jackson paper that Huntsman and Mcmeans is both one and that the grand jury of Weakley has given Huntsman a great vote but I have not taken the least alarm at it as I am writing a Circular to the District in which I comment largely on the Grand Jury election and the forged letter that have been published in the Jackson paper. I have let the editor know that he has to take responsibility for the forgery. I am determined to be imposed upon no longer by the poor devils. I have made an appeal to

the people that will Bring a reflection upon every honest man in the district; that forged letter has given me the best text in the world to comment upon and I am sure to use it. The poor miserable wretches cannot beat me by honesty, and they have resorted to forgery that no honest community will stand. I cannot be made to believe that it was not Huntsman that wrote the letter; however this, I will know when I get home, I will know all about it.

We are yet in a quandry about the frinch war. No report has been made by the committees of either house. When that is made we are to see how many Bloodhounds there is that is willing to plunge us in a war with one of the most powerful nations in the world. I see great efforts making to unite their party and to sustain Jackson and gratify his ambtion—[Here follows a line too indistinct to be read and then it goes on thus:]

Close our ports and we will soon bring them to terms. They can overpower us more than three to one in ships, and suppose they were to Blocade the mouth of the Mississippi and all our ports, what would become of the Western and Southern farmers? And besides it would Bring us under the needcessity of laying a tax for generations to come. This does not suit the South and the West, But the poor old fool does not know what he is about: he has destroyed the circulating medium of the country and destroyed all the prospects of internal improvements; he has destroyed the commerce and wants to bring on a war and go out with a Blaze of glory, and I am afraid that the people will say amen as usual. They will say it is all right, Jackson done it. If the people is ready to sustain him in this I am ready to give up the ship.

I still say as I have for the last four years, that if Martin Van Buren is elected I will leave the United States as soon as I can get out.

Give my love to mother and all the rest and all the neighbors, do write oftener. May God Bless you is the wish of your father.

David Crockett

John W. Crockett

Published in the (New Orleans) **Daily Picayune,** *March 16, 1884.*

This personal letter to Crockett's oldest son, John Wesley, is singular in its mention of Crockett's wife in the closing lines. Some Crockett biographers have claimed, with very little evidence, that the couple was estranged, but this letter indicates that was not the case.

*   *   *   *   *

LETTER TO CHARLES SHULTZ, DECEMBER 25, 1834.

Washington City
25th Decr 1834

Dear Sir

I wrote you a Short time ago and as I have caut a leasure moment I will write a gain although I can ad but little Times is still no report yet from the Committee of either house upon the French war recommendation I suspect when that report comes in to see the home Strings brake the western and Southern men dare not to Sustain Jackson in his mad Carear and when they refuse all the Blood hounds in the nation will be let loos on them

The time has come that men is expected to be transfarable and as negotiable as a promisary note of hand in these days of Glory and Jackson & reform & co—little Vann Sets in his chair and looks Sly as a red fox and I have no doubt but that he thinks Andrew Jackson has full powar to transfer the people of these united States at his will and I am truly afread that a majority of the free Citizens of these united States will Submit to it and Say amen Jackson done it it is right If we Judge by the past we can make no other Calculations

I have almost given up the Ship as lost I have gone so far as to declare that if he martin vanburen is elected that I will leave the united states for I never will live under his king dom before I will Submit to his government I will go to the wildes of Texes I will consider that government a Paradice to what this will be in fact at this time our Republican Government has dwindled almost into insignificancy our bosted land of liberty have almost Bowed to the yoke of [of] Bondage our happy days of Republican principles are near at an end and when a few is to transfer the many this is Vanburen principles there is more Slaves in New York and Pennsylvana then there is in Virginia and South Carolina and they are the meanest kind of Slaves they are Volunteer Slaves our Southern Slaves is of Some uses to the owner they will make Support for their masters and those others is of no other use than to make mischief I must close with a hope of Seeing better times

I am with great respects your friend & obt servt
David Crockett

Charles Shultz

PS will you get a paper from your editor that Contains the procedings of the days I Spent in your City last summer on my way home pleas to get it and enclose it to me as Soon as convenient and oblidge your friend
DC

David Crockett to Charles S[c]hultz, December 25, 1834, courtesy of the Gilder Lehrman Collection, GLC01162. Not to be reproduced without written permission.

Charles Shultz (or Schultz) was a resident of Cincinnati, Ohio, who likely met Crockett during his tour.

*   *   *   *   *

LETTER TO JOHN P. ASH, DECEMBER 27, 1834.

Washington City
27th Decr 1834

Dear Sir

Your friendly favor Came Safe to hand from two or three days ago And I would have answered it before this But I had a desire to informe you the feeling of the house upon the French question as you had a desire to know how parties Stands up on that question There is no report made yet to either house So that I can only give you my own oppinion

When the reports is made we will then See how many Blood hounds the hero of two wars will have to go with him Involving thirteen milions of Souls in a war with a people that have always been our best friend and in fact helped us to obtain the liberty we now enjoy when we know that the Executive of that nation is doing all in his powar to have the appropriation made the fact is I do think his measure was two rash If our minister Reeves had not Come home and boasted that he had over reached the French in the treaty and our papers got to Boasting about it to Show that Jackson had done more than Mr Adams Could do the french would not have objected to the pay ment at all

My own opinion is that the recommendation was made for no other purpose in the world than to rais an excitement to draw the Public attention from an envestigation of the abominable corrupt measures of this Adminestration they know that if the public were to get in possession of their inequitis acts and know the true Situation of this once happy Country it would Blow them all to the devil I do hope the people will view the measure as it deservs It Sertainly will a waken the people if any thing will—But I have almost lost all hopes from the late elections in New York & Pennsylvana It appears as if Jackson can do any thing he pleases and the people will Say it is right Jackson Says So—I am not Certain that the people will object to being transfered by Jackson over to that Political Judeas little Van If So I have sworn for the last four years that if Vanburen is our next President I will leave the united States I will not live under his king dom and I see no chance to beat him at present every thing apears favourable to him and I am sorry for it I have said for the last four years that I would vote for the devil against Van and any man under the Sun against Jackson and I have got no better yet

I expect in a few days to be able to Convey the good news to my District of the passage of my occupant land Bill The first Bill that will come up and I have no fears of its passage every member from Tennessee that I have talked to says it will pass if So it will Bless many a poor man with a home I See that they have got out Adam Huntsman & Mcmeans Both and if they run Both I am of opinion I will beat them I cannot tell I am determened to do my duty if I should niver see another Congress I must close by subscribing my self your friend and obt Servent

David Crockett
John P. Ash

University Archives and Special Collections, Sewanee: The University of the South.

The *(Dallas, Texas) Weekly Times Herald* **reprinted the letter on June 21, 1890, but misidentified John P. Ash as John B. Ashe and claimed the letter was from Fayetteville, North Carolina. The December 31, 1834, issue of the** *(Jackson) Southern Statesman* **published an anonymous letter from someone identified only as a Crockett constituent and supporter, which was likely the letter Ash had sent to Crockett. Crockett supplied that letter to the** *Statesman* **with his response, which was consistent with the published letter's contents.**

*   *   *   *   *

1835:

LETTER TO CAREY AND HART, JANUARY 1, 1835.

Washington City
1st January 1835

Mrrrs Cary & Hart

Gentle men I here enclose you the Title page of the new Book and it is my wish if it doesn't pleas you as you have the other Book and perhaps may think of something that may pleas you better you are at liberty to make any thing to suit your selves Mr Clark thinks this one will do though you know Best

I have given Mr. Clark my whole towar to the east and Back and I have no doubt but that it will make much more than Mr. Clark thinks it will do of this you can be the judge of when you see it

You wrote me that you would accept a draft at sixty days after date for 150 dollars If you could make it two hundred it would be a great accomodation to me at this time and I would feel under lasting obligations to you I do not wish to decieve any boddy on next tuesday I am compeld to pay the money and if you can send me your acceptince for what you can do it will save me the trouble of getting an indorser on it of this you are better acquainted with the nature of than I am I do not wish to put you to any inconvenience I hope you will have time to send it on to me by tuesday so that I may get my self out of this tite place

I enclosed you Mr Asguads letter a few days ago—and you shall have the whole of the work before the time agreed upon Mr Clark has been engaged in the Business of investigating the post office department so that he could not keep pace with me

I am preparing a Circular address to my constituents which I am of opinion would compose an enteresting part of my Book of this I will leave you to judge when you see it

I must close and remain with great respects your friend & obt servt

David Crockett

Courtesy, David Zucker Collection.

"Mr Asguads" is the artist Samuel Osgood. "Mr Clark" is another reference to Congressman William Clark of Pennsylvania, who was assisting Crockett with the book about his tour.

*　　*　　*　　*　　*

LETTER TO CAREY AND HART, JANUARY 8, 1835.

Washington City, 8th January 1835

Mssrs Cary & Hart

Gentlemen your favor enclosing the acceptance for two hundred dollars came safe to hand for which I feel under many obligations for I was with Mr Clark this morning and he red me what he had finished of the Book and I have no doubt of its filling your actpectation it must Sell

I am at prisent preparing an answer to Bentons letter to the convention of Mississippi I was asked by the same state to run for the Presidency and this gives me an excuse to answer him at length which will compose part of the Book and I will try and make it as interesting as any part of it you shall have it as soon as posable

I am with respects our obt servt

D Crockett

PS excuse my scrall I am in hast

Vertical File, H. Furlong Baldwin Library, Maryland Historical Society.

Early in 1834, a committee from Mississippi asked Crockett for permission to offer him as a candidate for the presidency. (See letter from "Two Citizens," January 12, 1834, and Crockett's reply of February 24, 1834.) He used the offer a year later to help lampoon the Jacksonians. Late in the fall of 1834, the Mississippi Convention asked Thomas Hart Benton, a senator from Missouri and a popular Jacksonian, to run for vice president on a ticket opposing Martin Van Buren, Jackson's hand-picked successor. Benton declined in a letter written on December 16, 1834, recommending that the convention support Van Buren for president, thus dashing any hope that Benton would support the Whigs.

On January 1, 1835, Van Buren's supporters published a letter asking that Benton explain his reasons for declining the invitation to run. This request was clearly a transparent ploy to get Benton's letter published, which provided

terrific anti-Whig fodder. Benton gladly replied the next day and also included his letter to the Mississippi Convention, which he said had been intended for publication. The Van Buren press widely ran all three letters.

The *National Banner and Nashville Whig* ran the Benton letters on January 21, 1835, followed by a set of matching parody letters, allegedly penned by Crockett, published on January 26. The parody letters had been published earlier in Gales & Seaton's *National Intelligencer.* Crockett does appear to have played some role in drafting the letters, but they were very likely a team effort by the Whigs.

*   *   *   *   *

LETTER TO ELIZABETH CROWDER, JANUARY 11, 1835.

Washington City, 11th January 1835

Dear Madam

Your letter of the first Inst came to hand by this days mail and I will hasten to answer it

You enquire of me relative to my mother and suppose her and you to be related this I have but little doubt but to the extent I cannot say My mother was a young woman when she left Maryland and I am of opinion that her fathers name was Nathan Hawkins But as to this I am not certain as he was dead long before my remembrance my mother had a Brother Aaron & John & Nicholes & Nathan Sisters Ruth & who married a man by the name of Webb in east Tennessee and she had another sister named Elizabeth that married a man by the name of Lewis—in the same neighbourhood as holston river This has been so long ago—that as to particulars I cannot say more But from what you write I have no doubt you an my self are related to some extent but what I cannot say My mothers relations moved to Kentucky & ohio many years ago and I do not know what have become of them as I have niver herd of them since they have left Tennessee I do not know what more to say upon the subject

I am with great respects your obt servt

David Crockett

Elizabeth Crowder

Davy Crockett to Elizabeth Crowder, MSS 6955, Clifton Waller Barret Library of American Literature, Special Collections, University of Virginia Library.

*   *   *   *   *

LETTER TO CAREY AND HART, JANUARY 12, 1835.

Washington City
12th Jany 1835

Mssrs Cary & Hart

Gentle men your favor & title page was received on yesterday I went imediately to Mr Clark and showed it to him and he told me to call this morning and he would have a package ready for me which I send you—and am sorry there is not more of it done I intend to try and have my part done this week or in the early part of next

Mr Clark has been engaged in the Post Office Committee so that he cannot keep pace with me But he sais he will soon be done and then he can in a few days finish you have stated that it is written by my self I would rather if you think it could sell as well that you had stated that it was written from notes furnished by my self But as to this I am not particular more than it will perhaps give some people a chance to cast reflections on me as to the correctness of it and as the design of it will be to make it as amusing as posable I thought I would sugest this Idea to you you can think of it and do as you think best—I hope you will answer this and let me know what you think of it what is prepared

I am with great respects your friend & obt servt

David Crockett

Courtesy of the New-York Historical Society, Misc. Mss. Crockett, David.

*   *   *   *   *

PARODY LETTER ADDRESSED TO CROCKETT, BURLESQUING A REQUEST SENT TO THOMAS HART BENTON, AND CROCKETT'S RESPONSE. *(WASHINGTON) DAILY NATIONAL INTELLIGENCER,* **JANUARY 12, 1835.**

Washington City, January 7, 1835

Hon. David Crockett,

Dear Sir: We have learned, because you secretly informed us, that you have declined permitting your name to be used as a candidate for the Presidency of the United States, and that you have addressed a letter to that effect, some time since, to the Committee of the Convention of Mississippi, by whom you were nominated for that high office. Upon a private understanding between you and ourselves, and a number of our friends held in a kind of caucus, it has been concluded that we should come out in a seeming open application for a copy of your letter, pretending that it is important that your friends else-where, as well as in Mississippi, may have an early opportunity of turning their attention to some other suitable person, but really to give you an occasion to play off upon the public one of your best efforts for effect, and to keep up the humbuggery of the Bank, Gold Currency, and all that sort of thing so necessary to blind the people, and keep our party together.

Yours, with great respect,

Nicholas Banks, of Pennsylvania
Andrew J. Bulion, of Indiana
Thos. B. Goldwire, of New Hampshire
Martin V. Trashmoney, of New York

[Crockett's tongue-in-cheek parody "response" to the above:]

To the Committee

Washington City, Jan. 8, 1835.

Gentlemen: I send you a copy of the letter you wish. It is not my wish to take advantage of any body. I never said I cared about being President now, and so I have writ to all my friends in private letters and when I talked about it I always talked that way. As Mississippi was the first State, (and I expected it would be the last) that nominated me for the "Government," I writ the letter and sent it there to be printed, to show that I did'nt go off half-cocked, and to keep people from thinking that I had refused before I was ready. But as I want another man elected in the north, that I may have a sort of a plea to come in next time myself from the South West, and as I see some people are going to try to hunt for themselves, and don't seem to be after the same game that I am, but are scouting all about to start other sport, and seem to be barking up the wrong sappling, I want to blow 'em off and put 'em on the right trail. But as we understand each other, I shan't say any more but just send you the letter, and am glad you mean to publish it.

Your friend,

David Crockett

To the Committee.

   The first Benton parody letter, fictionally dated January 7, 1835, spoofed the letter from Van Buren backers to Benton asking him to explain why he had declined to run with the Whigs. Here, however, a fictional group of Crockett backers ("Nicholas Banks," "Andrew J. Bullion," "Thomas B. Goldwire," and "Martin V. Trashmoney") asked Crockett to make public his letter to the Mississippi Convention. Crockett's satirical reply, dated January 8, 1835, explains that he declined to run because he believed that a northerner should be president, but that he might run the next time and noted that he had enclosed his letter to the Mississippi Convention. That letter, falsely (and deliberately) dated December 1, 1833, parodies Benton's letter to that body. The 1833 date was intended to make it look like Crockett had written it earlier, but was actually penned at the same time that the other two parody letters were. It appears below, out of date order, as Crockett appended it to those other letters. In fact, there is no evidence that Crockett was asked to run in 1833, nor has any authentic letter from that year been found. However, in 1834 two unidentified citizens from Lowndes County, Mississippi, did ask Crockett's permission to place his name in nomination, but Crockett politely turned them down (see letter dated January 12, 1834 from "Two Citizens" of Lowndes County, Mississippi, and Crockett's response to the Mississippi Congressional Delegation, dated February 24, 1834).

*   *   *   *   *

CROCKETT'S COMPLETE PARODY LETTER TO MISSISSIPPI CONVENTION. *(WASHINGTON) DAILY NATIONAL INTELLIGENCER*, JANUARY 12, 1835 (DELIBERATELY MISDATED DECEMBER 1, 1833).

Washington City
Dec. 1, 1833

Dear Sirs,

   I suppose the Democratic Convention is in earnest in recommending me to be the President of the U.S. There is so much trickery about that thing now a days, and so many sham nominations just to make people shew their hands, that I thought I would let you see that I know a thing or two myself, before I stated how thankful I am for your pitching on me for the Presidency. But I am sorry I don't want the office just now—I'm after another thing. I'm a very candid man, and when my mind is fixed upon a matter, you might as well try to stop gunpowder half blown up, as stop me. I can't agree to be President.

   The next election for President and Vice goes ahead of all the elections that ever took place in America, except when Jefferson and the present "Government" was elected. Them two beat all creation, because they fought for the "democratic principle." Now I should think the constitution quite gone unless the "democracy"—that is, our side, all the office holders in the country, and in Washington City, and at New York, and every where—carried the election in 1836. To win that election we must give item to one another. We must hang together like a pitch plaster to a bald pate. No flying off—no thinking for ourselves. One man must think for all. We mus'nt have but one candidate, and for that reason I won't go upon the list. I'll be a "voter," and this is a big character, able to shoulder a steamboat, and carry any candidate that the caucus at Baltimore may set up against the people. What's the people to a caucus? Nothing but a dead ague to an earthquake.

But, gentlemen, though I can't take the appointment myself, I will tell you who can, and you won't have to persuade him long neither. He will play shy at first, owing to his nature; but it ain't hard to bring him too. It is Mr. Martin Van Buren. Perhaps you never heard of him before. He never meddles in any body's business. I have known him a long time, and I can assure you he is all sorts of a great man. Where any other man has one good quality he has lots. We did'nt set in the same chair together more than two years, but fully half that time he was either in my lap or I in his, exchanging compliments, so that I know him better than a book, and can say, take him up one side and down the other, he is the most fitting man next to General Jackson, for the President, as any man that now hurrahs for hard money and the people. The way he is a Democrat, is a caution, all over. He is dyed in the wool, through and through, and comes as near to the red britches of Mr. Jefferson as a new patch upon an old garment can be made. As to ability, he himself don't know how much he knows; and if *he* don't, who can?

He ain't like any other living creatur; he can't be attacked—fights just as well behind as before—sees as well one way as another. They say his life is like a clean copy book; there is not a blot in any part of it; not a word nor letter scratched out, and every *i* dotted and every *t* crossed from one end to t'other. In his natral disposition, he is as tame as the present "government," and will just suit to come after it. The way his own State thinks of him outshines the yellar jackets. They have been stall-feeding him for 22 years, and have got him as slick as an ingon. His State is the biggest in the Union—has got two millions of people—42 members in Congress—the longest Canals—the largest ships—more banks – smaller notes—less cunning, and more honesty, than any State in the Union; and has never had a President yet—a great reason this for giving her one now. Though she has had three Vice Presidents out of seven, besides other high officers, from Alexander Hamilton down. But ignorant people, with a glib sort of tongue, says, what has he done? They ought to ask what has he not done? I would'nt answer the first question so far as the *people* is concerned, but for *his sake*, I will tell you what he has done. And not to get ahead of my story, I will go back to the time he began to be a politician. He set out with this rule—never to choose sides til he found out which was which, and if he happened to make a mistake, it was nothing to nobody, and things soon got straight. He never was wrong in any dispute if either side was right; that is, he was always right, unless both sides was wrong. He broke up a whole Legislatur in New York to support Mr. Madison in the war, and threatened to turn him out of his government, and put Mr. Clinton in; but failing in this, he turned over agin and tried to break down Mr. Clinton, in New York. All the time he was for the war, he was making the people believe Mr. Madison was not to be trusted; and there has been pieces printed from his speeches, and will be printed over, I suppose, shewing how he abused Mr. Madison's government. Then he praised Mr. Clinton, and afterwards turned right round and talked t'other way. He was all sorts of a member in the New York Legislatur. He was one of the litter of great men that was got by the *War* out of the *Old U.S. Bank*. He took sides with his father, and went his death against his mother. He was the very man for the times—talk—write—fight—bring in bills—laugh—make bows—draw State papers, which, finally made the federal party smell the patching that drove them from the field in April, 1814. This was a rale New Orleans scrape, and it was a long time before the people at Washington found out which was the biggest affair. But Mr. Van Buren always give up that Orleans was the greatest. Now, so much for the question, what has he done?

It is true, he voted for the Tariff of 1828, "that bill of abominations," as it was then called, but he was obliged to do that; his Legislature instructed him; but some have said, that they instructed him by his own request, for his friends have boasted that he has never seen the day for the last ten years, that he couldn't make a New York Legislature do as he wanted them. But this vote proves what I said before. He went against the Tariff at home, called the Harrisburgh Convention, while it was hatching this very Tariff bill of 1828, a trick and turn over to make a President, and then goes to Congress and votes for it. Don't this look like a man can't well be wrong that takes both sides? It looks a little curious that a man should go against a measure at home, speak in public, write agin it, abuse it as a fraud, and a trick and get elected under these circumstances and then get the very Legislature that elects him to tell him to vote against his own "graphic" speeches and for a "measure proceeding more from the CLOSET than from the WORKSHOP." This is the way he got the name of a MAGICIAN, and it looks a good deal like it to a man up in a tree.

Mr. Van Buren has been more scandalized than any man in the world, not excepting Mr. Jefferson. Every body has combined against him. He has never interfered with any body at all. If it hadn't been for this, he would have been Gen. Jackson's favorite, and he would have made him his successor. But they poured so much poison in the old man's ears about his conduct against the Seminoles, that he never could bear Van Buren any more. And he, poor man, gave up his Secretaryship, rather than have any fuss. He has never complained, and bore it all like a Christian. Now, some people have said, that he was first for Crawford, against Jackson, and Jackson's South Carolina friends; and then he was for Adams, and finally he came in at the eleventh hour for Jackson, got into the great nest of Jackson's first and last friends, rooted 'em out, took their place, and they even go so far as to say, that he is the choice of Gen. Jackson for President. But this ain't so; if it was, it would make him look again a little like a *Magician*.

He has been accused about the Safety Fund Banks in New York. Now, people don't know anything about these banks. Mr. Van Buren has always been in favor of "hard money," and he always obstinately refused to let any more than 150 banks be chartered at one time in New York; and then he said, and stood to it, they shouldn't issue notes lower than a *quarter of a dollar;* for if they went for notes under that, it would drive all the specie out of the country. And then again he provided, that for every sixty-three dollars issued in paper, there should be one dollar in silver; but, not satisfied with making the notes secure, by providing the above specie to take 'em up, he said that if one bank failed, all the others should make it good. Now, this is the Safety Fund system of New York. These banks are all in a league; and, to keep their privileges, and to keep up one another, and to keep up their party, they have a joint fund, that is always subject to party purposes, to pay for votes, for treating, for travelling, for printing, for handbills, and for every thing that is necessary to carry an election. All this is managed at Albany, and is called the Albany Regency. Now by this system New York has sound politics, sound morals, and *hard money*. How can any body blame him for the Safety Fund Banks?

Then too, he has gone with all his might against the U.S. Bank; but is in favor of its Branches, if they will put 'em in New York. Bad as the Bank is, he wrote for one to be put up in Utica, and his friends denied this till they proved it upon him by his letter, and because they happened to forget about his trying to get this Branch. His enemies want to make out that he rows one way and looks another, and this is the kind of proof that is to make a man a double dealer! a magician!

They call him non-committal, too, and this is because he always looks before he leaps. They say he never gives the measure of his foot. Now how can this be, when it is shewn that he speaks against the Tariff at home, and votes for it in Congress; goes for internal improvement by the General Government in New York, but against it out of it; goes against the Bank at Philadelphia, but in favor of it at Utica; goes for all the candidates for President in turn, Jackson last, notwithstanding which they say he is in higher favor there now than those that began before him. Went for the war, but went against Madison; wanted to turn out Madison, and put in Clinton, and then turned Clinton out from the little office he held in New York. Goes for gold and hard money, and has more rag money in his State than all the other States put together. Call you this non-committal? As well may you call the fingers of a watch non-committal, that goes regular round to every figure on its face.

I have gone through what they say against Mr. Van Buren, and now I must speak about our sticking together; every thing for Van Buren, nothing for nobody else—that is, nothing for Judge White; for to tell you the truth the whole of this letter is just intended to keep the people from opening their eyes. Some very good honest Jackson men are foolish enough to think they ought to have an opinion of their own, and talk about it quite grave. The words 'Magician,' 'little Magician,' 'non-committal,' 'safety fund,' 'Albany Regency,' 'New York tactics,' and such like have been named so often they begin to think there is something in it, and say, where there is so much smoke there must be fire, or, as we hunters used to say, where there is so much sign there must be game. Now Mr. Van and me, and the men that wrote to send 'em this letter to be published; and a good many of our folks, have all got together, and we think by making a great rush upon these free thinkers we can whip 'em back into the party, and make 'em stand up to their rack, fodder or no fodder. This letter is all for that purpose. I know, and we all know, that one half of it isn't true, and the other is trash. My friends said to me, your name sounds big, and if you come out and make believe that you don't want to be President, and talk about democracy, aristocracy, Jefferson, Madison, Crawford, persecution, the war, the Bank, gold currency, hard money, but, above all, Jackson and the Battle of New Orleans, and then hurra for union, harmony, concession, Van Buren, and the great State of New York; the seceders will tack and run back into the democratic republican fold, which means the Van Buren fold.

You must take notice that I am slabb'd off from the election, and am nothing but a "voter," and this gives me the right to dictate to the rest, and to tell them that I have no concern but to keep the democratic party united. Shallow-headed men won't see into this, and then I can go on to say you ought to elect Mr. Van Buren, because he is from the North. If we can keep things straight till we do this, the next time the President must come from the South-west, and then where do I stand? By that time the party will be so well drilled that they will take any body that the party says they must take, and, in the mean time, I think I can cry Bank! Bank! Monster! Corruption! Gold! Hard-money! Democracy! and all that, so that, if you will recommend me then, I'll be your man. If White should be elected now, that will be two Presidents from the South-west, and then I can't possibly get in; but take Van Buren, and by the time his term is up Judge White will never be in *my way*. It is true Judge White is as good a Jeffersonian as Martin Van Buren, but no better; and besides, he shouldered the musket, and fought bravely through the last war, (to say more might look like envy.) But if we elect him it will be greedy— look like we wanted all the Presidents. It would break up the democratic party—set the States together by the ears, and place the country in the frghtful situation in which it was situated when Virginia gave us four democratic Presidents—three hand running. It won't do. Let the next President come from the North, and then I go with all my heart for a South-west President, the time after, and that President shall be myself. Hoping that you will not forget me eight years hence, and that we can keep the People from thinking for themselves against a Caucus nomination,

I am your fellow-citizen,

David Crockett

*   *   *   *   *

LETTER TO THE *(JACKSON, TENNESSEE) TRUTH TELLER*, **EARLY JANUARY, 1835, PUBLISHED IN THE** *(WASHINGTON) NATIONAL INTELLIGENCER*, **FEBRUARY 20, 1835, TAKEN FROM THE** *LYNCHBURG VIRGINIAN* **(N.D.).**

Washington City
Early January 1835 [possibly January 13th]

I called last evening to see Judge White. Mr. Luke Lea, Mr. Bunch and Mr. Standifer all board at the same house with the judge. My business was to see a letter that Mr. Lea had received from the Judge, in answer to the one that the delegation from Tennessee had addressed to him, that is, all except two—Mr. Polk and Mr. Cave Johnson; and his honor, Mr. Grundy, refused to sign it. The balance of us, every one, signed it; and when I wrote you before, I did believe that not a member from the State would refuse; but as to that I was mistaken, for I find two Representatives and one Senator on the other side. But I cannot believe that their districts are with them, though this is none of my business—so I expect the best way is for every one to take care of his own.

The Judge says, in reply to us, as much as we could expect of him. He says the Presidency is a place that in no part of his life he ever wanted; nor did he ever believe himself qualified for the office; but that his services have been long before the people, and that he was in the hands of his friends; they could, if they choose, run his name, and if he was successful, it was an office that he could not decline; but if his friends choose to withdraw his, they would have his hearty approbation. This was as much as we could expect him to say. I do believe him the only man in the nation able to contend against little Van.

The office holders have got their champion, Mr. Benton, to come out in a long letter, which I will send you, and I sent you the paper on yesterday that contained my answer to it. The Van Buren party are sending off wagon loads of them, printed in pamphlet form. I do hope the people will not be duped by it. My letter was intended for a burlesque on it, and I hope it may have the desired effect. I am satisfied that his letter was intended to alarm Judge White and his friends, and drive them from the field; but I hope to see them stand firm—they cannot be beaten by the caucus system.

DAVID CROCKETT

Crockett and all the members of the Tennessee congressional delegation, save James Polk and Cave Johnson, petitioned Tennessee Senator (Judge) Hugh Lawson White to run for president in opposition to Martin Van Buren. Crockett further comments on the Benton parody letter.

In his January 8, 1835 letter to Carey and Hart, Crockett mentioned that he was preparing the parody, or burlesque of Benton's letters. In this letter he says that he had already sent the published parodies to the *Truth Teller*. Since the letters were published by the *Intelligencer* on January 12, the approximate date of this letter is January 13.

This transcript of the letter is taken from the *(Washington) National Intelligencer*, February 20, 1835, which states that it is reprinted from the *Lynchburg Virginian*, but gives no date. The *Virginian's* preface to the letter states that it was written "to the Editor of a paper published in [Crockett's] Congressional District." The *Macon Telegraph* of March 12, 1835, printed a truncated version of the letter and stated that the original was published in the *Truth Teller* on January 13, 1835, which seems too early if Crockett enclosed published material that had only appeared on January 12.

Luke Lea (1783–1851), Pryor Lea's brother, served as a congressman from Tennessee's Third Congressional District (1833-37) and as secretary of state of Tennessee (1835-39).

*   *   *   *   *

LETTER TO CAREY AND HART, JANUARY 22, 1835.

Washington City
22nd January 1835

Messrs Cary & Hart

Gentle men

Yours enclosing one to Mr Clark was red and I will hasten to answer it I have finished my part of the Book and am truly sorry that Mr Clark is hardly able to set up This you know I cannot help I took my manuscripts to Mr Clark on yesterday and he said if he was able to set up he could finish In a few days

I wrote on to Boston to Mr Abbot Lawrance to send me a full statement of one weeks work of all the manufactorys at Lowell I have recd a letter from him that he was preparing it for me and would send it on in a few days It is one metirial that I want in the Book

I regret that Mr Clark has been taken down as bad as you can I Just wint a head until I finished my part I will write a short article giving the idea that I am going over to put things to rights with Lewis – Philips and the king of england This is all I lack Mr Clark sais he can make as good a Book as you ever published out of the metirials that I have furnished to him

You say that it will not do to write little vans life this winter I am not going to give him a chance at me for a libel what I write will be true we will say no thing more on this I will write it and Bring it on as I go home then you can read it and Judge for your self and we can then talk more about that matter I will hurry Mr Clark all I can

I have a fight this morning between Mr Wise member of the H R and Mr Coke the former member from the Same District The news has come in that Wise is shot I cannot tell whether this is true or false

I am with great respects

Your friend and obt servt

David Crockett

David Crockett, ALS: Washington, D.C., to Carey & Hart, 1835 Jan. 22 (AMs 773/3), Rosenbach Museum & Library, Philadelphia, Pennsylvania.

Crockett comically boasts of his expertise in foreign affairs, and claims he will "put things to right" with Lewis-Philips, meaning Louis-Philippe I, king of France. Crockett mentioned his next proposal, a book about "little vans life," but Carey and Hart seemed reluctant to publish an unauthorized biography of Van Buren, written under Crockett's name, fearing charges of libel.

Henry Wise took Richard Coke Jr.'s Virginia congressional seat after a particularly nasty campaign in 1832. The animosity between the two men was undiminished after Wise's election, and on January 22, 1835, they fought a duel wherein Wise shot Coke through the right elbow. After receiving the nonfatal wound, Coke shook hands with Wise, ending their feud. Barton H. Wise, *The Life of Henry A. Wise* (New York: MacMillan, 1899), 36–41.)

*   *   *   *   *

LETTER TO UNKNOWN RECIPIENT, JANUARY 24, 1835.

Washington City
24th January, 1835

Dear Sir
  Your note of the 20th inst came to hand by this morning's mail and I hasten to answer its contents.
  You request me to send you my signature, which I do with Great pleasure, and I have no doubt if you wish a similar favor from any other member of either house they will fill your request by application.

I remain with great repect

Your obt. Servt.

David Crockett

Published in (Des Moines, Iowa) Daily State Register, *January 1, 1868.*

*   *   *   *   *

LETTER TO R. R. WALDRON, FEBRUARY 2, 1835 (PARTIAL TRANSCRIPT).

Washington City
February 2 1835

  We have had a small show for a French war, but it has blown over for the present and I am of the opinion not much to the credit of the President. A strange occurence took place here on last friday when the funeral procession of W. R. Davis was leaving the Capitol a man by the name of Rich'd Lawrence had prepared him self with two purcussion Pistols and snapped Both at the presidents Breast with in a few feet he was arested and is now in Joal it is said he is deranged and sais he is Richd the third and that Jackson is his servant and has usurped power . . . and that he will kill him—The President run a narrow escape Both Pistols has been examined and found to be well charged . . .

. . . We are about to run him against little *van*, if we do we will Beat down the drilld System of hirelands or Slaves . . .

Partial transcript from Charles Hamilton Auction Catalog, *September 22, 1966, item 62.*

  The description in the Hamilton catalog explains that in addition to the Jackson assassination attempt, the letter discusses John Quincy Adams, the Marquis de Lafayette, and Hugh Lawson White, to whom the last sentence above refers. The attempt on Jackson's life was made on January 8, 1835. Crockett was present and helped to restrain the would-be assassin.
  The letter is addressed to R. R. Waldron at Rio de Janeiro. Waldron was a purser in the navy serving on the U.S. schooner *Enterprise*, which was based out of Rio de Janeiro while exploring the East Indies. *Baltimore Gazette*, August, 22, 1835. Waldron's connection with Crockett is unclear.

*   *   *   *   *

LETTER TO LEVI WOODBURY, FEBRUARY 2, 1835.

H.R.
2nd Febry 1835

Will the Secratery of the navey examin the enclosed letter and ["with" crossed out] and Send me an answer that I can enclose to the applicant the earley attention to this will oblige your

obt servt

David Crockett

Hon. Levy Woodberry

Architectural Digest, December 1988, 156–59, 210–12, which cites Walter R. Benjamin Autographs, Inc., Hunter, N.Y.

Levi Woodbury (which Crockett has misspelled "Levy Woodberry") was elected to the U. S. Senate as a Jacksonian from New Hampshire and served from March 16, 1825, to March 3, 1831. He served as Jackson's Secretary of the Navy 1831-1834, and as Secretary of the Treasury 1834-1841, so he was not Secretary of the Navy when Crockett wrote this letter. Since Crockett asks "will the Secratery of the navey," rather than simply *"will you,"* it is possible that he wanted Woodbury to pass this request to his successor.

Woodbury was again elected to the U.S. Senate, as a Democrat, and served from March 4, 1841, to November 20, 1845. He was later appointed Associate Justice of the Supreme Court of the United States.

*   *   *   *   *

LETTER TO CAREY AND HART, FEBRUARY 6, 1835.

Washington City
6 February 1835

I regret Extremely that you have not got the work ready agreable to contract But I hope you will not think Hard of me as I had my part ready in time and if Mr Clark had not Benn taken down [ill] I have no doubt but that he would have his done I called on him…and he red me a letter from you speaking of the printed speech at Boston I had got Mr Sargent of Boston to procure it for me and… did not get it I have this morning sent to Genl Davis of Boston to procure a Coppy and enclose it to you as soon as posable The Genl was with me when I made the Speech and I hope he may get it and send it to you…Mr Clark sais he will finish in a few days and send it all on to you

I am with great respects
Your friend and obt servt

D Crockett

Christie's Auction Catalog, June 9, 1999, item 180.

The auction catalog partially quotes the letter and includes a photograph of a small section of the holograph; the present owner is unknown.

*   *   *   *   *

LETTER TO CAREY AND HART, FEBRUARY 9, 1835.

Washington City
9th Febry 1835

Mrrrs Cary & Hart

Gentlemen

I this day enclosed you two paikeges enclosed in one from Mr. Clark and he sais he will give me the amount of the gap which was lost by some of the neglect of the Post office

I am truly Sorry that Mr. Clark have not got on faster with it I cannot help him any more as I have given him all the notes and my Speech at Cincinati & at Louisville & Elizabeth Town on my way here I hope it may fill your expectation when done will you pleas to write me if you receive my printed Speech from Boston

Your friend
David Crockett

Sotheby Parke-Bernet Auction Catalog, February 27–28, 1974, Lot 261.

Crockett was referring to his forthcoming book *An Account of Col. Crockett's Tour to the North and Down East* (Baltimore, E. L. Carey and A. Hart: 1835), which was being composed by Pennsylvania Congressman William Clark from notes provided by Crockett. Clark, a member of the Anti-Masonic Party, served in the Twenty-third and Twenty-fourth Congresses (March 4, 1833-March 3, 1837).

*   *   *   *   *

LETTER FROM NICHOLAS BIDDLE TO CROCKETT, FEBRUARY 16, 1835.

Philad.
Feby 16th, 1835

Dear Sir

I have had the pleasure of receiving your favor of the 10th inst, and will be glad to do any thing in my power to accomodate you in the business to which it related.

Your note for $541.70 falls due at the Bank on the 19th of March next. It would be well at that time to pay what you can, if you cannot pay the whole. Suppose for instance you could reduce it to $400, then you might let it run to next Christmas. Let me know how much you can pay – and I will send you the notes for renewal, with the proper calculations.

Very truly

N Biddle

Hon. David Crockett

Manuscript Division, Library of Congress.

*   *   *   *   *

LETTER TO JAMES M. SANDERSON, FEBRUARY 18, 1835.

Washington City
18th February 1835

Dear Sir,

Your favor enclosing your advertisements and I will put up one in each of the great taverns in this city so that the people can read them and then be their own Judgez.

I will give you a Call on my way home. You wright me to say to you what kind of a Shot pouch to have made when I come on I will then Consult you upon that I expect to stay two or three days in your city and then I can get Such mitirials as I want

Rumer is afloat that there is news from france whether true or false I do not know

I am with great respects
your obt servt
David Crockett

Courtesy of the Phil Collins Collection.

For more information on James M. Sanderson see Crockett's June 25, 1834 letter to him.

*   *   *   *   *

LETTER TO CAREY AND HART, APRIL 16, 1835.

At home Weakley County Tennessee
April 16th 1835

Mrrrs Cary & Hart

Gentle men on yesterday I received the enclosed coppy write for the Book I forgot to get Mr Clark to send it to you But I hope it will make no differance

I had quite a pleasant trip home from Philadelphia and found all well I have commenced my canvass and have made three Speeches in three differant countys and I see nothing to dread I am told that Huntsman will run a gainst me Mcmeans has with drawn and I am still of opinion Huntsman will also with draw if he does not I have no doubt of beating him with ease I do believe I will get a better vote in the District than I ever got Jacksons will or his letter to parson Gwin has killed Jackson in this district the people here cannot be tranferred by the will of Andrew Jackson to little van The people here are all for Judge White and I go for him he could beat Jackson in this State The brightest day he ever Seen Judge White has been a favorite in Tennessee for the last twenty years

I have been looking for a letter from Judge Clayton in answer to the one I wrote him in your Store upon the subject of the other Book but have not yet recd any will you pleas to write me if you have had any answer from him and to what effect – I am anxious to here how he is coming on with the life of Van Pleas to answer this and direct your letter to Crocketts P O Gibson County Tennessee that is my nearest Post office get Mr Hart to write as I can read his writing best

I am with great respects your friend & obt servt

David Crockett

Haverford College Library, Haverford PA, Special Collections, Charles Roberts Autograph Letters Collection (collection 245).

"Parson Gwin" was the Reverend James Gwynn, of Nashville, who had written a letter, published in the *Nashville Republican* critical of Jackson's support for a political convention that would nominate candidates for president and vice-president. Gwynn argued that Jackson was attempting to take the elections out of the hands of the people and put the choice of candidates in the hands of a select group in order to secure the nomination of Martin Van Buren. Jackson defended his position in a response of February 23, 1835, and though he denied that he was attempting to rig the election, he admitted a preference for Van Buren without naming him. Jackson wrote, "All my friends must perceive, that to be consistent, my preference, as far as men are concerned, ought to be for him that is most likely to be the choice of the great body of Republicans; and yet, if this individual should not be Judge White, the editor of the Republican is ready to cry out, 'Dictation.'" (Reprinted in the *New-Bedford* [Massachusetts] *Mercury*, April 3, 1835.) Crockett and others jumped on Jackson's remark and held it up as evidence of foul play. Judge Clayton was Georgia Senator Augustin Clayton, whom Crockett had solicited to ghost-write his biography of Van Buren.

*   *   *   *   *

LETTER FROM ANDREW JACKSON TO JAMES K. POLK, MAY 3, 1835.

Washington
May 3d 1835

My Dear Sir,

I have been awaiting with some anxiety for your promised letter. I have become fearful that ill health or some other cause has prevented you from writing as you promised, for I am sure the little noise, and various meetings got up by the instrumentality of Mr Bell and Co. cannot have alarmed *you*.

I have been a constant observer of human nature since my youth and in the political world there is not an exception, whenever a political man has abandoned the principles he avowed, and which acquired him the confidence of the people, where the people did not abandon them—witness Mr. Clay, Calhoun & the unfortunate Burr. Just so in the present case Mr. Bell, Davy Crockett & Co. had placed judge White in the odious attitude of abandoning principle & party for office, and with the association of the nullifiers in Congress put his name up to carry the state of Virginia by the force of judge Whites name and popularity! How they have failed, and in what position have the[y] placed themselves and the judge! In the ranks of the opposition! The eyes of the people soon were opened to the wicked plan, to divide and conquer the Democracy of the union, prostrate the present administration by making it odious, by crying out corruption and misrule, and being supported by office holders and corruption, thereby to bring into power the opposition, recharter the United States Bank, destroy the republican government & substitute in its stead, a consolidated government under the controle and management of a corrupt monied monopoly, which would destroy our republican institutions and place us under the despotic & corrupt rule of the U. States Bank. Mr Bell & Co. have not succeeded. Virginia is erect again. Fifteen members, who support a national convention, have been elected to congress, a majority in the House of delegates, Virginia, of from 25 to 30 & twelve majority in the Senate. Leigh & Tyler will be instructed to vote for Col Bentons expunging resolution. I say *expunge,* for there is no other word that can meet the case, judge Whites amendment to strike it out, to the contrary notwithstanding.

I now ask you to look at the position Messers Bell & Co, *now* stand in—identified with the blue light federalists and modern *wiggs,* in the north, and the nullifiers, in the south. Does not common sense tell every one that they must become as odious to the virtuous yeomanry of Tennessee as those men do. Can any one believe that the republicans of Tennessee will abandon their principles, and party, to support any man, or set of men, who have abandoned their republican principles for office sake. I tell you, *I know the Tennesseans better,* and have too high an opinion of their virtue & honesty, to believe it. *It is a slander upon them.* The only lasting popularity, is based upon this rule—take truth, & principle for the guide & public good the end constantly in view, and the people will sustain the man that practises fearlessly upon it. Political demagogues, hypocrites, and apostates, may delude the people for a short time, but the moment the deception, and abandonment of principle, is discovered, the people will hurl them from their confidence, and the *recoil is overwhelming*. Just so with Mr. Bell, Davy Crockett and Co. The moment the people of Virginia discovered the wicked movement, not one member of congress who raised the White Whigg flagg, but Tolliver, was elected, and he beat Chinn 50 votes on Chinn's vote against the 3,000,000 for preparation for contingent defense. That you may have a bird eye view of Virginia, I send you the Richmond Enquirer. Judge White cannot get one vote except in So. Carolina & Tennessee and surely Tennessee will never put herself in the false position of joining the piedbald opposition of Whiggs nullifiers, blue light Federalist, and Hartford convention men. It cannot be—heaven and every principle of virtue and republicanism forbid it! How much better it would have been for our old friend judge White to have taken the advice of his real friends—*to have stuck to his party, and old republican principles* [. . .] thrown himself on a convention fresh from the people, (not upon the repudiated caucus of a few members of Congress with Davy Crockett in the midst) where his true merits would have been considered, and where, I have but little doubt, he would have been taken up at least, for vice president. But as he is, he has abandoned the republican fold, and is forever lost in their estimation. He has been placed by Mr. Bell & Co, as the candidate of the opposition under the odious imputation of abandoning his old republican principles & *party*, for office, and whether he has or not the world has taken up that opinion, and he never can regain the confidence of that party again. The opposition never intended that he should be elected, they meant to use him to divide, that they might conquor for Mr Clay who, you may rely, is to be their candidate at last. There is one use that the nullifiers, I mean Calhoun & Co, mean to make of judge Whites names if they can. That is to build up a Southern confederacy, and divide the union, but I hope judge Whites eyes may be opened and he will *now* see that he is in a false position and abandon Bell, Davy Crockett & Co, and withdraw himself from the odious attitude these intriguing apostates have placed him.

You and Grundy, (by the true Republicans in Congress) are looked to, to take a firm and open stand in favour of the republican principles, a *national convention by the people,* and in toto against nullification & disunion and against little cacuses, of a few apostate members of Congress, & preserve Tennessee from the disgrace of uniting with the piebald opposition to put down my *administration and my fame* with it, and give the reigns of government into the hands of those who have secretly conspired to recharter the Bank. Look at its extended loans to upwards of 14,000,000—extending its loans on stock for three years, two after the expiration of its charter when all its banking power cease on the 3rd of March next, and say whether these are not signs of its intension to make another panic, and regain a charter of *the Bank*—or as Mr. Bell says, *a Bank*. We fight for principle, and it is expected all will take an open and vigorous stand to perpetuate our glorious & happy republican system. Do your duty, (as you have here) *at home,* and you will stand high with the republicans every where. Connecticut and Rhode Island has faithfully done their duty. Rhode Island gives us a Senator, & Connecticut a full representation in congress, and can it be that Tennessee will abandon her republican principles and be ranked with apostates, nullifiers, & bluelight Federalist. Tristram Burges says she will. *Forbid it virtue, forbid it heaven.* Tennessee has sustained me thus far, and I trust she never will abandon her principles for any man. I write in great haste, and for your own eye, not for the papers. Present me & my household affectionately to your Lady & accept the same for yourself. . . .

Andrew Jackson

P.S. My health has been quite delicate, is better.
P.S. Say to col. Walker I have recd. his letter but ill health has prevented a reply.

In Herbert Weaver, editor, and Paul H. Bergeron, associate editor, **Correspondence of James K Polk, Volume 3, 1835–1836.** *(Knoxville, University of Tennessee Press, 1975,), 182–85.*

Jackson wrote "Private for your own eye—it is wrote in haste" at the top of the letter. The bracketed ellipsis [. . .] is present in Weaver and Bergeron's edition of Polk's correspondence, and evidently refers to an illegible word or words.

Jackson was particularly miffed at the Senate's censure of him and was insistent on having it expunged, lashing out at those who opposed that action. He was equally perturbed by the candidacy of Judge Hugh Lawson White for president and the support White had gained among most of the Tennessee congressional delegation, including Crockett and John Bell. White had opposed expunging the censure. Jackson's repeated mention of Crockett suggests that Jackson kept close track of what Crockett did and considered him a dangerous opponent of the administration's policies. In fact, Jackson had written to family and friends several times over the years complaining about Crockett's support of federal funding for internal improvements, his opposition to Jackson's Indian Removal Bill, and his recommendation against Jackson's nomination of his nephew, Stockley D. Hays, to be surveyor general for public lands "south of Tennessee."

It is ironic that both Crockett and Jackson invoke the word "principle" so often in defending their positions: Crockett in reference to his opposition to so many of Jackson's policies and what he considered the president's betrayal of his earlier principles, and Jackson to spew vitriol on anyone who did not share his view of what was in the best interests of the nation. The letter is an example of how unforgiving Jackson was of any opposition and how fawning he could be toward his loyal supporters, such as Grundy and Polk. While Jackson considered White's candidacy an act bordering on treachery, it was supported by those who favored a southern president over the president's chosen successor, Martin Van Buren, a northerner. Jackson's support for the concept of party loyalty over other considerations is the reverse image of Crockett's suspicion of such loyalties at the expense of principle.

Jackson's mention of the Bank's charter ending on March 3, 1836, is poignant; Crockett would find himself in the Alamo on that date, three days before the battle that took his life.

John Taliaferro was an anti-Jackson congressman from Virginia who became a Whig in 1835. He served in the Seventh, Twelfth, Eighteenth through Twenty-first, and Twenty-fourth through Twenty-seventh Congresses. Joseph W. Chinn was a Jacksonian representative in the Twenty-second and Twenty-third Congresses. *Biographical Directory of the United States Congress*, http://bioguide.congress.gov.

＊   ＊   ＊   ＊   ＊

LETTER TO THE *(JACKSON, TENNESSEE) TRUTH TELLER*, JUNE 5, 1835, PUBLISHED SAME DAY; REPRINTED IN THE *NASHVILLE BANNER AND WHIG*, JUNE 26, 1835.

Jackson, Ten, June 5th, 1835

To the Editor of the Truth Teller

Sir—Upon glancing over your paper of to-day, I discover an article addressed to myself and Mr. Huntsman, calling on us to state whether we are in favor of Col. John Bell, of Tennessee, for Speaker of the next Congress.

I am gratified to see this question before the country, as I conceive it one of great importance; and I do believe the next election for Speaker will have its influence in the next election for the Presidency, I can only say that I did support Mr. Bell for Speaker at the last Congress. Myself Mr. Peyton, Mr. Dickenson and Mr. Forrester were the only members from the State that did support Mr. Bell, as I understood and believe. I can also state that Mr. Bell more than filled expectation. He got what no other Speaker ever got since I have been in Congress—a unanimous vote of thanks. And I can say now, and at all times, that I will, if elected, vote for him against any man in the United States: I do consider him not only an honor to his District, but to the whole State of Tennessee.

I see that Mr. Van Buren and Col Johnson are nominated for President and Vice President by the Baltimore Convention; and we may expect to see the collar-dogs of *little Van* turned loose and set on Judge White and Mr. Bell. I now hope to see my countrymen do their duty, and stand by the country against dictation.

I remain your obedient servant,

David Crockett

*   *   *   *   *

LETTER TO CAREY AND HART, JULY 8, 1835.

At home Weakley County Tennessee
July 8th 1835

Messrs. Cary & Hart

gentlemen
    I have just returned from a two week Electionaring Canvass, and have spoken every day to large concourses of people with my competitor   I have him Badly Plagued   his name is Adam Huntsman   I tell him in my Speech that I have a great hope of writing one more Book and that shall be the second fall of Adam   I handle the administration with out gloves—and I do believe I will double my competitor   Jacksonism is dying here faster than I ever saw   I do believe he will be the most unpopular man in one more year that ever had any pretentions to the place he now fills
I recd your letter with your note for three hundred & fifty dollars and will go to town tomorrow to get it negotiated. I hope it may answer my purpose
    four weeks from tomorrow will end the dispute in our Elections   I do believe I will double my competitor and I have had an enteresting Canvass
Please to present me kindly to my friend george [?] & Mr. Biddle   tell them I am going a head and expects to see them and you this fall

I remain with great respects your friend & obt servt.

David Crockett

Courtesy of the Phil Collins Collection.

*   *   *   *   *

LETTER TO THE (*JACKSON, TENNESSEE*) *TRUTH TELLER*, **JULY 20, 1835.**

The Truth Teller
July 20th 1835

gentle men—
    I Some time Since made a Statement through the Paris paper Relative to a conversation that took place Between Judge Heskill and my self   I then stated the words as was stated to me by Judge Heskill and I have asked Esq Atckison to make a state ment through your paper if what was said to him by Judge Heskill and the word sent by him Atckison to me by Judge Heskell The Country can then Judge our State ments and decide as they may think proper
    I find in your paper an article signed by nine little gentle men two of which was certificate makers for Mr Fitzgerald four years ago when he beat me and all The Balance have at Every Election I ever had done all they could a gainst me and have Been Bussy in the present canvass

They say that I have made a Charge of Bribery & Corruption a gainst Gov Carroll and Call on me for proof I deny ever making any charge on Gov Carroll I mearly Stated what Judge Heskill had told me and I deny these <u>little gentle mens</u> the right to call on me for proof

I must pay a passing notice to his excellency Gov Carroll as he has made a direct Charge on me I will take the liberty to ask him two or three questions which are as follows I ask him if to Say whether or not he and Mr Vanburan did or did not walk hand and glove through the Capitol more than once last Spring was a year during the first session of the last Congress and whether or not he did or did not ride in Mr Van burans fine English Cariage with Mr Vanburan with his English horses and his white drivers with their gold & silver Band on their hats These are questions I ask Gov Carroll to answer as he sais he has had no letter from Mr VanBuran upon the subject of office or appointment these are questions I ask the Gov to answer for making the charge upon me in his late letter to Mr Mcmeans

Your comply and with this will obledge your obt servt

David Crockett

PS I also ask that Wm E Ball [?] and Samuel I Hayse to state through your paper whether or not they did or did not address a letter to Judge Heskill to admit or deny the state ment made in my letter to and whether or not they did not Sign a request to Colo John Read to come out and run for the Senate in opposition to Judge Heskill before the publication come out in answer to my letter—

David Crockett

Courtesy of the Gilder Lehrman Collection, GLC00631. Not to be reproduced without written permission.

"Judge Heskill" was Judge Joshua Haskell, a Crockett supporter. Crockett had publicly accused Gov. William Carroll, once a Crockett ally who had returned to the Jackson ranks, of being in league with Van Buren. Carroll's June 20 letter to James McMeans denying Crockett's charges was published in various newspapers. On July 12, Judge Haskell wrote a letter to the *Truth Teller* and denied that he had spoken of any collusion between Van Buren and Carroll. He wrote of Crockett, "The Colonel has fallen into the error by a misunderstanding or a misconstruction of the following conversation, &c, &c. (Here he goes on to state what he did say to Crockett, and Mr. C understood him)." Reprinted in the *Richmond (Virginia) Enquirer*, August 7, 1835.

*　　*　　*　　*　　*

LETTER TO THE *(WASHINGTON) NATIONAL INTELLIGENCER* AUGUST 10, 1835, PUBLISHED SEPTEMBER 2, 1835.

TO THE EDITORS
Weakley County,
Tennessee, August 10th, 1835

Messrs. Gales & Seaton:

As I have closed my canvass, and the result is known, I have concluded to drop you a line to inform you what I had to contend against. I had *Andrew Jackson* openly franking documents, and writing letters into my district. He even had my mileage and pay as a member of Congress drawn off, and franked it to the district, where it was published in a newspaper. His object was to hold out the idea to the People that I had taken pay for the same mileage that Mr. Fitzgerald did, when it is well known, all over the District, that Mr. Fitzgerald charged pay for thirteen hundred miles, and I charged for one thousand. The   *   *   *   *   *   *   stated that I ought to have charged but for seven hundred and fifty miles—a fact that he must know, every man that is acquainted with the district must know, is untrue.

The truth is, I do believe he is determined to expend every dollar of the Treasury, or make Van Buren his successor. I am determined to let the world know the means that have been resorted to for the purpose of defeating me. I had to contend against the whole popularity of Andrew Jackson and Governor Carroll, and the whole strength of the Union Bank. I have been told by good men that the managers of that Bank offered twenty-five dollars a vote for Mr. Huntsman. I had no Bank to aid me: I expected to have a fair race: but when the time came, and the polls opened, I found all Huntsman judges, and, in nearly all cases, Huntsman officers to hold the election. In fact I am astonished that I came as near beating him as I did. Men that were out of their County could vote for Mr. Huntsman, and, at the same place, when they would offer to vote for me, they were refused by the same judges. In fact, I see no hope. The People have almost given up to a *Dictator.* Andrew Jackson has franked loads of the extra Globe to every Post Office in this District, with a prospectus to get subscribers for it. Now I wish to ask the world a question, or the oldest man living, if they or he ever knew any President to serve out his time, and then to set down to open electioneering for his successor? The very paper franked by him, states that Judge White has sold himself to the Bank, and that there are no Jackson-White-men; that all must be Jackson-Van Buren-men. I have come to the conclusion, when the People will sanction the like of this, we have but little to hope, for I do believe Santa Ana's Kingdom will be a paradise, compared with this, in a few years. The People are nearly ready to take the yoke of bondage, and say "Amen! Jackson done it—it is all right!"

I have spoken what I thought, regardless of consequences, and have submitted to my fate without a murmur, and rejoice that I live in a district that has so near a majority of freemen in it. From the best information I can get, I will be beaten a few votes over two hundred in near ten thousand votes.

I am yours, &c.
DAVID CROCKETT

P.S. Correct errors, and publish this letter, and I take the responsibility.

[The good Colonel is so indignant at the arts by which his defeat has been effected, that he is not sparing of his rebuke of those who sit in high places. We have ventured indeed to soften his language in one or two passages, where it was rather too *energetic.* But the main fact stated by the Colonel is confirmed by publications in various Tennessee papers, and has indeed been admitted by the Official gazette, that the President of the United States has used his frank for the circulation, in the late canvass, of numbers of the Globe in the State of Tennessee. To this effect we find very direct and positive averments in an article in the Nashville Republican of the 10th instant, from which we extract the following: "it is a fact susceptible of proof, if denied—a fact within the knowledge of the People of a whole State—that numerous—not 'a *few only*—that hundreds, we believe we might safely add *thousands*, of Globes, containing the foulest slanders against Judge White and his leading friends, have been circulated, in this State, under the President's frank." Not only, we believe, has such a thing, never been done by any former President, but never has any thing like it been done by any President, or by his procurement. —*Nat. Intel.*]

Adam Huntsman refuted all of Crockett's charges in a long letter of September 23, 1835, to Gales and Seaton, published in the *Globe* on October 23, 1835. He ended his letter by writing "Now, I think if the Colonel and myself will weigh our grievances and compare notes together, we will come to the conclusion that they are about equal; and, as we passed through the canvass in friendship, we can mutually conclude that the reason why he lost the election was because he did not get votes enough."

*   *   *   *   *

LETTER TO CAREY AND HART, AUGUST 11, 1835.

Weakley County, Tennessee
August 11th 1835

Mrrrs Cary & Hart

    Gentle men I will now redeem my pledge to you my canvass is over and the result known I am beaton two hundred & thirty votes from the best infirmation I can get my object in writing you this letter is to inform you what I had to contend a gainst I had Mr Huntsman for my competitor aided by all the poppularity of both Andrew Jackson & Governer Carroll and the whole Strenth of the Union Bank at Jackson I have been told by good men that Some of the managers of the Bank on the day of the Election was herd say they would give 25 dollars a vote for votes enough to elect Mr Huntsman I have always believed Since Jackson removed the deposits that his whole object was to place the Treasury whare he could use it to influence elections and I do believe he is determened to sacrafise every dollar of the treasury or make the little flying doutchman his Successor I do know that for fourteen years Since I have been a candidate I never Saw Such means used to defeat any Candidate there was a disciplined band of Judges and officers to hold the election in all most every case Some officers held the election at the Same time had nearly all they was worth bet on Mr Huntsman I have no doubt that I was compleatly Raskeled out of my election I do regret that duty to my self & to my country compels me to expose such viloney

    Well might Gov Poindexter exclaim Oh my country what degradation though hast fallen in to Andrew Jackson was duren my election canvass franking the entre Globe with a prospectus in it to every post office in this district and upon one ocasion he had my miledge and pay as a member drawn of and Sent to this district to one of his minions to have it published Just a few days before the election he Stated that I had charged miledge for one thousand miles and that it was but Seven hundred & fifty miles and held out the Idea that I had to [illeg.] pay for the Same miledge that Mr Fitzgerald had taken when it was well known that he charged thirteen hundred miles from here to Washington and him and my self Both live in the same county The Genls Pet Mr Grundy charged for one thousand miles from Nashville to Washington and it was seanctined by the legislature I suppose because he would Huzzaw for Jackson and because I would not The Genl come out openly to Election a gainst me I now say that the oldest man living never herd of the president of a great nation to come down to open Electionaring for his successor We may truly say the poor old Superanuated man is surrounded by a poor Set of wretches using him to promote their own intrest in fact I do believe he is a perfect tool in their hands ready to be used to answer any purpose to either promote intrest or grattify ambition

    I come within 230 votes of being elected not withstanding I had to contend a gainst the greatest & best with the whole powar of the treasury a gainst me

    I am grattified that I have Spoken the truth to the people of my District regardless of Consequences I would not be compeld to bow to the Idol for a Seat in Congress during life I have never knew what it was to sacrafice my own Judgment to grattify any party and I have no doubt of the time being Close at hand when I will be rewarded for letting my tongue Speake what my hart thinks I have suffered my Self to be politically Sacrafised to save my country from ruin & disgrace and if I am never a gain elected I will have the grattification to know that I have done my duty

    I am in good health and hope these lines will find you & family in the alike I remain your obt servt

David Crockett

PS You may publish this letter it is the truth and I take the responsability in saying
DC

Vertical File, H. Furlong Baldwin Library, Maryland Historical Society.

*   *   *   *   *

LETTER DATED SEPTEMBER 30, 1835 TO FOURTEEN GENTLEMEN IN RESPONSE TO THEIR DINNER INVITATION.

Lagrange Fayette County
30th Sept 1835

Gentlemen
    In answer to our kind note inviting me to partake of a public dinner this day at the planters Hotel I am compeled to accept your invitation from a Since of Grattitude which I feel at all times willing to ac knowledge to my old friends & constituents
    I have anounced through the news papers that I never expect to offer my name a gain to the public for any office is one great reason of my acceptance of your kind offer I hope to Spend the evening in a Social manner leaving politicts out of the question as I hope never a gain middle my former political course is known to the public and I have not changed
    I am with great respects your friend & obt servt
David Crockett

Paris A Gorman
R. T Mahaffy
A B Gloster
F Hackney
H Atkinson
J.E Moody
E H Whitfield
Easton Morris
R J Sanford
R S Yancy
Thos B Firth
George Cossett
W Chase
D Jones

Provenance: "The White Mountain Collection," Matthew Bennett Sale #329, December 4, 2008, quoted by permission of the current owner.

*   *   *   *   *

LETTER TO GEORGE PATTON, OCTOBER 31, 1835.

Weakley County Tennessee
Octr 31st 1835

Dear Brother

I have concluded to drop you a line the whole Connection is well and I am on the eve of Starting to the Texes—on to morrow morning my self Abner Burgin and Lindsy K Tinkle & our Nephew William Patton from the lowar country this will make our Company we will go through Arkinsaw and I want to explore the Texes well before I return

I was greatly in hopes that you would have come out to court this week so that you Could have Answered the Bill and Seen your friends from the lowar Country Both William Patton and his brother in law Mr George W Harper Came to my house on Monday of Court and both went up and answered the Bill and if you had Come or Sent on your answer the Answers would all have been Complete They will take yours as Confessed

I am not the least uneasy about their gaining it Mr Burgin let William have a horse at one hundred dollars and I have paid Mr Harper one hundred & 25 dollars and I paid William a gun & Sadle and Some other things to the amount of Two-hundred-dollars—that I have paid them in all we have paid them three hundred They Brought Sufficient proof to Idintify them Selves—Mr george W Harper is a first rate Blacksmith and a Cleverer fellow you will be well pleased with him if you ever see him William will go with me and never return to that old woman again he is a fine fellow I am well pleased with them both

I will leave a recept from the date your note come due for the amount of $6..62 dollars or Credit your note with that amount You know if the will is not broke that there will be no difficulty They have never replyed to our answer as yet

george S Campbell has got a powar of attorny for that money ready to Send to you by Thos Foster george is in debt and wants his badly you will do him a good turn to Send it to him as Soon as posable I must close in hast your obt Servt

David Crockett

George Patton

Courtesy, David Zucker Collection.

George Patton was Crockett's brother-in-law. Crockett's father-in law, Robert Patton, had died, and Crockett and George Patton were named executors of Robert Patton's estate. Some family members contested the elder Patton's will, and a lawsuit was filed. See James Atkins Shackford, *David Crockett: The Man and the Legend*, John B. Shackford, ed. (Chapel Hill: University of North Carolina Press, 1956), 206-211.

*   *   *   *   *

1836:

CROCKETT LETTER TO WILEY AND MARGARET FLOWERS. PUBLISHED IN THE *DALLAS MORNING NEWS*, JUNE 1, 1913.

St. Augustine, Texas
Jan. 9th, 1836

My Dear Son and Daughter:

this is the first time I have had an opporttunity to write to you with convenience. I am now blessed with excellent health, and am in high spirits, although I have had many difficulties to encounter I have got through safe and have been received by every body with the open arms of friendship. I am hailed with a hearty welcome to this country, a dinner and a party of Ladys have honored me with an invitation to participate with them both at Nacogdoches and this place; the cannon was fired here on my arrival and I must say as to what I have seen of Texas it is the Garden spot of the world the best land and the best prospects for health I ever saw is here and I do believe it is a fortune for any man to come here; there is a world of country to settle, it is not required to pay down for your league of land; every man is entitled to make his headright of 4,438 acres; they may make the money to pay for it off the land. I expect in all probility to settle on the Bodark or Choctaw Bayou of Red River, that I have no doubt is the richest country in the world, good land and plenty of timber and the best springs and good mill streams, good range, clear water, and every appearance of health, game plenty. It is in the pass where the Buffalo passes from North to South and back twice a year, and bees and honey plenty. I have a great hope of getting the agency to settle that country and I would be glad to see every friend I have settle there, it would be a fortune to them all. I have taken the Oath of the Government and have enrolled my name as a volunteer for six months and will set out for the Rio Grande in a few days with the Volunteers of the United States, but all Volunteers is entitled to vote for a member of the Convention are to be voted for; and I have but little doubt of being elected a member to form the Consititution for this Province. I am rejoiced at my fate, I had rather be in my present situation than to be elected to a seat in Congress for life. I am in hopes of making a fortune for myself and family bad as has been my prospects; I have not wrote to William but have requested John to direct him what to do. I hope you show him this letter and also your brother John, as it is not convenient at this time for me to write to them. I hope you will all do the best you can and I will do the same, do not be uneasy about me, I am with my friends. I must close with great respects Your affection father, farewell,

David Crockett

*   *   *   *   *

CROCKETT LETTER TO WILEY AND MARGARET FLOWERS. COPY AT UNIVERSITY OF TENNESSEE, KNOXVILLE. (COPIES ALSO AT DRT LIBRARY AT THE ALAMO AND TENNESSEE STATE LIBRARY AND ARCHIVES.)

Saint Agusteen Texas
9th January 1836

My Dear Sone & daughter

This is the first I have had an opertunity to write to you with convenience I am now blessed with excellent health and am in high Spirits although I have had many difficulties to encounter I have got through Safe and have been received by everybody with the open cerimony of friendship I am hailed with a harty welcom to this country A dinner and a party of ladys have honored me with an invitation to partisapate both at Nacing doches and at this place The cannon was fired here on my arivil and I must say as to what I have seen of Texas it is the garden Spot of the world the best land and the best prospects for health I ever saw and I do believe it is a fortune to any man to come here There is a world of country here to Settle

It is not required here to pay down for your League of land every man is entitled to his head right of 4000–428 acres—they may make the money to pay for it on the land I expect in all probilaty to settle on the Bordar or Chactaw Bio of Red River that I have no doubt is the richest country in the world Good land and plenty of timber and the best springs & good mill streams good range clear water—and every appearance of good health and game plenty it is in the pass whare the Buffalo passed from North to South and back Twice a year and bees and honey plenty I have great hope of getting the agency to settle that country and I would be glad to see every friend I have settled thare It would be a fortune to them all I have taken the oath of government and have enrolled my name as a volunteer for [illegible] months and will set out for the Rio grand in a few days with the volunteers from the United States But all volunteers is intitled to a vote for a member to the convention or to be voted for and I have but little doubt of being elected a member to form a Constitution for this province I am rejoiced at my fate I had rather be in my present situation than to be elected to a seat in congress for life I am in hopes of making a fortune yet for myself and family bad as my prospect has been

I have not wrote to William but have requested John to direct him what to do I hope you will show him this letter and also Brother John as it is not convenient at this time for me to write to them I hope you will all do the best you can and I will do the same do not be uneasy about me I am among my friends—I must close with great respects Your affectionate father Farewell

David Crockett

Wily & Margaret Flowers

Margaret and Wiley Flowers were Crockett's daughter and son-in-law. The original letter has not been located.

The earliest mention of a personal Crockett letter from Texas that might be related to the Flowers letter was recorded in an unidentified newspaper interview with Crockett's daughter, Matilda Fields, in 1882. A typescript of that newspaper clipping was reprinted in the November 2006 issue of *The Crockett Chronicle*, no. 14, 4–5. Mrs. Fields recalled that "We did not know he intended to go into the army until he wrote mother a letter after he got to Texas."

No other letters from Crockett in Texas have been found, but the letter Mrs. Fields described contains at least some of the same information found in the letter to the Flowers.

The earliest specific mention of the Flowers letter was in the June 1, 1913, *Dallas Morning News*, which quoted the letter in full, but included some punctuation and spelling likely not found in the original. The article stated that the letter was transcribed from a copy owned by Martha M. Parks of Granbury, Texas.

Constance Rourke quoted this same letter in her book, *Davy Crockett* (New York: Harcourt, Brace, & Co., 1934),

171–72, and identified the letter's owner as Mrs. T. M. Hiner, of Granbury, Texas. In trying to locate an original copy of the letter, Crockett biographer James Shackford contacted Mrs. Hiner (and corrected her initials as "T. H."), but was informed that she had never owned an original of the letter, only a transcript copy. James Atkins Shackford, "The Autobiography of David Crockett: An Annotated Edition," Ph.D. dissertation, Vanderbilt University, 1948, 595.

Mrs. Hiner and Mrs. Parks were both granddaughters of David Crockett, and it is likely they both had copies of the same document.

On June 5, 1955, the *Memphis Commercial Appeal* ran a story about a hand-written copy of the Flowers letter and said the original was owned by J. D. Pate, a Crockett descendant from Martin, Tennessee. The article stated that the reverse of the letter was inscribed, "Memphis Feb. 3 Mr. Wiley Flowers, Crockett P.O. Gibson County, Tenn." The *Commercial Appeal* quoted the letter in full, but the text differs from the letter quoted in the *Dallas Morning News* forty-two years earlier. The transcript published in the *Commercial Appeal*, however, is nearly identical to the text found in photocopies of a handwritten Flowers letter that is in collections at the University of Tennessee, Knoxville; the DRT Library at the Alamo; and the Tennessee State Library and Archives.

The photocopy of the handwritten Flowers letter does not appear to be in Crockett's hand, but retains a lack of punctuation along with some misspellings and capitalization anomalies that are found in many of Crockett's holographs. Sections of the handwritten photocopy look as if they were over-written, perhaps in order to preserve a fading original document, but it is difficult to say with certainty if that is the case, since only photostats are available.

The second page of the photostat shows the "Crockett P.O." address noted above, so it is extremely likely that both the *Commercial Appeal* article and the photostat were copied from the same source. A photograph of the Pate letter that was published with the *Commercial Appeal* article provides further evidence that the letter owned by Pate was likely the source of the photostat, and that it may have been the original Crockett letter to Flowers, but the current location of this letter remains a mystery.

In 2007, another handwritten letter purporting to be the original Flowers letter was offered for sale to the Texas Historical Commission, which raised much controversy. The Historical Commission eventually declined to purchase the letter when Federal Forensic Associates, Inc., with whom they had contracted to analyze the document, was unable to confirm the letter's authenticity (see *Dallas Morning News*, December 8, 2007).

This letter bears no physical resemblance to the photocopies held by the University of Tennessee, Knoxville, and other institutions mentioned above, but the text is very similar to that of the letter printed in the 1913 *Dallas Morning News* article.

It is possible that all these versions of the Flowers letter are related, and the most logical explanation for the slight differences in content among the versions is that Crockett's original letter was copied and shared by family members shortly after its receipt.

The letters above are transcribed from the *Dallas Morning News* article and the photocopy of the Pate letter from the University of Tennessee, Knoxville, respectively.

*   *   *   *   *

JOHN WESLEY CROCKETT TO GEORGE PATTON, JULY 9, 1836.

Trenton
9th July 1836

Dear Sir:

You have doubtless seen the account of my Father's fall at the Alamo in Texas. He is gone from among us, and is no more to be seen in the walks of men but in his death like Sampson he slew more of his enemies than in all his life. Even his most bitter enemies here, I believe, have buried all animosity and joined the general lamentation over his untimely end.

I have been appointed administrator of your Father With his will annexed, since my Father's death and the object of this communication is to inform you that it will be necessary for me to bring the business of the estate to an im mediate close, and consequently it will be necessary for you to come or send out as soon as you possibly can and attend to settling up your interest in the Estate. Your note is here with Uncle's Peter and Abner as securities and is entitled to sundry credits if you will come out & have them allowed. Your own legacy & mothers are both to come out of it but If you dont attend to it in the Course of two or three months I shall be compelled, however it may conflict with my feelings, to proceed against your securities. This would be very far From my wish or feelings, as you must know, but the law points out my duties and I am compelled to go by it – we have no news of any importance. We are going ahead here for Judge White, and [illeg] you North Carolinians will join and assist us in resisting executive dictation. Please present me kindly to our family and permit me in conclusion to subscribe myself as ever

Your dearest Friend and obt servt
John W. Crockett

Capt. George Patton
Swannanoa
N.C.

From the Tennessee Historical Society Miscellaneous Files, courtesy of the Tennessee State Library and Archives.

*   *   *   *   *

LETTER FROM ISAAC N. JONES TO ELIZABETH CROCKETT, 1836. FROM (*JACKSON, TENNESSEE*) *TRUTH TELLER*, PRINTED IN *NATIONAL BANNER AND NASHVILLE WHIG*, AUGUST 12, 1836.

Lost Prairie, Ark's
1836

Mrs. David Crockett:

Dear Madam:
     Permit me to introduce myself to you as one of the acquaintances of your much-respected husband, Colonel Crockett. With his fate in the fortress, San Antonio, Texas, you are doubtless long since advised. With sincere feelings of sympathy I regret his untimely loss to your family and self – for if amongst strangers he constituted the most agreeable companion; he, doubtless, to his beloved wife and children, must have been a favorite peculiarly prized. In his loss, Freedom has been deprived of one of her bravest sons, in whose bosom universal philanthropy glowed with as genial warmth as ever animated the heart of an American citizen. When he fell, a soldier died. To bemoan his fate, is to pay a tribute of grateful respect to Nature – he seemed to be her son.
     The object of this letter, is to beg that you will accept the Watch which accompanies it. You will doubtless know it when you see it, and as it has his name engraved on its surface, it will no doubt be the more acceptable to you.
     As it will probably be gratifying to you to learn in what way I became possessed of it, permit me to state, that, last winter (the precise date not recollected by me,) Col. Crockett, in company with several other gentlemen, passed through Lost Prairie, on Red River, (where I live). The company, except the Colonel, he was a little behind, rode up to my house and asked accomodations for the night. My family being so situated, from the indisposition of my wife, that I could not accomodate them, they got quarters at one of my neighbor's houses. The Colonel visited me the next day and spent the day with me. He observed, whilst there, that his funds were getting short, and as a means of recruiting them, he must sell something. He proposed me to exchange watches. He priced his at $30 more than mine, which I paid him, and we accordingly exchanged.
     With his open frankness, his natural honesty of expression, his perfect want of concealment, I could not but be very much pleased. And with a hope that it might be an accommodation to him, I was gratified at the exchange, as it gave me a *keepsake* which would often remind me of an honest man, a

good citizen and a pioneer in the cause of Liberty, amongst his suffering brethren in Texas.

His military career was short. But though I deeply lament his death, I cannot restrain my American smile at the recollection of the fact that he died as a United States soldier should die, covered with his slain enemy, and, even in death presenting to them in his clenched hands, the weapons of their destruction.

We hope that the day is not far distant, when his adopted country will be freed from a savage enemy, and afford to yourself and children, a home, rendered in every way comfortable, by the liberal donations of her government.

Accept, dear madam, for yourself and family, the most sincere wishes for your future happiness, of Your most ob't servant and friend,

Isaac N. Jones

*   *   *   *   *

Part III

— DAVID CROCKETT POLITICAL CIRCULARS —

POLITICAL CIRCULAR, OCTOBER 25, 1824, MISCELLANEOUS FILES (T-100) BOX 3 – C 186 ½, TENNESSEE HISTORICAL SOCIETY, TENNESSEE STATE LIBRARY AND ARCHIVES.

Fellow-Citizens of the Counties of Humphreys, Perry, Henderson, Carroll, Madison, Gibson, Dyer, Tipton, Haywood, Hardeman, and Fayette.

The called session of the General Assembly having come to a close, I consider it my duty to inform my constituents, whose interest was entrusted to my care, in what manner I have acted, and some of my reasons for the course pursued. If my conduct while there shall prove satisfactory to you, I will be gratified; if not, I hope you will, in charity, attribute my errors to the head and not the heart. The principal subject for which the Legislature convened, was to correct an error in the Electoral Law, passed at the regular session: That has been done, and the time designated for the election of Electors is the first Thursday and Friday in November next. I hope my constituents will not fail to attend on those days, and shew to the world by their vote, an earnest desire to promote to the Presidency their own distinguished citizen, General Jackson. The nation owes him a debt of gratitude, which would in part be discharged by elevating him to the first office in the gift of the people.

A law has passed authorising the incorporation of a Turnpike Company, for a road from Nashville to Murfreesborough — I am a friend to internal improvement on land or water, and supported this measure as the commencement of a general system, which I hope to see prevail in time through the whole state. The people of all conditions are interested in good roads and navigable rivers — for each of those kind of improvements and conveniences add to the value of their produce, the value of their lands, and their general comfort and convenience.

I introduced a bill for the improvement of the navigation of Obion, Forked Deer, and Big Hatchie rivers, under the direction of three Commissioners for each river. The funds to defray the expense of these improvements, are to be raised by an annual tax of 12 ½ cents per hundred acres on all the lands in the section of country. The bill passed, and will, I hope, be carried into effect, to the great advantage of the citizens in general. By removing the obstructions, and improving the navigation of these rivers, all the necessary articles which the people are compelled to purchase, can be brought to them at a lower rate than at present — and in the single article of Salt, which is so indispensible, a considerable saving will be made. One of the most interesting subjects which engaged the attention of the Legislature, was a resolution authorising the Commissioner to adjudicate one hundred thousand acres of University Warrants, from North Carolina. I could not see the propriety of adjudicating those warrants, inasmuch as they did not appear to me to be clearly the property of the University but rather belonged to the United States — for this and other reasons satisfactory to me, I opposed the resolution, and it was rejected. At an early period of the session I introduced a bill for the location of a court of Chancery at Jackson — a general change of the Judiciary was afterwards proposed and adopted, which I hope will prove a benefit to the state — in this bill my first proposition was included, and we now have a Court of Chancery among us for the trial of our own Chancery business. I have no doubt that a future Legislature will, when the growth and population of the country requires it, give us also a Supreme Court. I did not consider it advisable at this time, to ask for a Supreme Court, fearing that if too much was asked, we would get nothing.

Fellow-Citizens —

I HAVE now served you during the last four years in the Legislature of Tennessee, and have during that time, been zealous in my exertions to advance your interests. I am not one of those who have had the opportunities and benefits of wealth and education in my youth — I am thus far the maker of my own fortunes. You have some knowledge of my services in the defence of our common country; for them I claim nothing, it was a duty, and I endeavored to perform it. If, in the discharge of my duties as your Representative, I have failed to exhibit the polished eloquence of men of superior education, I can yet flatter myself that I have, notwithstanding, been enabled to procure the passage of some laws and regulations beneficial to the interests of my constituents.

Fellow-Citizens of the Ninth Congressional District —
I now avail myself of the privilege common to every freeman, of offering myself as a candidate for a seat in the next Congress of the United States. It is not my design at this time to go into a detail of any of the subjects which may be expected to engage the attention of the next Congress, nor to discuss any of the public measures of the country — sufficient time will intervene between now and the period of election, to see and converse with many of you — all I will now undertake to say is, that I feel as much interest in your welfare, and if elected, will bestow as much labor in promoting your interests as any other.

I am, very respectfully, your obedient servant,

DAVID CROCKETT

Nashville, 25th October, 1824

*   *   *   *   *

POLITICAL CIRCULAR, SEPTEMBER 20, 1826, PUBLISHED IN THE *JACKSON (TENNESSEE) GAZETTE*, **OCTOBER 7, 1826.**

CIRCULAR

Fellow Citizens of the 9th Congressional District of the state of Tennessee. — You have already understood that I am a candidate to represent you in the 20th Congress of the United States. It becomes those who aspire to any office in the gift of the people, to make known to them their political creed. I am, Fellow-citizens, a plain farmer; my father was also a farmer; hence it is reasonable to suppose that to the agricultural class of the community, I am most tenderly attached. Whatever, then, will advance the interest of the farming class of the community, has ever received my warmest support, when honored with a seat in the Legislature of our state, and shall receive my devoted and continued attention, should I be so fortunate as to be your choice as representative in the national legislature. I shall therefore, with an eye on the interest of the Farmers of the Western District, be opposed to all restrictions put upon Commerce. Let it be as free as the breeze that wafts it along or the waters of the seas which support it and bring it to our shores. Whenever Great Britain can bring us her manufactures and other articles of comfort, and sell them at a cheaper rate than we can manufacture them, it is cruel to say to the American people, (by laying a heavy duty on them) "it shall not be your interest to purchase them: you shall purchase an article manufactured by the Yankees!!" inferior in quality, and at a higher price. This is the consequence of the last alarming Tariff. The effect of this course of policy, is to oppress the poor honest farmers, amongst whom I rank myself — To fatten the manufacturers of the East.

Fellow-citizens — I will oppose this narrow sighted policy, should I be the successful candidate. I will use unwearied exertions to procure a surrender of all the Land in this district, which shall belong to the general government, after satisfying the bona-fide claims of North Carolina. This land, if surrendered by Congress to the state of Tennessee, will be at the disposal of our state legislature; & will no doubt be disposed of for the purpose of establishing schools among us, where our children can recieve the advantages of education which otherwise must be denied them. This would be a matter of great importance — It would enable us to educate our children at home, without making it necessary for us to send them to a distance, to the colleges of the rich, where boarding and tuition are so high that we are unable to afford it.

I am in favor of such an amendment of the Constitution of the United States, as entirely to take the election of President from Congress, and let it remain with the people, who are as capable of making a final as a first choice. The President of this republic should be the choice of the people, and not forced upon them by the intrigue & management of a few demagogues at the Federal City. According to the present mode of choosing a President, there may be three candidates — no one of whom gets a majority of the whole electoral vote: they are all of course returned to Congress, and it devolves on that body to choose for us. Yet one of the candidates wanted but one vote of getting as many electoral votes as both the others. He is clearly the choice of the people. One of the candidates, when before the people, gets only the vote of the little state of Delaware; yet Congress has the power to make him the President, in open disregard of the expressed wish of the people. In this particular, the Constitution of the United States requires amendment. If the election goes to the House of Representatives, it will be decided as the last one was, by *bargain and barter,* and not according to the will of the people.

John Quincy Adams was, when a candidate for President, greatly in favor of giving the election to the People, by amending the constitution. He wrote powerfully in favor of it — His hireling papers were in favor of it. — He said that if the election continued to go to the House of Representatives that bargain and management would be the order of the day — and that this republic would come to ruin — But, fellow-citizens, this was when he thought Mr. Crawford was more popular in Congress than himself. Mr. Clay talked the same way. He was greatly in favor of amending the constitution, and of giving the election to the People — But when it was found that JACKSON was their choice, he entered into a corrupt bargain with John Quincy Adams which secured to him the office of Secretary of State, & to John Quincy, the Presidential chair.

When a resolution was afterwards offered to amend the constitution, so as to give the election to the People, they both came out with all their influence, in opposition to the very amendment which they had urged. Fellow-citizens, how can we account for this, but on the principle that they know they are not the choice of the people, and are afraid to delegate them with that power. I am opposed to Mr. Adams because he was a strong *Federalist;* opposed the Republicans at every step, until he found that his was the weak side, and not suited to his ambitious views, when he pretended to desert them: and as an excuse for doing so, said that he discovered they were about to separate the Union. I am opposed to Mr. Adams because he opposed the purchase of Louisiana, by Mr. Jefferson, which is viewed as one of the brightest acts of his administration. I am opposed to Mr. Adams because he opposed the admission of Louisiana into the Union, on an equal footing with the original states; which wicked opposition sprung from a wish to keep down the South and West, and keep the power in the Yankee states. I am opposed to Mr. Adams because he attempted to trade away the free navigation of the Mississippi, the great highway of the West, for a Yankee *Cod Fishery* — And I am opposed to Mr. Clay because he pushed Mr. Adams into the Presidential chair, who had done all he could to injure the West, in preference to General Jackson, who was the choice and glory of the American people; and whose greatness and goodness many of us witnessed, while fighting under his colors. That General Jackson was the choice of the American people, I presume no candid man will pretend to deny — If I mistake not, he received 99 electoral votes, while Mr. Adams received 86; and General Jackson received this handsome majority too, carrying all the time Henry Clay upon his back, who is admitted to have been a very bad rider, always endeavoring to reign *Old Hickory* out of the road, and distract the evenness and rapidity of his course. But, Fellow citizens, I am not only a friend to Gen. Jackson because he was the choice of the People, but on account of his great services and incorruptible integrity. His services are in the mouths of both old and young, from Maine to Mississippi — The British Lion crouched at his feet — Each man can boast of his state because *Jackson* is one of her citizens, and led her sons to victory — His integrity is incorruptible; he was tried at Washington City; the Presidential chair was offered to him, if he would wink at a corrupt arrangement; but his soul was too noble — His reply should be written in letters of gold — "BEFORE I WOULD GO INTO THE PRESIDENTIAL CHAIR BY BARGAIN AND BARTER, I WOULD SINK MYSELF AND THE WHOLE SET OF INTRIGUERS INTO OBLIVION!"

Fellow-Citizens, I *"speak of Gen. Jackson;"* I go for him; I do not pretend to be a great politician; you have my ideas in a plain homespun manner.

I am,
DAVID CROCKETT

Gibson County Sept. 20, 1826

*   *   *   *   *

POLITICAL CIRCULAR, JANUARY 15, 1829, *ADDRESS OF MR. CROCKETT, TO THE VOTERS OF THE NINTH CONGRESSIONAL DISTRICT OF THE STATE OF TENNESSEE; TOGETHER WITH HIS REMARKS IN THE HOUSE OF REPRESENTATIVES, JANUARY 5, 1829, ON HIS MOTION TO AMEND THE BILL "TO AMEND AN ACT, ENTITLED 'AN ACT TO AUTHORIZE THE STATE OF TENNESSEE TO ISSUE GRANTS AND TO PER-FECT TITLES TO CERTAIN LANDS THEREIN DESCRIBED, AND TO SETTLE THE CLAIMS TO VACANT AND UNAPPROPRIATED LANDS IN THE SAME,'" PASSED APRIL 18, 1806.* (WASHINGTON: PRINTED BY GALES & SEATON, JANUARY 15, 1829), RARE BOOKS DIVISION, LIBRARY OF CONGRESS.

Address, &c.

Washington City,
January 15, 1829.

TO THE INDEPENDENT VOTERS OF THE NINTH CONGRESSIONAL DISTRICT IN THE STATE OF TENNESSEE.

Fellow-Citizens, and, I may say, Fellow-Sufferers:

I have but little to write you; for, though Congress has been for a considerable time in session, nothing has been done sufficiently interesting in its character to merit a labored explanation.

When I say nothing has been done in which you would feel an interest, I merely mean to apply the remark to the mass of business which has been under consideration, and of which I give you no account in this letter.

Laying aside that description of business, I may say to you that much has been done, and that, too, greatly to your detriment and my dissatisfaction. It is due, both to you and to myself, that I should give you a brief history of the matter to which I allude.

It will be recollected that, during the last session of Congress, an attempt was made to procure a relinquishment of the title of the General Government to the lands in the Western District, and to vest them in the Legislature of Tennessee. I aided in this attempt, but not with the slightest hope that it would prove successful. I then believed, and still believe, that it would amount to an encroachment upon the rights of my constituents, to place it in the power of the Tennessee Legislature, or any other Legislature, to speculate upon the labor of the poor. I, surely, had no certain and fixed ground upon which to bottom the conclusion that your legislature would turn you out as houseless wanderers, by force and arms; but I was well satisfied, indeed I may say I was certain, that, if the title was once vested in them, your homes — if yours you continued to call them — would cost you still more toil and treasure. If any man wishes to know why I thought thus, I am neither afraid nor ashamed to answer him. Why, and how, did the Legislature of Tennessee interfere with your rights and your interests, when, without a shadow of claim to the land, they compelled you to have your lands laid off, plotted, and registered, without your own consent, and without the existence of the slightest necessity for it? Why, I ask, was this done? and what was the effect? The effect was, that it was placed in the power of a few deputy Surveyors to defraud you, by charging double prices for their labor, and often to sell the poor man's all to pay the fee. Seeing what I have seen, and feeling what I have felt, on account of this legislative error, I was unwilling to trust your homes to their mercy. I moreover knew that the weight of the State Legislature would stand, in a great measure, as the Tennessee delegation stands in Congress; that is, opposed to my proposition, which has been, and still is, dear to my heart. To make a short story of the whole affair, I wished you to have your homes directly from the hands of Congress, and then you could, with certainty, call them your own.

The Hon. Mr. Polk's proposition was the one which I have attempted to describe. I mean that its object was to relinquish the land to the State, as prayed for in the memorial of its Legislature. This I opposed, for the reasons before and hereafter given, and moved the following substitute, of the justice of which you will judge. It is in these words:

[Here Crockett inserted the text of his amendment to Polk's bill with his speech in support of it delivered in the House on January 5, 1829, which is transcribed in the section with selected speeches.]

Had the question at this time been taken, no doubt can exist but that I should have succeeded; but after several speeches had been made, Mr. Lea moved a postponement of the question, alleging, indirectly, the death of Mrs. Jackson as the cause why he was not then prepared to discuss the subject. It was postponed for eight days, which afforded the enemies of my measure time and opportunity to destroy it by their management.

When it was again called up, Mr. Lea opposed it in a lengthy and able speech. I must acknowledge that I regretted greatly that the time, and his talents, had not been devoted to some other object.

When he closed, I could not feel reconciled to see you stand without an advocate, and though I was a mere farmer, I replied as follows:

[Here Crockett inserted a revised version of remarks he had made in the House on January 12, 1829 (see *Register of Debates,* January 12, 1829, pp. 199–200). The essential meaning of his words is the same, but the speech has been heavily rewritten in the circular. These speeches are included in the section with selected speeches.]

Had the question here been taken, I should have proved successful. But speech elicited speech, until the House became utterly exhausted with the subject; and it may truly be said that it was spoken to death. A motion was made for the indefinite postponement of the subject - bill, and amendment, which was carried by a considerable majority. Thus have our prospects been covered with a cloud for the present; but I never will abate my exertions until that cloud is dispersed. I was utterly astonished at one thing. It was, that while gentlemen from other States were aiding me in what I consider so humane an attempt — an attempt to shelter the heads of defenceless widows and poor little orphans from the peltings of the pitiless storm - my own colleagues were bending all their powers against me. The measure met with no serious opposition, (with one exception,) which did not come from them. Whether in this matter they acted right or not, the people must determine. For myself, I am prepared to say that I was contending on the side of mercy; and I fought a good fight, though I had at last to yield.

Fellow-Citizens, you have this matter now before you; and I must close, or I should trespass on your patience. I beg you to receive my thanks for all your past favors. I have endeavored to deserve them, and shall continue to strive, so long as honored with your confidence.

I am, sincerely,

Your friend and servant,

DAVID CROCKETT

*   *   *   *   *

POLITICAL CIRCULAR, FEBRUARY 28, 1831, RARE BOOKS DIVISION, LIBRARY OF CONGRESS.

DAVID CROCKETT'S CIRCULAR.

To the Citizens and Voters of the Ninth Congressional District in the State of Tennessee.

Fellow Citizens:

It is expected by you that I should give you information of the proceedings of this session of Congress. At a very early day in the session the Senate proceeded to the trial of Judge Peck of Missouri, impeached by the House of Representatives, for an alleged illegal and oppressive exercise of his official duties. The Senate pronounced judgement of Not Guilty; and thus the impeachment ended. The House of Representatives suspended their business during a great part of the trial of the Judge. I was opposed to this. I thought that our House might as well go on with the public business, and leave it to our Managers to go on with the trial. I saw no reason why we should overlook our Managers. Owing to this trial very little has been done, except passing the appropriation bills, to carry on the operations of the government.

You know what a noise was made about Mr. Adams and Mr. Clay spending and wasting the public money, and that the friends of General Jackson made us believe, if they got in power, that they would reform the government, and retrench the expenses thereof. I am sorry to say that none of their promises have been performed; the expenses of every branch of the government have been increased; and all their boasted economy was a mere trap set for us — they caught us, and we put them in power; they now not only do what they denounced, but they push their waste of money further — the Appropriation Bills will show it. They have sent a Minister to Russia, paying him $9,000 outfit to furnish a house and $9,000 a year salary; and before he went, they granted him the right to leave here and go wherever he chose, and he went to England, staying in Russia but ten days or so. He is not going back to Russia; he is coming home, and has been announced a candidate for Congress, and I am told he says he was only sent out for one year. I may ask you what you think of this most unprincipled waste of your money, (to give it to a rich favourite) practised by men boasting of their political honesty and love of economy: search every department of the government from its commencement to the present time, and nothing like it can be found; this shows what little reliance can be placed on those who have the management of public affairs.

The men now in power used to argue in Congress that our Ministers abroad were too numerous, and paid too high. They have not reduced their number — they have tried to encrease their pay; and the Secretary of State, professing to act in obedience to the wish of the President, has recommended the most extravagant and splendid embassy that was ever dreamed of in this country. He recommends that a Minister should be sent to the Grand Turk at Constantinople, at an expense of nearly eighty thousand dollars for the first year; $50,000 of which are for the *Contingent Expenses,* to be laid out in presents for the Grand Seignor. The Secretary does not state how the $50,000 are to be laid out, that he has left to the discretion of the ambassador. The Clerks in the Departments, when Mr. Adams was in power, they said were too numerous and too lazy; now further pay is asked for them, and their number is too small! It appears, also, that the Post Office Department, instead of supporting its own expenses must now be supported by the Treasury.

I wish that the waste of public money and neglect of promises made by General Jackson, were the only charges that could be made against his Administration. My heart bleeds when I reflect on his cruelty to the poor unprotected Indians. I never expected it of him. Georgia has great weight in the councils of General Jackson; Mr. Van Buren, the Secretary of State, is the bosom friend of Mr. Crawford of Georgia. It is no longer matter of conjecture that Mr. Van Buren and Mr. Calhoun are striving each to succeed General Jackson; Mr. Calhoun was once in favour of protecting the Indians against Georgia — the President is against Mr. Calhoun — the President and his Cabinet are for Georgia against the Indians, and to gratify Georgia they deny to the weak Indians all the lands and rights secured to them by treaties made by every President since the commencement of the government. The government sent Preachers of the Gospel to teach them Christianity and the arts of civilized life, advised them to leave off hunting and to turn to farmers, and promised never to take their lands; the poor Indians took their advice, became cultivators of the soil and forgot the chase, and worshipped the god of the white man, and established order and civil subordination over their tribes. The government *invited* them again to become savages, to wander in the forests west of the Mississippi, in the precarious pursuit of the bear and the buffalo. The Indian refused, asking, "I have taken your advice; I have felt the blessings of certainty in procuring the means of living by cultivating the soil; I have built temples in which I worship your God; and I never will leave the land of my fathers." Georgia passes her jurisdiction and laws over them, drives them from working their own lands for gold, tries an Indian by her own laws for an offence committed within the limits of an Indian nation and against an Indian, and hangs the offender; and will not permit them to give evidence in a court of justice, altho' they do believe in a future state of rewards and punishments; and, finally will not suffer a Missionary to reside with them and preach the Gospel. The President, disregarding all the treaties made with them, the voice of humanity, and the honour of his country, flatters the pride and views of Georgia, by declaring to the Indians — "You must go, or submit to Georgia. I will not help you whatever Congress may have said. I am the President, and I say that all the laws and treaties are void. The State of Georgia may now wanton in her acts of wrong without fear of restraint from the President." I would to God that these were the only wrongs which the Indians had received from the President. It appears that he sent Commissioners among the Creek Indians to persuade them to emigrate west of the Mississippi, and promised to furnish them with provisions and land, and that the President would protect them from their chiefs if they would consent to go. They consented to go, and thus brought upon themselves the resentment of their chiefs, who, preferring to remain where they were, were displeased that any of their tribe should consent to emigrate. Having been thus seduced, to give their consent to emigrate, they omitted to plant their crops, or to make any preparation, for securing the means of living. They, at the appointed time, informed the agents of the government that they were prepared to emigrate, and claimed that the government should comply with the promises made to them, "to furnish the means of removing and subsistence," the government by its agents answered these just demands, by saying, "We will not help you go; we will not keep our promises to you; we will not give *you* the means of getting bread, unless *the whole tribe* consents to go." The President left them to suffer for bread — men, women and children, are alike the sufferers by this violation of the public faith.

The Indians petitioned Congress, stating these grievances: it was refereed to the Committee on Indian Affairs, the friends of General Jackson, and they have made no report upon it. It would seem that the sufferings of a hungering people excites no pity with our President; and that all the miseries of famine, brought on by his own acts, are to be used as the instruments for their extermination or removal.

Petitions from every part of the country against this inhuman policy towards the Indians have been sent to Congress. The President, relying on the strength of his popularity and on party spirit, persists in it, and thus brings shame and reproach on the American name; and nothing will stop this unfeeling career of treachery and cruelty but the ballot box, and it is now to be tried whether an honest adherence to treaties with defenceless tribes is to be sustained by you, against cruelty and bad faith. I have said much about this because I feel much about it.

Mr. Calhoun was the friend of Internal Improvements: General Jackson before he was elected was also its friend, and voted, over and over again, sums for it. He admits that he did so. Martin Van Buren, the Secretary of State, was opposed to it, and always voted against it — General Jackson now agrees in opinion with Martin Van Buren, and says he acted wrong when he voted to encourage, by the aid of Congress, the Internal Improvements of the country! Strange that so old a politician should have never seen the error of his ways, until he had Martin Van Buren for his counsellor. How wrong is it for General Jackson to disappoint the hopes of his friends who voted for him, because all his acts proved him to be the friend of Internal Improvements! How cruel to his country to sacrifice its great and permanent interests to the end that Martin Van Buren may get the votes of those States, which have all the advantages of water communication, and are therefore opposed to giving the public money to be expended in enabling the people to bring their produce to market. General Jackson is a western President, abandoning his old principles of Constitutional law, and sacrificing western interests that Martin Van Buren may be his successor!

The President, it is known to you all, recommended that an amendment should be made to the Constitution, so as to prevent members of Congress from being selected by the President for high offices. He said that this was the means employed by the Presidents to corrupt Congress, and that its practice would ruin the Republic; we all believed him, and we expected that under him such a practice would never be adopted. This was what he taught us, and it was patriotic; let us see what his practice was, when he came on and consulted with Martin Van Buren and others. He selected for his cabinet, members of Congress, Eaton, Ingham, Branch, and Berrien. This was the first unblushing departure from his doctrine. Of these, two were for Crawford against General Jackson. Van Buren has strengthened him self by giving all the first offices in the gift of the government to his friends. Rives, minister to France, McLane to London, Randolph to Russia, (all members of Congress,) Van Ness to Spain, and a host of others were all Crawford men, and against General Jackson. Thus General Jackson has, according to his own doctrine, attempted to corrupt Congress by selecting from them public ministers - and almost all the friends of Van Buren. Thus all his virtuous resolutions and patriotic views have yielded, and Martin Van Buren has benefited thereby. Surely this man must be very eloquent, who can change the General's opinions so much and so often.

General Jackson declared that a President should not serve longer than four years; he thought that a rotation in the office of President every four years was necessary to preserve the freedom of our institutions; he urged Congress to recommend such an amendment. Mr. McDuffie brought in such a resolution but before he could call it up, the newspapers favourable to Van Buren denounced Mr. McDuffie and his amendment — and it was published, by authority, that General Jackson was again a candidate for re-election.

General Jackson was for reform and retrenchment, before he was President. He has not practised either; but has permitted great waste of public money to reward his friends. General Jackson, before he was President, was the pure patriot who denounced the constitutional expediency of selecting Members of Congress for office; he has given to Members of Congress more appointments than all his predecessors. He *said*, before he was President, that no man ought to be President longer than four years; he is again a candidate. I thought with him, as he thought before he was President: he has altered his opinion — I have not changed mine. I have not left the principles which led me to support

General Jackson: he has left them and *me;* and I will not surrender my independence to follow his *new opinions,* taught by interested and selfish advisers, and which may again be remoulded under the influence of passion or cunning.

Having given you information on general subjects, I will now tell you what I attempted to do in relation to your own private interests.

The disposition of the public lands in our district has already been an object of great interest to you. I have laboured constantly and zealously to get such a disposition made of them, by Congress as would directly benefit you.

In my first Election, the question upon the disposition of the vacant land in my District, was one of great interest to the people. My object was to do the best I could for the occupants — but at the first session after I was elected, Mr. Polk took the advantage of me while I was confined to my bed with indisposition, and made a motion to dispose of the government land in the District, and had it referred to a Select Committee of which he was Chairman. I found his object was to have the whole of the land south and west of the congressional reservation line relinquished to the State of Tennessee, to be disposed of by the Legislature of the State in the same manner that he and my predecessor had effected the passage of a bill through the House of Representatives, at the Session previous to my coming in to Congress. That bill was not acted on in the Senate.

I did not agree in opinion with my colleague, Mr. Polk, for many reasons which I will mention; first I knew that if it was relinquished to the State, that it would be the interest of the State to put the highest possible price upon it that they could get; and I knew we the people, could not prevent them from setting a price upon it that would be out of the reach of the occupants. I knew, also, that we have but five members in the legislature from the whole western District, to contend against the 35 members from the balance of the State. I would ask any reasonable man, what chance our five members in the House of Representatives, would have to prevent a price being put upon that land, that would place it out of the reach of a large majority of the settlers, who have made valuable improvements upon the land. I knew the difficulties that these people had to labour under in settling the country; they have been driven from home to home, some of them several times, by the warrant holders; and have had their labour swept from them by a speculator, to raise a revenue to educate the children of the wealthy, is what I never can submit to while I am honoured with the confidence of those people.

I consider it unjust to oppress those people, and collect their money which they are not able to spare to give to the State of Tennessee, when, in fact, the State has no claim to it. My first object was to give it direct from the general government, to the occupants as a boon from that government — to the poor people who had settled the country through so many difficulties.

When my Colleagues found that there was a probability of my success in that attempt, they determined to defeat me by speaking the question to death, and they all arrayed themselves against me, and delivered no less than six set speeches against my proposition. There were six of the great Lawyers of Tennessee that took a hand against me, which was Mr. Bell, Mr. Polk, Mr. Blair, Mr. Isaacs, Mr. Mitchell, and Mr. Lea, and the other two were electioneering against my proposition. I supported the measure to the best advantage that I could, but finally the subject was laid on the table without the question being taken. I have always been of the opinion that if I could have gotten a vote on the bill, that I could have given it direct from Congress to the people.

At the last session, my Colleagues, after finding that I had made the proposition, and had the subject referred to a select committee of which I was Chairman, they proposed a compromise with me, that the people should pay twelve and one half cents per acre for the land, and give the people twelve months to pay that in, and the proceeds should go to the common school fund in the State of Tennessee. To this I agreed, and they were all to help me pass that bill; but when it come to the test, there was but one of them that raised his voice in favour of that measure, that was Colonel Johnson, and I was defeated a few votes.[1] I then went to Mr. Grenell and requested the favour of him to ask to re-consider the vote the next morning, he agreed to do so; I then prepared a substitute to offer in lieu of the whole bill which was to give a pre-emption right of two hundred acres to each occupant at twelve and a half cents per acre, and give the occupant two years to pay that in, to the Branch Bank of the United States at Nashville to be placed to the credit of the treasury of the United States, and legalized such acts of the Legislature of Tennessee, as to make good all surveys authorized by the statutes of the State, and made it the duty of the Surveyor to deliver to the occupant a plat and certificate upon which he could obtain his grant. By my proposition the people would have got the land, and the general government would get the proceeds, and our own officers would get the same fees as for similar services under the statutes of the State of Tennessee, and the State of Tennessee would get the revenue which I consider would be of more advantage to the State of Tennessee than any other way that it could be disposed of.

By my proposition to estimate, say ten thousand occupants at two hundred acres each would give the State of Tennessee the tax upon two millions of acres; and this measure was defeated for no other reason under heavens than that the eastern members voting for it, my colleagues made it a party question upon that ground and beat me three votes — with the whole delegation voting against me. The vote stood as follows — for the measure 89, and against it 92. If any two of my colleagues had voted with me, I have no doubt but I could have passed it; but instead of trying to aid me in procuring for the poor industrious occupant his home, they all united in running the influence of the Jackson party against me: it was the Jackson party that defeated the measure at the last session. When it has come to this, to defeat such a measure, merely to gratify the ambition of partizans, it is enough to make every lover of his country look down with indignation upon all such parties.[2]

I must, however, before I close this address, give you a statement of the expenditures of the government; from which you will all see clearly, that my foregoing statements relative to the increased extravagance of the present Administration are true. I present the following extract from a communication made by the Hon. James Clark, of Kentucky, to his constituents, which I have examined and found to be correct:

Among the numerous topics of animadversion in the last Administration, none was more clamorously urged, and none was more gratuitous, than the charge of extravagance in disbursing the public money. This is a subject that in every popular Government is deservedly and naturally, one of deep interest. The finances of a nation have so vital an influence on its prosperity, that the importance of their being judiciously managed, is obvious to the meanest capacity. It is a matter too in which every citizen feels himself to be directly concerned; and he readily considers every dollar improperly expended out of the national purse, as he would consider money wrongfully taken from his own. Intriguing politicians, in availing themselves of the natural temper of the public mind to further their own selfish and ambitious schemes, have often sedulously confounded the fact of expenditure with the guilt of extravagance, such persons tolerate no inquiry into the motives, the objects or the result of the expenditure. But their doctrines while they are struggling for power, are as different from their practice after they have attained it, as both their doctrines and their practice are different from sound principles. According to their *doctrines,* an Administration to merit public confidence must be parsimonious: according to their practice, an Administration which has once acquired public confidence is at liberty to violate every rule of economy. Now common sense and experience prove that economy is as essential to the well being of a People, as its opposites, parsimony and extravagance, are destructive to them. An eminent political writer has truly said, "Economy is a distributive virtue, and consists not in saving, but in selection. Parsimony requires no providence, no sagacity, no powers of combination, no comparison, no judgment." It may be added that it is the part of true economy both in individuals and in nations to keep their expenses within their income. In the paper already referred to, it was shown that the last Administration was emphatically *economical;* that it expended the public money only for the public interests, consistently with the public resources, and according to law; and that its expenditures in many important heads were even less in amount than corresponding expenditures under preceding Administrations. This last fact was, however, stated tin reply to some sweeping assertions of the party then in opposition, and not as a just criterion of the economy of that or of any other Administration. So many causes, which will readily present themselves to your minds, operate to produce unequal calls at different times on the public purse, that more money may be expended in one year than in another, and yet more economically, because more necessarily or more usefully expended. In remarking on the use made of the public money by the present Administration. I shall give them the full benefit of this consideration, though in their scuffle for office they were insensible to the justice of extending it to their predecessors. Let us first compare the public expenditure during the two periods, deducting from the expenses of each, the payments on account of the Public Debt, and those made under the Ghent Treaty:

Expenditure during Mr. Adams's Administration.

1825.	Whole expenditures,	$23,585,804.72
	Deduct payments on account of Public Debt,	12,095,344.78
	Leaves net expenses,	11,490,459.94
1826.	Whole expenditures,	$24,103,398.46
	Deduct payments on account of Pubic Debt,	11,041,082.19
	Leaves net expenses,	$13,062,316.27
1827.	Whole expenditures,	$22,656,764.04
	Deduct payments on account of Pubic Debt,	10,003,668.39
	Leaves net expenses,	$12,653,095.65
1828.	Whole expenditures,	$25,459,479.52
	Deduct payments on account of Pubic Debt,	12,163,438.07
		$13,296,041.45
	Deduct money paid under the Ghent Treaty	790,069.40
	Leaves net expenses,	$12,505,972.05

Expenditures under Gen. Jackson's Administration.

1829.	Whole expenditures,	$25,071,017.59
	Deduct payments on account of Pubic Debt,	12,383,800.77
		$12,687,216.82
	Deduct money paid under the Ghent Treaty	8,280.22
	Leaves net expenses,	$12,678,936.60

1830. I am saved the trouble of any calculation for this year as the President says, in his annual Message, (p. 24,) to Congress, December, 1830, "the total expenditure during the year, exclusive of the Public Debt, is estimated at $13,742,311.00.

The result of the preceding statement is, that the net expenses of the government during the last six years, have been, omitting the cents, as follows:

Mr. Adams's four years.
1825. $11, 490, 559
1826.   13,062,316
1827.   12,653,095
1828.   12,505,972

Gen. Jackson's two years.
1829. $12,678,936
1830.   13,742,311

So that if the President is right in estimating, as he does in his Message, the expenditure of the last year, he has during that year, spent nearly SEVEN HUNDRED THOUSAND DOLLARS more than Mr. Adams did in any one year of his Administration.

In the preceding comparative view of the public expenditures during the last and present Administrations, the payments under the Ghent Treaty, and those on account of the Public Debt, are deducted from the gross amounts, as not being part of the ordinary expenses of the nation. The payments under the Ghent Treaty were made out of a fund placed in our hands by Great Britain, according to a Convention, between her Government and our own, effected during the last Administration for the indemnification of certain citizens of the United States. The disbursement of it, dies not therefore fall within the ordinary public expenses. Payments on account of the Public Debt, are of the same extrinsic character. By the law of March 3d, 1817, the annual sum of ten millions of dollars, arising from duties on imposts and tonnage, internal duties, and from the sale of public lands, was appropriated and vested in the Commissioners of the sinking fund, for the payment of the Public Debt. Besides other provisions of that law, it exacted that in case of a surplus in the Treasury above the sums appropriated for the service of the year, so that a balance of two millions would remain to the end of the year, such surplus should be appropriated to the sinking fund. The principles on which the national debt is to be paid, were thus settled long before the birth of the present Administration, and advances, as rapid as the state of the country permitted, towards its extinguishment were made during the Administrations of Mr. Monroe and Mr. Adams. In the last Treasury report made while Mr. Adams was President, it was calculated by the Secretary that, assuming their payments beyond the stated appropriation of ten millions would be made in the same proportion in future years as *had been in the year* 1828, the debt would, in effect, be totally paid off in little more than four years. Two of these years have now come and gone, and they are the two first years of General Jackson's Administration. As a great credit is assumed by himself and his friends for *paying off* the Public Debt, and as his acts in this respect fall within the topic I am now treating of, I shall briefly examine the assumption. General Jackson has during his first two years, or had on the 1st of January last, paid on account of the Public Debt, the sum of $23,738,430. But in doing this, he used of money which Mr. Adams had accumulated and left as a surplus fund on hand, the sum of $1,152,654, for which amount Mr. Adams instead of General Jackson ought to have credit. It being therefore deducted from the amount, just mentioned, $23,738,430, the sum paid by General Jackson during his two first years, or on the 1st of January, last, on account of the Public Debt, is $22,585,776, which is at the rate of $11,292,888 a year, But Mr. Adams during his four years paid on account of the Public Debt, $45,303,533, making an average of $11,325,883 a year, besides accumulating a considerable surplus which was handed over to his successor. Thus Mr. Adams paid *more* on account of the Public Debt than General Jackson has paid, by an average yearly amount of THIRTY-TWO THOUSAND NINE HUNDRED AND NINETY FIVE DOLLARS! And at the close of the present year this average excess will probably be augmented as Mr. Ingham, the Secretary of the Treasury, in his Report (page 6) estimates that we shall be able to pay during the current year 1831, buy $10,000,000; which is a less sum than was paid by Mr. Adams in any one of his four years.

I will now present to you another aspect of this subject, viz. a view of the expenditures compared with the receipts of the country during Gen. Jackson's administration. From the letter of the Secretary of the Treasury, in December last, transmitting to Congress his annual Report on the Finances, it appears (see page 2) that the expenses of the year 1829, the first of Gen. Jackson's Administration, were $25,044,358.40 and that the receipts of that year from all sources amounted to, $24,827,627.38; Leaving an excess of expenditures over receipts for 1829, of 216,731.02. So that the *Reformers* instead of keeping their expenses within their income, during their first year, actually spent TWO HUNDRED AND SIXTEEN THOUSAND, SEVEN HUNDRED AND THIRTY-ONE DOLLARS more than they received! The document first referred to, informs us (see page 2, 3) of the stage at which Reform arrived during the next year. "The total estimated expenditures of the 'year' 1830, says Mr. Ingham, are $25,096,941.32. "The total estimated receipts of the 'year,' 1830 are, $24,161,018.179 Leaving an excess of expenditures over receipts for 1830, of, $935,922.53. So that the Reformers, improving on their first year, have during their second, spent NINE HUNDRED AND THIRTY-FIVE THOUSAND, NINE HUNDRED AND TWENTY TWO DOLLARS, more than they have received!! And, but for the money which Mr. Adams, whom they had denounced for extravagance, left in the Treasury when he retired from the Government, they could not have met these expenses without either borrowing money, or curtailing the payments on account of the Public Debt. This conclusion is inevitable, on inspection of the foregoing statements. I will now call your attention to the different manner, in which the finances of the country were managed by the last Administration. It appears from the Report of the Secretary of the Treasury, in December, 1825, that on the 31st December, 1824, two months before Mr. Adams' inauguration there was a balance in the Treasury of $1,946, 597.13. Instead of drawing on this balance left by his predecessor to help him out with his expenses, (as General Jackson has done with the balance left by Mr. Adams) he added to that balance from time to time, several millions of dollars, and finally left (as appears by Mr. Ingham's report, page 2) on the 1st of January, 1829, two months before Gen. Jackson took possession of the Government, a balance in the Treasury of $5,972,435.81, or nearly SIX MILLIONS OF DOLLARS. This sum Gen. Jackson, has according to his own showing, (see his Message to Congress, December, 1830, printed by order of Congress, page 24) in two years reduced to $4,819.781, which he says, will be the balance in the Treasury on the 1st January, 1831.

From the foregoing facts concerning the financial history of the present Administration, it is made manifest that they have spent more of the public money, and paid less of the Public Debt, than had been done by the last Administration, for equal times; and also that their expenses have exceeded their income. This is a startling attitude for public affairs to assume under the auspices of *"Reform and Retrenchment."* It may possibly be said that the censure which it undeniably deserves, should be borne, not by Executive officers, but by Congress for appropriating so much money to be expended. But this plea does not shift the responsibility from those who ought to fear it, because for the last two Congresses, there has been a decided majority of Gen. Jackson's political friends, in both Houses. Besides, the expenses which are within the special control of the Executive officers themselves, are marked by the same tendency to increase them, which is observable in the public expenditures generally, since Gen. Jackson came into power. By way of example, I subjoin, from the public documents, a statement of the expenses of the Executive Departments under the last and the present Administrations:

Mr. Adams' four years.

In 1825	$478,330
In 1826	489,776
In 1827	501,793
In 1828	506,873

Gen. Jackson's first year.

In 1829	530,172

For the years 1830, the Treasury Report gives the expenses of the three first quarters only, which amounted to,

	$412,332
Add for the remaining quarter, at the same rate,	137,444
And we have for 1830, Gen. Jackson's second year,	$549,776

We are now brought to the question what are the causes of the enormous expenditure of public money, which has characterized the present Administration? ave they spent the money necessarily or usefully? Have they spent it in improving the country, and in binding its several parts more firmly together by national works? Let the fate of the Maysville Road Bill, of the Frederick and Rockville Road Bill, of the Louisville and Portland Canal Bill, of the Light house Bill, answer this question. Let the qualification given by the executive to his approval of the bill in relation to the Cumberland Road, give a further answer to it, you all know that the *principle* of these bills has been over and over again settled by the People of the United States; you all know that the four first in the enumeration, after being passed by both Houses of Congress, were killed by General Jackson's *Veto;* and you all know on what reasons, in the several cases, his Veto was rested, though it would be ascribing to you more than human acumen, to suppose that you understand those reasons. Look at the money expended on Internal Improvements during the last Administration, which never exercised the *Veto* power; and look at the money expended by the present Administration under whose *Vetos,* Internal Improvements have been laid on a sick, perhaps a dying bed; and compare the total yearly expenditures of the two Administrations; and then see if there is any think in this great public interest, from which an excuse can be derived for the costly *"reforms"* and *"retrenchments"* of President Jackson. It will be equally vain to seek in any other object of national concern for an explanation of the extent to which he has advanced the expenditure of the public money. The true explanation is that he has administered the Government, not on public, but on party and personal principles. The enforcement of these principles has not only emptied the purse but has tarnished her character, violated the spirit of her institutions and retarded her march to prosperity and greatness.

The last subject to which I shall call your attention, is one which is near to my heart. It is one that awakens a solicitude in my bosom which language can never describe. I mean the situation of the occupants within the District; who undismayed by toil and difficulty, have settled themselves down, trusting to the justice and generosity of Congress, to secure to them their humble homes. In a previous part of this communication, I have treated of that subject — but since those remarks were penned, my attention has been called to it again by letters which I have received from gentlemen residing within the District. By them I am informed that a general alarm has been taken by the occupants; and that speculating warrant holders have taken advantage of that alarm, and in many instances practised the grossest frauds and impositions upon them. This I heard with deep regret. For I call upon my conscience to bear me witness when I assert, that no set of men on earth possess so great a share of my sympathetic regard, and my anxiety for their protection. It is asked why I have not done something to save them? Why I have not entered into some arrangement with my colleagues to secure the land to them? I can only reply that I thought I had done so. After it was ascertained that my first proposition would fail, I prepared a substitute for it, which I understood as being satisfactory — and which I again repeat I believe would have passed without difficulty, if they had not prevented me from getting the subject before the House.[3] Heaven knows that I have done all that a mortal could do, to save the people, and the failure was not my fault, but the fault of others. That you my fellow citizens, may be able to judge, whether I have been faithful or not — and whether or not my colleagues should have aided me, I here give you a copy of my substitute, in lieu of the original proposition:[4] —

"That each and every person, male and female, their heirs or assigns, who on or before the 1st day of December, 1830, had indicated a disposition to make a permanent settlement upon any of the vacant and unappropriated lands within the western district in the State of Tennessee, by erecting a house or clearing and enclosing one acre or more of land, shall be entitled to a right by pre-emption to two hundred acres of land, including the improvement so as aforesaid made; said occupant first paying into the Branch Bank of the United States, at Nashville, neither more nor less than the sum of twelve and a half cents per acre, for the land so located, to be placed to the credit of the Treasurer of the United States.

"Sec. 2. *And be it further enacted,* That in cases where surveys have been made, under the authority of the State of Tennessee, within the said western district, to wit, south and west of the congressional reservation line, the same shall be confirmed and held good and valid, on payment as aforesaid, to the occupant, his or her heirs or assigns as aforesaid, a certified plat and certificate of survey being properly registered, as is hereinafter required, or appearing already on the books of the surveyors. In no case, however shall the said pre-emption exceed two hundred acres, but shall, in every case, embrace in whole or in part the actual improvement of the occupant.

"Sec. 3. *And be it further enacted,* That in the event the aforesaid quantity of two hundred acres, embracing any improvement as contemplated by this act, cannot be had in and immediately around the same, it shall and may be lawful for the occupant as aforesaid subject to the provisions of the laws of Tennessee, to locate the same in one or two parcels upon any other vacant and unappropriated lands within the said western district, as in the whole not to exceed two hundred acres; and as much less as may be convenient for the occupant to locate and enter.

"Sec. 4. *And be it further enacted,* That in cases where surveys have been made under acts of the Tennessee Legislature, one passed in 1825, and another in the year 1829; or shall be made under this act, it shall be the duty of the surveyors who made or may make such survey to deliver to the occupant or person entitled to the same a certified plat and certificate thereof which being produced to the register of said district, he may receive and record the same; whereupon it shall and may be lawful for the register of said district, the purchase money aforesaid being first paid, to issue to such occupant, a grant or grants for his or her land so located and surveyed in one or more parcels as is hereinbefore authorized, the said grant being signed by the Governor, and countersigned in each case by the Secretary of the State of Tennessee.

"Sec. 5. *And be it further enacted,* That in the event of any occupant, or occupants not having had his, or her occupant claim or claims surveyed as authorized by the Statutes of the State of Tennessee, then and in that case, the said several surveyors in said District, are hereby authorized to cause such claim or claims, to be entered and surveyed in the same manner that occupant claims have been heretofore surveyed; under the laws of the State of Tennessee, and give a certificate thereof, and also that the actual possession of the occupants, prior to the 1st of December, 1830, shall be founded in all cases upon the testimony of at least two respectable witnesses, to be taken before said surveyor, for which said Surveyors shall be authorized to receive of said occupant, the same fees which are paid for similar services under the Statutes of the State of Tennessee.

"Sec. 6. *And be it further enacted,* That the fees allowed by this act to the Surveyors, Register and other officers shall be the same as those allowed for similar services, under the laws of the State of Tennessee.

"Sec. 7. *And be it further enacted,* That the time of two years from and after the passage of this act, be and the same is hereby allowed to said occupant settlers to make their entries, locations, and surveys, as contemplated by this act, and to file certificates thereof, with the register as hereinbefore required; during which time their improvements shall be secured against any and every other warrant, location, and entry made within that period.

"Sec. 8. *And be it further enacted,* That where two or more occupants hall have improvements so contiguous to each other as to prevent each from realizing the benefit of this act; in such case, the Surveyors shall divide as nearly as practicable the lands adjacent to their improvements between them, having due regard to quality and quantity, so as to interfere with the improvement of neither.

Who will or can say that this was unreasonable or unjust? No one would vote for you to enjoy your homes at all who could vote against your having them on the terms here proposed — and their object is now to hold out the idea to you that my obstinacy defeated the measure. They know this is not true. They were unwilling to let you have the land in any way except you got it from the Legislature of Tennessee; and to this I was opposed, because I knew that advantage would be taken of you; and that your rights would be sacrificed. Instead of being the cause of warrant-holders being let loose upon you, that is what I have been all along fighting against. I know, and you know too, that the Legislature has imposed upon you before, and I was afraid to trust them again. Of another thing I am certain in my own mind; it is, that Congress never would have passed the proposition of my colleagues — and therefore it is a mere imposition and a trick, to try to make you believe that you would have been secure in your homes if I had agreed to their arrangement. The object is too plain. It is to break me down — and destroy your confidence in me. If they can succeed in this, they perhaps may get a man in my place who will suit their purposes better; some one who will run at their bidding and do as they direct. This they know I wont do; and God is to be thanked that in a short time the people will find that they can't longer do so themselves. The party in power has opposed this measure, and so far defeated me — but now they are blowing up among themselves; and by another Congress will not be able to defeat any one. To occupants I say, hold fast to your possessions, and the justice of your country will yet secure you. The party in power, like Jonah's gourd, grew up quickly, and will quickly fall. They are all quarreling among themselves, and the people will turn away disgusted with them.

Fellow citizens; I am once more a candidate to represent you in Congress, I have met many disappointments, since I have been in your service, but I am not discouraged. I firmly believe that if I am again your choice, I shall meet a set of men in Congress, who will know how to feel for your situations, and will do you justice; and that I shall yet have the unspeakable pleasure, of seeing you seated by firesides which you can safely call your own. You know that I am a poor man; and that I am a plain man. I have served you long enough in peace, to enable you to judge whether I am honest or not — I never deceived — I never will deceive you. I have fought with you and for you in war, and you know whether I love my country, and ought to be trusted. I thank you for what you have done for me, and I hope that you will not forsake me to gratify those who are my enemies and yours.

With the best wishes for your prosperity and happiness, I am your friend and fellow citizen.

DAVID CROCKETT
Washington, February 28 1831.

[1] Cave Johnson actually spoke in favor of reconsidering the bill the next day, May 4, 1830, after it had been defeated the previous day.

[2] Crockett is, at best, being misleading here. The 89–92 vote was not on his bill, but rather a motion to bring the bill up for debate. Later in the circular he describes the vote more accurately.

[3] Here Crockett is more accurate in saying that the close 89–92 vote on May 4, 1830, was to reintroduce the bill, not a vote on the bill itself.

[4] This is the amended bill Crockett introduced on May 4, 1830, after his compromise bill had been defeated the previous day, and includes the new language drafted by Vinton. No official printed copy of the bill exists and it never came up for debate.

*   *   *   *   *

PART IV

— SELECTED SPEECHES OF DAVID CROCKETT —

JANUARY 5, 1829, IN THE HOUSE OF REPRESENTATIVES. SPEECH IN SUPPORT OF HIS AMENDMENT TO H.R. 27, POLK'S LAND BILL, INTRODUCED DECEMBER 24, 1827. *REGISTER OF DEBATES,* JANUARY 5, 1829, 162–63.

Mr. CROCKETT said that he had offered to the House the foregoing amendment to the bill, with the confident hope that, if he could succeed in convincing the House that this could not prove a precedent for its action in relation to other States, and that the land it proposed to give away would, if retained, be of no use or value to the General Government, they would adopt the amendment, and pass the bill. He regretted, on this subject, to be under the necessity of differing from his respectable colleague, [Mr. Polk] but the House would remember that his colleague and himself were very differently situated. They had received instructions from the Legislature of their State to ask Congress for a general grant of all the public lands remaining unpatented within its bounds for the purposes of education; and, having no prior obligation to conflict with those instructions, they were, of course, bound to obey them. He, it was true, as one of the Representatives of the State of Tennessee, was included within these instructions; but he had a higher authority, to which it was his duty and his pride ever to bow—his last instructions were from his own constituents, and these, in his estimation, took precedence of all others. The people who had honored him by making him their Representative, conceived that they were fairly entitled to the lands for which they had instructed him to ask this House, and which it was the object of his amendment to confer upon them. He asked this, however, not on the ground of strict legal right; he presented nothing in the shape of a demand; but he presented such a case as he believed and trusted would not fail to awaken the sympathies of this House, and effectually command its liberality. The persons in whose behalf he pleaded were the hardy sons of the soil; men who had entered the country when it lay in a state of native wildness; men who had broken the cane, and opened in the wilderness a home for their wives and children. The most of these enterprising and industrious settlers had once possessed other and better homes than they now enjoyed; they had entered on fertile lands, under titles which they believed to be good, and were successfully pushing their humble but independent fortune, when they were unexpectedly driven from their improvements by the appearance of a stranger, bringing a warrant of older date than theirs. Some of them had suffered this cruel disappointment more than once; they had been driven from improvement to improvement, and from home to home, till, in despair of ever realizing their early hopes, they had settled on lands that nobody would claim—on scraps and refuse fragments of the soil, which remained after all that was valuable had been first selected and occupied. The country where their humble homes were situated had been thrown open to warrant holders for eight years; floods of warrants had been issued, and armies of their holders had overspread the soil, picking and culling out all the good land as long as any was to be found; and it was the fractions, the odds and ends, the refuse which remained, in shapeless fragments, between the boundary lines of other tracts, that they now asked of Congress. The land was of poor quality, and of little value in itself; but it was dear to them, because it held their home, and was their all. The country thus situated formed but a small portion of the State, embracing the Congressional district from which he came, and part of another from which came his colleague on his right, [Mr. Polk.] The great mass of it lay in his own district, and, in fact, made up the whole of that district.

The House would, therefore, perceive how he was situated, and would appreciate the obligations under which he lay to press this amendment. It was impossible that the grant of fractions of land thus situated could ever operate as a precedent for grants in those States where the public lands were regularly laid out in townships and sections, by lines at right angles. This country had never been laid out at all. The General Government had never had a surveyor within its boundaries. It was thrown open in a mass for the satisfaction of the North Carolina warrants; and every man who had a warrant hunted out the best land he could find; and, in fixing his boundary lines, had respect only to the quality of the soil, and the quantity he had a right to take; and thus the tracts located were of every conceivable shape. On the intervals between these lines, the people for whom he was pleading had fixed their little homes. They had mingled the sweat of their brows with the soil they occupied, and by the hand of hard and persevering toil had earned the little comforts they possessed. Was it fair for the General Government to take away these humble cottages from them, and make a donation of the whole to the Legislature of the State, for the purpose of raising up schools for the children of the rich? I ask the House [said Mr. C.] if to do this will be an act of charity to the poor? It is asked by the State as charity: will it be so in practical effect? I ask some of it, but not for the State—not for the sons of the wealthy; but for the poor and industrious men who have given it all its value by their toil. Give it to them, and you will bind them to their Government by an indissoluble tie. Nothing makes a people love their Government like such acts of parental kindness. Sir, these people, though poor, are of inestimable value in a free republic. They are the bone and sinew of the land; they are its strength and its bulwark; they are its main reliance in the hour of danger, and the first to breast the onset of an enemy. Will you take away their little all and give it to the Legislature to speculate upon? Or will you make to each of these meritorious citizens the donation of his humble piece of land, where he has at last found a refuge from the pursuit of more successful warrant holders? It is dear to him, however humble; his children were born upon it; and there he has lived in peace and contentment. I ask you to give it him, and I ask with the confident hope that you will do it. Sir, my people think that those who live northeast of the dividing line have already made enough out of them. My district has had to pay one hundred thousand dollars towards the erection of colleges in the northeast part of the State. I think this is quite enough, but still more is now demanded, and I find myself under the necessity of defending one poor district against all the rest of the State of Tennessee. I shall do it; for I am dependent upon them for my station here; and so long as I hold a seat upon this floor I shall take their part against all who would exact upon them. Three hundred and five thousand acres of the best land in the district have already gone to satisfy warrants which I never believed to be just in principle. The compromise between the States of Tennessee and North Carolina required, indeed, the satisfying of these warrants, but they had been issued to Revolutionary soldiers, who were dead, and had no heirs living, and I ever viewed the arrangements as unjust and oppressive. When the measure was debated in the Legislature of my State, I opposed it to the best of my poor ability, but we were overruled and had to submit. According to that arrangement, the colleges got sixty thousand acres of our land. The University of North Carolina got one hundred and forty thousand acres more of it. After a little while, the demand for ninety-six thousand acres more was made. They demanded that this amount should be provided for and secured: that I also opposed. I could not, in my conscience, consent to it, because I did not think it right in principle. The measure, however, went into effect; and in a little while the ninety-six thousand acres had swelled to one hundred and five thousand. Yes, one hundred and five thousand acres taken out of one little district! You can readily believe that such a draught as that, made in twenty-five acre warrants, cut us up at an awful rate. The grant for the support of colleges drained us of fifty-two thousand five hundred dollars in cash. Ay, sir, in hard cash, wrung from the hands of poor men, who live by the sweat of their brow. I repeat, that I was utterly opposed to this: not because I am the enemy of education, but because the benefits of education are not to be dispensed with an equal hand. This College system went into practice to draw a line of demarcation between the two classes of society—it separated the children of the rich from the children of the poor. The children of my people never saw the inside of a college in their lives, and never are likely to do so. Those who passed the act well knew that we never should derive any good from it: but they insisted that the land should be given up, and they sent State surveyors to survey it. The expenses of that survey pressed heavily on my constituents—it drove some of them to their wit's end. Sir, I have seen the last blanket of a poor, but honest and industrious family, sold under the hammer of the sheriff, to pay for that survey. Ay, sir, the little furniture they had saved from better days, or earned by long and honorable toil, was torn from them to pay the fees of those surveyors. Exactions like these were made on men whose whole worldly estate consisted of some twenty or thirty acres of the poorest land. Sir, it is for such men that I plead. I ask, in my place, as their advocate and Representative, that you will make them a donation of that little property. Let it be their own. While they bedew it with the sweat of their faces, let them at least have the consolation of knowing that they may leave it to their own children, and not have it squandered on the sons of a stranger. Such fragments of miserable soil can be of no use or value to this Government. You will never insist on retaining it in your own hands. You will never sell it, for it will never bear the expense of surveying. You must do something with it. Will you not bestow it as a boon upon the unfortunate people who have nothing else in the world? There they are living in peace—they can there make shift to bring up their children. Some of them are widows, whose husbands fell while fighting your battles on the frontiers. None of them are rich, but they are an honest, industrious, hardy, persevering kind-hearted people. I know them [and] I know their situation. I have shared the hospitality of their cottages and been honored by their confidence with a seat in this assembly: and base and ungrateful indeed, must I be, when I cease to remember it. No, sir, I cannot forget it: and if their little all is to be wrested from them, for the purposes of State speculation; if a swindling machine is to be set up to strip them of what little the surveyors, and the colleges, and the warrant holders, have left them, it shall never be said that I sat by in silence, and refused, however humbly, to advocate their cause.

Crockett's January 15, 1829, circular (*Address of Mr. Crockett, to the Voters of the Ninth Congressional District of the State of Tennessee; Together with His Remarks in the House of Representatives, January 5, 1829* [Washington: Printed by Gales & Seaton, January 15, 1829], Rare Books Division, Library of Congress) includes some of this speech, with a few minor word changes, such as "on" instead of "upon." The only noticeable alteration in the circular is to the statement, "Sir, I have seen the last blanket of a poor, but honest and industrious family, sold under the hammer of the sheriff, to pay for that survey." The circular rephrased it to read, "Sir, I have seen the last article of property, which was subject to execution, of a poor, but honest and industrious family, sold under the hammer, by the Sheriff, to pay for that survey."

*   *   *   *   *

JANUARY 12, 1829, IN THE HOUSE OF REPRESENTATIVES. SPEECH IN SUPPORT OF HIS AMENDMENT TO H.R. 27, POLK'S LAND BILL, INTRODUCED DECEMBER 24, 1827, AND RESPONSE TO ATTACKS MADE ON HIM BY MEMBERS OF THE TENNESSEE DELEGATION. *THE REGISTER OF DEBATES IN CONGRESS*, JANUARY 12, 1829, 199–200.

Mr. CROCKETT then rose, and said that he felt it his duty to trouble the House with a few more observations in explanation of his views upon the subject before them, and particularly in reply to some remarks which had fallen from his honorable colleagues. He still remained unfixed in his opinion that, without the amendment which he had proposed, the bill could not possibly be productive of any good effects, and he therefore felt himself bound, both in justice to himself and to his constituents, to use every effort to carry it through that House. He had, during the last session of Congress, suggested to his colleague, [Mr. Polk] the Chairman of the Committee that had reported the bill brought into the House at that period, on the same subject as that which was then under consideration, the propriety of reporting a bill appropriating the proceeds of the land in question entirely for the benefit of the western district of Tennessee—for the benefit of those poor settlers, who had sat down, and occupied various small patches and fragments of the public domain, and established comfortable though humble homes. But he was sorry to say that that gentleman objected to his proposition, and preferred that bill of his own, which he subsequently introduced, and which ultimately failed. Mr. C. here observed that an explanation on one particular point might perhaps be considered due from him. He would shortly give it. He had on that occasion supported the original measure of his honorable friend, [Mr. Polk] while at the same time he perfectly knew that it would not be carried; he supported it under the hope that it would subsequently unite his colleagues of the Tennessee delegation with him in the support of his favorite measure—that of providing for the poor settlers of the western district. But he was sorry to find that he had been a very mistaken judge of policy indeed. Yes, [he repeated] he was well aware at the time that it could not succeed in passing the House, and he was of a similar opinion with respect to the present measure—he meant the original bill, which he was confident never would receive their sanction. It would be perceived by the House, that he was compelled to stand now in a very different attitude from that which he had assumed in the course of the last year's discussion of the subject. He felt himself called upon by a sense of duty to stand in opposition to the whole balance of the delegation from his own State; under the disadvantage also of having to contend with the arguments of three of the ablest members of the bar of that State. The House, he was sure, must fully appreciate the difficulties under which he labored in thus standing alone and unsupported; but he was strengthened in the task by the reflection that he was in the performance of his duty, and advocating the just claims of those poor, but honest, virtuous citizens who had sent him to that House to attend to their rights and interests. He could not conceive that, in submitting his amendment to the House, and soliciting them to sanction it by their vote, he had requested one particle which they ought not to grant, on every principle of charity and even of justice. to refer now to some observations of gentlemen upon that floor, relative to the operation of the amendment which he had proposed, one honorable gentleman [Mr. Polk] said it would act as a dangerous precedent; that other States would come forward, encouraged by the poor settlers of Tennessee, and claim every acre of the public domain. Now he [Mr. C] certainly could not see that such would be the necessary effect of the adoption of his amendment. Let other states be put in the same position as his State, and he would readily agree to grant them what Tennessee asked. Tennessee had received no public lands from the General Government; no United States surveyor had ever laid out lands in that State; she had a claim, and the worthy and honest citizens of his district had a claim— and a just claim it was, for it appealed to the best feelings of their hearts—to those lands. Was it then to be said that it would form a dangerous precedent to grant to those industrious and persevering men the miserable remnants and scraps of land which their toil alone could render desirable or valuable? Was it a dangerous precedent to grant to the poor and the needy the soil which they had reclaimed from the wilderness with the sweat of their brow? True, as had been said, those lands were of no value, but they were endeared to the settlers as being their homes—and to his own knowledge they were homes in which contentment and happiness reigned. But, if it were what they chose to consider so dangerous a precedent, he felt himself not the less bound to support it; his conscience told him he was right in doing so, and if that measure were adopted, the cries of those poor would resound in thanksgiving and gratitude before the throne of God. Another gentleman [Mr. Lea] had observed that, if the present claims were granted, they would at the next Congress come forward and ask for more. Now it did not appear to him that such would be the case: all that he wanted on behalf of his constituents was, that they should not be disturbed in the possession of the lands which they already occupied, and upon which depended their subsistence, by the holders of the North Carolina warrants. They asked Congress to grant them those lands, and those lands only; and if their request were complied with, the very utmost of their desires would be satisfied. The House, he was sure, must recollect that, when the subject was discussed last session, the gentleman from North Carolina and Tennessee had stated that some of the North Carolina warrants were in existence. He [Mr. C.] did not believe there did exist any; but, even supposing there were a number of them yet outstanding, were the holders of them to come and drive the settlers off their little patches of land, and reap the fruits of their years of toil and labor? He hoped the House would not sanction any measure fraught with so much cruelty and injustice. Besides, if those North Carolina warrants must be paid, there was good land enough in that State to meet them; and let them be satisfied out of that, without ejecting the indigent occupant in his district.

Mr. C. again expressed his full trust that gentlemen would properly appreciate the peculiar condition in which he was placed in that House respecting the subject before them, opposed as he was by the influence and talents of his honorable friends from Tennessee. With reference to the opposition which appeared to be entertained by the House to his amendment, he observed, that it was plain to him that it was wished to get rid of his proposition, together with the bill itself. He could see the tomahawk already lifted and impending over the head of the whole measure; and though it was of no importance to him personally, yet he could not view the prospect of its certain destruction without the deepest regret, for the sake of those poor people in whose behalf he was proud to rise up, either within this House or in any other place. One of his colleagues [Mr. Bell] had proposed to sell the land to the settlers at thirty-seven and a half cents per acre, whereas land as good as need be wished for could be purchased in the vicinity of the boundary line between Kentucky and Tennessee, a most fertile part of the State, in any quantities from six hundred and forty to one hundred and sixty acres, at fifty cents per acre. In fact, better lands than the patches occupied by his poor constituents could be bought as low as twenty-five cents. His honorable colleague's proposition, it would be seen by that, was indeed most bountiful. It went also to place the power of granting lands to actual settlers, after the liquidation of the North Carolina claims, in the Legislature of Tennessee; and it was assumed that the surplus lands would be gratuitously distributed; but he, [Mr. C.] would venture to pledge himself that, when they get the land into their hands, they would soon fix a price upon it. He repeated his conviction that it was designed to defeat the amendment, and the bill also, and to strangle the measure altogether: but he trusted the House would not suffer such a design to succeed.

Mr. C. concluded by thanking the House for the attention with which it had honored his humble efforts in support of his poor fellow-citizens in the Western district of Tennessee. He had addressed them in a style becoming what he was—a plain farmer; but, standing here, he reflected, with feelings of satisfaction, that whatever might be the decision of the House on the question, he had fulfilled his duty to the humble but virtuous men who had deputed him to represent them and their interests on that floor. He submitted the subject of his observations to the attentive consideration of that House.

Crockett included a heavily rewritten excerpt from this speech in his January 15, 1829, circular, although the essential meaning is unchanged. The version printed in the circular follows.

*　　*　　*　　*　　*

JANUARY 12, 1829 SPEECH IN THE HOUSE OF REPRESENTATIVES; ALTERNATE VERSION TRANSCRIBED FROM CROCKETT'S JANUARY 15, 1829 POLITICAL CIRCULAR, *ADDRESS OF MR. CROCKETT, TO THE VOTERS OF THE NINTH CONGRESSIONAL DISTRICT OF THE STATE OF TENNESSEE; TOGETHER WITH HIS REMARKS IN THE HOUSE OF REPRESENTATIVES, JANUARY 5, 1829* (WASHINGTON: PRINTED BY GALES & SEATON, JANUARY 15, 1829), RARE BOOKS DIVISION, LIBRARY OF CONGRESS), 10–12.

Mr. CROCKETT replied, and said that though he was sorry to trouble the House any farther on this subject, he felt it due to himself to make some explanation, in reply to so many attacks as had been made upon his unfortunate amendment. He had learned one lesson from the course of this debate; and that was, that he had been a poor judge of policy in the conducting of affairs in this House. At the last session, he had gone with his colleagues in support of this bill. (of the passage of which, however, he had then despaired,) in the form they approved; and he had done so with the hope that when it should come up at this session, his colleagues would in return lend their aid in giving it a form which might provide something for his constituents, and that the amendment he had offered would, at least, unite the Tennessee delegation. But he found he had made a very erroneous calculation: and he now found himself and his little amendment opposed by three of the ablest lawyers of his own State. He made no pretensions to literature or oratory, and felt the weight of such an opposition: he hoped the House would appreciate his situation. But, however opposed, he must do his duty. He had asked nothing of the House which they had not full power to grant. He was utterly astonished to find one of his colleagues [Mr. Polk] attempting to alarm the House with the danger of the precedent, and another [Mr. Lea] prophecying that as soon as what he asked should be given, more would be asked. Another of his colleagues was in trouble, lest enough land should not be left to satisfy those very *popular things called North Carolina warrants*. Such apprehensions came from a quarter that he had had no idea of. But, if it was so dangerous a thing to give those little scraps of poor land to poor but industrious men, he, as their Representative, was willing to bear all the blame of having proposed it: if he succeeded, their children would remember him in their appeals to the Throne of God for such an act of liberality to their parents; and this would be to him a sufficient reward. As to what a future Congress might do, he did not pretend to know any thing; possibly he could not see so far as some of his honorable colleagues; but they would surely recollect that both the Tennessee and North Carolina delegations had last session acknowledged that they knew of no more warrants yet to be satisfied: that point had been fully given up. Now, it seemed to have been brought up again; for what purpose he should not say. But, even if there should be more of these warrants, (for one, he thought there had been quite enough of them already,) still he hoped that the satisfying of these would not be a reason for taking away from his constituents the little homes they had earned by the sweat of their brow. There could be no necessity for sending the warrant-holder to pick and cull among their little improvements: there was land enough, and to spare, without this, as good as their warrants were honest; unless, indeed, the House would consent to give it all away at a stroke to the Tennessee Legislature. For his part, he urged no demands: he set up no claim: he only asked for an act of charity to the poor and needy. he had no faith in the system which had been proposed: he perceived the tomahawk drawn over his measure, and plainly enough saw what was the object intended: it was intended to defeat the grant to his constituents; and sooner than not accomplish this end, gentlemen were ready to give up the bill; but he cherished a hope that the House would show that they were determined these poor men should have a home. He still trusted that he should enjoy the satisfaction of sending them the good news that their little all was safe, and that the fruit of their toil should at last be made their own. The House, he knew, would have their thanks the longest day they had to live. But one of his honorable colleagues wanted to aid them in a very singular way: he would have them pay 37½ cents an acre for the land, with a view that a grand road should be made through their country from Memphis to the great National road from Zanesville to Florence, in Alabama; and, perhaps some gentlemen believed there was such a road. If any such grand national road was in existence, there might be more in the plan; but, as no such road existed any where, except in the imagination of gentlemen, he thought it would be best to wait till it had some existence elsewhere. Let us get the body, said Mr. C., before we talk about the limbs. A simple line alone divided his district from the adjoining State of Kentucky. On one side of this line the land was divided into sections and quarter sections, and whoever pleased might enter from a whole section down to 160 acres, at 50, and even he believed, at present, 25 cents, and this for as good land as any in his district; while, on his own side of the line, no such advantages were to be had, the warrant holders having culled out all the good land, and left nothing but the refuse. Surely his little act of charity was not so terrible a matter as it had been represented: it proposed nothing so very fatal or formidable to the State or to the United States. There was no design, no trick, nothing secret in the matter; but the amendment of his colleague, [Mr. Polk,] as first presented, and even as amended, was a perfect trap: it said they were to enter the land "without charge;" but he would be surety that the Legislature would exact the full value for the land. As to the North Carolina warrants, they were of a multiplying nature: they bred like rabbits; and if gentlemen wished more to come they had only to give encouragement to new demands, and no fear but they would have as many as their hearts desired. Mr. C. concluded by contrasting his own humble attainments with the array of talents opposed to him, but expressed his hope in the liberality of the National Legislature, relying most firmly upon the justice of the grounds which he had taken.

*   *   *   *   *

MAY 19, 1830 IN THE HOUSE OF REPRESENTATIVES, SPEECH IN OPPOSITION TO THE INDIAN REMOVAL BILL.

Two complete versions of this speech were published. The first, which appears to be closer to the original speech, was published in the *Jackson Gazette* on June 26, 1830. The second appeared in a collection of congressional speeches opposed to Indian removal, published in 1830.[1] The latter version appears to have been edited and slightly polished or revised, but there is no substantive difference between the two versions. The *Gazette* version is printed here, with the alternative wording in the second version footnoted.

INDIAN QUESTION.

SPEECH of Mr. Crockett, of Tennessee in the House of Representatives, on the 20th instant,[2] on the bill to provide for the removal of the Indians over the Mississippi.

Mr. Crockett said, that, considering his very humble abilities, it might be expected that he should content himself with a silent vote; but, situated as he was, in relation to his colleagues, he felt it to be a duty to himself to explain the motives which governed him in the vote he should give on this bill. Gentlemen had already discussed the treaty-making power; and had done it much more ably than he could pretend to do. He should not therefore enter on that subject, but would merely make an explanation as to the reasons of his vote. He did not know a man within 500 miles of his residence that would give a similar vote:[3] but he knew, at the same time, that he should give that vote with a clear conscience. He had his constituents to settle with, he was aware; and should like to please them as well as other gentlemen; but he had also a settlement to make at the bar of his God; and what his conscience dictated to be just and right he would do, be the consequences what they might. He believed that the people who had been kind enough to give him their suffrages supposed him to be an honest man, or they would not have chosen him. If so, they could not but expect that he should act in the way he thought honest and right. He had always viewed the native Indian tribes in this country[4] as a sovereign people. He believed they had been recognized as such from the very foundation of the Government;[5] and the United States were bound by treaty to protect them; it was their duty to do so. And as to giving the money of the American people for the purpose of removing them in the manner proposed, he would not do it. He would do that only for which he could answer to his God. Whether he could answer it before the people was comparatively nothing, though it was a great satisfaction to him to have the approbation of his constituents.

Mr. C. said he had served seven years[6] in a legislative body. But from the first hour he had entered a legislative hall, he had never known what party was in legislation; and God forbid he ever should. He went for the good of the country, and for that only. What he did as a legislator, he did conscientiously. He should love to go with his colleagues, and with the West and the South generally, if he could; but he never would let party govern him in a question of this great weight.[7]

He had many objections to the bill—some of them of a very serious character. One was, that he did not like to put half a million of money into the hands of the Executive, to be used in a manner which nobody could foresee, and which Congress was not to control. Another objection was, he did not wish to depart from the rule which had been observed towards the Indian nations from the foundation of the Government.[8] He considered the present application as the last alternative for these poor remnants of a once powerful people. Their only chance of aid was the hands[9] of Congress. Should its members turn a deaf ear to their cries, misery must be their fate. That was his candid opinion.

Mr. C. said he was often forcibly reminded of the remark made by the famous *Red Jacket,* in the rotundo of this building, when he was shown the pannel which represented in sculpture the first landing of the pilgrims,[10] with an Indian chief presenting to them an ear of corn, in token of friendly welcome. The aged Indian said "that was good." The Indian said, he knew that they came from the Great Spirit, and he was willing to share the soil with his brothers from over the great water. But when he turned round to another pannel representing Penn's treaty, he said "ah! all's gone now!"[11] There was a great deal of truth in this short saying; and the present bill was a strong commentary upon it.

Mr. C. said that four counties of his district bordered on the Chickasaw Country.[12] He knew many of their tribe; and nothing should ever induce him to vote to drive them west of the Mississippi. He did not know what sort of a country it was in which they were to be settled. He would willingly appropriate money in order to send proper persons to examine the country. And when this was done, and a fair and free treaty made with the tribes,[13] if they were desirous of removing, he would vote an appropriation of any sum necessary; but till this had been done, he would not vote one cent. He could not clearly understand the extent of this bill. It seemed to go to the removal of all the Indians in any State East[14] of the Mississippi river, in which the United States owned any land. Now, there was a considerable number of them still neglected; there was a considerable number of them in Tennessee, and the United States' Government[15] owned no land in that State, north and east of the congressional reservation line. No man could be more willing to see them remove than he was, if it could be done in a manner agreeable to themselves; but not otherwise. He knew personally that a part of the tribe of the Cherokees were unwilling to go. When the proposal was made to them they said, "No: we will take death at our homes.[16] Let them come and tomahawk us here at home; we are willing to die, but never to remove." He had heard them use this language. Many different constructions might be put on this bill.[17] One of the first things which had set him against the bill, was the letter from the Secretary of War to Col. Montgomery[18]—from which it appeared that the Indians had been intruded upon. Orders had been issued to turn them all off except the heads of the Indian families, or such as possessed improvements. Government had taken measures to purchase land from the Indians who had gone to Arkansas. If this bill should pass, the same plan would be carried farther;[19] they would send and buy them out, and put white men on[20] their land. It had never been known that white men and Indians could live together; and in this case, the Indians were to have no privileges allowed them, while the white men were to have all. Now, if this was not oppression with a vengeance, he did not know what was. It was the language of the bill, and its friends,[21] that the Indians were not to be driven off against their will. He knew the Indians were unwilling to go: and therefore he could not consent to place them in a situation where they would be obliged to go. He could not stand that. He knew that he stood alone, having, per-haps, none of his colleagues from his state agreeing in sentiment. He could not help that. He knew that he should return to his home glad and light in heart, if he voted against the bill. He felt that it was his wish and purpose to serve his constituents honestly, according to the light of his conscience. The moment he should exchange his conscience for mere party views, he hoped his Maker would no longer suffer him to exist. He spoke the truth in saying so. If he should stand alone amidst all the people of the United States, he should not vote otherwise;[22] and it would be a matter of rejoicing to him till the day he died, that he had given the vote. He had been told that he should be prostrated; but if so, he would have the consolation of conscience. He would obey that power, and glorified in the deed.[23] He cared not for popularity, unless it could be obtained by upright means.[24] He had been told that he did not understand English grammar. That was very true. He had never been six months at school in his life: he had raised himself by the labor of his hands. But he did not, on that account, yield up his privilege as the representative of forty thousand free men on this floor.[25] Humble as he was, he meant to exercise his privilege. He had been charged with not representing his constituents: if the fact was so,[26] the error (said Mr. C.) is here, (touching his head) not here (laying his hand upon his heart). He had never[27] possessed wealth or education, but he had ever been animated by an independent spirit, and he trusted to prove it on the present occasion.

Although Crockett's speech did not appear in the *Register of Debates in Congress*, which did not include all remarks made in Congress in any case, or in the *House Journal*, which included only brief summaries of debates, there is ample evidence to conclude that Crockett did, indeed, deliver this speech in the House of Representatives. The speech was reported and paraphrased in the *United States' Telegraph* on May 20, 1830, and Crockett himself wrote to the *Telegraph* the same day, complaining of inaccuracies in that paraphrasing, thus acknowledging that he had delivered it.[28] Several other newspapers repeated the *Telegraph's* account of Crockett's May 19th remarks: "Mr. Crockett also spoke in opposition to it, stating that, although four counties of his congressional district adjoined the Chickasaw nation of Indians, he was opposed in conscience to the measure; and such being the case, he cared not what his constituents thought of his conduct."[29]

---

[1] *Speeches on the Passage of the Bill for the Removal of the Indians* (Boston: Perkins & Marvin, 1830); 251–53, reprinted in Louis Filler and Allen Guttmann, eds., *The Removal of the Cherokee Nation: Manifest Destiny or National Dishonor?* (Lexington, Mass.: D. C. Heath and Company 1962), 39–41.

[2] This is an error in the date; all other sources give May 19 as the date of Crockett's speech.

[3] "He did not know whether a man* within 500 miles of his residence would give a similar vote;" (* "That is, a member of Congress."). The footnote clarifies that Crockett was referring to other congressmen, but he was equally aware that few of his constituents would support his vote against Indian removal.

[4] "Indian tribes of this country"

[5] "the very foundation of this government"

[6] "had served for seven years"

[7] "a question of this great consequence"

[8] "government"

[9] "was at the hands of Congress"

[10] "Pilgrims"

[11] "Ah! All's gone now." The two panels in the Capitol Rotunda that Crockett referred to are *William Penn's Treaty with the Indians* by Nicholas Gevelot and *Landing of the Pilgrims* by Enrico Causici. Architect of the Capitol website, http://www.aoc.gov/cc/capitol/rotunda.cfm.

[12] "country"

[13] "And when this had been done, and a fair and free treaty had been made with the tribes"

[14] "east"

[15] "government"

[16] "we will take death here at our homes"

[17] "upon this bill"

[18] "secretary of war to colonel Montgomery"

[19] "further"

[20] "upon"

[21] "and of its friends"

[22] "If he should be the only member of that House who voted against the bill, and the only man in the United States who disapproved it, he would still vote against it;"

[23] "and gloried in the deed"

[24] The second version adds a sentence here that is missing from the *Jackson Gazette* version: "He had seen much to disgust him here; and he did not wish to represent his fellow-citizens, unless he could be permitted to act conscientiously."

[25] "as the representative of freemen on this floor.* (*Colonel Crocket represents more voters than any member of Congress, except Mr. Duncan of Illinois. The reason is, the great influx of population since the State was formed into districts. There were 20,000 voters in Colonel Crockett's district more than a year ago. There are probably more than 22,000 now)." The change in wording and the explanatory footnote suggest that Crockett greatly overestimated the population of his district at some forty thousand, or perhaps represents no more than the difference in actual population compared to "voters," a substantially smaller number that included only adult white males.

[26] "his constituents. If the fact"

[27] "he never had"

[28] Crockett to the *United States Telegraph*, May 20, 1830, published May 25, 1830.

[29] Ibid.

*   *   *   *   *

FEBRUARY 24, 1831, IN THE HOUSE OF REPRESENTATIVES. SPEECH IN SUPPORT OF EXPENDITURES FOR INTERNAL IMPROVEMENTS AND AGAINST A MOTION TO RECOMMIT THE BILL. *REGISTER OF DEBATES*, FEBRUARY 24, 1831, 788-89.

Mr. CROCKETT said he was opposed to the motion to recommit, for several reasons. First, the object of the motion was to destroy the passage of the bill. It was late in the session, and, if recommitted, the bill could not be acted upon at the present session.

We expected to hear the doctrines advanced by that gentleman; we heard his sentiments a year ago upon the principle. For his own part, Mr. C. said, he had always supported the system of internal improvements, and, as he expected to be consistent, he should continue to support that system upon principle, at least until he was better informed than at present. Although, said Mr. C., our great man, at the head of the nation, has changed his course, I will not change mine. I would rather be politically dead than hypocritically immortalized. The more I become acquainted with the great value of the improvements in question, the more I am satisfied of their utility in a national point of view. I presume the improvement of the Ohio and Mississippi rivers is as much a work of national importance as any improvement in the country. At the commencement of that work it may have been slighted by the managers, but I am persuaded that no man acquainted with the mode now pursued can doubt the expediency of continuing it.

The gentleman from Virginia asks how long this appropriation is to be continued? I answer, as long as the Mississippi runs. What is money compared with the lives of the people engaged upon that river; or the appropriation compared with the amount of property which floats upon it? Sir, the produce of thirteen States finds its market by means of these rivers.

Those State rights gentlemen who are opposed to appropriations by the General Government for purposes of internal improvement, may think that the navigation of those rivers ought to be improved by the States. I should like to know what State is to take charge of the Mississippi, and to clear the obstructions of that river. Sir, I do hope the question will be taken, that we shall adopt the amendment of the gentleman from Kentucky, and pass the bill.

My colleague [Mr. Polk] says he hopes the appropriation for the surveys will be stricken out—I hope it will not. He says he has been a supporter of the present administration, and that he still supports it. I was also a supporter of this administration after it came into power, and until the Chief Magistrate changed the principles which he professed before his election. When he quitted those principles, I quit him. I am yet a Jackson man in principles, but not in name. The name is nothing. I support those principles, but not men. I shall insist upon it that I am still a Jackson man, but General Jackson is not; he has become a Van Buren man. I hope the motion to recommit will not prevail.

The House debated proposed expenditures of $50,000 for improving navigation of the Ohio and Mississippi Rivers, and $150,000 for improvement of the Ohio River. There was lengthy debate on the first measure, which Crockett spoke for "repeatedly." The speech quoted here was in support of the second measure. Crockett was objecting to a motion by his old foe Pryor Lea to delay action on the bill by recommitting it, which was defeated, along with a motion by Polk to strike out an appropriation of $25,000 for surveys.

Crockett clearly favored an activist central government with a national role that transcended states' rights. He was opposed by Jackson, who had supported internal improvements while in the Senate, but opposed them as president.

Polk was one of the staunchest opponents of federal funding of internal improvements. There is, however, a disconnect between Crockett's strong support of internal improvements and his consistent opposition to the federal tariff and support of cheap sale or free grants of federal land, since these were the only two sources of federal revenues that might pay for internal improvements.

*   *   *   *   *

SPEECH IN ABINGDON, VIRGINIA, NOVEMBER 18, 1833. *UNITED STATES' TELEGRAPH,* **DECEMBER 5, 1833.**

[The speech was preceded by six toasts, to: the President of the United States; the Federal Union; the 'Right of Instruction'; John Marshall, Chief Justice of the United States; the State of Alabama, and "Our worthy guest, Col. David Crockett. —His independent political course, and confidence in the integrity of his motives, have secured him the esteem of his countrymen." After the applause had subsided, Colonel Crockett rose and said,]

Gentlemen:—I am happy to meet with my fellow-citizens of Abingdon on this occasion.—To receive the approbation of those whose good opinion I highly prize, is at all times, and under all circumstances gratifying to me; and ought to be a sufficient reward to him who serves the public. But, Gentlemen: —on this occasion I am at a loss for language to express my gratitude for your kindness; and for the very flattering manner in which you have been pleased to allude to my public course. This, Gentlemen, is the first occasion of *this* nature, where I have felt myself called upon to address a public assembly. You well know how to appreciate those feelings, which this mark of your esteem and confidence is calculated to excite in my bosom. In the remarks which I may submit, I may be guilty of some error;—if so—you will know how to appreciate that error.

Although, Gentlemen, I was personally unacquainted with you, until circumstances threw me amongst you, and will cause me a temporary stay in your town; yet it was near your own Holston that I had my nativity. In early life I emigrated to the western wilds. I have never had the advantages of education, nor any of those refinements, by which man is polished and improved, and which will enable him to 'go ahead' among his fellow men. Unfortunately for me, these opportunities have been denied me. Thus thrown upon the world, I had to dictate my own course—to form and adopt my own principles and views, and to build up my own character. I have done so, and the people among whom I have settled have called upon me to discharge a public duty.

Their kindness brought me into public life. In 1831, I was elected to the Legislature of Tennessee. They favored me with their confidence—continued their support—and finally elected me to Congress. But I was so unfortunate in 1830, as to differ with the President: a man I had loved, honored, and supported. —I knew him well, and Gen. Jackson had the warmest feelings of my heart. I crossed the Tennessee river with him, the first time he ever fought the Indians. I served two campaigns of six months each, with him, in his Indian wars. I loved Gen. Jackson, and if any man could have been induced to cling to him from *personal* considerations, then would I still have been a Jackson man. But when I gave him my support for President, I did so upon *principles*. And when he *abandoned* those principles, I *abandoned* him. How could I have done otherwise? I never aspired to office. My people had kindly taken me up, and put me into political life. The President had departed from the principles upon which I supported him, and the alternative was now presented me, either to *act for myself,* or *for a party*—Gentlemen, I knew *no party.* I *never knew* a party. I had hoped ever to remain *the friend* of Jackson. But when he and my principles came in contact, I did not hesitate to choose which should receive the continuance of my support. I *gave up Jackson.* For *this* I was sentenced to "a two-years stay' at home. But I am happy, gentlemen, to inform you, that *my case* has been *reconsidered.*

In the late election in my district, I *opposed* Gen. Jackson, from principle. I well knew the mighty *power of his name,* but I determined, if beaten, to submit to my fate. I knew that his mighty name was like the vivid lightning that comes from Heaven, scorching and blasting every thing with which it comes in contact. But, gentlemen, in that election, I carried *both him,* and *all his influence* against the United States Bank, upon my shoulders. My constituents have again sent me to Congress as their Representative. But I am no *party man*—I go into public life as every man's representative—having in view the general welfare of our common country.

The next session of Congress will be an important one. Important measures will there have to be discussed and settled. Amongst other matters, the question of rechartering the Bank will be presented to our consideration. I was always in favor of the Bank, and shall support a bill to renew its charter. I am the only member from Tennessee that will do so. But I believe the Bank useful to the country, and shall support it from love of country, although I differ with the President on this subject.

But, Gentlemen,—we shall also have something to do with the removal of the deposites.—Our Government was wisely constructed, when the sword (subject to the control of Congress) was put into the President's hand; and the nation's purse into hands of another officer, the Secretary of the Treasury. But the time is come, when one man takes the sword in one hand, and the purse in the other, —puts forward his *own will* as the Law, and bids *defiance* to Congress and the nation. This is a new scene presented to the American people! Did any other President ever so act? No: —Gentlemen: all—presidents that ever wielded the destinies of this nation, have conferred with Congress, and have at all times received its aid in carrying into effect such measures as that body should deem proper and expedient. In all measures of this character, our Presidents have always had a majority of Congress with them. But this is not the case now. —In regard to the removal of the deposites, Gen. Jackson has gone directly contrary to the known wishes of Congress, and for so doing, 'takes the responsibility upon himself;' depending upon his popularity to sustain him in his arbitrary course. This, —Gentlemen, shows us the danger of having too popular a man at the head of our government. Could we have 'a peep behind the curtain,' we should then see into all that maneuvering, which has pushed Jackson forward in his bold and reckless course. Why such eagerness to remove the public deposites from the Bank of the U.S.? —it is, in my opinion, to effect *a particular* purpose. Caesar said, 'give me money and I can buy men, and give me men, and I can make power.' I do believe, gentlemen, that the sole object in removing the deposites, is to get 'the money' out of the iron chest, and put it into a little wooden box, so that they can get their hands upon it, and use it in making Mr. Van Buren the next President.

I ask, Gentlemen, shall this arbitrary course of the President be tolerated in a Government of free principles? Shall we tamely submit to the dictation of one man, and quietly yield up our liberties to the strong arm of Tyranny? If so, we must call things by their right name. Let us no longer talk of a free Government. —and let us give up the name of Republicanism.

Gentlemen, amongst the indications of a country's prosperity is the successful prosecution of works of internal improvement, of which I have ever been the friend and supporter; and it is with much gratification I see a handsome specimen of the liberal enterprise of the citizens of Abingdon, in the improvement of their streets, by their private means and exertions. Gentlemen, I give you the successful prosecution of your public work, and the health and happiness of your citizens.

Crockett's speech was followed by seven more toasts to Henry Clay; the Federal Constitution; the next Congress; the State of Virginia; the memory of Washington, Franklin, and Jefferson; Science; and the Fair Sex.

Crockett delivered this dinner speech at the invitation of citizens of Abingdon who hosted the dinner and said it was the first time he had been asked to serve as a dinner speaker. His mention of the nearby town of Holston as the place where "I had my nativity" is a reference to his father's tavern having been located along the Abingdon-Knoxville road, possibly near the Main Holston Road. As a youth, Crockett was hired out to Jacob Siler to work on a four-hundred-mile cattle drive to Rockbridge, Virginia, a route that took him through Abingdon. *David Crockett, A Narrative of the Life of David Crockett of the State of Tennessee,* **edited by James A. Shackford and Stanley J. Folmsbee (Knoxville: University of Tennessee Press, 1973), 22–27.**

*　　*　　*　　*　　*

SPEECH DELIVERED IN BOSTON, EARLY MAY, 1834. DAVID CROCKETT, *AN ACCOUNT OF COLONEL CROCKETT'S TOUR TO THE NORTH AND DOWN EAST* **(PHILADELPHIA: E. L. CAREY AND A. HART), 67-76.**

Gentlemen,

By the entire friendship of the citizens of Boston, as well as the particular friendship with which you have received me this evening, I have been brought to reflect on times that have gone by, and review a prejudice that has grown up with me, as well as thousands of my western and southern friends. We have always been taught to look upon the people of New England as a selfish, cunning set of fellows, that was fed on fox ears and thistle tops; that cut their wisdom teeth as soon as they were born; that made money by their wits and held on to it by natur[e]; that called cheatery mother-wit; that hung on to political power because they had numbers; that raised up manufactures to keep down the south and west; and, in fact, had much of the devil in all their machinery, that they would neither lead nor drive, unless the load was going into their own cribs, But I assure you, gentlemen, I begin to think different of you, and I think I see a good many good reasons for so doing.

I don't mean that because I eat your bread and drink your liquor, that I feel so. No; that don't make me see clearer than I did. It is your habits, and manners, and customs; your industry; your proud, independent spirits; your hanging on to the eternal principles of right and wrong; your liberality in prosperity, and your patience when you are ground down by legislation, which, instead of crushing you, whets your invention to strike a path without a blaize on a tree to guide you; and above all, your never-dying, deathless grip to our glorious constitution. These are the things that make me think that you are a mighty good people.—

(Here I had to stop for a while)

Gentlemen, I believe I have spoke the truth, and not flattery; I a'n't used to oily words; I am used to speak, what I think, of men and to men: I am perhaps more of a come-by-chance than any of you ever saw; I have made my way to the place I now fill, without wealth, and against education; I was raised from obscurity, and placed in the high councils of the nation, by the kindness and liberality of the good people of my district—a people whom I will never be unfaithful to, here or elsewhere; I love them, and they have honored me; and according as God has given me judgement, I'll use it for them, come of me what may.

These people once passed sentence upon me of a two years' stay-at-home, for exercising that which I contend belongs to every freeman in this nation: that was, for differing in opinion with the chief magistrate of this nation. I was well acquainted with him. He was but a man; and, if I was not before, my constituents had made a man of me. I had marched and counter-marched with him: I had stood by him in the wars and fought under his flag at the polls: I helped to heap the measure of glory that has crushed and smashed everything that has come in contact with it: I helped to give him the name of "Hero," which, like the lightning from heaven, has scorched and blasted everything that stood in its way—a name which, like the prairie fire, you have to burn against, or you are gone—a name which ought to be the first in war and the last in peace—a name, which, like 'Jack-o'-the-lantern,' blinds your eyes while you follow it through mud and mire.

Gentlemen, I never opposed Andrew Jackson for the sake of popularity. I knew it was a hard row to hoe: but I stood up to the rack, considering it a duty I owed to the country that governed me. I had reviewed the course of other presidents, and came to the conclusion that he did not of right possess any more power than those that had gone before him. When he transcended that power, I put down my foot. I knew his popularity; that he had come into place with the largest majority of anyone that had gone before him, who had opposition: but still, I did not consider this as giving him the right to do as he pleased, and construe our constitution to meet his own views.

We had lived the happiest people under the sun for fifty years, governed by the constitution and laws, on well established constructions: and when I saw the government administered on new principles, I objected, and was politically sacrificed: I persisted in my sins, having a clear conscience, that before God and my country, I had done my duty.

My constituents began to look at both sides; and finally, at the end of two years, approving of my course, they sent me back to Congress—a circumstance that was truly gratifying to me.

Gentlemen, I opposed Andrew Jackson in his famous Indian bill, where five hundred thousand dollars were voted for expenses, no part of which has yet been accounted for, that I have seen. I thought it was extravagant as well as impolitic. I thought the rights reserved to the Indians were about to be frittered away; and events prove that I thought correct. I had considered a treaty as the sovereign law of the land; but now saw it considered as a matter of expedience, or not, as it pleased the powers that be. Georgia bid defiance to the treaty-making power, and set at nought the Intercourse Act of 1802; she trampled it under foot; she nullified it: and for this she received the smiles and approbation of Andrew Jackson. And this was what induced South Carolina to nullify the tariff. She had a right to expect the president was favourable to the principle: but he took up the rod of correction, and shook it over South Carolina, and said at the same time to Georgia, 'You may nullify, but South Carolina shall not.'

This was like his consistency in many other matters. When he was a senator in Congress, he was a friend to internal improvements, and voted for them. Every thing then that could cement the states together, by giving them access the one to the other, was right. When he got into power, some of his friends had hard work to dodge, and follow, and shout. I called off my dogs, and quit the hunt. Yes, gentlemen, Pennsylvania, and Ohio, and *Tennessee*, and other states, voted for him , as a supporter of internal improvements.

Was he not a tariff man? Who dare deny it! When did we first hear of his opposition? Certainly not in his expression that he was in favour of a *judicious* tariff. That was supposed to be a clincher, even in New England, until after power lifted him above the opposition of the supporters of a tariff.

He was for putting down the monster 'Party,' and being the president of the people. Well, in one sense this he tried to do: he put down every one he could that was opposed to him either by reward or punishment; and could all have come into his notions, and bowed the knee to his image, I suppose it might have done very well, so far as he was concerned. Whether it would have been a fair reading of his famous letter to Mr. Monroe, is rather questionable.

He was to reform the government. Now if *reformation* consists of turning out and putting in, he did it with a vengeance.

He was, last of all, to *retrench the expenditures*. Well, in time, I have no doubt, this must be done; but it will not consist in the abolishing useless expenditures of former administrations. No, gentlemen; the spoils belonged to the victor; and it would never do to lessen the teats when the litter was doubled. The treasury trough had to be extended, and the pap thickened: kin were to be provided for; and if all things keep on as they are, his own extravagances will have to be retrenched, or you will get your tariff up again as high as you please.

I recollect a boy once, who was told to turn the pigs out of the corn-field. Well, he made a great noise, hallowing and calling the dogs—and came back. By-and-by his master said, 'Jim, you rascal! you didn't turn out the pigs.' — 'Sir,' said he, 'I called the dogs, and set them a-barking.'

So it was with that big Retrenchment Report, in 1828. Major Hamilton got Chilton's place as chairman—and called the dogs. Ingham worked honestly, like a beaver; Wickliff was as keen as a cutworm: all of them worked hard; and they did really, I suppose, convince themselves that they had found out a great deal of iniquity; or, what was more desirable, convinced the people that Andrew Jackson and his boys were the only fellows to mend shoes for nothing, and find their own candles. Everett and Sargeant, who made the minority report, were scouted at. What has come of all this? Nothing—worse than nothing. Jackson used these very men like dogs: they knew too much, and must be got rid of, or they would stop his profligacy too. They were greased and swallowed: and he gave them up to the torments of an anti-Jackson conscience.

Yes, gentlemen, as long as you think with him, very well; but if not—clear out; make way for some fellow who has saved his wind; and because he has just begun to huzzah, he has more wind to spare. General Jackson has turned out more men, for opinion's sake, than all other presidents put together, five times over: and the broom sweeps so low, that it reaches the humblest officer who happens to have a mean neighbour to retail any little story which he may pick up.

I voted for Andrew Jackson because I believed he possessed certain principles, and not because his name was Andrew Jackson, or the Hero, or Old Hickory. And when he left those principles which induced me to support him, I considered myself justified in opposing him. This thing of man-worship I am a stranger to; I don't like it; it taints every action of life; it is like a skunk getting into a house— long after he has cleared out, you smell him in every room and closet, from the cellar to the garret.

I know nothing, by experience, of party discipline. I would rather be a raccoon dog, and belong to a negro in the forest, than to belong to any party, farther than to do justice to all, and to promote the interests of my country. The time will and must come, when honesty will receive its reward, and when the people of this nation will be brought to a sense of their duty, and will pause, and reflect how much it cost us to redeem ourselves from the government of one man. It cost the lives and fortunes of thousands of the best patriots that ever lived. Yes, gentlemen, hundreds of them fell in sight of your own city.

I this day walked over the great battle-ground of Bunker's hill, and thought whether it was possible that it was moistened with the sacred blood of our heroes in vain, and that we should forget what they fought for.

I hope to see our happy country restored to its former peace and happiness, and once more redeemed from tyranny and despotism, which, I fear, we are on the very brink of. We see the whole country in commotion: and for what? Because, gentlemen, the true friends of liberty see the laws and constitution blotted out from the heads and hearts of the people's leaders: and their requests for relief are treated with scorn and contempt. They meet the same fate that they did before king George and his parliament. It has been decided by a majority of Congress, that Andrew Jackson shall be the Government, and that his will shall be the law of the land. He takes the responsibility, and vetos any bill that does not meet his approbation. He takes the responsibility and seizes the treasury, and removes it from where the laws had placed it; and now, holding purse and sword, has bid defiance to the Congress and to the nation.

Gentlemen, if it is for opposing those high-handed measures that you compliment me, I say I have done so, and will do so, now and for ever. I will be no man's man, and no party's man, other than to be the people's faithful representative: and I am delighted to see the noble spirit of liberty retained so boldly here, where the first spark was kindled; and I hope to see it shine and spread over our whole country.

Gentlemen, I have detained you much longer than I intended: allow me to conclude by thanking you for your attention and kindness to the stranger from the far West.

*　　*　　*　　*　　*

APPENDIX A: KNOWN MISSING CROCKETT CORRESPONDENCE AND CIRCULARS

LETTERS:
1828:
May 2, to Hon. S.L. Southard, secretary of the navy, recommending James Madison Lockert of Tennessee as midshipman; also signed by James K. Polk and three other legislators; auctioned November 6, 1969, by Charles Hamilton Autographs, Inc.

1830:
May 31, to Maj. William B. Lewis; introduction and recommendation for Thomas Graham; auctioned by Sotheby's, New York, October 3, 1989; California Book Auction Galleries, San Francisco, October 31, 1989; and Christie's, November 8, 1999.

December 16, to John Ross. Ross's January 13, 1831, letter to Crockett refers to "your favor of the 16th ult.," which included other "letters enclosed," a reference to letters of support for the Cherokee that Crockett had enclosed with his own letter to Ross, one of which was written by David L. Child. Crockett's letter to Ross has not been located.

1830 (no specific date), to William T. Barry, postmaster general, recommending Matthew Lyon for appointment as his clerk; also signed by Thomas Chilton and Joseph LeCompte; auctioned June 24, 1971, by Charles Hamilton Galleries/Autographs.

1834:
January 19, to Carey & Hart. This consists only of Crockett's free frank, postmarked January 19, 1834, suggesting that there probably is a lost Crockett letter of this date to Carey & Hart; auctioned December 10, 1999 by Christie's.

January 28, to Carey & Hart from Washington; auctioned June 7, 1907, by Stan V. Henkels. The auction catalog has none of the letter's contents or additional information.

February 17, to Levi Woodbury; recommendation for Isaac Brown for appointment as midshipman in the U.S. Navy; also signed by seven others. Very likely not in Crockett's hand or originated by him; auctioned November 29, 1967, by Parke-Bernet. The auction catalog has only a brief description of the letter, but no text or quotations.

May 11, to James M. Sanderson at the Exchange, Philadelphia, written from New York; with franked address sheet; making an appointment and stating that he was much pleased with his eastern tour. Auctioned January 15, 1930, by American Art Association and Anderson Galleries, Inc., from the estate of Joshua I. Cohen. Also, a letter cover franked and postmarked May 11, 1834, addressed by Crockett to Sanderson in Philadelphia was auctioned by Charles Hamilton Autographs September 22, 1966. Neither of these catalogs reprints any part of the letter. Sanderson was a Philadelphian who ordered a rifle made for Crockett as a gift from the Whigs of that city. Crockett wrote to Sanderson again on June 25, 1834, and February 18, 1835, regarding the rifle and other items.

August 20, from Weakley City [sic], Tennessee.; auctioned January 26, 1921, by Stan V. Henkels. Exact date of letter and recipient unknown, and no other information about the letter was included in the catalog listing.

September 30, to Committee of Invitation; auctioned February 6, 1998, by R. M. Smythe.

1835:
January 16, to Carey & Hart proposing to write a book about Martin Van Buren; auctioned March 18, 1913, by Stan V. Henkels. Shackford mentions the letter in *David Crockett: The Man and the Legend*, 186, and says that "Somewhere there exists a Crockett letter of January 16, 1835, to Carey & Hart 'proposing to write a Life of Martin Van Buren.'" Shackford cites a 1912 auction (probably the 1913 Henkels auction) and another held on December 23, 1923, at which the letter was offered, but adds that it had never been published (311, n. 16).

February 10, to Nicholas Biddle. Biddle's letter to Crockett of February 16, 1835, refers to Crockett's "favor the 10th inst.," but Crockett's letter has not been found.

June 26, to Carey & Hart from Mouth of Sandy, Henry County, Tennessee, auctioned May 10, 1910 by Merwin-Clayton, referring to his autobiography.

Date Unknown. There is a franked envelope sent by Crockett from Washington City to John McLean, Esq., Clark's Ferry, Pennsylvania, dated December 27 (year unknown) in the J. S. Cullinan Family Collection at the San Jacinto Museum of History. This is evidence of another missing Crockett letter.

CIRCULARS:

Crockett's circulars from 1833 and 1835 have not been found. In a letter of July 13, 1833 to the Editors of *Southern Statesman*, published on July 20, Crockett mentioned that he had sent the *Statesman* a circular a few days earlier, but it did not appear in that newspaper, and no copy has been located. Adam Huntsman responded to the circular in a letter dated July 23, 1833, published July 29 in the *Statesman*.

In a letter to his son, John Wesley Crockett, dated December 24, 1834, published in the *(New Orleans) Daily Picayune,* March 16, 1884, Crockett mentioned that he was preparing a new circular to be sent to residents of his district, but the circular has not been found.

APPENDIX B: DAVID CROCKETT'S YEARS IN OFFICE

Terms in the Tennessee Legislature's General Assembly:
Fourteenth General Assembly in Murfreesborough:
    First Session: September 17–November 17, 1821
    Special Session called by Gov. Carroll: July 22–August 24, 1822

Fifteenth General Assembly in Murfreesborough:
    First Session: September 15–November 29, 1823
    Second Session: September 20–October 22, 1824

Terms in the U.S. House of Representatives:

1825: Crockett lost his first race for the House.

1827: Crockett defeated Gen. William Arnold and Col. Adam Alexander.

Twentieth Congress:
    First Session: December 3, 1827–May 26, 1828
    Second Session: December 1, 1828–March 3, 1829

1829: Crockett was reelected to a second term

Twenty-First Congress:
    First Session: December 7, 1829–May 31, 1830
    Second Session: December 6, 1830–March 3, 1831

1831: Crockett was defeated in a close election by William Fitzgerald.

1833: Crockett defeated the incumbent Fitzgerald by 173 votes.

Twenty-Third Congress:
    First Session: December 2, 1833–June 30, 1834
    Second Session: December 1, 1834–March 3, 1835

1835: Crockett was defeated by Adam Huntsman by 252 votes.

APPENDIX C: HISTORY OF THE LAND BILL IN CONGRESS

H.R. 95: Polk's first bill, drafted in the Nineteenth Congress, dated February 9, 1826; the bill never came up for debate. Key provisions: Congress would cede to Tennessee all vacant lands in West Tennessee that remained after the North Carolina warrants were satisfied. This cession would partially make up for the deficiency in school lands. Tennessee would be authorized to sell the land at a price set by the legislature, with revenues used to fund schools.

H.R. 27: Polk's second bill, virtually identical to H.R. 95, introduced December 24, 1827; debated April 24, 29, 30, and May 1; tabled on May 1, 1828. Key provisions were the same as H.R. 95. During debate Polk reduced his request to an amount of public land equal to what he claimed the state was due for schools in proportion to the amount of land claimed by North Carolina warrants (one 640-acre section for each six square miles of public land used to satisfy the warrants).

H.R. 27 Amendments: Crockett introduced his amendment December 11, 1828. It was amended further later, but that version was not printed; it appears in the *Register of Debates* and Crockett's January 15, 1829, circular. It was debated January 5 and January 12–13, 1829, and tabled on January 13. John Bell of Tennessee proposed an amendment to H.R. 27 on January 5 and had it printed up as "Intended to be proposed," but it was never formally introduced or debated. Key provisions: Congress would grant title to plots of up to 160 acres to settlers who had improved their land, but held no legal title to it. No land would be ceded to the state, and no revenues would derive for schools or any other purpose.

H.R. 185: Crockett's new bill, dated January 29, 1830; debated and defeated on May 3, 1830. Although all of the Tennesseans voted for it, none but Crockett spoke for it. A motion to reconsider a drastically amended version of the bill was defeated by voice vote on May 4. Crockett made several subsequent, unsuccessful attempts to bring H.R. 185 up for debate. The dates of those attempts and the votes by which they were defeated were: December 23, 1830 (86-74), December 31, 1830 (97-69), and January 6, 1831 (92-89). Key provisions: The original bill, defeated on May 3, 1830, would have ceded to Tennessee land in the Western District equal to the amount that was to have been set aside for schools. Tennessee would be permitted to sell the land at any price, but not less than 12½ cents per acre, and sales would be made only in cash, with the proceeds used for a permanent fund for the establishment of common schools. Occupants who had made improvements to their land would receive a preemption of at least two hundred acres, including their improvements, for 12½ cents per acre.

H.R. 185 Amendments: Daniel Laurens Barringer of North Carolina added an amendment, which was accepted, requiring that North Carolina warrants be treated first, for a period of twelve months, before Tennessee could benefit from the sale of these lands. After the bill was defeated on May 3, 1830, Crockett attempted to have a drastically amended version reconsidered on May 4, which called for the sale only of the occupants' land, up to two hundred acres, with revenues going directly to the federal government instead of Tennessee. The remaining vacant lands would remain in federal hands. Tennessee would receive no land and no revenue, and there was no provision for school funds. This was very close to the amendment Crockett had proposed to H.R. 27 in the previous session.

H.R. 126: Crockett's final bill, introduced January 2, 1834, after he had been out of office for two years. The bill never came up for debate. Crockett tried to bring it up on February 20, 1835, but failed by a vote of 77-52. The bill was virtually identical to the version of H.R. 185 that was defeated on May 3, 1830. Key provisions: Land equal to the school deficiency would be ceded to Tennessee, and occupants would receive a preemption on two hundred acres for 12½ cents per acre, with proceeds going to a common school fund.

H.R. 528: Introduced December 17, 1840, by Crockett's son, John Wesley, who then worked with Isaac Edwin Crary of Michigan to produce a revised version, H.R. 607 (see below). Key provisions of H.R. 528: Tennessee would sell the vacant lands for 12½ cents per acre as agent for the federal government, which would receive all revenues. Occupants would receive a preemption on their land, also at 12½ cents per acre, with no acreage limit specified. North Carolina warrants would be honored for a period of one year, after which they could be redeemed for cash for an additional year.

H.R. 607: Introduced by Isaac Crary on January 16, 1841. The bill passed the House on February 15, 1841, and, after passage in the Senate, became law. It was a reworked version of H.R. 528 produced by Crockett and Crary. Key provisions: Tennessee acted as agent for the federal government, which received all revenues from land sales. North Carolina warrants would be honored for one year, after which they could be redeemed for 12½ cents per acre for one year. The warrants could not be used to claim lands where occupants had previously located. Occupants received a preemption on no more than two hundred acres for 12½ cent per acre. Tennessee would sell remaining vacant land for 12½ cents per acre.

BIBLIOGRAPHY

Manuscript Sources:

H. Furlong Baldwin Library, Maryland Historical Society
  Vertical File

Beinecke Rare Book & Manuscript Library,
  Yale University
    General Collection
    Yale Collection of Western Americana
      Thomas W. Streeter Collection of
      Texas Manuscripts

Boston Public Library, Rare Books
  David Crockett Letter

Buffalo and Erie County Historical Society Library
  and Archives
    David Crockett Letter

Columbia University Rare Book and
  Manuscript Library
    David Crockett Letter

Chicago History Museum
  David Crockett Collection

DRT Library at the Alamo
  David Crockett Letters

Bruce Gimelson
  David Crockett Letter

Haverford College Library Special Collections
  Charles Roberts Autograph Letters Collection

Historical Society of Pennsylvania
  David Crockett Letters

Hofstra University Libraries' Special Collections
  Department
    David Crockett Letter

Houghton Library, Harvard University
  Autograph File

Huntington Library, San Marino, California.
  David Crockett Letter

J. Y. Joyner Library, East Carolina University,
  Greenville, North Carolina
    John Heritage Bryan Papers (#147), Special
    Collections Department

Library of Congress, Manuscripts Division
  David Crockett Letter

Lilly Library Manuscript Collection, Indiana
  University, Bloomington, Indiana
    David Crockett Letter

Mississippi Department of Archives and History
  David Crockett Letter

New-York Historical Society
  B.V. Francis (Goelet) Collection
  Gilder Lehrman Collection
  Miscellaneous Manuscripts

New York Public Library
  Asher Durand Papers (microfilmed by the
    Archives of American Art, Smithsonian
    Institution)
  Carl H. Pforzheimer Collection of Shelley and
    His Circle
  David Crockett Miscellaneous File, Manuscripts
    and Archives Division
  Thomas Madigan Collection

Newberry Library
  Midwest Manuscripts

Phil Collins Collection
  David Crockett Letters

Pierpoint Morgan Library, Literary and Historical
  Manuscripts Department
    David Crockett Letters

Rosenbach Museum & Library
  David Crockett Letters

San Jacinto Museum of History
  J. S. Cullinan Family Collection

Sewanee: The University of the South, University
  Archives and Special Collections
    David Crockett Letter

Tennessee Historical Society, Miscellaneous Files
  David Crockett Letters

Tennessee State Library and Archives
  David Crockett Letters
  William Yeatman Letter

University of Rochester Library, Department of Rare
  Books and Special Collections
    David Crockett Letter

University of Tennessee Special Collections Library,
  Hoskins Library, University of Tennessee Libraries

University of Texas at Austin, Center for American
  History
    Crockett (David) Papers

University of Virginia Library, Special Collections
  Clifton Waller Barret Library of American
    Literature

U.S. National Archives and Records Administration
  Records of the U.S. House of Representatives
  Records of the U.S. Senate
  Revolutionary War Pension and Bounty-Land
    Application Files

Wilson Library, University of North Carolina
  Southern Historical Collection
    Calvin Jones Papers
Wisconsin Historical Society Archives
  David Crockett Letter
David Zucker Collection
  David Crockett Letters

Auction Catalogs:

Anderson Auction Co. and Galleries: June 1, 1904;
  March 13, 1914; April 16, 1914; December 15, 1914;
  February 26, 1917; December 2, 1918;
  January 15, 1930.

Christie's: December 5, 1991; May 17, 1996;
  December 5, 1997; June 9, 1999; November 8, 2001;
  June 17, 2003; December 3, 2007.

Charles Hamilton Autographs, Inc., and Charles
  Hamilton Galleries: September 22, 1966;
  March 20, 1969; November 6, 1969; June 24, 1971;
  December 6, 1973; May 2, 1974; May 20, 1982.

Leslie Hindman Auctioneers: January 15, 1984.

Matthew Bennett Sale: December 4, 2008.

Merwin-Clayton: April 5, 1910; May 10, 1910.

Parke-Bernet Galleries, Inc.: November 19, 1945;
  February 25, 1947; November 25, 1952;
  April 11, 1961; November 29, 1967.

Sotheby's: April 26, 1978; January 30, 1979;
  November 28, 1979; October 26, 1988;
  May 19, 1997.

Sotheby Parke-Bernet: February 28, 1974;
  December 16, 1994.

Smythe: February 26, 1998.

Swann Galleries, Inc.: May 19, 1960; March 14, 1991;
  June 8, 2000.

Stan V. Henkels: June 7, 1907; March 18, 1913;
  January 26, 1921; May 17, 1932.

Newspapers:

(Amherst, New Hampshire) Farmer's Cabinet
Augusta (Georgia) Chronicle and Georgia Advertiser
(Augusta, Maine) Age
Baltimore Gazette and Daily Advertiser
Baltimore Patriot and Mercantile Advertiser
(Bennington) Vermont Gazette
Brattleboro (Vermont) Messenger
(Brattleboro, Vermont) Independent Inquirer
(Brattleboro) Vermont Phoenix
(Chicago) Daily Inter Ocean
(Columbus) Ohio State Journal

(Concord) New Hampshire Patriot and State Gazette
Dallas (Texas) Morning News
(Dallas, Texas) Weekly Times-Herald
(Des Moines, Iowa) Daily State Register
(Dover) Delaware State Reporter
Easton (Maryland) Gazette
(Easton, Maryland) Republican Star and Daily Advertiser
(Hagers-Town, Marylan) Torch Light and Public Advertiser
(Hallowell, Maine) American Advocate
(Hartford) Connecticut Courant
(Hartford) Connecticut Mirror
(Hartford) Connecticut Patriot and Eagle
Hartford (Connecticut) Times
Jackson (Tennessee) Gazette
(Jackson, Tennessee) Southern Statesman
(Jackson, Tennessee) Truth Teller
(Keene) New Hampshire Sentinel
Knoxville(Tennessee) Journal
Knoxville (Tennessee) Register
Louisville (Kentucky) Journal
Lowell (Massachusetts)Daily Citizen and News
(Lowell) Massachusetts Sun
(Macon) Georgia Telegraph
Macon (Georgia) Telegraph
Nacogdoches (Texas) Chronicle
Nashville (Tennessee) Whig
(Nashville, Tennessee) National Banner
National Banner and Nashville (Tennessee) Whig
National Banner and Nashville (Tennessee) Advertiser
New Bedford (Massachusetts) Mercury
(Newport) Rhode Island Republican
(Norwich, Connecticut) Courier
(Philadelphia)Pennsylvania Inquirer and Daily Courier
Pittsfield (Massachusetts) Sun
(Portland, Maine) Eastern Argus Tri-Weekly
Portland (Maine) Advertiser
(Portsmouth) New Hampshire Gazette
Portsmouth (New Hampshire) Journal
(Poughkeepsie, New York) Independence
(Providence, Rhode Island) Cadet and Statesman
(Providence) Rhode Island American and Providence Gazette
Richmond (Virginia) Enquirer
(Rusk, Texas) Cherokee Sentinel
(Salem, Massachusetts) Essex Gazette
Salem (Massachusetts) Gazette
San Francisco (California) Bulletin
(San Antonio, Texas) Daily Express
(San Francisco, California) Evening Bulletin
Savannah (Georgia) Mercury
(Tallahassee) Floridian and Advocate
Urbana (Ohio) Record
(Washington) National Intelligencer

Congressional Publications:
Gales & Seaton's Register of Debates in Congress
Journal of the House of Representatives of the United States
Congressional Globe

Books:

American Book Prices Current. Various publishers, all volumes, 1901–99.

Abernethy, Thomas P. *From Frontier to Plantation in Tennessee*. Chapel Hill: University of North Carolina Press, 1932.

Arpad, Joseph John. "David Crockett, An Original Legendary Eccentricity and Early American Character." Ph.D. dissertation, Duke University, 1968.

Bassett, John Spencer. *The Life of Andrew Jackson*. New York: MacMillan, 1911, reprinted in 1925.

Belko, W. Stephen. *The Invincible Duff Green: Whig of the West*. Columbia, Missouri: University of Missouri Press, 2006.

Biddle, Nicholas. *Correspondence of Nicholas Biddle*. Edited by Reginald C. McGrane. Boston and New York: Hougton Mifflin Co., 1919.

Biographical Directory of the U.S. Congress. http://bioguide.congress.gov.

Blair, Walter. *Davy Crockett—Legendary Frontier Hero*. Springfield, Illinois: Lincoln-Herndon Press, Inc., 1955.

———. *Horse Sense in American Humor—From Benjamin Franklin to Ogden Nash*. Chicago: University of Chicago Press, 1942.

Borneman, Walter R. *Polk: The Man Who Transformed the Presidency and America*. New York: Random House, 2008.

Burstein, Andrew. *The Passions of Andrew Jackson*. New York: Vintage, 2004.

Carter, Clarence Edwin, ed., *Territorial Papers of the United States: Volume 5*. Washington, D.C.: Government Printing Office, 1937.

Catterall, Ralph C. H. *The Second Bank of the United States*. Chicago: University of Chicago Press, 1903.

Congressional Quarterly's Guide to U.S. Elections. Washington, D.C.: Congressional Quarterly Inc., 1994.

Corlew, Robert E. *Tennessee: A Short History*. Nashville: University of Tennessee Press, 1981.

Crockett, David. *An Account of Col. Crockett's Tour to the North and Down East*. Baltimore: E. L. Carey and A. Hart, 1835.

———. *Address of Mr. Crockett, to the Voters of the Ninth Congressional District of the State of Tennessee; Together with His Remarks in the House of Representatives,* *January 5, 1829*. Washington: Printed by Gales & Seaton, January 15, 1829. Rare Books Division, Library of Congress.

———. *David Crockett's Circular*, February 28, 1831. Rare Books Division, Library of Congress.

———. *A Narrative of the Life of David Crockett of the State of Tennessee*. Edited by Joseph J. Arpad. New Haven, Connecticut: College & University Press, 1972.

———. *A Narrative of the Life of David Crockett of the State of Tennessee*. Edited by James A. Shackford and Stanley J. Folmsbee. Knoxville: University of Tennessee Press, 1973.

Culp, Frederick M. and Robert E. Ross. *Gibson County: Past and Present*. Trenton, Tennessee: Gibson County Historical Society Publications, 1961.

Davis, James D. *History of the City of Memphis*. Memphis: Hite, Crumpton, & Kelly, 1873.

Davis, William C. *Three Roads to the Alamo: The Lives and Fortunes of David Crockett, James Bowie, and William Barret Travis*. New York: Harper Collins, 1998.

De Kay, James Tertius. *A Rage for Glory: The Life of Commodore Stephen Decatur, USN*. New York: Free Press, 2004.

Debo, Angie. *A History of the Indians of the United States*. Norman: University of Oklahoma Press, 1970.

Derr, Mark. *The Frontiersman: The Real Life and the Many Legends of Davy Crockett*. New York: William Morrow and Company, Inc., 1993.

Ehle, John. *Trail of Tears: The Rise and Fall of the Cherokee Nation*. New York: Anchor Press/Doubleday, 1988.

Ellis, Joseph J. *American Creation: Triumphs and Tragedies at the Founding of the Republic*. New York: Alfred A. Knopf, 2007.

Feller, Daniel. *The Public Lands in Jacksonian Politics*. Madison: University of Wisconsin Press, 1984.

Feller, Daniel, Harold D. Moser, Laura-Eve Moss, and Thomas Coens, eds. *The Papers of Andrew Jackson: Volume VII, 1829*. Knoxville: University of Tennessee Press, 2007.

Filler, Louis, and Allen Guttmann, eds. *The Removal of the Cherokee Nation: Manifest Destiny or National Dishonor?* Lexington, Massachusetts: D. C. Heath & Co., 1962.

French, James Strange. *Sketches and Eccentricities of Col. David Crockett, of West Tennessee*. New York: J. & J. Harper, 1833, New Edition. (Originally published anonymously.)

Goldman, Perry M., and James S. Young, eds. *United States Congressional Directories: 1789–1840*. New York: Columbia University Press, 1973.

Grund, Francis J. *Aristocracy in America*. London: Richard Benley, 1839.

Hargreaves, Mary W. M., and James F. Hopkins, eds. *The Papers of Henry Clay, Vol. 6, Secretary of State 1827*. Lexington: University Press of Kentucky, 1981.

Harper, Herbert L. (ed.), *Houston and Crockett: Heroes of Tennessee and Texas—an Anthology*. Nashville: Tennessee Historical Commission, 1986.

Hauk, Richard Boyd. *Davy Crockett: A Handbook*. Lincoln: University of Nebraska Press, 1986, reprint of *Crockett, a Bio-Bibliography*. Westport, Connecticut: Greenwood Press, 1982.

Heiskell, S.J. *Andrew Jackson and Early Tennessee History, Vol. 3*. Nashville: Ambrose, 1921.

Jackson, Andrew. *The Memoirs of General Andrew Jackson*. Auburn, New York: James C. Derby & Co., 1845.

Keating, J.M. *History of the City of Memphis, Tennessee*. Syracuse: D. Mason & Co., 1888.

Langsdon, Phillip. *Tennessee: A Political History*. Franklin, Tennessee: Hillsboro Press, 2000.

Leonard, Thomas M. *James K. Polk: A Clear and Unquestionable Destiny*. Wilmington, Delaware: Scholarly Resources Inc., 2001.

Lofaro, Michael A. ed., *Davy Crockett: The Man, the Legend, the Legacy, 1786-1986*. Knoxville: University of Tennessee Press, 1985.

Magliocca, Gerard N. *Andrew Jackson and the Constitution*. Lawrence: University Press of Kansas, 2007.

McBride, Robert M., and Owen Meredith, eds., *Eastin Morris' Tennessee Gazetteer 1834 and Matthew Rhea's Map of the State of Tennessee 1832*. Nashville: The Gazetteer Press, 1971.

McCormac, Eurgene Irving. *James K. Polk: A Political Biography*. Berkeley: University of California Press, 1922.

Meacham, Jon. *American Lion: Andrew Jackson in the White House*. New York: Random House, 2008.

Morgan, Robert. *Boone: A Biography*. Chapel Hill: Algonquin, 2007.

Moulton, Gary E., ed. *The Papers of Chief John Ross. Volume 1*. Norman: University of Oklahoma Press, 1985.

New Georgia Encyclopedia. http://www.georgia-encyclopedia.org.

Parrington, Vernon L. *Main Currents in American Thought, Volume Two, 1800–1860, The Romantic Revolution in America*. New York: Harcourt, Brace & Co., 1927.

Paulding, William I. *The Literary Life of James Kirk Paulding*. New York: Charles Scribner and Co., 1867.

Prucha, Francis Paul. *American Indian Policy in the Formative Years: The Indian Trade and Intercourse Acts 1790–1834*. Lincoln: University of Nebraska Press, 1962.

Remini, Robert V. *Andrew Jackson and the Bank War*. New York: W. W. Norton & Co., 1967.

———. *Henry Clay: Statesman for the Union*. New York: W. W. Norton & Co., 1991.

———. *The Legacy of Andrew Jackson: Essays on Democracy, Indian Removal, and Slavery*. Baton Rouge: Louisiana State University Press, 1988.

———. *The Life of Andrew Jackson*. New York: Penguin Books, 1988.

———. *Andrew Jackson and His Indians Wars*. New York: Penguin Books, 2001.

Ritchie, Donald A. *Press Gallery: Congress and the Washington Correspondents*. Cambridge: Harvard University Press, 1991.

Rothbard, Murray N. *The Panic of 1819: Reactions and Policies*. New York: Columbia University Press, 1962.

Rourke, Constance. *Davy Crockett*. New York: Harcourt, Brace & Co., Inc., 1934; reprint, Lincoln: University of Nebraska Press, 1998.

Saxton, Alexander. *The Rise and Fall of the White Republic*. London and New York: Verso, 2003.

Schlesinger, Arthur M., Jr. *The Age of Jackson*, abridged edition. New York: Mentor, New American Library, 1949.

Seigenthaler, John. *James K. Polk*. New York: Times Books, Henry Holt & Co., 2003.

Sellers, Charles Grier. *James K. Polk, Jacksonian, 1795–1843*. Princeton: Princeton University Press, 1957.

Shackford, James Atkins. "The Autobiography of David Crockett: An Annotated Edition." Ph.D. dissertation, Vanderbilt University, 1948.

Shackford, James Atkins; edited by John B. Shackford. *David Crockett: The Man and the Legend*. Chapel Hill: University of North Carolina Press, 1956.

Smith, Richard Penn. *"On to the Alamo," Col. Crockett's Exploits and Adventures in Texas*. Edited with an Introduction and Notes by John Seelye. New York: Penguin Classics, 2003.

Taylor, George Rogers, ed. *Jackson vs. Biddle's Bank*. Lexington, Massachusetts: D. C. Heath and Co., 1972.

Temin, Peter. *The Jacksonian Economy*. New York: W. W. Norton & Co., 1969.

Van Buren, Martin. *The Autobiography of Martin Van Buren*. Edited by John C. Fitzpatrick. Washington: U.S. Government Printing Office, 1920.

Wallace, Anthony F. C. *The Long, Bitter Trail: Andrew Jackson and the Indians*. New York: Hill and Wang, 1993.

Weaver, Herbert, ed., and Paul H. Bergeron, assoc. ed. *Correspondence of James K. Polk, Volume I, 1817–1832*. Nashville: Vanderbilt University Press, 1969.

———. *Correspondence of James K Polk, Volume 2, 1833–1834*. Knoxville: University of Tennessee Press, 1972.

———. *Correspondence of James K Polk, Volume 3, 1835–1836*. Knoxville: University of Tennessee Press, 1975.

Widmer, Ted. *Martin Van Buren*. New York: Henry Holt, 2005.

Wiener, Allen J., and William R. Chemerka. *Music of the Alamo: From 19th-Century Ballads to Big-Screen Soundtracks*. Houston: Bright Sky Press, 2009.

Williams, Emma Inman. *Historic Madison, The Story of Jackson and Madison County Tennessee, from Prehistoric Moundbuilders to 1917*. Jackson, Tennessee: Madison County Historical Society, 1946.

Williams, Samuel Cole. *Beginnings of West Tennessee: In the Land of the Chickasaws, 1541-1841*. Johnson City, Tenn.: The Watauga Press, 1930.

Wise, Barton H. *The Life of Henry A. Wise*. New York: MacMillan, 1899.

Articles:

Abernethy, Thomas P. "Andrew Jackson and the Rise of South-Western Democracy." *American Historical Review* 33, no. 1 (October 1927): 64–77.

———. "The Early Development of Commerce and Banking in Tennessee." *Mississippi Valley Historical Review* 14, no. 3 (December 1927): 311–25.

———. "The Origin of the Whig Party in Tennessee." *Mississippi Valley Historical Review* 12, no. 4 (March 1926): 504–22.

Adkins, Nelson F. "James K. Paulding's Lion of the West." *American Literature* 3, no. 3 (November 1931): 249–58.

Albanese, Catherine L. "Savage, Sinner, and Saved: Davy Crockett, Camp Meetings, and the Wild Frontier." *American Quarterly* 33, no. 5 (Winter 1981): 482–501.

Atkins, Jonathan M. "The Presidential Candidacy of Hugh Lawson White in Tennessee, 1832–1836." *Journal of Southern History* 58, no. 1 (February 1992): 27–56.

Bergeron, Paul H. "Tennessee's Response to the Nullification Crisis." *Journal of Southern History* 39, no. 1 (February 1973): 23–44.

Blair, Walter. "Six Davy Crocketts." *Southwest Review* 25, no. 4 (July 1940): 442–62.

Bogue, Allan G., and Mark Paul Marlaire. "Of Mess and Men: The Boardinghouse and Congressional Voting, 1821–1842." *American Journal of Political Science* 19, no. 2 (May 1975): 207–30.

Boylston, Jim. "Crockett, Boone, and the Chester Harding Matrix." *Crockett Chronicle* 1 (August 2003): 3–5.

Brown, Thomas. "Southern Whigs and the Politics of Statesmanship." *Journal of Southern History* 46, no.3 (August, 1980): 361–380.

Caldwell, Joshua W. "John Bell of Tennessee: A Chapter of Political History." *American Historical Review* 4, no. 4 (July 1899): 652–64.

Chemerka, William. "1882 Recollection of David Crockett by his Daughter Matilda Fields." *Crockett Chronicle* no.14 (November 2006): 4–5.

Conser, Walter H. Jr. "John Ross and the Cherokee Resistance Campaign, 1833–1838." *Journal of Southern History* 44, no. 2 (May 1978): 191–212.

Cooper, Texas Jim. "A Study of Some David Crockett Firearms." *East Tennessee Historical Society Publications* 38 (1968): 62–69.

Crowe, Charles. "The Emergence of Progressive History." *Journal of the History of Ideas* 27, no. 1 (January–March 1966): 109–24.

Currie, David P. "The Constitution in Congress: The Public Lands, 1829–1861." *University of Chicago Law Review* 70, no. 3 (Summer 2003): 783–820.

Davies, Caroline S. "A Yankee in the South." *New England Quarterly* 10, no. 1 (March, 1937): 63–83.

Davis, Curtis Carroll. "A Legend at Full-Length: Mr. Chapman Paints Colonel Crockett and Tells About It." *Proceedings of the American Antiquarian Society* 69 (1960): 69–170.

Dupre, Daniel. "Barbecues and Pledges: Electioneering and the Rise of Democratic Politics in Antebellum Alabama." *Journal of Southern History* 60, no. 3 (August 1994): 479–512.

Eriksson, Erik McKinley. "President Jackson's Propaganda Agencies." *Pacific Historical Review* 6, no. 1 (March 1937): 47–57.

Folmsbee, Stanley J. "David Crockett and West Tennessee." *West Tennessee Historical Society Papers* 28 (1974): 5–24.

Folmsbee, Stanley J., and Anna Grace Catron. "David Crockett: Congressman." *East Tennessee Historical Society's Publications* 29 (1957): 40–78.

———. "David Crockett in Texas." *East Tennessee Historical Society's Publications* 30 (1958): 48–74.

———. "The Early Career of David Crockett." *East Tennessee Historical Society's Publications* 28 (1956): 58–85.

Gatell, Frank Otto. "Spoils of the Bank War: Political Bias in the Selection of Pet Banks." *American Historical Review* 70, no. 1 (October 1964): 35–58.

Goldman, Perry M. "Political Virtue in the Age of Jackson." *Political Science Quarterly* 87, no. 1 (March, 1972): 46–62.

Hammond, Bray. "Jackson, Biddle, and the Bank of the United States." *Journal of Economic History* 7, no. 1 (May 1947): 1–23.

———. "The Second Bank of the United States." *Transactions of the American Philosophical Society, New Series,* 43, no.1 (1953): 80–185.

Heale, M. J. "The Role of the Frontier in Jacksonian Politics: David Crockett and the Myth of the Self-Made Man." *Western Historical Quarterly* 4, no. 4 (October 1973): 405–23.

Heidler, David S., and Jeannet Heidler. "'Not a Ragged Mob': The Inauguration of 1829." White House Historical Association, White House History #15; undated, http://www.whitehousehistory.org/08/subs/08_b15.html.

Hirsch, Mark. "Davy Crockett's Finest Hour." *American Indian* (Smithsonian Institution) (Winter 2007): 52–54.

Husch, Gail E. "'Poor White Folks' and 'Western Squatters': James Henry Beard's Images of Emigration." *American Art* 7, no. 3 (Summer 1993): 15–39.

Jones, Thomas B. "The Public Lands of Tennessee." *Tennessee Historical Quarterly* 28, no. 1 (Spring 1968): 13–36.

Latner, Richard B. "A New Look at Jacksonian Politics." *Journal of American History* 61, no. 4 (March 1975): 943–69.

Marshall, Lynn L. "The Strange Stillbirth of the Whig Party." *American Historical Review* 72, no. 2 (January 1967): 445–68.

Mason, Melvin Rosser. "'The Lion of the West': Satire on Davy Crockett and Frances Trolloppe." *South Central Bulletin* 29, no. 4 (Winter 1969): 143–45.

Mayo, Edward L. "Republicanism, Antipartyism, and Jacksonian Party Politics: A View from the Nation's Capital." *American Quarterly* 31, no. 1 (Spring 1979): 3–20.

Meerman, Jacob P. "The Climax of the Bank War: Biddle's Contraction, 1833–34." *Journal of Political Economy* 71, no. 4 (August 1963): 378–88.

Meyers, Marvin. "The Jacksonian Persuasion." *American Quarterly* 5, no. 1 (Spring 1953): 3–15.

Miles, Guy S. "David Crockett Evolves, 1821–1824." *American Quarterly* 8, no. 1 (Spring 1956): 53–60.

Mooney, Chase C. "The Political Career of Adam Huntsman." *Tennessee Historical Quarterly* 10, No. 2 (June 1951): 99–126.

Moore, Powell. "James K. Polk, Tennessee Politician." *Journal of Southern History* 7, no.4 (November, 1951): 493–516.

———. "The Revolt against Jackson in Tennessee, 1835–1836." *Journal of Southern History* 2, no. 3 (August 1936): 335–59.

Murphy, James Edward. "Jackson and the Tennessee Opposition." *Tennessee Historical Quarterly* 30, no. 1 (1971): 50–69.

Norman, Geoffrey. "The Cherokee." *National Geographic* 187, no. 5 (May 1995): 72–97.

Parsons, Lynn Hudson, "In Which the Political Becomes the Personal, and Vice Versa: The Last Ten Years of John Quincy Adams and Andrew Jackson." *Journal of the Early Republic* 23, no. 3 (Autumn 2003): 421–43.

Perkins, Edwin J. "Andrew Jackson, Lost Opportunities for Compromise in the Bank War: A Reassessment of Jackson's Veto Message." *Business History Review* 61, no. 4 (Winter 1987): 531–50.

Reising, Russell J. Reviews of Vernon Louis Parrington's *Main Currents in American Thought, Vol. 1: The Colonial Mind, 1620–1800; Vol. II: The Romantic Revolution in America, 1800–1860; and Vol. III: The Beginnings of Critical Realism in America, 1860–1920. American Quarterly* 41, no. 1 (March 1989): 155–64.

Remini, Robert V. "Andrew Jackson versus the Cherokee Nation." *American History* (August 2001): 48–56.

Scruggs, Thomas E. "Davy Crockett and the Thieves of Jericho: An Analysis of the Shackford-Parrington Conspiracy Theory." *Journal of the Early Republic* 19 (Fall 1999): 481–98.

———. "The Physical Stature of David Crockett: A Re-analysis of the Historical Record." *Journal of South Texas* 9, no. 1 (Spring 1996): 1–29.

Sellers, Charles Grier, Jr. "Banking and Politics in Jackson's Tennessee." *Mississippi Valley Historical Review* 14, no. 1 (June 1954): 61–84.

———. "Jackson Men with Feet of Clay." *American Historical Review* 62, no. 3 (April 1957): 537–51.

———. "Who Were the Southern Whigs?" *American Historical Review* 59, no. 2 (January 1954): 335–46.

Shockley, Megan Taylor. "King of the Wild Frontier vs. King Andrew I: Crockett and the Election of 1831." *Tennessee Historical Quarterly* 57, no. 3 (Fall 1997): 158–69.

Silbey, Joel H. "'Delegates Fresh from the People: American Congressional and Legislative Behavior." *Journal of Interdisciplinary History* 13, no. 4 (Spring 1983): 603–27.

Simon, John Y. "In Search of Margaret Johnson Erwin." *Journal of American History* 69, no. 4 (March 1983): 932–41.

Simpson, Jeffrey. "The Allure of Autographs." *Architectural Digest* 45, no. 12 (December 1988): 156–59, 210–12.

Sioussat, St. George Leakin. "Some Phases of Tennessee Politics in the Jackson Period." *American Historical Review* 14, no. 1 (October 1908): 51–69.

Tanenbaum, Miles. "Following Davy's Trail: A Crockett Bibliography." In Michael A. Lofaro and Joe Cummings, eds., *Crockett at Two Hundred: New Perspectives on the Man and the Myth*. Knoxville: University of Tennessee Press, 1989: 192–241.

Temin, Peter, "The Economic Consequences of the Bank War." *Journal of Political Economy* 76, no. 2 (March–April 1968): 257–74.

Voss, Frederick S. "Portraying an American Legend: The Likenesses of Davy Crockett." *Southwestern Historical Quarterly* 91, no. 4 (April 1988): 457–82.

Weisberger, Bernard A. "The Bank War." *American Heritage Magazine* 48, no. 4 (July–August 1997), viewable at www.americanheritage.com.

Wilentz, Sean. "On Class and Politics in Jacksonian America." *Reviews in American History* 10, no. 4 (December 1982): 45–63.

Williams, Emma Inman, ed. "Letters of Adam Huntsman to James K. Polk." *Tennessee Historical Quarterly* 6, no. 4 (December 1947): 337–69.

Wilson, Major. "Republicanism and the Idea of Party in the Jacksonian Period." *Journal of the Early Republic* 8, no. 4 (Winter 1988): 419–42.

Wyatt-Brown, Bertram. "Andrew Jackson's Honor." *Journal of the Early Republic* 17, no. 1 (Spring 1997): 1–36.

Zaboly, Gary S. "Crockett Goes to Texas: A Newspaper Chronology." *Journal of the Alamo Battlefield Association* 1, no. 1 (Summer 1995): 7–18.

INDEX OF KEY NAMES

Huntsman, Adam (aka "Black Hawk") 83, 85-6, 90, 118-19, 121-2, 125-6, 215, 221-3, 240, 255-6, 260-1, 263, 276, 279-80, 282-3, 327

I

Ingham, Samuel D. 190, 304
Isacks, Jacob C. 50, 55, 62-3, 150, 158, 180, 300

J

Jackson, Andrew 7-8, 15, 17-21, 23-5, 29, 31, 35-6, 39, 42-4, 46-7, 49, 51-5, 60, 64-75, 77-82, 84, 86-9, 91-110, 112-15, 119-23, 125-6, 146, 148, 151-5, 158, 160-1, 164-6, 169, 171, 174, 176, 187-9, 194, 196, 199-203, 206, 213, 216, 218-23, 225-8, 230-2, 234-5, 237, 240-5, 268, 283, 292, 294, 297-300, 303-5, 319, 324
Jefferson, Thomas 32, 65, 267-70, 294, 321
Johnson, Cave 51, 60-1, 63, 119, 178, 192-3, 271, 308
Jones, Calvin 84, 89, 217-18
Jones, Isaac N. 290
Jones, William 92
Junius Brutus 16, 82

K

Keller, John 225
Kendall, Amos 97, 102, 241
Kennedy, John 164
Knox, Henry 65

L

Lampkin, John W. 225
Lawrence, Richard 120, 273
Lea, Luke 53, 271
Lea, Pryor 35-6, 38, 41-2, 45-9, 51, 53-4, 59, 63, 81, 158, 160-1, 164-8, 170, 175, 177-8, 181, 196-7, 271, 296, 300, 313, 315, 319
Letcher, Robert P. 250
Levy, Lewis 241
Lewis, William B. 92, 105, 326
Lumpkin, Wilson 75

M

Marable, John H. 49, 51, 178
Marshall, John 70-1, 75, 196, 320
Mayo, Peter 225
McAllister & Co 146
McClung, Henry 80, 87, 194-5
McLane, Louis 98, 150, 201, 299
McLean, Charles D. 191-2
McLean, G.W. 234-5
McLean, John 228, 235, 327
McLemore, John C. 146
McMeans, James 121, 260, 263, 276, 281
McMillen, Davison 41-2, 54, 159-60
McMinn, Joseph 16, 24
McNairy, Boyd 24, 254-5

Miller, Pleasant 49, 55, 78, 179, 189
Mitchell, James C. 17, 24, 48, 54, 158, 175, 300
Moncrieff, William 52
Monroe, James 24, 65, 188, 303, 323
Moore, Thomas P. 250

N

Neilson, Hugh D. 58, 63, 153, 185
Newsam, Albert 124, 130

O

Osgood, Samuel S. 112, 124, 130, 238, 246, 260, 264
Overton, John 15, 18-21, 24-5, 78, 86, 92-7, 106, 120, 253

P

Partee, Hirom 156
Patton, George 49, 54-5, 84, 126, 162-3, 285, 288-9
Patton, Robert 13-15, 138-41, 285
Patton, William 122, 285
Paulding, James K. 80, 85, 87, 89, 109, 142, 194-5
Peale, Rembrandt 87, 128
Peck, James H. 202
Poe, Edgar A. 90, 121
Poindexter, George (U.S. Senator) 103, 120, 201, 226, 241, 283
Poindexter (of the Bank, first name unknown) 107, 254, 256-7
Polk, James K. 14, 18, 29-51, 53-5, 57-63, 80-1, 87, 91, 95, 97, 103-4, 113, 119, 125-6, 151, 154-6, 158-61, 165-6, 175, 178, 187-8, 193, 271, 277-9, 296, 300, 310, 312-13, 315, 319-20, 326, 328
Pounds, Daniel 63, 75, 88, 196

R

Randolph, John 123
Reed, William B. 108
Rice, Thomas 115
Rodgers, James 72, 225
Rodgers, William 63, 108, 229-30
Ross, John 71-2, 75, 198-200, 326

S

Sanderson, James M. 115, 118, 125, 253-4, 276, 326
Schultz, Charles 108, 125, 261-2
Seat, Robert 153, 161
Seaton, William 45, 48-9, 165, 167, 172, 177-8, 180, 217, 219, 236, 240, 247
Sergeant, John 114
Shegogue, James H. 129
Siler, Jacob 321
Smith, Richard 89, 100, 107, 219-20
Smith, Seba 110, 121
Smith, William 163
Sprigg, Michael 79, 87, 128, 176, 203-4

St. Claire Clarke, Matthew 90, 178
Standifer, James 193
Steele, Nathaniel 53
Stevenson, Andrew 151
Storrs, Henry 123, 231
Story, Joseph 75
Stuart, Charles Gilbert 133

T

Taliaferro, John 279
Taney, Roger 102
Thomas, Francis 252
Totten, James L. 150-3
Tyler, John 14, 220

U

Underwood, William H. 75

V

Van Buren, Martin 9, 14, 24, 53, 78, 81, 85-6, 91, 97, 99-101, 104-7, 110, 113, 119-21, 123, 186-8, 203, 213-14, 228, 239, 243, 245, 248-9, 261-5, 267-72, 277, 279, 281-2, 298-9, 319, 321, 325
Verplanck, Gulian 44, 53, 157-8
Vinton, Samuel 59-61, 63, 193

W

Waldron, R.R. 125, 273
Wallis, Joseph 124, 248
Washington, George 65, 73
Waterman, Albert G. 108, 228
Watson, Edward S. 225
Webster, Daniel 14, 82, 87, 96, 99, 102-4, 110, 118, 220, 253
White, Hugh Lawson 41, 46, 54, 92, 119, 165, 175, 270-1, 273, 276-9, 282, 289
Wickliffe, Charles Anderson 37, 165, 172-3, 175, 212, 323
Wilde, Richard H. 194
Wildfire, Nimrod 80, 85, 109, 117, 123, 194-5
Williams, John 18-19, 25, 92, 95, 105
Williams, Lewis 161, 173, 175
Winchester, Marcus B. 21-2, 86, 251
Wirt, William 24
Wise, Henry A. 272
Woodbury, Levi 274, 325
Worcester, Samuel 71, 75

Y

Yeatman, Thomas 96, 252-3
Yeatman, William 108, 252-3
Yell, Archibald 49, 54, 80, 87, 160